# Major Problems in

# American

**SECOND EDITION**

# Foreign

# Policy

DOCUMENTS AND ESSAYS

Volume I: To 1914

Edited by

## Thomas G. Paterson

UNIVERSITY OF CONNECTICUT

**D. C. Heath and Company** • Lexington, Massachusetts • Toronto

COVER ART: Detail from "Westward the Course of Empire Takes Its Way with McCormick Reapers in the Van." Lithograph. Chicago Historical Society.

Published simultaneously in Canada.

Printed in the United States of America.

International Standard Book Number: 0-669-06450-5

Library of Congress Catalog Card Number: 83-80923

1984

# Major Problems in American Foreign Policy

FOR *Aaron Matthew*

# Preface

The invitation to offer a second edition of this volume has afforded me the enviable opportunity to review the rich literature in diplomatic history. The goal remains: to provide students and instructors with the most distinguished, readable, and stimulating writing in the field. Since the first edition, the body of scholarly studies has grown tremendously, and new documents have become available to the curious historian. In this edition, new chapters appear, and many of the chapters carried over from the first edition have been revised to include new research, fresh and changed interpretations, recently declassified documents, and topics that have loomed in the last few years as especially helpful in understanding current foreign policy. At the same time, the core of the best scholarship from the first edition has been retained.

Each chapter addresses a major theme or question over which contemporaries and later scholars and writers have differed. The primary documents in each chapter introduce the problem, outline issues, reveal the flavor of the times, and convey the level of intelligence and intensity with which people held their positions and tried to persuade others. The questions were momentous—sometimes abstract, sometimes deadly concrete, but always consequential—and people like us defined and debated them. They suffered in their confusion and defeat, and they prospered in their success. This book attempts to capture and reveal that human dimension—that *people* struggled to make decisions. The essays in each chapter also reflect these qualities. Thus we learn not only *what* happened but *why* alternative policies were rejected. Joining studies by past masters are contributions by younger voices. Varying points of view are represented, and care has been taken to avoid contriving debates to fit a false either-or format. The chapter introductions and section headnotes set the readings in historical and interpretive perspective. Further Reading sections, highlighting recent scholarship, suggest other books and articles for continued research.

Many people have helped me prepare this anthology. My friend and colleague J. Garry Clifford, as always, gave valuable advice. For suggestions and other courtesies I thank Harold Barto, Richard Dean Burns, Bruce Cummings, Joe Decker, John Dobson, Michael Ebner, Gerald Gordon, Gregg Herken, James Hindman, Michael Hunt, Donald Johnson, Lawrence Kaplan, Warren Kimball, Melvyn Leffler, Douglas Little, James Matray, John Merrill, Charles Neu, Stephen Pelz, Carol Petillo, Sister Eileen Rice, Kenneth Shewmaker, Mark Stoler, William Stueck, and John Sylvester. My colleagues Karen Kupperman and Harry Stout shared their expertise with me, as did doctoral students Harlow Sheidley and Thomas Zoumaras. Ellen P. Kerley, an undergraduate History major, provided indispensable assistance. Jean Manter, my departmental secretary, assisted in many ways, and Holly Izard Paterson once again favored the book with her help.

TGP

# Contents

# 10 Late Nineteenth-Century Expansionism and Economics    324

# 11 The Spanish-American War and Empire    354

# 12 The Open Door Policy and China    388

# Diplomatic Historians
# and Their History

# 1

*It is a truism that history is as much the historian as the body of facts the historian weaves together to tell the story of the past. Historians, like all human beings, have their viewpoints that are shaped by parents, by personal experiences, by ideological preferences, and by myriad philosophers, scholars, politicians, and others. It is rare historical writing, indeed, that is free from the personal bias of the author. This does not make the writing less significant as a work of scholarship or as a viable interpretation. On the contrary, readers of history are enriched by knowing about and learning from an author's subjectivity. To overlook the historian's role in creating our image of the past is to miss an exciting part of the quest for knowledge and understanding.*

## ESSAYS

The following three essays, all by prominent diplomatic historians who have exerted considerable influence upon generations of scholars, help us to illustrate this truism. For example, Samuel Flagg Bemis, ardent nationalist, long-time professor of history at Yale University, mentor of talented students, and author of such major books as *Jay's Treaty* (1923) and *John Quincy Adams and the Foundations of American Foreign Policy* (1950), recalls his early days at Harvard as a graduate student undertaking historical research. Dexter Perkins, whose books on the Monroe Doctrine are considered classics, surveys his own life as a citizen as well as the events and leaders of his time that helped mold his "Wilsonian" view. And, finally, William Appleman Williams of Oregon State University, who has spoken in a powerful, critical voice through such works as *The Tragedy of American Diplomacy* (1959), *Empire as a Way of Life* (1980), and *The Roots of the Modern American Empire* (1969), delineates the influences that moved him toward a leftist, "revisionist" perspective.

Bemis, Perkins, and Williams have enjoyed different backgrounds, read different books, studied under different professors, argued with different students, and reached contrasting conclusions about the history of American diplomacy. The questions their autobiographies raise should be raised for every essay in this volume. It is debatable whether one has "to live through a period to understand it," as Professor Perkins claims in his essay, but certainly one must know about the viewpoint of the scholar to understand historical writing about any period.

---

# A Nationalist Education

### SAMUEL FLAGG BEMIS

Right away I found myself in Professor Channing's research seminar in American history. Edward Channing was then at the zenith of his lifework, his *History of the United States*. It remains the best attempt at a one-man, multi-volume history of the republic and its colonial background, documented by the best of published scholarship and his own research. As conceived by Channing, it was to cover the period from the discovery to the beginning of his own adult lifetime, that is, to the end of the nineteenth century. Channing died early in 1931 after finishing Volume VI that ended with the close of the Civil War. It was his method to organize his seminar about some central theme or period and to assign problems relating to that general subject to each student—I believe there were six of us that term. He had enough applicants so he didn't have to take in anyone who didn't want to work in this manner. Really it is the ideal way: teacher and disciples working together as fellow students on aspects of the same subject, each able to give and take; of course the instructor gave and the students took, but the latter could stimulate and occasionally rasp one another. It was all to the good for everybody.

I noticed that it was the custom of old students who dropped into the library to greet Channing by asking him what volume of the "great work" he was now working on. At my time he was writing Volume IV on the Federalist Period—dictating it little by little, so he would tell us casually, "after a cigar in the evening." For my seminar exercise I got the subject of Jay's Treaty with Great Britain of 1794, of which I had scarcely heard. Realizing that the subject had no adequate monograph based on investigation in the public and private archives of the negotiating countries, he thought that somebody some-

---
From "Harvard, 1913–1916." First published in *The New-England Galaxy* (Old Sturbridge Village), Volume XI, Winter 1970, pp. 13–15. "A Worcester County Student in Wartime London and Paris (via Harvard): 1915–1916." First published in *The New-England Galaxy* (Old Sturbridge Village), Volume XI, Spring 1970, pp. 15–16, 17–18, 19–23.

day should at least make a start in the foreign sources. It was my great luck that he threw that bone to me. Whether he realized how far it would take me, I often doubt.

Channing, Hart, and Turner were then the American history triumvirate at Harvard, joint compilers of the widely-known pioneer *Guide to American History.*

Channing would affect a singular, almost strutting pose (if one can strut in an armchair), and liked with students to take a poke at Hart now and then. But he never took a dig at Turner. Channing never wholly accepted Turner's famous frontier and sectional interpretation of American history and society; he took occasion to challenge it with other ideas, such as the pervasive centripetal and unifying force of nationalism overcoming sectionalism and states rights from colonial times to the present. I once unavoidably heard Channing and Haskins worrying about how they would keep Turner from going back to Wisconsin.

Channing would begin his seminar, which met only once a week, with a few informal lectures, or rather remarks. They were of a discursive and frequently personal nature—never reflecting any discredit on himself. (I never knew a teacher, including myself, who did. We are all vain.) These talks were mostly designed, I suspect, to take up time and keep the class together while the neophytes were getting immersed in their several researches. The most instructive feature of his teaching was the half-hour conference he had every week with each member of the seminar at his little desk in the library stacks, where he could reach for a special book or direct a student around the corner to a series in the stacks. Even in these conferences one had to hold Channing to one's own track of study: if you didn't he would get to worming personal information out of you, instead of imparting historical knowledge. As one of my friends who later took Channing's seminar said: "You had to knock it out of him." All this, I suspect, was the most subtle type of teaching. It was helping people to help themselves. Education is self-education: teachers and libraries are the means by which one educates oneself. Channing knew that; if his students didn't yet know it, they came to realize it.

The other principal feature of his seminar was the report of each student to the group. Channing wouldn't let you read it: all he would allow was a one-page outline of what you wanted to say, and no surreptitious glances at notes under the table. This required you to be so soaked up in your subject that you would have it at the end of your tongue. . . .

By the time I returned to Harvard in 1915 from my summer tutorial employment, my parents and younger brothers had moved down to Medford. I now enjoyed the Ozias Goodwin Memorial Fellowship and could devote all my time to my studies and preparation for my "generals." I could walk the three miles at least one way: across the Medway, over Winter Hill to East Cambridge, and to Harvard Square. After a hard day I could ride back on the subway and elevated to Sullivan Square and home, all still for a nickel, but it took, with changes, almost as much time as walking. More questionable exercise was walking for hours at night in the Fellsway, rehearsing and memorizing for my oral examination, an ordeal so dreaded by students that some of them collapse out of sheer anxiety.

At last came the day when I was to prove myself, whether I would be dropped out of the University or permitted to go on and present a thesis for the doctorate. I was not too scared or nervous until I saw Assistant Professor Johnston and Dr. Lord around the examiners' table; the others, as I remember, were Channing, Merriman, and McIlwain. Somehow I got through with McIlwain and Merriman. Then came R. M. Johnston's turn.

He asked a few questions about the significance of the French Revolution; then he wondered whether I might review the historiography of that great upheaval. I had read Mignet and Taine, a lot of Aulard, and some of Jaurès. Mr. Johnston himself had published a short volume for the aid of students summing up the subject, so I was able to run over the whole gamut of historians, not neglecting to mention Albert Sorel. The committee was impressed and Professor Johnston's eyes brightened. I should have stopped there, for he didn't seem to have any more to ask. "Then, of course," I added by way of a crowning touch, "there is your own little volume if I may mention it in the same list with these masters." Too late I realized what I had said, but my chagrin was lost in general laughter that went around the table; even R. M. Johnston joined in. "You may," he said, and I came back from the edge of the abyss and smiled sheepishly myself.

Then Channing turned to the youngest examiner, who had been called in as a man who had never had anything to do with my instruction and could size me up impersonally! "Any questions, Dr. Lord?" Dr. Lord had not gone to sleep during the session, as I had once done in my visit to his seminar, not for one second! He asked me a few questions, not at all vindictive, but I was by then so terrified by remembrance of my own snooze that I didn't field them very well, whatever they were. I knew by then I must be sunk.

It was Channing who ended the exam and came to my rescue. He asked me some questions as easy for me as pop flies for a third baseman, though perhaps a little recondite to the committee.

I passed—over Dr. Lord's dissenting vote. His negative voice was not undeserved, if only on the basis of my answers to his questions.

"What did you have against *me?*" Channing asked me a little gruffly, next time I saw him. "We were only trying hard to pull you through."

I had nothing but the greatest gratitude! I guess that I must have looked a little truculent after Lord had got through with me. . . .

At first glance Jay's Treaty, that Channing had assigned me, must seem to be a rather unattractive and uninspiring subject. Actually it lay at the very heart of the new nationality of the United States under the Constitution of 1787, when American foreign policy was taking shape and party politics were crystallizing under the rival leadership of Alexander Hamilton and Thomas Jefferson during the administrations of President George Washington. It was, in fact, the first treaty, aside from a consular convention with France, to be ratified by the Senate of the United States. The negotiation involved the whirlpool of international politics during the wars of the French Revolution and the attitude of the United States toward them: isolation and neutrality under sufferance of the British navy for the benefit of American commerce and tariff revenues so indispensable to the support and credit of the new national government of the United States under the Hamiltonian system. Jay's Treaty of 1794 with Great Britain therefore exposed the very foundations of American foreign policy soon to be spelled out in Washington's Farewell Address of 1796.

Though I did not realize it then, the preparation of this doctoral dissertation launched me on a career at home and abroad of historical writing and teaching nothing less than the history of the foreign policy of the United States, from the beginning, where I started my research, to—I will not say to the end—to the present year 1970 of this terrible yet magnificent twentieth century. Before the First World War it was quite possible for a young man to encompass everything that had been written on the diplomatic history of the United States up to and including his own times. Channing had hitched me up to something big while I was still in my early twenties.

At the time of Jay's Treaty, and indeed until the end of the Napoleonic Wars, foreign policy ruled American politics. For a century afterward American domestic politics ruled foreign policy, so far as the Old World was concerned, during a hundred years of peace on the great oceans. As I set forth for Europe, in October 1915, on the neutral Dutch liner *Nieuw Amsterdam,* Europe was again convulsed on the Continent and engulfed in war at sea. Foreign policy again was agitating and would soon dominate American politics during the Great War of 1914–1918. Another passenger on the *Nieuw Amsterdam* was the Austrian Ambassador Constantine Dumba, whom President Wilson had just expelled from the United States for saying that the President's *Lusitania* notes to Germany were only intended for domestic consumption.

Where I spent the first night in darkened London I cannot remember, but next day an advertisement in the *Times* took me to a boarding house in Finsbury Park at 30 Adolphus Road, the home of a Mr. and Mrs. Kay and their two amiable daughters, Jennie and Lettie, one of whom, Jennie, the elder, succeeded in advancing my German to an imperfect speaking ability. The elder Kays were naturalized British subjects born in Germany, as Mrs. Kay was careful to explain before I engaged room and board. The family, with the possible exception of Mrs. Kay, were violently anti-German. They had changed their names legally from Kaiser to Kay, just as our good neighbors back in Worcester were to change Hamburg St. to Genesee St. after the United States entered the war, and American schools dropped the German language from their curricula. Probably, this was one reason why I obtained such reasonable rates at the Kay's, the sterling equivalent of about five dollars a week. I lived pleasantly with this family all the time I was in London. It was within twenty minutes by tube from the Public Records Office and the British Museum.

Next morning I betook myself to the Records Office, equipped with the required introduction from the American Ambassador. At the head of Chancery Lane was a huge hole, the size of my bedroom, in the street, about six or eight feet deep, made by a Zeppelin bomb dropped the night before I arrived in London. A recruiting officer was signing men up from a scaffolding that had been erected over the hole. The Zeppelins did not do much real damage during the First World War—aerial bombardment was in its infancy and the huge ships were easy targets for anti-aircraft guns. There was not another raid all that winter, but there was many an alarm and blackout, the night sky constantly crisscrossed by searchlights, and much toing and froing in the obscured streets by clanging fire apparatus and mobile artillery, bedlam on foggy nights. . . .

The solemn music and grave ceremony of a wartime service at Westminster Abbey still haunts my mind. . . .

In a few months I finished my work in London and mailed to Professor Channing a typescript of my dissertation. It could still be touched up by some investigation in the archives of the French Foreign Office at the Quai d'Orsay. That part of my requirement for the degree was over, as I booked passage for France and checked my steamer trunk through to Paris. With me I carried a suitcase and a leather Boston bookbag stuffed with the notes I had taken in England.

Those were the days of diplomatic debate between President Wilson and the German Imperial Government over submarine warfare, which had subsided a little, at least in respect to "unarmed passenger vessels."

"Any trouble lately with submarines?" I asked at the London ticket office.

"Not on this line," replied the impassive agent at the window.

The cross-Channel ship *Sussex,* on which I embarked early on the afternoon of March 24, 1916, was a small, unarmed passenger vessel flying the flag of France, on the route Dover to Calais. I had a second-class ticket. For such a short passage I could wait for dinner until we got in to Calais, although the *Sussex* had a dining room up forward, where some passengers were already taking tea. I had not become wholly addicted to the English custom of afternoon tea, so I went back to the stern deck.

The sea was very calm. The flag had been taken down from the rear mast. As I looked out over the water from the port side, I noticed that we were wallowing through drifting bales and flotsam that looked like remnants of wreckage. Suddenly a passenger exclaimed, excitedly, "What's that?"

I was looking in the right direction. "That" was the straight and swirling wake of something just beneath the surface, rapidly shooting toward the ship. I realized what it meant, but before I could shout "torpedo!" it had crashed into the port bow. The submarine never surfaced. According to the log of the submarine commander, preserved in the German archives, it was exactly 2:55 p.m. European time.

A tremendous explosion threw to the deck some of those who happened to be standing. The entire bow was blown off and with it the people who were in the dining room. The ship began slowly to sink forward. Crew and passengers scrambled toward the lifeboats. The boats had not been swung out on their davits to be let down quickly in case of emergency. There had been no lifeboat drill. The ropes were all gummed up and difficult to loosen. I and others tore at them in vain with our cold fingers. Finally the crew were able to lower some boats, loaded principally with women. I don't remember having seen any children about. In one case the ropes stuck at a davit, letting one end of the boat go down while holding up the other. The occupants simply slid into the sea, some with lifebelts that could hold them up for possible rescue.

By this time I began to look about for a lifebelt for myself. All those stored in and about the deck had been taken during the rush, but inside the second-class saloon I found a rotten fragment of one and managed to tie on that much with a chance piece of rope. The boats were all away by now. I resolved to get into a position from which I could swim for something as the ship went down bow first. I took off my shoes, climbed over the rail, and found a temporary perch above the propeller on a cleat that ran around the stern just above the water line. A few minutes before I had seen a man in the sea clinging to the end of the log-line like a fish on a hook; he was no longer there; the rope payed out slack behind the slowly sinking ship. In a moment a lifeboat crowded with people warped around the stern and I stepped off into it. I stepped from the lifeboat to an emergency life-raft, good for one person, that was floating along in touch. Astride this thing, about the size of a child's coffin, I gradually floated out to sea. After a while the ship stopped sinking. The lifeboats remained clustered around her, their occupants waiting to see what would happen. By a miracle the explosion that blew away the bow and perhaps the forward third of the vessel had blasted the remainder inwards, so that it kept afloat in the calm weather. But there was I, drifting farther and farther away from a chance of rescue. I caught hold of some wreckage including a steamer chair, from which with my jackknife I cut the canvas into strips and tied things together to make a raft of sorts, big enough to hold me mostly out of the chilling water.

Riding along in this jolly way, I noticed a singular, almost ridiculous, little coincidence of traffic in the English Channel. Floating close along, bobbing up and down in the easy sea, never quite within reach, was one of my shoes that I had abandoned on the deck of the ship, sailing quite upright, nicely enough to please Old Mother Hubbard herself. I never did recover it, nor its mate wherever that was.

As I looked back at the slowly receding *Sussex* and its cluster of lifeboats I saw on the horizon another ship: a three-masted, full-rigged sailing vessel, sails spread wide to catch the breeze. It soon disappeared. Soon I met a fellow navigator, not too lucid, a Swiss about my own age, who like me was astride a raft of his own. We came within reach of each other and I tied our two seahorses together, so that in that quiet sea we were fairly well out of the water.

It was now getting dusk. We were perhaps a mile or so from the ship. Suddenly we spied a lifeboat making our way. The captain of the *Sussex* had sent it out, manned by two sailors, to pick up anybody still afloat. What a noble Frenchman, to whom we certainly owed our lives!

"Gee!" said my new-found companion, in impeccable English, "I hope they see us. If they pick us up I'll give them five dollars in gold each."

As I have suggested, he was a little delirious.

Back on the *Sussex* when we arrived, people were cheering up. The vessel was floating securely, at least for the time being, though nobody knew for how long, or whether to expect another torpedo; and the wireless was busy. Several bodies were laid out on the starboard deck.

I found my suitcase and bookbag of notes intact where I had left them. From the suitcase I got a pair of beaded Indian moccasins, put them on my cold wet feet, and sat down on the bench inside the saloon, to wait and see. Beside me was a young woman, sad and still dry-eyed. Just before the crash her husband had left her momentarily for some purpose forward. He never came back. Forlornly in her lap she held his Belgian officer's cap. They had just been married and were on their way to Belgium for their honeymoon.

Presently some of the lights turned on, enough to see about the cabin. I began to shiver in my wet clothing. A woman with a lunchbox offered me a leg of chicken, which I accepted, not knowing where or whether the next meal was coming from. Attracted by a warmer current of air, I found my way to the boiler room. The boilers were still warm and I sat down above them. My clothes dried and I stopped shaking.

Some hours after dark we survivors were all rescued. Some eighty-four lives were lost, including that of the famous composer, Granados, whom I had seen walking about the ship in his coat and cap of Astrakhan fur. A British mine-sweeper came alongside to take us off. What crisp and rapid commands that officer snapped out, how the crew responded promptly: "Aye, aye, sir!"

"Passengers will come on without baggage!"

I had my bag of precious notes in my hand when I joined the line to go down the ladder. It was only a little bag, but I treasured it more than my trunk and suitcase. I stepped out of line, went a few yards to the right or left, and tossed it, well strapped up, down to the deck of the minesweeper. In the pre-occupation and excitement of the moment nobody noticed, and I stepped back to another place in line. Later I found the bag safe and intact on the rescue ship and hugged it to myself all the way into the port of Boulogne.

How and when we passed the rest of the night ashore I forget completely, and indeed everything until we got off the train at the *Gare du Nord* in Paris. At the platform to greet us was a young attaché from the American Embassy. Me he taxied in my dishevelment, wet moccasins and all, to the American Embassy, where Ambassador William Graves Sharp took me into his own residence. I have been a guest in many embassies since, but this first experience was the most welcome of all. A valet conducted me to a guest room on the top floor and equipped me with shoes from the wardrobe of the Ambassador's own son. They fitted just fine.

"The Ambassador will be expecting you down to lunch right away," said the valet, as he left me to my own devices for a moment.

I didn't know what to do with those soggy moccasins. The room opened on an inside balcony that ran around an ornamental central hallway rising four stories from the first floor below, where the dining room and reception parlors were. I stepped to the banister and dropped the moccasins overboard, hoping some servant would pick them up and take care of them. They hit the marble floor below with a squishy sound. When I got downstairs they were nowhere to be seen, but the Ambassador was standing by the entrance to the dining room. "I know what that plomp was," he said jovially, as he took me in to luncheon and introduced me to Mrs. Sharp. "It was those moccasins!"

# The Wilsonian Influence

DEXTER PERKINS

As I look back and reflect upon the evolution of my views in the field of foreign policy (a field which has, as the reader knows, occupied much of my teaching and writing), what impresses me is how typical of many an American my own development has been. The innocence of youth has faded; faith in a simple remedy for the appeal to violence has been dimmed; the magnitude of the problem becomes apparent. Above all, and this I shall have to say frankly at the outset, pacifism as gospel seems to me illusory and dangerous. Peace, if it comes, will rest upon organized force, not upon innocent good will. Reinhold Niebuhr has put the matter in a nutshell: "Love without power" (I paraphrase) "will in the long run, or perhaps the short run, be overcome by power without love." I was a long time coming to this view; I reproach myself, student that I was of international affairs, that I awakened slowly to this essential truth; but perhaps just because this is true, what I have to say here may have some value for my readers.

I grew up in an era when the dominant mood of America was peace. Since 1815 there had been no large-scale conflict in Europe. Since 1865 there had been no large-scale conflict in the Americas, save for a bloody struggle in Paraguay—hardly noticed in the United States. True, we had fought a war with Spain in 1898, but this was hardly more than a military picnic. In Europe in the first decade of the twentieth century there were ominous signs for those who knew how to read them, most especially, the growth of German nationalism. But at the time of the first Moroccan crisis (1905) the possibility of a European war on a grand scale seemed to have been exorcised by the Conference of Algeciras. Austria's annexation of the Turkish province of Bosnia Herzegovina in 1908 passed without a conflict, despite the hostility it aroused among the South Slavs. When I graduated from college in 1909, men were dwelling on the folly of war. They were preparing not long after to celebrate a century of peace between the United States and Great Britain. The Hague Conferences of 1899 and 1907, however little they may have accomplished, seemed another happy augury. Norman Angell's *The Great Illusion,* which was published in 1910 and which I read not very long after, confidently predicted that the economic interest of the world in stability would prevent armed conflict. Leading Americans like Charles William Eliot and David Starr Jordan exuded confidence in the pacific character of the future.

It was easy for me, an idealistic youth, to believe in goodness and to minimize the forces of evil in the world. In these years I dreamed that a way might be found to abolish war between civilized nations. And in my senior year in college I took a course in international law, and in an immature way came to the conclusion that here was an answer to the problem of power and that I wanted to teach the subject. Part of my graduate work was in this field. When I got my fellowship to study in France in the fall of 1911, one of the inducements was that at the École des Sciences Politiques, which I was to attend, was Louis Renault, one of the most renowned international lawyers of the period. When I got my first job in Cincinnati in 1914, I stipulated that I was to have an opportunity to teach a half-course in the law of nations.

In the summer of 1914 came the First World War. I remember very well the day that the newspaperman came up the drive with the Sunday papers, the first of August, 1914, and the look on my father's face as he read that Germany had declared war on Russia. He looked as if the skies had fallen in. And what is striking to me now is that though I had taken an interest in contemporary diplomacy, although indeed I had been in France in 1911 and 1912, and had an opportunity to observe the growth of the war spirit in France, I was by no means prepared for the outburst of hostilities. I resembled most Americans in believing that we had progressed beyond the point where a world war was possible.

In the policy of neutrality which Wilson followed I was strongly behind the President. As I look back, I think I saw the struggle through his eyes. As we now know, Wilson was not indifferent to the idea of a German victory. But he cherished the hope that the war might be brought to an end through American mediation, and he placed in the forefront of his thought the maintenance of legal principle. Did he, as later critics were to insist, discriminate in favor of the Allies? In one sense, yes. He avoided a sharp challenge to Great Britain and France; he responded sharply to German violations of law. But there was a world of difference between Allied and German conduct. The Western powers were interfering with trade; the Germans, in initiating the submarine warfare against merchant vessels, were infringing on the long-established principle that such vessels, whatever their cargo, could not be sunk without making provision for the safety of their passengers and crew. This infringement, to one trained in international law as I had been, seemed a serious breach in the legal order, on a wholly different plane than interference with commerce, with regard to which it is fair to say that the principles of law were somewhat cloudy.

It is not strange, then, that I supported the President, at the same time cherishing the hope that he could avoid a direct confrontation with Germany. When the *Lusitania* went down in May 1915, with the loss of over one hundred American lives, I was behind Wilson in his protest, and also in his exercise of patience. It is not always remembered that after a long period of notewriting that provoked the scorn of such nationalists as Theodore Roosevelt, the President secured the actual suspension of the U-boat war in the spring of 1916.

One day that spring Dr. Rhees called me in and asked if I wanted to attend a dinner meeting at Washington of a new organization called the League to Enforce Peace. The principle on which this organization was based was that the nations of the world would act collectively to put down an aggressor. We have learned today that things do not work out just that way. Very regretfully, but entirely clearly, I have come to the conclusion that collective security, in the broadest sense, is impracticable, that so varied are the interests of nations, and so widespread the desire to keep out of trouble if one can, that it has not been possible to rally all governments against a law-breaking state. But fifty years ago the idea did not seem impractical; it seemed an excellent specific for the evil of war. You may imagine, then, my feelings that evening when I sat in the great ballroom on the top floor of the Willard, and heard the President, in a dry, thin voice, but in precise language, commit himself and his administration to the central idea of the League to Enforce Peace. I can see that scene now. Former President Taft presided. And as the President came to the crux of his argument, while cheers broke out all over the room, Taft lifted his huge bulk, and waved his napkin enthusiastically. It was easy to believe that a new and great idea had been born.

I have already indicated my passionate interest in the election of Wilson in the campaign of 1916. After the election I continued to hope for peace. And I read with enthusiasm the "peace without victory" address of January 1917.

Then came the breach with Germany, the severance of diplomatic relations as Berlin declared unrestricted submarine warfare. Even then, my fundamental aversion to war led me to hope that an all-out conflict could be avoided. Events, of course, were to prove me wrong.

There are two incidents in the winter of 1917 that deserve recollection. Though my father was an orthodox Republican, he and my mother generously offered to take my fiancée and me to the inauguration. When we got to Washington we learned that the President's request to Congress to authorize the arming of the merchant ships of the United States had been filibustered to death in the Senate. And that night, as we were having dinner in our hotel, Senator Robert La Follette, one of the filibusterers, came in with a company of friends and sat down at the table near us. The band struck up the Star-Spangled Banner. At La Follette's table most of his friends remained seated. But the Senator, with the saddest and grimmest expression that I have ever seen, rose while the strains of the national anthem died away.

In the middle of March came the first Russian Revolution. One afternoon I bought the newspaper and read that the tsar had been dethroned. I cannot remember my own reaction, but writing in the historical vein, I have often wondered whether this was not a substantial factor in leading the President to the decision for war. It seems to me that ideologically it cleared the air. It had been difficult to depict the war as an out-and-out struggle of democracy against autocracy with the Russians fighting on the allied side. But the March revolution changed all that, and I know that Wilson, no doubt naively but surely, felt that a new and democratic Russia might rise from the ruins of the old. Another point. The chances of allied victory, it could be perceived, were diminished with the change of government in Russia. Could she, would she, continue the war? Was it not more than ever necessary for the United States to enter the struggle, if the democratic nations of the West were to win? These thoughts were not stressed by the President in that eventful period. But for many Americans, I am sure, they constituted a reason for entering a conflict which these same Americans had been anxious to avoid.

In April came war. I was in Boston visiting my parents at the time. I read the President's request for a declaration of hostilities with complete conviction that he had done all he could to avoid the struggle. It was hard to believe that it had come, and that not improbably I would be in it, but the issue seemed to me inescapable. . . .

The events which I have just described suggest some analysis of my later historical judgment of the period. No one of our wars has left behind more divergent interpretations among the historians. There are those who hold that Wilson's attitude was too rigid, and that war might have been avoided had he been more flexible. On the other hand, with the passage of time the view has been put forward that the United States had a profound security interest in preventing the victory of Germany, and that since the President's policy tended to that end it is to be commended. And there are those, including the most distinguished students of the Wilson period, who believe that no chief executive could possibly have failed to defend the rights which Germany challenged.

No one can tell what would have been the outcome had the United States not entered the war. Time and time again I have had occasion in my teaching to assert that confident judgment on the history that never happened is risky business for the historian. The events in the international scene are so complicated that it is best not to be dogmatic. We simply cannot reconstruct history by hypothesis.

Without our intervention would Germany have won an all-out victory? Would she have dominated the Continent, but failed to bring British seapower to its knees? Would a stalemate have postponed revolution in Russia with all its tremendous consequences? These are all important questions to which a definitive answer is impossible. But recently a young scholar in a noteworthy book has underlined, more strikingly than ever before, the scope of German ambition, and therefore the dangers of German success.

In my interpretation of the period, on which I have lectured for many years, I am thrown back on the facts, as distinguished from the speculations. What are these facts? In taking his stand on the submarine issue the President was supported by the majority opinion of the nation. This was true partly because the legal issue bulked important in the thought of many people, and because it was fortified by the disposition of the majority of the American people to sympathize with the cause of the Allies. The issue of national safety did not bulk large in people's minds by comparison. On this question the nation was divided. There were powerful elements who did not accept it, large numbers of German-Americans as well as large numbers of Irish-Americans who had their eyes on the repression practiced by Britain in Ireland at the same time that she was defending the principles of democracy in war. There were also large numbers of Americans who hoped fervently that the United States could avoid involvement, who remembered, perhaps vaguely but nonetheless with conviction, the principle of nonentangling alliances, and who would have seen direct intervention on the allied side as a violation of American tradition. Wilson acted from conviction, in choosing the ground that he did choose, and his position was, in my judgment, that position which best maintained the unity of the American people, and made it possible, when war came, to enter the struggle with the maximum amount of national unity. This I have maintained for many years.

Nonetheless, subsequent generations, and especially the college generation of the twenties and thirties, often found it hard to accept the necessity of enforcing a legal principle. Why not warn Americans off the merchant ships of the Allies? Why contend for a principle in view of the risks involved? The question has been asked me time and time again, and, as we shall see, it was reflected in wide segments of opinion in the nineteen thirties. It provides an interesting example of the inability of one generation to understand the motives and rationale of another. Intellectually, it is easy for men in time of peace to recoil from the kind of decision that may mean war. Such people cannot reconstruct the emotional suppositions that actually governed action, or the feelings of horror, to make the point more concrete, that filled many American breasts at the time of the sinking of the *Lusitania*. You have to live through a period to understand it. . . .

In the early twenties one leading theme was reduction of armaments. This was not only an obeisance to the peace spirit generated by Wilson, but it was also dictated by prevailing economic notions as to the necessity of frugality in government, and of reduction of swollen expenditures.

At the outset there was what looked like a brilliant success in this field at the Washington Arms Conference of 1921 and 1922. Secretary Hughes managed to bring about an agreement for the restriction of capital ships and aircraft carriers based on existing ratios. The longer view was to prove this achievement a very temporary one. In the second place, the reparations question, which had seemed vexing at the time of the Treaty of Versailles, yielded to treatment. By the terms of the treaty, impossible burdens were assessed on Germany. But in the agreements of 1924 (the Dawes Plan) and 1929 (the Young Plan) progress seemed to have been made in dealing with the problem. Thereby the Locarno treaties and the admission of Germany to the League were other happy omens for the future. The proposal of the Harding and Coolidge administrations for American adhesion to the protocol creating a World Court, though not accepted by the Senate in satisfactory form, nonetheless made it appear that the United States was moving in the right direction. With these various steps I, of course, sympathized, and used my editorial pen to support them.

In two respects, however, I was not in accord with the trend of the times. I did not share the increasing body of opinion which was sharply critical of the Treaty of Versailles. The reparation clauses I thought harsh, and I severely condemned the French occupation of the Ruhr in 1923. But the longer view suggested that these terms would be modified. As to the territorial arrangements in Europe, they seemed to me, on the whole, to be based upon the principle of nationality, and therefore acceptable. I would have admitted that there were exceptions—the prohibition of Austrian union with Germany except by vote of the Council of the League, the incorporation in the newborn state of Czecho-Slovakia of the large German-speaking area of the Sudetenland, and the Italian occupation of the Tyrol. But at the time these did not seem to threaten peace.

What I overlooked was the climate in which the peace treaty was negotiated, a climate which little recognized the necessity for considering German pride and German feeling. The manner in which the Versailles pact was imposed on the new Reich was humiliating. The attempt to fix Germany with total responsibility for the war was bound to be resented. And the territorial terms, however judged, were not likely to be accepted if Germany regained her military power. In not taking account of this latter possibility, the peace treaty was based on sand. None of these things did I see at the time.

On the other hand, I was not captivated by the negotiation in 1928 of that extraordinary document known as the Kellogg-Briand Pact, for the outlawry of war, which was negotiated by Secretary Kellogg, and signed with great fanfare by most of the nations of the world in a great meeting at Paris in the summer of 1928. . . .

What was my own view at the time? I was, I repeat, not a bit seduced by the pact. I was far too good a Wilsonian for that. But I nourished the hope (an extravagant hope, as appeared in the sequel) that it might be the stepping stone to some closer association with the League. In part, therefore, I shared the euphoria with which this extraordinary document was surrounded. . . .

To revert to the period of the thirties, these years provide an interesting example of the way in which foreign policy is—or at any rate may be—formed in the United States. People have the idea, some people, at any rate, that the President is all-powerful. But in the first six years of the Roosevelt administration, one of the strongest of our chief executives was compelled to accept policies which he secretly deprecated, and which were contrary to his own view of the national interest. Perhaps one of the reasons why I never developed for Roosevelt the enthusiasm that I had had for Woodrow Wilson may lie in the fact that he proved so ineffectual in guiding public opinion during these years.

The story of revisionism, as it was called, has often been told, but deserves recapitulation. One of the first important books which hinted at the idea that Wilson was lured into a war which might have been avoided was C. Hartley Grattan's *When War Came.* A famous article in *Fortune* in 1934 laid the foundation for the widening belief that wicked war profiteers had had a good deal to do with American policy. An arms investigation in the Senate, headed (for reasons difficult to explain), by a North Dakota Senator, Gerald P. Nye, fed the flames of the revisionist movement, condemning Wilson for failure to observe the true principles of neutrality. A Yale law professor, Edwin Borchard, wrapped the argument in legal phraseology. And in 1935 Walter Millis, in a book disastrously well written—and therefore quite influential—presented in appealing fashion the thesis that it was all a muddle from beginning to end.

This indictment I never accepted, and do not accept today. That the history of the First World War should be rewritten was perhaps to be expected; every generation sees the problems of the past in a different perspective from that of the generation preceding. To repeat what I have already said, there is a fundamental reason for this, especially when it comes to the history of war. War is passion; it springs from passion and ends in passion. Thus it is not strange that a new generation fails to understand the emotions and the accompanying rationalizations out of which the conflict sprang. This much, it seems to me, is to be admitted.

Nonetheless, there are things strangely wrong with regard to the revisionist judgment of the war period, and of the treaty which followed it. A capital error in revisionism is the assumption that had another course been followed, a happier and better world would have resulted. To make such a judgment ought to be deemed impossible for a mind disciplined to rigorous thinking. The facts of history are far too complicated to permit *any* confident generalization as to what would have happened if that which did not happen had happened! We cannot project with mathematical certainty an alternative course of action. It is foolish to try.

How seriously the revisionist gospel affected the course of politics in the thirties it is, of course, impossible to say. It has been argued that it encouraged Hitler in his ambitious projects, giving him assurance that the United States would keep out of a world struggle. But this is by no means certain. Though sometimes ignorant of and contemptuous of American power, Hitler knew enough not to provoke the American government, and it was only with the Japanese attack on Pearl Harbor that he accepted a direct confrontation with the United States.

In the repeal of the neutrality legislation of the thirties I had a small part. But I was no militant, even in 1940 and 1941. As a teacher, as a radio commentator, by participation in such agencies as the Foreign Policy Association, I sought to do my bit to enlighten public opinion. In general I supported the Roosevelt administration in its European policy and was lukewarm in its attempts to bring pressure on Japan. With Pearl Harbor, of course, I became a complete supporter of the war.

There has been a revisionist movement with regard to the policy of Roosevelt, as there was one with regard to Wilson. It has been claimed that he wished war with Japan, and that he wilfully exposed the American fleet at Pearl. This is nonsense. Roosevelt's object was to "baby" the Japanese along. He did, indeed, give aid to the Nationalists in China, and he gradually restricted, and finally cut off aid to Nippon. In this he was propelled by public opinion. But to him the European struggle was the central matter. And rightly so. Just imagine the kind of world that would have been born if the psychopath who led the German people had attained victory, had found the secret of the bomb, and had made the whole world the object of his ruthless ambition!

I cannot say that in the period of the war I was one who foresaw the kind of world that would come after. I was overoptimistic of the possibilities of understanding with the Soviet Union. I still hoped, more than time has justified, for a major role for the United Nations. But many people felt that way. It was only with 1945 that the international climate began to change, and that there was ushered in one of the most extraordinary periods in the history of mankind. For the last quarter of a century my task, as writer and teacher, and as citizen, has been to try to describe that world, and on occasion, to add my voice to others in the formulation of policy. Twice I have been offered important posts in Washington; but always I have preferred the role which I have just described. Rightly or wrongly, my choice has always been the classroom, the press, and the forum rather than government service.

## The Open Door Interpretation

### WILLIAM APPLEMAN WILLIAMS

Allow me first to comment directly on the prospects of revisionism.

Go back fifty years.

You will find a youngish doctor in New Jersey who is writing poems, essays, and novels during the moments between-and-after treating his patients. One of his books is a collection of subtle Freudian commentaries on key figures in early American history; and perhaps the best of those pieces, entitled "The Virtue of History," is a revisionist interpretation of Aaron Burr.

The doctor's name is William Carlos Williams. The work is called *In the American Grain*.

Now return to the present.

Go across the river from New Jersey. There you will find an extremely talented gentleman named Gore Vidal who has platinum-plated his literary reputation by offering a brilliant revisionist novel about Aaron Burr. Mr. Vidal does not mention the once-young-and-now-dead poet in New Jersey.

So go the prospects of revisionism.

Well, not quite.

After all, Korea, Cuba, Vietnam, Cambodia, and Chile did happen. So did Jackson State and Kent State. And now we have Watergate and San Clemente, and the cruel games being played in the name of national security and the energy crisis. There is no way to deny the revisionist insight into any of those issues.

Beginning with my first appearance before this honorable trade association as a freshman PhD, I have responded to many critics in candor and in length: orally and in writing, and directly and indirectly. I have not answered others because they have been redundant or incidental; because their primary thrust has been non- or anti-intellectual; or because in general I have been more concerned with getting on with my life.

I am here today in the hope that we can open a dialogue about History, as well as about particular parts of history: a dialectic involving our different strategies of intellectual inquiry. I have chosen the idiom of confession because it offers the most direct way of confronting three important matters: acknowl-

William Appleman Williams, "Confessions of an Intransigent Revisionist," *Socialist Revolution,* 17 (1973), 89–98. Reprinted by permission of the publisher and author.

edging mistakes, bearing witness to the truth, and stating one's considered view of the world.

Having taken notes on thousands of primary and secondary documents (and during interviews with hundreds of protagonists), and having many times revised my first drafts, I assume as part of being human that I have made these kinds of mistakes:

1. I have miscopied, or incorrectly transcribed, such documents;

2. In making summaries or abstracts, I have used language that became unclear or ambivalent when I returned to my notes; and

3. I have not always perfectly transferred an initially accurate note or summary into my final draft.

I am also certain, for two reasons, that I have not corrected all those mistakes during the process of publication:

1. I respect my own typing, linotype operators, computer print-outs, and copy editors, but I also know that each make their own kind of mistakes; and that all of them make mistakes correcting mistakes (and thereby produce some very strange results).

2. I am a poor proofreader. By the time I receive galley proof (let alone page proof) I am satiated with the sight of my mind as it existed eight to twelve months earlier. I cope with that situation as I learned to deal with the blindness of the egg checker. After you have candled so many eggs, they all look good or they all look bad. So you turn the job over to someone else while you go off to plow a field, lay in the hay, or catch some catfish. But all of us are susceptible to the blindness of the egg checker—thus there are some mistakes in my work that can be interpreted by those who do not understand such human frailty as proof of crimes that never entered my head, and would in any event be utterly beyond my interest or my patience.

I have always become intellectually excited in the course of any project—researching and writing history has been one of my favorite highs. That has probably led to a higher incidence of the kind of mistakes that I have just described, and has certainly prompted me to present much of my work too cryptically. I have too often written to myself, so to speak, during moments of intellectual exhilaration.

Moving on to a different kind of mistake, and given the orthodoxy that guides this trade, I have erred in not devoting my life to one subject or to one period. Thus all that I have written is subject to modification simply because I do not know everything about everything that I have written about. I have wandered as an historian because I explored many aspects of life before I became an historian, and because I think that it is only rarely that the belated discovery of new documents revolutionizes some part of history.

Here we come in a preliminary way to the heart of the matter about revisionism. *The revisionist is one who sees basic facts in a different way and as interconnected in new relationships.* He is a sister and a brother to those who use old steel to make a zipper, as contrasted with those who add new elements to make a better steel.

I have also mistakenly assumed that everyone engaged in the serious study of human affairs understands that the urge to power is a significant, but nonetheless routine, element of life. Hence I have considered it more important to concentrate on why individuals or groups want power, what happens when they get it and use it for their purposes, and how they respond to changes in order to keep power. It is of course important to study the special case of those who seek power for its own sake; but neither my personal nor historic experience has convinced me that mankind—and hence History—can be understood in those terms.

In a similar way, I have mistakenly assumed that we all know that some psychological orientation informs the work of every historian; but that if psychology is your thing, then you become a psychologist. I am obviously a Gestaltian who does not think that Freud or Jung or Adler wiped the slate clean of Dilthey or James—or even Marx.

I have likewise been mistaken in assuming that my personal dedication to freedom and equality *within a community* is unequivocally documented in my teaching, my writing, and in the way that I live my life. I disagree with those who assert that such a commitment can only be established by perpetual outrage against the faults of other societies. It is easy to construct an academic (even public) career by moralizing about the failures of other countries. It is also a cheap shot—*bush*. There are moments when serious protest promises consequences, and in those instants I have signed my name, written a private letter, walked the streets, or sent my money.

But whether I am writing about American History, or trying as a citizen to change America, I must first understand America. And I confess that in my lifetime—from the Great Depression to Watergate—that task has absorbed most of my intelligence, my guts, and my energy. I do not approve of imperial actions by Russia *or* by Israel, and I do not approve of repression in Brazil *or* in France; but most of all I like them least by and in my own America.

Finally, I am sure that I am mistaken, *within my chosen framework,* in some of my reconstructions, analyses, and interpretations. I take it as given that most of you who look at the world from another perspective think that I am mostly wrong. Neither truth traumatizes my ego. I learned a lifetime ago that I could not sink every shot or make every finesse, read every book in every library, memorize every document in every archive, or answer every question that I asked myself in the first light of dawn to the satisfaction of myself—let alone to the plaudits of everyone else.

Yet, granted such mistakes, and speaking very softly, I confess that I must say these things:

1. I do not think that my mistakes subvert the value of my work;
2. My critics have yet to respond to fundamental issues that I have raised; and
3. I am sure that a number of my reconstructions, analyses, and interpreta-

tions—granted their weaknesses—have informed and challenged your minds. I never entertained the slightest thought of doing more.

Here permit me to be blunt.

1. I have never engaged in an intellectual conspiracy.
2. I have never wilfully distorted a document.
3. I have never invented evidence.
4. I have protected the confidentiality of primary sources in the United States, Russia, England, and Cuba. I will continue to protect them until they choose to enter the public arena with their information. . . .

Here we confront the central questions: how one perceives the evidence, and how one presents one's perceptions. For the primary issue between me as a revisionist and my serious critics involves our different theories of knowledge—our antithetical conceptions of reality. An honest and potentially creative conflict.

I came to History after ten years of sustained involvement in mathematics and the physical sciences. That education and experience inherently included the serious study of such giants as Aristotle, Descartes, Spinoza, Leibniz, Kant, Whitehead, and Russell. Confronted with such conflicting theories of knowledge, I was inexorably drawn into the process of choosing how I would make sense of the world.

Surprising as it may seem, I did not follow Descartes into a universe composed of discrete positivistic and atomistic elements sometimes connected to each other in a mechanistic fashion. Instead, I chose Spinoza. I thought he was far more realistic in positing one organic world in which seemingly separate parts are in reality always internally related to each other; a universe in which an ostensibly positivistic fact is in truth a set of relationships with all other facts and therefore with the whole.

From the moment I encountered him, therefore, I responded to Marx. For, despite his extensive empirical research, which gives him the appearance of being a super-positivist, I recognized him as a fellow Spinozian. Hence I read him then, as I read him now, as a genius in social history and political economy—and not at all as an early computer offering the date for the birth of Utopia.

I remain exhilarated by his capacity for seeing in one piece of evidence a set of relationships that reveal an economic truth, a truth about an idea, a social verity, and a political truth. I also think that there is more psychological insight in his analysis of our alienation from our Humanity under western capitalism than there is in all but a one-foot shelf of contemporary psychohistory.

Spinoza and Marx proceed from the assumption that everything is internally related to everything else. Thus the problem is not whether or how $a$ may be related to $d$ or $p$ or $v$, but instead the question of how $a$ and $d$ and $p$ and $v$ reveal as microcosms the nature of the macrocosm. Or, conversely, how the macrocosm reveals the character of $a$ and $d$ and $p$ and $v$. Reality is not an issue of economics versus ideas, or of politics versus either; it is not even defined by coefficients of correlation between voting records and geographic location, or by a mathematical model that proves that what was done was wrong. Reality instead involves how a political act is also an economic act, of how an economic decision is a political choice, or of how an idea of freedom involves a commitment to a particular economic system. Lukács said it all in three sentences.

> It is not the primacy of economic motives in historical explanation that constitutes the decisive difference between Marxism and bourgeois thought, but the point of view of totality. Whatever the subject of debate, the dialectical method is concerned always with the same problem: knowledge of historical process in its entirety. This means that "ideological" and "economic" problems lose their mutual exclusiveness and merge into one another.

Granted all that, my confidence in the Spinozian-Marxian strategy of intellectual inquiry was severely tested by Fred Harvey Harrington. He pushed the positivistic, interest-group approach to its furthest limits. He could dissect any decision, event, or movement into its constituent parts with a subtle, loving ruthlessness that earned him the nicknames of Mr. Cold, and The Fish Eye. And he understood the techniques of quantification and statistical correlation, though he chose to translate them into the King's English.

After a time, however, the mathematician in me realized that neither he nor anyone else of his persuasion had developed either a scale for weighting the various atomistic factors, or a system of differential equations that could reintegrate the parts into the whole. In the usual course of events, that is to say, discrete atomism, or sophisticated scientism, does nothing more than turn Carl Becker on his head: every historian becomes his own man, and hence there is no dialectical encounter between theories of knowledge. There is only an endless argument about which factor is most important—or endless evasion in the name of multiple causation.

At this point, Hans Gerth took me by the hand. As a brilliant (though neglected) member of the Frankfurt School, he teased and pushed me into a confrontation with the central problem: how does an historian hone the Spinozian-Marxian theory of reality into a manageable intellectual tool? Which is to say: who mediates between our ordinary selves and genius?

Guided by Gerth, I became deeply involved with Hegel, Dilthey, Adorno, Horkheimer, and Lukács. I enjoyed the ensuing dialectical tension: that coming apart at the seams at midnight, and then the stitching it back together in a sentence or two at 3 A.M. Dilthey ultimately taught me the concept of *Weltanschauungen,* the sense of three dialectically interacting world views: a workable version of Spinoza's organic reality, and a realistic limit on relativism.

Foreign relations seemed to offer the most promising arena for the deployment of that intellectual strategy. Indeed, if there is a Spinozian whole for an historian, then it has to involve foreign policy and the periodization of history. My first book was the result of an effort to lay an empirical foundation for developing a set of internal relations that would make it possible to conceptualize the organic sense of reality entertained by American policy-makers (and, by indirection, by the American body politic). I chose relations with Russia because it struck me that such a *Weltanschauung* was apt to reveal itself with particular clarity during a confrontation with a different view of the world.

Out of that effort came my concept of Open Door Imperialism as the *Weltanschauung* of twentieth-century American foreign policy. I began with three atomistic documents: Secretary of State Hay's circular letters of September 6, 1899, and July 3, 1900, and his note to the Germans of October 29, 1900. I next conceptualized those documents as the basic formulation of a general outlook that was amplified and applied to other areas of the world, as in Secretary of State Root's instructions of November 28, 1905, to the American delegation to the Algeciras Conference.

I concluded, at the end of that intellectual voyage, that the Open Door Policy was a vast network of internal relations in the sense meant by Spinoza and Marx—and therefore a *Weltanschauung* in the sense meant by Dilthey. Viewed in that way, it is a conception of reality that integrates economic theory and practice, abstract ideas, past, present and future politics, anticipations of Utopia, messianic idealism, social-psychological imperatives, historical consciousness, and military strategy.

As formulated by the protagonists at the turn of the century, the *Weltanschauung* of the Open Door was an integrated set of assumptions that guided elitist *and* popular thinking (and responses), and that defined bureaucratic perceptions and actions. It then became an ideology (even theology), and ultimately a reification of reality that is finally being subverted by a new reality.

It is so easy to illustrate this with the likes of Hay, Conant, Root, Wilson, Culbertson, Hughes, Hull, and Stimson that the challenge lies with those like Hoover and Acheson. Hoover is fascinating because of his instinct to transcend the orthodoxy. Acheson is particularly revealing because he crystallized the discussion of the 1890s in his 1944 testimony before the congressional committee on postwar planning and policy.

To avoid "a very bad time," Acheson warned, meaning "the most far-reaching consequences upon our economic and social system," "you must look to foreign markets." True, "you could probably fix it so that everything produced here would be consumed here, but that would completely change our Constitution, our relations to property, to human liberty, our very conceptions of law. And nobody contemplates that. Therefore, you find you must look to other markets and those markets are abroad. . . ."

The issue here is not economic motives, and certainly not the kind of economic determinism that Marx would have scorned as absurdly simplistic. The first point is the network of internal relationships in Acheson's mind between foreign markets and everything that he treasures. Or, conversely, the inability to imagine freedom and welfare in a non-capitalistic framework. Secondly, we have a conception of markets that involves American predominance. That is not trade in the classic sense of give-and-take. It is the imperial dynamic of we need, you give.

Having crystallized, Acheson began to reify. As in National Security Council Document No. 68: freedom and welfare can be secured only through "the virtual abandonment by the United States of trying to distinguish between national and global security." And then the ultimate distillation: "We are willing to help people who believe the way we do, to continue to live the way they want to live." Acheson was not present at the creation of a policy—he merely presided over the reification of a *Weltanschauung*.

All of which brings me back to Spinoza. Acheson provides us with a fact that contains the whole, and a whole that contains every fact. So if I condense the evidence about Russian policy on reparations at Potsdam into one introductory paragraph that summarizes Moscow's comments of earlier years, and at the same time provides a preview of the Kremlin's final posture, I have not distorted history. I have done my best to encapsulate the history that I then explore: that is the definition of an essay.

Just as when I seem redundant in *The Roots of the Modern American Empire,* it is because I am trying to explore and reveal all the internal relationships that give meaning to a group of positivistic facts.

Ah, so.

I make my final confession. I have fallen between upteen stools. So be it. All I can do is to echo Wright Morris: *What A Way To Go!*

But, in a final effort to explicate the text, let me offer you a proposition taken from William Carlos Williams' essay on Aaron Burr.

> Near the end of his life a lady said to him: "Colonel, I wonder if you were ever the gay Lothario they say you were." The old man turned his eyes, their lustre still undiminished, toward the lady—and lifting his trembling finger said in his quiet, impressive whisper: "They say, they say, they say. Ah, my child, how long are you going to continue to use those dreadful words? Those two little words have done more harm than all others. Never use them, my dear, never use them."

That is why, warts and all, I remain, faithfully yours, an intransigent revisionist.

*Bibliographical Note*

This has been an excursion rather than a monograph. Hence my sources are designed to take you along the same great circle route. Or, in other words, a Bowditch for this voyage.

A. G. A. Balz: *Idea and Essence in the Philosophy of Hobbes and Spinoza.*

K. E. Boulding: *The Image, Knowledge in Life and Society.*

Wilhelm Dilthey: *The Essence of Philosophy.* Translated into English by S. A. Emery and W. T. Emery.

H. F. Hallett: *Benedict De Spinoza: The Elements of His Philosophy.*

H. A. Hodges: *The Philosophy of Wilhelm Dilthey.*

M. Jay: *The Dialectical Imagination: A History of the Frankfurt School and the Institute of Social Research, 1932–1950.*

W. Kluback and M. Weinbarum: *Dilthey's Philosophy of Existence: Introduction to Weltanschauungslehre.*

G. Lukács: *History and Class Consciousness.*

K. Müller-Vollmer: *Towards a Phenomenological Theory of Literature: A Study of Wilhelm Dilthey's* Poetik.

B. Ollman: *Alienation: Marx's Conception of Man in Capitalist Society.*

G. H. R. Parkinson: *Logic and Reality in Leibniz's Metaphysics.*

L. Roth: *Spinoza;* and *Spinoza, Descartes, and Maimonides.*

B. Russell: *A Critical Exposition of the Philosophy of Leibniz.*

---

## FURTHER READING

Thomas A. Bailey, "Confessions of a Diplomatic Historian," *Society for Historians of American Foreign Relations Newsletter,* 6 (1975), 2–11

Samuel Flagg Bemis, "American Foreign Policy and the Blessings of Liberty," *American Historical Review,* 67 (1962), 291–305

Barton J. Bernstein, ed., *Towards a New Past* (1968)

Warren I. Cohen, *The Revisionists* (1967)

Jerald A. Combs, *American Diplomatic History: Two Centuries of Changing Interpretations* (1982)

Marcus Cunliffe and Robin Winks, eds., *Pastmasters: Some Essays on American Historians* (1969)

Alexander DeConde, ed., *Encyclopedia of American Foreign Policy,* 3 vols. (1978)

Frances FitzGerald, *America Revised: History Schoolbooks in the Twentieth Century* (1979)

Gerald K. Haines and J. Samuel Walker, eds., *American Foreign Relations: A Historiographical Review* (1981)

Simon G. Hanson, "Dexter Perkins on the Caribbean," *Inter-American Economic Affairs,* 1 (1948), 46–54

John Higham, "The Cult of the 'American Consensus': Homogenizing Our History," *Commentary,* 27 (1959), 93–100

———, *History* (1965)

Walter LaFeber, " 'Ah, If We Had Studied It More Carefully': The Fortunes of American Diplomatic History," *Prologue,* 11 (1979), 121–131

Lester Langley, "The Diplomatic Historians: Bailey and Bemis," *History Teacher,* 6 (1972), 51–70

Christopher Lasch, "William Appleman Williams on American History," *Marxist Perspectives,* 1 (1978), 118–126

Richard W. Leopold, "The History of United States Foreign Policy," in Charles F. Delzell, ed., *The Future of History* (1976)

Francis L. Loewenheim, ed., *The Historian and the Diplomat* (1967)

Charles S. Maier, "Marking Time: The Historiography of International Relations," in Michael Kammen, ed., *The Past Before Us* (1980)

Thomas J. McCormick, "Drift or Mastery?" *Reviews in American History,* 10 (1982), 318–330

———, "The State of American Diplomatic History," in Herbert J. Bass, ed., *The State of American History* (1970)

Richard A. Melanson, "The Social and Political Thought of William Appleman Williams," *Western Political Quarterly,* 31 (1978), 392–409

Dexter Perkins, "American Foreign Policy and Its Critics," in Alfred H. Kelley, ed., *American Foreign Policy and American Democracy* (1954)

"Symposium: Responses to Charles S. Maier, 'Marking Time,' " *Diplomatic History,* 5 (1981), 353–371

J. A. Thompson, "William Appleman Williams and the 'American Empire,'" *Journal of American Studies,* 7 (1973), 91–104
Robert W. Tucker, *The Radical Left and American Foreign Policy* (1971)
William A. Williams, *The Great Evasion* (1968)
————, *History as a Way of Learning* (1973)

# The Origins of American Foreign Policy

# 2

*Americans were once proud members of the British Empire. For over 150
years that membership brought good profit at low cost and protection against
the French in North America. But in the 1760s, after victory in the French
and Indian War, the mother country began to impose new taxes and regulations that shattered the relationship. In 1776 the American colonials chose
independence through revolution. They selected that dangerous course not
only because of perceived British perfidy, but also because of their own
New World sense of themselves as different from—indeed, superior to—
the Old World of monarchy, relentless international rivalry, and corrupted
institutions.*

*Geographical isolation from Europe helped spawn such notions of excep-
tionalism, as did the American doctrine of mission and God-favored destiny
the Puritans had etched on American memory. Colonials from New England
to Georgia had also become accustomed to making their own decisions, governing themselves at the local level in what one historian has tagged "island
communities," and expanding their landholdings and commerce without
much interference from the British Crown and Parliament. Yet when the
founding fathers declared independence and then worked to gain and preserve it in a doubting and hostile world, they felt compelled to appeal for
help from Europe, particularly France. They became conspicuously uneasy
about calling upon the decadent Old World to save their fresh New World
experiment, because the linkage so violated what some scholars have labeled
American "isolationism." At the same time, however, American leaders
saw in their new treaties and nationhood the opportunity to reform traditional world politics to ensure the country's safety and prosperity.*

*As children of empire, early national leaders naturally dreamed of a new and ever-expanding American empire. They recognized the obstacles to expansion: Native Americans, European powers, and their own sectional and political differences. In fact, many of the nation's founders thought that internal squabbling and the absence of a strong central government threatened not just expansionism but independence itself. A persuasive argument for the Constitution, ratified in 1789, was that it would permit the new United States to devise a coherent and respected foreign policy.*

*Historians have debated the relative importance of isolationism, expansionism, imperialism, and idealism as characteristics of early American foreign policy. And they have wondered to what extent American leaders understood and exercised power in eighteenth-century world affairs. But they have agreed that Americans ardently claimed that their upstart republic held a unique international position that would transform the world community. Why Americans came to think so is explained by the documents and essays in this chapter.*

## DOCUMENTS

John Winthrop, the first governor of Massachusetts Bay, defined the Puritan mission in a lay sermon of June 1630, aboard ship off the New England coast. The second document, from John Adams' diary of late 1775, recounts this founding father's case for alliance with France, but cautions against entanglement in Europe's wars. Thomas Paine, who had moved from England to Philadelphia just two years before independence was declared, invigorated the revolutionary spirit with his popular 1776 tract *Common Sense,* wherein he demanded severance from the British Empire. The Declaration of Independence of July 4, 1776, outlined American grievances against the mother country. The two treaties with France provided not only for alliance, but also for principles that would govern foreign commerce. The seventh document is a celebratory statement by Ezra Stiles, president of Yale College. Delivered as a Connecticut election sermon in May 1783, the message reveals the American penchant for seeing the new United States as the best hope for mankind. America's birth certificate, in preliminary form, was signed by British and American emissaries on November 30, 1782. The final Treaty of Peace was signed in Paris on September 3, 1783, and ratifications were exchanged on May 12, 1784. The last document presents the parts of the United States Constitution of 1789 that cover foreign policy.

# John Winthrop's City Upon a Hill, 1630

Now the onely way to avoyde this shipwracke and to provide for our posterity is to followe the Counsell of Micah, to doe Justly, to love mercy, to walke humbly with our God, for this end, wee must be knitt together in this worke as one man, wee must entertaine each other in brotherly Affeccion, wee must be willing to abridge our selves of our superfluities, for the supply of others necessities, wee must uphold a familiar Commerce together in all meekenes, gentlenes, patience and liberallity, wee must delight in eache other, make others Condicions our owne rejoyce together, mourne together, labour, and suffer together, allwayes haveing before our eyes our Commission and Community in the worke, our Community as members of the same body, soe shall wee keepe the unitie of the spirit in the bond of peace, the Lord will be our God and delight to dwell among us, as his owne people and will commaund a blessing upon us in all our wayes, soe that wee shall see much more of his wisdome power goodnes and truthe then formerly wee have beene acquainted with, wee shall finde that the God of Israell is among us, when tenn of us shall be able to resist a thousand of our enemies, when hee shall make us a prayse and glory, that men shall say of succeeding plantacions: the lord make it like that of New England: for wee must Consider that wee shall be as a Citty upon a Hill, the eies of all people are uppon us; soe that if wee shall deale falsely with our god in this worke wee have undertaken and soe cause him to withdrawe his present help from us, wee shall be made a story and a by-word through the world, wee shall open the mouthes of enemies to speake evill of the wayes of god and all pro-fessours for Gods sake; wee shall shame the faces of many of gods worthy servants, and cause theire prayers to be turned into Cursses upon us till wee be consumed out of the good land whether wee are going: And to shutt upp this discourse with that exhortacion of Moses that faithfull servant of the Lord in his last farewell to Israell Deut. 30. Beloved there is now sett before us life, and good, deathe and evill in that wee are Commaunded this day to love the Lord our God, and to love one another to walke in his wayes and to keepe his Commaundements and his Ordinance, and his lawes, and the Articles of our Covenant with him that wee may live and be multiplyed, and that the Lord our God may blesse us in the land whether wee goe to possesse it: But if our heartes shall turne away soe that wee will not obey, but shall be seduced and worshipp other Gods our pleasures, and proffitts, and serve them, it is propounded unto us this day, wee shall surely perishe out of the good Land whether wee passe over this vast Sea to possesse it;

> Therefore lett us choose life,
> that wee, and our Seede,
> may live; by obeyeing his
> voyce, and cleaveing to him,
> for hee is our life, and
> our prosperity.

# John Adams on Connection with France, 1775

Some Gentlemen doubted of the Sentiments of France, thought She would frown upon Us as Rebells and be afraid to countenance the Example. I replied to these Gentlemen, that I apprehended they had not attended to the relative Situation of France and England. That it was the unquestionable Interest of France that the British continental Colonies should be independent. That Britain by the Conquest of Canada and their naval Tryumphs during the last War, and by her vast Possessions in America and the East Indies, was exalted to a height of Power and Preeminence that France must envy and could not endure. But there was much more than pride and Jealousy in the Case. Her Rank, her Consideration in Europe, and even her Safety and Independence was at stake. The Navy of Great Britain was now Mistress of the Seas all over the Globe. The Navy of France almost annihilated. Its Inferiority was so great and obvious, that all the Dominions of France in the West Indies and in the East Indies lay at the Mercy of Great Britain, and must remain so as long as North America belonged to Great Britain, and afforded them so many harbours abounding with Naval Stores and Resources of all kinds and so many Men and Seamen ready to assist them and Man their Ships. That Interest could not lie, that the Interest of France was so obvious, and her Motives so cogent, that nothing but a judicial Infatuation of her Councils could restrain her from embracing Us. That our Negotiations with France ought however, to be conducted with great caution and with all the foresight We could possibly obtain. That We ought not to enter into any Alliance with her, which should entangle Us in any future Wars in Europe, that We ought to lay it down as a first principle and a Maxim never to be forgotten, to maintain an entire Neutrality in all future European Wars. That it never could be our Interest to unite with France, in the destruction of England, or in any measures to break her Spirit or reduce her to a situation in which she could not support her Independence. On the other hand it could never be our Duty to unite with Britain in too great a humiliation of France. That our real if not our nominal Independence would consist in our Neutrality. If We united with either Nation, in any future War, We must become too subordinate and dependent on that nation, and should be involved in all European Wars as We had been hitherto. That foreign Powers would find means to corrupt our People to influence our Councils, and in fine We should be little better than Puppetts danced on the Wires of the Cabinetts of Europe. We should be the Sport of European Intrigues and Politicks. That therefore in preparing Treaties to be proposed to foreign Powers and in the Instructions to be given to our Ministers, We ought to confine ourselves strictly to a Treaty of Commerce. That such a Treaty would be an ample Compensation to France, for all the Aid We should want from her. The Opening of American Trade, to her would be a vast resource for her Commerce and Naval Power, and a great Assistance to her in protecting her East and West India Possessions as well as her Fisheries: but that the bare dismemberment of the British Empire, would be to her an incalculable Security and Benefit, worth more than all the Exertions We should require of her even if it should draw her into another Eight or ten Years War.

# Thomas Paine's *Common Sense*, 1776

I have heard it asserted by some, that as America has flourished under her former connection with Great Britain, the same connection is necessary towards her future happiness, and will always have the same effect. Nothing can be more fallacious than this kind of argument. We may as well assert that because a child has thrived upon milk, that it is never to have meat, or that the first twenty years of our lives is to become a precedent for the next twenty. But even this is admitting more than is true; for I answer roundly, that America would have flourished as much, and probably much more, had no European power taken any notice of her. The commerce by which she hath enriched herself are the necessaries of life, and will always have a market while eating is the custom of Europe.

But she has protected us, say some. That she hath engrossed us is true, and defended the continent at our expense as well as her own, is admitted; and she would have defended Turkey from the same motive, *viz.* for the sake of trade and dominion.

Alas! we have been long led away by ancient prejudices and made large sacrifices to superstition. We have boasted the protection of Great Britain, without considering, that her motive was *interest* not *attachment;* and that she did not protect us from *our enemies on our account;* but from *her enemies* on *her own account,* from those who had no quarrel with us on any *other account,* and who will always be our enemies on the *same account.* Let Britain waive her pretensions to the continent, or the continent throw off the dependance, and we should be at peace with France and Spain, were they at war with Britain. The miseries of Hanover's last war ought to warn us against connections. . . .

But Britain is the parent country, say some. Then the more shame upon her conduct. Even brutes do not devour their young, nor savages make war upon their families; wherefore, the assertion, if true, turns to her reproach; but it happens not to be true, or only partly so, and the phrase *parent* or *mother country* hath been jesuitically adopted by the king and his parasites, with a low papistical design of gaining an unfair bias on the credulous weakness of our minds. Europe, and not England, is the parent country of America. This new world hath been the asylum for the persecuted lovers of civil and religious liberty from *every part* of Europe. Hither have they fled, not from the tender embraces of the mother, but from the cruelty of the monster; and it is so far true of England, that the same tyranny which drove the first emigrants from home, pursues their descendants still.

In this extensive quarter of the globe, we forget the narrow limits of three hundred and sixty miles (the extent of England) and carry our friendship on a larger scale; we claim brotherhood with every European Christian, and triumph in the generosity of the sentiment. . . .

Much hath been said of the united strength of Britain and the colonies, that in conjunction they might bid defiance to the world. But this is mere presumption; the fate of war is uncertain, neither do the expressions mean any thing; for this continent would never suffer itself to be drained of inhabitants, to support the British arms in either Asia, Africa or Europe.

Besides, what have we to do with setting the world at defiance? Our plan is commerce, and that, well attended to, will secure us the peace and friendship of all Europe; because it is the interest of all Europe to have America a free port. Her trade will always be a protection, and her barrenness of gold and silver secure her from invaders. . . .

Europe is too thickly planted with kingdoms to be long at peace, and whenever a war breaks out between England and any foreign power, the trade of America goes to ruin, *because of her connection with Britain.* The next war may not turn out like the last, and should it not, the advocates for reconciliation now will be wishing for separation then, because neutrality in that case would be a safer convoy than a man of war. Every thing that is right or reasonable pleads for separation. The blood of the slain, the weeping voice of nature cries, 'TIS TIME TO PART. Even the distance at which the Almighty hath placed England and America is a strong and natural proof that the authority of the one over the other, was never the design of heaven. . . .

Small islands not capable of protecting themselves are the proper objects for government to take under their care; but there is something absurd, in supposing a Continent to be perpetually governed by an island. In no instance hath nature made the satellite larger than its primary planet; and as England and America, with respect to each other, reverse the common order of nature, it is evident that they belong to different systems. England to Europe: America to itself. . . .

O! ye that love mankind! Ye that dare oppose not only the tyranny but the tyrant, stand forth! Every spot of the old world is overrun with oppression. Freedom hath been hunted round the globe. Asia and Africa have long expelled her. Europe regards her like a stranger, and England hath given her warning to depart. O! receive the fugitive, and prepare in time an asylum for mankind. . . .

In almost every article of defence we abound. Hemp flourishes even to rankness, so that we need not want cordage. Our iron is superior to that of other countries. Our small arms equal to any in the world. Cannon we can cast at pleasure. Saltpeter and gunpowder we are every day producing. Our knowledge is hourly improving. Resolution is our inherent character, and courage has never yet forsaken us. Wherefore, what is it that we want? Why is it that we hesitate? From Britain we can expect nothing but ruin. If she is once admitted to the government of America again, this continent will not be worth living in. Jealousies will be always arising; insurrections will be constantly happening; and who will go forth to quell them? Who will venture his life to reduce his own countrymen to a foreign obedience? The difference between Pennsylvania and Connecticut, respecting some unlocated lands, shows the insignificance of a British government, and fully proves that nothing but continental authority can regulate continental matters. . . .

I shall conclude these remarks, with the following timely and well-intended hints. We ought to reflect, that there are three different ways by which an independency may hereafter be effected; and that *one* of those *three,* will, one day or other, be the fate of America, viz. By the legal voice of the people in Congress; by a military power; or by a mob: It may not always happen that our soldiers are citizens, and the multitude a body of reasonable men; virtue, as I have already remarked, is not hereditary, neither is it perpetual. Should an independency be brought about by the first of those means, we have every opportunity and every encouragement before us, to form the noblest, purest constitution on the face of the earth. We have it in our power to begin the world over again. A situation, similar to the present, hath not happened since the days of Noah until now. The birthday of a new world is at hand, and a race of men, perhaps as numerous as all Europe contains, are to receive their portion of freedom from the events of a few months. The reflection is awful, and in this point of view, how trifling, how ridiculous, do the little paltry cavilings of a few weak or interested men appear, when weighed against the business of a world. . . .

## The Declaration of Independence, 1776

When, in the course of human events, it becomes necessary for one people to dissolve the political bonds which have connected them with another, and to assume, among the powers of the earth, the separate and equal station to which the laws of nature and of nature's God entitle them, a decent respect to the opinions of mankind requires that they should declare the causes which impel them to the separation.

We hold these truths to be self-evident: That all men are created equal; that they are endowed by their Creator with certain unalienable rights; that among these are life, liberty, and the pursuit of happiness; that, to secure these rights, governments are instituted among men, deriving their just powers from the consent of the governed; that whenever any form of government becomes destructive of these ends, it is the right of the people to alter or to abolish it, and to institute new government, laying its foundation on such principles, and organizing its powers in such form, as to them shall seem most likely to effect their safety and happiness. Prudence, indeed, will dictate that governments long established should not be changed for light and transient causes; and accordingly all experience hath shown that mankind are more disposed to suffer, while evils are sufferable, than to right themselves by abolishing the forms to which they are accustomed. But when a long train of abuses and usurpations, pursuing invariably the same object, evinces a design to reduce them under absolute despotism, it is their right, it is their duty, to throw off such government, and to provide new guards for their future security. Such has been the patient sufferance of these colonies; and such is now the necessity which constrains them to alter their former systems of government. The history of the present King of Great Britain is a history of repeated injuries and usurpations, all having in direct object the establishment of an absolute tyranny over these states. To prove this, let facts be submitted to a candid world.

He has refused his assent to laws, the most wholesome and necessary for the public good.

He has forbidden his governors to pass laws of immediate and pressing importance, unless suspended in their operation till his assent should be obtained; and, when so suspended, he has utterly neglected to attend to them.

He has refused to pass other laws for the accommodation of large districts of people, unless those people would relinquish the right of representation in the legislature, a right inestimable to them, and formidable to tyrants only.

He has called together legislative bodies at places unusual, uncomfortable, and distant from the depository of their public records, for the sole purpose of fatiguing them into compliance with his measures.

He has dissolved representative houses repeatedly, for opposing, with manly firmness, his invasions on the rights of people.

He has refused for a long time, after such dissolutions, to cause others to be elected; whereby the legislative powers, incapable of annihilation, have returned to the people at large for their exercise; the state remaining, in the mean time, exposed to all the dangers of invasions from without and con-vulsions within.

He has endeavored to prevent the population of these states; for that pur-pose obstructing the laws for naturalization of foreigners; refusing to pass others to encourage their migration hither, and raising the conditions of new appropriations of lands.

He has obstructed the administration of justice, by refusing his assent to laws for establishing judiciary powers.

He has made judges dependent on his will alone, for the tenure of their offices, and the amount and payment of their salaries.

He has erected a multitude of new offices, and sent hither swarms of officers to harass our people and eat out their substance.

He has kept among us, in times of peace, standing armies, without the consent of our legislatures.

He has affected to render the military independent of, and superior to, the civil power.

He has combined with others to subject us to a jurisdiction foreign to our constitution, and unacknowledged by our laws, giving his assent to their acts of pretended legislation:

For quartering large bodies of armed troops among us;

For protecting them, by a mock trial, from punishment for any murders which they should commit on the inhabitants of these states;

For cutting off our trade with all parts of the world;

For imposing taxes on us without our consent;

For depriving us, in many cases, of the benefits of trial by jury;

For transporting us beyond seas, to be tried for pretended offenses;

For abolishing the free system of English laws in a neighboring province, establishing therein an arbitrary government, and enlarging its boundaries, so as to render it at once an example and fit instrument for introducing the same absolute rule into these colonies;

For taking away our charters, abolishing our most valuable laws, and altering fundamentally the forms of our governments;

For suspending our own legislatures, and declaring themselves invested with power to legislate for us in all cases whatsoever.

He has abdicated government here, by declaring us out of his protection and waging war against us.

He has plundered our seas, ravaged our coasts, burned our towns, and destroyed the lives of our people.

He is at this time transporting large armies of foreign mercenaries to complete the works of death, desolation, and tyranny already begun with circumstances of cruelty and perfidy scarcely paralleled in the most barbarous ages, and totally unworthy the head of a civilized nation.

He has constrained our fellow-citizens, taken captive on the high seas, to bear arms against their country, to become the executioners of their friends and brethren, or to fall themselves by their hands.

He has excited domestic insurrection among us, and has endeavored to bring on the inhabitants of our frontiers the merciless Indian savages, whose known rule of warfare is an undistinguished destruction of all ages, sexes, and conditions.

In every stage of these oppressions we have petitioned for redress in the most humble terms; our repeated petitions have been answered only by repeated injury. A prince, whose character is thus marked by every act which may define a tyrant, is unfit to be the ruler of a free people.

Nor have we been wanting in our attentions to our British brethren. We have warned them, from time to time, of attempts by their legislature to extend an unwarrantable jurisdiction over us. We have reminded them of the circumstances of our emigration and settlement here. We have appealed to their native justice and magnanimity; and we have conjured them, by the ties of our common kindred, to disavow these usurpations, which would inevitably interrupt our connections and correspondence. They, too, have been deaf to the voice of justice and of consanguinity. We must, therefore, acquiesce in the necessity which denounces our separation, and hold them, as we hold the rest of mankind, enemies in war, in peace friends.

We, therefore, the representatives of the United States of America, in General Congress assembled, appealing to the Supreme Judge of the world for the rectitude of our intentions, do, in the name and by the authority of the good people of these colonies, solemnly publish and declare, that these United Colonies are, and of right ought to be, FREE AND INDEPENDENT STATES; that they are absolved from all allegiance to the British crown, and that all political connection between them and the state of Great Britain is, and ought to be, totally dissolved; and that, as free and independent states, they have full power to levy war, conclude peace, contract alliances, establish commerce, and do all other acts and things which independent states may of right do. And for the support of this declaration, with a firm reliance on the protection of Divine Providence, we mutually pledge to each other our lives, our fortunes, and our sacred honor.

## Treaty of Amity and Commerce with France, 1778

**Article 2.** The most Christian King, and the United States engage mutually not to grant any particular Favour to other Nations in respect of Commerce and Navigation, which shall not immediately become common to the other Party, who shall enjoy the same Favour, freely, if the Concession was freely made, or on allowing the same Compensation, if the Consession was Conditional. . . .

**Article 19.** It shall be lawful for the Ships of War of either Party & Privateers freely to carry whithersoever they please the Ships and Goods taken from their Enemies, without being obliged to pay any Duty to the Officers of the Admiralty or any other Judges; nor shall such Prizes be arrested or seized, when they come to and enter the Ports of either Party; nor shall the Searchers or other Officers of those Places search the same or make examination concerning the Lawfulness of such Prizes, but they may hoist Sail at any time and depart and carry their Prizes to the Places express'd in their Commissions, which the Commanders of such Ships of War shall be obliged to shew: On the contrary no Shelter or Refuge shall be given in their Ports to such as shall have made Prize of the Subjects, People or Property of either of the Parties; but if such shall come in, being forced by Stress of Weather or the Danger of the Sea, all proper means shall be vigorously used that they go out and retire from thence as soon as possible. . . .

**Article 25.** . . . And it is hereby stipulated that free Ships shall also give a freedom to Goods, and that every thing shall be deemed to be free and exempt, which shall be found on board the Ships belonging to the Subjects of either of the Confederates, although the whole lading or any Part thereof should appertain to the Enemies of either, contraband Goods being always excepted. It is also agreed in like manner that the same Liberty be extended to Persons, who are on board a free Ship, with this Effect, that although they be Enemies to both or either Party, they are not to be taken out of that free Ship, unless they are Soldiers and in actual Service of the Enemies.

**Article 26.** This Liberty of Navigation and Commerce shall extend to all kinds of Merchandizes, excepting those only which are distinguished by the name of contraband; And under this Name of Contraband or prohibited Goods shall be comprehended, Arms, great Guns, Bombs with the fuzes, and other things belonging to them, Cannon Ball, Gun powder, Match, Pikes, Swords, Lances, Spears, halberds, Mortars, Petards, Granades Salt Petre, Muskets, Musket Ball, Bucklers, Helmets, breast Plates, Coats of Mail and the like kinds of Arms proper for arming Soldiers, Musket rests, belts, Horses with their Furniture, and all other Warlike Instruments whatever. These Merchandizes which follow shall not be reckoned among Contraband or prohibited Goods, that is to say, all sorts of Cloths, and all other Manufacturers woven of any wool, Flax, Silk, Cotton or any other Materials whatever; all kinds of wearing Apparel together with the Species, whereof they are used to be made; gold & Silver as well coined as uncoin'd, Tin, Iron, Latten, Copper, Brass Coals, as also Wheat and Barley and any other kind of Corn and pulse; Tobacco and likewise all manner of Spices; salted and smoked Flesh, salted Fish, Cheese and Butter, Beer, Oils, Wines, Sugars and all sorts of Salts; & in general all Provisions, which serve for the nourishment of Mankind and the sustenence of Life; furthermore all kinds of Cotton, hemp, Flax, Tar, Pitch, Ropes, Cables, Sails, Sail Cloths, Anchors and any Parts of Anchors; also Ships Masts, Planks, Boards and Beams of what Trees soever; and all other Things proper either for building or repairing Ships, and all other Goods whatever, which have not been worked into the form of any Instrument or thing prepared for War by Land or by Sea, shall not be reputed Contraband, much less such as have been already wrought and made up for any other Use; all which shall be wholly reckoned among free Goods: as likewise all other Merchandizes and things, which are not comprehended and particularly mentioned in the foregoing enumeration of contraband Goods: so that they may be transported and carried in the freest manner by the Subjects of both Confederates even to Places belonging to an Enemy such Towns or Places being only excepted as are at that time beseiged, blocked up or invested. . . .

## Treaty of Alliance with France, 1778

**Article 1.** If War should break out betwan france and Great Britain, during the continuence of the present War betwan the United States and England, his Majesty and the said united States, shall make it a common cause, and aid each other mutually with their good Offices, their Counsels, and their forces, according to the exigence of Conjunctures as becomes good & faithful Allies.

**Article 2.** The essential and direct End of the present defensive alliance is to maintain effectually the liberty, Sovereignty, and independance absolute and unlimited of the said united States, as well in Matters of Gouvernement as of commerce. . . .

**Article 5.** If the united States should think fit to attempt the Reduction of the British Power remaining in the Northern Parts of America, or the Islands of Bermudas, those Contries or Islands in case of Success, shall be confederated with or dependant upon the said united States.

**Article 6.** The Most Christian King renounces for ever the possession of the Islands of Bermudas as well as of any part of the continent of North america which before the treaty of Paris in 1763. or in virtue of that Treaty, were acknowledged to belong to the Crown of Great Britain, or to the united States heretofore called British Colonies, or which are at this Time or have lately been under the Power of The King and Crown of Great Britain.

**Article 7.** If his Most Christian Majesty shall think proper to attack any of the Islands situated in the Gulph of Mexico, or near that Gulph, which are at present under the power of Great Britain, all the said Isles, in case of success, shall appertain to the Crown of france.

**Article 8.** Neither of the two Parties shall conclude either Truce or Peace with Great Britain, without the formal consent of the other first obtain'd; and they mutually engage not to lay down their arms, until the Independence of the united states shall have been formally or tacitly assured by the Treaty or Treaties that shall terminate the War. . . .

**Article 11.** The two Parties guarantee mutually from the present time and forever, against all other powers, to wit, the united states to his most Christian Majesty the present Possessions of the Crown of france in America as well as those which it may acquire by the future Treaty of peace: and his most Christian Majesty guarantees on his part to the united states, their liberty, Sovereignty, and Independence absolute, and unlimited, as well in Matters of Government as commerce and also thair Possessions, and the additions or conquests that their Confédération may obtain during the war, from any of the Dominions now or heretofore possessed by Great Britain in North America, conformable to the 5th & 6th articles above written, the whole as their Possessions shall be fixed and assured to the said States at the moment of the cessation of their present War with England. . . .

# Ezra Stiles' "The United States Elevated to Glory and Honour," 1783

Already does the new constellation of the United States begin to realize this glory. It has already risen to an acknowledged sovereignty among the republicks and kingdoms of the world. And we have reason to hope, and I believe to expect, that God has still greater blessings in store for this vine which his own right hand hath planted, to make us "high among the nations in praise, and in name, and in honour." The reasons are very numerous, weighty, and conclusive.

In our civil constitutions, those impediments are removed which obstruct the progress of society towards perfection: Such, for instance, as respect the tenure of estates, and arbitrary government. The vassalage of dependent tenures, the tokens of ancient conquests by Goths and Tartars, still remain all over Asia and Europe. In this respect, as well as others, the world begins to open its eyes. One grand experiment in particular has lately been made. The present Empress of Russia, by granting lands in freehold in her vast wilderness of Volkouskile, together with religious liberty, has allured and already draughted from Poland and Germany a colonization of six hundred thousand souls in six years only, from 1762 to 1768.

Liberty, civil and religious, has sweet and attractive charms. The enjoyment of this, with property, has filled the English settlers in America with a most amazing spirit, which has operated, and still will operate, with great energy. Never before has the experiment been so effectually tried, of every man's reaping the fruits of his labour and feeling his share in the aggregate system of power. The ancient republicks did not stand on the people at large; and therefore no example or precedent can be taken from them. Even men of arbitrary principles will be obliged, if they would figure in these states, to assume the patriot so long that they will at length become charmed with the sweets of liberty.

Our degree of population is such as to give us reason to expect that this will become a great people. It is probable that within a century from our independence the sun will shine on fifty million of inhabitants in the United States. This will be a great, a very great nation, nearly equal to half Europe. Already has our colonization extended down the Ohio and to Koskaseah on the Mississippi. And if the present ratio of increase should be rather diminished in some of the elder settlements, yet an accelerated multiplication will attend our general propagation and overspread the whole territory westward for ages. So that before the Millennium, the English settlements in America may become more numerous millions than that greatest dominion on earth, the Chinese empire. Should this prove a future fact, how applicable would be the text, when the Lord shall have made his American Israel "high above all nations which he hath made," in numbers, "and in praise, and in name, and in honour!"

I am sensible some will consider these as visionary Utopian ideas. And so they would have judged had they lived in the apostolick age and been told that by the time of Constantine the empire would have become christian. As visionary that the twenty thousand souls which first settled New-England should be multiplied to near a million in a century and a half. As visionary that the Ottoman empire must fall by the Russian. As visionary to the Catholicks is the certain downfall of the Pontificate. As Utopian would it have been to the loyalists, at the battle of Lexington, that in less than eight years the independence and sovereignty of the United States should be acknowledged by four European sovereignties, one of which should be Britain herself. How wonderful the revolutions, the events of Providence! We live in an Age of Wonders. We have lived an age in a few years. We have seen more wonders accomplished in eight years than are usually unfolded in a century. . . .

This great American revolution, this recent political phenomenon of a new sovereignty arising among the sovereign powers of the earth, will be attended to and contemplated by all nations. Navigation will carry the American flag around the globe itself and display the Thirteen Stripes and New Constellation at Bengal and Canton on the Indus and Ganges, on the Whang-ho and the Yang-tse-kiang; and with commerce will import the wisdom and literature of the east. That prophecy of Daniel is now literally fulfilling—there shall be an universal travelling "too and fro, and knowledge shall be increased." This knowledge will be brought home and treasured up in America: and being here digested and carried to the highest perfection, may reblaze back from America to Europe, Asia and Africa, and illumine the world with TRUTH and LIBERTY. . . .

Little would Civilians have thought ages ago that the world should ever look to America for models of government and polity. Little did they think of finding this most perfect polity among the poor outcasts, the contemptible people of New-England, and particularly in the long despised civil polity of Connecticut; a polity conceived by the sagacity and wisdom of a Winthrop, a Wyllys, a Ludlow, Haynes, Hopkins, Hooker, and the other first settlers of Hartford, in 1636. And while Europe and Asia may hereafter learn that the most liberal principles of law and civil polity are to be found on this side of the Atlantick, they may also find the true religion here depurated from the rust and corruption of ages, and learn from us to reform and restore the church to its primitive purity. It will be long before the ecclesiastical pride of the splendid European hierarchies can submit to learn wisdom from those whom they have been inured to look upon with sovereign contempt. But candid and liberal disquisition will sooner or later have a great effect. Removed from the embarrassments of corrupt systems, and the dignities and blinding opulence connected with them, the unfettered mind can think with a noble enlargement, and with an unbounded freedom go wherever the light of truth directs. Here will be no bloody tribunals, no cardinals inquisitors-general, to bend the human mind, forcibly to control the understanding, and put out the light of reason, the candle of the Lord, in man; to force an innocent Galileo to renounce truths demonstrable as the light of day. Religion may here receive its last, most liberal, and impartial examination. Religious liberty is peculiarly friendly to fair and generous disquisition. Here deism will have its full chance; nor need libertines more to complain of being overcome by any weapons but the gentle, the powerful ones of argument and truth. Revelation will be found to stand the test to the ten thousandth examination.

There are three coetaneous events to take place whose fruition is certain from prophecy, the annihilation of the Pontificate, the reassembling of the Jews, and the fulness of the Gentiles. That liberal and candid disquisition of Christianity, which will most assuredly take place in America, will prepare Europe for the first event, with which the other will be connected, when especially on the return of the twelve tribes to the Holy Land, there will burst forth a degree of evidence hitherto unperceived and of efficacy to convert a world. More than three quarters of mankind yet remain heathen. Heaven put a stop to the propagation of Christianity when the church became corrupted with the adoration of numerous deities and images, because this would have been only exchanging an old for a new idolatry. Nor is Christendom now larger than it was nine centuries ago. The promising prospects of the *Propaganda fide* at Rome are coming to nothing: and it may be of the divine destiny that all other attempts for gospelizing the nations of the earth shall prove fruitless, until the present Christendom itself be recovered to the primitive purity and simplicity. At which time, instead of the Babel confusion of contradicting missionaries, all will harmoniously concur in speaking one language, one holy faith, one apostolick religion to an unconverted world. At this period, and in effecting this great event, we have reason to think that the United States may be of no small influence and consideration. It was of the Lord to send Joseph into Egypt, to save much people, and to shew forth his praise. It is of the Lord that "a woman clothed with the sun, and the moon under her feet," and upon "her head a crown of twelve stars," (not to say thirteen) should "flee into the wilderness, where she hath a place prepared of God" (Rev. xii. 1 & 6), and where she might be the repository of Wisdom, and "keep the commandments of God, and have the testimony of Jesus." It may have been of the Lord that Christianity is to be found in such great purity in this church exiled into the wilderness of America; and that its purest body should be evidently advancing forward, by an augmented natural increase and spiritual edification, into a singular superiority—with the ultimate subserviency to the glory of God, in converting the world.

# Treaty of Peace, 1783

**Article 1st.** His Britannic Majesty acknowledges the said United States, viz. New-Hampshire Massachusetts Bay, Rhode-Island & Providence Plantations, Connecticut, New York, New Jersey, Pennsylvania, Delaware, Maryland, Virginia, North Carolina, South Carolina & Georgia, to be free sovereign & Independent States; that he treats with them as such, and for himself his Heirs & Successors, relinquishes all Claims to the Government Propriety & Territorial Rights of the same & every Part thereof.

**Article 2d.** [boundaries]

**Article 3d.** It is agreed that the People of the United States shall continue to enjoy unmolested the Right to take Fish of every kind on the Grand Bank and on all the other Banks of New-foundland, also in the Gulph of St. Lawrence, and at all other Places in the Sea where the Inhabitants of both Countries used at any time heretofore to fish. And also that the Inhabitants of the United States shall have Liberty to take Fish of every Kind on such Part of the Coast of New-foundland as British Fishermen shall use, (but not to dry or cure the same on that Island) And also on the Coasts Bays & Creeks of all other of his Britannic Majesty's Dominions in America, and that the American Fishermen shall have Liberty to dry and cure Fish in any of the unsettled Bays Harbours and Creeks of Nova Scotia, Magdalen Islands, and Labrador, so long as the same shall remain unsettled but so soon as the same or either of them shall be settled, it shall not be lawful for the said Fishermen to dry or cure Fish at such Settlement, without a previous Agreement for that purpose with the Inhabitants, Proprietors or Possessors of the Ground.

**Article 4th.** It is agreed that Creditors on either Side shall meet with no lawful Impediment to the Recovery of the full Value in Sterling Money of all bona fide Debts heretofore contracted.

**Article 5th.** It is agreed that the Congress shall earnestly recommend it to the Legislatures of the respective States to provide for the Restitution of all Estates, Rights and Properties which have been confiscated belonging to real British Subjects. . . . And that Persons of any other Description shall have free Liberty to go to any Part or Parts of any of the thirteen United States and therein to remain twelve Months unmolested in their Endeavours to obtain the Restitution of such of their Estates Rights & Properties as may have been confiscated. . . .

And it is agreed that all Persons who have any Interest in confiscated Lands, either by Debts, Marriage Settlements, or otherwise, shall meet with no lawful Impediment in the Prosecution of their just Rights.

**Article 6th.** That there shall be no future Confiscations made nor any Prosecutions commenc'd against any Person or Persons for or by Reason of the Part, which he or they may have taken in the present War, and that no Person shall on that Account suffer any future Loss or Damage, either in his Person Liberty or Property; and that those who may be in Confinement on such Charges at the Time of the Ratification of the Treaty in America shall be immediately set at Liberty, and the Prosecutions so commenced be discontinued.

**Article 7th.** There shall be a firm and perpetual Peace between his Britannic Majesty and the said States and between the Subjects of the one, and the Citizens of the other, wherefore all Hostilities both by Sea and Land shall from henceforth cease: All Prisoners on both Sides shall be set at Liberty, and his Britannic Majesty shall with all convenient speed, and without causing any Destruction, or carrying away any Negroes or other Property of the American Inhabitants, withdraw all his Armies, Garrisons & Fleets from the said United States, and from every Port, Place and Harbour within the same; leaving in all Fortifications the American Artillery that may be therein: And shall also Order & cause all Archives, Records, Deeds & Papers belonging to any of the said States, or their Citizens, which in the Course of the War may have fallen into the Hands of his Officers, to be forthwith restored and deliver'd to the proper States and Persons to whom they belong.

# Foreign Policy Powers in the Constitution, 1789

**Article I**

*Section 8.* The Congress shall have power

To lay and collect taxes, duties, imposts, and excises, to pay the debts and provide for the common defense and general welfare of the United States; but all duties, imposts and excises shall be uniform throughout the United States;

To borrow money on the credit of the United States;

To regulate commerce with foreign nations, and among the several States, and with the Indian tribes;

To establish an uniform rule of naturalization, and uniform laws on the subject of bankruptcies throughout the United States;

To coin money, regulate the value thereof, and of foreign coin, and fix the standard of weights and measures; . . .

To define and punish piracies and felonies committed on the high seas and offenses against the law of nations;

To declare war, grant letters of marque and reprisal, and make rules concerning captures on land and water;

To raise and support armies, but no appropriation of money to that use shall be for a longer term than two years;

To provide and maintain a navy;

To make rules for the government and regulation of the land and naval forces;

To provide for calling forth the militia to execute the laws of the Union, suppress insurrections, and repel invasions;

To provide for organizing, arming, and disciplining the militia, and for governing such part of them as may be employed in the service of the United States, reserving to the States respectively the appointment of the officers, and the authority of training the militia according to the discipline prescribed by Congress;

To exercise exclusive legislation in all cases whatsoever, over such district (not exceeding ten miles square) as may, by cession of particular States, and the acceptance of Congress, become the seat of government of the United States, and to exercise like authority over all places purchased by the consent of the legislature of the State, in which the same shall be, for erection of forts, magazines, arsenals, dock-yards, and other needful buildings;—and

To make all laws which shall be necessary and proper for carrying into execution the foregoing powers, and all other powers vested by this Constitution in the government of the United States, or in any department or officer thereof. . . .

*Section 10.* No State shall enter into any treaty, alliance, or confederation; grant letters of marque and reprisal; coin money; emit bills of credit; make anything but gold and silver coin a tender in payment of debts; pass any bill of attainder, ex post facto law, or law impairing the obligation of contracts, or grant any title of nobility.

No State shall, without the consent of Congress, lay any imposts or duties on imports or exports, except what may be absolutely necessary for executing its inspection laws: and the net produce of all duties and imposts, laid by any State on imports or exports, shall be for the use of the treasury of the United States; and all such laws shall be subject to the revision and control of the Congress.

No State shall, without the consent of Congress, lay any duty of tonnage, keep troops or ships of war in time of peace, enter into any agreement or compact with another State, or with a foreign power, or engage in war, unless actually invaded, or in such imminent danger as will not admit of delay. . . .

**Article II**

*Section 2.* The President shall be commander in chief of the army and navy of the United States, and of the militia of the several States, when called into the actual service of the United States; he may require the opinion, in writing, of the principal officer in each of the executive departments, upon any subject relating to the duties of their respective offices, and he shall have power to grant reprieves and pardons for offenses against the United States, except in cases of impeachment.

He shall have power, by and with the advice and consent of the Senate, to make treaties, provided two-thirds of the Senators present concur; and he shall nominate, and by and with the advice and consent of the Senate, shall appoint ambassadors, other public ministers and consuls, . . .

## Article III

*Section 1.* The judicial power of the United States shall be vested in one Supreme Court, and in such inferior courts as the Congress may from time to time ordain and establish. . . .

*Section 2.* The judicial power shall extend to all cases, in law and equity, arising under this Constitution, the laws of the United States, and treaties made, or which shall be made, under their authority;—to all cases affecting ambassadors, other public ministers and consuls;—to all cases of admiralty and maritime jurisdiction;—to controversies to which the United States shall be a party;—to controversies between two or more States;—*between a State and citizens of another State;*—between citizens of different States;—between citizens of the same State claiming lands under grants of different States, and between a State, or the citizens thereof, and foreign states, citizens or subjects.

In all cases affecting ambassadors, other public ministers and consuls, and those in which a State shall be party, the Supreme Court shall have original jurisdiction. . . .

## Article IV

*Section 3.* The Congress shall have power to dispose of and make all needful rules and regulations respecting the territory or other property belonging to the United States; and nothing in this Constitution shall be so construed as to prejudice any claims of the United States, or of any particular State. . . .

## Article VI

This Constitution, and the laws of the United States which shall be made in pursuance thereof; and all treaties made, or which shall be made, under the authority of the United States, shall be the supreme law of the land; and the judges in every State shall be bound thereby, anything in the Constitution or laws of any State to the contrary notwithstanding. . . .

## ESSAYS

The principles of early American foreign policy are the subject of Max Savelle's essay. Long a professor at Stanford University and the University of Washington, Savelle has explored the subject in a number of articles and books, including *The Origins of American Diplomacy* (1968). Finding that American ideas—

such as the doctrines of isolation and the two spheres—took shape well before the Declaration of Independence, Savelle discovers their source in the environment of North America and the American interaction with English and European diplomacy. William Appleman Williams of Oregon State University is also curious about ideas (such as the doctrine of mission), but he is especially interested in how these ideas influenced Americans to exercise power to build an often exploitative empire. For Williams, the essence of American foreign policy was imperialism, because Americans came to believe that therein lay greatness and that continued expansion was essential to the maintenance of their well-being and freedom.

---

# Early American Diplomatic Principles

### MAX SAVELLE

In a survey of the "permanent bases" of American diplomacy, published a few years ago, Mr. John W. Davis lists six doctrines which, as he says, "seem to have run with reasonable persistence throughout the course of American diplomacy." These are, according to Mr. Davis, the doctrine of isolation, the Monroe Doctrine, the doctrine of non-intervention, the freedom of the seas, the open door, and the pacific settlement of disputes. The first four Mr. Davis classifies as "negative" principles; the other two he calls "positive." For the purposes of this paper, Mr. Davis's classification will be used.

Now, in the words of Mr. James Brown Scott, "the foreign policy of a state or nation necessarily pre-supposes its existence as a political body." Historians of American foreign policy have, therefore, generally begun their story with the appointment of a Committee of Secret Correspondence by the second Continental Congress and the sending of Silas Deane abroad as the agent of the colonies on the eve of American independence. Deane and the American commissioners who followed him to Europe went with instructions which show that the basic principles of subsequent American diplomacy were already well developed in the minds of the American leaders in the Congress. Whence came the diplomatic principles embodied in the instructions of the American representatives abroad? Were they formulated, as it were, out of nothing, and without antecedents, to meet the need of the moment, or did they have some other, more remote origin? It is the purpose of this paper to suggest that the ideas underlying the permanent bases of American diplomacy were already old, even traditional, long before the time of American independence; that those ideas are as old as European settlement in America, because they arose out of needs which were inherent in the geographic situation of the colonies here; and that they developed simultaneously in America and in Europe, out of the intercolonial relations of English, Spanish, Dutch and French colonies,

---

Max Savelle, "Colonial Origins of American Diplomatic Principles," *Pacific Historical Review*, 3 (1934), 334–350. Reprinted by permission of the Pacific Coast Branch of the American Historical Association.

on the one hand, and out of the adaptation of European diplomacy to the new international situation presented by the appearance of colonial empires in the western hemisphere, on the other.

The doctrine of isolation, the first of these basic principles, probably dates from the beginning of Anglo-Saxon colonization in North America. The idea of escape from the entanglements of Europe, international, moral, religious and economic, appears in the thinking of the earliest permanent settlers, especially those who built their homes on the shores of Massachusetts Bay. "There never was a generation," wrote Increase Mather in 1677, "that did so perfectly shake off the dust of Babylon both as to ecclesiastical and civil constitution, as the first generation of Christians that came into this land for the gospel's sake." William Bradford and Edward Winslow both express this feeling in explaining the move of the Pilgrims from Leyden to America, and the same theme is repeated again and again in the history of Massachusetts Bay. The Massachusetts General Court, for example, in 1651 reminded Oliver Cromwell that it was to escape Europe that the founders of that colony came to America, and justified their feeling on the ground that "We know not any country more peaceable and free from Warre . . ." than this. Francis Daniel Pastorius, speaking, perhaps, for thousands of the Germans who came to the middle colonies in the next century, expressed the same feeling when he said that "After I had sufficiently seen the European provinces and countries, and the threatening movements of war, and had taken to heart the dire changes and disturbance of the Fatherland, I was impelled through a special guidance from the Almighty, to go to Pennsylvania."

This deeply rooted feeling of escape from the turmoil of Europe, an escape guaranteed by three thousand miles of ocean, is the negative side of the colonial doctrine of isolation. The doctrine also had its positive side, which took the form of refusal, on occasion, to be drawn into European conflicts. Thus, for example, during the first Anglo-Dutch war, Governor Peter Stuyvesant of New Netherland proposed to the New England Confederation that the English and Dutch colonies maintain a policy of neutrality in the war between their "Nations in Europe." At the same time, Massachusetts, who did not share Connecticut's prospect for territorial gain at the expense of the Dutch, was blocking the entrance of the New England Confederation into the war, because, as it seemed to the Massachusetts General Court, "it was most agreeable to the gospel of peace which we profess, and safest for these colonies at this season, to forbeare the use of the sword."

The real reason for these actions by New Netherland and Massachusetts was probably less the gospel of peace than the fact that there was a very profitable intercolonial trade going on between them, which must inevitably have suffered in war. Their isolation was thus based largely upon self-interest; but the ideas inherent in the action are, none-the-less, the basic ideas of the doctrine of isolation, as subsequently developed. The geographic situation of the English and Dutch colonies not only took them outside the stream of European conflict, in this case, but had actually created interests for them which made for the maintenance of peace.

Nor was this an isolated case. Similar situations arose, from time to time, during the intercolonial wars of the eighteenth century; and the unwillingness of such colonies as New Jersey and Pennsylvania to contribute men or money for those wars, because their interests were not directly involved, is notorious. Furthermore, as a part of the doctrine of the two spheres, the principle of American isolation from European conflict was recognized and encouraged by the mother countries by treaty, as, for example, in the Anglo-French treaty of Whitehall, of 1686.

John Adams expressed no new idea, therefore, when he formulated the American doctrine of isolation in 1776, to the effect that "we should make no treaties of alliance with any European power . . . [but] that we should separate ourselves, as far as possible and as long as possible, from all European politics and wars." Rather, he was expressing in terms of high policy a sentiment which was already a tradition in the American colonies, based upon a deep-seated feeling of escape from Europe and a strong tendency, encouraged by European diplomacy, to avoid becoming entangled in European conflict, whenever it was to their interest to do so.

Similarly, the ideological origins of the Monroe Doctrine, which is complementary to that of isolation, are to be traced far back into the beginnings of the colonial period. The basic theme in the Monroe Doctrine is the idea that "the political system of the allied powers [of Europe] is essentially different . . . from that of America . . . [and] we should consider any attempt on their part to extend their system to any portion of this hemisphere as dangerous to our peace and safety." This is, in itself, a re-statement of the old international doctrine that America is a new world, separate and distinct from Europe, to which the European system of politics and diplomacy does not apply. In expressing his doctrine, Monroe thus falls back upon the older European principle of the two spheres, which had found both doctrinal expression and contractual implementation before the end of the sixteenth century.

As early as 1532, Francisco de Vittoria proclaimed the inviolability of America. It is true, of course, that Vittoria's argument is very different from that of Monroe. Vittoria based his principle upon the fact that the Indians had a civilization of their own, were the rightful owners of the new lands, and, therefore, could not legally be dispossessed, whereas Monroe based his doctrine upon the existence of an European-American civilization in America which had developed since the beginning of European settlement. They do have, however, a common premise, and that is that America is a new, different and independent world, over which Europe has no legal right to extend its control.

Vittoria's philosophical pronouncement of the doctrine of the two spheres was not, however, the interpretation of that doctrine carried into the practice of European diplomacy. The early diplomatic application of this principle is to be seen, rather, in the practical dogma that "there is no peace beyond the Line." That is to say, to the diplomatists of the sixteenth and seventeenth centuries, Europe was one world and America, lying beyond the Line, was another; and piracy, territorial plundering, or intercolonial wars might take place in that new sphere without disturbing the peace and friendly relations of the mother countries in Europe. Likewise, under certain treaties, the reverse was true.

Such was the principle of the two spheres inherent in the oral agreement with regard to colonial affairs between French and Spanish diplomats at Cateau-Cambrésis, in 1559, and embodied in many subsequent treaties, notably the Anglo-Spanish treaty of 1604. This was also the principle underlying the Anglo-French treaty of Whitehall, of 1686. In this latter case, however, the doctrine is a doctrine of peace, not war. For Article XVII of this treaty provides that hostilities between the French and English colonies in America shall not be made a cause of war between the mother countries, and Article XVIII provides that war between England and France shall not be a cause of war in America; but that "true and firm peace and neutrality shall continue in America between the . . . French and English nations, in the same manner as if no such rupture had occurred in Europe."

The clearest example, perhaps, of the legal embodiment of the doctrine of the two spheres is the Hispano-Portuguese treaty of 1750. Not only is it provided in this treaty that the Spanish and Portuguese colonies shall remain neutral in case of war between the two nations in Europe, but, also, the treaty provides that, should either party to the treaty make an alliance with a third nation, the party making such an alliance, nevertheless, will not permit its ally to use its American ports or territories as bases of operations against the other party to the treaty or its colonies. In other words, even though enemies in Europe, they are to remain effectual allies for the maintenance of the *status quo* in America. This treaty is significant, not only as showing the importance of the doctrine of the two spheres in European diplomacy, but, also, because it shows that the diplomats of Spain and Portugal, at least, were coming to think of the territorial *status quo* in America as fixed, and not subject to further change.

It thus seems clear that the principle of the two spheres was well established when John Adams and his colleagues embodied the idea in the form of treaties prepared for the American representatives abroad, in 1776. The interpretation now given to this principle, however, was new. Hitherto, the European treaties based upon the doctrine of the two spheres had legalized a system for America which was distinct from the system of Europe, in matters of commerce, territories, and war. But Adams went one step farther, and, while assuming the basic principle of the two spheres, claimed for the young United States a deciding voice in the disposition of territories in North America still in the possession of Great Britain.

At this point, a new factor enters into any consideration of the old doctrine of the two spheres. Basically, the doctrine remains the same; but henceforth affairs in the western sphere are not to be determined by the diplomats of Europe. On the contrary, there has now appeared in the western world a new and independent nation which may be expected to assume a decisive position in affairs pertaining to America. It was only a short step further that Monroe was to go, when, the Spanish colonies having, in the meantime, achieved their independence, he proclaimed the predominant interest of the United States, not only in any territorial change that might, in the future, take place, but in blocking, once and for all, the possibility of further change in the direction of extending European possessions in the entire western hemisphere.

It should be borne in mind, of course, that Monroe did not, necessarily, draw upon European precedents to justify his interpretation of the doctrine of the two spheres. The ingrained American sentiment of isolation produced, in its normal growth, the determination not only to stay out of European complications, but, also, to keep European complications out of America. The doctrine of isolation is the negative American aspect of the principle of the two spheres; the Monroe doctrine is the positive American aspect of that same principle. It is sufficient for us to note that both the European doctrine of the two spheres and the American doctrine of isolation, culminating in the Monroe Doctrine, have a common origin and kinship in the elemental facts of the geography of the new world.

In a similar, if, perhaps, a more local and specific sense, the principle of non-intervention may be said to have grown out of the exigencies of colonial life in America. Perhaps the earliest opportunity for interference in the affairs of another nation or colony, and an occasion which demands the formulation of a policy, presented itself to the Commonwealth of Massachusetts Bay in the struggle of Charles de la Tour and the Sieur d'Aulnay Charnisé for the control of Acadia, in the fourth and fifth decades of the seventeenth century.

The merchants of the Bay were already trading for furs with La Tour when he made his first proposal for an alliance with Massachusetts in 1641. His emissaries were unsuccessful, and La Tour himself came to Boston in June, 1643, to propose, for the third time, an alliance with Massachusetts in his fight against d'Aulnay. The legislature was not at the moment in session; so, probably at the prompting of the merchants in Boston, Governor John Winthrop, on his own responsibility, allowed La Tour to hire such men and ships as were willing to go with him. This enabled La Tour to take out of Boston a filibustering expedition of four ships and a pinnace, with seventy land soldiers, although there was no alliance.

This action by the governor aroused an immediate storm of disagreement in the Bay towns, and three of the magistrates, together with several other leading men of the colony, wrote Winthrop a strong letter of protest. The burden of the argument in this, the so-called "Ipswich letter," was that the governor's action was tantamount to intervention in an internal quarrel between two factions in the territory of the King of France, the merits of which the governor could not know. Not only was this a breach of intercolonial neighborliness, but it was positively dangerous. D'Aulnay was strong, he would certainly protest against the aid given to La Tour, and he was liable to be supported against the colony of Massachusetts Bay by the armed forces of France. And, they said, "He that loseth his life in an unnecessary quarrel dyes the Devill's martyr."

Here is a clear, if homely expression of the doctrine of nonintervention, generated, as it were, not out of pure thought or precedent, but, rather, out of the actual circumstances of a particular situation. There can be no doubt, either, that it represents the feeling of the majority of the people of the colony and of New England. It was certainly effective, for it caused Governor Winthrop very carefully to repudiate, in a letter to d'Aulnay, all responsibility for the actions of La Tour's volunteers, while at the same time stoutly maintaining the right of the Massachusetts merchants to trade with whomsoever they would. As the governor disingenuously put it, "we thought not fit to give him [La Tour] aid, as being unwilling to intermeddle in the wars of any of our neighbors, yet considering his urgent distress, we could not in Christianity or humanity deny him liberty to hire for his money any ships in our harbor . . . And whereas some of our people were willing to go along with him . . . We had charged them to labor by all means to bring matters to a reconciliation . . . and . . . that if they [should] do or attempt anything against the rules of justice and good neighborhood, they must be accountable therefor unto us at their return." One might well have asked the governor for what purpose they were permitted to go, anyway.

Massachusetts was very careful, thereafter; and the Commissioners for the United Colonies, at the time of ratifying the commercial treaty later made between Massachusetts and d'Aulnay, wrote the doctrine of non-intervention into the records of the New England Confederation in unmistakable terms.

In the case of the doctrine of non-intervention, then, we may say that its American origin lies in a practical situation in the experience of the colonies themselves. That is to say, after meddling rather gingerly in the civil strife in Acadia, and considering the possible consequences, the colony and the Confederation finally arrived at the conclusion that it was best not to intervene at all, except insofar as to claim the right of the "Bastonnais" to trade with both sides.

Out of this same episode with La Tour and d'Aulnay may be seen arising the beginnings of American diplomatic interest in the freedom of the seas. From the first, New England's major interests lay upon the sea; and when d'Aulnay protested against the Massachusetts trade with La Tour and threatened to seize the "Bastonnais" ships, the magistrates sent him a "sharp answer," asserting the right of the English colonists to travel the seas freely, trading with whomsoever they would. Winthrop had already voiced this principle in his reply to the "Ipswich letter": "it is lawful," he wrote, "for the owners and masters of shipps, and is in the way of their calling, to be hyred by laTour . . . But if our shipps shall be opposed in their lawfull course, the justice of their cause will lye in that: as for example: a man travailing in a wagon in England, and carrying his goods with him, his creditor sets upon the wagon to take his debtors goods from him by force, the wagoner may defend him and his goods, [the traveller] being now in his charge without any respect to the former ingagement; for the justice of his cause ariseth upon another ground."

Here Winthrop distinguishes between aid to La Tour and the mere carrying of La Tour and his goods. In the first case, he is arguing for the right of the citizens of Massachusetts to hire themselves and their ships to anyone who will pay them their price, which is essentially the argument of freedom of trade. In the other case, the emphasis is placed upon the right of the neutral carrier to carry his customer and the customer's goods without molestation by the customer's enemy. The justice of the neutral carrier's cause arises from the fact that he is not a party to the quarrel, and, therefore, may not be attacked by either party to it. This argument for the rights of neutral carriers, growing, as it did, out of the necessity for some expression of policy to meet the situation of the moment, voices a fundamental principle of later American diplomacy.

Now, while Winthrop's principle arose out of an immediate local need, the incident took place at a time when the question of the freedom of the seas was coming greatly to occupy the minds of European thinkers on international law. It is true that Francis I hurled his challenge to the Hispano-Portuguese monopoly of the seas of the new world in 1541, and that, from that time forward, the international relations of Europe were full of the claims of the non-monopolizing nations, England, France and Holland, to the right to sail the seas beyond the Line without molestation. But it was not until 1609 that Grotius wrote his *Mare Liberum,* and it was 1635 when John Selden published his *Mare Clausum* in reply. It is hardly probable that Governor Winthrop had seen either of these books; if not, it seems apparent that the local need induced the principle, independently of the development of the principle in Europe. In any case, the question of the freedom of the seas is an important one in European diplomacy at least from the middle of the seventeenth century on.

Of particular interest to Americans, with regard to this principle, are the articles in the "Treaty of Navigation and Commerce" between England and France, signed at Utrecht, 11 April, 1713, that deal with the rights of neutrals on the high seas, the definition of contraband, and the doctrine that free ships make free goods. These articles applied to the colonies as well as to the mother country, of course, and satisfied the needs of the colonies for such diplomatic protection. It is no wonder, therefore, that they were copied verbatim in the form of treaties prepared for the American commissioners to France in 1776, and were embodied in the treaty of commerce with France signed 6 February, 1778.

That is to say, the commercial interests of the colonies, which had appeared by the third decade of English settlement, coincided, to a degree, with the commercial interests of the mother country in 1713. In 1776, their commercial interests remaining the same, the United States, now independent, could appropriate bodily to their own use that part of the mother country's diplomatic policy which had served them so well as colonies. The history of this growing body of ideas with regard to the freedom of the seas furnishes an interesting case of a principle which originated simultaneously in Europe and America, but whose first legal expression as an American principle is not American at all, but British.

Turning now to the "positive" doctrines of American foreign policy, we find their evolution may be traced to similar beginnings. The principle of the freedom of trade, which now goes under the name of the "open door," goes back at least to that day in 1541 when Francis I espostulated against the Hispano-

Portuguese monopoly of the land and commerce of the world: *"Le soleil luit pour moi comme pour les autres; je voudrais bien voir la clause du Testament d'Adam qui m'exclut du partage du monde."*

But this principle, too, has an independent origin in the needs and the experiences of the British colonies in the new world. As early as 1627 we find the Pilgrim governors at Plymouth negotiating with an emissary from the Dutch colony of New Amsterdam for "mutual commerce and trading in such things as our countries afford." And the chief provision in the treaty between the Commonwealth of Massachusetts and Governor d'Aulnay, of Acadia, in 1644, was that "it shalbe lawfull for all their people, aswell French as English, to trade each with other . . . provided alwayes that the governor and Majestrates [of Massachusetts] aforesaid bee not bound to restrayne their Merchants from tradeing with the[ir] ships with what people soever, whether French or others, in what place soever inhabiting." Here is a guarantee of the open door in Acadia; for one of the specific aims of this treaty, so far as Massachusetts was concerned, was to prevent the closing of the lucrative trade between the Boston merchants and La Tour, d'Aulnay's rival.

A similar treaty was made at Jamestown, in the year 1660, between the English colony of Virginia and the Dutch colony of New Netherland, in flat defiance of the British Navigation Act of 1651. And the freedom of trade provided by the treaty of Jamestown was further established, in Virginia, by legislation, in the Act of March, 1660, to the effect that "all strangers of what Xpian nation soever in amity with the people of England shall have free liberty to trade with us, for all allowable commodities . . . and shall have equall right and justice with our own nation in all courts of judicature." If England closed the door to Virginia, Virginia itself would open the door, to the Dutch and to all others, by treaty and by act of Assembly. Thus did the colony defy the mother country because the colony's economic interests ran counter to those of England; thus, also, did Virginia give expression to a principle, which Virginia was not able to maintain, it is true, in the face of the later Acts of Trade, but which has remained one of the permanent bases of American foreign policy.

Meanwhile, the "most favored nation" clause, itself a diplomatic lever for opening closed commercial doors, was making its appearance in European diplomacy, and was embodied in the Anglo-French commercial treaty of Utrecht. This principle, too, was adopted for its own use by the United States, and embodied in the Franco-American commercial treaty of 1778; but it was inserted there only because it was found impossible to get from France that unrestricted freedom of commerce with France and the French colonies which was the dearest wish of the young American nation, whose past growth and whose future prosperity were predicated upon an expanding commerce.

Finally, the principle of peaceful settlement of disputes, as all these other permanent bases, has its origins both in the practices of European diplomacy with regard to the colonies and in the experiences themselves. As early as 1655, Oliver Cromwell made a treaty with France which dealt, in part, with the issues raised in the informal war then going on between the two countries and with the seizure of Acadia by Major Sedgwick's expedition in 1654. This treaty provided for the establishment of a joint claims commission, composed of three appointees on each side, which was empowered, also, to settle the dispute with regard to the ownership of Acadia. In case the commissioners failed to agree, the disputes between the two countries were to be submitted to the city of Hamburg for arbitration. The provisions for arbitration were not carried out; but the principle of the arbitration of colonial disputes was clearly recognized, and was embodied later, notably in the Anglo-French treaty of Whitehall, 1686.

Meanwhile, in the colonies themselves, this principle had been established by the intercolonial treaty of Hartford, 1650. For two decades the boundary line between the English and the Dutch in Connecticut and Long Island had been in dispute. Various suggestions had been made, on both sides, that the dispute be settled by arbitration, but no action was taken until Peter Stuyvesant journeyed to Hartford in 1650 and negotiated with the Commissioners of the United Colonies a treaty which provided for the determination of the boundary by four commissioners, two to be appointed on each side.

Thereafter, the principle of settlement of colonial disputes by arbitration or joint commission was given lip-service in the treaties of Whitehall (1686), Utrecht (1713), and Aix-la-Chapelle (1748); and an attempt was actually made to settle the dispute over the Acadian boundary by peaceful methods after 1749. This attempt collapsed, however, with the outbreak of the Seven-years War, and, apparently, there is no record of a successful application of this method of settling intercolonial disputes after the treaty of Hartford. The principle was, none-the-less, recognized; and it was embodied, as a principle by no means new, in the Jay Treaty of 1794, upon the basis of which certain disputes between the United States and Great Britain were actually settled.

We have now considered certain suggestions with regard to the origins of the ideas underlying the six permanent bases of American diplomacy. In noting the existence and application of those ideas very early in the colonial period of American history, it has appeared that they were drawn from three sources. First, certain ideas were developed in the practical experiences of the colonies in America, in the course of their natural economic and political development and the relations of the French, Dutch and English colonies with each other. Second, we have seen that certain other ideas which later found a place in American diplomacy grew out of the relationships of the English colonies with the mother country; as, for example, those ideas and practices which underlie the doctrine of isolation. Third, we have seen that certain ideas later embodied in American diplomacy are drawn from European diplomacy, and, particularly, from the relations of England with other European nations, with regard to colonial commerce and related subjects. It is to be remembered, also, that the ideas underlying the six major doctrines we have discussed developed simultaneously in America and in Europe, sometimes with very little connection between the developments in Europe and those in America, and, sometimes, with a large amount of dependence by America upon Europe.

Looked at in this light, early United States diplomacy becomes a synthesis of American, English and European elements. This means, also, that the history of American diplomatic ideas does not really begin in 1776. On the contrary, it begins with the discovery of America and the appearance of the international doctrine of the two spheres. The permanent bases of American foreign policy are those concepts which grew out of the experiences of the European nations and the colonies in their efforts to direct the international destiny of the new world. They were laid down in the course of the first two centuries of exploration, annexation and settlement in North America.

So far as the colonies themselves were concerned, they contributed very little to the evolution of an American diplomatic system after the Stuart restoration of 1660. The reason for this fact is to be seen in the increasing importance of the colonies to the mother country, and the resultant increasingly important part the affairs of the colonies play in the determination of British foreign policy. From this time forward, British diplomacy is, largely, colonial diplomacy. On the other hand, however, the experiences of the colonies during the first five decades of their history, when they were most completely free from the political control of the mother country, were peculiarly like the experiences of the United States just after independence. They forecast, in unique fashion, the diplomatic needs of the United States, and the rudimentary policies then evolved similarly forecast the policies of the new republic. The mother country, after 1660, merely undertook to conduct the diplomacy of the colonies for them. It was not always conducted as the colonies would have liked; but, in so far as the British policies did satisfy the aspirations of the colonies, those policies were continued after independence without a break.

It is precisely in this first half-century of settlement, therefore, that the peculiarly American policies may be said most clearly to have had their origin. If the evolution of American diplomatic ideas paralleled the development of similar ideas in Europe, and if United States diplomacy adopted *in toto* certain doctrines of European diplomacy as its own, it is because the needs of America, arising out of its natural environment, were similar, in respect to the problems dealt with by such borrowed doctrines, to European needs.

Finally, we are to draw from this discussion one more suggestion. If it be true that the permanent bases of American diplomacy are rooted in the geography of North America, it becomes easy to understand why they remain consistent throughout the whole course of American history, and, therefore, come to be called traditional. Further, if this be a valid explanation of their traditional nature, it follows that they may be expected to remain the permanent bases of American foreign policy until, perhaps by mechanical agencies, the nature of the geographic relationship of North America to the rest of the world be changed or modified.

# Born and Bred of Empire
## WILLIAM APPLEMAN WILLIAMS

The 19th- and 20th-century empire known as the United States of America began as a gleam in the eyes of various 16th-century critics of, and advisers to, Elizabeth I; and not improbably as a thought in Her Majesty's own mind. In the language of our time, England was then a backward and underdeveloped small island: poor, weak, and constantly torn by internal social conflict. Many other countries dismissed it as a pathetic excuse for a nation and raided its commerce with impunity. The frontier of Rome had become a leftover enclave.

Looking out upon the world in 1550, even the most unimaginative Englishman could see that the Portuguese, the Spanish, and the French—even the Dutch—were exploring and expropriating much of the newly discovered world. The English faced a choice: they could concentrate their resources, energy, and will to organize and develop themselves as a small but dynamic and creative community, or they could galvanize themselves to join the scramble for the globe.

It was not a hypothetical choice. Throughout human history various peoples have resisted the temptations of empire. One thinks here, for example, of the Japanese during many centuries of their development; or of the Chinese deciding to break up and burn the great fleets of Admiral Cheng-Hô that had reached the east coast of Africa long before the Portuguese. For that matter, some British and American imperial spokesmen have been candid enough to acknowledge the virtues of the other option. A smaller, non-imperial society enjoys not inconsiderable rewards. "Human problems can be truly perceived which in larger social structures must more or less necessarily be sacrificed. . . . People were conscious of what can be named serenity or dignity of human nature."

Thus empire as a way of life was never, even in the beginning, the only alternative open to us as Americans. Indeed, various minorities (and occasionally pluralities) amongst us have from time to time argued and agitated for a non-imperial outlook. And a significant number of those who chose the imperial option, such as James Madison, were excruciatingly aware that they were challenging an older, awesome wisdom. But the historian must record that America was born and bred of the British Empire.

The difficult labor of creating that empire occupied the English for many generations, and in the beginning they struggled primarily to impose order upon their own island. It was a painful process that involved asserting London's power over Scotland and Wales, *the creation of an empire within the island,* and the development of a dynamic economy. None of it was easy, and Britain remained divided, poor, weak, and backward well into the 16th century. The economic progress that did occur—as in textiles—was uncoordinated and characterized by serious and costly fluctuations, and agriculture was chronically sick. A boom in the wool trade from 1550 to 1552, for example, shortly collapsed and the society once again faced economic stagnation and social violence.

Over the years, various monarchs had tried to promote economic growth and social stability by decrees and laws designed to encourage, direct, and integrate the system. Thus Edward I (r. 1272–1307) terminated some foreign enterprises and focused the wool trade on exports to Antwerp; and Edward III extended those efforts as he dealt with domestic unrest and waged a long (1333–60) war with France. The Ordinance of Labourers and the Statute of Labourers were attempts to control wages and prices in an equitable relationship, for example, as well as measures to put every man to work and thereby help agriculture. And Richard II's Navigation Act of 1381 favored British traders and shippers against their foreign competitors. The profits of commerce were viewed as capital for domestic improvement.

Such fitful, even fumbling, efforts to build a system were refined, extended, and integrated by Elizabeth I and her successors. In its most general meaning, the term *system* bespeaks the arrangement of things to form a whole. Thus the various organs of the body constitute a system once their interrelationships are understood. But here, and elsewhere in this essay, the word, and concept, *system* is also used to describe an attitude of mind. One is reluctant to interpret Elizabeth's dramatically discreet visit to the London docks to knight Francis Drake as a cost-effective pirate who hijacked and brought home large amounts of Spanish gold; but we do need to comprehend her outlook and her purpose.

Psychologists and other students of human behavior have demonstrated that most people concentrate their attention, even vision, on one or a few of the elements that are parts of a whole. This is nicely demonstrated, for example, in the lack of composition in most people's snapshots. Their awareness of interrelationships is limited. This is particularly true when they confront a complex subject like society or culture. In a similar (and related) way, such people are inclined to think about society in terms of random action and chance.

Another group of people, however, do see the whole, and do conceptualize and think in terms of multiple inter-relations and a system. Queen Elizabeth I and her senior advisers, and others who later exercised power, were such people. They were not content to rely on the *chance* that random, uncoordinated activity by individuals or groups would produce the general welfare. Their philosophical resistance to that idea was reinforced by their knowledge of English history and their contemporary pragmatic experience. They simply could not take seriously the proposition that random activity somehow produced a coherent, consequential result. Most of them believed in God, or Some Power Out There, but they did not think it likely that He—or It—had either the time or the inclination to save fools who did not look after themselves. They did not share the belief, later to be so popular, that some Hidden Hand would coordinate random and self-interested activity to produce the common good. They sought instead to coordinate—*even to plan*—their efforts to realize their desired goals. They were in truth concerned to create a system through a conscious effort to integrate disparate elements into a purposeful pattern. They did not deny the reality of chance—and random activity, but sought instead to absorb them within their purpose.

Such coordination can occur in two principal ways. The government asserts its will in an attempt to define and enforce various relationships designed to realize a program. Or private individuals and groups join hands—openly or covertly—to accomplish their objectives. As we shall see, both kinds of system building have been an integral part of American history. But here let us observe the efforts by Elizabeth I and others to create an imperial system.

Those who followed her in that labor were more knowledgeable about the intricacies of such an effort, but she exuded imperial verve and style. She encouraged and rewarded the dashing forays by Drake and others against the Spanish and the French. And she knew that when she touched the sword to Drake's shoulder that she was honoring a hero of a nasty business. Take from them to honor us and I will honor you. An honest and forceful imperial leader.

Karl Marx later cut through the romance of such activity and described it bluntly for what it was. To knight a pirate, he explained, is to legitimatize the primitive accumulation of the wealth that is essential to generate capitalist growth in a poor society. Small wonder, as one observer noted during Drake's heyday, that Mercury was christened the English "God of trade and theft." But such entrepreneurs had to be controlled, as well as encouraged, if the system was to create the general welfare. That was not only desirable in the social and moral sense, it was also necessary to prevent the imbalances that generated unrest or revolution.

"It stands not with the policy of the State," Sir Francis Bacon warned as early as 1601, "that the wealth of the Kingdom should be engrossed into a few graziers' hands." For in that case, Sir Edward Sandys explained, "the rich will eat out the poor." As a result, English leaders gradually created a pattern of legislation and other regulations that was designed to control the giants of the marketplace, improve the position of agriculture, and in general maintain balance and equity in the domestic side of the political economy.

But all those efforts were predicated upon imperial expansion. That was the engine of the system. No one stated the principle more candidly than Bacon. "The rebellions of the belly are the worst. The first remedy or prevention, is to remove, by all means possible that material cause of sedition, which is want and poverty in the estate. To which purpose serveth the opening and well balancing of trade; the cherishing of manufacturers; the banishing of idleness. . . . The increase of any estate must be upon the foreigner, for whatsoever is somewhere gotten is somewhere lost." William Lane added a pithy amplification: the point of such expansion was "we to lyve off them and they not off us."

That imperial outlook and strategy were not seriously challenged by the coalition of interests and classes which between 1640 and 1649 made the English Revolution and created a republican Commonwealth led by Oliver Cromwell. It is conceivable, but highly improbable, that if the Levellers and other radicals within the revolutionary movement had won control of the country they would have freed the American colonies, ended other imperial ventures, and settled down to cultivate their domestic commonwealth. Not only were they children of the imperial way of life, but they were also vigorous envangelists of *their* particular truths. And, as the United States was to demonstrate, there is neither a logical nor a pragmatic connection between more freedom at home and less empire abroad.

As for Cromwell, he was a crusader and an imperialist. He assaulted his fellow-Protestant Dutchmen, as well as the Catholic Irish and Spanish, in the course of establishing the Rights of Free Englishmen. He was arrogantly confident that England's ideal constitution would claim "the patronage of the world." His judgment of other societies and cultures was classically imperial: they were "all sick." And his imperial legislation, such as the act forbidding the importation of goods except in English ships (or those of the nation producing the items), was explicitly designed to control world trade.

The English Revolution unquestionably strengthened the Rights of Free Englishmen and created a strong momentum toward more representative and responsible government. But it did not solve the problems of backwardness and underdevelopment, and hence British leaders continued and extended their efforts to rationalize and expand a centrally directed imperial system. The resulting tension between freedom, order, and prosperity created a paradox perhaps most strikingly symbolized in the thought and career of John Locke.

Locke was at the center of English politics, both as an adviser to high officials and as a philosopher who evoked wide public response, from 1660 to the end of the century. He is important in the development of empire as a way of life not because he was unique, but because he expressed the contradictions of the imperial outlook with a special verve, clarity, and style, and because he influenced large numbers of Americans.

Englishmen on both sides of the Atlantic responded to him, for he expressed and clarified the basic elements of their attitudes and thoughts: the concern with responsible, balanced (even limited) liberty; the assumption that progress depended upon coordinated, even planned, action; and the belief that—given the finite nature of the world—domestic welfare and social peace required vigorous imperial expansion. "Riches do not consist in having more Gold and Silver, but in having more in proportion than the rest of the World, or than our Neighbours, whereby we are enabled to procure to ourselves a greater Plenty of the Conveniences of Life than comes within the reach of Neighbouring Kingdoms and States."

Locke also provided a model for colonial Englishmen who sought power in the name and exercise of freedom. In a crucial sense, as historian Merle Curti pointed out many years ago, Locke offered something to everybody.

A yeoman, artisan, or mechanic could cite him in praise of liberty. A merchant, squire, or politician could quote him on the necessity of balance and order. And all of them shared his concern with expansion.

Locke and other post-revolutionary leaders moved vigorously to enlarge and integrate the American colonies as an essential part of the empire. Their objective was to create a system ruled with a combination of firmness and permissiveness that honored the principles of an imperial commonwealth. There was never any question about London setting basic policy, or ensuring the English metropolis a favorable balance of trade (and allocation of resources). But the colonies were granted a significant degree of local autonomy, were protected militarily, and were granted economic favors (and opportunities) that guaranteed consequential profits and growth.

It is very easy to document the lack of perfection in the reality of the evolving empire. There were significant inequalities within the colonies, and in England; as well as a growing discrepancy in the pace and balance of development between the colonies and the British metropolis. Even so, the imperial way of life provided important gains for increasing numbers of Englishmen. And in the larger sense the most significant aspect of the empire was the success in transforming the American colonies from tiny, insecure outposts into dynamic societies generating their own progress. Whatever its costs, both then and later, the empire functioned effectively during the century after the English Revolution.

On the one hand, the American colonies prospered as part of the British Empire, and their developing strength, self-consciousness, and confidence were essential in moving them to *think* of revolution and in translating that idea into action. On the other hand, the successes of the Empire produced vast changes within Great Britain which led to the confrontation with the colonies. That dialectical process provides a classic example not only of the nature of change, but of the interaction between economic activity and political, intellectual, and social developments. It also produced another culture based on the proposition that expansion was the key to freedom, prosperity, and social peace.

Locke said it as well as anyone and more honestly than most: empire as a way of life involves taking wealth and freedom away from others to provide for your own welfare, pleasure, and power. Even so, others like Henry VII were respectably candid. Elizabeth I may have been discreet in knighting Drake, but her general directive was straight to the point: conquer any "remote heathen and barbarous lands" and impose proper government upon such savages. And in 1607 the directors of the Virginia Company of London were properly blunt. Knowing the purpose of settlement, they warned their colonists that "you cannot carry yourselves so toward them [the First Americans] but they will grow discontented with your habitation."

In the broader sense, however, the English and other European empire builders developed a contradictory and convoluted (if at times sophisticated) argument that justified their imperial activities in India, Africa, Asia, and

America. That elaborate ideology was not simply or only a callous or cynical rationalization. Whatever their roots in the mundane realities of greed, such overarching systems of ideas take on a life of their own and function (and become accepted) as engines of action.

Thus it is revealing and useful to explore them on their own terms. My emphasis here is on the English confrontation with the established seaboard, but it applies with equal force to the subsequent enslavement of Africans and the destruction of the First Americans west of the Appalachian Mountains. Both were the motifs of the imperial coin.

Karl Marx once remarked, in a phrase that illuminates his exasperated outburst that he was not a Marxist, that the past weighs like an Alp upon the brain of the living. Old ideas influence a new reality. One could have great fun, and perhaps make a contribution to wisdom, by arguing that therein lies the genesis of psychoanalysis. But let us here use Marx's insight as a guide to exploring the origins and character of the imperial characterization of its victims. How we perceive our victims tells us much indeed about ourselves. Such overarching ideologies are inherently complicated, giving rise to different emphases and interpretations among historians, sociologists, anthropologists, political theorists, and ethnohistorians. We can properly begin, therefore, by outlining two of those arguments.

The problem confronting the English (and other European) empire builders was very simple. Even by their own rules, the unilateral, uninvited, and unprovoked intrusion over thousands of miles by one culture into the life and affairs of another could not be explained or justified by an appeal to self-defense. That primal right could plausibly be invoked, even at best, *only after the initial penetration had occurred and was revisited.* Hence the initial invasion must be justified by some other logic. Over the years, scholars dealing with that problem have tended to separate into two groups: one emphasizes the importance of color (blacks and browns are inferior); the other stresses Christianity (heathens are agents of the Devil and so must be converted or destroyed).

Now in truth those explanations are less contradictory or exclusive than mutually supportive and reinforcing of empire as a way of life. Whatever its origins in the eastern Mediterranean, Christianity became a European phenomenon and, despite the brownish hue of some Mediterranean Catholics and Orthodox believers, they were generally lighter—"whiter" than the uninformed or unpersuaded in India, Asia, Africa, and America. Heathens were on sight generally darker than converts, and hence visually tainted by the domestic force of the Devil who was always presented as black.

That evidence, such as it was, was reinforced by other kinds of proof. Europeans were highly conscious—one might even say hypersensitive—of having come through an extremely difficult and perilous time of troubles. Not only had they been challenged by Islamic and other non-believers, but the infidels had probed close to the vitals of their own way of life. They had also been tested in horrendous trials by disease and other disasters. But they *had* survived. It was more than a bit like death and resurrection. Given their Christianity, that was understandably interpreted as a sign of the Grace of God. Their disputations and wars with each other about the nature of the true faith were tactical not strategic: not about the faith, but only about how best to interpret and extend it.

Thus it is important to realize that Jennings's perceptive remark about the Holy Church has to do with secular as well as religious ideology. It was not only that Christianity was the true religion. The faithful had survived and were moving toward the assertion of their superiority. They had developed better ships and more deadly weapons to subdue the Eastern infidels. They had triumphed over pestilence and poverty to build cities. They had controlled dissidence through the creation of centralized instruments of government. And they had organized economic activity well enough to generate a growing surplus (well, at least for some).

To employ the science and the language of a later century, there was a non-articulated social Darwinism in all of that: a preview of the sense, if not the theory, of the superiority inherent in mere survival and continuation. It was not formulated in those terms, or with those footnotes, but it was nevertheless a very real and present and powerful element of the developing imperial way of life. There was, in short a secular Holy Church with its own doctrine of superiority.

Those complementary dogmas, sacred and secular, did not immediately or inevitably produce a hard-line racist outlook. There emerged instead a spectrum of attitudes, among both religious and lay thinkers, that can usefully be described in terms of two contradictory images: the Noble Savage and the Ignoble Savage. The former, a combination of romanticism and superciliousness, developed as the faith and idiom of the more humane group of English and American imperialists. They considered themselves superior, and justified the imposition of imperial power on that basis, but they modified such arrogance in several respects.

To begin with, they acknowledged that some aspects of "savage" life were worth serious consideration and perhaps even emulation. They were impressed, for example, by the significantly (even statistically) lower incidence of violence within First American societies, and by the limits generally imposed by those cultures upon inter-societal warfare. They responded favorably —or at least thoughtfully and tolerantly—to the more relaxed attitudes about sex, marriage, and divorce, and to the different idioms of personal hygiene (as in daily bathing) and medical treatment. And they recognized, however cautiously, that the religion of the First Americans—including its emphasis on dreams—bespoke a sense of awe and wonder that was related to their own belief in spirits and miracles.

Those more relaxed or benevolent imperialists also acknowledged the impressive skills of the First Americans. Not only were they good farmers (who cleared enough land to let half lie fallow), but they demonstrated a sophisticated understanding of how to create and sustain a symbiotic relationship with the land. They did not graze cattle or pigs, to be sure, but they did create pasture for deer. They also displayed an ability to organize a division of labor, both within and between cultures, that led to a remarkable system of trade over long distances that involved food, metals, and other commodities.

For all those reasons, the group of English people (and later Americans) that we can usefully call the soft imperialists—religious and secular—did not become racists. They were arrogant, supercilious, and patronizing, but they did separate themselves from the racists on three vital issues. First, they considered the First Americans human. Second, they acknowledged their achievements. And, third, on those grounds, they considered it possible and desirable to elevate the Noble Savage into at least partial civilization. They left the future open.

It would be pleasant, and surely uplifting, to report that such soft imperialists carried the day. They did not. Indeed not. But even so the soft imperialists were and remained important. If nothing else, they now and again prevented the hard-line imperialists from plunging joyfully into disaster. American historians, along with their fellow intellectuals, display their imperial temperament by cataloging people according to two categories: imperialists and anti-imperialists. It is a less than helpful filing system. We Americans, let alone our English forefathers, have produced very, very few anti-imperialists. Our idiom has been empire, and so the primary division was and remains between the soft and the hard.

It all comes down to the question of whether one conquers to transform the heathen into lower-class members of the empire or simply works them to death for the benefit of the imperial metropolis. Even if the softies win, empire is still the way of life.

But the truth of it is that the hard-liners won. And so in that sense, at any rate, the question of racism is secondary. The primary question has always been the control of wealth and the liberty for some to do as they choose. Racism, the product of the image of the Ignoble Savage, began and survived as the psychologically justifying and economically profitable fairy tale. It provided the gloss for the harsh truth that empire, soft or hard, is the child of an inability or an unwillingness to live within one's own means. Empire as a way of life is predicated upon having more than one needs.

Think of it this way: the English-American empire builders went first for the land cleared and cultivated by the First Americans. It was simply too much hard work to chop those trees and root those stumps. Easier by far to take the land already cleared by the heathens. And take their food to survive. We have all heard, as children of children of children, how our ancestors in Virginia and Massachusetts were saved by the surplus produce from the gardens cultivated by those Ignoble Savages. And it is true. Hence it cannot be true that they were nomads who misused the land. John Winthrop of Massachusetts, churchman though he was, was simply wrong—if not worse—when he said that the First Americans "inclose noe land neither have any settled habitation." They treasured and cherished all the land they shared in common.

But, good Christian imperial lawyer that he was, Winthrop was making the best case for grabbing the land. After all, as Cromwell had said, all others were "sick." And you were sick if you did not sit on it all the time. No fences and no cattle meant "noe other but a naturall right to those countries." Hence, "if we leave them sufficient for their use we may lawfully take the rest." The "rest" meant wherever they were not located at any given moment, and the law was imperial fiat. Winthrop was a soft imperialist in that he hoped to convert the heathen to embrace their doom, but a hard imperialist in acquiring the loot. . . .

The British triumph over the French in the long war from 1754 to 1763, which delivered Canada into their hands, posed a tricky problem for the victors. The State needed money. The economic giants at home demanded ever more freedom and profit for themselves by limiting the freedom of the American colonies. And yet the Americans were becoming strong enough— and self-conscious enough—to resist the measures that would satisfy the Crown and the metropolitan behemoths.

If we step back from the bones and dust and blood of the cockpit of daily politics, we can see that the British mercantilists were reaping the troubles of their successes. There is no question that empire provides benefits for a few of the people all of the time, and even for all of the people some of the time—including various groups in the colonies. The difficulty arises when the powers-that-be in the metropolis insist upon economic or political policies that antagonize or threaten the elite in the provinces. For that enables the element within the upper class that wants independence to lead (and manipulate) the masses. They can thus isolate or overpower those members of their class who are reluctant to break the umbilical cord that has provided ideological, political, and social security—and economic sustenance.

Think only of Joseph Galloway of Pennsylvania and Samuel Adams of Massachusetts. Galloway was a thoughtful member of the elite who wanted to temporize: compromise contemporary differences, grow stronger, and bank the profits and the power of the natural course of events. Adams, an anticolonial politician with a master's degree from Harvard, urged action before the imperial metropolis asserted ever stronger controls over the American political economy. He was hot for revolution in the name of liberty and the conquest of Canada.

We can begin to unravel the Adams paradox by examining the wisdom of Benjamin Franklin. His perceptive essay "Observations Concerning the Increase of Mankind, Peopling of Continents, etc." (1751) was perhaps the first integrated secular argument by a colonial that linked expansion with prosperity, social peace, and freedom. Given the propensity of people to procreate, he wrote, surplus land was essential to generate sustenance and wealth through agriculture and commerce. Furthermore, a crowded country became socially and politically corrupt and unstable. Thus there were two possibilities: North America, including Canada, could divide into several nations; or it could develop as the metropolis of a vastly more powerful British Empire.

When he wrote that analysis, and for many years thereafter, Franklin favored the second course of action. Compromise, woo the British, and become the metropolis. And, not surprisingly, he cast himself for a major role as one of the people who would be "properly called *Fathers*" of that grand empire. Along with those like Galloway, Franklin labored long hours to persuade his fellow colonists, and leaders in London, to accept his strategy. During the Albany Conference in 1754, for example, he proposed a coalition between the elites in London and America to handle the problems of expansion (Indians, taxes, armies, and the like) on a partnership basis; and he pushed the essentials of his plan, such as joint economic development, down to the eve of the revolution. But the British feared that such a policy would lead to the loss of control and profits, and Americans increasingly asserted their own claims to their own empire.

Near the end of the ensuing confrontation, Franklin adroitly presented himself as an advocate of independence and joined Sam Adams in agitating for the conquest of Canada—and added his own arguments for taking the Floridas and the West Indies. It was not so much that Adams and his street politics had proved superior to Franklin's theory as it was that the British failed to see the power of Franklin's argument that they could continue to rule indefinitely by moving London to the Ohio River Valley. One cannot resist wondering whether Franklin enjoyed a chuckle when, centuries later, the London Bridge was sold to a private real-estate developer in Arizona.

Adams and Franklin are less to be understood as adversaries than as powerful protagonists of the different elements that created the American version of empire as a way of life. For, despite all his denial of upper-class ties, his plotting in the back room of his favorite inn in Boston, and his militant rhetoric about liberty, Adams was a man who honored and sustained the Puritan tradition of *ordered* freedom. Like many later Americans who thought of themselves as radicals (even liberals), Adams was a crusader who wanted to save his fellow citizens in the course of reforming the world and creating an empire.

If we consider the mix of religion, natural rights philosophy, capitalist political economy, and cultural superiority, then Adams is properly honored as a symbol as well as an organizing genius of the emerging American empire. He was a master of arousing, coordinating, focusing, and energizing those attitudes, beliefs, and ambitions into a political movement. And he knew how to pick effective associates, like Joseph Warren, and give them a loose rein. If he was not the father of the Revolution, he was surely the midwife.

But Adams did not, probably could not, synthesize all those ideas into an imperial philosophy. That was very largely the labor of two Virginians, Thomas Jefferson and James Madison. The point here is not elitist: those two dear friends and neighbors of the slave-owning aristocracy did not invent and then impose an imperial way of life upon their fellow Americans. After all, Daniel Boone and his unremembered but no less adventurous allies were the facts behind the ideas. Jefferson and Madison simply put it all together in a way that excited true believers and persuaded doubters.

We need to begin, therefore, with the bricks with which they built the imperial foundation. Winthrop's faith in America as a City on the Hill and then as another Israel was echoed in the remark by Jonathan Edwards "that God might in [America] begin a new world in a spiritual respect." Edwards was in some ways highly skeptical of imperial ventures and tried to devise a working compromise with the First Americans, and hence his crusading hope is all the more revealing of the underlying attitudes. Other New Englanders stressed the secular Holy Church. James Otis, only slightly less important than Sam Adams, rhapsodized about "so glorious an empire." . . .

Winning the Revolutionary War solved one problem but created many difficulties. Once free of the British, the American colonies slipped backward toward an earlier stage of capitalist development. To that extent, History *is* reversible, and we can learn by observing how different peoples deal with such situations. The colonies emerged victorious from their seven-year war, but they no longer enjoyed their preferential position within the empire (the vital West Indies trade, for example, was now closed to them), and they were divided, weak, and floundering without an integrated system. They were not as backward as England under Elizabeth I but they were certainly far less coherent and dynamic than they had been just prior to the battle for independence against the British metropolis. . . .

Weak and troubled, many Americans increasingly turned back to their imperial heritage for a solution. As George Washington phrased it in 1783, perhaps more in hope than certainty, the not-so-united states were "a rising empire." Franklin had never changed his basic argument for expansion, and others like the Revolutionary leader Samuel Adams continued to argue the need for taking Canada. Southerners sought the Floridas and supported the western drive for the Mississippi and New Orleans. William Henry Drayton of South Carolina, a planter and politician of considerable importance, put it this way: "a new Empire, stiled the United States of America. . . . That bids fair, by the blessing of God, to be the most glorious of any upon Record." Still others stressed the need to move against the First Americans and the British in the Ohio Valley and Great Lakes region. And men of all sections grew ever more concerned about the need for a strong and effective trading and commercial policy in the world marketplace.

Those issues (and the related fears) prompted a group of leaders from the middle and southern states to gather in Annapolis, Maryland, to discuss the organization of a regional economic system. Instead, they quickly decided to create a new and far stronger national government. Under the leadership of Madison, the ensuing convention of 1787 in Philadelphia produced (behind locked doors) the Constitution. Both in the mind of Madison and in its nature, the Constitution was an instrument of imperial government at home and abroad. . . .

As with many intellectual revolutions, Madison made his with ruthless simplicity. He simply turned conventional wisdom upside down, or inside out. The Revolutionary generation was impressively literate and knowledgeable about history and political theory (and literature); and the symbol of its understanding of the relationship between size, power, and freedom was based on Montesquieu's principle that liberty could exist only in a small state. Madison boldly argued the opposite: that empire was essential for freedom.

He explained it very clearly in a personal letter to Thomas Jefferson, an intimate friend he was most concerned to persuade to accept and support the new empire. "It may be said that the new Constitution is founded on different principles, and will have a different operation. I admit the difference to be material. . . . This form of government, in order to effect its purpose, must operate not within a small but an extensive sphere." The reason was simple. "Extend the sphere, and you take in a greater variety of parties and interests; you make it less probable that a majority of the whole will have a common motive to invade the rights of other citizens; or if such a common motive exists, it will be more difficult for all to feel it . . . to act in unison with each other."

Madison was nothing if not comprehensive. He was arguing that surplus social space and surplus resources were necessary to maintain economic welfare, social stability, freedom, and representative government. That was implicit in his related judgment that agrarian citizens were "the best basis of public liberty"; and explicit in his concern for a strong central government to acquire the land required for such people, and to protect and expand their export trade and to encourage their manufactures, shipping, and even finance. Not only was the Constitution grounded in an imperial logic, but it created a government armed with typically mercantilist powers over the political economy.

The latter point has often been overlooked, largely because of the different circumstances in which Madison operated, and because mercantilist doctrine had become far more sophisticated by the 1780s than it had been during earlier centuries. But the Constitution's provisions concerning money and finance, domestic and foreign commerce, foreign policy, the President as commander in chief, and the control of undeveloped territories were in truth examples of classic mercantilist theory and practice.

Madison's contemporary critics missed none of those essential features of the Constitution. Robert Yates, for example, saw immediately that it would create an empire of the existing states—an American version of the United Kingdom. Others, like "An Old Whig" and "A Federalist," who offered their views in newspapers and pamphlets, recognized the imperial nature of Madison's logic and prophesied the biggest "consolidated empire" in history. "We are vain, like other nations," another observer noted in sadness. "We wish to make a noise in the world. . . . We are also, no doubt, desirous of cutting a figure in History. Should we not reflect," he concluded, "[that] . . . extensive empire is a misfortune to be depreciated."

Even so, most of the critics wanted the land and the markets—and the domestic stability—that the Constitution was designed to provide through its imperial powers. As a result, they were trapped in a wrenching predicament: accept the Constitution or risk more social unrest (like Shays's Rebellion in Massachusetts) and economic difficulties—or domination by the more advanced political economy of Great Britain. The "Old Whig," for example, understood the dilemma perfectly, but could do no more than plead for a slightly weaker central government and explicit guarantees for the Natural Rights of Free Americans. Only a few like George Clinton of New York explicitly reasserted the validity of Montesquieu's thesis, but even he accepted the need to control domestic social unrest and admitted that the states would become an empire.

Perhaps the most revealing part of the story lies in the subsequent behavior of the critics. The overwhelming number rapidly embraced both the principles and the powers of the Constitution once they had lost the battle against adoption. Madison and his supporters had made their revolution: the logic and the instrument of empire had become the foundation of American society and the means to realizing the Future of liberty, freedom, opportunity, stability, and material welfare. Paraphrasing Washington's projection of hope into reality, Jedediah Morse asserted in 1789 that the erstwhile colonies "had risen into empire." He added that "it is well known that empire has been travelling from east to west. Probably her last and broadest seat will be America."

Thomas Hutchins, the geographer to the government, simply assumed that America would acquire the continent. That would enable the United States "to possess, in utmost security, the dominion of the sea throughout the world." That concern to create a maritime as well as a territorial empire also nibbled at the minds of Jefferson, Madison, and other southerners. Madison, for example, insisted as early as 1784 on the importance of controlling the coastline of the Gulf of Mexico. Jefferson (as well as Franklin) floated the idea that the eastern boundary of the United States was the far edge of the Gulf Stream. That argument presumably grew out of his new American system of natural rights: "the right to use a thing comprehends a right to the means necessary to its use." Jefferson would later carry that logic to its imperially absurd conclusion. In the meantime, the Kentucky Convention of 1788 reminded the new government of "the natural right of the inhabitants of this country to navigate the Mississippi."

Empire as a way of life steadily gathered momentum. Citing Jefferson's proposal to have the Great Seal of the United States depict the children of Israel being guided by a pillar of light, Weinberg concluded that "the doctrine of America's mission developed rather quickly into a dogma of special delegation." Ezra Stiles, the president of Yale University, would probably have applauded Weinberg's analysis. Stiles was certain, as early as 1783, that the Good Lord would raise America "high above all nations which he has made." But perhaps it is said best of all in Federalist Paper No. XI. Let us "concur in erecting one great American system, superior to the control of all trans-Atlantic force or influence, and able to dictate the terms of the connection between the old and new world." Truly, a manifesto of empire as a way of life. . . .

The appeal and influence of Madison's rational argument for imperial republicanism were steadily reinforced by individuals and groups who struggled to acquire ever more land and trade, and by other ideas and emotions. One of the most powerful of those forces was a belief from the past that was gradually adapted to the new realities of America. For the early religious sense of mission, so eloquently expressed in Governor Winthrop's phrase— "wee shall bee as a City upon a Hill"—did not lose its power.

Many Americans, poor as well as powerful, and agricultural as well as urban, viewed themselves as agents of God's will and purpose. There is no reason, for example, to doubt the sincerity of John Quincy Adams of Massachusetts when he described the United States as "a nation, coextensive with the North American Continent, destined by God and nature to be the most populous and powerful people ever combined under one social compact."

As that example suggests, ordained missionaries were not the only people motivated (even driven) by that religious spirit to carry America's truth on across the Pacific to Asia, or back across the Atlantic to the Middle East. One cannot escape a strong sense, in this connection, that even though God has been pronounced dead in many different ways since the Reformation, He was still very much alive. One of the most sophisticated ways of transforming Him involved secularizing Him by equating Godliness with individual or collective success on earth. As one perceptive observer has noted, that meant that Christianity became increasingly "self-centered and ego-directed."

Thus the successful way becomes the Lord's way, and Everyman becomes a missionary of the American Dream in dealing with the Indians and others who are not following the American Way. If such people refuse to "open their minds to the idea of improvement," they are agents of the Devil who must be dealt with by force. Or, as phrased by Lewis Henry Morgan, the father of American anthropology, they must be educated to American conceptions of the "rights of property, and rights of citizenship, which are common to ourselves." Such examples, and they can be cited *ad infinitum,* remind one of Horace Walpole's caustic observation of 1762 that "every age has some ostentatious system to excuse the havoc it commits."

That comment serves to underscore the point that the secularization of God affected groups (and even an entire society) as well as individuals. If the person's sense of calling was transformed from honoring God's laws to prospering in the marketplace, then the nation's calling was changed from being a City on a Hill to being the active crusader to reform the world according to the American Dream.

That process, which continued throughout the 19th century, was greatly reinforced by the wholly secular idea that the American Revolution (including the conception and implementation of the Constitution) represented the perfect revolution. Americans came very quickly to view themselves as having discovered the ultimate solution to mankind's long search for the proper way to organize society. Jefferson encapsulated the outlook in his famous remark that America was "the world's best hope."

That belief had two imperial consequences. First, the behavior of other peoples (including their revolutions) was judged by its correspondence with the American Way. The weaker the correlation, the greater the urge to intervene to help the wayward find the proper path to freedom and prosperity. Second, the faith in America's uniqueness coupled with the failure of others to copy the perfect revolution generated a deep sense of being *alone*. Americans considered themselves perpetually beleaguered, an attitude that led on to the conviction that military security was initially to be found in controlling the entire continent—and ultimately prompted them to deny *any* distinction between domestic and foreign policy.

Here again we can learn from Weinberg, an extremely subtle historian who offers sophisticated examples of how psychology can inform our understanding of what happened in the past and of who we are in the present. He suggests, for example, that the failure to conquer Canada during the Revolutionary War transformed acquisitiveness (or greed) into a trauma of insecurity. An irrational concern for "security for the future." He then ties that to the conviction of beginning the world over again: "a feeling of preordained right to ideal security." And so, "subordinating to their own right to security another people's right to liberty and equality, Americans apparently considered that no natural right of another was inalienable upon occasion—that on which it conflicted with the always inalienable rights of Americans themselves."

But even Franklin, that sly imperialist, had the sense to set limits. "To desire the Enemies whole country," he warned in 1760, "upon no other Principle but that otherwise you cannot secure your own, is turning the Idea of mere Defence into the most dangerous of all Principles. It is leaving no medium between Safety and Conquest."

But Americans increasingly defined safety in terms of conquest—or at any rate domination.

---

## FURTHER READING

Samuel Flagg Bemis, *The Diplomacy of the American Revolution* (1935)

I. R. Christie, *Crisis of Empire* (1966)

Gerald Clarfield, "John Adams: The Marketplace and American Foreign Policy," *New England Quarterly*, 52 (1979), 345–357

Jonathan R. Dull, *The French Navy and American Independence* (1976)

Felix Gilbert, *To the Farewell Address: Ideas of Early American Foreign Policy* (1961)

Ronald Hoffman and Peter J. Albert, eds., *Diplomacy and Revolution: The Franco-American Alliance of 1778* (1981)

James J. Hutson, *John Adams and the Diplomacy of the American Revolution* (1980)

Lawrence S. Kaplan, ed., *The American Revolution and "A Candid World"* (1977)

Walter LaFeber, "Foreign Policies of a New Nation," in William A. Williams, ed., *From Colony to Empire* (1972)

Frederick W. Marks, *Independence on Trial: Foreign Affairs and the Making of the Constitution* (1973)

Richard Morris, *The Peacemakers* (1965)
Max Savelle, *Empires to Nations: Expansion in America, 1713–1824* (1974)
———, *The Origins of American Diplomacy* (1968)
William Stinchcombe, *The American Revolution and the French Alliance* (1969)
Gerald Stourzh, *Benjamin Franklin and American Foreign Policy* (1969)
Richard Van Alstyne, *The Rising American Empire* (1960)
———, *Empire and Independence* (1965)
John Edward Wilz, "American Isolationism: Its Colonial Origins," *Amerikastudien/American Studies,* 21 (1976), 261–280

# The Great Debate of the 1790s

# 3

The peace with Britain ending the American Revolution, and the alliance
with France that helped achieve independence, presented the United States
with its first diplomatic problems as a new nation. Through the 1780s and
into the early 1790s, the British refused to leave fortified posts on American
soil or to negotiate a commercial treaty to protect American foreign trade.
The 1778 alliance with France became an encumbrance in 1792–1793 when
the French Revolution entered a violent and stormy stage that initiated war
between republican France and monarchical Europe. Conservative Americans
recoiled from what they identified as the excesses of republicanism. Alexander
Hamilton, Federalist Party leader and Secretary of the Treasury in the administration of George Washington, especially denounced France and urged
better relations with Great Britain as a bastion of conservatism and as
America's chief trading partner. On the other hand, James Madison and
Thomas Jefferson led a faction called the Republican Party. They applauded
the French Revolution as a notable triumph for freedom from tyranny and
for the ideas expressed in the American Revolution. They argued also that the
United States, because its foreign trade was so dependent upon the British,
was compromising its sovereignty by favoring Great Britain.

The Jay Treaty of 1794, signed with Britain, defused Anglo-American
tensions, especially over the occupied forts, but it ignited a heated debate at
home. George Washington tried to cool political passions and summarize
American diplomatic principles in his Farewell Address of 1796. But debate
persisted, and not until 1800 did France and the United States temper their
relations after years of quasi-war on the high seas by signing an agreement
terminating the 1778 alliance. Like other great debates in the history of

*American foreign policy, that of the 1790s illuminated profound questions and helped Americans define their future.*

## DOCUMENTS

At stake in the 1790s, thought many, was the survival of the fledging republic itself. President Washington asked Treasury Secretary Hamilton and Secretary of State Jefferson to provide answers to some tough questions: Should the United States proclaim formal neutrality? Should the minister from republican France be received? Was the United States still bound by the 1778 alliance? In April 1793, as the first two documents demonstrate, the articulate Cabinet members responded with strikingly different views. The Jay Treaty, signed on November 19, 1794, and ratified on June 22, 1795, by a 20–12 Senate vote, became the focal point for a spirited public debate. The next document, a letter from James Madison to Robert Livingston, dated August 10, 1795, reveals the Virginia congressman's political outrage over Jay's Treaty. George Washington's Farewell Address stands as a key document in the record of American diplomacy because it spoke not only to the immediate dangers of factionalism, but also to those American beliefs he hoped would guide diplomats in the future.

## Alexander Hamilton on the Alliance with France, 1793

Are the United States bound, by the principles of the laws of nations, to consider the treaties heretofore made with France as in present force and operation between them and the actual governing powers of the French nation? or may they elect to consider their operation as suspended, reserving also a right to judge finally whether any such changes have happened in the political affairs of France as may justify a renunciation of those treaties?

It is believed that they have an option to consider the operation of those treaties as suspended, and will have eventually a right to renounce them, if such changes shall take place as can *bona fide* be pronounced to render a continuance of the connections which result from them disadvantageous or dangerous.

There are two general propositions which may be opposed to this opinion: 1st. That a nation has a right, in its own discretion, to change its form of government—to abolish one, and substitute another. 2d. That *real* treaties (of which description those in question are) bind the NATIONS whose governments contract, and continue in force notwithstanding any changes which happen in the forms of their government.

The truth of the first proposition ought to be admitted in its fullest latitude. But it will by no means follow, that, because a nation has a right to manage its own concerns as it thinks fit, and to make such changes in its political institutions as itself judges best calculated to promote its interests, it has therefore a right to involve other nations, with whom it may have had connections, *absolutely* and *unconditionally,* in the consequences of the changes which it may think proper to make. This would be to give to a nation or society not only a power over its own happiness, but a power over the happiness of other nations or societies. It would be to extend the operation of the maxim much beyond the *reason* of it, which is simply, that every nation ought to have a right to provide for its own happiness. . . .

All general rules are to be construed with certain reasonable limitations. That which has been just mentioned must be understood in this sense, that changes in forms of government do not of course abrogate *real* treaties; that they continue absolutely binding on the party which makes the change, and will bind the other party, unless, in due time and for just cause, he declares his election to renounce them; that in good faith he ought not to renounce them, unless the change which happened does really render them useless, or materially less advantageous, or more dangerous than before. But for good and sufficient cause he may renounce them.

Nothing can be more evident than that the existing forms of government of two nations may enter far into the motives of a real treaty. . . .

Two nations may form an alliance because each has confidence in the energy and efficacy of the government of the other. A revolution may subject one of them to a different form of government—feeble, fluctuating, and turbulent, liable to provoke wars, and very little fitted to repel them. Even the connections of a nation with other foreign powers may enter into the motives of an alliance with it. If a dissolution of ancient connections shall have been a consequence of a revolution of government, the external political relations of the parties may have become so varied as to occasion an incompatibility of the alliance with the Power which had changed its constitution with the other connections of its ally—connections perhaps essential to its welfare.

In such cases, reason, which is the touchstone of all similar maxims, would dictate that the party whose government had remained stationary would have a right, under a *bona-fide* conviction that the change in the situation of the other party would render a future connection detrimental or dangerous, to declare the connection dissolved.

Contracts between nations as between individuals must lose their force where the considerations fail.

A treaty pernicious to the state is of itself void, where no change in the situation of either of the parties takes place. By a much stronger reason it must become *voidable* at the option of the other party, when the voluntary act of one of the allies has made so material a change in the condition of things as is always implied in a radical revolution of government.

## Thomas Jefferson on the Alliance with France, 1793

I proceed, in compliance with the requisition of the President, to give an opinion in writing on the general Question, Whether the U.S. have a right to renounce their treaties with France, or to hold them suspended till the government of that country shall be established? . . .

I consider the people who constitute a society or nation as the source of all authority in that nation, as free to transact their common concerns by any agents they think proper, to change these agents individually, or the organisation of them in form or function whenever they please: that all the acts done by those agents under the authority of the nation, are the acts of the nation, are obligatory on them, & enure to their use, & can in no wise be annulled or affected by any change in the form of the government, or of the persons administering it. Consequently the Treaties between the U.S. and France, were not treaties between the U.S. & Louis Capet, but between the two nations of America & France, and the nations remaining in existence, tho' both of them have since changed their forms of government, the treaties are not annulled by these changes. . . .

Compacts then between nation & nation are obligatory on them by the same moral law which obliges individuals to observe their compacts. There are circumstances however which sometimes excuse the non-performance of contracts between man & man: so are there also between nation & nation. When performance, for instance, becomes *impossible,* non-performance is not immoral. So if performance becomes *self-destructive* to the party, the law of self-preservation overrules the laws of obligation to others. . . .

But Reason, which gives this right of self-liberation from a contract in certain cases, has subjected it to certain just limitations.

The danger which absolves us must be great, inevitable & imminent. Is such the character of that now apprehended from our treaties with France? What is that danger. . . . Obligation is not suspended, till the danger is become real, & the moment of it so imminent, that we can no longer avoid decision without forever losing the opportunity to do it. . . .

The danger apprehended, is it that, the treaties remaining valid, the clause guarantying their West India islands will engage us in the war? But Does the Guarantee engage us to enter into the war in any event?

Are we to enter into it before we are called on by our allies? Have we been called on by them?—shall we ever be called on? Is it their interest to call on us?

Can they call on us before their islands are invaded, or imminently threatened?

If they can save them themselves, have they a right to call on us?

Are we obliged to go to war at once, without trying peaceable negotiations with their enemy?

If all these questions be against us, there are still others behind.

Are we in a condition to go to war?

Can we be expected to begin before we are in condition?

Will the islands be lost if we do not save them? Have we the means of saving them?

If we cannot save them are we bound to go to war for a desperate object?

Will not a 10 years forbearance in us to call them into the guarantee of our posts, entitle us to some indulgence?

Many, if not most of these questions offer grounds of doubt whether the clause of guarantee will draw us into the war. Consequently if this be the danger apprehended, it is not yet certain enough to authorize us in sound morality to declare, at this moment, the treaties null. . . .

Is the danger apprehended from the 22nd Art. of our treaty of commerce, which prohibits the enemies of France from fitting out privateers in our ports, or selling their prizes here. But we are free to refuse the same thing to France, there being no stipulation to the contrary, and we ought to refuse it on principles of fair neutrality.

But the reception of a Minister from the Republic of France, without qualifications, it is thought will bring us into danger: because this, it is said, will determine the continuance of the treaty, and take from us the right of self-liberation when at any time hereafter our safety would require us to use it. The reception of the Minister at all (in favor of which Col. Hamilton has given his opinion, tho reluctantly as he confessed) is an acknolegement of the legitimacy of their government: and if the qualifications meditated are to deny that legitimacy, it will be a curious compound which is to admit & deny the same thing. But I deny that the reception of a Minister has any thing to do with the treaties. There is not a word, in either of them, about sending ministers. This has been done between us under the common usage of nations, & can have no effect either to continue or annul the treaties.

But how can any act of election have the effect to continue a treaty which is acknoleged to be going on still? For it was not pretended the treaty was void, but only voidable if we chuse to declare it so. To make it void would require an act of election, but to let it go on requires only that we should do nothing, and doing nothing can hardly be an infraction of peace or neutrality.

But I go further & deny that the most explicit declaration made at this moment that we acknolege the obligation of the treaties could take from us the right of non-compliance at any future time when compliance would involve us in great & inevitable danger.

I conclude then that few of these sources threaten any danger at all; and from none of them is it inevitable: & consequently none of them give us the right at this moment of releasing ourselves from our treaties.

# The Jay Treaty, 1794

**Article II.** . . . His Majesty will withdraw all His Troops and Garrisons —from all Posts and Places within the Boundary Lines assigned by the Treaty of Peace to the United States. This Evacuation shall take place on or before the first Day of June One thousand seven hundred and ninety six. . . .

**Article III.** It is agreed that it shall at all Times be free to His Majesty's Subjects, and to the Citizens of the United States, and also to the Indians dwelling on either side of the said Boundary Line freely to pass and repass by Land, or Inland Navigation, into the respective Territories and Countries of the Two Parties on the Continent of America (the Country within the Limits of the Hudson's Bay Company only excepted) and to navigate all the Lakes, Rivers, and waters thereof, and freely to carry on trade and commerce with each other. But it is understood, that this Article does not extend to the admission of Vessels of the United States into the Sea Ports, Harbours, Bays, or Creeks of His Majesty's said Territories; nor into such parts of the Rivers in His Majesty's said Territories as are between the mouth thereof, and the highest Port of Entry from the Sea, except in small vessels trading bona fide between Montreal and Quebec, under such regulations as shall be established to prevent the possibility of any Frauds in this respect. Nor to the admission of British vessels from the Sea into the Rivers of the United States, beyond the highest Ports of Entry for Foreign Vessels from the Sea. The River Mississippi, shall however, according to the Treaty of Peace be entirely open to both Parties; And it is further agreed, That all the ports and places on its Eastern side, to whichsoever of the parties belonging, may freely be resorted to, and used by both parties, in as ample a manner as any of the Atlantic Ports or Places of the United States, or any of the Ports or Places of His Majesty in Great Britain. . . .

**Article VI.** Whereas it is alleged by divers British Merchants and others His Majesty's Subjects, that Debts to a considerable amount which were bónâ fide contracted before the Peace, still remain owing to them by Citizens or Inhabitants of the United States. . . . It is agreed that in all such Cases where full Compensation for such losses and damages cannot, for whatever reason, be actually obtained had and received by the said Creditors in the ordinary course of Justice, The United States will make full and complete Compensation for the same to the said Creditors. . . .

**Article XII.** His Majesty Consents that it shall and may be lawful, during the time hereinafter Limited, for the Citizens of the United States, to carry to any of His Majesty's Islands and Ports in the West Indies from the United States in their own Vessels, not being above the burthen of Seventy Tons, any Goods or Merchandizes, being of the Growth, Manufacture, or Produce of the said States, which it is, or may be lawful to carry to the said Islands or Ports from the said States in British Vessels, and that the said American Vessels shall be subject there to no other or higher Tonnage Duties or Charges, than shall be payable by British vessels, in the Ports of the United States; and that the Cargoes of the said American Vessels shall, be subject there to no other or higher Duties or Charges than shall be payable on the like Articles, if imported there from the said States in British vessels.

And His Majesty also consents that it shall be lawful for the said American Citizens to purchase, load and carry away, in their said vessels to the United States from the said Islands and Ports, all such articles being of the Growth, Manufacture or Produce of the said Islands, as may now by Law be carried from thence to the said States in British Vessels, and subject only to the same Duties and Charges on Exportation to which British Vessels and their Cargoes are or shall be subject in similar circumstances.

Provided always that the said American vessels do carry and land their Cargoes in the United States only, it being expressly agreed and declared that during the Continuance of this article, the United States will prohibit and restrain the carrying any Meolasses, Sugar, Coffee, Cocoa or Cotton in American vessels, either from His Majesty's Islands or from the United States, to any part of the World, except the United States, reasonable Sea Stores excepted. Provided, also, that it shall and may be lawful during the same period for British vessels to import from the said Islands into the United States, and to export from the United States to the said Islands, all Articles whatever being of the Growth, Produce or Manufacture of the said Islands, or of the United States respectively, which now may, by the Laws of the said States, be so imported and exported. And that the Cargoes of the said British vessels, shall be subject to no other or higher Duties or Charges, than shall be payable on the same articles if so imported or exported in American Vessels.

It is agreed that this Article, and every Matter and Thing therein contained, shall continue to be in Force, during the Continuance of the war in which His Majesty is now engaged; and also for Two years from and after the Day of the signature of the Preliminary or other Articles of Peace by which the same may be terminated. . . .

**Article XIII.** His Majesty consents that vessels belonging to the citizens of the United States shall be admitted and hospitably received in all the seaports and harbors of the British territories in the East Indies. And that the citizens of the said United States may freely carry on a trade between the said territories and the said United States, in all articles of which the importation or exportation respectively, to or from the said territories shall not be entirely prohibited. . . . But it is expressly agreed that the vessels of the United States shall not carry any of the articles exported by them from the said British territories to any port or place, except to some port or place in America. . . . It is also understood that the permission granted by this article is not to extend to allow the vessels of the United States to carry on any part of the coasting trade of the said British territories; . . .

**Article XIV.** There shall be between all the dominions of His Majesty in Europe and the territories of the United States a reciprocal and perfect liberty of commerce and navigation. . . .

**Article XV.** It is agreed, that no other or higher Duties shall be paid by the Ships or Merchandize of the one Party in the Ports of the other, than such as are paid by the like vessels or Merchandize of all other Nations. Nor shall any other or higher Duty be imposed in one Country on the importation of any articles, the growth, produce, or manufacture of the other, than are or shall be payable on the importation of the like articles being of the growth, produce or manufacture of any other Foreign Country. Nor shall any prohibition be imposed, on the exportation or importation of any articles to or from the Territories of the Two Parties respectively which shall not equally extend to all other Nations. . . .

**Article XVIII.** In order to regulate what is in future to be esteemed Contraband of war, it is agreed that under the said Denomination shall be comprized all Arms, and Implements serving for the purposes of war . . . as also Timber for Shipbuilding, Tar or Rosin, Copper in Sheets, Sails, Hemp, and Cordage, and generally whatever may serve directly to the equipment of

Vessels, unwrought Iron and Fir planks only excepted, and all the above articles are hereby declared to be just objects of Confiscation, whenever they are attempted to be carried to an Enemy.

And Whereas the difficulty of agreeing on the precise Cases in which alone Provisions and other articles not generally contraband may be regarded as such, renders it expedient to provide against the inconveniences and misunderstandings which might thence arise: It is further agreed that whenever any such articles so becoming Contraband according to the existing Laws of Nations, shall for that reason be seized, the same shall not be confiscated, but the owners thereof shall be speedily and completely indemnified; and the Captors, or in their default the Government under whose authority they act, shall pay to the Masters or Owners of such Vessels the full value of all such Articles, with a reasonable mercantile Profit thereon, together with the Freight, and also the Demurrage incident to such Detension. . . .

**Article XXIV.** It shall not be lawful for any Foreign Privateers (not being Subjects or Citizens of either of the said Parties) who have Commissions from any other Prince or State in enmity with either Nation, to arm their Ships in the Ports of either of the said Parties, nor to sell what they have taken, nor in any other manner to exchange the same, nor shall they be allowed to purchase more provisions than shall be necessary for their going to the nearest Port of that Prince or State from whom they obtained their Commissions.

**Article XXV.** It shall be lawful for the Ships of war and Privateers belonging to the said Parties respectively to carry whithersoever they please the Ships and Goods taken from their Enemies without being obliged to pay any Fee to the Officers of the Admiralty, or to any Judges whatever; nor shall the said Prizes when they arrive at, and enter the Ports of the said Parties be detained or seized, neither shall the Searchers or other Officers of those Places visit such Prizes (except for the purpose of preventing the Carrying of any of the Cargo thereof on Shore in any manner contrary to the established Laws of Revenue, Navigation or Commerce) nor shall such Officers take Cognizance of the Validity of such Prizes; but they shall be at liberty to hoist Sail, and depart as speedily as may be, and carry their said Prizes to the place mentioned in their Commissions or Patents, which the Commanders of the said Ships of war or Privateers shall be obliged to shew. No Shelter or Refuge shall be given in their Ports to such as have made a Prize upon the Subjects or Citizens of either of the said Parties; but if forced by stress of weather or the Dangers of the Sea, to enter therein, particular care shall be taken to hasten their departure, and to cause them to retire as soon as possible. Nothing in this Treaty contained shall however be construed or operate contrary to former and existing Public Treaties with other Sovereigns or States. But the Two parties agree, that while they continue in amity neither of them will in future make any Treaty that shall be inconsistent with this or the preceding article. . . .

**Article XXVIII.** It is agreed that the first Ten Articles of this Treaty shall be permanent and that the subsequent Articles except the Twelfth shall be limited in their duration to Twelve years. . . .

# James Madison's Criticism of the Jay Treaty, 1795

... Indeed, the Treaty from one end to the other must be regarded as a demonstration that the Party to which the Envoy [Jay] belongs & of which he has been more the organ than of the U. S., is a British party systematically aiming at an exclusive connection with the British Govern$^t$ & ready to sacrifice to that object as well the dearest interests of our commerce as the most sacred dictates of National honour. This is the true Key to this unparalleled proceeding, & can alone explain it to the impartial & discerning part of the Public. The leaders of this Party stand *self condemned* in their efforts to paliate [sic] the Treaty by magnifying the necessity of the British commerce to the U. S. & the insufficiency of the U. S. to influence the regulation of it. You will find on turning to a Pamphlet addressed to your people by Mr. Jay when the Federal Constitution was before them, that he then could see our power under such a Constitution to extort what we justly claimed from G. B., & particularly to open the W. India ports to us. As an Agent for the Constitution he now voluntarily abandons the very object which as an advocate for the Constitution he urged as an argument for adopting it,—read also the Paper N°. XI in the Publication entitled the Federalist for the view of the subject then inculcated by another advocate,—it is with much Pleasure I assure you that the sentiments & voice of the People in this State, in relation to the attempt to Prostrate us to a foreign & unfriendly Nation, are as decided & as loud as could be wished. Many, even of those who have hitherto rallied to the most exceptionable Party measures, join in the general indignation ag$^{st}$ the Treaty....

# George Washington's Farewell Address, 1796

The period for a new election of a citizen to administer the Executive Government of the United States being not far distant, and the time actually arrived when your thoughts must be employed in designating the person who is to be clothed with that important trust, it appears to me proper, especially as it may conduce to a more distinct expression of the public voice, that I should now apprise you of the resolution I have formed to decline being considered among the number of those out of whom a choice is to be made....

I have already intimated to you the danger of parties in the State, with particular reference to the founding of them on geographical discriminations. Let me now take a more comprehensive view, and warn you in the most solemn manner against the baneful effects of the spirit of party generally.

This spirit, unfortunately, is inseparable from our nature, having its root in the strongest passions of the human mind. It exists under different shapes in all governments, more or less stifled, controlled, or repressed; but in those of the popular form it is seen in its greatest rankness and is truly their worst enemy.

The alternate domination of one faction over another, sharpened by the spirit of revenge natural to party dissension, which in different ages and countries has perpetrated the most horrid enormities, is itself a frightful despotism. But this leads at length to a more formal and permanent despotism. The disorders and miseries which result gradually incline the minds of men to seek security and repose in the absolute power of an individual, and sooner or later the chief of some prevailing faction, more able or more fortunate than his competitors, turns this disposition to the purposes of his own elevation on the ruins of public liberty.

Without looking forward to an extremity of this kind (which nevertheless ought not to be entirely out of sight), the common and continual mischiefs of the spirit of party are sufficient to make it the interest and duty of a wise people to discourage and restrain it.

It serves always to distract the public councils and enfeeble the public administration. It agitates the community with ill-founded jealousies and false alarms; kindles the animosity of one part against another; foments occasionally riot and insurrection. It opens the door to foreign influence and corruption, which find a facilitated access to the government itself through the channels of party passion. Thus the policy and the will of one country are subjected to the policy and will of another. . . .

Observe good faith and justice toward all nations. Cultivate peace and harmony with all. Religion and morality enjoin this conduct. And can it be that good policy does not equally enjoin it? It will be worthy of a free, enlightened, and at no distant period a great nation to give to mankind the magnanimous and too novel example of a people always guided by an exalted justice and benevolence. Who can doubt that in the course of time and things the fruits of such a plan would richly repay any temporary advantages which might be lost by a steady adherence to it? Can it be that Providence has not connected the permanent felicity of a nation with its virtue? The experiment, at least, is recommended by every sentiment which ennobles human nature. Alas! is it rendered impossible by its vices?

In the execution of such a plan nothing is more essential than that permanent, inveterate antipathies against particular nations and passionate attachments for others should be excluded, and that in place of them just and amicable feelings toward all should be cultivated. The nation which indulges toward another an habitual hatred or an habitual fondness is in some degree a slave. It is a slave to its animosity or to its affection, either of which is sufficient to lead it astray from its duty and its interest. Antipathy in one nation against another disposes each more readily to offer insult and injury, to lay hold of slight causes of umbrage, and to be haughty and intractable when accidental or trifling occasions of dispute occur.

Hence frequent collisions, obstinate, envenomed, and bloody contests. The nation prompted by ill will and resentment sometimes impels to war the government contrary to the best calculations of policy. The government sometimes participates in the national propensity, and adopts through passion what reason would reject. At other times it makes the animosity of the nation subservient to projects of hostility, instigated by pride, ambition, and other sinister and pernicious motives. The peace often, sometimes perhaps the liberty, of nations has been the victim.

So, likewise, a passionate attachment of one nation for another produces a variety of evils. Sympathy for the favorite nation, facilitating the illusion of an imaginary common interest in cases where no real common interest exists, and infusing into one the enmities of the other, betrays the former into a participation in the quarrels and wars of the latter without adequate inducement or justification. It leads also to concessions to the favorite nation of privileges denied to others, which is apt doubly to injure the nation making the concessions by unnecessarily parting with what ought to have been retained, and by exciting jealousy, ill will, and a disposition to retaliate in the parties from whom equal privileges are withheld; and it gives to ambitious, corrupted, or deluded citizens (who devote themselves to the favorite nation) facility to betray or sacrifice the interests of their own country without odium, sometimes even with popularity, gilding with the appearances of a virtuous sense of obligation, a commendable deference for public opinion, or a laudable zeal for public good the base or foolish compliances of ambition, corruption, or infatuation.

As avenues to foreign influence in innumerable ways, such attachments are particularly alarming to the truly enlightened and independent patriot. How many opportunities do they afford to tamper with domestic factions, to practice the arts of seduction, to mislead public opinion, to influence or awe the public councils! Such an attachment of a small or weak toward a great and powerful nation dooms the former to be the satellite of the latter. Against the insidious wiles of foreign influence (I conjure you to believe me, fellow-citizens) the jealousy of a free people ought to be *constantly* awake, since history and experience prove that foreign influence is one of the most baneful foes of republican government. But that jealousy, to be useful, must be impartial, else it becomes the instrument of the very influence to be avoided, instead of a defense against it. Excessive partiality for one foreign nation and excessive dislike of another cause those whom they actuate to see danger only on one side, and serve to veil and even second the arts of influence on the other. Real patriots who may resist the intrigues of the favorite are liable to become suspected and odious, while its tools and dupes usurp the applause and confidence of the people to surrender their interests.

The great rule of conduct for us in regard to foreign nations is, in extending our commercial relations to have with them as little *political* connection as possible. So far as we have already formed engagements let them be fulfilled with perfect good faith. Here let us stop.

Europe has a set of primary interests which to us have none or a very remote relation. Hence she must be engaged in frequent controversies, the causes of which are essentially foreign to our concerns. Hence, therefore, it must be unwise in us to implicate ourselves by artificial ties in the ordinary vicissitudes of her politics or the ordinary combinations and collisions of her friendships or enmities.

Our detached and distant situation invites and enables us to pursue a different course. If we remain one people, under an efficient government, the period is not far off when we may defy material injury from external annoyance; when we may take such an attitude as will cause the neutrality we may at any time resolve upon to be scrupulously respected; when belligerent nations, under the impossibility of making acquisitions upon us, will not lightly hazard the giving us provocation; when we may choose peace or war, as our interest, guided by justice, shall counsel.

Why forego the advantages of so peculiar a situation? Why quit our own to stand upon foreign ground? Why, by interweaving our destiny with that of any part of Europe, entangle our peace and prosperity in the toils of European ambition, rivalship, interest, humor, or caprice?

It is our true policy to steer clear of permanent alliances with any portion of the foreign world, so far, I mean, as we are now at liberty to do it; for let me not be understood as capable of patronizing infidelity to existing engagements. I hold the maxim no less applicable to public than to private affairs that honesty is always the best policy. I repeat, therefore, let those engagements be observed in their genuine sense. But in my opinion it is unnecessary and would be unwise to extend them.

Taking care always to keep ourselves by suitable establishments on a respectable defensive posture, we may safely trust to temporary alliances for extraordinary emergencies.

Harmony, liberal intercourse with all nations are recommended by policy, humanity, and interest. But even our commercial policy should hold an equal and impartial hand, neither seeking nor granting exclusive favors or preferences; consulting the natural course of things; diffusing and diversifying by gentle means the streams of commerce, but forcing nothing; establishing with powers so disposed, in order to give trade a stable course, to define the rights of our merchants, and to enable the Government to support them, conventional rules of intercourse, the best that present circumstances and mutual opinion will permit, but temporary and liable to be from time to time abandoned or varied as experience and circumstances shall dictate; constantly keeping in view that it is folly in one nation to look for disinterested favors from another; that it must pay with a portion of its independence for whatever it may accept under that character; that by such acceptance it may place itself in the condition of having given equivalents for nominal favors, and yet of being reproached with ingratitude for not giving more. There can be no greater error than to expect or calculate upon real favors from nation to nation. It is an illusion which experience must cure, which a just pride ought to discard.

---

# ESSAYS

The 1793 debate between Hamilton and Jefferson over the alliance with France was just one of their many verbal skirmishes in the 1790s. As the following essays illustrate, the Founding Fathers grappled with weighty questions about the national interest, and scholars differ in their interpretations of the answers the beleaguered Fathers gave.

Professor Paul A. Varg of Michigan State University gently chides Thomas Jefferson and James Madison for excessive idealism and applauds the tough-minded realism of Hamilton, who saw the economic necessity of amicable ties with Britain. Lawrence Kaplan of Kent State University, on the other hand, finds a healthy blend of realism and idealism in Jefferson and points out similarities with Hamilton. The closing essay by Alexander DeConde of the University of California, Santa Barbara, takes another tack, which is outside the idealism versus realism debate. DeConde stresses the often selfish political partisanship of both Hamiltonians and Jeffersonians and suggests that the inflated, glorified image of Washington era leaders as great statesmen requires revision.

# The Virtues of Hamiltonian
# Realism over Jeffersonian Idealism

### PAUL A. VARG

Foreign policy questions during the presidency of George Washington became the focal point of political debate and contributed in a major way to the rise of political parties. The Constitution did not envision parties, and George Washington was strongly averse to their becoming a part of the American political scene, but as Joseph Charles has shown in *The Origins of the American Party System,* the debate over foreign policy, culminating in the crisis over the question of ratification of the Jay Treaty, brought about the division of the people into two divergent groups.

It has usually been overlooked that the issues at stake in the debate over that treaty emerged in the first session of the first Congress. James Madison was then a leader in the House of Representatives, and he sought to carry out what he deeply believed had been the mandate of the public in establishing the new government, namely a change from the helpless posture in foreign affairs to a position of effective bargaining. His program centered on commercial relations and sought to extend commerce with nations other than Great Britain and thereby to free the republic from being a mere appendage of the British economy. He viewed British economic influence by means of close commercial ties as exceedingly dangerous to the cherished republican ideals. James Madison is usually associated with the states rights position in domestic history, but he was a highly sensitive nationalist whose patriotism rested on a deep commitment to the principles of the Revolution.

His opponent in the long controversy was Alexander Hamilton, another nationalist, with whom he had been a colleague in the Constitutional Convention and with whom he joined, along with John Jay, in writing the *Federalist Papers.* They were on cordial terms at the convention and the views they expressed in their written defense of the Constitution show a close harmony. The split between them arose over Madison's foreign commercial policy. Thereafter Madison became an ardent opponent of the views expressed by

Paul A. Varg, *Foreign Policies of the Founding Fathers* (East Lansing, Mich.: Michigan State University Press, 1963), pp. 70–79, 83, 95–97, 105–107, 111–113, 145–147.

Hamilton in the famous reports he prepared as Secretary of the Treasury. Hamilton expressed surprise when he found Madison opposing him on the measures he recommended and he recalled that his opponent had expressed sympathy with similar proposals in 1787. There is evidence that Madison's essential disagreement with Hamilton was on foreign policy rather than the domestic measures. A recent writer, E. James Ferguson, raises questions concerning the genuineness of Madison's opposition to Hamilton's funding measures and suggests that political expediency rather than considerations of justice caused Madison to oppose Hamilton's proposal. This conclusion, of course, lends added weight to the view that the basic cause of the split between the two ardent nationalists was a difference in foreign policy.

Their differences on foreign policy are more than adequate to explain the struggle that developed. These differences went down to the very roots where every serious debate over foreign policy issues must inevitably find itself. Hamilton was above all a realist who fatalistically accepted the existing framework, and dedicated himself to obtaining the best bargain possible. He did not object to the *realpolitik* of balance of power diplomacy, chose to regard treaties as convenient arrangements binding on the parties until they no longer served the purposes of one or the other, accepted British dominance as a simple fact of life, and dismissed as dangerous embarking on goals that the limited power of the country could scarcely hope to achieve. His own limited aim in foreign relations was to guarantee access to what he considered the prime need of a nation that desperately needed capital for the development of its tremendous resources so that it might one day emerge as a major power.

James Madison exemplifies the idealist in foreign policy. He spoke often of the rights of the republic and of what was just in international affairs but never felt it necessary to balance goals with the power available. At the base of his nationalism was a moralistic view that the new republic would be false to its mission in the world if it compromised its ideals. To remain true to its mission the nation must free itself from British dominance over the carrying trade and from the marketing of its goods through the British mercantile houses because British influence through these channels would strengthen monarchical principles and jade the lustrous principles of republicanism.

When the administration of George Washington took office in March, 1789, the basic dilemma confronting the nation was not yet clear. The United States was allied to France not only by treaty but by sentiment; it was tied to Great Britain in terms of markets, sources of manufactures, and credit. The rivalry of these two nations, soon to break forth in war, imposed on the new nation issues that threatened to tear it apart. In these issues lies the thread of American diplomacy from 1789 to 1812.

In the first session of Congress Madison presented a program for a commercial system that would give the United States economic independence. He explained that "the commerce between America and Great Britain exceeds what may be considered its natural boundary." British dominance, he said, was due to "the long possession of our trade, their commercial regulations calculated to retain it, their similarity of language and manners, their conformity of laws and other circumstances—all these concurring have made their commerce with us more extensive than their natural situation would require it to be."

Madison's program called for discriminatory tonnage duties on British ships. France and other nations that had entered into commercial treaties were to be rewarded with preferential rates. The opposition quickly pointed out that the higher rates on non-British ships could only mean higher prices on the goods Americans bought. Madison replied that the patriotism of Americans would cause them to make the necessary sacrifice, and that Americans could be induced to build a merchant marine in a short time as American ships would have an advantage over all foreign ships. He admitted that he would much prefer to see a completely free system. "But," he said, "we have maritime dangers to guard against, and we can be secured from them no other way than by having a navy and seamen of our own; these can only be obtained by giving a preference." "I admit it is a tax," he continued, "and a tax upon our produce; but it is a tax we must pay for the national security."

A nationalistic tone pervaded Madison's discourse on commerce. The economic advantages sought seemed at times less important than to command the respect of Great Britain. "We have now the power to avail ourselves of our natural superiority," he said, "and I am for beginning with some manifestation of that ability, that foreign nations may or might be taught to pay us that respect which they have neglected on account of our former imbecility." It was all important to show that "we dare exert ourselves in defeating any measure which commercial policy shall offer hostile to the welfare of America." He defended his program against the charge that it was a tax that the people would pay by asserting that his measures would "secure to us that respect and attention which we merit." Great Britain, he charged, "has bound us in commercial manacles, and very nearly defeated the object of our independence."

Madison's nationalism led him to place a high estimate on the strength of the new nation. He had no fear of British recriminations for "her interests can be wounded almost mortally, while ours are invulnerable." The British West Indies, he maintained, could not live without American foodstuffs, but Americans could easily do without British manufactures. This same faith led him to the conclusion "that it is in our power, in a very short time, to supply all the tonnage necessary for our own commerce."

Enamored with democratic ideals and absorbed with the need for markets for the ever richer flow of agricultural produce, James Madison set forth a foreign policy that would enable the new nation to carry on its experiment in republican principles and promote the economic well being of the farmers who constituted ninety per cent of the population. Like true agrarians they believed that the world lived by the produce of the farm; like true Americans they also believed that American farms were the most important in meeting the needs of the world's markets. Therein, they thought, lay the new nation's opportunity to influence world affairs.

Farmers had an eye for markets that would enter into competitive bidding for their ever expanding supplies. Dependence on Great Britain, they said, reduced them to a hostage of that country. British merchants took almost half of their exports and furnished three-fourths of the imports. Their patriotism rebelled at the sense of dependence that British economic connections fostered. How much better to trade with all the world. That others wanted their wheat, flour, and rice seemed self-evident. The other nations would gladly buy from them if only the dependence on British ships could be overcome. British ships funnelled everything through England's entrepôts, and then redistributed large amounts to other nations. How much better if a direct trade with consuming countries could be opened up. What a great advantage it would be if the United States could have its own merchant marine. That merchant marine would serve as a great nursery for seamen and would enable the nation to build a navy to protect the routes to markets. And what a sense of freedom would be imparted by the absence of the ubiquitous British creditor who stalked through the South collecting his debts. Virginians alone owed British merchants £2,300,000 (pounds sterling).

James Madison, and the new Secretary of State, Thomas Jefferson, who soon joined him, called for legislative measures to emancipate the country from economic bondage to Great Britain and the fostering of closer economic ties with other nations. France naturally attracted attention. Capable of absorbing large amounts of produce both at home and in her West Indies colonies, and also able to supply many of the needed manufactures, France seemed to offer the best counterpoise to England. Together the two nations could break the overwhelming British economic power that held Europe in its control.

The prospect took on a new glow when, in 1789, France embarked on revolution. Now it seemed that the two nations would complement each other politically as well as economically. Thomas Jefferson alone among foreign diplomats in Paris welcomed the event. "I have so much confidence in the good sense of man, and his qualifications for self-government," he wrote, "that I am never afraid of the issue where reason is left free to exert her force; and I will agree to be stoned as a false prophet if all does not end well in this country. Here is but the first chapter of the history of European liberty." To Madison he observed that members of the French Assembly looked to America as their model and viewed American precedents as they would the authority of the Bible, "open to explanation but not to question."

The kinship between the two nations received symbolic expression in Jefferson's assistance in the drafting of the Declaration of the Rights of Man. And in the last days of August, 1789, the leaders of the new government met in Jefferson's apartment to settle their differences on the degree of power to be exercised by the king. Four years later the French Jacobins made James Madison an honorary citizen of France. Madison gloried in the thought that France ignored the traditional national fences that had divided humanity into hostile camps.

On August 28, two days after the French presented to the world the Declaration of the Rights of Man, Jefferson wrote to Madison expressing the hope that the United States would take steps to assist France and not be content to place the French "on a mere footing with the English."

> When of two nations, the one has engaged herself in a ruinous war for us, has spent her blood and money to save us, has opened her bosom to us in peace, and received us almost on the footing of her own citizens, while the other has moved heaven, earth, and hell to exterminate us in war, has insulted us in all her councils in peace, shut her doors to us in every port where her interests would admit it, libelled us in foreign nations, endeavored to poison them against the reception of our most precious commodities, to place these two nations on a footing, is to give a great deal more to one than to the other if the maxim be true that to make unequal quantities equal you must add more to the one of them than the other.

At first all classes and parts of the country hailed the Revolution. George Washington, after learning of the developments in France in the summer of 1789, expressed fear that it "is of too great a magnitude to be effected in so short a space" but what had taken place struck him as "of so wonderful a nature, that the mind can hardly realize the fact." If it should end as recent events indicated "that nation will be the most powerful and happy in Europe." Gouverneur Morris, who was in Paris, found it difficult "to guess whereabouts the flock will settle, when it flies so wild," but he too approved of the overthrow of the old order. He advised Washington: "I say, that we have an *interest* in the liberty of France. The leaders here are our friends. Many of them have imbibed their principles in America, and all have been fired by our example. Their opponents are by no means rejoiced at the success of our revolution, and many of them are disposed to form connexions of the strictest kind, with Great Britain."

The revolution in France merely strengthened convictions that Jefferson and Madison had held since 1783. As minister to France since 1785 Jefferson had worked industriously to promote commerce between the two countries. And when the new government took office in 1789 Madison earnestly believed that a leading motive in its establishment had been to achieve a degree of reciprocity with England and to extend the trade with other countries.

Congress did establish discriminatory duties on foreign ships, but it rejected Madison's proposal for further discrimination against ships of nations that had failed to enter into a commercial treaty. Those involved in trade saw no great hope of developing a trade with France, a nation they considered as staunch an adherent of the old exclusive mercantile system as the British. Madison would make his proposals another day when the country faced a dangerous foreign situation. By then he faced the hard fact that Alexander Hamilton had committed the nation to a foreign and domestic policy that ran directly counter to the most cherished ideals of the agrarians and tied the United States to England.

Hamilton boldly asserted that foreign policy must serve the ends set forth by national economic policy. Foreign capital constituted the great economic need of the United States, and, true to his principles, Hamilton fought desperately to make foreign policy an instrument for meeting that need. Concerning the value of foreign capital, he wrote that it ought to be "considered as a most valuable auxiliary, conducing to put in motion a greater quantity of productive labor, and a greater portion of useful enterprise, than could exist without it." In an underdeveloped country like the United States, "with an infinite fund of resources yet to be unfolded, every farthing of foreign capital" invested in internal improvements and in industry, "is a precious acquisition."

The value he placed upon it appeared in more eloquent fashion in the measures he put through. Capital would be available if the new nation demonstrated that it was friendly to capitalists and not ready to bend to the whims of an ignorant public guided by passion and by hostility to privileged classes. His program as the Secretary of the Treasury met all the requirements. Foreign, national domestic debts, and state debts were met with an alacrity that invited the fullest confidence of the creditor class. The funding system provided an opportunity for profitable investment guaranteeing to creditors an attractive rate of interest over a long period of time. The United States Bank added to the circulating media and thereby promoted business, but it had the added advantage of providing capitalists with a good investment opportunity. And Hamilton's leadership in the Washington administration approximated that of a British prime minister who steered Congress at will and reduced popular distempers to harmless frustration.

Hamilton's financial system necessitated a policy of friendship toward Great Britain. Only British capital could guarantee the economic leap that the Secretary of Treasury envisioned. Only duties on imports would meet the financial obligations the new government assumed, and three-fourths of the imports came from Great Britain. Any interruption of that trade would deprive the new government of its major source of revenue. National interest, then, dictated good relations with Great Britain.

The great danger facing Hamilton's financial structure lay in the anti-British feelings of the people and their readiness to accept revolutionary France as a sister nation fighting for the rights of man. Of these two hazards, the feeling of kinship for the French revolutionary leaders posed the greatest threat. Hamilton viewed with alarm the French messianic rhetoric and a mass psychological outburst in the name of liberty, equality and fraternity that suggested the immediate emancipation of mankind from the thralldom of the past. The French leaders startled the world with appeals to people everywhere to revolt against their masters. The powerful and deeply ingrained democratic sentiments of Americans provided a fertile soil for such appeals, and Hamilton lived in mortal dread of the excited multitude driving their representatives into a pro-French policy that would alienate the British and perhaps even pull the nation into partnership with France against Great Britain in war. . . .

What had been a rift became a deep cleavage in 1793. Two developments sharpened the differences. In February of that year Great Britain and France went to war and forced the United States to give careful thought to its obligations under the French alliance. The Washington administration no sooner came to grips with that issue than Citizen Genêt arrived with a proposal for a new commercial treaty and instructions to promote the use of American manpower, port facilities, and produce. The merchant group made shrewd use of both to strengthen their political hold.

In April Washington's cabinet debated the question of the relationship of the United States to the two belligerents. The issue was not neutrality as much as it was the kind of neutrality. Hamilton contended that the treaty with France was no longer binding. He argued that the justice of Louis' execution appeared doubtful, that it remained to be seen whether the new government would prove stable, that it was guilty of taking extreme measures and of being the aggressor in the war, that it had violated all rights in seeking to promote revolutions abroad, and that it was undertaking military and naval operations involving risks never contemplated at the time the treaty was negotiated. Hamilton, the advocate of *realpolitik,* held that a nation's first duty was to uphold its own interests and that treaty obligations must always be subordinate to that duty. Jefferson expressed disgust at the expediency of the Secretary of the Treasury. "Would you suppose it possible," he wrote to Madison, "that it should have been seriously proposed to declare our treaties with France void on the authority of an ill-understood scrap in Vattel and that it should be necessary to discuss it?"

Jefferson refused to throw off the treaty, but this did not prevent him from firmly resolving on a policy of neutrality. It must be a "manly neutrality" as opposed to Hamilton's "abject principles" and willingness to offer "our breech to every kick which Great Britain may choose to give." He was equally determined to stand firm against any French violations of American neutrality. "I wish," he wrote to James Monroe, "we may be able to repress the spirit of the people within the limits of a fair neutrality." A "fair neutrality" would yield no more privileges to France than to England. Jefferson gave the treaty with France a strict interpretation and narrowed the rights of that country to a minimum. He confided to Madison, "I fear that a fair neutrality will prove a disagreeable pill to our friends, tho' necessary to keep us out of the calamities of a war."

Jefferson's "fair neutrality" gained the support of President Washington. He issued a proclamation warning citizens against unneutral acts. The tone of the proclamation disturbed the incorruptible Madison whose sense of moral obligation winced at the sacrifice of principle to what appeared to be national self interest. He disliked the use of the term "impartial" in the President's proclamation. "Peace," wrote Madison, "is no doubt to be preserved at any price that honor and good faith will permit." "In examining our own engagements under the Treaty with France," he wrote, "it would be honorable as well as just to adhere to the sense that would at the time have been put on them." "The attempt to shuffle off the Treaty altogether by quibblings on Vattel is equally contemptible." The difference between Hamilton's approach to a treaty and the approach of Jefferson and Madison was symbolic of the wide gulf that separated their broader concept of foreign relations.

The Secretary of State soon complained that his colleagues in the administration leaned toward England. "We are going on here in the same spirit still," he wrote. "The Anglomania has seized violently on three members of our council," said the Secretary of State. Jefferson saw that the "natural aristocrats" of the larger towns, the merchants trading in British capital, the "paper men," and all the "old tories" supported the English side on every question. The farmers, tradesmen, mechanics, and merchants trading on their own capital took the other side. The same groups who supported Hamilton's fiscal policy followed him on the question of foreign affairs. Not all discerned the intimate relation between the recently adopted financial program and the question of what attitude to take toward Great Britain, but the connection by no means escaped such leaders in Congress as William Smith of South Carolina and Fisher Ames and Theodore Sedgwick of Massachusetts. Nor did the fact that domestic policy and foreign policy were essentially one and the same escape Jefferson and Madison. The latter saw in the "errors" of the administration a wound to national honor, a disregard of the obligations to France, and an injury to public feeling "by a seeming indifference to the cause of liberty." But it was not the cause of liberty in Europe alone but in the United States as well that both Jefferson and Madison had in mind. What they did not understand was that Hamilton put national interest above all other considerations. . . .

The debate over relations with Great Britain became inextricably involved with the question of which of the two emerging parties was to control the federal government for the next four years. The Jay Treaty was a reasonable give-and-take compromise of the issues between the two countries. What rendered it so assailable was not the compromise spelled out between the two nations but the fact that it was not a compromise between the two political parties at home. Embodying the views of the Federalists, the treaty repudiated the foreign policy of the opposing party. The Anti-Federalists saw in their party's foreign policy a set of principles of fundamental importance not only in relation to the outside world but also basic to the very nature of the kind of society they were seeking to establish at home. They were likewise intent on taking control of the government in the approaching election. Tied to the question of the ratification of the treaty was the question of the future prospects of the two camps of political leaders.

The British expected their rivals to fight. If they didn't, observed Henry Adams, they looked upon them as cowardly or mean. Alexander Hamilton's determination not to offend Great Britain invited a high handed and callous disregard that nettled the American agrarians. The United States had turned its breeches to receive British kicks. So it seemed to Jefferson.

The list of grievances against Great Britain included retention of the military posts in the Northwest, at least indirect encouragement to the Indians who had launched a costly and troublesome war, the carrying away of several thousand Negro slaves at the close of the Revolution without making compensation, and a policy of extorting the most out of American trade without offering reciprocal advantages. For two years Jefferson invited negotiation of the issues without gaining any response. To this frustrating experience George Hammond, the British minister, added a tone of conversation that convinced Jefferson and

Madison that the British planned to make war. A speech by Lord Dorchester, Governor General of Canada, encouraging the Indians to make war, and the building of a new fort at Maumee by Governor Simcoe, strengthened this view.

The British game poorly prepared the way for American acceptance of British rulings as to commerce on the high seas upon the outbreak of hostilities between Great Britain and France in February, 1793. On June 8 Lord Grenville issued orders to naval commanders to seize all ships carrying corn, flour, or meal bound for a port in France or any port controlled by the armies of France. Hammond, the British minister, defended the order with the dubious assertion that the law of nations sanctioned the treatment of all provisions as contraband and subject to confiscation "where the depriving an enemy of these supplies, is one of the means intended to be employed for reducing him to reasonable terms of peace." Jefferson jumped upon the British contention with the eagerness of one who believed that the prospective enemy had overreached himself. In an instruction to Thomas Pinckney, American minister in London, Jefferson damned the measure as "so manifestly contrary to the law of nations, that nothing more would seem necessary, than to observe that it is so."

Jefferson carefully outlined the dangerous implications of the British contention for the United States. "We see, then, a practice begun, to which no time, no circumstances, prescribe any limits, and which strikes at the root of our agriculture, that branch of industry which gives food, clothing and comfort, to the great mass of inhabitants of these States," he stated. "If any nation whatever has a right," he said, "to shut up, to our produce, all the ports of the earth, except her own, and those of her friends, she may shut up these also, and confine us within our limits." "No nation," he proclaimed, "can subscribe to such pretensions; no nation can agree, at the mere will or interest of another, to have its peaceable industry suspended, and its citizens reduced to idleness and want."

The question likewise involved, said Jefferson, the right of the American government to defend itself against involuntary involvement in war. To put the United States into a position in which it furnished supplies to one belligerent and not to the other could only be deemed a cause for war by the latter. There was no difference, he explained, in the United States restraining commerce with France and her suffering Great Britain to prohibit it. France would consider the latter a mere pretext. To permit Great Britain to bar commerce with France would impose on the United States a neutral duty to likewise withhold supplies from Great Britain. "This is a dilemma," he said, "which Great Britain has no right to force upon us, and for which no pretext can be found in any part of our conduct."

Jefferson's firm posture contrasted with the note of supplication that so characterized Hamilton's every intrusion into foreign affairs when these involved Great Britain. Jefferson and Madison meant to demand respect. Privately, Jefferson confessed to Madison that he had no hope of Great Britain revoking her measures. These two architects of the republic aimed at impressing the British with the fact that they could not deal with the United States with impunity. . . .

In April the battle raged on another front. President Washington appointed

John Jay special envoy to Great Britain. No appointment would have proved popular with the Republicans who much preferred to take economic measures before entering upon negotiations. The naming of Jay convinced them that further appeasement was to be expected. Jay had been ready to agree to the closing of the Mississippi in 1786 in return for a commercial treaty with Spain. His critics predicted that he would yield to the merchants again and negotiate a treaty that sacrificed the true national interest. The Republican societies engaged at once in a campaign of vilification of the envoy. This did not deter the Senate, always on the side of the executive branch, from confirming the appointment.

The instructions carefully spelled out the grievances, spoliations, violations of the peace treaty, and the restrictions on trade. No commercial treaty should be negotiated unless American ships gained the right to enter the British West Indies. But the firm tone of the instructions did not obscure the fact that the governing group at home desperately needed some kind of a treaty that would put an end to the dangerous tendency to take hostile measures toward England. Jay thought as did Hamilton and the merchants, and one paragraph of his instructions undoubtedly carried a special significance to him. That paragraph read: "You will mention, with due stress, the general irritation of the United States at the vexations, spoliations, captures, &c. And being on the field of negotiation you will be more able to judge, than can be prescribed now, how far you may state the difficulty which may occur in restraining the violence of some of our exasperated citizens." And besides his formal instructions Jay carried with him the letters from Hamilton urging a settlement and outlining its nature. . . .

In July Lord Grenville gave to Jay a draft of the proposed treaty altering somewhat the one submitted by Jay a few days earlier. Grenville's project probably reached Philadelphia in late August. Hamilton examined it and found two major weaknesses. He took strong exception to placing British vessels in American ports on the same basis as American vessels. He objected to Article XII dealing with the right of American vessels to enter the ports of the West Indies because the privilege was limited to two years and because it would have prohibited Americans from transporting produce of any of the West Indies to any other part of the world than the United States.

Edmund Randolph, Jefferson's successor as Secretary of State, scrutinized Grenville's draft with an equally critical eye. The refusal of the British to make compensation for the slaves taken at the close of the Revolution disturbed him more than any other aspect. He too considered Article XII unsatisfactory. He likewise objected to postponing British evacuation of the Northwest posts until June, 1796.

The criticisms of Hamilton and Randolph did not reach Jay until the treaty had been signed. Jay held that the treaty represented the utmost that could be expected in dealing with a nation so proud and so powerful. The fact that Article XII contained a two year limitation and prohibited the United States from engaging in the all important carrying trade from the West Indies struck Jay as less important than the fact that a wedge had been driven into the British barrier against American vessels.

The essence of Jay's defense of the treaty lay in his explanation to Edmund Randolph. "Perhaps it is not very much to be regretted that all our differences are merged in this treaty, without having been decided; disagreeable imputations are thereby avoided, and the door of conciliation is fairly and widely opened, by the *essential* justice done, and the conveniences granted to each other by the parties," he reflected. The treaty removed the most serious apprehensions concerning British intentions in the West. The two boundary disputes in the Northwest and the Northeast were to be settled by commissions. A *modus vivendi* assuring Americans of compensation for the losses on the high seas removed some of the ignitive quality from the controversy over neutral rights. The Hamiltonians, anxious about what war would do to the fiscal system and dreading a war in which they would inevitably become the allies of France considered these two as the great gains of the treaty.

The final treaty arrived in Philadelphia on March 7, 1795. Washington and Randolph decided at once not to make it public. The Senate received it in June and approved the treaty but without a vote to spare and subject to the removal of Article XII. The President delayed ratification, finding serious objections to the document that Jay had signed. During the anxious months of indecision he weighed two notably thoughtful papers prepared by Alexander Hamilton and Edmund Randolph. Both recommended favorable action, but Randolph made his approval subject to the British withdrawal of a recently issued order for the seizure of all corn, grain and flour destined for France. Washington agreed to the condition laid down by his Secretary of State.

Hamilton's paper for the President, *Remarks on the treaty of amity, commerce, and navigation, made between the United States and Great Britain,* placed the treaty under a microscope. With a tough mindedness that deserves notice Hamilton dealt with the objections that had been put forward against the treaty with as much honesty as he did with the advantages. Concerning the first ten articles, the only permanent ones, he concluded: "They close the various matters of controversy with Great Britain, and, upon the whole, they close them reasonably." Article XII was objectionable. Article XVIII left something to be desired, a stricter list of contraband. It likewise suffered from the failure to define clearly by what special circumstances noncontraband might become contraband. This lack of precision, due to a failure to reach agreement, could become "the pretext of abuses on the side of Great Britain, and of complaint on that of France. . . ." "On the whole," wrote Hamilton, "I think this article the worst in the treaty, except the 12th, though not defective enough to be an objection to its adoption."

Hamilton then hammered home the major argument for ratification of the treaty. The "truly important side of this treaty" as he saw it, lay in the fact that it closed the "controverted points between the two countries."

Jefferson contended for the ideal of "free ships make free goods" that had been incorporated in previous treaties of the United States. Both he and Madison held that the ideal was a part of the "law of nations." Hamilton rejected this. A majority of treaties did not incorporate this principle. No nation had gone to war in defense of it. The United States, yet weak, could scarcely find it advisable to contend for it at the price of war entailing economic ruin and probable loss of territory. . . .

The Jay Treaty pinched the Jeffersonians at three points. It committed the United States not to establish discriminatory duties against the British. Thereby it forced the agrarians to lay aside their whole foreign policy program and to accept that of the opposition.

Secondly, the treaty offended the nationalistic and democratic sentiments of the agrarians. Jefferson lamented: "The rights, the interest, the honor and faith of our nation are so grossly sacrificed. . . ." He wrote to Madison: "Where a faction has entered into a conspiracy with the enemies of their country to chain down the legislature at the feet of both; where the whole mass of our constituents have condemned this work in unequivocal manner, and are looking to you as their last hope to save them from the effects of the avarice and corruption of the first agent. . . ." Both Jefferson and Madison believed that a majority of the people opposed the treaty and that the popular will had been denied. When it became clear that the House of Representatives would appropriate the funds for putting the treaty into effect, Madison attributed it to the pressure of business interests.

Jefferson's and Madison's denunciations of the treaty are also better understood if one takes into account that in their eyes the treaty surrendered a major principle in the "Law of Nations." That term—"Law of Nations"—had all the aura of the Age of Enlightenment. It had no well defined meaning and certainly few generally accepted points, but to Jefferson and Madison it connoted justice and reason. They never doubted that their own broad interpretation of neutral rights accorded with the "Law of Nations" and the welfare of mankind.

This approach, one of the central threads of their foreign policy from 1789 to 1812, owed something to the fact that American interests would have benefitted tremendously by a universal acceptance of their interpretation of neutral rights. It owed quite as much to an idealistic view of what would benefit mankind. They desperately wanted a world order in which the innocent by-stander nations would not be made to suffer because a few major powers engaged in the folly of war. Jefferson and Madison overlooked the fact that Great Britain could not accept such an ideal without granting victory to its enemies.

In the situation confronting the United States in the spring of 1796 the surrender of the ideal had an additional and more grievous meaning for Jefferson's followers. To yield to British dictates on control of the seas meant that France would be denied access to American supplies. The United States would provide Great Britain with supplies at a time when the traditional friend, France, was struggling for liberty.

In September, 1796, George Washington delivered his Farewell Address. The President, finding himself amid the dissensions of heated party strife, had striven manfully to avoid falling into the hands of either faction. In 1793 he had, to a great degree, followed Jefferson's advice in meeting the dangers brought on by the war between Great Britain and France. Throughout the heated debates he had retained a sense of gratitude toward France and a sincere desire to deal with her justly. In the summer of 1795, he had resisted the pressure of Hamilton to ratify the Jay Treaty at once and had deliberated long before making his decision to ratify it. To be sure he could not participate in the feelings experienced by Jefferson and Madison because he did not share their philosophical outlook and their intense concern for their particular political ideals. On the other hand, he found it more difficult than Hamilton to make the concessions necessary to preserve harmony with Great Britain. The President found himself in an isolated position.

When the time came to deliver a farewell address, he called on Hamilton to draft it, and the message warned against party spirit and against a passionate attachment to one nation. To the more extreme elements in the more extreme Republican societies the counsel was applicable, but it scarcely applied to Jefferson and Madison whose pro-French feelings were rigorously subordinated to American nationalism.

Their nationalism posed a danger for they confused their American view of the world with their proclaimed universal view of justice and right reason. Their strong desire to make their republic an example of what could be achieved by noble aspiration set free to apply reason made them impatient and particularly so concerning Great Britain's financial influence and arbitrary dicta as to how far the seas were to be open to a free exchange of goods. That they were misunderstood, that their views were dubbed theoretical, is not surprising. Idealists in the realm of foreign affairs trying to establish a program that would reconcile national interests and idealistic considerations were to find themselves in a difficult position many times in the future. . . .

Historians, pointing to the modest changes that ensued in domestic policies, usually reject Jefferson's judgment that his election [in 1800] constituted a revolution. Jefferson's own yardstick, a change in attitude and spirit, does justify the term. It was a revolution in terms of a buoyant spirit unencumbered by traditional fatalism. Jefferson expressed the new attitude as he observed the beginnings of the French Revolution: "I have so much confidence in the good sense of man, and his qualifications for self-government that I am never afraid of the issue where reason is left free to exert her force."

The change from Federalism to Republicanism initiated a new approach to foreign policy of notable significance. Whereas Hamilton was distinguished by a tough-minded realism, by prudence, by a disciplining of the national spirit, and by sober calculation of available power, Jefferson and Secretary of State James Madison exhibited an assertiveness, a keen sensitivity to presumed slights, and a full confidence in the nation's capacity to defend its interests and uphold justice. Hamilton and the Federalists started their formulations with a recognition of the existing system of international relations and were willing to work within the framework of current practice. Jefferson and Madison began by rejecting existing realities and sought to implement an ideal.

To understand Jefferson and Madison in foreign affairs one has to begin by making their full faith in the natural rights political theory central to their approach. In every society man was endowed with the natural rights of life, liberty, and the pursuit of happiness. The ideal government was one which served to uphold these rights and the ideal citizen was one who jealously guarded his rights which rested in the natural order of the universe and were above existing man-made contrivances. Only in the United States had the ideal been transformed into practice and embodied in political institutions. This system had its counterpart in international relations. A nation possessed rights that had their origin in the natural order, and these were no less rights because the existing system ignored them. It was the first duty of an enlightened citizen and of an enlightened nation to uphold these rights against the forces of darkness.

Thereby entered the moralistic approach to foreign policy. What was right and justifiable was to be determined by standards derived from an ideal and not by the standards of existing systems. With it entered the imperious assumption that American concepts of what was right and wrong possessed a universal validity. This is what made the American approach to foreign relations unique and in the light of this we better understand both its strength and weaknesses.

The attitude expressed itself spontaneously and Americans never found it necessary to explain its intellectual basis. An interesting illustration of the approach is found in the report of a committee of Congress drafted in 1803 when it was proposed that two million dollars be appropriated for the purchase of the Floridas. The committee observed:

> The Government of the United States is differently organized from any other in the world. Its object is the happiness of man; its policy and its interest, to pursue right by right means. War is the great scourge of the human race, and should never be resorted to but in cases of the most imperious necessity. A wise government will avoid it, when its views can be attained by peaceful measures. Princes fight for glory, and the blood and the treasure of their subjects is the price they pay. In all nations the people bear the burden of war, and in the United States the people rule.

High purpose and selfish material interests were thereby blended into foreign policy. The upholder of the higher law inevitably became the uncompromising defender of national interests without suffering any wracking doubts concerning the identity of national interests and international justice. Jefferson and Madison gave expression to widely held views and their approach to foreign policy became the American approach that found its culmination in the moralizing of Woodrow Wilson at Versailles and Cordell Hull's moral and legalistic expositions in behalf of an ideal international order based on law rather than force.

## Jefferson as Idealist-Realist

### LAWRENCE S. KAPLAN

No statesman of the revolutionary and early national periods made a more substantial contribution to the development of American foreign policy than Thomas Jefferson. From his magnificent synthesis of eighteenth-century political theory in the Declaration of Independence to his death fifty years later,

"Thomas Jefferson: The Idealist as Realist," by Lawrence S. Kaplan, is reprinted, with the permission of Charles Scribner's Sons, from *Makers of American Diplomacy*, edited by Frank Merli and Theodore A. Wilson. Copyright © 1974 Frank J. Merli and Theodore A. Wilson.

Jefferson's idealism, tempered by pragmatic regard for practical realities, played a key role in defining a distinctively American position toward the external world. No one, it might be said, ever blended the moralistic yearnings of the young Republic for a new international order with the practical pursuit of national self-interest more effectively than he.

Examination of Jefferson's amazingly varied career and multiple talents highlights the renaissance quality of his mind and work. For another man any one of his accomplishments would have assured the homage of posterity. Over a span of eighty-three years Jefferson pursued an astonishing range of activities: he was largely responsible for founding the University of Virginia; he was an architectural innovator who helped bring classical forms to the New World; he was an agronomist experimenting with transplantations of rice and silk to the South; he was a theologian who attempted to harmonize Christianity with the temper of the Enlightenment. Above all, he was a scholar in the art of government whose ideas spread through the nation as Jeffersonian democracy. The prestige conferred by authorship of the Declaration of Independence and the power of the presidency ensured dissemination of his ideas in a manner rarely available to political theorists. If his virtuosity did not encompass an appreciation for the intricacies of finance, that shortcoming stemmed less from a lack of understanding the techniques of moneymaking than from a taste that placed spending above getting. Against the bankruptcy of his Monticello estate must be weighed the credit of a life-style that warmed guests in the beautiful mansion with their host's hospitality as much as with fine French wines.

This westerner belonged to an aristocratic family, the Randolphs of Virginia. His father had improved his status by a wealthy marriage. As a member of the governing elite of the colony, Jefferson early experienced British and European influences flowing across the ocean to Tidewater and Piedmont, Virginia. While there may have been few artists or scientists at the College of William and Mary in the colonial capital, there were sufficient men and books to initiate the youthful Jefferson into the life of the eighteenth-century liberal mind. He enjoyed the best of both the Old and the New World, sharing the excitement of European ideas that ranged from Arthur Young's tracts on scientific farming to the disputed poems of Ossian. Books and papers from European centers found their way to Jefferson's library and to the drawing rooms of Williamsburg and Philadelphia. He was very much a member of the international fraternity of literati that pumped liberal ideas into the courts of Europe and the coffeehouses of America—ideas that ultimately pushed both along the road to revolution. Jefferson's intimacy with such scholarly men as Professor William Small of William and Mary and George Wythe, his law teacher at Williamsburg, and with such sophisticated men of the world as Francis Fauquier, lieutenant governor of Virginia during his student days, were experiences he repeated in Philadelphia and Paris in later years. True, the above names almost exhausted the roster of interesting people in colonial Virginia, but the point is that his circle of acquaintances included some of the broadest intellectual interests there; his six years at the village capital provided him with an extraordinary range of ideas.

At the same time, perhaps more than any contemporary, Jefferson captured the best elements in the transatlantic civilization of the colonies. As an American living close to the frontier he appreciated the richness of his environment and recognized the advantages of a land with few people and abundant resources. The agrarian society he so valued bred equality among its members, fostered self-reliance, and opened opportunities for individual growth that the Old World could never provide; his experiences encompassed facets that Europeans could not share unless they came to America. . . .

For him, as for all the Founding Fathers, the central event of life was the creation of a nation out of thirteen disparate British colonies. Every step in making the Revolution and in securing it afterwards involved foreign affairs. In such a context, conventional divisions between domestic and foreign affairs lost meaning. In the first generation of the Republic no national leader could escape awareness of the hostile outside world. Europe intruded in every way, inspiring fear of reconquest by the mother country, offering opportunity along sparsely settled borderlands, arousing uncertainties over the alliance with a great power. Unless the new nation settled for a subsistence economy its prosperity rested upon trade with the Old World; the European market held the American economy captive, and no political theory could alter that fact of economic life. There could be no escape from such concerns, any more than from the language Americans spoke, the customs they followed, or the ideas they circulated.

Anglo-American relations dominated American history in the early years of the Republic. Despite a successful military separation, the economic links of tradition proved more enduring than the political, even though many people, Jefferson included, wished it to be otherwise. If an alternative to a British connection existed, it was not to be achieved by retreating into autarchy but by shifting the economy toward France, the wartime ally; it was to France that those leaders suspicious or fearful of British designs turned during the administrations of George Washington and John Adams. . . .

The record clearly reveals the Jeffersonian involvement in foreign affairs. His service as delegate to both Continental Congresses, as wartime governor of Virginia, and as commissioner to France at the end of the war were all linked to French and British influences in American life. During the Confederation period he represented the United States in Paris, attempting to mobilize support for its continued independence. Upon [his] return to America he became secretary of state, the first in the revitalized union, absorbed in assuring survival of the nation in a hostile world. The French Revolution and its subsequent wars dominated his years as vice-president and president. The magnificent acquisition of Louisiana, though not wholly his doing, deservedly is credited to him; and the disastrous embargo of 1807, though not wholly his mistake, if mistake it was, appropriately is identified with him. Success or failure, Jefferson the public man was of necessity a maker of diplomacy.

Jefferson's enemies of every generation make much of what they consider his deficiencies in character. Most dwell on his inconsistency, pointing out that he shifted from one position to another at critical moments out of fear of consequences, instability of judgment, or passion for power. Thus, his movement from strict to loose construction of the Constitution, from agrarianism to support of manufacturing, from fear of executive power to abuse of it in office, from a love of France to distrust and finally to dependence upon that country under Napoleon have all been used by enemies who would dismiss him as weak, cowardly, opportunistic, or worse. His Francophilism has been interpreted as a personality quirk with dire consequences for the country.

Much of the familiar Federalist criticism of Jefferson withers in the face of close examination. A far better case may be made of excessive consistency, of an allegiance to a conception of society long after it had become obvious that the ideal could not be sustained, or of reliance upon economic weapons against Europe after those weapons were turned against him. Jefferson never questioned what he wanted for America; he envisioned a society of cultivated, independent men on terms of equality with one another, keeping government as close to the local level as possible, living on farms rather than in cities because the agrarian life best propagated the good life. Expansionism became part of the plan because an American empire would remove the corrupt and dangerous model of Europe, as it would if the pattern of international commerce could also be reorganized to incorporate the American alternative to mercantilism, free trade. He identified urban commercial society with class conflict, with oligarchic manipulation of politics, and with European financial control over America, most especially Great Britain's economic interests in its former colonies. To combat such dangers, he believed that right reason applied to the right environment would create a society embodying the best blend of the Enlightenment with the frontier.

He never abandoned his vision of the good society. Apparent deviations were responses to external pressures or were expedients, temporary tactical retreats. He shared with other Founding Fathers a belief that alliances with European powers were unnecessary and potentially dangerous to American independence. His musings about a relationship with Europe "precisely on the footing of China," while fanciful, were genuine; and he knew that in an imperfect world less desirable choices sometimes had to be made to attain more desirable ends. Thus, an alliance with France might be made if Britain threatened the nation's independence; the danger of a connection with Europe had to be balanced against the greater damage that defeat or accommodation with Britain might bring. . . .

Part of the explanation of Jefferson's flexibility lies in his early recognition of the importance of the external world in American affairs and in his firm belief in the permanent hostility of Great Britain. Preservation of the new nation from the baneful effects of those realities required statecraft; if Jefferson sometimes overrated the efficacy of diplomacy, he seldom underestimated the danger of involvement in transatlantic affairs. Ultimately, of course, Americans sought a solution in withdrawal from the European arena into their own empire, into a peculiarly American isolationism wherein obligations to Europe did not exist. In one way or another nearly every American statesman worked to free the nation from dependence upon Europe.

When Jefferson was secretary of state in the 1790s, his countrymen differed violently about the direction of foreign affairs, especially about the American response to the French Revolution and its subsequent wars. The powerful commercial interests of New England and the seaboard towns looked to Great Britain as a necessary business partner, at least until a viable domestic economy could be created. Many of its leaders equated a pro-British policy with freedom from French ideology and French imperialism. Jefferson and his followers never accepted such views. They believed, at least until after the War of 1812, that Britain intended to reduce America to a position of permanent inferiority in an economic relationship more suffocating than the political connection had been before independence. Like their opponents the Federalists, Jeffersonians responded emotionally to events in France, but they read their import differently. They believed that if the French republic collapsed in its war with monarchical Britain, monarchy if not British rule would return to America.

Jefferson's anti-British animus had deep roots. It grew in part from wartime experiences and received repeated reinforcement during his career. At times his fears approached obsession, but he directed these sentiments more to particular institutions and proponents of policy than to Englishmen per se or to the benign aspects of British culture. However flawed, the British political system surpassed any in Europe; and even when in France desperately seeking help during the Confederation period, Jefferson could in good conscience recommend to French friends that they follow the British political model. If Frenchmen kept in view the example of their cross-Channel neighbor, he told Lafayette, they might advance "step by step towards a good constitution." His feelings for English friends remained as warm as his feelings for Frenchmen. He admired the liberal English reformers whose Anglo-Saxon traditions in law and language he claimed for America—indeed, he who had paraphrased Locke's political philosophy could hardly do otherwise. . . .

To effect a new relationship with France and to break the old one with Britain required a centralized government strong enough to command the respect of its peers in the international arena. In this view Jefferson was at one with John Jay and Alexander Hamilton. Like the former (who had been secretary for foreign affairs under the Confederation) he believed that if Europeans saw an efficient and well-administered national government, with its trade and finances prudently regulated, they would be disposed to cultivate American friendship rather than risk its resentment. This theme, which Jay stressed in the third *Federalist,* found a harmonious response in Jefferson, and he could even join with Hamilton when the New Yorker asserted in the eleventh *Federalist* that "a steady adherence to the Union" might allow the new nation to tip the scales of European competition in the New World for the benefit of Americans. Thus, a commonly recognized impotence in foreign affairs provided a powerful stimulus for strengthening the powers of the central government. The Founding Fathers, even when they could agree on little else, all sought to exploit European disadvantage for America's advantage.

Historians have not always recognized that Hamilton and Jefferson shared belief in a strong executive able to resist congressional encroachments upon its power in foreign affairs. Jefferson earlier had expressed approval of the constitutional device that freed the central government from the interference of state assemblies on matters of taxation; now with the new government in operation, he thought that the federal legislature's natural tendency to interfere with presidential responsibilities must be resisted. In a memorandum to Washington, presented shortly after taking office, the new secretary of state questioned the propriety of presidential consultation with the Senate about diplomatic exchanges. Arguing that there was no constitutional requirement for such solicitation and that the practice would create an unfortunate precedent, Jefferson interpreted senatorial powers as extending no further than approval or disapproval of nominees. Even then, he envisioned the decision as basically presidential—almost exclusively so, "except as to such portions of it as are specially submitted to the Senate. Exceptions are to be construed strictly." Jefferson's rigid construction of the Constitution in 1790 was hardly distinguishable from that of the Hamiltonians around him, including the secretary of the treasury himself.

If the Jeffersonian vision of American foreign policy began with an executive free of congressional constraints and the shortcomings of the Confederation, it included other elements customarily identified with his great rival, Hamilton: repayment of obligations to foreign creditors through assumption of the debts of previous governments and the promotion of American shipping through an effective navigation system. New England merchants and Philadelphia creditors welcomed these facets of the Hamiltonian program, and, to a point, so did Madison and Jefferson. While it is true that from the outset Jefferson had many reservations about his cabinet colleagues, especially when he suspected them of monarchical tendencies, he could work with them during the early years of Washington's administration. He could tolerate Treasury intrusion into his department by Hamilton's involvement in consular affairs, as long as he believed that Jeffersonian views received a fair hearing. His rivals in the cabinet in those early years were "good men and bold men, and sensible men."

Not even the Nootka Sound affair in the summer of 1790 fully revised that judgment. Although Jefferson strongly opposed Hamilton's wish to grant a British request for the passage of troops through American territory in the event of war between Spain and Britain over the Pacific Northwest, he had no knowledge of Hamilton's intimate connections with British agents. Nor did he adamantly oppose concessions to the British per se. His point simply was that concessions ought to be reciprocal; the United States ought not surrender a bargaining weapon in advance. In their first cabinet debate on foreign affairs Hamilton and Jefferson differed more on tactics than on ideology.

Of course, Hamilton's early hostility to discriminatory legislation against British shipping did evoke criticism from Madison and Jefferson, but not the deep emotional response it was to arouse in 1793–94. Hamilton, after all, had a navigation system, and that was a step in the right direction. It took time before Jefferson's mind converted Hamilton's behavior into a dangerous passion for monarchy and a fatal dependence on Britain.

In part, at least, Jefferson's tolerance for failure of punitive measures against the British may have flowed from the concurrent insensitivity toward America displayed by the liberal regime in France. While the revolutionists had reformed their government under the National Assembly, nothing in those reforms served the interests of the United States. To his chagrin, Jefferson realized that the new bourgeois rulers of France had no more intent than the mercantilists of the old regime to permit liberal terms for American goods in French markets. That realization caught him between anger and embarrassment, for it coincided with a contretemps in relations between the two nations. Madison's navigation law (which failed to discriminate between ships of countries with commercial treaties and those without them) had given rise to a French protest, to which Jefferson normally would have been sympathetic. He recognized that in spirit, if not in letter, it was unfair that British and French ships would receive equal treatment in American ports, and he wished Congress to make special concessions to the French in return for the concessions they had made during his ministry; but French intransigence threatened to undermine support for such an arrangement.

Still, Jefferson sought to exploit the situation. The behavior of the National Assembly freed him from some inhibitions over past French favors and permitted him a degree of flexibility. That France did not see its own advantage in at least removing prerevolutionary restrictions from the West Indian trade seemed incredible to him. His impatience flared into anger when the French consul in New York insisted upon the recall of two consuls whom Congress had sent to the French islands. Jefferson resisted that demand, ultimately winning a minor victory when the American consuls were permitted to remain as "commercial agents." That success signified little and the secretary knew it; he harbored no illusions that an entente had been established between the two countries.

Much of his distress in office, then, stemmed less from the Francophobic character of the Hamiltonians than from the fact that the French refused friendly gestures when they were offered. Neither Madison's persistent attempts in Congress to fashion a navigation system that would benefit French commerce nor Jefferson's illuminating reports on the whale oil and codfish industries (with their clear invitation to France to replace those who had built "their navigation on the ruin of ours") struck responsive chords in Paris. Assuming the impossibility of weaning Americans from British ties, the French middle-class leaders of the Revolution wrote off American commerce. They even revoked the minor concessions that Jefferson had so painfully extracted during his ministry in France. The arrival in 1791 of a new French minister, Jean Baptiste Ternant, did not help matters. Ternant found Hamilton more congenial than Jefferson, so when the latter presented a plan for exchanging with the French full privileges of natives in each other's ports, the negative response did not surprise him. To the minister, free trade seemed to reward Britain at the expense of France.

War in Europe, particularly between France and Britain in 1793, changed the immediate course of Franco-American relations. It revived Jefferson's hopes for a new identity of interests between the two countries, although he recognized the danger of American involvement in the European conflict through obligations incurred in the alliance of 1778. For all his rising anger against Federalists and Britons, Jefferson did not envisage American troops or ships fighting alongside the French in the West Indies or anywhere else any more than did Hamilton. Yet the opportunity for exploiting a new French mood to strike out at British suzerainty over trade and arrogance over maritime claims proved too glittering to resist. The republican government of France opened West Indian ports to American ships and dispatched a more amiable minister to negotiate a liberal commercial treaty based precisely on Jefferson's scheme of mutual naturalization. Small wonder that the secretary's expectations outweighed fears as Europe plunged into the wars of the French Revolution.

There was a link between the worsening of Jefferson's relations with Hamiltonians at home and improvement of his relations with France. From 1793 to the end of the decade, first as secretary of state and then later as vice-president, he saw the Republic in peril in America and the Republic in peril in Europe. France's part as warrior against British monarchy and imperialism sharpened his antagonism toward British agents in America; increasingly, he saw the Federalist faction as a tool of British interests seeking to restore monarchy to America. Such a goal explained the uses to which Hamiltonian power would be put; it explained the failure of his own efforts to reduce British influence and enhance the interests of American democrats. The whole Hamiltonian program—from funding the national debt and establishing a national bank to Anglo-American reconciliation and a pro-British trade policy—became in his mind part of an enormous invisible conspiracy against the national welfare. The European war unmasked Hamilton's real purpose. Such was the Jeffersonian image of Federalism; of course there was a mirror image of Jeffersonians in the minds of their opponents.

Naturally, this Jeffersonian angle of vision enhanced the importance of France as a counterweight to domestic and foreign enemies. While hardly a new position, its urgency intensified after 1793, and introduced a new and ugly dimension into American debates on foreign affairs and domestic politics. The French republic took on symbolic overtones. According to Jeffersonians, France struggled for more than its own survival—the survival of liberty everywhere was at stake. A British victory would reimpose its rule in America, either directly or through Britain's faithful American servants. Many of Jefferson's friends perished in the struggle for republicanism in France; although he deplored the losses, he endured them stoically, even philosophically, regarding his friends as soldiers fallen in the battle for universal liberty. "My own affections have been deeply wounded by some of the martyrs to this cause," he told William Short on 3 January 1793, "but rather than it should have failed I would have seen half the earth desolated; were there but an Adam to an Eve left in every country. Left free, it would be better than it now is." Written a month before France declared war on Britain, this letter expressed Jefferson's deep commitment to the cause of revolutionary republicanism. Given that predisposition, his fear of counterrevolutionary Britain and its supposed American agents intensified. The mild challenge raised by Britain in the Nootka Sound affair of 1790 had become three years later a matter of the life and death of a society.

The immediate problem for Washington's advisers, however, was the position of the United States toward the belligerents. To resolve that difficulty, Jefferson laid down a precedent for recognition of foreign governments: *de facto* control by the government in power. Possession of domestic power and ability to fulfill international obligations were the tests of legitimacy. Even before Washington raised the question of recognition in the cabinet, Jefferson had spelled out his position in a letter to the American minister in France. "I am sensible," he told Gouverneur Morris on 12 March 1793, "that your situation must have been difficult during the transition from the late form of government to the reestablishment of some other legitimate authority, that you may have been at a loss to determine with whom business might be done. Nevertheless when principles are well understood, their application is less embarrassing. We surely cannot deny to any nation that right whereon our own government is founded, that every one may govern itself according to whatever form it pleases, change these forms at its own will; that it may transact its business with foreign nations through whatever organ it thinks proper, whether King, Convention, Assembly, Committee, President, or anything else it may use. The will of the nation is the only thing essential to be regarded." Jefferson never questioned that the republican government of France should have its minister received, its financial claims honored, and its role as an ally affirmed; when Washington raised these questions after the execution of the French king and the extension of the European war, the secretary of state immediately perceived the mind of Hamilton guiding the president. It outraged him that America seemed more cautious in its support of a republic than it had been in its allegiance to a monarchy. With feeling he asked, "Who is the American who can say with truth that he would not have allied himself to France if she had been a republic?"

In defending the alliance Jefferson marshaled evidence from many authorities on international law of the seventeenth and eighteenth centuries, from Grotius to Vattel. He won his case, at least over recognition and legitimacy of treaties, if not over neutrality. If his position was based on the moral worth of republicans expressing the will of the people rather than on *de facto* control of France by the Girondists, realism needs redefinition. The scholars of international law help little in understanding the Jeffersonian position, for they can be cited either way, as Jefferson himself did when he dismissed that "ill understood scrap in Vattel" that Hamilton had used to deny recognition and then a few months later cited that same Vattel to refute the French minister's demand for a more friendly neutrality. For both Hamiltonians and Jeffersonians the nub of the matter seems to have been the legitimacy of a revolutionary transfer of power. For the former destruction of a hereditary monarchy by revolution stripped from the usurpers all international obligations owed to their predecessors; for the latter, revolutionists merely made legitimate what had been doubtful before by exercising a natural right to alter the form of government. . . .

Belief in Federalist subversion of America's republican experiment dominated Jefferson's mind for the remainder of the decade. Obsession with Hamiltonian maleficence led him at times to startling judgments couched in picturesque language. Washington appeared elliptically as one of the "Samsons in the field & Solomons in the council . . . who have had their heads shorn by the harlot England." On another occasion he prepared to leave Monticello for a visit to London (which he expected to find under French occupation) to "hail the dawn of liberty and republicanism in that island." His conviction that the Federalists had accepted a British definition of neutral rights and an inferior position in the British Empire merged with the conviction that they also planned a monarchical government for America. Washington was their captive, and while John Adams resisted Hamiltonian pretensions, the second president was also an adherent of a form of society inimical to Jeffersonian values. So the world seemed to Jefferson, retired in Virginia from 1794 to 1796 and then isolated in the vice-presidency during Adams's administration. A quasi-war with France coupled with assaults upon the liberties of Republicans lent credence to a nearly paranoid view of America that Jefferson did not alter until he became president.

Yet even in his moments of deepest despair over the direction of American policy under the Federalists, Jefferson resisted his natural impulses to expand the relationship with France, for he knew the limits of counterbalance. Even as he tangled with his rival over neutrality in 1793, Jefferson had no wish to bring the United States into the European war. His opponents were far less fastidious on isolation when Britain was involved. What Jefferson wanted was a benevolent neutrality that would assist France rather than Britain; with it he wished to pressure the British for commercial concessions in return for abstention from the conflict. He failed. Once a proclamation of neutrality had been issued, the possibilities for manipulating it to the advantage of Britain passed to Hamilton, and he made the most of them. There is, however, no evidence that for all his unhappiness Jefferson would have risked a war with Britain. He, rather than Adams, might have reaped the unhappy consequences of Jay's Treaty— and he might have handled them less well.

Jefferson's disavowal of Minister Edmond Genêt during his last year in office and subsequent willingness to let the French alliance lapse at the beginning of his presidency provide an appropriate frame for the comment of France's minister in 1796, Pierre Adet, that Jefferson was an "American and, as such, he cannot be sincerely our friend. An American is the born enemy of all the European peoples." Adet recognized a basic Jeffersonian premise, that in the midst of war and revolution he had given his fervent blessings to the French cause—but France essentially was an instrument of policy rather than an object of it. Its society, its people, its culture all evoked a genuine Francophilism. In Jefferson's statecraft with France, however, there were always *arrières pensées*. . . .

The primacy of American independence from the Old World remained a ʌstant in Jefferson's thinking. He preferred an agrarian society to an indus-ial one; but if he had to accept the latter, he wished for an industrial America ⊃ut loose from British controls, performing the role France had failed to provide. To ensure insulation from Europe's troubles he pressed for westward and southern expansion to free American borders from the anxieties of war and to make room for the growth of the Republic. Jefferson's early encounters with division and disunity in the Revolution and Confederation had qualified his dedication to states' rights; his major involvement with them was when he felt impotent to control the central government. While he never denied the virtues he had celebrated in limited government, his early advice to Washington and his own behavior during his presidency suggest that when opportunities for vital action by the executive offered themselves the president ought not to be inhibited by excessive deference to congressional or state authority.

The pragmatic strain in Jefferson's management of foreign affairs, which permitted him to accept conditions inhibiting his freedom of action, also permitted him to shape those conditions to his ideas of the needs of the nation. If commercial ties with Europe were indispensable—and they were—he wished them to be conducted with minimal political entanglements as he preached in his first inaugural. He shed no tears for the demise of the French alliance. If developments abroad served the interests of a small maritime power, he could exploit them without surrendering either American interests or principles. Philosophers of the Old World might be enlisted in the American cause, just as the conflicts among European states might serve American trade or territorial advances. Such sentiments marked Jefferson's view of France and his policy toward it.

Whether Europe or America derived more gain from his dalliances remains debatable. What is certain is Jefferson's consistent belief in the justice of his policies; they were moral by virtue of their American character. For all his expediency he never separated national self-interest from morality in the management of foreign affairs. His determination to recognize the French republic in 1793 rested on justice as well as on utility. Recognition appeased his moral sense while it appealed to his practical streak, much as did his ideas on neutral rights and free trade. A characteristic American approach to international relations has been the casting of national interests on a moral base; Jefferson's contribution was to shape this conceit and to seek a relationship with the external world that followed from it.

## Political Opportunism and Statesmanship

ALEXANDER DECONDE

What significance do the crucial Washington years have in American political and diplomatic history?

Alexander DeConde, *Entangling Alliance: Politics and Diplomacy under George Washington.* (Durham, N. C.: Duke University Press, 1958), pp. 502–507, 508–510. Copyright © 1958 by Duke University Press.

If these pages shed any light on the question, they show that the traditional picture of the beginnings of our national history which has heretofore been painted in bold strokes remains firm in the main outline but that some major details should be modified. These first years under the federal government have been depicted as "our Golden Age," as "the classic age of American statecraft," an era which produced men of "heroic stature," particularly among the statesmen who molded foreign policy. While the founding fathers were undeniably men of rare ability, above the average of succeeding generations of politicians, they do not emerge in this study "men of talents and genius on a scale perhaps unexampled in the history of the world." Instead, like all men, they appear mortal, with human strengths and weaknesses, with petty faults, at times with heroic virtues.

The statesmen of the Washington era, to some extent, played their politics and diplomacy by ear. They were marked too often in their attitudes by selfish, irrational behavior; too often they placed political advantage above national welfare. Jefferson, and, to a greater degree, Hamilton, in their political pursuits and in their connivance with agents of foreign powers committed acts which in the mid-twentieth century would appear treasonable.

While recognizing that the Washington administrations were distinguished at times by remarkable foresight and brilliant statesmanship, we should not overlook the political opportunism and partisan strife over foreign policy of the time, seldom if ever equaled in our history. Statesmen of our generation are often compared to the founding fathers of the Washington years as pygmies to giants. Such comparisons are unfair and unjust; recent statesmen in their own context have blundered as badly, but have at times performed just as brilliantly.

Being men, the founding fathers were not infallible. Yet succeeding generations of Americans have, in worship of the past and in seeking guidance for their own pressing problems, glorified them and have accepted them as infallible guides in foreign policy. To assume that Washington's Farewell Address, basically a statement of the partisan political philosophy of Alexander Hamilton, established long-enduring principles to guide the nation in foreign policy for generations to come is to endow Washington with powers reserved for the gods of Olympus. It is to assume that the United States for over a century and a half was capable of pursuing a foreign policy of its own choosing, free from the caprices of party and the foibles of other more powerful nations. Actually, in the 1790's the United States was relatively so insignificant in the scale of international power that in any struggle in which the major maritime powers took a real interest it could be little more than a pawn. In relations with the great powers Federalist statesmen were fortunate; they were able to use the opportunities that fell their way. The nation was then led by men who showed real ability in capitalizing on the misfortunes of Europe.

Chance, then as now, played a vital role in the course of our foreign policy. Even though England had most of the advantages in the Washington years, relations with France and England might have gone either way. A stroke of fortune, aided by the vital tie of blood, of culture, and of similar institutions, perhaps more than anything else, thrust us on England's side to the abandonment of the French alliance. Without the support and prestige of Washington and under a more democratic electorate, might not Americans have overthrown the Hamiltonian system and cast America's lot with the French alliance and Republican France? As it was, Federalists and Republicans in their struggle over foreign policy were motivated by self-interest. Each party was convinced that its program, its foreign policy, was in the national interest. The founding fathers were divided on almost every important issue, on the basic philosophies of politics and foreign policy. Who could say, in the context of the times, which side was wrong?

Many students of American foreign policy accept the view that under the American democratic system the orientation and conduct of foreign policy reflects domestic political patterns. To succeed, they say, foreign policy must have the support of the Executive, of the Congress, and of the public. In the Washington years foreign policy conformed to no such criterion. In this period, in relation to the French alliance, we have an example of foreign policy being conducted despite a hostile public opinion until that opinion changed or partially changed. Washington's foreign policy in relation to Great Britain and France was a partisan foreign policy, a foreign policy of one political party, perhaps a minority party.

In assuming that foreign policy reflected the public sentiment of the time, men have often interpreted the Washington era as spawning principles of isolationism. Yet the period was far from isolationist. While it was true that many, regardless of party, nourished the illusion that the United States could isolate and immunize itself from the politics of Europe, other Americans took the opposite view. They tried to thrust the United States into European affairs. Basically, American attitudes toward Europe and toward isolation were, as they have always been, mixed. Some men believed that "the causes which create war among European powers, do not here exist," while others "were too ready to play a part among the nations of Europe; and to involve themselves in the interests of foreign powers, from which nature had most happily separated them."

To quote selected passages from the founding fathers giving voice to hopes and unrealized sentiments without analyzing the actions of the same men, which often were in direct opposition to their isolationist phrases, gives an inaccurate picture of these men and their time. Which best reflects a man's attitudes, his words written to influence other men, or his deeds committed to realize definite objectives?

Although the era of Washington did not in practice set the precedent for a foreign policy of isolationism, there is no denying that it was an age of precedent making in politics and foreign policy. It was not, however, an era in which precedents were established with majority agreement and approval; Washington (even though he may have thought he did) never had a nonpartisan foreign policy. The precedents he left in foreign policy and politics are not clear-cut, having evolved often from political expediency or *ad hoc* diplomatic expediency rather than from exalted principle. As in most periods of stress and storm and as a result of their practical origins, the precedents are mixed and contradictory. What has come to be accepted as binding precedent has gained acceptance because of the authority of time and of the reverence which has blanketed the figure of Washington and also the sacred group denominated founding fathers.

The principle of avoidance of entangling alliances, like most else in Washington's administration, was based on partisan politics, the child of Hamilton's fecund brain. Since the Hamiltonians were anti-French, in their view the French alliance was entangling. Ironically, they saw no evil in close connections with Great Britain; under the circumstances, in Federalist eyes there could be no "entanglement," with its evil connotations, with Great Britain. If cooperation with Great Britain was just and proper, the French alliance alone, as has been maintained, could not have shown by example the danger of entanglement in European international politics. Fears of French entanglement reflected Federalist rationalization, universalized for political consumption.

Whether or not it be entangling has little to do with the real value of an alliance. By definition, an alliance entangles. To have value to both parties, to survive stresses and strains, an alliance should be based on mutual interests; paper bonds alone do not tie effectively. If an alliance is to prove reliable, both parties should continue to fear the contingency or party against whom the alliance was originally directed. There must be, moreover, reasonable hope or assurance that together the allies are capable of meeting the contingency with success. Above all, the alliance should serve the interests of both parties.

After the peace of 1783 the French alliance met none of these conditions. With the exception of the brief war scare of 1793–94 which preceded the Jay treaty, the strength of American animosity toward Great Britain (notably on the part of the Washington administration) was not sufficient to demonstrate the mutual interests of France and the United States under the alliance. The alliance, in fact, became a major source of Franco-American friction. As has often been the case, the stronger party in an alliance usually incites suspicion and jealousy in the weaker country, particularly if the government of the weaker country is antagonistic to it and believes that the alliance entails acceptance of domination by the stronger power. In the Washington period this fear of the French connection was present from the beginning; but more important, Federalists exploited it for political purposes in support of the Hamiltonian system.

Since French statesmen wished to manipulate their ally, they spoke often of gratitude being the binding cement of the alliance. Yet they recognized that mutual benefits gave real adhesion; they understood the partisan source of American opposition to the alliance. Reflecting eighteenth-century concepts, they believed that an alliance cannot be permanent except among natural allies. The Franco-American alliance, they maintained before consummation of the Jay treaty, was natural because of the position of the two countries; it could do neither country harm. Realizing that the proper measure of an alliance is the importance of its advantages to either party, they came to recognize that to Americans, notably to the Federalists, the alliance had lost its advantages; that Americans under the alliance would defend their own interests, but that they would not make war to succor an ally, particularly one distrusted by the powerful political and financial elements in the community.

When a people take such a stand, the French concluded, it is useless to cultivate their friendship as an ally in time of war. This was one reason why the French never implemented the alliance. In spite of these obstacles, certain French officials believed up to the end of the Washington years that the alliance would triumph in the United States because it had the support of the masses who they believed were still pro-French.

Within the sweep of history, the quarrel with France and the party bitterness in the Washington years had in them the same elements found in similar situations in later years. Undoubtedly, as some have seen it, the conflict with France had in it elements of friction between rival nationalisms. Yet Federalists and Republicans successfully suppressed their national feelings—if they had any independently of their politics—when dealing with the foreign power they preferred. The political struggle over foreign policy had in it elements which later became important factors in our political history: sectionalism, antiforeignism, appeal to the past, and defense of the *status quo* by those in power. . . .

From the beginning, Washington's foreign policy was a partisan policy in keeping with the Hamiltonian system; in sum, it was Hamilton's foreign policy. No important foreign policy decision was made without Hamilton having a part in it. Almost all the important ideas, almost all the significant measures under Washington originated with Hamilton. The Hamilton "engine of government" was all pervasive, touching all aspects of administration and policy. But Washington was essential to the system. Without his unquestioning support, without the backing of his awesome prestige and opposition-smothering popularity, it could never have been carried into effect. Washington the popular hero was far more potent politically than his party or the all-encompassing ideas of Hamilton.

Used as a tool by Hamiltonians and convinced that opposition to Federalism was personal opposition and "faction," Washington in his last years became intensely partisan without knowing it. As Jefferson remarked just before the General retired, "his mind has so long been used to unlimited applause that it could not brook contradiction, or even advice offered unasked." Under the circumstances and in view of Hamilton's *de facto* dominance in the government, Jefferson "long thought therefore it was best for the republican interest to soothe him [Washington] by flattering where they could approve of his measures, & be silent where they disapprove . . . in short to lie on their oars while he remains at the helm, and let the bark of state drift as his will and a superintending providence shall direct."

Since it has long been known that Hamilton, perhaps aided by "a superintending providence," guided the helm of the bark of state during most of the Washington era, it is difficult to account for the efforts of posterity equipped with critical methodology to conjure Washington into a statesman of far-seeing vision and ability. Much easier to understand, but perhaps just as difficult to explain, is the veneration he won from his own people as a statesman. Far from being a statesman of wide grasp, Washington lacked the broad intellectual qualities capable of constructing the all-embracing Hamiltonian program with its sweeping domestic and foreign policy objectives. Slow of mind, he took his ideas and theories, without much question, from Hamilton. Grounded though it was in the broad principles of Hamilton's system, Washington's foreign policy in implementation was *ad hoc* and often governed by political expediency; each policy, while conforming to the over-all philosophy of Alexander Hamilton, was a specific response to a specific situation.

Given the politics, the Hamiltonian theory, and the context of the Washington era, we can see that it was not a period when government on the basis of lofty principle sought to follow a policy of isolation and nonentanglement. It was, instead, a period wherein one party took control of the new national government, supported by men of wealth and position, and successfully attempted to change the foreign policy orientation of the nation. At the end of eight years the government had reversed the basic foreign policy alignment of the nation so that a former enemy was an ally and an ally-in-name was in a state of open hostility, almost of undeclared war. Under the circumstances, the French alliance was doomed from the beginning of the new national government, because of its capture by Washington and Hamilton.

This era of Washington was a crucial time, and Hamiltonians knew it; they knew that in implementing Hamilton's system what they did would form precedents for the future. In giving Hamilton dominance in his government, in accepting the Hamiltonian system as the philosophical foundation of his government, Washington had made his government incompatible with the French alliance. By so doing, from the viewpoint of American responsibility, he planted the seeds of war with France; the roots of the Quasi-War (1797–1800) with France gained nourishment in the Washington administrations.

---

## FURTHER READING

Harry Ammon, *The Genêt Mission* (1973)
Samuel Flagg Bemis, *Jay's Treaty* (1962)
———, *Pinckney's Treaty* (1960)
George A. Billias, *Elbridge Gerry* (1979)
Albert H. Bowman, "Jefferson, Hamilton and American Foreign Policy," *Political Science Quarterly*, 71 (1956), 18–41
———, *The Struggle for Neutrality: Franco-American Diplomacy During the Federalist Era* (1974)
Julian P. Boyd, *Number 7: Alexander Hamilton's Secret Attempts to Control American Foreign Policy* (1964)
Irving Brant, *James Madison*, 6 vols. (1941–1961)
Ralph A. Brown, *The Presidency of John Adams* (1979)
Joseph Charles, *The Origins of the American Party System* (1956)
Gerald H. Clarfield, *Timothy Pickering and the American Republic* (1981)

Jerald A. Combs, *The Jay Treaty* (1970)

Alexander DeConde, *The Quasi War* (1966)

Lawrence S. Kaplan, *Colonies into Nation* (1972)

——, *Jefferson and France* (1963)

Ralph Ketcham, *James Madison* (1971)

Walter LaFeber, "Foreign Policies of a New Nation," in William A. Williams, ed., *From Colony to Empire* (1972)

Gilbert Lycan, *Alexander Hamilton and American Foreign Policy* (1970)

Dumas Malone, *Jefferson and the Ordeal of Liberty* (1962)

Drew R. McCoy, "Republicanism and American Foreign Policy: James Madison and the Political Economy of Commercial Discrimination, 1789 to 1794," *William and Mary Quarterly,* 31 (1974), 633–646

Forrest McDonald, *The Presidency of George Washington* (1979)

John C. Miller, *Alexander Hamilton* (1959)

Merrill D. Peterson, "Thomas Jefferson and Commercial Policy, 1783–1793," *William and Mary Quarterly,* 22 (1965), 584–610

——, *Thomas Jefferson and the New Nation* (1970)

Charles Ritcheson, *Aftermath of Revolution: British Policy Toward the United States, 1783–1795* (1969)

William Stinchcombe, *The XYZ Affair* (1981)

Richard Van Alstyne, *The Rising American Empire* (1960)

Arthur P. Whitaker, *The Spanish-American Frontier, 1783–1795* (1927)

Marvin R. Zahniser, *Charles Cotesworth Pinckney* (1967)

# The Louisiana Purchase

# 4

In 1803 the United States purchased from Napoleonic France a territory, then without precise boundaries, totalling about 828,000 square miles. At a sale price of $15 million, the vast expanses of land were quite inexpensive— about 3 cents an acre. Behind the negotiations in Paris lay years of interest in and worry over Louisiana. In 1800 Spain secretly retroceded Louisiana to France, although the arrangement was not consummated until 1802. Americans bristled at this transaction. The administration of Thomas Jefferson attempted to persuade France to abandon the large colony. On April 30, French and American emissaries signed a treaty turning Louisiana over to the United States. "You have made a noble bargain," French Minister of Foreign Affairs Talleyrand remarked, "and I suppose you will make the most of it."

Historians differ over the degree to which the United States followed an active, forceful diplomacy and over whether this purchase was a lucky windfall made possible by Napoleon's European troubles or a much-pursued, successful example of America's imperial quest. In either case, the territorial bargain extended the young nation's border far westward, abutting other lands claimed by Spain and Britain.

## DOCUMENTS

The following documents demonstrate the Jefferson administration's profound concern with Louisiana. Jefferson himself, in a letter of April 1802, appreciated the value of New Orleans to the American export trade and the detrimental international consequences of French rule there. Robert R. Livingston, a New Yorker serving as

American Minister to France, recounted in an April 1803 letter to Secretary of State James Madison the steps leading to the purchase.

---

# Thomas Jefferson on Louisiana, 1802

The cession of Louisiana and the Floridas by Spain to France, works most sorely on the United States. On this subject the Secretary of State has written to you fully, yet I cannot forbear recurring to it personally, so deep is the impression it makes on my mind. It completely reverses all the political relations of the United States, and will form a new epoch in our political course. Of all nations of any consideration, France is the one which, hitherto, has offered the fewest points on which we could have any conflict of right, and the most points of a communion of interests. From these causes, we have ever looked to her as our *natural friend,* as one with which we never could have an occasion of difference. Her growth, therefore, we viewed as our own, her misfortunes ours. There is on the globe one single spot, the possessor of which is our natural and habitual enemy. It is New Orleans, through which the produce of three-eighths of our territory must pass to market, and from its fertility it will ere long yield more than half of our whole produce, and contain more than half of our inhabitants. France, placing herself in that door, assumes to us the attitude of defiance. Spain might have retained it quietly for years. Her pacific dispositions, her feeble state, would induce her to increase our facilities there, so that her possession of the place would be hardly felt by us, and it would not, perhaps, be very long before some circumstance might arise, which might make the cession of it to us the price of something of more worth to her. Not so can it ever be in the hands of France: the impetuosity of her temper, the energy and restlessness of her character, placed in a point of eternal friction with us, and our character, which, though quiet and loving peace and the pursuit of wealth, is high-minded, despising wealth in competition with insult or injury, enterprising and energetic as any nation on earth; these circumstances render it impossible that France and the United States can continue long friends, when they meet in so irritable a position. They, as well as we, must be blind if they do not see this; and we must be very improvident if we do not begin to make arrangements on that hypothesis. The day that France takes possession of New Orleans, fixes the sentence which is to restrain her forever within her low-water mark. It seals the union of two nations, who, in conjunction, can maintain exclusive possession of the ocean. From that moment, we must marry ourselves to the British fleet and nation. We must turn all our attention to a maritime force, for which our resources place us on very high ground; and having formed and connected together a power which may render reinforcement of her settlements here impossible to France, make the first cannon which shall be fired in Europe the signal for the tearing up any settlement she may have made, and for holding the two continents of America in sequestration for the common purposes of the United

British and American nations. This is not a state of things we seek or desire. It is one which this measure, if adopted by France, forces on us as necessarily, as any other cause, by the laws of nature, brings on its necessary effect. It is not from a fear of France that we deprecate this measure proposed by her. For however greater her force is than ours, compared in the abstract, it is nothing in comparison of ours, when to be exerted on our soil. But it is from a sincere love of peace, and a firm persuasion, that bound to France by the interests and the strong sympathies still existing in the minds of our citizens, and holding relative positions which insure their continuance, we are secure of a long course of peace. Whereas, the change of friends, which will be rendered necessary if France changes that position, embarks us necessarily as a belligerent power in the first war of Europe.

## Robert R. Livingston on the Negotiations in Paris, 1803

I have just come from the Minister of the Treasury. Our conversation was so important, that I think it necessary to write it, while the impressions are strong upon my mind; and the rather, as I fear I shall not have time to copy and send this letter, if I defer it till morning.

By my letter of yesterday, you learned that the Minister had asked me whether I would agree to purchase Louisiana, &c. On the 12th, I called upon him to press this matter further. He then thought proper to declare that his proposition was only personal, but still requested me to make an offer; and, upon declining to do so, as I expected Mr. Monroe the next day, he shrugged up his shoulders, and changed the conversation. Not willing, however, to lose sight of it, I told him I had been long endeavoring to bring him to some point; but, unfortunately, without effect: that I wished merely to have the negotiation opened by any proposition on his part; and, with that view, had written him a note which contained that request, grounded upon my apprehension of the consequence of sending General Bernadotte without enabling him to say a treaty was begun. He told me he would answer my note, but that he must do it evasively, because Louisiana was not theirs. I smiled at this assertion, and told him I had seen the treaty recognizing it; that I knew the Consul had appointed officers to govern the country, and that he had himself told me that General Victor was to take possession; that, in a note written by the express order of the First Consul, he had told me that General Bernadotte was to treat relative to it in the United States, &c. He still persisted that they had it in contemplation to obtain it, but had it not. I told him that I was very well pleased to understand this from him, because, if so, we should not commit ourselves with them in taking it from Spain, to whom, by his account, it still belonged; and that, as we had just cause of complaint against her, if Mr. Monroe concurred in opinion with me, we should negotiate no further on the subject, but advise our Government to take possession. He seemed alarmed at the boldness of the measure, and told me he would answer my note, but that it would be evasively. I told him I should receive with pleasure any communication from him, but that we were not disposed to trifle; that the times were critical, and though I did not know what instructions Mr. Monroe might bring, I was perfectly satisfied that they would require a precise and prompt notice; that I was very fearful, from the little progress I had made, that my Government would consider me as a very indolent negotiator. He laughed, and told me that he would give me a certificate that I was the most importunate he had met with. . . .

I told him that the United States were anxious to preserve peace with France; that, for that reason, they wished to remove them to the west side of the Mississippi; that we would be perfectly satisfied with New Orleans and the Floridas, and had no disposition to extend across the river; that, of course, we would not give any great sum for the purchase; that he was right in his idea of the extreme exorbitancy of the demand, which would not fall short of one hundred and twenty-five millions; that, however, we would be ready to purchase, provided the sum was reduced to reasonable limits. He then pressed me to name the sum. I told him that this was not worth while, because, as he only treated the inquiry as a matter of curiosity, any declaration of mine would have no effect. If a negotiation was to be opened, we should (Mr. Monroe and myself) make the offer after mature reflection. This compelled him to declare, that, though he was not authorized expressly to make the inquiry from me, yet, that, if I could mention any sum that came near the mark, that could be accepted, he would communicate it to the First Consul. I told him that we had no sort of authority to go to a sum that bore any proportion to what he mentioned; but that, as he himself considered the demand as too high, he would oblige me by telling me what he thought would be reasonable. He replied that, if we would name sixty millions, and take upon us the American claims, to the amount of twenty more, he would try how far this would be accepted. I told him that it was vain to ask anything that was so greatly beyond our means; that true policy would dictate to the First Consul not to press such a demand; that he must know that it would render the present Government unpopular, and have a tendency, at the next election, to throw the power into the hands of men who were most hostile to a connection with France; and that this would probably happen in the midst of a war. I asked him whether the few millions acquired at this expense would not be too dearly bought?

He frankly confessed that he was of my sentiments; but that he feared the Consul would not relax. I asked him to press this argument upon him, together with the danger of seeing the country pass into the hands of Britain. I told him that he had seen the ardor of the Americans to take it by force, and the difficulty with which they were restrained by the prudence of the President; that he must easily see how much the hands of the war party would be strengthened, when they learned that France was upon the eve of a rupture with England. He admitted the weight of all this: "But," says he, "you know the temper of a youthful conqueror; everything he does is rapid as lightning; we have only to speak to him as an opportunity presents itself, perhaps in a crowd, when he bears no contradiction. When I am alone with him, I can speak more freely, and he attends; but this opportunity seldom happens, and is always accidental. Try, then, if you can not come up to my mark. Consider the extent of the country, the exclusive navigation of the river, and the importance of having no neighbors to dispute you, no war to dread." I told him that I considered all these as important considerations, but there was a point beyond which we could not go, and that fell far short of the sum he mentioned. . . .

I speak now without reflection, and without having seen Mr. Monroe, as it was midnight when I left the Treasury Office, and is now near 3 o'clock. It is so very important that you should be apprized that a negotiation is actually opened, even before Mr. Monroe has been presented, in order to calm the tumult which the news of war will renew, that I have lost no time in communicating it. We shall do all we can to cheapen the purchase; but my present sentiment is that we shall buy. Mr. Monroe will be presented to the Minister to-morrow, when we shall press for as early an audience as possible from the First Consul. I think it will be necessary to put in some proposition to-morrow: the Consul goes in a few days to Brussels, and every moment is precious.

---

## ESSAYS

Lawrence S. Kaplan of Kent State University, an expert on the foreign policy of Thomas Jefferson, places the purchase of Louisiana in the context of a concept made famous by Samuel Flagg Bemis: Europe's distresses worked to America's advantage. In other words, Kaplan tends to emphasize external factors and to suggest a defensive, reactive, even expedient, posture on the part of the United States. France threatened American commerce and security. In his essay, Alexander DeConde, who teaches at the University of California, Santa Barbara, discusses the Louisiana Purchase within the general interpretive framework of American imperial expansion. Thus, to him, the Louisiana "affair" sprang from a self-generated, traditional, ideological American quest for landed empire. He depicts not a defensive reaction, but an aggressive American behavior that followed the dictates of the imperial thrust.

---

## America's Advantage from Europe's Distress

### LAWRENCE S. KAPLAN

Although France intended to conceal the fact of the Treaty of San Ildefonso until Louisiana had been fully secured, a secret involving such stakes was impossible to keep for long. Rumors of the transaction flew all over Europe, notably into the hands of the British enemy, who in turn relayed them to the Americans. Rufus King, the Federalist Minister to England, whom Jefferson was in no hurry to discharge, reported in March, 1801 the news that a double disaster awaited the United States: cession of Louisiana and the Floridas to France, and negotiation of a Franco-British peace which would enable Bonaparte to take advantage of his new property. When these tidings reached the United States, Jefferson confided to his friends the ominous implications that the transfer of Louisiana would have for American security.

From the moment he heard the news he began to wrestle with the problem of living next door to a new neighbor in control of New Orleans. It was an unhappy prospect he faced, filled with opportunities for violence in the event the French attempted to build an empire in America. Even if they did not intend to violate American territory, their probable interference with American commerce on the Mississippi would drive the Westerners either to war or to desertion of the Union. The solution for the United States lay only in Jefferson's ability to thwart fulfillment of the agreement between Spain and France. Such was his object.

War with France was one solution to the problem of Louisiana, but it was an unpalatable response for the President, considering his distaste for the cost of maintaining a large military establishment and considering his fear of a military caste which would thrive on war. The solution had to be a peaceable one, and in order to win time for working out a policy he appeared willing to accept the fiction that Louisiana was still Spanish. If he did not have to recognize the existence of a transfer, he would not have to take any immediate steps until France actually secured possession of the territory. In the meantime, it was conceivable that something could arise that would nullify the Franco-Spanish deal. Hence his annual message to Congress in the fall of 1801 contained no reference to the Louisiana problem. The President in that year had made every effort to maintain friendly ties with France even though it involved the acceptance of Bonaparte's conditions for the ratification of the Convention of 1800 and might require the reception of French envoys Laforest and Otto whom he considered to be anti-republican if not anti-American.

By 1802 the melancholy observations of Robert Livingston on France's imperial plans induced Jefferson to announce not only his knowledge of the Treaty of San Ildefonso but also his opposition to it. Pichon reported the change. Shortly after the President had assured the French Minister of his faith in France's disclaimers about Louisiana, he began to hint at a rupture between the two countries that would take place as soon as war was resumed in Europe. To avoid this state of affairs, Jefferson suggested that France provide Americans with favorable commercial concessions on the Mississippi. He had apparently decided to face the fact of French imperialism without waiting for French troops on American soil to rouse him to action.

The President's aim now was to persuade France by intimidation to give up her ambitions in America. The price of America's friendship would be more than economic favors from the new masters of Louisiana; France would have to cede New Orleans, the Floridas, all the territory that she received from

Spain. If France should refuse his request, he predicted, she would lose the territory the moment the perennial troubles of Europe distracted her attention from the New World. France would be wiser to give up the land voluntarily and retain the good will of the United States. The alternative for Americans was an alliance with Britain. Dramatically, almost theatrically, Jefferson warned that "the day that France takes possession of N. Orleans, fixes the sentence which is to restrain her forever within her low-water mark. It seals the union of two nations, who in conjunction, can maintain exclusive possession of the ocean. From that moment we must marry ourselves to the British fleet and nation."

The President wrote these often quoted words in a letter to the American Minister to France for the beneficial effect he hoped they would have upon its bearer, Pierre Samuel Du Pont de Nemours, a distinguished physiocrat and a friend for almost twenty years. Although Du Pont was then a resident of the United States and was departing for France for what he thought would be only a brief stay, Jefferson saw an opportunity to exploit the economist's contacts with the French government by having him publicize the seriousness with which the United States regarded the Louisiana cession. Lest the Livingston letter fail in its purpose, the President sent Du Pont a note in which he asked him to impress upon his fellow countrymen the importance of ceding all French territory in America, not just New Orleans.

The unofficial emissary of America served faithfully the task which Jefferson had chosen for him, but he did not accept it until his pride as a Frenchman had been appeased. The President's tactics, he thought, would antagonize rather than intimidate the French. It would be better for the United States to help the French win Canada in exchange for the surrender of Louisiana, for such a gesture would permit the arrangement to appear reciprocal. If this plan were impossible, he advised, Jefferson should offer a reasonable price for the territory at issue, in language that would not offend Bonaparte.

While appreciating the spirit of friendship evidenced by Du Pont's reply to his suggestion, the President was not at all pleased with the idea of purchasing Louisiana. He had anticipated France's compliance with his wishes on the strength of his threats and on the hope of new conflicts in Europe. Only when his alternatives seemed to be purchase or war did Jefferson turn to the Du Pont plan. The world situation in general and his political fortunes in particular allowed no other solution in 1802. Abroad, the Peace of Amiens had been made in the very month in which he had made overtures to Du Pont, and Rufus King reported that Britain, despite her interest in the disposition of Louisiana, would not bring the Louisiana question into her negotiations with France. Edward Thornton, the British Chargé d'Affaires in Washington, even suggested that if the French should occupy Louisiana, the British would have greater influence over a frightened United States. Bonaparte was therefore free to complete his plans for the occupation of the territory. At home, the President had to contend with the rising anger of the Westerners over the prospect of having their rights of deposit in New Orleans taken away by the new rulers of the Mississippi. Pinckney's Treaty with Spain in 1795 had given the United States the right to navigate the Mississippi from its source to the sea, and to deposit its goods at New Orleans for transshipment to ocean-going vessels. Spain suspended this right in October, 1802, and France was immediately blamed for the affront. Federalists were able to use Western discontent to embarrass the administration by demanding redress from France and posing as the new champions of the West.

The President responded to these challenges by employing a weapon that his predecessors had used successfully a few years before: a special mission empowered to settle a special problem. He chose James Monroe to be Minister Plenipotentiary and Envoy Extraordinary to France to help Livingston win Louisiana from the French. Jay's mission in 1794 had postponed Republican attacks until a treaty with Britain had been made; Monroe, a popular figure in the West, might have the same success, not only in silencing the Federalists but also in dampening the ardor of the West for war. Jefferson authorized the two envoys to purchase New Orleans and the Floridas alone for a price slightly less than what was finally paid for the entire Louisiana territory, and to guarantee if necessary the rest of the territory to the French. Should France appear hostile, they were to open talks with the British about the possibility of cooperating in a joint venture against French Louisiana. . . .

Inasmuch as France never completed her empire in America, there can be no certainty as to the extent to which Jefferson might have gone to counter the moves of Bonaparte. During the difficult days of 1802 his fears often dented the armor of confidence he had built out of hopes that the troubles of the Old World would in some way prove to be his salvation. On such occasions he would be convinced that France would force the United States into the arms of Britain, and so he took pleasure in noting every manifestation of friendship on the part of the British. But generally Jefferson's dallying with Britain was so half-hearted and so palpably self-seeking that Thornton, with whom he attempted to ingratiate himself in gloomy moments, distrusted his sudden appreciation of British merits and claimed that he seemed to tax "his imagination to supply the deficiency of his feeling." Thornton was right. When Jefferson's mood of despair lifted, he trusted in the intervention of a *deus ex machina*—war in Europe, revolution in the West Indies, or financial difficulties in France—to make France see the light and to keep his country out of the clutches of Britain. Months before he had seen any of his hopes realized, the President railed against those Americans who would have the United States take immediate action on Louisiana. Nothing but dire necessity, he asserted, could force the country out of neutrality and into the orbit of Britain. And such a crisis looked distant as reports began coming in about the restoration of American rights of deposit in New Orleans, the imminence of war in Europe, and the difficulties that Leclerc's French armies were having in occupying the island of Santo Domingo. The President's willingness to guarantee Louisiana to France as well as his talk of a British alliance must be weighed against his knowledge that the future of the territory irrevocably belonged to the rising West and against his conviction that British services should never be used to help obtain it.

When all Louisiana and not just New Orleans fell into the hands of the surprised envoys in May 1803, the event took place in the manner that Jefferson had predicted. Bonaparte had to sacrifice his imperial ambitions in the New World, temporarily at least, before the altar of a new war in Europe. Since British sea power would have prevented him from occupying his American empire, he deemed it advisable to sell the entire territory to the United States, despite the dubious legality of such a transaction, and receive in return funds to carry on his European ventures. Other explanations for the First Consul's actions are available. George Dangerfield has recently pointed out that failure in Santo Domingo made war in Europe inevitable: Bonaparte needed a new arena in which to recoup his losses. Whatever may have been the ultimate factor in the decision, Jefferson had a right to feel that he had won complete success. He had vindicated not only the policy of nonentanglement advocated by Washington and Adams but also the assumption he had made as Secretary of State: America's advantage from Europe's distress.

## An American Imperial Thrust

### ALEXANDER DECONDE

*Imperialism,* usually a nation's use of power to acquire territory belonging to others, is an emotionally charged word that implies undesirable behavior. So Americans and their historians have seldom employed the term to describe the growth of their country, and most rarely have they applied it to the formative years of the republic. They have preferred to use *expansion, mission,* or other more flattering terms. According to conventional historical theory, American imperialism or something akin to it developed suddenly in the 1840s under a vague but basically beneficent concept called Manifest Destiny. In the era of the Civil War this imperialism virtually disappeared, but it or something like it came to life again in the 1890s to create an empire overseas.

Modern scholarship has just about demolished the idea that the new Manifest Destiny, or imperialism, of the late nineteenth century was an aberration or something really new in the American experience. In most of the histories dealing with expansion in the early years of the republic, however, the conventional wisdom still prevails. It portrays Americans, at least until mid-nineteenth century, as a peaceful people who shunned the militarism, power politics, and imperialism of European countries but who nonetheless expanded by chance, without much opposition and without causing genuine harm to anyone. They were a people with a sense of mission who when they gobbled territory did so to extend the domain of democracy, to build an empire for liberty, and not to exploit others.

In this interpretation imperialism has no place in the unfolding of early American history. In it the paradigm of peaceful, democratic, fortuitous ex-

Excerpt from *This Affair of Louisiana* by Alexander DeConde is reprinted by permission of Charles Scribner's Sons. Copyright © 1976 Alexander DeConde.

pansion is the affair of Louisiana. What followed in the nation's history, however, sometimes diverged from the model. In noting this divergence, one scholar argues, for instance, "that Manifest Destiny and imperialism were traps into which the nation was led in 1846 and 1899." This conventional thesis has not reigned without challenge. A diverse group of scholars have depicted imperialism, or expansionism, as a main theme, even as a determining force, in the history of the United States. They contend that from the beginning the leaders of the republic had the imperial urge and that the founding fathers intended the United States to possess adjacent and even distant lands.

In this book the process of analyzing expansionism takes the questioning of the conventional interpretation a step further. It places the origin of the imperial thrust in the colonial period and in Europe, but especially in England, and hence American expansionism fits into a context wider than that depicted in most histories. If we separate rationale from true motivation and from events, or from what happened in the New World since the time of the first European settlements, we can discern the Europeans as venturesome expansionists. We can, in the large context, perceive American expansionism as part of the rise of Western nationalism and imperialism. We can note also that the Anglo-Americans brought with them from England an especially compelling imperialist creed. For example, the eminent English philosopher Francis Bacon stressed the importance of "imperial expansion" as a duty for a people who sought "greatness."

The powerful national states of western Europe pursued imperial greatness in the New World by planting colonies. In the process they systematically reduced, absorbed, or annihilated tribal or other native peoples. In no other people was the racism implicit in this imperial process more deeply rooted than among Anglo-Americans. The sixteenth-century Oxford geographer Richard Hakluyt and others maintained that Englishmen, like the Romans of the ancient world, were predestined to take over, colonize, and rule the New World. Imbued with the concept that native Americans were an inferior people who had to give way before a superior race, Anglo-Americans felt no compunctions in dispossessing Indians. They did all this while using the rationale that they were advancing the frontier of civilization and doing so more capably than any other people.

So it was that descendants of those who settled Jamestown, Plymouth, and Massachusetts Bay inherited an imperialist ideology along with their language, politics, religion, and culture. Motivated by a tough, ruthless acquisitiveness that drove them westward in an unrelenting quest for empire, they accepted territorial expansion in conflict with Indians as an intrinsic part of their experience. Considering themselves a chosen people, the Puritans of New England even rationalized their conquest of Indians in the place of converting them to Christianity as the will of God. Two of the leading Puritan divines, Increase and Cotton Mather, defended wars against Indians and Frenchmen, too, as just and proper. Sometimes these Anglo-American colonists were more aggressively expansionist than were the policy makers of empire in London.

The imperial ideology that accompanied the Anglo-American experience runs through the thinking of a number of pre-Revolutionary leaders, but it stands out most vividly in the thought of Benjamin Franklin, the foremost believer in the idea of an expanding American empire. Another who shared this idea, John Adams, spoke in 1755 while not yet twenty of a time when Anglo-Americans would transfer "the great seat of empire into America. It looks likely to me," he added, "for if we can remove the turbulent Gallicks, our people, according to the exactest computations, will in another century become more numerous than England itself."

Three years later Brigadier General James Wolfe, the British hero of the French and Indian War, was impressed with the presence of this imperial urge and with the general aggressiveness in the Anglo-American colonies. He thought that they had acquired "the vices and bad qualities of the mother country." Nonetheless, he prognosticated that those colonies "will some time hence, be a vast empire, the seat of power and learning, . . . and there will grow a people out of our little spot, England, that will fill this vast space, and divide this great portion of the globe with the Spaniards."

After benefiting from the British conquests in the French and Indian War, Anglo-Americans expanded their horizon in their quest for imperial greatness. Even college students could join in praising such a quest. At the Princeton commencement of 1771 two seniors envisioned the time

> . . . when we shall spread
> Dominion from the north, and south, and west,
> Far from the Atlantic to Pacific shores,
> And people half the convex of the main!—
> A glorious theme!—

The patriot victories of the American Revolution enhanced this imperial view of the future, which now became part of the heritage of the new nation. At the Paris peace negotiations in 1782 and 1783 Benjamin Franklin sought, along with England's recognition of the independence of the United States, acquisition of Canada and the Floridas, or essentially all of continental British North America. He was convinced that eventually all this territory must become part of the empire of the United States. Like Franklin and other Revolutionary leaders, J. Hector St. John de Crèvecoeur, the popular French observer of the American scene, took for granted the indefinite westward expansion of American society. "Who can tell how far it extends?" he wrote. "Who can tell the millions of men whom it will feed and contain?"

Immediately after independence the leaders of the new nation fixed their eyes on Louisiana. They replaced British policy makers and their Anglo-American representatives as the prime imperialists in the Mississippi Valley. Independent Americans were confident that the imperial thrust that had brought them possession of the trans-Appalachian West would make the territory west of the Mississippi the heartland of the American empire.

Those in the ruling establishment, as well as other Americans, unabashedly thought of themselves as expansionists and proudly tried to justify their imperialist ideology with pious assertions of a hazy continental destiny. Their foes, whether Indians, Spaniards, Frenchmen, or Englishmen, also considered them aggressive expansionists, essentially imperialists. Through infiltration, immigration, and trade, American hunters, farmers, and merchants began dominating parts of Spanish Louisiana and West Florida. Retaining their loyalty to the United States, these settlers not only refused allegiance to Spain but also brought with them an undisguised contempt for the Spanish rulers of their new homeland. More than the rhetoric or theories of statesmen, the inexorable pressure of these Americans expanding into the Ohio and Mississippi valleys and then into the territory held by Spain gave substance to the imperial thrust.

While this American vanguard moved across Louisiana's frontiers, prominent and well-to-do men of the republic in 1787 framed a new constitution that could or could not sanction imperialism, depending on the attitude of the interpreter. James Madison, one of the Constitution's most perceptive original interpreters, viewed it as congenial to empire building. In support of this view he advanced a theory that justified American territorial expansion as a means of extending the boundaries of freedom. In discussing the advantages of a republic over a democracy, for example, he argued that "the greater the number of citizens and extent of territory," the less the oppression and the more the security for republican government. "Extend the sphere," he said, "and . . . you make it less probable that a majority of the whole will have a common motive to invade the rights of other citizens." This kind of government required, in his analysis, a strong union or "one great, respectable, and flourishing empire." So he married the idea of freedom with that of expansionism, a duality that American leaders such as Thomas Jefferson used often in the quest for empire.

This theme, taken from the words of the founding fathers themselves, formed a foundation for the conventional wisdom. It gave historians a ready-made analysis based on original sources. They could depict American expansion in moral terms as the peaceful extension of democracy into wilderness or into sparsely settled land and as bringing considerable benefit to lesser peoples. What the expounders of this thesis often overlook or put aside is that early continental expansionism had behind it a thrust of force, a coercive energy, something that its victims—mainly Indians and Spaniards—well understood.

Actually, the thinking of early national leaders as it pertained to empire was less altruistic and tougher than is usually depicted in the conventional analysis. Patrick Henry, for one, argued that "Some way or other we must be a great and mighty empire; we must have an army, and a navy, and a number of things." Publicists stressed the same aggressive theme. Jedidiah Morse, a New Englander, in 1789 published a widely read *American Geography* in which he anticipated American expansion across the Mississippi into Louisiana. Since these were not "merely the visions of fancy," he wrote, "we cannot but anticipate the period, as not far distant, when the AMERICAN EMPIRE will comprehend millions of souls, west of the Mississippi. . . . the Mississippi was never designed as the western boundary of the American empire."

Federalist leaders in the 1790s supported the westward push of "pioneers" and were willing to coerce a weak Spain into relinquishing at least part of Louisiana and the Floridas. A western publicist predicted in 1792 that "posterity will not deem it extraordinary, should they find the country settled quite across to the Pacific ocean, in less than another century."

Eager to extend American dominion toward the Pacific, Federalists debated the various means of acquiring Louisiana. In 1796 Federalist newspapers expressed hope that the United States could someday obtain the province "by purchase or amicable means." Other Federalist shapers of opinion, such as Alexander Hamilton, were willing, even eager, to conquer for empire.

When the Republicans gained control of the federal government, they thought and acted toward Louisiana as had their Federalist predecessors, but they showed more caution in pressuring powerful France than in badgering weak Spain. Despite their periods of restraint, these Jeffersonian leaders, too, were confident expansionists, men with an unquestioning faith in America's destined right to conquer, whether by sword or diplomacy. They played power politics, as they saw it, from a position of strength because they were convinced that the future belonged to them. They viewed the United States as a "rising power," and looked down on rivals such as Spain as "declining powers." Those in decline had no choice. The reality of power compelled them, as it had forced Indian tribes, to recognize the predominance of the United States in North America and to give way before it.

Regardless of the contradictions and inconsistencies in the expansionist ideology, few of the leaders of American society, whether Federalist or Republican, questioned it. They justified their land hunger as the dictate of highest morality. Yet their actions, rather than their rhetoric, indicated that anything goes in constructing an empire for liberty.

According to the conventional view, Thomas Jefferson, the builder of the empire for liberty, was a man who considered war the "greatest scourge of mankind," believed only in defensive measures, and sought peaceful solutions to all foreign problems. Yet historians point out his willingness to use offensive tactics to gain territory. They call him "the greatest of American expansionists," "the architect of orderly expansion," "the first apostle of Manifest Destiny," "the grand agrarian imperialist," the "expansionist of freedom, not of empire," and "America's first great expansionist." Regardless of the accuracy or flaws in the conventional view, he clearly thought in imperial terms.

Unlike contemporaries who often used the rhetoric of expansion without having power, Jefferson as president possessed power; he had the opportunity to act decisively as well as to talk. Continuing desire, ideology, a rhetoric and a program of expansion, no matter how widespread, do not necessarily translate into national policy. A program that becomes policy and a foreign policy that produces imperialist action are shaped by definable forces, usually by men in positions of power.

In the case of Louisiana both external and internal forces, men of power in Europe and America, brought about the acquisition. In the United States Jeffersonians felt the expansionist ideology with such intensity that they considered the transformation of rhetoric and policy into action as the working of Providence. In their thinking the Indians, the French, and the Spaniards held Louisiana temporarily as trustees. Jeffersonians saw themselves as taking rightful possession, regardless of the clouded legal title, of what had been destined to be theirs anyway. With their program of deliberate expansionism, these confident activists merely hastened the work of this inevitable destiny.

In working out this program, Jefferson took over the ideas of Benjamin Franklin, John Adams, James Madison, and other founding fathers, fused expansion with destiny and freedom, and rationalized the whole process as the building of an empire for liberty. Capitalizing on the westward surge of population and using a mixture of threat and restraint in diplomacy, he never lost sight of his desired objective: territory. With the acquisition of Louisiana he converted the idea of empire into reality and made it the finest achievement of his presidency. Henry Adams, a historian often critical of Jefferson, called this affair of Louisiana an unparalleled piece of diplomacy, "the greatest diplomatic success recorded in American history." He ranked its importance "next to the Declaration of Independence and the adoption of the Constitution."

The Jeffersonian concept of empire did not emerge suddenly or haphazardly a full-blown success. It reflected a well-developed expansionist tradition and a conscious vision of a national future. Yet the immediate circumstances of the president's decision to try to buy New Orleans and of Bonaparte's decision to sell Louisiana give the appearance of stemming more from expediency than from plan. So the conventional wisdom usually depicts Louisiana as coming to the Jeffersonians unexpectedly, "out of the blue," as "an accident of fate," a "diplomatic miracle," as being suddenly thrust upon "indifferent hands," virtually "forced on the United States," or tossed "into the lap of Americans." This aspect of conventional history echoes Federalist reactions. Federalists wanted to deny Jefferson credit for the achievement, and so they argued that he really did nothing more than profit from fortuitous circumstances.

Jefferson's political maneuvering lends credence to this thesis. Although committed to a doctrine of expansion, he appeared to act more to placate aggressive Westerners, to preserve his party's power, and perhaps to prevent disunion than to carry out a national mission. Destiny may work in strange, but not necessarily inexplicable, ways. If the president and his advisers had not been heirs of an imperial tradition and believers in an expansionist ideology, they probably would not have acted as they did when they did.

American policy makers and opinion makers and others had long coveted Louisiana, had schemed to obtain it, had within a decade converted at least part of the province into an economic dependent, and had all along assumed that it was destined in the long pull for no hands but their own. When the prize appeared within their grasp, they did not hesitate; they moved swiftly and confidently to possess it.

Bonaparte, too, had a commitment to a concept of western empire. Chance and expediency, according to conventional interpretations, forced him to abandon that commitment. He found it expedient to sell Louisiana to the United

States rather than lose it in war to England. Chance, shaped by the struggle for power in Europe, brought him suddenly to the decision to sell.

Actually, the idea of the sale to the United States had many antecedents. Federalists discussed the possibility of purchase as well as of conquest; Joseph Bonaparte hinted at selling it in 1802; Jefferson alluded to it after hearing of the retrocession to France; and Robert R. Livingston suggested purchase to Bonaparte before Pierre Samuel Du Pont de Nemours and Jefferson had discussed it.

The evidence also suggests that the First Consul decided to sell because of the pressure Americans exerted on him as much as for any other reason. Jefferson, his advisers and diplomats, and Congress all joined the campaign against the French. The Jeffersonians threatened to use force if Bonaparte did not offer concessions in Louisiana, and the evidence indicates they meant it. Bonaparte's own diplomats and advisers, as well as the Jeffersonian leaders, pointed out to him that his plan of empire in North America was turning a friend into an enemy. At the least it was driving the United States into an alliance with England.

Despite this American pressure, according to some scholars, Bonaparte did not have to sell to the United States. He could have disposed of Louisiana in some other way. Actually, he had little real choice. If he had held on, either England or the United States would have conquered the province. Why not turn it over to the United States in exchange for profit and goodwill? He knew that Americans were driven, as much as he was, by a virtually compulsive expansionism. Sooner or later they would take Louisiana anyway. Why not "spare the continent of North America from the war that threatened" to erupt because of clashing French and American imperialisms?

Even the actions of James Monroe and Livingston stemmed more from dedication to the imperial concept than from mere expediency. They committed their government to buy Louisiana, even though they had no authority to do so, because they instantly recognized a great bargain, knew it fitted the American program of empire, and were convinced that the Jeffersonian leadership would support them. They did not think that the affair of Louisiana all hinged on chance. Nor did other Jeffersonian partisans. They gave credit to the president's "wise & firm tho moderate measures," or his masterly statesmanship, as the essential factor that influenced Bonaparte to sell.

Jefferson himself, in retrospect, stressed the inevitability of Louisiana's fate. "I very early saw that Louisiana was indeed a speck in our horizon which was to burst in a tornado," he said. Napoleon's "good sense" in perceiving this as well as the unavoidable sequence between "causes and effects," he added, "saved us from that storm." The acquisition of Louisiana, as the frontier historian Frederick Jackson Turner hypothesized, was thus "no sudden or unrelated episode. . . . It was the dramatic culmination of a long struggle" that began in the colonial era.

The president's shift in constitutional principles can also be viewed as culminating in his desire to gain and hold Louisiana. Since his strict-constructionist principles clashed with his imperial concept, he switched to broad construction, or to the use of implied powers of government to justify the acquisition. This shift, the argument goes, exemplifies gross expediency, or that the end justifies the means. There is truth in this assessment, but in addition the evidence suggests that Jefferson moved as he did not just out of expediency but also because he felt that now he could carry out the imperial idea that had been important in his thinking for years. He never really retreated from his expansionist program; he never questioned the acquisition or considered relinquishing it. He merely sought the best constitutional means of carrying it out, especially a formula that would blunt the criticism of Federalists and anti-expansionists. In doing so, he established a precedent for use of the Constitution as an instrument sanctioning, even sanctifying, expansionism.

This constitutional sanction helped make the Jeffersonian empire for liberty successful and lasting. Independence had given the United States a sound foundation for growth in the trans-Appalachian West. Louisiana provided Americans with room for more growth with a sense of legal and physical security. Its acquisition not only removed "a fearful cause of war with France" and eliminated a powerful barrier to expansion, but also placed the force of the Constitution behind the imperial thrust. American society and institutions, as a result, fashioned no lasting legal barriers to the absorption of nearly a million square miles to the national domain. This area, larger than Great Britain, France, Germany, Italy, Spain, and Portugal lumped together, doubled the size of the nation.

There were, of course, initial difficulties. To the consternation of the Jeffersonians, the Creoles for a while preferred Spanish sovereignty to incorporation within the benevolent empire for liberty. So the president violated the principle he had himself inscribed in the Declaration of Independence—that governments derive "their just powers from the consent of the governed." He used troops in ruling the new empire.

Some critics feared that such tactics, the apparatus of imperial government, or just expansion itself would endanger American democracy as it was evolving within existing geographical limits. In his second inaugural address Jefferson took note of such criticism and restated his old imperial argument. "I know that the acquisition of Louisiana has been disapproved by some from a candid apprehension that the enlargement of our territory would endanger its union," he said. "But who can limit the extent to which the federative principle may operate effectively? The larger our association, the less will it be shaken by local passions; and in any view, is it not better that the opposite bank of the Mississippi should be settled by our own brethren and children than by strangers of another family?"

Disputes within the American family over the governing and status of Louisiana did produce long-lasting political strain and recurring conflicts over constitutional interpretation. Despite these problems, the enlarged nation, as Jefferson hoped, did hold together. Out of the western empire eventually came the states of Louisiana, Arkansas, Missouri, Nebraska, North and South Dakota, Oklahoma, and much of Kansas, Minnesota, Colorado, Montana, and Wyoming. The difficulty of fitting these territories into the nation's previous sectional pattern, however, contributed to the coming of the Civil War.

Regardless of the internal difficulties that Louisiana stimulated, Jefferson considered it—the largest acquisition in the nation's history—a personal and national triumph, a proper monument to the imperial idea. When he left office, he expressed an old desire, expansion into the Floridas, Cuba, Mexico's provinces, and Canada. Then, he said, "we should have such an empire for liberty as she has never surveyed since the creation." He was convinced that his fellow Americans had fashioned an instrument of government uniquely suited for this continuing imperial thrust. "I am persuaded," he added, "no constitution was ever before so well calculated as ours for extensive empire and self-government."

More than a decade later John Quincy Adams, who believed that all of North America was "destined by Divine Providence to be peopled by one *nation*," the United States, looked back upon this affair of Louisiana and expressed similar sentiments. Within it he saw "an assumption of implied power greater in itself and more comprehensive in its consequences than all the assumptions of implied powers in the twelve years of the Washington and Adams Administrations put together."

In even broader perspective, with the acquisition of Louisiana the Jeffersonians carried on the imperial creed of their Anglo-American forefathers. With it they accelerated the dismantling of Spain's New World empire and the emergence of the United States as one of the truly powerful nations in the world. Although the United States did not immediately achieve the status or influence of a great power, its size and wealth after the incorporation of Louisiana were such that other nations could not ignore it or threaten it with impunity in its own North American neighborhood.

While anchored in the past of the Anglo-American imperial tradition, this affair of Louisiana also faced the future. It fitted comfortably within the nationalistic and expansionist ideology of America's political leaders, regardless of party affiliation, and met the desires of the many Americans who felt that sooner or later the entire North American continent must be theirs. With minor variations it gave form to the idea of Manifest Destiny and served as a model for future expansion.

# FURTHER READING

Albert H. Bowman, "Pichon, the United States, and Louisiana," *Diplomatic History*, 1 (1977), 257–270

George Dangerfield, *Chancellor R. Livingston of New York, 1746–1813* (1960)

Arthur B. Darling, *Our Rising Empire* (1940)

Robert M. Johnstone, Jr., *Jefferson and the Presidency* (1978)

E. Wilson Lyon, *Louisiana in French Diplomacy, 1759–1804* (1934)

———, *The Man Who Sold Louisiana: The Career of François Barbé-Marbois* (1942)

Dumas Malone, *Jefferson the President* (1970)
Merrill D. Peterson, *Thomas Jefferson and the New Nation* (1970)
Marshall Smelser, *The Democratic Republic, 1801–1815* (1968)
Richard Van Alstyne, *The Rising American Empire* (1960)
Paul A. Varg, *Foreign Policies of the Founding Fathers* (1970)
Arthur P. Whitaker, *The Mississippi Question, 1795–1803* (1934)
Marvin R. Zahniser, *Uncertain Friendship* (1975)

# The War of 1812

# 5

In 1803 Europe once again exploded in war. England and France battled
furiously and, once again, the United States became ensnarled. As a neutral
trading nation, America was the target of economic warfare, because each
antagonist attempted to halt the flow of American goods to the other. France
declared a Continental System to close Europe to British products and to
force neutrals to cease trade with Britain. The British issued Orders-in-
Council to blockade France and to curb neutral trade with Napoleon's
nation. America's neutral rights and foreign commerce suffered. Jefferson
and Madison tried retaliatory measures—embargo and non-intercourse
acts—to no avail. War with England came in 1812.

Historians have offered several explanations for the causes of the War of
1812: national honor, defense of neutral rights, British impressment of
American sailors, injury to commerce, hunger for land (Florida and Canada),
eradication of the Indian menace, fear of continued economic depression,
and the efforts of Republican Party leaders to strengthen their political power.
Some scholars have emphasized the leadership of James Madison, which
they find inept. The following readings address these issues.

## DOCUMENTS

The vital importance to the United States of foreign commerce and maritime
issues in the early nineteenth century became evident when Napoleonic France, in
the Berlin Decree of November 21, 1806, attempted to shut down trade with
Britain completely. American ships were also endangered by the British Order-in-

Council of November 11, 1807, designed to sever trade with France and its colonies. The retaliatory American Embargo Act of December 22, 1807, became an abortive attempt to protect American vessels against capture, to avoid inevitable diplomatic disputes over neutral rights, and to deny the belligerents the benefits of American commerce. "War hawk" Congressman Henry Clay of Kentucky delivered a stirring anti-British speech, reprinted as the fourth document, on December 11, 1811. On June 1 of the following year, President James Madison asked Congress to declare war against Britain. His message, reprinted here, listed a host of grievances. The final document emanated from the convention of New Englanders who met in Hartford, Connecticut, from December 15, 1814, to January 5, 1815, to protest the War of 1812 and its damage to their commerce. The delegates recommended several constitutional amendments to diminish the federal power to regulate foreign commerce and to make wars.

## Napoleonic Decree (Berlin), 1806

**Art. I.** The British islands are declared in a state of blockade.

**Art. II.** All commerce and correspondence with the British islands are prohibited. In consequence, letters or packets, addressed either to England, to an Englishman, or in the English language, shall not pass through the post-office and shall be seized. . . .

**Art. VI.** No vessel coming directly from England, or from the English colonies, or having been there since the publication of the present decree, shall be received into any port.

**Art. VIII.** Every vessel contravening the above clause, by means of a false declaration, shall be seized, and the vessel and cargo confiscated, as if they were English property.

## British Order-in-Council, 1807

Whereas certain orders, establishing an unprecedented system of warfare against this kingdom, and aimed especially at the destruction of its commerce and resources, were sometime since, issued by the government of France, by which "the British islands were declared to be in a state of blockade," thereby subjecting to capture and condemnation all vessels, with their cargoes, which should continue to trade with his majesty's dominions:

And whereas, by the same order, "all trading in English merchandise is prohibited, and every article of merchandise belonging to England, or coming from her colonies, or of her manufacture, is declared lawful prize:" . . .

His majesty is therefore pleased, by and with the advice of his privy council, to order, and it is hereby ordered, that all the ports and places of France and her allies, or of any country at war with his majesty, and all other ports or places in Europe, from which, although not at war with his majesty, the British flag is excluded, and all ports or places in the colonies belonging to his majesty's enemies, shall, from henceforth, be subject to the same restrictions in point of trade and navigation . . . as if the same were actually blockaded by his majesty's naval forces, in the most strict and rigorous manner: And it is hereby further ordered and declared, that all trade in articles which are of the produce or manufacture of the said countries or colonies, shall be deemed and considered to be unlawful; and that every vessel trading from or to the said countries or colonies, together with all goods and merchandise on board, and all articles of the produce or manufacture of the said countries or colonies, shall be captured and condemned as prize to the captors. . . .

And whereas countries not engaged in the war have acquiesced in these orders of France, prohibiting all trade in any articles the produce or manufacture of his majesty's dominions; and the merchants of those countries have given countenance and effect to those prohibitions by accepting from persons, styling themselves commercial agents of the enemy, resident at neutral ports, certain documents, termed "certificates of origin," being certificates obtained at the ports of shipment, declaring that the articles of the cargo are not of the produce or manufacture of his majesty's dominions, or to that effect. . . .

His majesty is therefore pleased . . . to order . . . that if any vessel, after reasonable time shall have been afforded for receiving notice of this his majesty's order, at the port or place from which such vessel shall have cleared out, shall be found carrying any such certificate or document as aforesaid, or any document referring to or authenticating the same, such vessel shall be adjudged lawful prize to the captor, together with the goods laden therein, belonging to the persons by whom, or on whose behalf, any such document was put on board.

# The Embargo Act, 1807

*Be it enacted by the Senate and House of Representatives of the United States of America in Congress assembled,* That an embargo be, and hereby is laid on all ships and vessels in the ports and places within the limits or jurisdiction of the United States, cleared or not cleared, bound to any foreign port or place; and that no clearance be furnished to any ship or vessel bound to such foreign port or place, except vessels under the immediate direction of the President of the United States: and that the President be authorized to give such instructions to the officers of the revenue, and of the navy and revenue cutters of the United States, as shall appear best adapted for carrying the same into full effect: *Provided,* that nothing herein contained shall be construed to prevent the departure of any foreign ship or vessel, either in ballast, or with the goods, wares and merchandise on board of such foreign ship or vessel, when notified of this act.

*Sec. 2. And be it further enacted,* That during the continuance of this act, no registered, or sea letter vessel, having on board goods, wares and merchandise, shall be allowed to depart from one port of the United States to any other within the same, unless the master, owner, consignee or factor of such vessel shall first give bond, with one or more sureties to the collector of the district from which she is bound to depart, in a sum of double the value of the vessel and cargo, that the said goods, wares, or merchandise shall be relanded in some port of the United States, dangers of the seas excepted, which bond, and also a certificate from the collector where the same may be relanded, shall by the collector respectively be transmitted to the Secretary of the Treasury. All armed vessels possessing public commissions from any foreign power, are not to be considered as liable to the embargo laid by this act.

## Henry Clay on Grievances Against Britain, 1811

What are we to gain by war, has been emphatically asked? In reply, he would ask, what are we not to lose by peace?—commerce, character, a nation's best treasure, honor! If pecuniary considerations alone are to govern, there is sufficient motive for the war. Our revenue is reduced, by the operation of the belligerent edicts, to about six million of dollars, according to the Secretary of the Treasury's report. The year preceding the embargo, it was sixteen. . . .

He had no disposition to swell, or dwell upon the catalogue of injuries from England. He could not, however, overlook the impressment of our seamen; an aggression upon which he never reflected without feelings of indignation, which would not allow him appropriate language to describe its enormity. Not content with seizing upon all our property, which falls within her rapacious grasp, the personal rights of our countrymen—rights which forever ought to be sacred, are trampled upon and violated. The Orders in Council were pretended to have been reluctantly adopted as a measure of retaliation. The French decrees, their alleged basis, are revoked. England resorts to the expedient of denying the fact of the revocation, and Sir William Scott, in the celebrated case of the Fox and others, suspends judgment that proof may be adduced of it. And, at the moment when the British Ministry through that judge, is thus affecting to controvert that fact, and to place the release of our property upon its establishment, instructions are prepared for Mr. Foster to meet at Washington the very revocation which they were contesting. And how does he meet it? By fulfilling the engagement solemnly made to rescind the orders? No, sir, but by demanding that we shall secure the introduction into the Continent of British manufactures. England is said to be fighting for the world, and shall we, it is asked, attempt to weaken her exertions? If, indeed, the aim of the French Emperor be universal dominion (and he was willing to allow it to the argument,) what a noble cause is presented to British valor. But, how is her philanthropic purpose to be achieved? By scrupulous observance of the rights of others; by respecting that code of public law, which she professes to vindicate, and by abstaining from self-aggrandizement. Then would she command the sympathies of the world. What are we required to do by those who would engage our feelings and wishes in her behalf? To bear the actual cuffs of her arrogance, that we may escape a chimerical French subjugation! We are invited, conjured to drink the potion of British poison actually presented to our lips, that we may avoid the imperial dose prepared by perturbed imaginations. We are called upon to submit to debasement, dishonor, and disgrace—to bow the neck to royal insolence, as a course of preparation for manly resistance to Gallic invasion! What nation, what individual was ever taught, in the schools of ignominious submission, the patriotic lessons of freedom and independence? Let those who contend for this humiliating doctrine, read its refutation in the history of the very man against whose insatiable thirst of dominion we are warned. . . .

He contended that the real cause of British aggression, was not to distress an enemy but to destroy a rival. A comparative view of our commerce with England and the continent, would satisfy any one of the truth of this remark. . . . It is apparent that this trade, the balance of which was in favor, not of France, but of the United States, was not of very vital consequence to the enemy of England. Would she, therefore, for the sole purpose of depriving her adversary of this commerce, relinquish her valuable trade with this country, exhibiting the essential balance in her favor—nay, more; hazard the peace of the country? No, sir, you must look for an explanation of her conduct in the jealousies of a rival. She sickens at your prosperity, and beholds in your growth —your sails spread on every ocean, and your numerous seamen—the foundations of a Power which, at no very distant day, is to make her tremble for naval superiority.

## James Madison's War Message, 1812

I communicate to Congress certain documents, being a continuation of those heretofore laid before them on the subject of our affairs with Great Britain.

Without going back beyond the renewal in 1803 of the war in which Great Britain is engaged, and omitting unrepaired wrongs of inferior magnitude, the conduct of her Government presents a series of acts hostile to the United States as an independent and neutral nation.

British cruisers have been in the continued practice of violating the American flag on the great highway of nations, and of seizing and carrying off persons sailing under it, not in the exercise of a belligerent right founded on the law of nations against an enemy, but of a municipal prerogative over British subjects. British jurisdiction is thus extended to neutral vessels in a situation where no laws can operate but the law of nations and the laws of the country to which the vessels belong. . . .

The practice, hence, is so far from affecting British subjects alone that, under the pretext of searching for these, thousands of American citizens, under the safeguard of public law and of their national flag, have been torn from their country and from everything dear to them; have been dragged on board ships of war of a foreign nation and exposed, under the severities of their discipline, to be exiled to the most distant and deadly climes, to risk their lives in the battles of their oppressors, and to be the melancholy instruments of taking away those of their own brethren.

Against this crying enormity, which Great Britain would be so prompt to avenge if committed against herself, the United States have in vain exhausted remonstrances and expostulations, and that no proof might be wanting of their conciliatory dispositions, and no pretext left for a continuance of the practice, the British Government was formally assured of the readiness of the United States to enter into arrangements such as could not be rejected if the recovery of British subjects were the real and the sole object. The communication passed without effect.

British cruisers have been in the practice also of violating the rights and the peace of our coasts. They hover over and harass our entering and depart-ing commerce. To the most insulting pretensions they have added the most lawless proceedings in our very harbors, and have wantonly spilt American blood within the sanctuary of our territorial jurisdiction. The principles and rules enforced by that nation, when a neutral nation, against armed vessels of belligerents hovering near her coasts and disturbing her commerce are well known. When called on, nevertheless, by the United States to punish the greater offenses committed by her own vessels, her Government has bestowed on their commanders additional marks of honor and confidence.

Under pretended blockades, without the presence of an adequate force and sometimes without the practicability of applying one, our commerce has been plundered in every sea, the great staples of our country have been cut off from their legitimate markets, and a destructive blow aimed at our agricultural and maritime interests. In aggravation of these predatory measures they have been considered as in force from the dates of their notification, a retrospective effect being thus added, as has been done in other important cases, to the unlawful-ness of the course pursued. And to render the outrage the more signal these mock blockades have been reiterated and enforced in the face of official com-munications from the British Government declaring as the true definition of a legal blockade "that particular ports must be actually invested and previous warning given to vessels bound to them not to enter."

Not content with these occasional expedients for laying waste our neutral trade, the cabinet of Britain resorted at length to the sweeping system of block-ades, under the name of orders in council, which has been molded and managed as might best suit its political views, its commercial jealousies, or the avidity of British cruisers.

To our remonstrances against the complicated and transcendent injustice of this innovation the first reply was that the orders were reluctantly adopted by Great Britain as a necessary retaliation on decrees of her enemy proclaiming a general blockade of the British Isles at a time when the naval force of that enemy dared not issue from his own ports. She was reminded without effect that her own prior blockades, unsupported by an adequate naval force actually applied and continued, were a bar to this plea; that executed edicts against millions of our property could not be retaliation on edicts confessedly impos-sible to be executed; that retaliation, to be just, should fall on the party setting the guilty example, not on an innocent party which was not even chargeable with an acquiescence in it.

When deprived of this flimsy veil for a prohibition of our trade with her enemy by the repeal of his prohibition of our trade with Great Britain, her cabinet, instead of a corresponding repeal or a practical discontinuance of its orders, formally avowed a determination to persist in them against the United States until the markets of her enemy should be laid open to British products, thus asserting an obligation on a neutral power to require one belligerent to encourage by its internal regulations the trade of another belligerent, contradicting her own practice toward all nations, in peace as well as in war, and betraying the insincerity of those professions which inculcated a belief that, having resorted to her orders with regret, she was anxious to find an occasion for putting an end to them.

Abandoning still more all respect for the neutral rights of the United States and for its own consistency, the British Government now demands as pre-requisites to a repeal of its orders as they relate to the United States that a formality should be observed in the repeal of the French decrees nowise necessary to their termination nor exemplified by British usage, and that the French repeal, besides including that portion of the decrees which operates within a territorial jurisdiction, as well as that which operates on the high seas, against the commerce of the United States should not be a single and special repeal in relation to the United States, but should be extended to whatever other neutral nations unconnected with them may be affected by those decrees. . . .

It has become, indeed, sufficiently certain that the commerce of the United States is to be sacrificed, not as interfering with the belligerent rights of Great Britain; not as supplying the wants of her enemies, which she herself supplies; but as interfering with the monopoly which she covets for her own commerce and navigation. She carries on a war against the lawful commerce of a friend that she may the better carry on a commerce with an enemy—a commerce polluted by the forgeries and perjuries which are for the most part the only passports by which it can succeed.

Anxious to make every experiment short of the last resort of injured nations, the United States have withheld from Great Britain, under successive modifications, the benefits of a free intercourse with their market, the loss of which could not but outweigh the profits accruing from her restrictions of our commerce with other nations. And to entitle these experiments to the more favorable consideration they were so framed as to enable her to place her adversary under the exclusive operation of them. To these appeals her Government has been equally inflexible, as if willing to make sacrifices of every sort rather than yield to the claims of justice or renounce the errors of a false pride. Nay, so far were the attempts carried to overcome the attachment of the British cabinet to its unjust edicts that it received every encouragement within the competency of the executive branch of our Government to expect that a repeal of them would be followed by a war between the United States and France, unless the French edicts should also be repealed. Even this communication, although silencing forever the plea of a disposition in the United

States to acquiesce in those edicts originally the sole plea for them, received no attention. . . .

In reviewing the conduct of Great Britain toward the United States our attention is necessarily drawn to the warfare just renewed by the savages on one of our extensive frontiers—a warfare which is known to spare neither age nor sex and to be distinguished by features peculiarly shocking to humanity. It is difficult to account for the activity and combinations which have for some time been developing themselves among tribes in constant intercourse with British traders and garrisons without connecting their hostility with that influence and without recollecting the authenticated examples of such interpositions heretofore furnished by the officers and agents of that Government.

Such is the spectacle of injuries and indignities which have been heaped on our country, and such the crisis which its unexampled forbearance and conciliatory efforts have not been able to avert. It might at least have been expected that an enlightened nation, if less urged by moral obligations or invited by friendly dispositions on the part of the United States, would have found in its true interest alone a sufficient motive to respect their rights and their tranquillity on the high seas; that an enlarged policy would have favored that free and general circulation of commerce in which the British nation is at all times interested, and which in times of war is the best alleviation of its calamities to herself as well as to other belligerents; and more especially that the British cabinet would not, for the sake of a precarious and surreptitious intercourse with hostile markets, have persevered in a course of measures which necessarily put at hazard the invaluable market of a great and growing country, disposed to cultivate the mutual advantages of an active commerce.

Other counsels have prevailed. Our moderation and conciliation have had no other effect than to encourage perseverance and to enlarge pretensions. We behold our seafaring citizens, still the daily victims of lawless violence, committed on the great common and highway of nations, even within sight of the country which owes them protection. We behold our vessels, freighted with the products of our soil and industry, or returning with the honest proceeds of them, wrested from their lawful destinations, confiscated by prize courts no longer the organs of public law but the instruments of arbitrary edicts, and their unfortunate crews dispersed and lost, or forced or inveigled in British ports into British fleets, whilst arguments are employed in support of these aggressions which have no foundation but in a principle equally supporting a claim to regulate our external commerce in all cases whatsoever.

We behold, in fine, on the side of Great Britain a state of war against the United States, and on the side of the United States a state of peace toward Great Britain.

Whether the United States shall continue passive under these progressive usurpations and these accumulating wrongs, or, opposing force to force in defense of their national rights, shall commit a just cause into the hands of the Almighty Disposer of Events, avoiding all connections which might entangle it in the contest or views of other powers, and preserving a constant readiness to concur in an honorable reestablishment of peace and friendship, is a solemn question which the Constitution wisely confides to the legislative department of the Government. In recommending it to their early deliberations I am happy in the assurance that the decision will be worthy the enlightened and patriotic councils of a virtuous, a free, and a powerful nation.

Having presented this view of the relations of the United States with Great Britain and of the solemn alternative growing out of them, I proceed to remark that the communications last made to Congress on the subject of our relations with France will have shewn that since the revocation of her decrees, as they violated the neutral rights of the United States, her Government has authorized illegal captures by its privateers and public ships, and that other outrages have been practiced on our vessels and our citizens. It will have been seen also that no indemnity had been provided or satisfactorily pledged for the extensive spoliations committed under the violent and retrospective orders of the French Government against the property of our citizens seized within the jurisdiction of France. I abstain at this time from recommending to the consideration of Congress definitive measures with respect to that nation, in the expectation that the result of unclosed discussions between our minister plenipotentiary at Paris and the French Government will speedily enable Congress to decide with greater advantage on the course due to the rights, the interests, and the honor of our country.

## The Hartford Convention, 1814–1815

The next amendments proposed by the convention relate to the powers of Congress in relation to embargo and the interdiction of commerce.

Whatever theories upon the subject of commerce have hitherto divided the opinions of statesmen, experience has at last shown that it is a vital interest in the United States, and that its success is essential to the encouragements of agriculture and manufactures, and to the wealth, finances, defence, and liberty of the nation. Its welfare can never interfere with the other great interests of the State, but must promote and uphold them. Still, those who are immediately concerned in the prosecution of commerce will of necessity be always a minority of the nation. They are, however, best qualified to manage and direct its course by the advantages of experience and the sense of interest. But they are entirely unable to protect themselves against the sudden and injudicious decisions of bare majorities, and the mistaken or oppressive projects of those who are not actively concerned in its pursuits. Of consequence, this interest is always exposed to be harassed, interrupted, and entirely destroyed upon pretence of securing other interests. Had the merchants of this nation been permitted by their own government to pursue an innocent and lawful commerce, how different would have been the state of the treasury and of public credit! How short-sighted and miserable is the policy which has annihilated this order of men, and doomed their ships to rot in the docks, their capital to waste unemployed, and their affections to be alienated from the government which was formed to protect them! What security for an ample and unfailing revenue can ever be had, comparable to that which once was realized in the good faith, punctuality, and sense of honor which attached the mercantile class to the interests of the government! Without commerce, where can be found the aliment for a navy, and without a navy what is to constitute the defence and ornament and glory of this nation! No union can be durably cemented in which every great interest does not find itself reasonably secured against the encroachment and combinations of other interests. When, therefore, the past system of embargoes and commercial restrictions shall have been reviewed, when the fluctuation and inconsistency of public measures, betraying a want of information as well as feeling in the majority, shall have been considered, the reasonableness of some restrictions upon the power of a bare majority to repeat these oppressions will appear to be obvious.

The next amendment proposes to restrict the power of making offensive war. In the consideration of this amendment it is not necessary to inquire into the justice of the present war. But one sentiment now exists in relation to its expediency, and regret for its declaration is nearly universal. No indemnity can ever be attained for this terrible calamity, and its only palliation must be found in obstacles to its future recurrence. Rarely can the state of this country call for or justify offensive war. The genius of our institutions is unfavorable to its successful prosecution, the felicity of our situation exempts us from its necessity. In this case, as in the former, those more immediately exposed to its fatal effects are a minority of the nation. The commercial towns, the shores of our seas and rivers, contain the population whose vital interests are most vulnerable by a foreign enemy. Agriculture, indeed, must feel at last, but this appeal to its sensibility comes too late. Again, the immense population which has swarmed into the West, remote from immediate danger, and which is constantly augmenting, will not be averse from the occasional disturbances of the Atlantic States. Thus interest may not unfrequently combine with passion and intrigue to plunge the nation into needless wars and compel it to become a military rather than a happy and flourishing people. These considerations, which it would be easy to augment, call loudly for the limitation proposed in the amendment. . . .

*Resolved,* That the following amendments of the Constitution of the United States be recommended to the States represented as aforesaid, to be proposed by them for adoption by the State legislatures, and in such cases as may be deemed expedient by a convention chosen by the people of each State. . . .

*Third.* Congress shall not have power to lay any embargo on the ships or vessels of the citizens of the United States, in the ports or harbors thereof, for more than sixty days.

*Fourth.* Congress shall not have power, without the concurrence of two-thirds of both Houses, to interdict the commercial intercourse between the United States and any foreign nation, or the dependencies thereof.

*Fifth.* Congress shall not make or declare war, or authorize acts of hostility against any foreign nation, without the concurrence of two-thirds of both Houses, except such acts of hostility be in defence of the territories of the United States when actually invaded.

## ESSAYS

The following essays explain the coming of the War of 1812 differently. Julius Pratt, noting the desire of Americans in the Western states and territories for war, stresses the Indian menace. Pratt does not deny that maritime issues helped to cause war, but he does argue that without Western grievances there would have been no declaration of war. He suggests, further, a "sectional bargain" between the Northwest, which sought Canada, and the Southwest, which coveted Spanish Florida. Bradford Perkins of the University of Michigan acknowledges Western hawkishness, but he concludes that war came because Americans wished to recover the respect they had lost over the preceding years when the Europeans trampled upon their neutral rights. The war, then, was a matter of national honor. The last essay, by J.C.A. Stagg of the University of Auckland, New Zealand, looks anew at the intense American interest in Canada. He suggests that Canada was a target largely because American seizure of the valuable British colony might force the British to accept United States maritime principles.

## Western Demands and War

### JULIUS W. PRATT

That the United States went to war with Great Britain in 1812 at the insistence of western and southern men, and over the opposition of the Northeast, is a fact about which there has never been any doubt. There was a paradox here which apparently gave little concern to the older historians. If the real grievances which caused the war were interference by Great Britain with American commerce and the rights of American sailors, why was war to redress those grievances opposed by the maritime section of the nation and urged by the inland section, which they scarcely affected? The old answers, that New England was Anglophile, and that the West and South had developed a more aggressive and martial spirit, which felt the humiliation if not the pecuniary loss occasioned by the British measures, were in a measure true, but hardly sufficient. For some years past, historians have been turning to new explanations.

In this field, as in almost every other in American history, it is easy to see the profound influence of Professor F. J. Turner. Before the publication in 1893 of his essay, "The Significance of the Frontier in American History," the frontier had been regarded as little more than a picturesque phase in the national development. Since that event, the frontier—the "West"—has come to be recognized as the source of many aspects of American character and the determining factor in many American policies. It was natural, therefore, that students of the War of 1812 should come to view the West—particularly the Northwest—with more careful scrutiny. The result of such examination has been the placing of new emphasis upon the western demand for the annexation of Canada, which is seen to have arisen in large part from the conviction that the British were in league with the northwestern Indians and that only by destroying that alliance could the Northwest continue its career of expansion.

The war found its sponsors, however, not only in the Northwest but along the whole frontier from New Hampshire round about to Georgia. For the states south of Kentucky, there was little to be gained by the conquest of Canada, and, since the divergence of interests between North and South was already evident, there was reason for southern states to fear the political effect of a large addition to northern territory. Why, then, did the Southwest support the war? The answer to this question has been suggested, but has never been worked out with anything approaching completeness. The examination made in the course of this study reveals an ardent expansionist sentiment already at work along the whole southern and southwestern border, varying in scope from the relatively modest proposal for the annexation of the Floridas to the more visionary idea of seizing all the Spanish possessions on the continent of North America. The link between the designs of the Southwest and those of the Northwest was the existence of the alliance between Great Britain and Spain. It was widely assumed that war with Great Britain would mean war with Spain, and that thus expansion at the north and at the south would proceed *pari passu*.

The purposes of the present study have been: to examine the development in the Northwest of the demand for the conquest and annexation of Canada; to trace the rise in the South and Southwest of the plan to annex the Floridas and possibly Mexico; to discover the relations of these two proposals to each other and to the question of war with Great Britain; to determine the position of the executive branch of the United States government (especially of Madison and his Secretary of State, Monroe) toward the plans for expansion, north and south; and finally, to determine the causes for the failure, all along the line, of the expansionist hopes with which the war began.

The principal conclusions arrived at may be summarized as follows:

1. The belief that the United States would one day annex Canada had a continuous existence from the early days of the War of Independence to the War of 1812. From 1783 to about 1810 such annexation was thought of only as a matter for an indefinite future, the nation during those years having neither the strength, nor any sufficient motive, for taking Canada by force. The rise of Tecumseh, backed, as was universally believed, by the British, produced an urgent demand in the Northwest that the British be expelled from Canada. This demand was a factor of primary importance in bringing on the war.

2. The South was almost unanimous in its demand for the Floridas, for agrarian, commercial, and strategic reasons, and in the spring of 1812 appeared to be in a fair way to accomplish its purpose. In the Southwest, at the same time, there was a lively interest in Mexico and a widely prevalent opinion that it was ready to fall into American hands.

3. Even within the Republican party, there was already a distinct sectional rift between North and South, and neither section was anxious to see the other

increase its territory and population. But if both could gain at the same time, and in something like equal proportion, such objections would be obviated on both sides. There is good evidence that, before the declaration of war, northern and southern Republicans came to a definite understanding that the acquisition of Canada on the north was to be balanced by the annexation of the Floridas on the south. Thus the war began with a double-barrelled scheme of territorial aggrandizement.

4. Both Madison and Monroe, especially the latter as Secretary of State, were wholly in sympathy with the proposal for annexing Florida. The invasion of East Florida by General Mathews in March and April, 1812, was effected with the full knowledge of the administration. Special circumstances forced the government to repudiate Mathews, but the territory he had taken from the Spanish was held for over a year, until Congress had twice refused to sanction the occupation. At the same time, Monroe's official correspondence shows that he never really desired or expected the annexation of Canada.

5. It appears that in the all round failure of the expansionist plans, sectional feeling played a larger part than is commonly supposed. The sectional bargain with which the war had begun broke down. Opposition from northern Republicans combined with Federalists forced the abandonment of East Florida. On the other hand, it is evident that in the utter failure of the efforts to take Canada, not only want of skill and preparation, but also a lack of enthusiasm on the part of the administration and of certain southern men in Congress played a part.

6. Finally, in the expansionist program with which the war opened, we have the first general appearance of the idea which later received the name of "Manifest Destiny." Although enthusiasts like Jefferson had dreamed years before of a nation destined to embrace the continent, the date usually given for the dawn of "Manifest Destiny" is about 1830. Yet both in the Congressional debates of 1812 and in the contemporary press, particularly that of the Southwest, we find the idea repeatedly expressed. "Where is it written in the book of fate," asked the editor of the Nashville *Clarion* (April 28, 1812), "that the American republic shall not stretch her limits from the Capes of the Chesapeake to Nootka sound, from the isthmus of Panama to Hudson bay?"

Two explanations are due, with respect to the scope and proportions of this study. First, it makes no effort to give a full account of the causes of the War of 1812, but deals with one set of causes only. The exclusion from all but briefest mention of the maritime grievances against Great Britain is with no wish to belittle them. Without them, it is safe to say, there would have been no war, just as the writer feels safe in saying that without the peculiar grievances and ambitions of the West there would have been no war. One set of causes was perhaps as essential as the other. . . .

Throughout the year 1811, alarm at the menace of Tecumseh's confederacy and conviction that the British were instrumental in its formation and support grew rapidly among government officials and the people of the West. Governor Harrison wrote in February to the Secretary of War: "If the intentions of the British Government are pacific, the Indian department of Upper Canada have not been made acquainted with them: for they have very lately said every thing to the Indians, who visited them, to excite them against us."

In July a group of citizens of Knox County, Indiana, met at Vincennes and adopted resolutions demanding that the Indian settlement at Tippecanoe—one hundred and fifty miles up the Wabash—be broken up. The wish was natural, in view of the serious menace which the Prophet's town held over the heads of the Knox County settlers; but it was significant that the British were charged with responsibility for the whole situation. "We are fully convinced," said the resolutions, "that the formation of the combination, headed by the Shawanee prophet, is a British scheme, and that the agents of that power are constantly exciting the Indians to hostilities against the United States." Similar views were reflected in resolutions adopted by residents of St. Clair County, Illinois, which mentioned "the seditious village of Peoria, the great nursery of hostile Indians and traitorous British Indian traders."

Meanwhile the *Kentucky Gazette* was warning its readers of the British-Indian menace in outspoken language:

"It would seem from the attitude of the Indians—the combination of the Northern and Southern tribes—the conference at Malden—the circumstances attendant on the mission of *Foster*—the late arrival of regular troops in Canada, that the British ministry were planning '*another expedition.*' ...

"From the friendly course pursued by Mr. Jefferson, towards our red neighbors, and which has been followed by Mr. Madison, we had supposed the Indians would never more treat us otherwise than as brethren. But we have been mistaken—British intrigue and British gold, it seems, has greater influence with them of late than American justice and benevolence. . . . We have in our possession information which proves beyond doubt, the late disturbances to be owing to the too successful intrigues of British emissaries with the Indians."

Governor Harrison, representative of "American justice and benevolence" toward the Indians, was at this time planning to open the way to a military career by an attack on the Indian village at Tippecanoe. But he knew that war with England was probable, and suspected that the regiment of regular troops now on their way to him from Pittsburgh, were destined "to our frontiers bordering on Upper Canada." More important than his own ideas on the subject was his estimate of the spirit of the western people, whom he knew if any one knew them. "The people of this Territory [Indiana] and Kentucky," he wrote, "are extremely pressing in offers of their service for an expedition into the Indian Country. Any number of men might be obtained for this purpose or for a march into Canada."

Early in September it was reported to Harrison "that defection is evidenced amongst all the Tribes from the Wabash to the Mississippi and the Lakes. That the Indians of the Wabash, Illinois, etc., have recently visited the British agent at Malden. That they are now returning from thence with a larger supply of goods than is ever known to have been distributed to them before. That rifles or fusees are given to those who are unarmed and powder and lead to all. And that the language and measures of the Indians indicate nothing but war." Harrison passed on the information to the War Department a few days later

(September 17, 1811), with additional details of the extent of British subsidies: "A trader of this country was lately in the King's store at Malden, and was told that the quantity of goods for the Indian department, which has been sent out this year, exceeded that of common years by £20,000 sterling. It is impossible to ascribe this profusion to any other motive than that of instigating the Indians to take up the tomahawk; it cannot be to secure their trade, for all the peltries collected on the waters of the Wabash, in one year, if sold in the London market, would not pay the freight of the goods which have been given the Indians."

Harrison, however, went on to say that, "although I am decidedly of opinion that the tendency of the British measures is hostility to us, candor obliges me to inform you, that, from two Indians of different tribes, I have received information that the British agent absolutely dissuaded them from going to war against the United States." That the compulsion of candor was necessary to bring the governor to pass on this last bit of information is an interesting commentary on his state of mind; but the information itself is perfectly consistent with the other facts of the situation. General Brock wrote, after Harrison's battle with the Indians, that the latter had been "implicitly told not to look for assistance from us," but the phrase occurs in a letter whose main purpose was to point out how the effective aid of the Indians was to be secured and used against the Americans. Throughout the period of the rise of Tecumseh, the British had dissuaded the Indians from beginning a war against the United States; but the purpose of this policy was to allow time for the consolidation of the confederacy, that the aid of the Indians might be the more effective when needed.

Early in November came Harrison's badly managed campaign ending in the battle of Tippecanoe. From the facts already presented it is clear that the blood there shed would be added to the grievances already existing against the British and would bring the West to an eagerness for war without precedent in the entire controversy. *"The blood of our murdered countrymen must be revenged,"* wrote Andrew Jackson to Harrison. "I do hope that Government will see that it is necessary to act efficiently and that this hostile band which must be excited to war by the secret agents of Great Britain must be destroyed." The battle of Tippecanoe gave inestimable support to the war party in the Twelfth Congress, now assembled in Washington for its first session.

The war party, composed of western men and "radical, expansionist, malcontent politicians of the east," which had existed in Congress since 1810 at least, found itself in full control when the Twelfth Congress met. Clay, the most prominent of the "war hawks," came now to the House of Representatives, where he was at once chosen speaker. He was supported in his warlike policy by members from the frontier sections of the northern states, such as Peter B. Porter of New York and John A. Harper of New Hampshire; by almost the entire delegation of the western states—Worthington of Ohio and Pope of Kentucky, both in the Senate, were the only important exceptions— by a fair proportion of the members from Pennsylvania, Virginia, and North Carolina; and by a very able and aggressive group of young men from South

Carolina and Georgia—Calhoun, Cheves, Lowndes, Crawford, Troup, and others—men who had reasons of their own for promoting a war of expansion.

It was soon apparent that the war to which this party was committed was to be no such purely defensive war as the Tenth Congress had contemplated, but that it was to be waged aggressively and with the conquest of Canada as a major object. Some Easterners might agree with Monroe that Canada might be invaded, "not as an object of the war but as a means to bring it to a satisfactory conclusion," but the West was more of the mind of a correspondent of the Philadelphia *Aurora,* "who wrote that if England were to restore all impressed seamen and make compensation for all her depredations we should listen to no terms that did not include Upper Canada."

President Madison's annual message, delivered to Congress on November 5, contained language that could plainly be interpreted as meaning war. After touching upon the obdurate persistence of Great Britain in attacking American commerce, he went on to say: "With this evidence of hostile inflexibility, in trampling on rights which no independent nation can relinquish, Congress will feel the duty of putting the United States into an armor and an attitude demanded by the crisis, and corresponding with the national spirit and expectations." To deal with that part of the message concerned with foreign relations, Speaker Clay appointed a select committee, upon which he placed a group of the most reliable war men—Porter, Calhoun, Grundy, Harper, and Desha. The committee reported on November 29 a set of six resolutions recommending an increase of ten thousand men for the regular army, a levy of fifty thousand volunteers, the outfitting of all vessels of war not in active service, and the arming of merchant vessels.

It was in the House debate on these resolutions that the war party frankly revealed their designs upon Canada. Mr. Porter, chairman of the committee, speaking on December 6, explained that in addition to the injury which American privateers could inflict upon British commerce, "there was another point where we could attack her, and where she would feel our power still more sensibly. We could deprive her of her extensive provinces lying along our borders to the north. These provinces were not only immensely valuable in themselves, but almost indispensable to the existence of Great Britain, cut off as she now in a great measure is from the north of Europe. He had been credibly informed that the exports from Quebec alone amounted during the last year, to near six millions of dollars, and most of these too in articles of the first necessity—in ship timber and in provisions for the support of her fleets and armies. By carrying on such a war as he had described . . . we should be able in a short time to remunerate ourselves tenfold for all the spoliations she had committed on our commerce."

Grundy of Tennessee, three days later, dwelt upon the peculiar advantage to the Westerner to be derived from war. "We shall drive the British from our Continent—they will no longer have an opportunity of intriguing with our Indian neighbors, and setting on the ruthless savage to tomahawk our women and children. That nation will lose her Canadian trade, and, by having no resting place in this country, her means of annoying us will be diminished."

Rhea of Tennessee was equally explicit upon the object of the war—"That all that part of North America which joins the United States on the Northeast, North, and Northwest, shall be provided for in a mode which will forever thereafter put it out of the power of Great Britain, or of any British agent, trader, or factor, or company of British traders to supply Indian tribes with arms or ammunition; to instigate and incite Indians to disturb and harass our frontiers, and to murder and scalp helpless women and children."

Two members of the House, one from Kentucky and one from New Hampshire, expounded the doctrine of Manifest Destiny. "I shall never die contented," announced R. M. Johnson, "until I see her [Great Britain's] expulsion from North America, and her territories incorporated with the United States. ... In point of territorial limit, the map will improve its importance. The waters of the St. Lawrence and the Mississippi interlock in a number of places, and the great Disposer of Human Events intended those two rivers should belong to the same people." "The northern provinces of Britain are to us great and valuable objects," proclaimed Harper of New Hampshire. "Once secured to this Republic, and the St. Lawrence and the Lakes become the Baltic, and more than the Baltic to America; north of them a population of four millions may easily be supported; and this great outlet of the northern world should be at our command for our convenience and future security. To me, sir, it appears that the Author of Nature has marked our limits in the south, by the Gulf of Mexico; and on the north, by the regions of eternal frost."

While Congress debated, reports continued to come in of British agents at work among the Indians. As a matter of fact, it would appear that presents to the Indians, and particularly ammunition, were less at this time than previously. Claus wrote General Brock from Amherstburg in June, 1812, that during the last six months the Indians had received only 1211 pounds of powder— "nineteen hundred and twenty-one pounds less than at former periods—of lead, not one ounce has been issued to them since last December." But a letter from Fort Wayne in February stated that two British emissaries had recently passed that way on a mission to the Prophet, and that "their business was to invite all the Indians to meet at Malden very early in the spring." Any event of this kind would of course receive the most unfavorable interpretation. The same letter gave other disturbing reports: "The Pottawatomy chief, Marpack, has been in the neighborhood of Malden since August last. ... He has about one hundred and twenty of the best warriors in this country with him. ... I know this chief is hostile inclined towards the United States, and have no hesitation in saying, that he is kept at that place by the British agents at Malden."

If their relations with the Indians constituted a standing reason for driving the British from Canada, a special reason was furnished by the publication of the Henry Letters, for Henry had been in the employ of the Governor-General of Canada. "Can any American, after this discovery," wrote Congressman Desha to a friend in Kentucky, "doubt the propriety of ousting the British from the continent, or hesitate in contributing his proportionable part of the expense which will necessarily be incurred in the laudable undertaking."

The West no longer needed any such prompting from its representatives in Washington. The rise of Tecumseh and the Prophet, the battle of Tippecanoe, the outspoken position of their congressmen together with the current belief that the British were behind all their Indian troubles, had resulted in an insistent demand from the Westerners for the conquest of Canada. The Lexington *Reporter* published in January a *"Franklinian Prescription—To cure Indian hostilities, and to prevent their recurrence:* Interpose the American arm between the hands of the English and their savage allies. This done, the occupation of the Canadas, New Brunswick and Nova-Scotia, would give us perpetual concord with the Indians; who would be obliged *to depend upon us* for supplies of Blankets, knives, gunpowder, etc."

The Kentucky Legislature, which in the crisis of 1807–1808 had made no official mention of the border question, in its resolutions of February, 1812, added to Great Britain's violations of American rights at sea her practice of "inciting the savages (as we have strong reasons to believe) to murder the inhabitants of our defenseless frontiers—furnishing them with arms and ammunition lately, to attack our forces; to the loss of a number of our brave men."

Another indication of public opinion in Kentucky is the character of the toasts proposed at a Washington's Birthday dinner in Lexington. The banqueters drank to such toasts as *"Great Britain, when she comes to her senses —If she continues lunatic, Canada and our arms!"* or *"The American Congress—If* they barter the nation's honor under the false idea of temporary popularity, may they meet with the just scorn of an indignant people!"

Public opinion in Ohio paralleled closely that of Kentucky. The Circleville *Fredonian* declared the "indignant spirits" of Americans could be appeased only "by the restoration of our rights, or the conquest of Canada." Correspondents of Senator Thomas Worthington believed that if war came, "we would attack [and] conquer Cannady & humble their overbearing pride," or hoped that American troops would "sever Upper Canada from the British without delay."

As the year advanced, the tone of the press grew even more determined. The *Fredonian* saw no hope of peace and security from the savages until "another WAYNE shall force *them* to become our friends, and another WASHINGTON exterminates from the Canadas, the base remains of royal perfidy." The British "must be for ever driven from all their possessions in America." The same paper professed itself eager to undertake a war against both France and Great Britain when it appeared that neither nation was willing to recognize American rights. In April the *Kentucky Gazette* stated: "Great Britain has determined not to recede, and Congress seem at last to have got in earnest, and appear disposed to prepare for war. . . . The recruiting service has been actually commenced in various places, and large bodies of militia are to be raised to march for Detroit and other parts of our frontier. This is all preparatory to the invasion of Canada, now more than ever necessary, as presenting whilst in the possession of Britain, a never failing source of Indian hostility. Until those civilized allies of our Savage neighbors, are expelled from our continent, we must expect the frequent recurrence of the late scenes on the Wabash."

The same paper could not suppress its wrath when the *National Intelli-*

*gencer,* reputed to be the administration organ, hinted that war might yet be avoided. "Notwithstanding a mass of evidence of this kind [i.e. as to captures, impressment, Henry plots, etc.], the Intelligencer may talk of *negociation* and *'honorable accommodation'* with England; but when we view the effects of her policy in the *West*—when we hear of the tragic scenes that are now acting on our frontiers, after the slaughter of Tippecanoe, it is really surprising to hear that there is any doubt about the *'active preparations for warlike operations'* . . . We will only add, at this time, that we should much like to know the price which the 'Intelligencer' would receive as a compromise for the scalps of *Western Farmers.*"

On May 26, three weeks before the declaration of war, the *Gazette* gave what appears like a parting injunction to Congress: "Can it be expected that those savage butcheries will have an end until we take possession of Malden and other British forts on the Lakes? And must the settlements in our territories be entirely destroyed, and the blood of the women and children drench the soil before this can be done? . . . What will our Congress say?" In similar tone the *Reporter* of May 30 declared: "Britain has commenced war in the Western Country, equally so as France would have done, was she to burn New York. The citizens of the Eastern States, and members in Congress, may abandon 7,000 seamen—they may term it, a *trifling impropriety* on the part of England, but the old Revolutionary Heroes here are not to be deceived by the misrepresentations of any man whatever. The Government MUST not abandon the Western Country to the British."

Thus by the end of the spring of 1812, the whole frontier country from New Hampshire to Kentucky was insisting that the British must be expelled from Canada. The demand had been of slow growth. Taking its origin from the ideas of Revolutionary statesmen, it was fed from various sources—from jealousy of the British fur trade, from exasperation at British contempt for the American flag at sea, from the alluring vision of a continent destined to recognize a single sovereignty—but unquestionably most of all from the conviction that the British in Canada were in unholy alliance with the western Indians, and that only by cutting off the Indians from British support could the West gain peace and security. Only thus could the Westerner be free to continue that policy of "justice and benevolence" toward the Indians, which consisted in pushing the boundaries of the white settlements ever farther into the Indian country. Other motives—commercial, political, punitive—played a part; but the overmastering desire of the people of the Northwest was to feel free to develop their country without peril from those Indian conspiracies which were universally believed to have their origin in British Canada. . . .

If the frontiersman of the Northwest demanded war with Great Britain as indispensable, his kinsman of the southern border at least saw in it a means of fulfilling his expansionist dreams. The past two years had done much to give him what he thought his territorial rights, but much remained to be gained. The Spanish still held Mobile and Pensacola, St. Mark's and St. Augustine, and the American troops that held the country between the St. John's and the St. Mary's rivers were, it was supposed, about to be withdrawn.

The demand for the annexation of all Florida was more insistent than ever.

Georgians like Floyd, Mitchell, Troup, and Crawford—the last two influential members of the war party in Congress—held the acquisition of East Florida essential to the prosperity, to the very safety, of their state. The Augusta *Chronicle* . . . hoped for "some new measures for the purpose of placing the whole of that colony under the control of the United States." Out in Mississippi Territory, the news of the occupation of East Florida aroused a lively hope of similar action farther west. "There is no doubt," wrote a recent settler at St. Stephens, to a friend in the East, "but Mobille and Pensacola will share the same fate in a few weeks, which no doubt will occation considerable action in this quarter during this summer, and all the citizens in this part of the country are much gratified at the Idea of the United States getting Possession of this Southern Coast, as it is certainly of all importance to the citizens of this country." The Nashville *Clarion,* quoting at length from the Congressional Report of 1803 on the navigation of the southern rivers, and explaining in detail how Tennessee's transportation difficulties would be solved by the opening of the Alabama and Tombigbee, declared that "No part of the union can be so much interested in the acquisition of West Florida as the State of Tennessee. . . . The Floridas will soon be occupied by American troops."

But if the whole southern border was eager to take what remained of Florida, war with England seemed to afford a perfectly clear occasion for doing so. Spain was England's ally in the European war, and it was safe to assume that Spanish harbors in America would be open to British fleets and armies. As a simple measure of self-defense, the occupation of Florida seemed to many indispensable, and it was commonly assumed at the South that war with England meant war with Spain, or at least the forcible occupation of all Florida.

The notion of a war at once against England and Spain had been broached by Jefferson in 1807, in which case, he declared, "our southern defensive force can take the Floridas." Mathews had alluded to a similar connection when he instructed the "discontents" of East Florida "not to expect that prompt and efficient aid from the United States, if our negotiation with the British Minister terminates auspiciously for us, that they might in the other event expect." Expansionists like Clay and Harper, when they hurled defiance at Great Britain, had spoken in one breath of the nation's prospective conquests on the St. Lawrence and the Gulf of Mexico. Grundy of Tennessee, in the war debate in December, 1811, stated that he felt anxious "not only to add the Floridas to the South, but the Canadas to the North of this empire," and he wrote to Jackson that in case of war "the Canadas & Floridas will be the Theatres of our offensive operations."

Jackson himself, when shortly after the declaration of war he called upon his division of Tennessee militia to be in readiness, assured them that it was in West Florida that their arms should find employment. Jefferson, writing of the mustering of the militia in his Virginia county in June, 1812, said that "the only inquiry they make is whether they are to go to Canada or Florida."

In Georgia it was generally assumed that war with Great Britain would mean the certain seizure of all of Florida that remained unoccupied. "Had we no other claim on Florida or Spain," said the Augusta *Chronicle* in May, "sound policy would dictate the propriety as well as necessity of retaining possession of it till the close of the war we are now on the eve of commencing with an ally of that country." On the day preceding the declaration of war, the Republican citizens of Milledgeville passed resolutions approving the war measures against Great Britain, and declaring their belief that with war in prospect the occupancy of East Florida was "essential to the interests of the country and the safety of our southern frontier." A letter from Milledgeville dated July 8, 1812, reported that Governor Mitchell, who was at St. Mary's, had received news of the declaration of war, and, "considering that the Spaniards and British are in alliance both offensive and defensive, and that the vital interests of this state and the honor of the United States are implicated and will be hazarded by suffering the occupancy of East Florida by the banditti now in possession"— not the "patriots" evidently, to whom the term might have been applied, but the Spanish governor and his negro and Indian auxiliaries—"he will be detained until the reinforcements he has sent for and which are now assembling on the Oconee River, are received." Mitchell himself explained later to the Georgia legislature the light in which, prior to the declaration of war, he had viewed the situation. "The confidence with which I anticipated the declaration of war against Great Britain," said the governor, "led me with equal confidence to anticipate an enlargement of the powers of the President, by congress, as the necessary consequence, having for its object the entire occupancy of East and West Florida."

War with Great Britain, then, meant, to the average Southerner, war also with Spain, and the completion of the annexation of the Floridas. To the people of the Southwest it meant the possibility of even greater things. The old dream of revolutionizing Mexico and, if not actually annexing it to the United States, at least profiting by its agricultural, mineral, and commercial wealth, revived with new vigor. The Southwest tried to persuade itself that the Federal government favored such plans, quoting cryptic passages from "prints known to be in the interest of the administration," and citing the promotion of Colonel Pike, an avowed annexationist, and his position then in command of the troops on the border, as evidence that an invasion was contemplated. A writer signing himself "Americus" contributed to the Nashville Clarion of April 28 a long article in which "Manifest Destiny" ran riot.

"The Canadas," wrote Americus, "freed from the chains of an European master, shall take the rank of an independent state; or, too weak for sovereignty, shall hover under the wings of the American eagle. . . . The Floridas will sink into the confederation of American states. . . . Whilst our eastern and southern brethren are purchasing renown in arms, and extending the limits of the republic, are we condemned to remain inactive . . . ? No, citizens of the West! a destiny still more splendid is reserved for you. Behold the empire of Mexico, a celestial region, whose valiant sons are now struggling for their liberties as we struggled for ours thirty years ago. . . . Here it is that the statesman shall see an accession of Territory sufficient to double the extent of the republic; where the merchant shall see commercial resources unrivalled in other countries, the farmer, a luxuriant soil and delicious climate, where the financier shall be dazzled with gold and silver mines; while the ardent and generous mind, in the idea of establishing a new republic . . . shall deliver himself up to an enthusiasm of glory. . . . Besides, where is it written in the book of fate that the American republic shall not stretch her limits from the capes of the Chesapeake to Nootka sound, from the isthmus of Panama to Hudson bay?"

Thus while the Northwesterner expected to take Canada as a result of war with Great Britain, southern men generally expected to complete the seizure of Florida from Great Britain's ally, Spain, while the more ambitious expansionists of the Southwest dreamed of further aggressions upon the Spanish territories, which should end in making the United States coextensive with the continent of North America.

# A Question of National Honor

## BRADFORD PERKINS

The war continued for two and a half years, and for nearly 150 years it has challenged those who seek to explain its coming. Contemporary Federalists found a simple explanation in alleged Republican subserviency to France. A New York dominie declared God had brought on war so that the young republic might chastise the British government, "a *despotic usurpation—A superstitious combination of civil and ecclesiastic power—A branch of the grand antichristian apostacy—Erastian in its constitution and administration—*and *Cruel in its policy.*" Actually, neither God nor Napoleon seems an adequate explanation for the war, and historians have sought to establish the importance of more mundane influences.

Most nineteenth-century historians emphasized British outrages against American commerce. Admiral Mahan said that the orders "by their enormity dwarfed all previous causes of complaint, and with the question of impressment constituted a vital and irreconcilable body of dissent which dragged the two states into armed collision." Henry Adams apparently considered this maritime emphasis inadequate, but, as Warren Goodman suggests in an able historiographical article, he modified rather than abandoned the traditional view, although he did hint that Canadian-directed imperialism played a part. Despite a dislike of Jefferson and Madison so bitter that he sometimes doctored the evidence, Adams' volumes remain the most complete, often the best written, and, when used with proper caution, the most useful survey of the entire period. After a lapse of some years, A. L. Burt reëmphasized maritime causes in a graceful summary of the era.

For two decades before the appearance of Burt's work in 1940, scholars sought to explain the motives of the West, the section that most unanimously supported war. Louis M. Hacker, then in a Marxist phase, suggested that a greedy desire for fertile Canadian farm land lay behind the façade of argu-

Bradford Perkins, *Prologue to War: England and the United States, 1805–1812*, pp. 421–437. Copyright © 1961 by The Regents of the University of California; reprinted by permission of the University of California Press.

ments for national honor. Julius W. Pratt contradicted Hacker's position, largely by disproving the central hypothesis, that there was no longer good agricultural land on the American side of the frontier. Then, following a line already sketched by Dice R. Anderson, Pratt in his turn suggested a bargain between frontiersmen and Republicans of the North, who desired Canada, and Southerners, who wanted to absorb Florida. Sectional jealousies, Pratt concluded, broke down this alliance only after it had brought on war. Pratt found it difficult to demonstrate a real bargain, and there is reason to believe that the South did not almost universally desire the acquisition of Florida, as he maintained. But not without merit is Pratt's thesis that Western Anglophobia was stirred by the menace of Indian warfare believed to be inspired by Canadian authorities. Finally, George R. Taylor put forward the argument that the West, economically overextended and suffering from depression from 1808 onward, blamed its troubles on the restrictive edicts of Europe and advocated war to break down this barrier to prosperity. In April, 1812, Augustus J. Foster anticipated this interpretation: "The Western States having nothing to lose by war, . . . [are] clamorous for it, . . . being likely even to gain in the Exports of their produce while the exportation of that of the Atlantic shall be impeded." Moreover, there was always the chance that war, or even the threat of war, would drive England to surrender the orders.

Hacker billed his suggestion "a conjecture," and Pratt and Taylor specifically noted that they were dealing, in the former's words, "with one set of causes only." Still, despite Pratt's coördinate interest in Southern ambitions for Florida, the researches of these scholars concentrated attention upon the West. The war came to bear the mark of the West, although only nine congressmen—a mere one of each nine voting for war—came from Western states. Taylor's suggestion that the West sought war to regain an export market might just as legitimately have been applied to other agricultural areas of the country, particularly the South, as Goodman, Burt, and Margaret K. Latimer have recently noted. Studies of Western motivation, despite the caveats of their authors, have distorted the image of events leading to the War of 1812.

In his biography of the President, Irving Brant attempts to refurbish Madison's reputation. Attention is so narrowly concentrated on the President and on events with which he dealt that many important developments in Europe and America are slighted. Brant clearly shows the President's technical diplomatic ability. He does not equally clearly disprove Henry Adams' contention that, by emphasizing America's right to demand repeal of the orders as a consequence of alleged French repeal,

> Madison had been so unfortunate in making the issue that on his own showing no sufficient cause of war seemed to exist. . . . Great Britain was able to pose before the world in the attitude of victim to a conspiracy between Napoleon and the United States to destroy the liberties of Europe. Such inversion of the truth passed ordinary bounds, and so real was Madison's diplomatic mismanagement that it paralyzed one-half the energies of the American people.

As Brant claims, Madison recognized that peace might become impossibly costly, but in 1812 he abandoned with great reluctance what Samuel Flagg

Bemis has perceptively called his "strategy of auctioning the great belligerents out of their respective systems of retaliation." Perhaps Napoleon and Perceval acted foolishly in rejecting the bids Madison put forward during the auction; perhaps the President calculated more accurately the mutual benefits of accommodation. Still, it is one of the supreme functions of the statesman to weigh the intangibles as well as the tangibles, to expect illogical and prejudiced reactions along with coolly calculated ones. When Irving Brant declares that "President Madison to be successful . . . needed to deal with men whose understanding matched his own," he really confesses the political failure of his hero.

Madison never firmly controlled the Congress; he often lost command of his own Cabinet; frequently he seemed to drift rather than to direct policy. John Adams, fiercely challenged during the disintegration of Federalism, at least remained firm. In the spring of 1812 the congressional delegate from Mississippi Territory wrote that "the Executive is much censured by all parties for the tardiness of its advances to meet the *tug of war,* and the tenure of Mr. Madison's continuance in the presidential chair, in my opinion, depends upon the success of our hostile preparations." Yet the President did not forcefully support the cause of those whose loyalty had to be preserved for the impending election, nor did he speak out in favor of a course that might have maintained the peace he cherished. He reigned but he did not rule. After the declaration of war Jonathan Roberts wrote: "The world are pleased to suppose I am on good terms at the White House which by the way is no advantage for the cry of mad dog is not more fatal to its victim than the cry of executive connexion here." Madison won reëlection, but he was the least respected victor the country had yet known.

The war came, not because of the President, but despite him. The war came, not for any single reason, but from the interplay of many. The nation did not want war, and surely it did not embark gleefully on a great crusade. Tired of the self-flagellation and the disgrace that had marked the years since 1805, propelled by the fear of ridicule for inconsistency and by an honest interest in the nation's honor, a sufficient number of congressmen allowed themselves to support war. Justification for a declaration of war was not wanting, and the long-term results were probably beneficial. Still, the war came just when the United States might have enjoyed without a struggle the immense benefits of the neutrality in which so much Christian forbearance (or cowardice) had been invested. Neither side sought the War of 1812, and in the short run it was tragically unnecessary.

The United States did not go to war to add new states to the Union. A very few ebullient men from the North may have desired this. For sectional reasons the South and the West opposed it. A few advance agents of manifest destiny believed, as the Reverend McLeod put it in 1815, that the war was "a contest, not only to prevent the recolonization of these states, but also in the Providence of God for extending the principles of *representative democracy*—the blessings of liberty, and the rights of self-government, among the colonies of Europe." Even McLeod counted more on the imperialism of ideas than on military conquest. For most Americans Canada was but a means to an end, "a blow that might have given a speedier termination to the controversy," as Niles put it. At most, the occupation of the British provinces seemed the best means to reduce the enemy's power. A loyal Republican paper in Virginia commented:

> The great advantages to be derived from the acquisition of those possessions will not accrue so much from the tenure of them as a conquest, . . . but from the very important consequences which their loss will occasion to Britain; and among these consequences we may reckon the suppression of a great deal of smuggling, the curtailment . . . of the British fur trade and the disseverance of the West India Islands from Great Britain.

So feeble was the desire for permanent incorporation of Canada within the Union that within six weeks after the destruction of British power in Upper Canada at the battle of the Thames in 1813, the Western militia had returned to their homes.

From the opening of the war session, both supporters and enemies of war proclaimed that an attack upon Canada would be the principal American offensive. Congress ostensibly tailored the new army to the requirements of this campaign. All the Republicans, at least, believed that even the slightest effort would result in victory. "In four weeks from the time that a declaration of war is heard on our frontier," John C. Calhoun declared, "the whole of Upper and a part of Lower Canada will be in our possession." When Federalists complained that their opponents sought to establish a standing army that might menace American liberties, Trenton's *True American* replied, "It will be a *moving, fighting, conquering,* army—and as soon as its duty is done, it will be disbanded." Had Bermuda or Jamaica been vulnerable to attack by a flotilla of Jefferson's gunboats, the War Hawks would have been equally satisfied to invade them.

Even Indian warfare did not inspire important demands for Canadian conquest in the winter of 1811–12. "Much of that resentment against the British, which prevailed so strongly in the western states," a Kentucky historian of the war stated, ". . . may fairly be attributed to this source." Even this Western chronicler, however, declared that the Orders in Council became more intolerable than any other source of complaint against England. After Tippecanoe desultory warfare took place along the frontier, but most Indian tribes remained at peace until General Hull surrendered his army to Isaac Brock in the summer of 1812. Although Grundy and the Lexington *Reporter* remained irate, the Indian menace played a comparatively minor part in congressional debates until the very end of the session, when all complaints against Britain were being brought together to support a declaration of war. At that time congressmen emphasized Britain's interference in American affairs rather than the material consequences to one section.

The most important, most justified American complaints against England sprang from Britain's exercise of her maritime power. Substantively, through the loss of seamen, ships, and cargoes, America suffered greatly from impressment, blockades, and the Orders in Council. The sovereign spirit and the self-respect of the American nation suffered perhaps even more every time a seaman was removed from beneath the Stars and Stripes or a merchant vessel was haled to trial before an admiralty court that paid scant heed to international law. The penalties of neutrality are often dear, and perhaps only the weak, the phlegmatic, or the noble are capable of enduring them. Jefferson and Madison might fit into one or the other of these categories. Ultimately the nation felt taxed beyond endurance. However necessary to British prosecution of the contest with Napoleon impressment and attacks upon neutral commerce might be, they finally brought war with America. Fortune rather than justice postponed the outbreak of war beyond the gloomiest days of Britain's struggle, when American entry might well have played an important part.

Impressment, Frank A. Updyke has observed, was "the most aggravating and the most persistent" American grievance. By 1812 the press gangs had been at work for twenty years. In many instances—probably even the majority —the British forcibly recalled a king's subject to his allegiance rather than kidnapped an American. More often than was generally admitted, the Admiralty released mariners mistakenly seized. Still, impressment formed an ultimately intolerable insult to national sovereignty. When, during the war, the Federalist legislature of Massachusetts undertook an investigation to show that very few seamen had been impressed, John Quincy Adams angrily and accurately declared the question irrelevant:

> No Nation can be Independent which suffers her Citizens to be stolen from her at the discretion of the Naval or military Officers of another. . . . The State, by the social compact is bound to *protect* every one of its Citizens, and the enquiry how many of them a foreign Nation may be allowed to rob with impunity is itself a humiliation to which I blush to see that the Legislature of my native state could defend. . . . The principle for which we are now struggling is of a higher and more sacred nature than any question about taxation can involve. It is the principle of personal liberty, and of every social right.

Failures of American arms and a European peace that halted impressment caused Adams, along with Madison and Monroe, to accept a peace silent on impressment. In principle, however, he was correct. America might well have gone to war on this issue, perhaps at the time of the *Chesapeake* affair.

Although officially the American government made very little of impressment from 1808 onward, the people could not forget it. During the war session, and particularly in the spring, impressment aroused more and more heat. *Niles' Register,* which began publication in 1811, rallied opinion on this issue. "Accursed be the American government, and every individual in it," an imprecation ran, "who . . . shall agree to make peace with Great Britain, until ample provision shall be made for our impressed seamen, and security shall be given for the prevention of such abominable outrages in the future." A Quid and a Republican who hoped to avoid war told Foster this was the most ticklish problem to explain to their constituents, and even the stanchly antiwar senator, Thomas Worthington, found impressment almost impossible to tolerate. "He says," Foster wrote in his diary, "he would rather live on a Crust in the Interior than live degraded." Foster, who repeatedly suggested that modification of the orders would prevent a declaration of war, nevertheless recognized the renewed importance accorded to impressment. On April 23 he wrote, "Very inflammatory paragraphs and letters on the subject . . . have lately been circulated in the American papers, and as the causes of war become more closely canvassed, that arising out of the practice of impressment seems to be dwelt upon with considerable vehemence." When war approached, the War Hawks had a singularly effective propaganda point in this violation of the rights of individual Americans who deserved better of their country.

Both the British government and the Federalists later complained that the President only resuscitated the impressment issue after the Orders in Council had disappeared. They pointed out that, particularly in the Erskine negotiations, the administration had allowed impressment to pass in silence. In 1813 Lord Castlereagh described it as "a cause of war, now brought forward as such for the first time." These criticisms showed only that the administration had been backward in defending the rights of citizens, or that the President and Congress had been willing for a time to exchange the kidnaping of Americans for the benefit of neutrality. Neither Lord Castlereagh nor Timothy Pickering, who as secretary of state had himself vehemently protested the practice, should have been surprised that the American people considered impressment an insult.

Even more than impressment, with which congressmen and newspaper editors often coupled them, the Orders in Council showed Britain's contemptuous disdain for American protests against her use of sea power. The forcible enlistment of seamen could be expressed in dramatic human terms. The Orders in Council more massively and more selfishly assaulted the United States. Their material cost was impressive. Although the number of seizures actually fell after 1808, the year beginning in October, 1811, saw an increase of nearly 50 per cent. The orders and the *Essex* case had long since reduced the reëxport trade to a shadow of its former size. After a spurt stimulated by Macon's Bill #2 and the Cadore letter, the export of native American produce fell drastically after the spring of 1811. By far the greatest proportion of this decline came in exports to Britain, particularly because return cargoes were forbidden and the United Kingdom suffered from glut. Agriculturists and plantation owners, some shipowners, and the average congressman ascribed the decline to Britain's Orders in Council, which prevented Americans from developing the presumably lucrative Continental market. At the same time, particularly because the British permitted their own subjects to trade with Europe under license, the Orders in Council seemed humiliating. Since at least November, 1807, the English had presumed to legislate not only for their own people but also for the commercial world. Economic necessity and national right alike cried out against the Orders in Council.

Everyone in Washington during the months from November to June placed the Orders in Council at the head of the list of American grievances. Louis Sérurier and Augustus Foster, Federalists and Republicans were in agreement. When the British minister asked Chauncey Goodrich, a Federalist senator, "what was required of us by Men of fair Views, he replied, take off the Orders in Council and come to some Arrangement about Impressment." In November President Madison considered British maritime policy the transcendent issue between the two countries. Porter's report declared that the orders "went to the subversion of our national independence" and were "sapping the foundation of our prosperity." Throughout the winter congressmen assailed the orders, drowning out the "whip-poor-will cry" for Canada of which John Randolph spoke. Repeal, Madison noted years later, would have postponed war and led to renewed negotiations on impressment "with fresh vigor & hopes, under the auspices of success in the case of the orders in council." The orders, he told Jared Sparks in 1830, were the only issue sturdy enough to bear a declaration of war.

The strength of this issue depended in part upon the reinforcement provided by impressment and other grievances, the flying buttresses of the central structure. Had the orders stood alone as a British challenge, war would probably not have come in 1812. But they became the key to the drive for war. No other factor, not even impressment, which most directly affected Northeasterners, struck all sections so impartially. Not even impressment exceeded the orders as a threat to America's position as a sovereign power. The Orders in Council were four years old when the Twelfth Congress met, going on five when America declared war. Why this delay? A natural desire to escape war partly explains it. Unreal faith in the power of trade boycotts, more justified expectations from the Erskine agreement, optimism engendered by the Cadore letter, hope that the Prince of Wales would replace his insane father's ministers with more friendly men, the anticipated impact of American measures of preparedness in Great Britain—all these counseled delay. When war ultimately came in June, 1812, the Orders in Council were the central issue. The requirements of consistency and a growing realization that American honor had been nearly exhausted were the immediate precipitants.

Since at least 1806 the United States government, and more particularly Republican congressmen, had proclaimed that America would not settle for whatever neutral trade the belligerents chose to let her enjoy. Profitable as such trade might be (and it often was extremely rewarding), the United States would demand its rights. Of course Jefferson, and especially Madison, did not demand utter surrender from their opponents, and they did not press certain claims they considered comparatively insignificant. In principle, however, they insisted that Britain and France recognize American rights and tailor their policies to them. Commercial pressure failed, political bargaining did not succeed, pleas for justice rebounded hollowly across the Atlantic. Still America maintained her claims, and the only remaining weapon to secure them was military power. The War Hawk Congress initiated preparedness, and the administration discreetly encouraged it, in the hope that England would surrender to this weapon what she had denied to boycotts, bargaining, and complaint.

Once embarked upon this course it became almost impossible to turn back. Many who voted for military measures without wanting war found it difficult to recede from the ground they had taken. The 10,000-man army proposed by the House of Representatives had an ostensible military purpose, but its supporters valued it chiefly as a demonstration of American determination. "We are not at war yet tho' David R. Williams hopes in god we soon shall be. Till we are at war I shall not go above 10,000 additional troops," Jonathan Roberts wrote in December. As time passed, Roberts became more and more bellicose. In February he wrote, "There seems to be no disposition to relax our war measures but I believe every body would be exceeding glad to remain at peace." A month later he stated, "I am well convinced we have no hope of peace but by vigorous preparations for War," but he added that he was ready to vote for war. As the spring passed, Roberts found his Quaker principles weakening, and he attended meetings very infrequently. In May and June this man, who had come to Washington determined that affairs should be forced to a solution and yet still hopeful war could be avoided, found himself more and more firmly committed to the cause of the War Hawks. The logic of the situation carried the Pennsylvanian and many of his colleagues forward.

In May John Randolph declared that, although many members of the majority would not follow the same course if they had it to do over again, "they have advanced to the brink of a precipice, and not left themselves room to turn." John Smilie admitted as much, arguing that while he would have preferred a further attempt at commercial coercion he now felt it necessary to go on toward war, since "if we now recede we shall be a reproach among nations." Willis Alston of North Carolina told Foster in March that Congress "should have originally taken another Course, now too late. It would have been better to protest against the belligerents & let Commerce thrive, this should have been done from the Beginning." Alston voted with the War Hawks on every important roll call. Speaker Clay and his supporters counted on and made frequent, effective reference to consistency in the closing months of the session. "After the pledges we have made, and the stand we have taken," Clay asked his colleagues, "are we now to cover ourselves with shame and indelible disgrace by retreating from the measures and ground we have taken?" Remembering the reputation of the Tenth Congress, many representatives felt that the answer was as obvious as Clay pictured it. Thus legislators who were really "scarecrow men" came to support a declaration of war. James A. Bayard, one Federalist who had foreseen this danger from the beginning, chided a friend for his shortsightedness, saying, "You have thought the thing all along a jest & I have no doubt in the commencement it was so, but jests sometimes become serious & end in earnest." So it was in 1812.

Consistency in congressmen, in a party, or in an administration became national honor when applied to the country as a whole. Since the acquisition of Louisiana in 1803, America had endured a steady diet of diplomatic humiliation. Jefferson, Madison, and the Congress of their time attempted to reverse European policy by applying economic pressure. This tactic failed because Congress lacked staying power and Republican leaders underestimated the strength of emotions abroad. Defeats continued. Napoleon's announcement of repeal merely worsened the situation, for his cynical contempt and the gullibility of the American administration soon became apparent. Republicans had jeopardized the national character and the reputation of the United States; they had created a situation from which war was almost the only honorable escape; they had encouraged England, where unfortunately such encouragement was too little needed, to act almost as though Lord Cornwallis had won the battle of Yorktown. "We have suffered and suffered until our forbearance has been pronounced cowardice and want of energy," a friend wrote Jonathan Roberts. Although talk of honor perhaps came too easily to the lips of some patriotic orators, the danger was real. When John C. Calhoun asserted that "if we submit to the pretensions of England, now openly avowed, the independence of this nation is lost. . . . This is the second struggle for our liberty," he scarcely exaggerated. When a Republican Fourth of July meeting at Boston toasted "The War—The second and last struggle for national freedom—A final effort to rescue from the deep the drowning honor of our country," the sentiment was apt.

In his first annual message after the outbreak of war, President Madison declared:

> To have shrunk under such circumstances from manly resistance would have been a degradation blasting our best and proudest hopes; it would have struck us from the high rank where the virtuous struggle of our fathers had placed us, and have betrayed the magnificent legacy which we hold in trust for future generations. It would have acknowledged that on the element which forms three-fourths of the globe we inhabit, and where all independent nations have equal and common rights, the Americans were not an independent people, but colonists and vassals.

A year after the war ended, Henry Clay similarly stressed the theme of national honor and self-respect. "We had become the scorn of foreign Powers, and the contempt of our own citizens," he said. ". . . Let any man look at the degraded condition of this country before the war; the scorn of the universe, the contempt of ourselves. . . . What is our present situation? Respectability and character abroad—security and confidence at home. . . . our character and Constitutions are placed on a solid basis, never to be shaken." Years later, Augustus J. Foster philosophically wrote: "This war was certainly productive of much ill-blood between England and America, but in the opinion of the Speaker, Mr. Clay, and his friends it was as necessary to America as a duel is to a young naval officer to prevent his being bullied and elbowed in society. . . . Baleful as the war has been, I must confess that I think in this respect something has been gained by it." The President, the Speaker, and the envoy, who stood at the center of affairs during the war session, effectively summarized the one unanswerable argument for war. All the insults suffered by the United States, even the most important of them all, the Orders in Council, posed a greater threat in the realm of the spirit than in the world of the accountant and the merchant, the seaman and the frontiersman.

That war became imperative in June, 1812, does not mean that the American people desired it or that it could not have been avoided by greater wisdom in earlier years. Castlereagh's statement, in 1813, that "Great Britain has throughout acted towards the United States of America, with a spirit of amity, forbearance, and conciliation," was simply preposterous. While the policy of England was far less rigid than Americans often suggested, the self-righteous spirit of messianism engendered by the Napoleonic wars and a woeful underestimation of the price of American good will combined to prevent a reconciliation Jefferson and Madison eagerly desired. In America, most of the Federalists served their country ill, for, blinded by their own hatred of Napoleon and their inveterate contempt for the politicians who had displaced them, they sabotaged peaceful American resistance to British outrages and repeatedly declared that the Republicans lacked the fortitude to go to war. Roberts wrote in his memoirs, "There had all along been an idea cherish'd by the opposition, that the majority would not have nerve enough to meet war. This I believe, mainly induc'd Britain to persist in her aggressions. If she could have been made to believe . . . that we were a united people, & would act as such, war might have been avoided." The *Independent Chronicle* complained with a good deal of justice, "In every measure of government, the federal faction have rallied in opposition, and urged the Ministry to persist in their Orders. They forced the United States to the alternative, either to *surrender their independence,* or *maintain it by War.*" American disunion was clear enough, the desire to avoid war quite obvious. Despite the temporary and transparent policy advocated by Quincy, the Federalists contributed to that disunion and to British stubbornness.

Still, the Republican chieftains must bear primary responsibility for the war and the factionalism that made it an almost fatal test of the sturdiness of the nation they themselves had done so much to build. Whereas Washington and Adams kept objectives and means in harmony with one another, their successors often committed the United States to seek absolute right with inadequate weapons. Compromise, when sought, was usually offered at an impossible time. The justice of American demands is nearly undeniable, but the two Virginians, who prided themselves on the coolness of their logic, failed to perceive that justice was not a weapon in itself. They provided it with insufficient support, and they expected warring powers to view collateral problems with the same coolness that America exhibited. Economic warfare rested upon a rigid, mechanical conception of international trade. Although it was, of course, felt by the belligerents, it proved far more harmful to America, economically and morally, and served chiefly to convince Europe of the cowardice of the United States.

The two presidents secured not one important diplomatic objective after 1803. They scarcely challenged the development of factionalism within the Republican party, factionalism that deprived Congress of any real sense of direction. They provided public opinion with far too little leadership. They and their followers often spoke loudly and carried no stick at all. When at last a small group of congressmen declared that the time for half measures had ended and carried a majority with them down the road toward war, neither Great Britain nor the American people believed the destination would be reached. Thus British concession was discouraged and national union made impossible. In a state of military and psychological unpreparedness, the United States of America embarked upon a war to recover the self-respect destroyed by Republican leaders. Old John Taylor of Caroline wrote to the Secretary of State on the day of the declaration of war, "May God send you a safe deliverance."

# Coercing Great Britain by Conquering Canada

### J. C. A. STAGG

During the War of 1812 the United States invaded Canada to obtain redress for injuries suffered on the high seas from the Royal Navy's enforcement of British maritime policies. Some fifty years ago, Julius W. Pratt attempted to account for this strategy by arguing that the American concern with Canada in 1812 originated in a complex combination of resentment by frontier congressmen at British links with the northwestern Indians, an incipient sense of "Manifest Destiny," and a tacit sectional bargain that traded off the promise of northern expansion into Canada against the prospect of southern expansion into Spanish East Florida. Many of the elements in Pratt's explanation have now been discarded as unconvincing or have not been given the same emphasis that Pratt gave to them, but in rejecting the "expansionist" thesis historians have lost sight of the larger problem that it addressed: the nature of the American interest in Canada in 1812 and its relationship to the maritime grievances that the second war with Great Britain was intended to settle. Most historians now seem satisfied with the explanation of American policy offered by Secretary of State James Monroe in a letter of June 1812 that "it might be necessary to invade Canada, not as an object of the war but as a means to bring it to a satisfactory conclusion."

Monroe's statement, however, explains very little about Canada's role in the War of 1812. Possibly, the secretary of state meant to suggest that the United States, lacking the naval power to challenge its enemy on the seas, had to take advantage of Canada's proximity and vulnerability, and seize the region in order to use it as a bargaining point in negotiations that might secure British respect for American maritime rights. If so, the logic of the argument seems plausible, but it did not satisfy John Taylor of Carolina, the recipient of Monroe's letter. Taylor had written to Monroe in May 1812 to state his reasons for opposing the impending war, among them his conviction that Great Britain would never sacrifice its maritime policies to save Canada from an American invasion. He argued that as Britain had been unwilling to renounce any of its maritime and imperial pretensions during the Revolutionary War in order to preserve its American colonies, it was unlikely now to surrender its methods of commercial and naval warfare in a much more desperate struggle with Napoleonic France simply to retain Canada, a collection of colonies that were of far less value to the empire than the lost thirteen had been. Taylor's argument thus exposed some very

From "James Madison and the Coercion of Great Britain: Canada, the West Indies, and the War of 1812." First published in the *William and Mary Quarterly*, 38 (January, 1981), 3–13. Reprinted by permission of the author.

large assumptions in the American strategy of invading Canada as a means of coercing Great Britain. When Monroe's response ignored the objection, Taylor repeated in a second letter that the war "may gain Canada and nothing beneficial."

Taylor's views were echoed by most opponents of the War of 1812, and his doubts were shared even by some advocates of the conflict. Senator Jesse Franklin of North Carolina, for example, supported both the preparations for war and its declaration, yet he privately confessed in February 1812 that he could not see how the seizure of Canada would "settle the dispute about which we are now like to get to war, that is our *Commercial Rights*." As for territory, he added, "God knows we [have] enough already." Americans who questioned the wisdom of administration policies would, no doubt, have been even more concerned had they been aware of Monroe's instructions to the American chargé d'affaires in London, Jonathan Russell, shortly after the war began. The secretary of state told Russell to warn the British government that a successful American war against Canada would "present very serious obstacles on the part of the United States to an accommodation which do not now exist," and he predicted that it might be "difficult to relinquish territory which had been conquered." The Madison administration thus seems to have presumed that the occupation of Canada in 1812 would be sufficient to bring Great Britain to terms. The question is why, especially when so many Americans were not convinced that it would do so but believed that the possession of Canada would scarcely repay the cost of acquiring it.

The purpose of this essay is to suggest an answer to that question. It will proceed on the assumption that the motive for the War of 1812 was not so much to enlarge the boundaries of the United States as to deprive Great Britain of Canada in the expectation that this action would affect Britain's capacity to exercise its commercial and naval powers against Americans in harmful ways that they could not otherwise control. The essay will try to demonstrate that assumption by reconstructing, as far as possible, President James Madison's understanding of the potential impact of the loss of Canada on the British empire. The focus on Madison is justified on the ground that he was, after all, the commander-in-chief and the official most responsible for conceiving a war strategy. Moreover, he has enjoyed a deserved reputation as a systematic thinker who was ever conscious of the relationship between the ends and means of politics; accordingly, it is difficult to imagine that he gave no thought at all to how a Canadian war might relieve the United States from the effects of British maritime policies, especially when he had spent much of his public career studying those policies as they had operated against the interests of his country. The task of reconstructing Madison's thinking, though, is by no means easy, principally because the president seldom made comments in his correspondence during the war years that directly addressed the issue in point.

Among the reasons why Madison's surviving correspondence is silent here is the fact that the war failed to produce the military victories necessary for

Madison to engage in successful diplomatic bargaining with Great Britain over the problems of maritime rights; as a consequence, the president's wartime statements invariably centered on problems of a different order. Furthermore, whenever he sought to explain his conduct during the war he was usually more preoccupied with demonstrating to Americans the malignant nature and consequences of the British policies he wished them to resist than he was with revealing his strategic view of the effect of a Canadian war. Nonetheless, Madison's papers contain a number of statements on Canada, and these are most suggestive about his understanding of the role that Canada played in Anglo-American relations. Indeed, the context in which these statements occur makes it evident that Madison, as a close observer of British affairs, was well aware of Canada's significance in the minds of the most determined defenders in Great Britain of the anti-American aspects of that nation's maritime policies. It was against these men that Madison's Canadian war was really waged, and he had good reason to believe that, had the war been successful, the British government would have been compelled to pay greater respect to American maritime rights.

The argument of this essay accordingly depends less on anything that Madison wrote or said during the War of 1812—as distinct from what he tried to do—than on the thesis that the American attempt to conquer Canada was both a logical sequel to Madison's entire mode of thinking about the relationship between the United States and the British empire after 1783, and a natural reaction to the problems he encountered in trying to translate that thinking into effective policy. Once the problem of Canada has been placed in a longer-term perspective, it becomes apparent that there was considerable continuity in the assumptions underlying all the policies that Madison attempted to pursue toward Great Britain throughout his long public life between 1779 and 1817. And, paradoxical though it may seem, Madison's decision to make war on Canada was not basically inconsistent—as historians have so often supposed—with the reasons for the belief he held before 1812 that the diplomacy of commercial restriction would enable the United States to avoid hostilities with Britain. In fact, given the circumstances Madison had to confront by 1812, the policy of a Canadian war followed logically from his previous diplomatic strategies that assumed that efforts to restrict British access to vital American resources would be instrumental in compelling Britain to moderate its anti-American policies. For by 1812, Canada had become an integral part of the larger question of British access to American resources, and Madison could therefore believe that to strip Britain of its North American possessions was a reasonable response to the maritime disputes that had long disturbed Anglo-American relations.

Underlying most of the disputes that led to the war was the problem of how far British merchants and shippers should enjoy access to American markets, natural resources, and agricultural produce. The dimensions of this problem were clearly defined in 1783 by the British decisions—embodied particularly in the Order in Council of July 2 of that year—to deny the United States any of their former commercial privileges in the trade of the empire, especially the West Indian trade, as well as by the polemical arguments put forward in defense of those decisions by John Baker Holroyd, first earl of Sheffield, in his pamphlet *Observations on the Commerce of the American States*. The outline of most of Lord Sheffield's ideas is well known, particularly his assertion that the United States were by definition not a nation and his peculiar notion that America had no future, while its independence was for Great Britain a blessing in disguise. Less appreciated has been the distinctive impact on an entire generation of Englishmen, Canadians, Americans, and West Indians of Sheffield's defense of the navigation system after 1783 and his vision of how to reconstruct the economy of the empire. This impact was central to Madison's understanding of the problems of Anglo-American relations, and his policy of commercial restriction was conceived very much in response to it.

In the *Observations* Sheffield developed a number of justifications for attempting to keep the United States commercially subordinate. These he put forward in an analysis of commerce under two main headings. British exports to America and American exports to Britain. Many of the goods, Sheffield believed, that Britain had traditionally sent to the United States, notably manufactures, would continue to be bought by Americans because they had no alternative supply and could not manufacture them locally. Even where Americans could establish manufactures, Sheffield dismissed them as expensive, shoddy, incapable of competing with British products in cost and quality. American exports to Britain, largely bulky raw materials, posed more difficulty, but Sheffield claimed that tobacco alone had appreciable value, and then only as an item in Britain's entrepôt trade. Other important raw materials, such as timber, naval stores, pipe staves, and even wheat, Sheffield believed would soon be in short supply in the United States, and for this reason he argued that it would be better for Britain to obtain them from alternative sources, either from other parts of the empire or from the Baltic region.

This line of argument led to a discussion of American trade with the British West Indies, designed by Sheffield to support the claim that after 1783 the empire could be reconstituted as a self-sufficient economic unit. Crucial to this claim was Sheffield's belief that Canada could be developed to fill the role previously played by the revolted colonies. Nowhere was the need for a substitute for the American contribution to empire greater than in the matter of West Indian supply, and Sheffield attempted to demonstrate in detail that Canada could produce the timber, livestock, fish, and other provisions that the islands needed in order to furnish the mother country with the greatly valued staples of sugar and coffee. Indeed, so optimistic was his vision of Canada's future that he even predicted substantial northward emigration from the United States. Many of his writings on British maritime rights through to 1809 continued to assert Canada's economic potential in the most fulsome tones. The means for developing Canada were basically simple; Sheffield believed that the enforcement of the navigation laws against the United States, together with some bounties on Canadian exports, would be sufficient.

Yet, as Sheffield made abundantly clear, more than rivalry for trade and development was at stake. His primary goal in advocating the application of the navigation laws against the United States was to preserve the effectiveness of those laws as the basis of Great Britain's naval power. Few Englishmen seriously questioned that the navigation laws, by augmenting British shipping and the nation's pool of trained seamen, did serve this function, though some—of whom the earl of Shelburne was the most prominent—were prepared by 1783 to consider loosening parts of the system in order to guarantee American supplies to the West Indies and to inaugurate a new era of Anglo-American harmony and cooperation. Sheffield, however, believed that relaxation of the laws would permit ruinous competition for trade that would ultimately destroy Great Britain as a naval power. This fear drove him to argue that the empire could—indeed, must—function as a coherent economic unit despite the loss of the American colonies. His claims were made all the more attractive to his countrymen by his prediction that Britain could continue to dominate the American market by carrying its trade there.

Nor did Sheffield expect that the United States were capable of demonstrating any of his views to be ill founded, mainly because their government under the Articles of Confederation was no more effective than the Diet of Germany. He dismissed as ridiculous the idea that they might close their markets or withhold their produce in protest. Even if such attempts were made, he saw Britain's possession of Canada as the means to undermine them. Many of the northern parts of the United States had little option but to trade with Canada through the St. Lawrence River as a means of reaching the outside world, while control of that waterway would also enable Britain to transport its exports into the American interior.

The restrictive policies of Great Britain after 1783, as well as the arguments of Lord Sheffield, provoked strong reactions on both sides of the Atlantic, resulting in a sizeable polemical literature not unlike that produced by the controversy over annexing Canada or Guadaloupe after 1760. Among the best-known pamphlets published in Britain were those by Edward Long and Bryan Edwards, both writing as spokesmen for the West India planters. The most comprehensive assault on Sheffield's doctrines was written by Richard Champion, a Bristol china manufacturer of liberal opinions who had been deputy paymaster of the forces in the early 1780s until he resigned his office in disgust at the Treaty of Paris and moved, in 1784, to South Carolina. In the United States, Tench Coxe's seven essays, assembled as *A Brief Inquiry into the Observations of Lord Sheffield,* were the most extended American response. Madison, too, had been in the forefront of protests against the British decision to subject the American states to the navigation laws, both with his sponsorship of the Virginia Port Bill of 1784 and with his support of attempts to strengthen the powers of the Continental Congress to regulate foreign trade. The failure of Congress or the states to achieve significant commercial reform after 1783 led Madison to support the more sweeping changes put forward in the Constitutional Convention of 1787. One of the first duties of the new government, he declared to George Washington in 1788, would be to pass a retaliatory navigation act, and he introduced in Congress between 1790 and 1794—as an accompaniment to Thomas Jefferson's reports on the state of American fisheries and commerce—a series of discriminatory duties against nations, principally Great Britain, that refused to trade with the United States on reciprocal terms.

Madison's arguments in his public defense of this course were shaped to a considerable degree by his reactions to Sheffield's views. Alarmed by the appearance of the *Observations* so soon after the establishment of American independence, Madison noted that the pamphlet's prescriptions, put into effect, would preclude Anglo-American commercial harmony. His alarm was tempered, however, by his awareness that many of Sheffield's more extreme claims were not very plausible: to the extent that they were erroneous he concluded that British commercial policies were based on false premises. In reaching this position, Madison was clearly influenced by the polemical writings that the *Observations* had provoked—especially those by Champion, Coxe, and Edwards—from which he frequently lifted statistical information and key ideas, integrating these with opinions derived from his wider reading and experiences in public affairs. In particular, he was greatly offended, as were all American nationalists in the 1780s, by Sheffield's belief that the United States was a weak nation condemned by diminishing economic resources to a bleak future, including the loss of both trade and population to Canada. It was for this reason, no doubt, that Madison heartily approved of Coxe's detailed refutation of Sheffield's arguments on this score and made a considerable effort to send a copy of Coxe's pamphlet to England, possibly in the hope that Sheffield would see it.

Of greatest importance in shaping Madison's diplomacy was his response to Sheffield's argument that Canada could replace the United States in the West Indian trades. This point attracted the most attention in the polemical controversies after 1783, and the majority of pamphleteers took very strong issue with Sheffield. In fact, the notion that Canada could ever be as valuable as America had already been rejected, even before American independence, by many British political economists who had stressed the vital economic contribution of the American colonies to British commercial and naval power. From this viewpoint, it seemed illogical for Sheffield to suggest that Britain had less need of American trade after independence than before, and no one was quicker to develop this objection than the West Indian planters. Those planters found no substance in the claim that Canada could provide them with timber and provisions, and even Sheffield himself could publish trade figures for only one year—1774—that demonstrated Canada's ability to produce a surplus of wheat for export. Equally vulnerable was Sheffield's tacit admission that exploitation of Canada's resources of timber would require more capital, people, and shipping than the region possessed. For these reasons, West Indians, especially after the hardships they had suffered from starvation, hurricanes, and trade disruption during the Revolution, were most reluctant to risk relying on Canada for supply, and their demands that the United States be exempted from the navigation laws for that purpose were accordingly presented as a sustained assault on Lord Sheffield's political economy and vision of Canada.

The planters' polemic depicted Canada as an ice-bound, snow-covered, windy, foggy desert where crops froze in the ground and agricultural surpluses could not be produced. As Bryan Edwards bluntly declared, "Canada is shut up six months of the year and the other six months is devoted to everlasting sterility." So outraged were the planters at being asked, as they believed, to risk starvation and ruin for the Canadian fantasies of a man who understood nothing of their situation that, led by Edwards, they continued their attacks on Sheffield and the navigation laws well into the early nineteenth century. In successive editions of his voluminous history of the West Indies, Edwards offered the dead bodies of thousands of slaves as evidence for the folly of Sheffield's attempts to promote Canada, while he produced trade figures for the years after 1783 to prove that Canada was unable to provide the surplus wheat that Sheffield had predicted. Even Richard Champion, who did not have the same personal stake in the issue as the West Indians, agreed that Sheffield's views were both "extravagant" and "mischievous." "Till we can force Nature to make," he added, "a free and open navigation and to soften the climate, we will not derive any advantage from Canada or Nova Scotia in any degree equal to the hopes that are held out to us."

Madison was thoroughly familiar with this criticism of Sheffield, and many of his notes as well as his speeches in Congress indicate that he assimilated it into the arguments he put forward in favor of commercial discrimination from 1790 to 1794. He revealed his doubts about the ability of Canada to replace the United States in the West Indian trade by including in his preparation for a major speech in 1790 a rhetorical question aimed at the defenders of Sheffield's system: how had the West Indies fared for supply during the Revolution? The answer, as Madison pointed out on several occasions, was "very badly indeed," and he noted also that the planters had to divert labor "to less profitable cultivation to avoid starving." Madison also knew from Coxe's pamphlet that trade between Canada and the West Indies did not increase significantly in the years immediately after 1783, and that to cope with this situation the British government, especially during wartime, had to exempt the islands from the navigation laws in order to allow them to receive supplies in American bottoms. Indeed, at times the situation in the Canadian provinces themselves seemed so unpromising, even in the Newfoundland fishery, that Canadians had to import food from the United States. It is hardly surprising therefore that Madison observed, in 1790, that should Britain ever be forced to attempt to supply the islands during wartime without American aid, "she could not afford to keep them." . . .

Pursuing the conclusions he had reached in the 1790s, Madison suggested in March 1805 that the United States demand reciprocity with Great Britain in its West Indian trade, and stated his belief that Britain could not resist the demand because its Canadian colonies seemed no more prosperous than they had been a decade earlier and could not therefore be an alternative source of supply. He then extended the logic of this thinking to advocate by September 1805 an embargo on American trade to the Caribbean islands. "If indeed a commercial weapon can be shaped for the executive hand," he argued to Jefferson, "it is more and more apparent to me that it can force all nations having colonies in this quarter of the globe to respect our rights." That Britain might react by "forcing the growth of the Continental provinces of Nova Scotia etc" and thus risking the sources of "wealth and power" that the West Indies contributed to the "revenue, commerce, and navigation of the parent state," Madison had already dismissed as simply "preposterous."

Jefferson's response to this suggestion—reflected in the nonimportation law of April 1806 and in the decision to continue negotiations with Great Britain even after his rejection of the Monroe-Pinkney treaty—was less forceful than Madison would have liked, but he remained constant in his view that the problems of the West Indies should be exploited as the key British weakness. Issuing instructions in May 1807 for the American ministers in London, James Monroe and William Pinkney, Madison observed that it was within the power of the United States to destroy the value of the West Indies to the British empire since it could no longer be unknown, even "to the most sanguine partisan of the colonial monopoly that the necessaries of life and cultivation can be furnished to those Islands from no other source than the United States, [and] that immediate ruin would ensue if this source were shut." The course of events after the *Chesapeake* incident of June 1807, culminating in the adoption of the embargo in December, then created a situation where Madison's views were to receive a fair trial. As early as October 1807 the administration had learned—from the receipt of parliamentary reports on the West India trade—that Britain was contemplating new and drastic measures against neutral commerce, and when the Orders in Council of November 1807 went into effect, along with the Berlin and Milan decrees of France, Madison was successful in his advocacy of an embargo as the American response.

Madison's colleagues, particularly Jefferson, appear to have accepted the embargo, at least initially, for its value in preserving American commerce from the danger of seizures by the European belligerents, but the secretary of state's emphasis was rather different. Believing that Britain's policies posed a more serious threat to American neutral rights than did those of France, Madison hoped, if the editorials in the *National Intelligencer* are to be believed, that the embargo would "coerce the settlement of long-standing and complicated accounts." The administration journal predicted that Great Britain would feel the effects of the loss of American trade "in her manufactures, in the loss of naval stores, and above all in the supplies essential to her colonies." On the basis of Madison's previous arguments, the embargo would achieve these effects provided that Britain lacked alternative sources for the supplies it needed. So far as Madison could see, Canada, all Lord Sheffield's hopes notwithstanding, had failed to develop sufficiently, while by the end of 1807 the Baltic region—the only other source from which Britain might draw grain, timber, and naval stores—had been closed to

British trade by the decision of Alexander I to join Napoleon's Continental System.

In these circumstances, Madison's confidence in the coercive efforts of an embargo seemed reasonably well founded, and throughout 1808, he calmly waited for the measure to accomplish its purpose. Indeed, he could scarcely believe that Britain would adhere to the Orders in Council so far as to jeopardize the foundations of the West Indian commercial system; as early as May 1808, and again in July, he predicted the repeal of the Orders because of "distress" in the West Indies. By August, however, the embargo was in serious difficulty, mainly because Madison and his colleagues had miscalculated both its popularity in the northern states and the problems of enforcement there. Beginning in March with the Treasury Department's attempts to cut off all exports by land, there developed down the St. Lawrence and Richelieu rivers a massive clandestine trade, principally in timber, provisions, and potash, much of which ultimately found its way through Canada to Great Britain and the West Indies. To stop this traffic, Treasury Secretary Albert Gallatin first demanded a "little army on the lakes," but by August he had come to believe that the embargo had failed in this region and should therefore be abandoned. . . .

These developments distressed Madison, who found himself in the unenviable position of having to respond to British maritime policies with commercial and diplomatic weapons that he regarded as inadequate. A return to his favored policy of the embargo was, he reluctantly admitted, out of the question since popular prejudice and enforcement problems had "incapacitated [it] for future use." The Non-Intercourse law was increasingly evaded by Great Britain through an entrepôt trade opened to Americans in Amelia Island off the coast of Georgia, in Halifax in Nova Scotia, and even in Montreal in Lower Canada itself. Nor did the practical consequences of the nonimportation clauses of Macon's Bill #2—which Madison invoked in November 1810 in response to Napoleon's offer of the Cadore letter and which Congress enacted into law on March 2, 1811—at first seem any better. The United States was now attempting to alter British maritime policies largely by coercing that nation's manufacturing interests, and Madison, although quite willing to try this tactic, was somewhat doubtful about its prospects, probably because it would take time for the manufacturers to organize an effective campaign against the better-represented shipping and West Indian interests that supported the Orders in Council. Aided by a severe depression in Great Britain, nonimportation, ironically, did finally bring down the Orders in Council in June 1812, but long before that date Madison, for a variety of reasons, had concluded that the policy was ineffective and had shifted, after July 1811, toward preparations for war. As with the embargo, the roots of the apparent failure of nonimportation could be traced back to Canada.

The difficulties of enforcing nonimportation throughout 1811 were felt in two areas: the first was in the trade from Passamaquoddy through Eastport and from there to other major American ports; the second, in the region between lakes Ontario and Champlain. A growing number of American merchants sailed to Eastport to import British merchandise under fraudulent bills of lading for local plaster of paris, while British West Indian rum was extensively smuggled into the United States as Spanish produce, especially in New England where there was sudden absence of experts to testify in the courts as to its true British origins. Equally serious was the smuggling of British manufactures from Montreal through the lakes region, a business which the Treasury reported gave all the indications of having a determined and large-scale organization behind it. Only one officer of the Treasury Department—Peter Sailly at Champlain—showed any zeal in enforcing the law; the others lacked either the will or the means to stop the smuggling. By October 1811, Gallatin felt compelled to report to Madison, as he had done to Jefferson three years earlier, that nonimportation could not be enforced without considerable expansion of the numbers of customs officers and of their powers, including the right to search private houses. The administration's attorney general, Caesar A. Rodney of Delaware, also urged this course.

Madison did not oppose these suggestions, though he may have doubted their effectiveness. He was well aware of the difficulties of implementing nonimportation and had regretted as early as May 1811 that Congress had not banned American exports to Nova Scotia to lessen the inducements for British merchants to come there with imports. By the end of the year, too, he knew that Britain had decided to assist further the smugglers of both British manufactures and West Indian produce by throwing open some free ports in Canada to American shipping. Moreover, these problems would worsen over the winter of 1811–1812 as the freezing of roads and rivers multiplied the opportunities for smugglers to evade customs officers, and it promised to be a nice question how those officers were going to do their duty without running the risk of being shot as highwaymen by Americans who were obviously determined to trade with Canada. There was, moreover, the undesirability of tolerating a situation where Britain could encourage American citizens to flout American laws to the detriment of republican virtue. Madison also believed that widespread smuggling encouraged Britain to resist America's demands for redress of its maritime grievances. As he told the Twelfth Congress when it met to consider war in November 1811, "the practice of smuggling . . . is odious," especially "when it blends with a pursuit of ignominious gain a treacherous subserviency in the transgressors, to a foreign policy adverse to that of their own country," and he called on Congress to pass whatever measures were necessary to suppress all forms of illicit trade.

Following this injunction, Gallatin requested from Congress at the end of November 1811 several laws to tighten nonimportation, including authorization of customs collectors to search private houses and the creation of an additional district court on the New York frontier. But by now the administration was committed to preparing for war, and it could have hardly escaped Madison's notice that belligerency, too, was another way of dealing with the difficulties of enforcing restraints on trade. Indeed, the president may have concluded that the occupation of Canada was the only way to seal off the North American continent from British trade, though he did not publicly justify the War of 1812 on this ground. To have done so, given the disfavor into which commercial restrictions had fallen by late 1811, would have been politically unwise and would have weakened his case for war against Britain. Shortly after the war ended, however, Madison pointed out to Monroe that "interested individuals," presumably in Britain, had "dwelt much on [Canada's] importance to G. Britain as a channel for evading and crippling our commercial laws"; as such, he continued, Canada "must ever be a source of collision between the two nations." To remove these and other causes of friction, he stressed, was "in truth the only reason we can have to desire Canada." The fact, however, that Madison was willing to call for war after the summer of 1811 strongly suggests that he had reached the conclusion that Canada was of considerable value to Great Britain as a vent for trade long before he made this written admission to Monroe. If so, a war in Canada had become necessary in order to reinforce restrictive policies by which Madison had originally intended to avoid resorting to such a drastic remedy for the nation's grievances.

Madison's belief that the United States should seize Canada in 1812 emerged from concerns that were broader than the practical problems of enforcing commercial restrictions. These concerns, which centered on Canada's position in the British empire, reflected the fact that after 1808 Madison could no longer be confident that Sheffield's predictions about the Canadian contribution to the empire were as erroneous as he had initially supposed. Sheffield had continued to assert his claims for Canada, and after the resumption of the Anglo-French war in 1803 he was again one of the earliest pamphleteers to warn of the dangers in making concessions to Americans in the West Indian trades. At this time, though, he came to appreciate that the West India interest—toward which his earlier feelings had been somewhat ambivalent—could provide some important allies in his campaign to uphold the navigation acts. He therefore endorsed warmly in 1806 James Stephen's pamphlet *War in Disguise,* while many of the pamphleteers for the West India interest, particularly the merchants, in return adopted Sheffield's enthusiasm for Canada to assist their argument for driving neutral commerce out of the colonial trades. . . .

As Madison himself recalled some years later, there had swiftly developed after 1807 "in the portion of the United States connected with the [St. Lawrence] and the inland seas a world of itself" where patterns of trade and personal allegiances cut across political boundaries. And it was in this "world" that the policies of embargo and nonimportation were failing. If anything, American restrictive policies, with the enormous boost they gave to smuggling, stimulated rather than retarded the Canadian economy. Canadian officials and merchants boasted to British companies that it would be business as usual during the nonimportation period, while the withdrawal of American vessels from the sea during the embargo gave Canadian shippers a strong incentive to develop a trade with the West Indies. And despite the heavy demands made on Canadian shipping to carry timber to Great Britain, Canadian navigation to the West Indies did increase significantly, albeit with some fluctuations, after 1807, so that the British North American provinces began to supply the islands to a greater degree than they had done before. The president of the Board of Trade, Earl Bathurst, produced figures in Parliament in February 1809 demonstrating that the commerce between British North America and the West Indies "was in a rapid state of increase," and both Lord Sheffield and William Knox at last had the satisfaction of seeing their predictions begin to come true. As Knox wrote in 1808: "I applaud Jefferson very much, as an Englishman and especially as a New Brunswick Agent and Planter, for the measure of the embargo, as it . . . raises our continental colonies at the expense of the American States. I hope it will continue during the war with France." Sheffield, it hardly need be pointed out, was equally delighted.

The beginning of Canada's transition from a "few acres of snow" to a collection of "respectable" colonies was a development of considerable significance for Anglo-American relations, and Madison, in the years after 1815, explicitly stated his belief that this growth encouraged Britain to resist claims for more liberal definitions of American maritime rights. From the outset, moreover, he was aware of the changing nature of Canada's contribution to the empire, having been warned by Pinkney in June 1808 that one way Britain intended to evade the effects of American commercial restrictions was "to look to the carriage from New Brunswick etc to the British Islands of commodities previously smuggled, in violation of our embargo, from the United States." Very probably, Madison at first dismissed this possibility as he had done on a number of occasions in the past, but the dispatches to the State Department from American consuls throughout the Caribbean during the embargo period left little doubt that Canadian-West Indian trade had grown very rapidly and that the impact on the islands of the withdrawal of American shipping was not as severe as Madison had predicted. The consul in Kingston, Jamaica, for example, reported at the beginning of 1809 that while the embargo had caused the planters some hardship, "the Canadas [had] furnished through the navy of Quebec flour to a greater magnitude than anticipated as also the article of lumber which comprises the implement of conveyance of the produce of the colonies to the mother country."

Admittedly, many of these new Canadian exports, especially in 1808, were American rather than Canadian in origin, but Madison could have derived little comfort from that fact. He had long been aware that even if Canada itself seemed to lack potential for development, the waterway of the Great Lakes and the St. Lawrence had the capacity to command much of the trade of the American interior, and as early as 1780, he had predicted that should the commerce of the American hinterland ever be channeled down the St. Lawrence the commercial benefit to Great Britain would be enormous. "So fair a prospect," he then wrote, "could not escape the commercial sagacity of that nation [and] she would embrace it with avidity [and] cherish it with the most studious care." If Britain did succeed in fixing America's inland commerce in the St. Lawrence "channel," Madison added, "the loss of her exclusive possession of the trade of the United States might prove a less decisive blow to her maritime pre-eminence and tyranny than has been calculated." The failure of the embargo and the consequences of that failure turned this prediction into a growing reality. After 1808 Gallatin began to collect statistics on the trade of Quebec, and these confirmed other reports of rising exports in lumber and provisions as well as a steady growth in Canadian tonnage and seamen. In fact, the figures on Canadian trade compiled by John Jacob Astor for the Treasury Department in 1810 were higher than those reported to the British Foreign Office by Francis James Jackson.

Additional news about the rising prosperity of Canada, moreover, was readily available in the United States, and it is inconceivable that Madison was not familiar with this information. Many Republican congressmen after 1809, as well as several American newspapers such as the *National Intelligencer,* made references to the growth of Canada, speculated on its importance to Great Britain, and hinted that the United States should lose no time in depriving that nation of such a vital resource. The editor of the Philadelphia *Aurora General Advertiser,* William Duane, after denouncing Britain's encouragement of smuggling from Canada, predicted in October 1811 that the British government would never renounce its anti-American policies voluntarily and suggested that his readers consult the pamphlets of Sheffield and Stephen for the reason. At the same time, the Richmond *Virginia Argus* claimed that "many of the effects of a successful naval warfare would result to us from the conquest of the British provinces adjacent to us," though the editor hastened to add that this did not mean that the United States would have any territorial ambitions in a war with Britain. In Washington, the administration journal reported that some of the assemblies of the West Indian islands—which had usually been as skeptical as Madison about the claims made for Canada's economic potential—were now considering resolutions that they should rely in future on Canadian rather than American timber. Furthermore, it was apparent that after 1807 the British government was far less disposed to grant West Indian governors the powers to exempt American shipping from the navigation laws. Among the indications of this hardening attitude were the decisions in 1809 to authorize all West Indian assemblies to adopt discriminatory duties against American produce and to institute an enlarged convoy system to protect Canadian-West Indian trade from French privateers. Finally, in an Order in Council dated September 6, 1811, Britain excluded American salt fish from the West Indies and imposed heavy duties on all other articles imported into the islands from the United States. As the *National Intelligencer* observed, this measure could only have been designed to promote Canadian-West Indian trade at the expense of the United States.

Discussing the Order in Council of September 6, the administration newspaper, on November 2, 1811, argued that the West Indies could only be supplied from the United States, but the significance of the growth of Canada after 1808 was not to be mistaken, and the *National Intelligencer* admitted as much very shortly afterwards. In a series of articles in late November and early December 1811, the *Intelligencer* commented at length on the problem of Canada. To remove any impression among the members of the Twelfth Congress—who were on the point of considering a report from the House Foreign Relations Committee on preparations for war—that the comments were merely occasional pieces, the editor stated that they came from a "valuable correspondent whose sources of information are unquestioningly correct and whose statements may therefore be relied on." More significantly, that correspondent, after providing detailed discussions of the economy, soils, waterways, and population of Canada, noted that his information about the Canadians was "the more necessary as it is intimately connected with their reduction and affiliation with the United States." Admitting that former ideas about Canada as a "sterile" region, useful only in so far as it produced furs, had been proved "erroneous" by Canada's rise to "wealth and importance," the author declared that "in the present state of the world" Canada was "of more vital importance to Great Britain than one half her West India colonies." This rapid rise in Canada's value he attributed to recent changes "effected by settlements, by commerce, and by war," particularly the growing needs of Britain's West India colonies, the exclusion of that nation's trade from the "north of Europe" by France and Russia, the operation of "our embargo and other restrictive laws," and, above all, the expansion of American settlements, especially in New York, "to those places which naturally communicate with Canada." This last cause, he feared, "will continue to increase the trade down the St. Lawrence till it will be equalled only by that of the Mississippi," and he added the warning that should the growth of Canada go unchecked and "should Great Britain be allowed to retain possession of [it] she may laugh at any attempts to distress her West Indies or exclude her from the Baltic, for she will have more than a Baltic of her own."

These editorials were the closest that Madison's administration ever came to admitting openly by word, as distinct from deed, that the growth of Canada had the potential to destroy the very basis of Madison's diplomacy of commercial restriction—the assumption that Britain and its empire were dependent on the United States for "necessaries." Without such dependence between the two nations, the United States, as Madison understood its position, would have few means of bringing effective pressure on Britain other than by trying to build up its own naval and military forces to match those of the enemy. This would not have been an attractive proposition for Madison, and, given the considerations that he knew had justified British policies toward the United States since 1783, it was entirely logical for him to conclude by 1812 that the time had come to deprive Britain of Canada. As he recalled on more than one occasion after the War of 1812, a developing Canada presented "serious difficulties . . . in self-denying contests with Great Britain for commercial objects." To Tench Coxe, who like Madison, had dismissed Sheffield's claims for Canada in the 1780s and 1790s, he observed in 1820 that "the supplies attainable *from* Canada and from the contiguous parts of the United States, now become so productive *through* Canada, may render the contest [between Great Britain and the United States] more obstinate than might have happened at periods when the dependence of the Islands on our exports was more acutely felt." With this remark, and others like it, Madison tacitly conceded that events in Canada had undermined the diplomacy of commercial restriction and, as he pointed out to Churchill C. Cambreleng in 1827, that "future contests" between the two nations would have to take "a different character."

The British government, as it took steps to foster the growth of Canada after 1808, also counted on being able to draw increasing amounts of grain, timber, and naval stores from the Baltic region as the nations there struggled to break away from Napoleon's Continental System, but it was the belief of many Americans, including Madison and his minister to Russia, John Quincy Adams, that Napoleon would probably succeed in 1812 in excluding British commerce from the north of Europe. This development promised to leave Britain almost wholly dependent on Canada for resources that were essential for maintaining its navigation system, and it was for this reason that Madison could believe that a Canadian war would be an effective solution to the problem of compelling British respect for American maritime rights. American victory in Canada would leave little alternative but to accept American terms for trade if Britain wished to preserve the remnants of its empire and its naval power from further damage. The defenders of the navigation system, such as Lord Sheffield, could have presented critics of that system, both in America and in Britain, with no answer to the argument that the empire, without Canada, would be unquestioningly dependent on the resources of the United States. It was therefore by no means unreasonable for James Monroe to explain American policy to John Taylor of Carolina and Jonathan Russell as he did in June 1812. To the former he could state in good faith that the republic was not going to war for the sake of territorial expansion, while to the latter he could give authority to warn the British government that if it did not speedily make a settlement with the United States, American forces would have to occupy Canadian soil and then refuse to relinquish it.

## FURTHER READING

Irving Brant, *James Madison*, 6 vols. (1941–1961)

Roger Brown, *The Republic in Peril: 1812* (1964)

A. L. Burt, *The United States, Great Britain, and British North America* (1940)

Harry L. Coles, *The War of 1812* (1965)

Clifford L. Egan, *Neither Peace Nor War: Franco-American Relations, 1803–1812* (1983)

———, "The Origins of the War of 1812: Three Decades of Historical Writing," *Military Affairs*, 38 (1974), 72–75

Jeffrey A. Frankel, "The 1807–1809 Embargo Against Great Britain," *Journal of Economic History,* 52 (1982), 291–308.

Warren H. Goodman, "The Origins of the War of 1812: A Survey of Changing Interpretations," *Mississippi Valley Historical Review,* 28 (1941), 171–186

Donald R. Hickey, "American Trade Restrictions During the War of 1812," *Journal of American History,* 68 (1981), 517–538

Reginald Horsman, *The Causes of the War of 1812* (1962)

Ralph Ketcham, *James Madison* (1971)

Alfred Thayer Mahan, *Sea Power in Its Relations to the War of 1812* (1905)

Drew R. McCoy, *The Elusive Republic: Political Economy in Jefferson America* (1980)

Bradford Perkins, *The First Rapprochement* (1955)

Norman K. Risjord, "1812: Conservatives, War Hawks, and the Nation's Honor," *William and Mary Quarterly,* 18 (1961), 196–210

Robert A. Rutland, *Madison's Alternatives* (1975)

Marshall Smelser, *The Democratic Republic: 1800–1815* (1968)

Burton Spivak, *Jefferson's English Crisis* (1979)

J. C. A. Stagg, "James Madison and the 'Malcontents': The Political Origins of the War of 1812," *William and Mary Quarterly,* 33 (1976), 557–585

Patrick C. T. White, *A Nation on Trial* (1965)

# le Monroe Doctrine

ნ

On December 2, 1823, President James Monroe gave his Annual Message to
Congress. Therein he stated principles that became lasting guides to American
diplomacy. He declared that the Western Hemisphere was no longer open to
European colonization, that the New and Old Worlds were so different that the
United States would abstain from European wars, and that the European powers should not intervene forcefully in the two Americas in an attempt to deny
them their independence. These three points—non-colonization, two spheres,
and non-intervention—were designed to warn the monarchies of Europe
against crushing the independence of the new states of Latin America which
had broken from the Spanish Empire.

Britain, which had profited commercially from the break-up of the Spanish
mercantile system and, therefore, did not welcome a restoration of Spanish rule
in South America, approached the United States with the idea of issuing a joint
declaration warning against European intervention. North Americans, who
also realized economic benefits from the dismantling of the Spanish Empire and
who sympathized with the Latin American independence movements, also
grew worried about the apparent European threat. Monroe's "doctrine"
constituted the American answer to this menace.

## DOCUMENTS

The first document is British Foreign Secretary George Canning's August 1823
appeal to the United States to unite with Great Britain in a joint declaration
against European intervention in the newly independent Latin American nations.

President Monroe consulted his Cabinet about the proposal; he also asked the advice of two former Presidents, Thomas Jefferson and James Madison. Jefferson's counsel is reprinted here, as is an entry from the diary of Secretary of State John Quincy Adams, who vigorously opposed cooperative action with Britain and won his point. The final selection is Monroe's famous message to Congress of December 2, 1823.

## George Canning's Overture for a Joint Declaration, 1823

*My Dear Sir:* Before leaving Town, I am desirous of bringing before you in a more distinct, but still in an unofficial and confidential, shape, the question which we shortly discussed the last time that I had the pleasure of seeing you.

Is not the moment come when our Governments might understand each other as to the Spanish American Colonies? And if we can arrive at such an understanding, would it not be expedient for ourselves, and beneficial for all the world, that the principles of it should be clearly settled and plainly avowed?

For ourselves we have no disguise.

1. We conceive the recovery of the Colonies by Spain to be hopeless.

2. We conceive the question of the recognition of them, as Independent States, to be one of time and circumstances.

3. We are, however, by no means disposed to throw any impediment in the way of an arrangement between them, and the mother country by amicable negotiation.

4. We aim not at the possession of any portion of them ourselves.

5. We could not see any portion of them transferred to any other Power, with indifference.

If these opinions and feelings are as I firmly believe them to be, common to your Government with ours, why should we hesitate mutually to confide them to each other; and to declare them in the face of the world?

If there be any European Power which cherishes other projects, which looks to a forcible enterprize for reducing the Colonies to subjugation, on the behalf or in the name of Spain; or which meditates the acquisition of any part of them to itself, by cession or by conquest; such a declaration on the part of your government and ours would be at once the most effectual and the least offensive mode of intimating our joint disapprobation of such projects.

It would at the same time put an end to all the jealousies of Spain with respect to her remaining Colonies—and to the agitation which prevails in those Colonies, an agitation which it would be but humane to allay; being determined (as we are) not to profit by encouraging it.

Do you conceive that under the power which you have recently received, you are authorized to enter into negotiation, and to sign any Convention upon this subject? Do you conceive, if that be not within your competence, you could exchange with me ministerial notes upon it?

Nothing could be more gratifying to me than to join with you in such a work, and, I am persuaded, there has seldom, in the history of the world, occurred an opportunity when so small an effort, of two friendly Governments, might produce so unequivocal a good and prevent such extensive calamities.

I shall be absent from London but three weeks at the utmost: but never so far distant but that I can receive and reply to any communication, within three or four days.

## Jefferson's Advice to James Monroe, 1823

Dear Sir, The question presented by the letters you have sent me, is the most momentous which has ever been offered to my contemplation since that of Independence. That made us a nation, this sets our compass and points the course which we are to steer through the ocean of time opening on us. And never could we embark on it under circumstances more auspicious. Our first and fundamental maxim should be, never to entangle ourselves in the broils of Europe. Our second, never to suffer Europe to intermeddle with cis-Atlantic affairs. America, North and South, has a set of interests distinct from those of Europe, and peculiarly her own. She should therefore have a system of her own, separate and apart from that of Europe. While the last is laboring to become the domicile of despotism, our endeavor should surely be to make our hemisphere that of freedom. One nation, most of all, could disturb us in this pursuit; she now offers to lead, aid, and accompany us in it. By acceding to her proposition, we detach her from the bands, bring her mighty weight into the scale of free government, and emancipate a continent at one stroke, which might otherwise linger long in doubt and difficulty. Great Britain is the nation which can do us the most harm of any one, or all on earth; and with her on our side we need not fear the whole world. With her then, we should most sedulously cherish a cordial friendship; and nothing would tend more to knit our affections than to be fighting once more, side by side, in the same cause. . . .

But we have first to ask ourselves a question. Do we wish to acquire to our own confederacy any one or more of the Spanish provinces? I candidly confess, that I have ever looked on Cuba as the most interesting addition which could ever be made to our system of States. The control which, with Florida Point, this island would give us over the Gulf of Mexico, and the countries and isthmus bordering on it, as well as all those whose waters flow into it, would fill up the measures of our political well-being. Yet, as I am sensible that this can never be obtained, even with her own consent, but by war; and its independence, which is our second interest, (and especially its independence of England,) can be secured without it, I have no hesitation in abandoning my first wish to future chances, and accepting its independence, with peace and the friendship of England, rather than its association, at the expense of war and her enmity.

I could honestly, therefore, join in the declaration proposed, that we aim not at the acquisition of any of those possessions, that we will not stand in the way of any amicable arrangement between them and the Mother country; but that we will oppose, with all our means, the forcible interposition of any other power, as auxiliary, stipendiary, or under any other form or pretext, and most especially, their transfer to any power by conquest, cession, or acquisition in any other way. I should think it, therefore, advisable, that the Executive should encourage the British government to a continuance in the dispositions expressed in these letters, by an assurance of his concurrence with them as far as his authority goes; and that as it may lead to war, the declaration of which requires an act of Congress, the case shall be laid before them for consideration at their first meeting, and under the reasonable aspect in which it is seen by himself.

## John Quincy Adams' Account of the Cabinet Meeting of November 7, 1823

Washington, *November 7th.*—Cabinet meeting at the President's from half-past one till four. Mr. Calhoun, Secretary of War, and Mr. Southard, Secretary of the Navy, present. The subject for consideration was, the confidential proposals of the British Secretary of State, George Canning, to R. Rush, and the correspondence between them relating to the projects of the Holy Alliance upon South America. There was much conversation, without coming to any definite point. The object of Canning appears to have been to obtain some public pledge from the Government of the United States, ostensibly against the forcible interference of the Holy Alliance between Spain and South America; but really or especially against the acquisition to the United States themselves of any part of the Spanish-American possessions.

Mr. Calhoun inclined to giving a discretionary power to Mr. Rush to join in a declaration against the interference of the Holy Allies, if necessary, even if it should pledge us not to take Cuba or the province of Texas; because the power of Great Britain being greater than ours to *seize* upon them, we should get the advantage of obtaining from her the same declaration we should make ourselves.

I thought the cases not parallel. We have no intention of seizing either Texas or Cuba. But the inhabitants of either or both may exercise their primitive rights, and solicit a union with us. They will certainly do no such thing to Great Britain. By joining with her, therefore, in her proposed declaration, we give her a substantial and perhaps inconvenient pledge against ourselves, and really obtain nothing in return. Without entering now into the enquiry of the expediency of our annexing Texas or Cuba to our Union, we should at least keep ourselves free to act as emergencies may arise, and not tie ourselves down to any principle which might immediately afterwards be brought to bear against ourselves.

Mr. Southard inclined much to the same opinion.

The President was averse to any course which should have the appearance of taking a position subordinate to that of Great Britain. . . .

I remarked that the communications recently received from the Russian Minister, Baron Tuyl, afforded, as I thought, a very suitable and convenient opportunity for us to take our stand against the Holy Alliance, and at the same time to decline the overture of Great Britain. It would be more candid, as well as more dignified, to avow our principles explicitly to Russia and France, than to come in as a cock-boat in the wake of the British man-of-war.

This idea was acquiesced in on all sides, and my draft for an answer to Baron Tuyl's note announcing the Emperor's determination to refuse receiving any Minister from the South American Governments was read.

## Monroe's Annual Message, 1823

At the proposal of the Russian Imperial Government, made through the minister of the Emperor residing here, a full power and instructions have been transmitted to the minister of the United States at St. Petersburg to arrange by amicable negotiation the respective rights and interests of the two nations on the northwest coast of this continent. . . . In the discussions to which this interest has given rise and in the arrangements by which they may terminate the occasion has been judged proper for asserting, as a principle in which the rights and interests of the United States are involved that the American continents, by the free and independent condition which they have assumed and maintain, are henceforth not to be considered as subjects for future colonization by any European powers. . . .

It was stated at the commencement of the last session that a great effort was then making in Spain and Portugal to improve the condition of the people of those countries, and that it appeared to be conducted with extraordinary moderation. It need scarcely be remarked that the result has been so far very different from what was then anticipated. Of events in that quarter of the globe, with which we have so much intercourse and from which we derive our origin, we have always been anxious and interested spectators. The citizens of the United States cherish sentiments the most friendly in favor of the liberty and happiness of their fellow-men on that side of the Atlantic. In the wars of the European powers in matters relating to themselves we have never taken any part, nor does it comport with our policy so to do. It is only when our rights are invaded or seriously menaced that we resent injuries or make preparation for our defense. With the movements in this hemisphere we are of necessity more immediately connected, and by causes which must be obvious to all enlightened and impartial observers. The political system of the allied powers is essentially different in this respect from that of America. This difference proceeds from that which exists in their respective Governments; and to the defense of our own, which has been achieved by the loss of so much blood and treasure, and matured by the wisdom of their most enlightened citizens, and under which we have enjoyed unexampled felicity, this whole nation is devoted. We owe it, therefore, to candor and to the amicable relations existing between the United States and those powers to declare that we should consider any attempt on their part to extend their system to any portion of this hemisphere as dangerous to our peace and safety. With the existing colonies or dependencies of any European power we have not interfered and shall not interfere. But with the Governments who have declared their independence and maintained it, and whose independence we have, on great consideration and on just principles, acknowledged, we could not view any interposition for the purpose of oppressing them, or controlling in any other manner their destiny, by any European power in any other light than as the manifestation of an unfriendly disposition toward the United States. In the war between those new Governments and Spain we declared our neutrality at the time of their recognition, and to this we have adhered, and shall continue to adhere, provided no change shall occur which, in the judgment of the competent authorities of this Government, shall make a corresponding change on the part of the United States indispensable to their security.

The late events in Spain and Portugal shew that Europe is still unsettled. Of this important fact no stronger proof can be adduced than that the allied powers should have thought it proper, on any principle satisfactory to themselves, to have interposed by force in the internal concerns of Spain. To what extent such interposition may be carried, on the same principle, is a question in which all independent powers whose governments differ from theirs are interested, even those most remote, and surely none more so than the United States. Our policy in regard to Europe, which was adopted at an early stage of the wars which have so long agitated that quarter of the globe, nevertheless remains the same, which is, not to interfere in the internal concerns of any of its powers; to consider the government *de facto* as the legitimate government for us; to cultivate friendly relations with it, and to preserve those relations by a frank, firm, and manly policy, meeting in all instances the just claims of every power, submitting to injuries from none. But in regard to those continents circumstances are eminently and conspicuously different. It is impossible that the allied powers should extend their political system to any portion of either continent without endangering our peace and happiness; nor can anyone believe that our southern brethren, if left to themselves, would adopt it of their own accord. It is equally impossible, therefore, that we should behold such interposition in any form with indifference.

---

# ESSAYS

Dexter Perkins has traced the origins and evolution of the Monroe Doctrine in a series of scholarly volumes. In the first selection, he acknowledges that Americans were thinking about their commercial stakes when they decided to speak out for the non-colonization principle, but he argues that American republican sympathies for the anti-colonial rebellions to the south lay behind the non-intervention clause. William Appleman Williams does not see the Monroe Doctrine in any way as a defensive measure, but as a United States attempt to establish its commercial supremacy in the Western Hemisphere.

# The Defense of Commerce and Ideals

## DEXTER PERKINS

The famous declaration of December 2, 1823, which has come to be known as the Monroe Doctrine, had a dual origin and a dual purpose. On the one hand, it was the result of the advance of Russia on the northwest coast of America, and was designed to serve as a protest against this advance and to establish a general principle against Russian expansion. Referring to this question of the northwest, President Monroe laid down the principle in his message to Congress that "the American continents, by the free and independent condition which they have assumed and maintain, are henceforth not to be considered as subjects for future colonization by any European powers." On the other hand, the message was provoked by the fear of European intervention in South America to restore to Spain her revolted colonies, and was intended to give warning of the hostility of the United States to any such intervention. "With the governments [that is, of the Spanish-American republics] who have declared their independence, and maintained it," wrote the President, "and whose independence we have, on great consideration and just principles, acknowledged, we could not view any interposition for the purpose of oppressing them, or controlling in any other manner their destiny, by any European power, in any other light than as the manifestation of an unfriendly disposition toward the United States." . . .

Russian interest in the northwest coast of America goes back to the second quarter of the eighteenth century, to the days of the renowned navigator Vitus Behring, who discovered in 1727 the Straits that now bear his name, and fourteen years later the Alaskan coast in the neighborhood of latitude 58. Behring's explorations were followed by the voyages of fur traders and by the establishment of trading posts on the islands off the American mainland. After years of demoralizing competition on the part of private individuals, the Tsar determined to create a commercial monopoly for the exploitation of the rich fisheries to be found in that part of the world. By the ukase of July 8, 1799, the Russian-American Company was constituted, and to this company were granted exclusive trading rights and jurisdiction along the coast as far south as latitude 55, and the right to make settlements on either side of that line in territory not occupied by other powers.

From an early date the operations of this Russian corporation were impeded by interlopers, very largely American. American vessels sold arms and ammunition to the natives, and secured a considerable part of the fur trade. As early as 1808 and 1810 complaints on the part of the Russian government began to be made to the government at Washington. There was, obviously enough, a situation that might lead to serious friction. . . .

On September 4/16, 1821, the Tsar Alexander I, acting at the instigation

Reprinted by permission of the publishers from *The Monroe Doctrine, 1823–1826* by Dexter Perkins, Cambridge, Massachusetts: Harvard University Press, Copyright © 1927 by the President and Fellows of Harvard College, © 1955 by Dexter Perkins.

of the Russian monopoly, promulgated an imperial decree which renewed its privileges and confirmed its exclusive trading rights. This time the southern limit of these rights on the American coast was set, not at 55, but at 51 degrees. And in addition, all foreign vessels were forbidden, between Behring Straits and 51 degrees, to come within 100 Italian miles of the shore, on pain of confiscation. A Russian warship was dispatched to the northwest coast to enforce this remarkable decree, and every intention was manifested of barring all other nations from any participation whatever in the trade or fisheries of the region. Such a course of action very naturally provoked a protest, not only on the part of the United States, but also on the part of Great Britain. At this time the two Anglo-Saxon powers had joint ownership, under the convention of 1818, of the territory north from 42 degrees to a line yet to be determined, and the Russian claims of exclusive jurisdiction as far south as 51 degrees could hardly fail to be disquieting. Both from London and from Washington, therefore, came strong diplomatic remonstrance, and thus began a controversy which was to have the closest relationship to the famous pronouncement of 1823.

It is neither necessary nor desirable, in connection with this narrative, to trace the negotiations on the northwest question in all their details. What is of special interest here is the evolution of the non-colonization principle in the course of the discussions, the reception which it met at the hands of the interested powers, and the effect which it produced upon the diplomatic interchanges themselves. . . .

These discussions, begun in 1822, assumed little importance till the late spring of 1823. By that time it had been agreed that the question should be threshed out at St. Petersburg. In June the cabinet discussed the instructions which were to be sent to Mr. Middleton, American minister at the court of the Tsar. The Secretary of State declared it to be his conviction that the United States ought to contest the right of the Russian government to any territorial establishment on the American continents. Apparently this point of view did not pass unchallenged. It was pointed out that Russia would have little reason to accept such drastic doctrine. The United States, in maintaining it, would be asking everything, and conceding virtually nothing. A compromise was suggested and agreed upon by which this country would recognize the territorial claims of the Tsar north of 55 degrees. On this basis, the negotiations were actually to be conducted.

But Adams, with a curious inconsistency, did not on this account surrender the principle which was taking shape in his mind. At the very moment when he was perfecting the instructions to Middleton along the lines agreed upon in the cabinet, he declared himself to Tuyll, the Russian minister at Washington, in language very much more sweeping.

> I told him specially [he writes in his diary, alluding to an interview of July 17, 1823], that we should contest the right of Russia to *any* territorial establishment on this continent, and that we should assume distinctly the principle that the American continents are no longer subjects for *any* new European colonial establishments.

In this statement, almost five months before the appearance of the President's message, we have the non-colonization principle full-fledged, no longer merely a subject of cabinet debate, but explicitly put forward to the minister of another power, to the minister of the power perhaps most concerned in denying it. . . .

We have another statement of the non-colonization dogma almost contemporaneous with the interview with Tuyll. This is found in the instructions to Richard Rush, American minister at the Court of Saint James's. As England had an interest in the northwest controversy, it was obviously desirable that the diplomatic representative of the United States at London should be informed of the views of his government on the subject. Accordingly, on July 22, Adams sent forward a long and careful dispatch, in which he set forth his new theory in greater detail than at any other time. That dispatch will claim our special attention later. . . .

Adams secured Monroe's assent to his new principle in July. . . . Whether that assent was cordial and positive, or whether it was given as a mere matter of routine, we have no way of knowing. The President may have warmly approved the non-colonization doctrine; he may, on the other hand, have been little aware of its significance or its implications. On this point his writings provide us with no illumination. But at any rate, he *did* accept it. When, therefore, the Secretary of State drew up in November, the customary sketch of the topics of foreign policy which might interest the President in connection with the preparation of the forthcoming message, he naturally included in the paragraph on the Russian negotiations a reference to the new dogma. That paragraph was taken over almost without verbal change by Monroe, and thus it appeared in his communication to the Congress. These facts are clear, for we have the actual manuscript of Adams's outline of the diplomatic matters which he wished to draw to the attention of the President, and the language of that outline, so far as the non-colonization principle is concerned, corresponds almost exactly with the language of the message itself.

There was, apparently, no consideration of the principle in the cabinet discussion preceding the publication of the President's declaration. On this point Calhoun, then Secretary of War, was to testify many years later, and the silence of Adams's diary at the time confirms this testimony. There is, after all, nothing strange in such a circumstance. For the question of the hour, in November, 1823, was not the dispute with Russia, but the menace offered by the Holy Alliance to the independence of the States of South America. It was on these problems that all the debates turned; so, very naturally, the other problem was crowded out. . . .

Having thus examined the origins of the non-colonization clause in the message of 1823, we must now turn back to discuss the viewpoint and the reasoning which lay behind it. What was the motive in promulgating such a sweeping theory? What was the logic by which it might be supported?

In later interpretations of this part of the President's declaration, the emphasis has frequently been laid on the dangers involved in bringing the intrigues and conflicting territorial ambitions of Europe across the seas and into the New World. The United States, the argument has run, would thus be swept into the vortex of European politics, and exposed to the wicked influences for which those politics are notorious. Or it has been maintained that the new European territorial establishments would endanger American security, and ought to be opposed on these grounds.

These were not the bases, however, on which John Quincy Adams, in 1823, rested his opposition to colonization. The territorial aspects of colonization were not uppermost in his mind. He was thinking (and the point has been all too little emphasized) primarily of the commercial interests of the United States. In the history of American diplomacy, the principle of non-colonization has a certain affinity with the principle of the open door, asserted three quarters of a century later. It was based on immediate economic factors, not on vague fears of the future. It was because the colonial system meant commercial exclusion that the Secretary of State proclaimed its banishment from the American continents.

A close examination of Adams's point of view makes this clear. The principle of equality of commercial opportunity was one for which he contended with the utmost vigor, not only in the northwest controversy, but in other fields. He fought vigorously against the narrow policy of Great Britain in the British West Indies. He instructed the ministers to the South American states, when they set out in 1823, to contend for the principle that the new republics should treat all nations on the same footing, and that they should give no preferences, not even to their former mother country. The right to which he held most tenaciously in the dispute with Russia was not the right to full possession of the territory on the northwest (on this, as we have seen, it had been agreed to compromise on the line of 55 degrees); the right which he deemed of most importance was the right to trade, and this Middleton was instructed stoutly to maintain. In Adams's opinion the notion of European colonization was flatly opposed to the maintenance of these economic interests. The colonizing methods of the Old World, he told Stratford Canning in November, 1822, had always involved a more or less complete commercial monopoly. "Spain had set the example. She had forbidden foreigners from setting a foot in her Colonies, upon pain of death, and the other colonizing states of Europe had imitated the exclusion, though not the rigor of the penalty." From the very beginning, therefore, the Adams doctrine was knit up with the commercial interests of the United States. And so it remained throughout this early period of its development. Nothing shows this more clearly than the important dispatch of July 22, 1823, to Richard Rush, in which the whole theory of the doctrine found most careful expression. After declaring that the American continents will henceforth no longer be subjects for colonization, the American Secretary of State goes on to say:

> Occupied by civilized independent nations, they will be accessible to Europeans and to each other on that footing alone, and the Pacific Ocean in every part of it will remain open to the navigation of all nations, in like manner with the Atlantic. . . . The application of colonial principles of exclusion, therefore, cannot be admitted by the United States as lawful upon any part of the northwest coast of America, or as belonging to any European nation.

In these clear-cut and precise phrases, the innermost connection of the new dogma with American trading rights stands revealed.

It need not be contended, of course, that there was no more to it than this. It would be a clear exaggeration to say that Adams was contending for trading rights alone. He was thinking also of territorial settlement, as the very dispatch just quoted helps to make clear.

> It is not imaginable [he declared] that, in the present condition of the world, *any* European nation should entertain the project of settling a *colony* on the northwest coast of America. That the United States should form establishments there, with views of absolute territorial right and inland communication, is not only to be expected, but is pointed out by the finger of nature.

But these comments were made with an eye to the future. What was interesting in the immediate sense, "the only useful purpose to which the northwest coast of America" had been or could be made "subservient to the settlement of civilized men," was that of trade and of the fishery. The rights of the United States in this regard it was vital to maintain. On the territorial question there might be compromise; this we have already seen. But on the commercial question there ought to be none. "The right of carrying on trade with the natives throughout the northwest coast they [the United States] cannot renounce." Clearly, it was antagonism to commercial restriction that lay at the basis of the Secretary of State's famous dictum. . . .

The revolt of the Spanish-American colonies followed hard upon the Napoleonic conquest of Spain. From the very beginning, the sympathies of the United States appear to have been engaged upon the side of the revolutionists. American sentiment was distinctly favorable to a movement for independence which had at least a superficial resemblance to that of 1776, and which could easily be regarded as an effort to throw off an odious tyranny and establish throughout the greater part of the New World the blessings of republican government. Fellow feeling in a struggle for liberty and independence was an essential element in forming the policy of the United States with regard to South America.

It was indeed, to all appearances, a far more important element than any hope of material gain. In the formative period of this country's relations with the new states of South America, certainly down to 1822, there is little evidence of the working of economic interest. In the absence of exact statistics for much of the period, and in view of the paucity of references to trade with the Spanish colonies, it is difficult to speak with precision. But certain general observations may safely be made. In the first place, the trade with Cuba and with Spain itself was far more important than the trade with the new republics of the South. A diplomatic policy favorable to the South-American states might jeopardize or even sacrifice commercial interests superior to those which it would promote. If economic reasons were to be regarded as shaping political developments, there were more reasons for a cautious than for an active line of policy. In the second place, there was not, as in the case of Great Britain, any powerful pressure from the commercial classes in favor of colonial independence. The evidence on this point is partly negative, it is true, but it is negative evidence of the strongest kind. One can hardly imagine that the existence of such pressure would pass unnoticed in the debates in Congress, and in such contemporary records as the diary and writings of Adams, and the correspondence of Monroe. But it is not necessary to depend upon this fact alone. Statistics indicate that as late as 1821 only 2.3 per cent of American exports and 1.6 per cent of American imports were South American in destination or origin. In March of the same year Adams could tell Henry Clay that he had little expectation of any commercial advantages from the recognition of the new states. And even later, in 1823, the Secretary of State speaks of commercial development as a matter of hope for the future rather than a present accomplishment. That hope may, of course, have counted for something from the beginning. But, all things considered, it seems highly probable that political sympathy, not economic self-interest, lay at the root of American policy so far as it revealed itself as favorable to the new states of South America.

From the very beginnings of the South American struggle this sympathy asserts itself. As early as 1810, the American government, then headed by Madison, sent agents to South America—Joel R. Poinsett to La Plata and Chile, and Robert Lowry to Venezuela. At the end of 1811, James Monroe, then Secretary of State, thought seriously of raising the question of the recognition of the new states, and of exerting American influence in Europe to secure like action from the principal European powers. He also entered into informal relations with agents from at least one of the revolted provinces. And in Congress, at the same time, in response to the sympathetic language of the President's message, a resolution was passed, expressing a friendly solicitude in the welfare of these communities, and a readiness, when they should become nations by a just exercise of their rights, to unite with the Executive in establishing such relations with them as might be necessary. Thus, very early in the course of the colonial struggle, the general bent of American policy was made plain.

But it was some time before the South-American question became a matter of really first-rate importance. In the years 1810 to 1815, the prime concern of the administration at Washington lay in the preservation of American neutral rights, and, from 1812 to 1814, in the prosecution of the war with Great Britain. Moreover, the course of events in the overseas dominions of Spain was for some time hardly favorable to the revolutionists. In 1814 and 1815, indeed, it seemed entirely possible that the revolutionary movements might be snuffed out. In the north, in Venezuela and Colombia, the army of the Spanish general, Morillo, won victory on victory, and drove the leader of the revolutionists, Bolívar, into exile. In the south, in Chile, Osorio reëstablished the power of the mother country, and in Buenos Aires the struggles of contending factions weakened the new government that had been set up. Under such circumstances, prudence would have dictated a policy of reserve on the part of the United States, even if its government had not been preoccupied with other and more pressing matters.

With the year 1817, however, a change takes place in the status of the colonial question. In the case of one, at any rate, of the new states, the struggle was virtually over. The republic of La Plata had declared its independence and successfully maintained it, so that not a Spanish soldier remained upon its territory; even more, it had dispatched its great general, San Martín, across the Andes, and, with the victory of Chacabuca, taken a great step toward the final liberation of Chile. Perhaps as a result of these developments, interest in favor of the recognition of the new state began to develop in the United States; there were numerous newspaper articles in the summer of 1817, notably the discussions of Lautaro in the Richmond *Enquirer;* and the affairs of South America became a matter of debate both in the councils of the administration and in the halls of Congress.

It is interesting, in the light of later events, to examine these developments. So far as the administration was concerned, the point especially to be emphasized is the warm sympathy of the President himself with the South American cause. There has been a tendency in some quarters, in connection with the evolution of the Monroe Doctrine, to ascribe a very slight importance to the views of the very man who promulgated it. Mr. Monroe has been pictured as "slow-moving and lethargic," as prodded forward only by the more vigorous mind and more determined will of John Quincy Adams, his Secretary of State. But as a matter of fact, Monroe was at all times quite as much interested in the colonial cause, and in as full sympathy with it, as Adams. From the very beginning of his presidency, he showed his concern with regard to it. As early as May, 1817, some months before Adams took office, the President had determined upon a mission of inquiry to the provinces of La Plata, and as early as October he questioned his cabinet on the expediency of recognizing the government of that region. He raised the problem again in the succeeding May, even suggesting the possibility of sending an armed force to the coast of South America, to protect American commerce, "and to countenance the patriots." His views, it is true, were to be overruled or modified by his advisers. But his interest in positive action was very real, and is quite consistent with the character of the man whose flaming sympathy with French republicanism had been so obvious in his earlier career. . . .

In the discussions upon the northwest controversy, as has been seen, trading influences contributed very materially to the stand which was taken by the administration. But it would be difficult to prove anything of the kind with regard to the warning given to Europe against intervention in South America. This is not to say that such influences necessarily played no rôle at all. John Quincy Adams, of course, came from the great shipping section of the Union. In his instructions to the American ministers sent out to Colombia and La Plata in the spring of 1823, he had laid a very considerable emphasis upon freedom of commercial opportunity, though he was by no means exuberantly optimistic as to the possibilities of the South American trade. In the cabinet discussions of November, he had, on one occasion, brought forward as a reason for action the fact that if the United States stood aside and Great Britain alone vetoed the designs of the Continental powers, the latter country would gain great commercial advantages. It is worth noting, too, that our commerce with the Spanish-American states was considerably more important in 1823 than it had been two or three years before. But these facts would be a slender foundation on which to base an "economic interpretation" of the Monroe Doctrine. And they are offset by many others. Whoever reads the pages of Adams's diary will find it hard to believe that trading considerations played a very considerable rôle in his mind. The distaste produced by the homilies of the Tsar, a genuine and robust disapproval of the trend of European politics, a desire to set forth the political doctrines of the United States in opposition to those of the Alliance, these are the factors that bulked largest in his thought. Economic considerations there may have been in the background. But it was a profound political antagonism that gave force to the action which he advocated in the councils of President Monroe.

With the President himself, this antagonism was even more keenly felt. The letter to Jefferson, written early in June, seems to express his point of view pretty accurately. He was anxious to strike a blow for liberty, and the situation in the fall of 1823 offered him an excellent opportunity. To this must be added the fact that Monroe, like Calhoun, feared that an assault upon the liberties of the Spanish Americans would be dangerous to the safety of the United States itself. It was these considerations, beyond a doubt, that sharpened his pen as he wrote the declaration of December 2. . . .

Monroe's belief in the superiority of American institutions, his conviction that the extension of European dominion would be dangerous to our peace and safety—these are propositions that are hardly capable of rigorous demonstration. Perhaps their strength lies in just that fact. Yet there is, I think, one thing more to be said for them. In resting his opposition to European intermeddling in Spanish America on the "peace and safety" of the United States, the President was taking up a strong position from the legal and moral point of view. For he was basing American policy on the right of self-preservation, a right that is and always has been recognized as fundamental in international law. If in very truth the interposition of the Holy Alliance in South America imperilled the peace and safety of the United States, then the President's right to protest against it was obvious. Nor was it to be expected that as to the reality of the peril he would accept the conclusions of European statesmen. He stood secure in his own conviction and on his own ground.

# Manifesto of the American Empire

## WILLIAM APPLEMAN WILLIAMS

Though it is generally treated as the cornerstone of American diplomacy, most analyses of the doctrine emphasize its negative aspects. It is thus presented as a defensive statement of the territorial and administrative integrity of North and South America: no further colonization, no transfer or extension of exist-

From pp. 215–218 in *The Contours of American History* by William Appleman Williams (World Publishing Co., 1961). Reprinted by permission of the author.

ing claims, and in return America would not interfere in European affairs. This standard interpretation neglects three major facts: the men who formulated it were concerned as much with European commercial and economic expansion as with its schemes for colonization; they viewed it as a positive, expansionist statement of American supremacy in the hemisphere, and Monroe actually intervened in European politics with the very same speech in which he asserted that Europe should stay out of American affairs.

Aware that the political economy of the United States was established, and properly interpreting the results of the War of 1812 as being fundamentally favorable to its position in the hemisphere, American leaders reached an obvious conclusion. If they could exclude further European penetration as Spain's authority collapsed, then the United States would remain as the predominant power in the hemisphere. Monroe thus reasserted the expansionist thesis at the end of his message of December 2, 1823, which announced the doctrine. Having urged further support for manufactures and internal improvements, as well as warning Europe off Latin America while he encouraged the Greek revolution, he concluded with this well-nigh classic paraphrase of Madison's theory. "It is manifest that by enlarging the basis of our system, and increasing the number of States, the system itself has been greatly strengthened in both its [state and national] branches. Consolidation and disunion have thereby been rendered equally impracticable."

As one who was equally familiar with Madison's theory of expansion (he mentioned it specifically in his eulogy of Madison), Adams fully expected the United States to acquire Cuba, Texas, and other tidbits of territory in North America. But he was at least as concerned with establishing American commercial supremacy as he was with blocking further colonial experiments by European nations. This balanced expansionist sentiment behind the Monroe Doctrine was well revealed in the congressional discussions about Oregon which some thought was threatened by Russia as well as by England. Francis Baylies of Massachusetts might have been expected to concern himself with the "magnificent prospects" of the Pacific commerce, but he also quoted Napoleon to emphasize his support for territorial expansion: he "never uttered words of more wisdom than when he said, 'I want ships, commerce, and colonies.'" Robert Wright of Maryland called for expansion because "there is less danger of separatism in a confederacy of 20 or 30 States than in one of a smaller number."

Senator James Barbour agreed. "Our advance in political science has already cancelled the dogmas of theory. We have already ascertained . . . that republics are not necessarily limited to small territories. . . . Whether America is capable of indefinite extent, must be left to posterity to decide." And speaking for a growing consensus, John Floyd of Virginia accurately concluded that "all contemplate with joy" continued westward expansion. It would provide land for farmers, "procure and protect the fur trade," "engross the whale trade," and "control the South Sea trade. . . . All this rich commerce could be governed, if not engrossed, by capitalists at Oregon."

Adams shared such commercial interest in the Northwest, and it contributed to his thinking about the Monroe Doctrine. Even more in his mind, however, was the importance of trade with Latin America. By 1820, when Adams, in his instructions to American agents, described it as "deserving of particular attention," this trade had developed into a significant commerce that vigorous European intervention would curtail and perhaps even destroy. Baltimore specialized in flour and furniture, but Salem, New York, Philadelphia, and even New Orleans, shipped shoes, cotton textiles, fertilizer, pitch, and lumber into such cities as Rio de Janeiro. The carrying trade was also important. American shippers carried Asian goods to Chile, Argentine beef to Cuba, and European items to the entire region. British agents reported to Foreign Secretary George Canning that Americans controlled the Argentine flour market, that their tonnage in Uruguay was "greater than that of any other nation," and that Peru's commerce with Asia "has been entirely engrossed by the North Americans."

Aware of this strong position, Henry Clay predicted that in half a century Americans, "in relation to South America," would "occupy the same position as the people of New England do to the rest of the United States." The implications of Clay's remark unquestionably disturbed some southerners in 1820 as much as the validity of his prediction was to upset Latin Americans in the 20th century. His enthusiastic campaign to establish an American System embracing the hemisphere was important for several reasons. Promising "mercantile profits," an influx of Spanish gold, and markets for the farmers and other entrepreneurs of the Mississippi west, he also assured his countrymen that the expansion of America's ideological principles would provide military as well as economic security. Being like the United States, he argued, the new countries would not be prone to oppose its basic policies.

Adams was wary of Clay's rambunctious ideological assertiveness, but he was fully agreed on the importance of commercial activity. His instructions of May 27, 1823, to an American agent who was being sent to Colombia left no doubt about his basic strategy. The American political economy was now strong enough to take advantage of its great relative superiority over the emerging new nations. "As navigators and manufacturers, *we* are already so far advanced in a career upon which *they* are yet to enter," he explained, "that we may, for many years after the conclusion of the war, maintain with them a commercial intercourse, highly beneficial to both parties, as *carriers* to and for them of numerous articles of manufacture and foreign produce."

---

## FURTHER READING

Harry Ammon, *James Monroe* (1970)
———, "The Monroe Doctrine: Domestic Politics or National Decision?" *Diplomatic History*, 5 (1981), 53–70
Samuel Flagg Bemis, *John Quincy Adams and the Foundations of American Foreign Policy* (1949)

George Dangerfield, *The Awakening of American Nationalism, 1815–1828* (1965)
————, *The Era of Good Feelings* (1952)
Lester D. Langley, *Struggle for the American Mediterranean* (1976)
J. A. Logan, *No Transfer* (1961)
Ernest R. May, *The Making of the Monroe Doctrine* (1975)
Bradford Perkins, *Castlereagh and Adams* (1964)
Dexter Perkins, *A History of the Monroe Doctrine* (1955)
Armin Rappaport, ed., *The Monroe Doctrine* (1964)
J. Fred Rippy, *Rivalry of the United States and Great Britain over Latin America, 1808–1830* (1929)
E. H. Tatum, Jr., *The United States and Europe, 1815–1823* (1926)
A. P. Whitaker, *The United States and the Independence of Latin America, 1800–1830* (1941)

# Westward Expansion
# and Indian Removal

# 7

Americans have often spoken of their impressive movement westward in the nineteenth century as if they were inexorably moving into empty lands. Of course, the rich territory along the frontier was inhabited by aborigines or Native Americans—Indians. The story of expansion is thus also the story of Indian removal, sometimes by white man's disease, sometimes by wars and massacres, and sometimes by treaties, honored and unhonored. Whites wanted Indian lands for their own, and they got them. In the process, whites defined Indians as inferiors, dehumanizing them and demanding their submission to a superior civilization. Indian ways seemed strange: their property was held communally, not privately; their economies were oriented to subsistence rather than profit; their non-Christian religions were "heathen," too resistant to the missionary's call for conversion. Although there was great diversity among the many tribes of North America, white Americans lumped them together as uncivilized "savages" with painted faces and feathered bonnets or as children needing a firm fatherly hand. They overlooked Indian achievements in social and political organization, farming, hunting, and transportation. The interaction between whites and reds changed the latter more than the former. Some Americans worked to assimilate the Indian into white culture, but on the western frontier extermination and segregation became the practice.

After the 1780s, federal policy treated each tribe as a sovereign entity capable of signing treaties with the United States. Although federal officials dealt with the tribes as separate nations, they assumed at the same time that the Indians ultimately would be "Americanized." But as American pioneers relentlessly pushed westward into the trans-Appalachian territory, they clashed with Native American populations that held treaty-guaranteed lands. Moreover, in the War of 1812, Indians in the Northwest led by the Shawnee chieftain Tecumseh joined British soldiers to battle American forces. The Indians were defeated, and their European ally—Britain—retired. Soon they were punished for their resistance to white advancement: the federal government ordered them moved to the trans-Mississippi West. In the 1820s, the Kickapoos, Sacs, Foxes, Chippewas, Sioux, Potawatomis, Winnebagos, and others reluctantly trekked to lands beyond the Mississippi River. The tribes of the Southwest—Cherokees, Choctaws, Creeks, Seminoles, and Chickasaws—also met white pressure; they fell victim especially to President Andrew Jackson's demand that they remove themselves from the Southern states. He engineered the Indian Removal Act of 1830. West of Iowa, Missouri, and Arkansas, an Indian Territory was set aside for the many tribes.

The Cherokees resisted, going to court to overturn Georgia laws that restricted their freedoms on tribal lands. The Supreme Court claimed that it did not have constitutional jurisdiction, but in an 1832 ruling it stated that the Cherokees were immune from Georgia state laws. Jackson then refused to enforce the court's decision and warned the Indians to leave for the Indian Territory. Some Cherokees departed, but others desperately held on. In 1838, under the guns of federal troops and Georgia state militia, the Cherokee Trail of Tears began. Hundreds died en route, never to reach the Indian Territory. American expansionists had advanced the American frontier by destroying a people. Why and how this tragedy occurred is the subject of this chapter.

## DOCUMENTS

Historians agree that the Removal Act of May 28, 1830, doomed Indians to the dictates of whites, despite the legislation's language suggesting a fair "exchange" of lands. The second document is President Andrew Jackson's First Annual Message to Congress of December 8, 1830, in which he argued that "benevolent" removal served all parties. On February 14, 1831, Congressman Edward Everett of Massachusetts delivered an impassioned speech against the cruelties and dishonor of broken treaties and removal. The Supreme Court's ruling in *Cherokee Nation* v. *the State of Georgia* (1831) addressed the question of whether tribes could be treated as "foreign nations." Counting them as wards of federal authority, the justices nonetheless ruled that the Cherokees would have to redress their wrongs somewhere else. The last document constitutes the surrender speech of Black Hawk, the leader of Sac and Fox Indians. In mid-1832, Black Hawk and his debilitated followers were captured in Wisconsin by white militiamen. His words in defeat bespoke the Indian experience.

## The Removal Act, 1830

*An Act to provide for an exchange of lands with the Indians residing in any of the states or territories, and for their removal west of the river Mississippi.*
*Be it enacted by the Senate and House of Representatives of the United*

*States of America, in Congress assembled,* That it shall and may be lawful for the President of the United States to cause so much of any territory belonging to the United States, west of the river Mississippi, not included in any state or organized territory, and to which the Indian title has been extinguished, as he may judge necessary, to be divided into a suitable number of districts, for the reception of such tribes or nations of Indians as may choose to exchange the lands where they now reside, and remove there; and to cause each of said districts to be so described by natural or artificial marks, as to be easily distinguished from every other.

*And be it further enacted,* That it shall and may be lawful for the President to exchange any or all of such districts, so to be laid off and described, with any tribe or nation of Indians now residing within the limits of any of the states or territories, and with which the United States have existing treaties, for the whole or any part or portion of the territory claimed and occupied by such tribe or nation, within the bounds of any one or more of the states or territories, where the land claimed and occupied by the Indians, is owned by the United States, or the United States are bound to the state within which it lies to extinguish the Indian claim thereto.

*And be it further enacted,* That in the making of any such exchange or exchanges, it shall and may be lawful for the President solemnly to assure the tribe or nation with which the exchange is made, that the United States will forever secure and guaranty to them, and their heirs or successors, the country so exchanged with them; and if they prefer it, that the United States will cause a patent or grant to be made and executed to them for the same: *Provided always,* That such lands shall revert to the United States, if the Indians become extinct, or abandon the same.

*And be it further enacted,* That if, upon any of the lands now occupied by the Indians, and to be exchanged for, there should be such improvements as add value to the land claimed by any individual or individuals of such tribes or nations, it shall and may be lawful for the President to cause such value to be ascertained by appraisement or otherwise, and to cause such ascertained value to be paid to the person or persons rightfully claiming such improvements. And upon the payment of such valuation, the improvements so valued and paid for, shall pass to the United States, and possession shall not afterwards be permitted to any of the same tribe.

*And be it further enacted,* That upon the making of any such exchange as is contemplated by this act, it shall and may be lawful for the President to cause such aid and assistance to be furnished to the emigrants as may be necessary and proper to enable them to remove to, and settle in, the country for which they may have exchanged; and also, to give them such aid and assistance as may be necessary for their support and subsistence for the first year after their removal.

*And be it further enacted,* That it shall and may be lawful for the President to cause such tribe or nation to be protected, at their new residence, against all interruption or disturbance from any other tribe or nation of Indians, or from any other person or persons whatever.

*And be it further enacted,* That it shall and may be lawful for the President to have the same superintendence and care over any tribe or nation in the country to which they may remove, as contemplated by this act, that he is now authorized to have over them at their present places of residence: *Provided,* That nothing in this act contained shall be construed as authorizing or directing the violation of any existing treaty between the United States and any of the Indian tribes.

*And be it further enacted,* That for the purpose of giving effect to the provisions of this act, the sum of five hundred thousand dollars is hereby appropriated, to be paid out of any money in the treasury, not otherwise appropriated.

## Andrew Jackson's Case for Removal, 1830

It gives me pleasure to announce to Congress that the benevolent policy of the Government, steadily pursued for nearly thirty years, in relation to the removal of the Indians beyond the white settlements is approaching to a happy consummation. Two important tribes have accepted the provision made for their removal at the last session of Congress, and it is believed that their example will induce the remaining tribes also to seek the same obvious advantages.

The consequences of a speedy removal will be important to the United States, to individual States, and to the Indians themselves. The pecuniary advantages which it promises to the Government are the least of its recommendations. It puts an end to all possible danger of collision between the authorities of the General and State Governments on account of the Indians. It will place a dense and civilized population in large tracts of country now occupied by a few savage hunters. By opening the whole territory between Tennessee on the north and Louisiana on the south to the settlement of the whites it will incalculably strengthen the southwestern frontier and render the adjacent States strong enough to repel future invasions without remote aid. It will relieve the whole State of Mississippi and the western part of Alabama of Indian occupancy, and enable those States to advance rapidly in population, wealth, and power. It will separate the Indians from immediate contact with settlements of whites; free them from the power of the States; enable them to pursue happiness in their own way and under their own rude institutions; will retard the progress of decay, which is lessening their numbers, and perhaps cause them gradually, under the protection of the Government and through the influence of good counsels, to cast off their savage habits and become an interesting, civilized, and Christian community. These consequences, some of them so certain and the rest so probable, make the complete execution of the plan sanctioned by Congress at their last session an object of much solicitude.

Toward the aborigines of the country no one can indulge a more friendly feeling than myself, or would go further in attempting to reclaim them from their wandering habits and make them a happy, prosperous people. I have endeavored to impress upon them my own solemn convictions of the duties and powers of the General Government in relation to the State authorities. For the justice of the laws passed by the States within the scope of their reserved powers they are not responsible to this Government. As individuals we may entertain and express our opinions of their acts, but as a Government we have as little right to control them as we have to prescribe laws for other nations.

With a full understanding of the subject, the Choctaw and the Chickasaw tribes have with great unanimity determined to avail themselves of the liberal offers presented by the act of Congress, and have agreed to remove beyond the Mississippi River. Treaties have been made with them, which in due season will be submitted for consideration. In negotiating these treaties they were made to understand their true condition, and they have preferred maintaining their independence in the Western forests to submitting to the laws of the States in which they now reside. These treaties, being probably the last which will ever be made with them, are characterized by great liberality on the part of the Government. They give the Indians a liberal sum in consideration of their removal, and comfortable subsistence on their arrival at their new homes. If it be their real interest to maintain a separate existence, they will there be at liberty to do so without the inconveniences and vexations to which they would unavoidably have been subject in Alabama and Mississippi.

Humanity has often wept over the fate of the aborigines of this country, and Philanthropy has been long busily employed in devising means to avert it, but its progress has never for a moment been arrested, and one by one have many powerful tribes disappeared from the earth. To follow to the tomb the last of his race and to tread on the graves of extinct nations excite melancholy reflections. But true philanthropy reconciles the mind to these vicissitudes as it does to the extinction of one generation to make room for another. In the monuments and fortresses of an unknown people, spread over the extensive regions of the West, we behold the memorials of a once powerful race, which was exterminated or has disappeared to make room for the existing savage tribes. Nor is there anything in this which, upon a comprehensive view of the general interests of the human race, is to be regretted. Philanthropy could not wish to see this continent restored to the conditions in which it was found by our forefathers. What good man would prefer a country covered with forests and ranged by a few thousand savages to our extensive Republic, studded with cities, towns, and prosperous farms, embellished with all the improvements which art can devise or industry execute, occupied by more than 12,000,000 happy people, and filled with all the blessings of liberty, civilization, and religion?

The present policy of the Government is but a continuation of the same progressive change by a milder process. The tribes which occupied the countries now constituting the Eastern States were annihilated or have melted away to make room for the whites. The waves of population and civilization are rolling to the westward, and we now propose to acquire the countries occupied by the red men of the South and West by a fair exchange, and, at the expense of the United States, to send them to a land where their existence may be prolonged and perhaps made perpetual. Doubtless it will be painful to leave the graves of their fathers; but what do they more than our ancestors did or than our children are now doing? To better their condition in an unknown land our forefathers left all that was dear in earthly objects. Our children by thousands yearly leave the land of their birth to seek new homes in distant regions. Does Humanity weep at these painful separations from everything, animate and inanimate, with which the young heart has become entwined? Far from it. It is rather a source of joy that our country affords scope where our young population may range unconstrained in body or in mind, developing the power and faculties of man in their highest perfection. These remove hundreds and almost thousands of miles at their own expense, purchase the lands they occupy, and support themselves at their new homes from the moment of their arrival. Can it be cruel in this Government when, by events which it can not control, the Indian is made discontented in his ancient home to purchase his lands, to give him a new and extensive territory, to pay the expense of his removal, and support him a year in his new abode? How many thousands of our own people would gladly embrace the opportunity of removing to the West on such conditions! If the offers made to the Indians were extended to them, they would be hailed with gratitude and joy.

And is it supposed that the wandering savage has a stronger attachment to his home than the settled, civilized Christian? Is it more afflicting to him to leave the graves of his fathers than it is to our brothers and children? Rightly considered, the policy of the General Government toward the red man is not only liberal, but generous. He is unwilling to submit to the laws of the States and mingle with their population. To save him from this alternative, or perhaps utter annihilation, the General Government kindly offers him a new home, and proposes to pay the whole expense of his removal and settlement....

May we not hope, therefore, that all good citizens, and none more zealously than those who think the Indians oppressed by subjection to the laws of the States, will unite in attempting to open the eyes of those children of the forest to their true condition, and by a speedy removal to relieve them from all the evils, real or imaginary, present or prospective, with which they may be supposed to be threatened.

## Congressman Edward Everett's Protest, 1831

I cannot disguise my impression, that it is the greatest question which ever came before Congress, short of the question of peace and war. It concerns not an individual, [but] entire communities of men, whose fate is wholly in our hands, and concerns them—not to the extent of affecting their interests, more or less favorably, within narrow limits. As I regard it, it is a question of inflicting the pains of banishment from their native land on seventy or eighty thousand human beings, the greater part of whom are fixed and attached to their homes in the same way that we are. We have lately seen this House in attendance, week after week, at the bar of the other House, while engaged in solemn trial of one of our own functionaries, for having issued an order to deprive a citizen of his liberty for twenty-four hours. It is a most extraordinary and astonishing fact, that the policy of the United States toward the Indians—a policy coeval with the revolution, and sanctioned in the most solemn manner [on] innumerable occasions—is undergoing a radical change, which, I am persuaded, will prove as destructive to the welfare and lives of its subjects, as it will to their rights; and that neither this House, nor the other House, has ever, even by resolution, passed directly upon the question.

But it is not merely a question of the welfare of these dependent beings, nor yet of the honor and faith of the country which are pledged to them—it is a question of the Union itself. What is the Union? Not a mere abstraction; not a word; not a form of Government; it is the undisputed paramount operation, through all the States, of those functions with which the Government is clothed by the constitution. When that operation is resisted, the Union is in fact dissolved. I will not now dwell on this idea; but the recent transactions in Georgia have been already hailed in the neighboring British provinces as the commencement of that convulsion of these United States, to which the friends of liberty throughout the world look forward with apprehension, as a fatal blow to their cause. . . .

The Secretary of War tells us that a new era has within a few years arisen in relation to our Indian affairs. He does not indicate precisely what marks the new era; but, in one respect, there has unquestionably arisen a new era in this department, that of substituting Executive decision for congressional enactment. Formerly the Executive only carried into effect our laws and treaties made by the treaty-making branch of the Government. Now the President, 1st, permits the States to annul the treaties, and proceed on their declared want of validity, and, 2d, annuls the laws himself, and permits his Secretary to come down to Congress, with an argument to prove that a law substantially coeval with the Government is unconstitutional. I am willing to receive the Secretary's argument for what it is worth; but really, sir, I have studied the constitution unsuccessfully, if the mere opinion of a Secretary, with or without an argument, renders a law unconstitutional, and makes it cease to be obligatory. But to this I shall return, only repeating, now, that the assumption of these two principles in our Indian affairs does, indeed, constitute a new era. . . .

Sir, the Secretary says a new era has arisen in our Indian affairs. This is true. Up to the year 1828, the course of proceeding in our Indian affairs is well known, at least in reference to all the tribes whose rights are now in controversy. The United States had negotiated treaties with all the Southwestern tribes. Our relations with them, and the boundary between them and us, were regulated by treaty; and by the intercourse law framed in pursuance of the same policy. A limited and qualified sovereignty, sufficient to enable them to contract these treaty obligations, was conceded to the tribes. No State had pretended to extend her laws over either of these tribes till the year 1828. . . .

While the Secretary of War announces this new era, the President in his message at the opening of the session informed us, that "the benevolent policy of the Government, steadily pursued for nearly thirty years, in relation to the removal of the Indians beyond the white settlements, is approaching to a happy consummation." This statement appears to me at variance with that which was made in the annual message of the last year. In that document, we were told that "it has long been the policy of Government to introduce among Indians the arts of civilization, in the hope of gradually reclaiming them from a wandering state." This is certainly a benevolent policy: and this is the policy which has been steadily pursued for nearly thirty years. But last year, the President added:

> This policy has, however, been coupled with another, wholly incompatible with its success. Professing a desire to civilize and settle them, we have, at the same time, lost no opportunity to purchase their lands, and thrust them further into the wilderness. By this means, they have not only been kept in a wandering state, but have been led to look upon us as unjust and indifferent to their fate. Thus, though lavish in its expenditures on the subject, Government has constantly defeated its own policy.

Last year the benevolent policy of settling and civilizing them had been thwarted by another, that of removal to the West, declared to be incompatible with its success. This year the removal to the West is declared to be the benevolent policy which has been steadily pursued. In my judgment, the view taken in the message of last year is the sounder.

But the policy of removal has, I grant, been pursued steadily for thirty years, but never in the same manner as now. It was never thought of, that all the treaties and laws of the United States protecting the Indians could be annulled, and the laws of the States extended over them; laws of such a character that it is admitted, nay urged, that they cannot live under them. The policy of removal has been pursued by treaty, negotiated by persuasion, urgency, if gentlemen please, with importunity. But the compulsion of State legislation, and of the withdrawal of the protection of the United States, was never before heard of. . . .

Georgia led the way. In 1828, she passed a summary law, to take effect prospectively, extending her jurisdiction, civil and criminal, over the Indian tribes within her limits. In 1829, this law, with more specific provisions, was re-enacted, to take effect on the 1st day of June, 1830. This example of Georgia was imitated by Alabama and Mississippi. By these State laws, the organization previously existing in the Indian tribes was declared unlawful, and was annulled. It was made criminal to exercise any function of Government under authority derived from the tribes. The political existence of these communities was accordingly dissolved, and their members declared citizens or subjects of the States. What a contrast, in two or three years! In 1826, after many days' debate, the Legislature of Mississippi decided that it had no right to pass a law to pursue its own citizens, being fugitive debtors, into the Indian country. In 1829, the same State extends all its laws over the Choctaws, abrogates their Government, and denounces the punishment of imprisonment on any person who should exercise any office under the authority of the tribe.

The Indians, as was natural, looked to the Government of the United States for protection. It was the quarter whence they had a right to expect it—where, as I think, they ought to have found it. They asked to be protected in the rights and possessions guarantied to them by numerous treaties, and demanded the execution, in their favor, of the laws of the United States governing the intercourse of our citizens with the Indian tribes. They came first to the President, deeming, and rightly, that it was his duty to afford them this protection. They knew him to be the supreme executive officer of the Government; that, as such, he had but one constitutional duty to perform toward the treaties and laws—the duty of executing them. The President refused to afford the protection demanded. He informed them that he had no power, in his view of the rights of the States, to prevent their extending their laws over the Indians; and the Secretary of War, in one of his communications to them, adds the remark, that the President had as little inclination as power to do so. . . .

Here, at the centre of the nation, beneath the portals of the capitol, let us solemnly auspicate the new era of violated promises, and tarnished faith. Let us kindle a grand council-fire, not of treaties made and ratified, but of treaties annulled and broken. Let us send to our archives for the worthless parchments, and burn them in the face of day. There will be some yearnings of humanity as we perform the solemn act. They were negotiated for valuable considerations; we keep the consideration, and break the bond. One gave peace to our afflicted frontier; another protected our infant settlements. Many were made when we were weak; nearly all at our earnest request. Many of them were negotiated under the instructions of Washington, of Adams, and of Jefferson—the fathers of our liberty. They are gone, and will not witness the spectacle; but our present Chief Magistrate, as he lays them, one by one, on the fire, will see his own name subscribed to a goodly number of them.

## Cherokee Nation v. the State of Georgia, 1831

Mr. Chief Justice Marshall delivered the opinion of the Court:

This bill is brought by the Cherokee nation, praying an injunction to restrain the state of Georgia from the execution of certain laws of that state, which, as is alleged, go directly to annihilate the Cherokees as a political society, and to seize, for the use of Georgia, the lands of the nation which have been assured to them by the United States in solemn treaties repeatedly made and still in force.

If courts were permitted to indulge their sympathies, a case better calculated to excite them can scarcely be imagined. A people once numerous, powerful, and truly independent, found by our ancestors in the quiet and uncontrolled possession of an ample domain, gradually sinking beneath our superior policy, our arts and our arms, have yielded their lands by successive treaties, each of which contains a solemn guarantee of the residue, until they retain no more of their formerly extensive territory than is deemed necessary to their comfortable subsistence. To preserve this remnant, the present application is made.

Before we can look into the merits of the case, a preliminary inquiry presents itself. Has this court jurisdiction of the cause?

The third article of the constitution describes the extent of the judicial power. The second section closes an enumeration of the cases to which it is extended, with "controversies" "between a state or the citizens thereof, and foreign states, citizens, or subjects." A subsequent clause of the same section gives the supreme court original jurisdiction in all cases in which a state shall be a party. The party defendant may then unquestionably be sued in this court. May the plaintiff sue in it? Is the Cherokee nation a foreign state in the sense in which that term is used in the constitution?

The counsel for the plaintiffs have maintained the affirmative of this proposition with great earnestness and ability. So much of the argument as was intended to prove the character of the Cherokees as a state, as a distinct political society, separated from others, capable of managing its own affairs and governing itself, has, in the opinion of a majority of the judges, been completely successful. They have been uniformly treated as a state from the settlement of our country. The numerous treaties made with them by the United States recognize them as a people capable of maintaining the relations of peace and war, of being responsible in their political character for any violation of their engagements, or for any aggression committed on the citizens of the United States by any individual of their community. Laws have been enacted in the spirit of these treaties. The acts of our government plainly recognize the Cherokee nation as a state, and the courts are bound by those acts.

A question of much more difficulty remains. Do the Cherokee constitute a foreign state in the sense of the constitution?

The counsel have shown conclusively that they are not a state of the union, and have insisted that individually they are aliens, not owing allegiance to the United States. An aggregate of aliens composing a state must, they say, be a foreign state. Each individual being foreign, the whole must be foreign.

This argument is imposing, but we must examine it more closely before we yield to it. The condition of the Indians in relation to the United States is perhaps unlike that of any other two people in existence. In the general, nations not owing a common allegiance are foreign to each other. The term foreign nation is, with strict propriety, applicable by either to the other. But the relation of the Indians to the United States is marked by peculiar and cardinal distinctions which exist no where else.

The Indian territory is admitted to compose a part of the United States. In all our maps, geographical treaties, histories, and laws, it is so considered. In all our intercourse with foreign nations, in our commercial regulations, in any attempt at intercourse between Indians and foreign nations, they are considered as within the jurisdictional limits of the United States, subject to many of those restraints which are imposed upon our own citizens. They acknowledge themselves in their treaties to be under the protection of the United States; they admit that the United States shall have the sole and exclusive right of regulating the trade with them, and managing all their affairs as they think proper; and the Cherokees in particular were allowed by the treaty of Hopewell, which preceded the constitution, "to send a deputy of their choice, whenever they think fit, to congress." Treaties were made with some tribes by the state of New York, under a then unsettled construction of the confederation, by which they ceded all their lands to that state, taking back a limited grant to themselves, in which they admit their dependence.

Though the Indians are acknowledged to have an unquestionable, and, heretofore, unquestioned right to the lands they occupy, until that right shall be extinguished by a voluntary cession to our government; yet it may well be doubted whether those tribes which reside within the acknowledged boundaries of the United States can, with strict accuracy, be denominated foreign nations. They may, more correctly be denominated domestic dependent nations. They occupy a territory to which we assert a title independent of their will, which must take effect in point of possession when their right of possession ceases. Meanwhile, they are in a state of pupilage. Their relation to the United States resembles that of a ward to his guardian.

They look to our government for protection; rely upon its kindness and its power; appeal to it for relief to their wants; and address the president as their great father. They and their country are considered by foreign nations, as well as by ourselves, as being so completely under the sovereignty and dominion of the United States, that any attempt to acquire their lands, or to form a political connexion with them, would be considered by all as an invasion of our territory, and an act of hostility.

These considerations go far to support the opinion, that the framers of our constitution had not the Indian tribes in view, when they opened the courts of the union to controversies between a state or the citizens thereof, and foreign states.

In considering this subject, the habits and usages of the Indians, in their intercourse with their white neighbours, ought not to be entirely disregarded. At the time the constitution was framed, the idea of appealing to an American court of justice for an assertion of right or a redress of wrong, had perhaps never entered the mind of an Indian or of his tribe. Their appeal was to the tomahawk, or to the government. This was well understood by the statesmen who framed the constitution of the United States, and might furnish some reason for omitting to enumerate them among the parties who might sue in the courts of the union. Be this as it may, the peculiar relations between the United States and the Indians occupying our territory are such, that we should feel much difficulty in considering them as designated by the term foreign state, were there no other part of the constitution which might shed light on the meaning of these words. But we think that in construing them, considerable aid is furnished by that clause in the eighth section of the third article; which empowers congress to "regulate commerce with foreign nations, and among the several states, and with the Indian tribes."

In this clause they are as clearly contradistinguished by a name appropriate to themselves, from foreign nations, as from the several states composing the union. They are designated by a distinct appellation; and as this appellation can be applied to neither of the others, neither can the appellation distinguishing either of the others be in fair construction applied to them. The objects, to which the power of regulating commerce might be directed, are divided into three distinct classes—foreign nations, the several states, and Indian tribes. When forming this article, the convention considered them as entirely distinct. We cannot assume that the distinction was lost in framing a subsequent article, unless there be something in its language to authorize the assumption.

The counsel for the plaintiffs contend that the words "Indian tribes" were introduced into the article, empowering congress to regulate commerce, for the purpose of removing those doubts in which the management of Indian affairs was involved by the language of the ninth article of the confederation. Intending to give the whole power of managing those affairs to the government about to be instituted, the convention conferred it explicitly; and omitted those qualifications which embarrassed the exercise of it as granted in the confederation. This may be admitted without weakening the construction which has been intimated. Had the Indian tribes been foreign nations, in the view of the convention; this exclusive power of regulating intercourse with them might have been, and most probably would have been, specifically given, in language indicating that idea, not in language contradistinguishing them from foreign nations. Congress might have been empowered "to regulate commerce with foreign nations, including the Indian tribes, and among the several states." This language would have suggested itself to statesmen who considered the Indian tribes as foreign nations, and were yet desirous of mentioning them particularly.

It has been also said, that the same words have not necessarily the same meaning attached to them when found in different parts of the same instrument: their meaning is controlled by the context. This is undoubtedly true. In common language the same word has various meanings, and the peculiar sense in which it is used in any sentence is to be determined by the context. This may not be equally true with respect to proper names. Foreign nations is a general term, the application of which to Indian tribes, when used in the American constitution, is at best extremely questionable. In one article in which a power is given to be exercised in regard to foreign nations generally, and to the Indian tribes particularly, they are mentioned as separate in terms clearly contradistinguishing from each other. We perceive plainly that the constitution in this article does not comprehend Indian tribes in the general term "foreign nations," not we presume because a tribe may not be a nation, but because it is not foreign to the United States. When, afterwards, the term "foreign state" is introduced, we cannot impute to the convention the intention to desert its former meaning, and to comprehend Indian tribes within it, unless the context force that construction on us. We find nothing in the context, and nothing in the subject of the article, which leads to it.

The court has bestowed its best attention on this question, and, after mature deliberation, the majority is of opinion that an Indian tribe or nation within the United States is not a foreign state in the sense of the constitution, and cannot maintain an action in the courts of the United States.

A serious additional objection exists to the jurisdiction of the court. Is the matter of the bill the proper subject for judicial inquiry and decision? It seeks to restrain a state from the forcible exercise of legislative power over a neighbouring people asserting their independence; their right to which the state denies. On several of the matters alleged in the bill, for example on the laws making it criminal to exercise the usual powers of self-government in their own country by the Cherokee nation, this court cannot interpose; at least in the form in which those matters are presented.

That part of the bill which respects the land occupied by the Indians, and prays the aid of the court to protect their possession, may be more doubtful. The mere question of right might perhaps be decided by this court in a proper case with proper parties. But the court is asked to do more than decide on the title. The bill requires us to control the legislature of Georgia, and to restrain the exertion of its physical force. The propriety of such an interposition by the court may be well questioned. It savours too much of the exercise of political power to be within the proper province of the judicial department. But the opinion on the point respecting parties makes it unnecessary to decide this question.

If it be true that the Cherokee nation have rights, this is not the tribunal in which those rights are to be asserted. If it be true that wrongs have been inflicted, and that still greater are to be apprehended, this is not the tribunal which can redress the past or prevent the future.

The motion for an injunction is denied.

## Black Hawk's Surrender Speech, 1832

You have taken me prisoner with all my warriors. I am much grieved, for I expected, if I did not defeat you, to hold out much longer, and give you more trouble before I surrendered. I tried hard to bring you into ambush, but your last general understands Indian fighting. The first one was not so wise. When I saw that I could not beat you by Indian fighting, I determined to rush on you, and fight you face to face. I fought hard. But your guns were well aimed. The bullets flew like birds in the air, and whizzed by our ears like the wind through the trees in the winter. My warriors fell around me; it began to look dismal. I saw my evil day at hand. The sun rose dim on us in the morning, and at night it sunk in a dark cloud, and looked like a ball of fire. That was the last sun that shone on Black Hawk. His heart is dead, and no longer beats quick in his bosom. He is now a prisoner to the white men; they will do with him as they wish. But he can stand torture, and is not afraid of death. He is no coward. Black Hawk is an Indian.

He has done nothing for which an Indian ought to be ashamed. He has fought for his countrymen, the squaws and papooses, against white men, who came, year after year, to cheat them and take away their lands. You know the cause of our making war. It is known to all white men. They ought to be ashamed of it. The white men despise the Indians, and drive them from their homes. But the Indians are not deceitful. The white men speak bad of the Indian, and look at him spitefully. But the Indian does not tell lies; Indians do not steal.

An Indian who is as bad as the white men, could not live in our nation; he would be put to death, and eat [sic] up by the wolves. The white men are bad school-masters; they carry false looks, and deal in false actions; they smile in the face of the poor Indian to cheat him; they shake them by the hand to gain their confidence, to make them drunk, to deceive them, and ruin our wives. We told them to let us alone; but they followed on and beset our paths, and they coiled themselves among us like the snake. They poisoned us by their touch. We were not safe. We lived in danger. We were becoming like them, hypocrites and liars, adulterers, lazy drones, all talkers, and no workers.

We looked up to the Great Spirit. We went to our great father. We were encouraged. His great council gave us fair words and big promises, but we got no satisfaction. Things were growing worse. There were no deer in the forest. The oppossum and beaver were fled; the springs were drying up, and our squaws and papooses without victuals to keep them from starving; we called a great council and built a large fire. The spirit of our fathers arose and spoke to us to avenge our wrongs or die. . . . We set up the war-whoop, and dug up the tomahawk; our knives were ready, and the heart of Black Hawk swelled high in his bosom when he led his warriors to battle. He is satisfied. He will go to the world of spirits contented. He has done his duty. His father will meet him there, and commend him.

Black Hawk is a true Indian, and disdains to cry like a woman. He feels for his wife, his children and friends. But he does not care for himself. He cares for his nation and the Indians. They will suffer. He laments their fate. The white men do not scalp the head; but they do worse—they poison the heart, it is not pure with them. His countrymen will not be scalped, but they will, in a few years, become like the white men, so that you can't trust them, and there must be, as in the white settlements, nearly as many officers as men, to take care of them and keep them in order.

Farewell, my nation. Black Hawk tried to save you, and avenge your wrongs. He drank the blood of some of the whites. He has been taken prisoner, and his plans are stopped. He can do no more. He is near his end. His sun is setting, and he will rise no more. Farewell to Black Hawk.

---

## ESSAYS

In the first essay, Robert F. Berkhofer, Jr., of the University of Michigan explains the ideological and economic importance of land to white Americans and traces federal policy toward Native Americans. He analyzes the white American justification for "expansion with honor," the contradictions of that policy that led to imperial conquest, and the notions of individualism and tribalism that clashed— all at the expense of the Indian. Robert V. Remini of the University of Illinois, Chicago Circle, a chronicler of Andrew Jackson's life, concentrates on the President's reasons for urging removal. He stresses the inevitability of removal because of white advance, but also places the issue in the context of American security and politics. That is, Jackson, a man of the frontier himself, worried about military security; and as an advocate of states' rights, the President felt compelled to restrain federal authority when it conflicted with state preferences. Like most historians, Remini is critical of American mistreatment of the Indians, but he defends the President by arguing that an anguished Jackson, locked in dilemma, did not intend their destruction.

---

# The White Advance Upon Native Lands

### ROBERT F. BERKHOFER, JR.

Given the perspective of the time, land played an important role in the preservation as well as the fulfillment of what had been achieved in America. To leading Americans of the Revolutionary generation, agriculture was the preferred (as well as the predominant) means of existence for the vast majority of the population, because it provided the best economic foundation for the political and social arrangements considered ideal in the new nation. If a citizen was economically independent, he would be politically autonomous in their opinion. Under republican ideals of the period, property was connected with life and liberty because its ownership was the surest guarantee of those other inalienable rights. To perpetuate the social hierarchy leading Americans deemed desirable to preserve public virtue as well as to provide the stake in society thought necessary for responsible decision making, republican constitutions restricted the franchise to property holders.

Widespread ownership of property was also believed to afford the basis for the social equality believed so prevalent at the time. Americans as well as Europeans thought the vast majority of (White) inhabitants of the United States belonged to the middle ranks of society, neither rich nor poor but a "happy mediocrity" as they said, due to the extensive property ownership in the new nation. This combination of substantial land ownership and new political system made for the historical uniqueness of America in the eyes of Ezra Stiles, president of Yale. In his sermon of 1783, "The United States Elevated to Glory and Honor," he observed, "But a Democratical polity for millions, standing upon a broad basis of the people at large, amply charged with property, has not hitherto been exhibited." From our vantage point, only the existence of cheap, readily available land for the general populace allowed the reconciliation of the general equality of condition with equality of opportunity. Without cheap lands and access to them, the paradox, or even conflict, of these two sides of American political and economic liberalism would have become apparent. If republican institutions and social structure constituted the ideal America in the opinion of the era's leaders and its people, then the future of that America depended upon the continued availability of cheap lands as the population increased.

Thus geography took on a moral as well as an economic dimension under the ideology of Americanism that had direct implications for Native American occupancy. First, to preserve the American political and social system, certain ways of using the land were preferred to others, and the idea of the Indian and his way opposed these modes. According to the imagery, Indians were hunters and Americans were farmers or at least industrious in other ways in transforming nature into property. As John Quincy Adams queried in 1802 in words that were to haunt him decades later during the removal debate: "What is the right of a huntsman to the forest of a thousand miles over which he has accidentally ranged in quest of prey? . . . Shall the fields and vallies, which a beneficent God has formed to teem with the life of innumerable multitudes, be condemned to everlasting barrenness?" The deficient Indian, as usual in this doctrine of uses, possessed more land than he could utilize in approved fashion. Second, American ways of life were fated to expand within the boundaries of the United States and even beyond in accord with the ideas of progress and destiny.

If national destiny at this time was not as manifest as it would become when premised upon assumptions of evolutionism and racism in the second third of the nineteenth century, its course and implications were evident enough to Jedidiah Morse in his *American Geography* of 1789. He discussed whether American citizens venturing beyond the Mississippi River, which was the western boundary of the United States under the peace treaty of 1783, would be lost to the nation's commerce and to Americanism as they came under Spanish rule. After some practical arguments upon the matter, he ended with a peroration premised upon an ideal of America that expressed clearly what United States expansion meant in terms of who would use the land and how they would use it:

> Besides, it is well known that empire has been traveling from east to west. Probably her last and broadest seat will be America. Here the sciences and the arts of civilized life are to receive their highest improvement. Here civil

and religious liberty are to flourish, unchecked by the cruel hand of civil or ecclesiastical tyranny. Here Genius, aided by all the improvements of former ages, is to be exerted in humanizing mankind—in expanding and inriching their minds with religious and philosophical knowledge, and in planning and executing a form of government, which shall involve all the excellencies of former governments, with as few of their defects as is consistent with the imperfection of human affairs, and which shall be calculated to protect and unite, in a manner consistent with the natural rights of mankind, the largest empire that ever existed. Elevated with these prospects, which are not merely the visions of fancy, we cannot but anticipate the period, as not far distant, when the AMERICAN EMPIRE will comprehend millions of souls, west of the Mississippi. Judging upon probable grounds, the Mississippi was never designed as the western boundary of the American empire. The God of nature never intended that some of the best part of this earth should be inhabited by the subjects of a monarch, 4000 miles from them. And may we not venture to predict, that, when the rights of mankind shall be more fully known, and the knowledge of them is fast increasing both in Europe and America, the power of European potentates will be confined to Europe, and their present American dominions, become, like the United States, free, sovereign and independent empires.

In not discussing the effects this "empire for liberty," to use Jefferson's phrase, would have for Native American occupancy, Morse presumed that the natural increase of the White American population, the intentions of Providence, and the spirit of progress all would overwhelm the Indian like the Spaniard. For him, as for so many other leading intellectuals and politicians in the new United States, American nationality, defined as allegiance to American ideals and institutions, excluded the "foreigner" and the Indian as aliens. As a result many wished to deny asylum to immigrants presumed still loyal to foreign, i.e., un-American, values and institutions, and they thought the Indian should and would inevitably be replaced by proper Americans upon the lands Native Americans inhabited as the United States fulfilled its destiny.

Under these impressions of the future of the American empire, what would and could United States policy makers do for the Indian in accord with both the ideals of the new nation and the necessities of the situation? Indians constituted but one part of the problem of the West the Continental Congress inherited from England. In a diplomatic coup, the United States negotiators obtained an area, ranging from the Appalachian settlements of the Americans to the shores of the Mississippi River, that the new national government could not control so long as the English retained forts and soldiers within its boundaries and the Native Americans who dwelt there opposed occupation. So the West and the Indians posed both a military and diplomatic problem for the American leaders. Since many of the original states claimed lands within this trans-Appalachian region according to their colonial charter boundaries, their leaders challenged the right of the Continental Congress to set policy for the region and therefore made Indian policy another matter of conflict between the states and the central government.

Even if these states ceded their claims in this region to the central government, Congress faced the additional problems of, first, how to settle this area while raising desperately needed revenue for the empty Confederation treasury and, secondly, how to govern this huge area so far removed from the original states. Would a strong military force be necessary in the West to preserve law and order among the settlers and to keep peace between them and the Indians? Such a solution, however, violated republican prejudices against a standing army inherited from the conflict with England's troops of occupation before the Revolution. All these problems appeared connected in the minds of the new nation's policy makers, and so Indian policy influenced the solutions to the others and vice versa.

In efforts to resolve some of these problems, the Continental Congress bequeathed to posterity a new kind of colonial and land system in line with both the ideals of the era and the necessities of the moment. Congress laid the foundations for the American public land system in the Ordinance of 1785. After survey according to the now familiar rectangular coordinates, the national public domain was to be sold to individuals in fee simple, the most liberal land tenure of the time, without any further quitrents as had been collected by the crown and proprietors in the colonial period. This method of land disposal sought to settle the huge Western regions in an orderly fashion with industrious republican farmers at the same time that the sales raised revenue for the depleted central treasury.

The Continental Congress created a new kind of colonial system with the Northwest Ordinance of 1787, which set up territorial government for those who settled the West. What had once been proposed as colonies under the crown now were to become new states under the ordinance after spending some period as territories under control of Congress. To allow for the independent spirit of the settlers fostered by the distant trans-Appalachian environment, this system provided for the addition of new states equal to the old in the Confederation. Since the frontier produced lawlessness and civic irresponsibility as well in the eyes of good republicans, the period spent as a territory would teach lessons in public virtue under the tutelage of Congress. After recapitulating in brief the history of the original states, these territories were to become their coequals in the Confederation. And so the American empire was to expand according to a novel colonial system, which came to, be called "territorial" to distinguish it from the old imperial type. Both of these important ordinances presumed the solution of the Indian and other problems of the West, because they provided for the settlement and goverance of Americans on lands still under native occupancy at the time.

What Indian policy was depended upon who managed it. As part of the centralization of imperial administration before the Revolution, English officials had sought to remove the control of Indian trade and policy and the purchase of native lands from the hands of colonial legislatures. In a series of proclamations and instructions to colonial governors and through treaty negotiations by their agents, English home officials had defined and bounded for the first time an Indian country in which colonial settlement was prohibited and the sole right of land purchase reserved to the crown. With the appointment of officials responsible to London to grease the wheels of Indian diplomacy, the English officials also had hoped to restrict the trade malpractices that irked the Indians as much as the advances of White settlers upon their lands. The colonists had objected to these efforts to restrict their expansion and their profits from speculation and trade. Once the colonists had declared their independence, they watched warily any attempt to re-create such central authority over their affairs. States with claims to trans-Appalachian lands opposed giving too much power over Indian affairs to the Continental Congress in the Articles of Confederation. After the war, New York challenged the authority of Congress to negotiate a peace treaty with the Iroquois, over whom it claimed jurisdiction, and the Southern states opposed congressional authority over Indian tribes within or near their borders.

Perhaps because of such controversial implications, the federal Constitution barely mentions the Indian. Although the founding fathers meant to strengthen the central government at the expense of the states, the only power expressly granted Congress under the Constitution to control Indian policy is the brief mention in the commerce clause: "to regulate Commerce with Foreign Nations, and among the several States, and with Indian Tribes." Whether the authority to manage Indian affairs in general derived from that specific clause or the power to make treaties or to promote the general welfare, the new federal government acted as if it possessed such authority in full. State leaders questioned the federal government's right to set policy at times as it applied to tribes in which they asserted particular interest. Differ as the two sides might over the ultimate authority over Indian affairs, both state and federal officials assumed that the United States as a nation possessed full sovereignty according to international law over its territory, regardless of whether they actually had military control over the region between actual White settlement and the boundaries of the nation upon the Mississippi.

Both of the men who laid down the principles of the new nation's Indian policy, George Washington as the first President under the federal Constitution and his Secretary of War, Henry Knox, looked beyond the immediate hostilities inherited from the Confederacy with the trans-Appalachian tribes to a permanent solution to Indian affairs. In summarizing the lessons of the Confederation experience for long-range policy, Knox ruled out destruction of the Indians in favor of conciliation. To defeat let alone wipe out the Indians with the small military forces at the command of the United States had proved impossible and, besides, would cost the poverty-stricken republic too much money. Moreover, Knox reasoned such a policy was as unnecessary as it was inconsistent with the new nation's honor in light of the natives' future. The importance of the image of the Indian in coming to these conclusions can be seen from his actual argument:

> When it shall be considered that the Indians derive their subsistence chiefly by hunting, and that, according to fixed principles, their population is in pro-

portion to the facility with which they procure their food, it would most probably be found that the expulsion or destruction of the Indian tribes have nearly the same effect: for if they are removed from the usual hunting grounds, they must necessarily encroach on the hunting grounds of another tribe, who will not suffer the encroachment with impunity—hence they destroy each other.

In formulating the principles proper for an enlightened federal policy, Knox assumed that White advance upon native lands was as unpreventable as it was inevitable, but it should be restrained and regulated in the interests of keeping peace with the Indians. Given the republican image of frontier inhabitants and the lessons of previous experience, illegal White intrusion upon native territory had to be curbed in the short run in order to achieve relatively peaceful, and therefore cheap, expansion in the long run.

To conciliate and attach the Indians to the United States as opposed to England or Spain required the recognition of native occupancy rights and their transfer through purchase, for the attempt by the Continental Congress to gain cessions through mere expropriation in the treaties after the Revolution had failed in practice. In arguing this point, Knox suggested why Indian affairs ought to be considered the province of the new federal government rather than of the states. Careful reading of his actual words indicates that his argument for Indian sovereignty aimed to restrict state authority in favor of federal control, not to declare that tribal governments possessed sovereignty vis-à-vis the United States as such:

> It would reflect honor on the new Government, and be attended with happy effects, were a declarative law to be passed, that the Indian tribes possess the right of the soil of all lands within their limits, respectively, and that they are not to be divested thereof, but in consequence of fair and bona fide purchases, made under the authority, or with the express approbation, of the United States.
>
> As the great source of all Indian wars are disputes about their boundaries, and as the United States are, from the nature of the government, liable to be involved in every war that shall happen on this or any other account, it is highly proper that their authority and consent should be considered as essentially necessary to all measures for the consequences of which they are responsible.
>
> No individual State could, with propriety, complain of invasion of its territorial rights. The independent nations and tribes of Indians ought to be considered as foreign nations, not as the subjects of any particular State. Each individual State, indeed, will retain the right of pre-emption of all lands within its limits, which will not be abridged; but the general sovereignty must possess the right of making all treaties, on the execution or violation of which depend peace or war.

So the ascendancy of the federal government over the states through the treaty power of the Constitution as well as the honor of the nation prompted an enlightened policy based upon principles consistent with the ideals of the new republic.

Expansion could be achieved with honor if the United States offered American civilization in return for native lands. This policy would redound to the future reputation of the nation at the same time that it contributed to the acquisition of native lands according to Knox's image of the Indian, for the advance of White civilization brought the inevitable demise of the Indian. Federal policy could only hope to mitigate this decline. . . .

If assumptions of progress and environmentalism offered hope of "civilizing" the Indian, the image of the "dying Indian" and progress made such a hope a close contest with native disappearance through laws seemingly as inevitable in their operation as those that pushed the frontier people westward. Regardless of the outcome of the program, Knox recognized that the certain demise of the Indian in a relatively short time would make the price of their lands a bargain while the effort to do them some good according to White definition made the policy honorable in the view of posterity. Thus were national interests reconciled with national ideals in a federal Indian policy that can be called, for short, expansion with honor. . . .

In line with these larger policy considerations, Congress enacted a series of laws "to regulate trade and intercourse with Indian tribes, and to preserve peace on the frontiers," as the first summary codification of 1802 phrased the intent. Designed at first to supplement and to uphold the treaty obligations of the United States with various Indian tribes, these laws came more and more to embody the legal framework of federal Indian policy. Thus, from the initial laws licensing traders, prohibiting private purchase of Indian lands, and punishing murder and other crimes committed by Whites on native lands, Congress increasingly tried to control both sides of Indian-White relations. It went on to regulate, and even conduct from 1796 to 1822, trade with Indians. It at first restricted, then prohibited liquor in the Indian country in 1832 and provided more generally for the punishment of crimes in Indian country and native crimes committed outside that area. After 1819 Congress began to finance the education and "civilization" of Indians. By defining and bounding an "Indian country," regulating trade, and reserving to the federal government the preemption, or exclusive right, to purchase land, Congress adopted the program England had attempted before the Revolution. By continuing the negotiation of treaties for the establishment of peace and for the purchase of lands, Congress continued colonial and Confederation policy. In any case, peace and expansion with honor depended upon the federal government's ability to implement these laws and treaties as much as on the correctness of Knox's and other White leaders' assumptions about the nature of Indian life. . . .

Enforcement of the trade and intercourse acts as well as the maintenance of peace in the Indian country depended upon the power of the army. Indian superintendents and agents had to call upon the military establishments in their area to remove Whites who intruded upon native lands or to apprehend Whites who murdered or stole from Indians on those lands. But Congress denied the army the right of summary punishment so many officers thought desirable in favor of civilian courts. Although both the Indian office and the army were branches of the same executive department, the military commandants resented orders from civilians, whether they came from Washington, the territorial governor, or the agents. In many cases, the officers thought that another Indian policy should have been pursued rather than the official one from Washington, and these men believed, moreover, that Indian policy on the frontier should be under military control. Civil-military conflict over Indian policy and its control lasted throughout the nineteenth century.

If maintenance of peaceful Indian relations hinged upon the power of the army, then Congress frustrated this end in the pursuit of other goals. As a result of their pre-Revolutionary experience, Americans distrusted a standing army in times of peace as dangerous to their civil liberties and freedom. This attitude plus the tendency of Congress to economize on the appropriations for the military kept the army small in size and inadequate to frontier needs. In fact, Congress only supported an army in "peace time"—a phrase that discounted battles with Native Americans as mere police actions and not full-fledged wars with foreign powers—as a result of Indian hostilities. Congress, at the same time, funded too few troops to be effective in preventing White depredations against Native Americans or in maintaining peaceful relations with and among tribes. A cordon of forts followed the frontier westward in the nineteenth century, but neither Red nor White peoples could count upon the army to preserve peace and expansion with honor.

For the apprehension and prosecution of White and Indian crimes committed outside the Indian country, the agents had to rely upon the local law-enforcement agencies and judicial systems. Besides being inadequate to the task, local agencies and courts refused frequently to find White criminals guilty when committing crimes against Indians. Superintendents and agents in the field reported numerous times that White murderers and thieves went scot-free after the clearest evidence of their guilt, to the great disgust of Native Americans. On the other hand, the local militia rushed out all too often to punish Indians presumed to be murderers and thieves and, in their trigger-happy haste, killed innocent as well as guilty Indians. As the actions of the local militia and the decisions of local juries suggest, frontier state and territorial citizens often opposed federal policy. These people saw little reason not to violate Indian country or to kill Native Americans at will, justifying their actions by summoning up the image of the Indian as horrible savage. In this way they were as bloodthirsty and as lawless as the image republican leaders held of the frontier inhabitant. On the other hand, frontier Americans justified their actions ultimately upon the same grounds as the federal policy: the laws of nature and nations and the principle of higher uses. As the governor of frontier Tennessee argued in 1798: "By the law of nations, it is agreed that no people shall be entitled to more land than they can cultivate. Of course no people will sit and starve for want of land to work, when a neighbouring nation has much more than they can make use of."

The territorial system, in fact, by continually creating new territories that would eventually become states in the union, only added new voices in Congress for native land cessions and war. It thereby counteracted the whole policy of peaceful relations with Indians at low cost and expansion with honor. Thus the oft-quoted third article of the Northwest Ordinance, which was readopted by the first federal Congress, expresses an ideal made less attainable by the very territorial system the law created:

> The utmost good faith shall always be observed towards the Indians; their lands and property shall never be taken from them without their consent; and in their property, rights and liberty, they never shall be invaded or disturbed, unless in just and lawful wars authorized by Congress; but laws founded in justice and humanity shall from time to time be made, for preventing wrongs being done to them, and for preserving peace and friendship with them.

Given the sensitivity of Congress to special interests, nineteenth-century committees on Indian Affairs in the two houses soon contained members and even chairmen from frontier states and, in the House of Representatives, delegates from territories. The constant addition of new states to the Union and their representatives in Congress meant that, as the older frontier became the East and new areas became the West, the traditional East-West conflict over Indian policy continued throughout the nineteenth century. That conflict concerned not so much the ultimate ends of Indian policy as the speed and method of its execution. Citizens of both the older and newer areas of the country agreed on the desirability of White expansion upon native lands, for both held the same basic image of the Indian, and on the desirability and, indeed, inevitability of progressive American individuals and institutions replacing the Indian tribes and their ways upon native lands. What separated Eastern and Western leaders in Washington and in home capitals were the issues of how fast and by what means such supersession should take place. Both sides envisaged national interests in the long run in the same way but differed over their accomplishment in the short run. They also differed about the desirability as well as possibility of achieving expansion with honor if this end had to wait for the "civilization" of the Indians. Frontier people doubted whether Indians were capable of such a drastic transformation. The ambivalence of legislative policy produced by this dual vision found its counterpart in the dilemma of the territorial governor who, according to his instructions, must civilize and protect the Indians from White intrusion but also must gain new cessions as quickly as possible to extend White settlements.

To transform the Indian into a White-approved model citizen was an integral part of the expansion-with-honor program from the beginning, but the means to its accomplishment barely existed until after the War of 1812. Most of the monies appropriated for Indian affairs by Congress in the first three decades paid agents in the field and bought presents for chiefs. The agents and factory traders supposedly exemplified civilized life for Indian imitation, and some chiefs' gifts and annuity monies went for White agricultural implements. Some treaties in this early period provided blacksmiths for certain tribes, and the Indian office funded a few persons to teach farming to native men and spinning and weaving to native women. Before the War of 1812, few missionaries served among the Indians. Only after that war did national missionary societies arise with sufficient treasuries to support extensive establishments and numerous missionaries among the tribes.

Congress, beginning in 1819, appropriated ten thousand dollars annually "for the purpose of providing against the further decline and final extinction of the Indian tribes adjoining the frontier settlements of the United States, and for introducing among them the habits and arts of civilization," but only after arguing about the possibility of ever achieving such an unlikely goal. Thomas McKenney, who headed Indian Affairs in the War Department at that time, used the money to subsidize missionary societies in the establishment of schools and the instruction of Indians in agriculture and domestic arts. Soon afterward, newly negotiated treaties contained articles appropriating tribunal annuities to the same agencies for the same purposes.

The close relationship between state and church in this endeavor was mutually advantageous to both parties: the missionary societies received some money to support the secular side of their stations and the federal government obtained civilization agents at low cost. Given the lack of occupational specialization, government policy makers had to support missionaries in these tasks until after the Civil War if the Indians were to be acculturated at all by anyone. Such an arrangement saved the government money, moreover, through sharing costs. In this deal so dependent upon the realities of American society and economy at the time, the missionaries received some federal money and moral support, the Indians supposedly obtained "civilization," and the government leaders salved the American conscience while they hoped soon to acquire native lands no longer needed by their transformed inhabitants.

As the federal support of mission activities indicates, the separation of church and state in the United States was never meant by its proponents to eliminate the moral and spiritual foundations of American society. Government officials joined missionaries and their patrons in subscribing to the same basic version of Christian civilization to be promulgated among the Indians. Americanism rested upon a firm religious and moral groundwork in the opinion of all policy makers, and so naturally religion, preferably Protestantism, was presumed to be an inextricable part of the acculturation process for Indians. Whether missionaries favored civilizing or Christianizing their charges first, erecting small stations and day schools or building large manual labor boarding schools, they sought to re-form the Indian into a model American husband or wife, who farmed his private property, attended church faithfully, could read and write and keep accounts, and participated in government as an American citizen. Regardless of denomination, missionaries in the early period, placing their faith in millennial hopes and perhaps environmental theory, expected the rapid conversion of Indian tribes to White civilization and Christianity. Since the superiority of the American Way of Life appeared self-evident to them, they thought that Indians too would see it in their immediate self-interest to adopt the habits and beliefs of the (good) White American after a brief demonstration. . . .

Even as the immediate future revealed the gulf between these hopes and the actual accomplishment of missionaries, their societies and the government affirmed the possibility of Indian transformation and eventual acculturation and assimilation through the increasing support and staff thrown into the process. As Enlightenment belief in the rationality of all people and the environmental theory of human behavior and diversity gave way to romantic racism and democracy, missionary societies and governmental officials continued to urge civilizational transformation of the Indian as the last best hope of peaceful expansion with honor and the preservation of an otherwise doomed race. As one missionary to the Eastern Sioux exclaimed in 1846: "*As tribes and nations the Indians must perish and live only as men!* With this impression of the tendency of God's purposes as they are being developed year after year, I would labor to prepare them to fall in with *Christian Civilization* that is destined to cover the earth." Missionaries more than other persons tended to believe Christianity and civilization were in direct conflict with Indianness, but all White policy makers subscribed to this fusion of religion and lifestyle. For the missionaries the goal of Christian civilization justified their increasingly larger budgets and numbers. For government officials, Christian civilization increasingly became the only pacific method of dealing with the Indian problem in the nineteenth century. So an old policy inherited from colonial times continued to be espoused in the midst of changing intellectual currents and new social and economic institutions, in a United States whose territory as well as population were expanding. Only now larger sums of money, better organization, and more missionaries carried out the old aims with much the same results as before.

From even this brief survey of the formative period of United States Indian policy, the contradictions built into the system emerge clearly. Who should formulate and execute Indian policy? What should be its specific methods and who should carry them out? At what rate should land cession and White settlement proceed? Whose view of the Indian should prevail? These questions point to some of the consistent inconsistencies of United States Indian policy that prevailed throughout the nineteenth century and made honorable, peaceful, and inexpensive expansion difficult or impossible.

Less apparent but equally important were the contradictions at the very heart of the policy of expansion with honor. The preemption doctrine presumed that Indian tribes would be ready to sell whenever Whites were ready to buy. By making American expansion contingent upon Indian consent, government policy makers predicated a delicate balance of conditions and a certain set of assumptions about the Native American as Indian. First, the policy implied that Indians possessed more land than they could or would use and that the Indians would readily surrender those lands to Whites for relatively small amounts of money and gifts. The Indians would cede the lands wanted by Whites because they (1) could withdraw westward easily and resume their migratory ways, or (2) would die of disease or other natural causes as White society approached, or (3) would become "civilized" and thus disappear as Indians. Since all Indians were presumed alike, policy makers thought that a tribe could easily roam westward before the White advance and continue their hunting without difficulty upon the large amounts of land underutilized in the same manner by other tribes. When Congress, for example, first bounded the Indian country in 1796, only an eastern line of separation was stipulated, apparently under this assumption. If most members of a tribe died off as usually happened when White civilization approached, then surely the remainder needed less territory than the whole tribe originally claimed. If the Indians switched from hunting to farming, the policy makers supposed they would use the soil more intensively than previously and thus be able to surrender the large amount of surplus land. For this reason, White policy makers viewed civilization transformation useful to expansion as well as good for the Indian per se. All in all, the basic policy of expansion with honor rested upon the assumption that Indians would not cede more lands than their changing status encouraged or required them to, and that Whites would not ask for more land than the orderly advance of the frontier necessitated or stimulated them to require. The policy, moreover, optimistically presumed that cessions could be obtained from the various tribes before White expansion overwhelmed them, and that presupposed in turn a relatively slow speed of White settlement advance westward.

Under such a policy, whatever was good for the White American was assumed good for the Native American also, even if the Indians had to be manipulated against their own inclinations for the larger good as the Whites saw it. How much cajolery, disingenuousness, bribery, or even coercion this justified remained a matter of practice, of the means available, and of White morality. The last persons presumed to know their own larger interests were the Indians, and policy makers therefore assumed a stewardship over native interests in the American scheme of things. Whether ethnocentrism, racism, high idealism, or sheer self-interest prompted such stewardship made little difference to Native Americans as they felt its effects.

On the other hand, what was good for the Indian under the expansion-with-honor policy was not necessarily good for White society, given the paradoxical assumptions of Americanism. How would and should Indians be accepted into American society as a whole? Would and should they be assimilated as individuals or as whole tribes? Would and should White Americans welcome them as full-fledged citizens? Would they allow their children to marry Indians? To raise these problems of social incorporation, cultural assimilation, and marital amalgamation points beyond the inconsistencies of Indian policy to the great consistencies among nineteenth-century American values and institutional arrangements. . . .

The changing intellectual currents of the nineteenth century made the Indian and the American more antithetic than ever in theory if not in actual practice. As the ideal of democracy replaced republicanism, old words took on new meaning and new words came into use to characterize newer concepts basic to Americanism. Foremost among these semantic shifts was the word *democracy* itself, which was lifted out of its narrow and often disparaging political context in the days of the early nation and broadened to embrace that peculiar fusion of social equality and political freedom that

Americans believed they lived. Whether grounded on the romantic absolutes of the decades before the Civil War or the naturalism of the late nineteenth century, American democracy designated a belief in the goodness of majority rule, a minimal government supposedly beneficial to all alike, and free enterprise—in short, the classic liberalism of the age.

America became the symbol to Europeans as well as to its own citizens of what the future of liberal democracy would be in the world, as Alexis de Tocqueville expounded it in his famous analysis of the United States in the 1830s. To describe the effects of American liberalism on the inhabitants of the United States, Tocqueville employed the word *individualism,* and the word was introduced into the English language through the translation of his *Democracy in America.* Americans had long prided themselves upon their individualism without having a word for it, but in the decades before the Civil War romantic connotations of dynamism and potentiality infused new meaning into the concept of the free individual, different from what the republican founding fathers understood or meant. Now individuals needed more than uncoerced options to have freedom; they also had to have the opportunity to develop their natural talents to the fullest in order to realize their inner potential. Only a liberal government beneficial to all in theory and an untrammeled economy offered equal opportunity to every American, and conversely all good Americans ought to take advantage of their opportunities because they supposedly could. With the artificial barriers of class privilege presumably removed under the new regime, the self-made person became the ideal American. Therefore, if every American did not become a success it was his own fault. If Black slavery violated more than ever an individual's freedom under these democratic and romantic assumptions of human potentiality, so too White failure to achieve material success indicated a defect in personality or ambition. Liberal institutions supposedly offered the chance and individualism afforded the motive under this theory. Freedom of opportunity under liberalism had as its goal the freedom to become unequal in wealth and position, all in the name of equal rights.

Democracy, liberalism, and individualism possessed important implications for understanding frontiersmen and Indians. The frontier acquired greater symbolic importance than ever as the place offering upward social mobility through the acquisition of property and the exploitation of resources at low cost. Moreover, the White frontier population gained new respectability under the assumptions of democracy and racism. From the lawless image of republican days, they personified increasingly as the century passed the self-help and self-reliance considered so desirable in a good American. By the end of the century they represented, to historian Frederick Jackson Turner, the people who had made American history American.

With the rise of racism, whether based upon romantic principles or upon "scientific" research, Americans became ever more aware of the biological basis of their ideal society. Measured by their ideal of individualism and the liberalism of American institutions, they found other nationalities deficient in or opposed to American values and customs. Apprehensive about the impact of foreign immigration upon American society, leading politicians and intellectuals more and more linked Americanism to Anglo-Saxonism, especially in images of Manifest Destiny. The laws of progress and the biology of racism combined with the self-image of Americanism to justify continental expansion of the truly American populace against Indians within the enlarging boundaries of the United States and against Mexicans and others to enlarge those boundaries. . . .

The emphasis on individualism and liberal institutions, moreover, placed Indian tribalism in direct opposition to Americanism even more under democracy than under republicanism. Indians must join American society as individuals in the liberal state and economy rather than as tribes. Cultural assimilation, likewise, must proceed according to the values of individualism and not those of tribalism. What the proper White individual should be and therefore what the proper Indian individual must be represented an absolute antithesis to how Americans assumed Indians lived as tribal members. By definition, the tribal Indian lacked the industry, the self-reliance, and the material desires and success appropriate to the good American. Throughout the nineteenth century, missionaries and philanthropists, government officials in Washington and on the frontier, military officers and Western settlers measured the tribal Indian by their standard of Americanism and found him wanting, according to the traditional deficiency image.

While American thought changed during the nineteenth century, so too did American social, political, and economic organization. Of these latter changes, three major developments affected the formulation and execution of Indian policy as much as, or more than, the altered intellectual climate. In the economy, the improved means of transportation not only speeded up settlement of the West but also integrated those who settled there into a national economic system at a faster pace. Better roads, the building of canals, and, most important of all, the expansion of railroads brought to the West at increasing rates Eastern and European farmers, merchants, speculators, and others seeking their fortune, and once there, these people could find ever bigger markets through the same transportation modes in the evolving industrial economy. In the political system, the development of permanent party organization made Indian policy a partisan issue like any other question before the politicians. Party voting, once thought disreputable in the republican era of the new nation, now became one of the foundation stones of a democracy based on majority rule. Partisan affiliation and individual conscience made strange alliances under the auspices of party brokerage in Congress and the executive. Accompanying the changing economy and politics was the third major development: the proliferation of voluntary associations devoted to philanthropy, religion, education, and reform. Not only did some leaders of these many organizations participate directly in either formulating or executing Indian policy, but they also through the mobilization of public opinion as represented by their members brought pressure to bear on the political process in that formulation. In turn, reform leaders' opinions and positions became just another aspect of partisanship under the political party system. . . .

Although Thomas Jefferson in 1803 originated the idea of exchanging lands west of the Mississippi River for Indian lands in the East, the policy of removal only developed as a "permanent" solution to the Indian problem in the 1820s during the administration of James Monroe. For Jefferson, removing the Indians into the newly acquired Louisiana Purchase was, like his plan for colonizing emancipated Blacks in Africa, a way of expelling from within the nation those influences he believed deleterious to the American spirit and the continued vitality of American institutions. For his fellow Virginian James Monroe, the Tennessean Andrew Jackson, and others in the period after the War of 1812, however, removal offered a solution to pressing practical problems, in addition to being the only method calculated in their opinion to preserve the Indian from total extinction. Citizens of states and territories with rapidly growing populations demanded further cession of native lands and preferably the expulsion of all Indians from within their borders. States and territories to the west of these states not only demanded the same policy but in addition did not want to be the homeland for Indian emigrants displaced from areas to the east.

Under these circumstances, only allotment in severalty [the division of tribal properties into individual holdings] and native assimilation in the places where Indians lived or removal to an area not desired by White settlers in the immediate future offered any hope for solving the twin problems of further land cessions for the frontier Whites and the preservation of the Indian from intrusion and decimation. Some of the treaties negotiated by Jackson and other United States commissioners after the War of 1812 contained provisions for the exchange of lands and financial aid to Indians in the move beyond the Mississippi. A few treaties with Southern tribes provided in addition for allotments of 640 acres in trust to those Indians who wished to remain in their native lands and become citizens.

Not until the end of his administration, however, did Monroe recommend to Congress the enactment of a law providing for the general removal of tribes east of the Mississippi. Although impelled by the urgent demand of Georgia for the United States government to fulfill its part of the compact of 1802 (in which the state surrendered its claim to western territory beyond its boundaries in return for the federal government's extinguishing the title to Indian lands within its borders), Monroe laid down principles upon which he thought the new policy could be achieved with honor to the United States and still promote the "welfare and happiness" of the Indians. Fearing their "degradation and extermination" if they remained in the East, Monroe proposed that removal might be made honorable to the United States and attractive to the Indians if Congress guaranteed the emigrant Indians a permanent title to their Western lands, organized some kind of government among the removed tribes to protect their territory from intrusion, preserved peace among the tribes native to the West and the emigrant tribes, and continued funding of civilization agents among them to prevent further "degeneracy."

Monroe thought such a program not only made removal practical but offered a positive boon to the Indians while it served the ideals and basic interests of the American people:

The digest of such a government, with the consent of the Indians, which should be endowed with sufficient power to meet all the objects contemplated—to connect the several tribes together in a bond of amity and preserve order in each; to prevent intrusions on their property; to teach them by regular instruction the arts of civilized life and make them a civilized people—is an object of very high importance. It is the powerful consideration which we have to offer to these tribes as an inducement to relinquish the lands on which they now reside and to remove to those which are designated. It is not doubted that this arrangement will present considerations of sufficient force to surmount all their prejudices in favor of the soil of their nativity, however strong they may be. Their elders have sufficient intelligence to discern the certain progress of events in the present train, and sufficient virtue, by yielding to momentary sacrifices, to protect their families and posterity from inevitable destruction. They will also perceive that they may thus attain an elevation to which as communities they could not otherwise aspire....

It may fairly be presumed that, through the agency of such a government, the condition of all the tribes inhabiting that vast region may be essentially improved; that permanent peace may be preserved with them, and our commerce be much extended.

So once again Indians were offered civilization for land as a boon supposedly to both parties, but now assimilation was to be achieved through segregation. Both the rationale and the basic principles of guaranteed land title, preservation of peace, organization of government, and the funding of civilization agents were embodied in the program proposed by Andrew Jackson after he entered the presidency.

## Andrew Jackson and Indian Removal

### ROBERT V. REMINI

It is an awesome contradiction that at the moment the United States was entering a new age of economic and social betterment for its citizens—the industrial revolution underway, democracy expanding, social and political reforms in progress—the Indians were driven from their homes and forced to seek refuge in remote areas west of the Mississippi River. Jackson, the supreme exponent of liberty in terms of preventing government intervention and intrusion, took it upon himself to expel the Indians from their ancient haunts and decree that they must reside outside the company of civilized white men. It was a depressing and terrible commentary on American life and institutions in the 1830s.

The policy of white Americans toward Indians was a shambles, right from the beginning. Sometimes the policy was benign—such as sharing educational advantages—but more often than not it was malevolent. Colonists

Abridgement of "Brothers, Listen ... You Must Submit" (Chap. 15) in *Andrew Jackson and the Course of American Freedom, 1822–1832,* Vol. II, by Robert V. Remini. Copyright © 1981 by Robert V. Remini. Reprinted by permission of Harper & Row, Publishers, Inc.

drove the Indians from their midst, stole their lands and, when necessary, murdered them. To the colonists, Indians were inferior and their culture a throwback to a darker age.

When independence was declared and a new government established committed to liberty and justice for all, the situation of the Indians within the continental limits of the United States contradicted the ennobling ideas of both the Declaration and the Constitution. Nevertheless, the Founding Fathers convinced themselves that men of reason, intelligence and good will could resolve the Indian problem. In their view the Indians were "noble savages," arrested in cultural development, but they would one day take their rightful place beside white society. Once they were "civilized" they would be absorbed.

President George Washington formulated a policy to encourage the "civilizing" process, and Jefferson continued it. They presumed that once the Indians adopted the practice of private property, built homes, farmed, educated their children, and embraced Christianity these Native Americans would win acceptance from white Americans. Both Presidents wished the Indians to become cultural white men. If they did not, said Jefferson, then they must be driven to the Rocky Mountains.

The policy of removal was first suggested by Jefferson as the alternative to the "civilizing" process, and as far as many Americans were concerned removal made more sense than any other proposal. Henry Clay, for example, insisted that it was impossible to civilize these "savages." They were, he argued, inferior to white men and "their disappearance from the human family would be no great loss to the world."

Despite Clay's racist notions—shared by many Americans—the government's efforts to convert the Indians into cultural white men made considerable progress in the 1820s. The Cherokees, in particular, showed notable technological and material advances as a result of increased contact with traders, government agents, and missionaries, along with the growth of a considerable population of mixed-bloods.

As the Indians continued to resist the efforts to get rid of them—the thought of abandoning the land on which their ancestors lived and died was especially painful for them—the states insisted on exercising jurisdiction over Indian lands within their boundaries. It soon became apparent that unless the federal government instituted a policy of removal it would have to do something about protecting the Indians against the incursions of the states. But the federal government was feckless. It did neither. Men like President John Quincy Adams felt that removal was probably the only policy to follow but he could not bring himself to implement it. Nor could he face down a state like Georgia. So he did nothing. Many men of good will simply turned their faces away. They, too, did nothing.

Not Jackson. He had no hesitation about taking action. And he believed that removal was indeed the only policy available if the Indians were to be protected from certain annihilation. His ideas about the Indians developed from his life on the frontier, his expansionist dreams, his commitment to states' rights, and his intense nationalism. He saw the nation as an indivisible unit whose strength and future were dependent on its ability to repel outside foes. He wanted all Americans from every state and territory to participate in his dream of empire, but they must acknowledge allegiance to a permanent and indissoluble bond under a federal system. Although devoted to states' rights and limited government in Washington, Jackson rejected any notion that jeopardized the safety of the United States. That included nullification and secession. That also included the Indians.

Jackson's nationalism, a partial product of his expansionist ideals, and his states' rights philosophy, a product of his concern for individual liberty, merged to produce his Indian policy.

He formally proposed removal to the Congress in his first message. The reaction startled him. It generated a storm of protest whose intensity and power caught him completely off guard. Directed by the American Board of Commissions for Foreign Affairs under the prodding of Jeremiah Evarts, this storm descended on both the Congress and the administration. It sent cries of outrage reverberating in the House and Senate. It gained strength by its religious fervor. How could supposedly decent and civilized men send helpless Indians to certain death in the wastelands beyond the Mississippi? How could they face themselves and their families knowing they had condemned innocents to torment and destruction?

The power and suddenness of this protesting storm delighted the National Republicans. At last they could identify with popular feeling. They immediately accused the administration of betraying the Indians and the many promises given them in the past. Their accusations produced instantaneous results. Petitions opposing removal flooded into Congress.

Under the direction of the President the Democratic leaders in both houses maneuvered to ram a removal bill through Congress. The matter was appropriately sent to the respective committees on Indian affairs in the House and Senate, both of which favored the measure. Jackson had personally arranged the membership of the House committee. In addition, two Tennesseans, John Bell and Hugh Lawson White, headed the committees. As added protection the administration looked to Speaker Andrew Stevenson to break any tie votes and, as it turned out, he was required to do so on three separate occasions to save the removal bill from defeat.

On February 22, 1830, the Senate committee reported the first bill, and two days later the House committee reported the second. As might be expected, given Jackson's interest, the two bills were remarkably alike. Fundamentally they recommended establishing an area west of the Mississippi to be divided into enough districts to accommodate as many tribes as might choose to go west, and removing them there. The scheme also involved an exchange of land for all the tribes residing in the east. Both bills triggered heated debate over the constitutional and moral implications of the exchange and eventually questioned the President's unwarranted extension of executive power.

The Senate bill touched off several wild exchanges when it came up for debate on April 6. Senator Theodore Frelinghuysen of New Jersey led the opposition forces and spoke for three days, for a minimum of two hours each day. A deeply religious man with a proven record of humanitarian concern for the Indians, he attacked what he called the hypocrisy of the Democrats. He insisted that the true purpose of the bill was the ultimate removal of all Indians—not just the southern tribes—or their complete abandonment to the tender mercies of state law and jurisdiction. The Indians had a right to refuse to surrender their lands, he said. To threaten or harass them only invited violence and bloodshed. He pronounced Georgia's dispute with the Cherokees a simple violation of Indian treaty rights. The United States was obligated to protect the civil and political rights of the Indians against all transgressors, including sovereign states.

In the course of his remarks Frelinghuysen noted the intrusion of the President himself in trying to resolve the problem. It was done, he asserted, "without the slightest consultation with either House of Congress, without any opportunity for counsel or concert, discussion or deliberation, on the part of the co-ordinate branches of the Government, to despatch the whole subject in a tone and style of decisive construction of our obligations and of Indian rights." For an administration that spoke so grandly about liberty and the abuse of power by the central government, this action against the Indians was hardly consistent. "We must," he thundered, "firmly protest against this Executive disposition of these high interests." Apart from that, he continued, the Indians themselves have known nothing but our cupidity and greed as we committed one crime after another against them. They listened to "our professions of friendship." We called them brothers and they believed us. They yielded millions of acres to our demands "and yet we crave more. We have crowded the tribes upon a few miserable acres of our Southern frontier: it is all that is left to them of their once boundless forests: and still, like the horse-leech, our insatiated cupidity cries, give! give! give!"

John Forsyth of Georgia responded with savage sectional rage. Frelinghuysen's "speech was plain enough," he said. "The Indians in New York, New England, Virginia etc etc are to be left to the tender mercies of those States, while the arm of the General Government is to be extended to protect the Choctaws, Chickasaws, Creeks and especially the Cherokees from the anticipated oppressions of Mississippi, Alabama and Georgia." What the north and east have already gotten away with is now to be denied the south. Robert Adams of Mississippi seconded Forsyth's argument. He insisted that everyone living within the boundaries of a particular state is subject to the laws of that state. Otherwise chaos reigns. Or has a new set of rights been discovered? In addition to federal and state rights we will now have "Indian rights." What folly! Peleg Sprague of Maine spoke against the bill and charged the Senate with its responsibility to carry out the treaties signed with the Indians. Protection had been "solemnly promised" and we can provide nothing less. Have we not done the Indians enough harm? he wearily asked. Have we not taken enough of their land?

Some Senators asked for an amendment that would guarantee proper negotiations with the Indians in providing for removal, but this was rejected. Frelinghuysen also proposed that removal be delayed until Congress could determine whether the western lands were adequate to the needs of the Indians. Again this was rejected. Finally on April 26, 1830, the bill came up for a final vote and passed by the count of 28 to 19 along fairly strict party lines.

In the House of Representatives both the bill and President Jackson took a worse pounding. Removal came close to defeat. The opposition never really expected to kill the measure in the Senate where the Democrats outnumbered and outmaneuvered them. What they hoped to do in the upper house was arouse public sympathy for the plight of the Indian and the terrible wrong removal involved. But in the House, the National Republicans looked for a triumph. The Democrats in the House were not as well disciplined as those in the Senate, and many of them feared reprisals from certain religious groups like the Quakers if they voted for the bill. Removal might remove *them* from office.

Serious debate on the bill began on May 15, when Henry R. Storrs of New York took dead aim on the White House and fired a powerful salvo. He accused Jackson of attempting to overthrow the constitutional securities of the states and their authority as well as assume the power of Congress to abrogate existing treaties in cases of necessity or war. The friends of states' rights who are such strong supporters of the administration ought to see this, he facetiously remarked. Already the President has given notice that his administration will be one of aggressive action by the central government to address problems and resolve them—with or without the co-operation of Congress. The "military chieftain" is about to demonstrate what his brand of leadership is like. "If these encroachments of the Executive Department," said Storrs, "are not met and repelled in these halls, they will be resisted nowhere. The only power which stands between the Executive and the States is Congress. The states may destroy the Union themselves by open force, but the concentration of power in the hands of the Executive leads to despotism, which is worse. Of the two evils, I should prefer the nullifying power in the States—it is less dangerous." . . .

The Indian Removal Act of 1830 authorized Jackson to carry out the policy outlined in his first message to Congress. He could exchange unorganized public land in the trans-Mississippi west for Indian land in the east. Those Indians who moved would be given perpetual title to their new land as well as compensation for improvements on their old. The cost of their removal would be absorbed by the federal government. They would also be given assistance for their "support and subsistence" for the first year after removal. An appropriation of $500,000 was authorized to carry out these provisions.

This monumental piece of legislation spelled the doom of the American Indian. It was harsh, arrogant, racist—and inevitable. It was too late to acknowledge any rights for the Indians. As Frelinghuysen remarked, all the white man had ever said to the Indian from the moment they first came into contact was "give!" Once stripped of his possessions the Indian was virtually abandoned.

Of the many significant predictions and warnings voiced during the debates in Congress that eventually came true, two deserve particular attention. One of them made a mockery of Jackson's concern for freedom. The President insisted that the Indians would not be forced to remove. If they wished to reside within the state they might do so but only on condition that they understood they would be subject to state law. He would never force them to remove, never compel them to surrender their lands. That high and noble sentiment as interpreted by land-greedy state officials meant absolutely nothing. Fraud and deception also accompanied the exchange of land. Jackson himself tried desperately to discourage corruption among the government agents chosen to arrange the removal, but the events as they actually transpired ran totally opposite to what he expected and promised.

The other prediction that mocked Jackson's commitment to economy was the cost of the operation. In the completed legislation the Congress had appropriated $500,000 but the actual cost of removal is incalculable. For one thing the process extended over many years and involved many tribes. Naturally some Indians resisted Jackson's will and the government was required to apply force. The resulting bloodshed and killing and the cost of these Indian wars cannot be quantified. For a political party that prized economy above almost everything else the policy of Indian removal was a radical departure from principle. Still many Democrats argued that the actual cost was a small price to pay for the enormous expanse of land that was added to the American empire. In Jackson's eight years in office seventy-odd treaties were signed and ratified, which added 100 million acres of Indian land to the public domain at a cost of roughly $68 million and 32 million acres of land west of the Mississippi River. The expense was enormous, but so was the land-grab.

Andrew Jackson has been saddled with a considerable portion of the blame for this monstrous deed. He makes an easy mark. But the criticism is unfair if it distorts the role he actually played. His objective was not the destruction of Indian life and culture. Quite the contrary. He believed that removal was the Indian's only salvation against certain extinction. Nor did he despoil Indians. He struggled to prevent fraud and corruption, and he promised there would be no coercion in winning Indian approval of his plan for removal. Yet he himself practiced a subtle kind of coercion. He told the tribes he would abandon them to the mercy of the states if they did not agree to migrate west.

The Indian problem posed a terrible dilemma and Jackson had little to gain by attempting to resolve it. He could have imitated his predecessors and done nothing. But that was not Andrew Jackson. He felt he had a duty. And when removal was accomplished he felt he had done the American people a great service. He felt he had followed the "dictates of humanity" and saved the Indians from certain death.

Not that the President was motivated by concern for the Indians—their language or customs, their culture, or anything else. Andrew Jackson was motivated principally by two considerations: first, his concern for the military safety of the United States, which dictated that Indians must not occupy areas that might jeopardize the defense of this nation; and second, his commitment to the principle that all persons residing within states are subject to the jurisdiction and laws of those states. Under no circumstances did Indian tribes constitute sovereign entities when they occupied territory within existing state boundaries. The quickest way to undermine the security of the Union, he argued, was to jeopardize the sovereignty of the states by recognizing Indian tribes as a third sovereignty.

But there was a clear inconsistency—if not a contradiction—in this argument. If the tribes were not sovereign why bother to sign treaties (requiring Senate approval) for their land? Actually Jackson appreciated the inconsistency, and it bothered him. He never really approved of bargaining or negotiating with tribes. He felt that Congress should simply determine what needed to be done and then instruct the Indians to conform to it. Congress can "occupy and possess" any part of Indian territory, he once said, "whenever the safety, interest or defence of the country" dictated. But as President, Jackson could not simply set aside the practice and tradition of generations because of a presumed contradiction. So he negotiated and signed treaties with dozens of tribes, at the same time denying that they enjoyed sovereign rights.

The reaction of the American people to Jackson's removal policy was predictable. Some were outraged, particularly the Quakers and other religious groups. Many seemed uncomfortable about it but agreed that it had to be done. Probably a larger number of Americans favored removal and applauded the President's action in settling the Indian problem once and for all. In short, there was no public outcry against it. In fact it was hardly noticed. The horror of removal with its "Trail of Tears" came much later and after Jackson had left office. . . .

Jackson expected to meet with the Indian chiefs of the Chickasaw and Choctaw nations in Franklin [Tennessee] around the middle of August [1830]. He communicated with various government agents to the tribes and instructed them to use their influence with the Indians to encourage their chiefs to come to Franklin and meet with him and Eaton and Coffee. "I beg of you to say to them," he wrote to one such agent, "that their *interest happiness* peace and prosperity depend upon their removal beyond the jurisdiction of the laws of the State of Mississippi." Congress had provided the "liberal appropriations" whereby they might remove "comfortably" and with a minimum of difficulty. "It was a measure I had much at heart and sought to effect because I was satisfied that the Indians could not possibly live under the laws of the States. . . . I feel conscious of having done my duty to my red children."

The President assumed that the Chickasaws would arrive on the nineteenth and the Choctaws on the twenty-fifth. The Chickasaws did appear on schedule, but the Choctaws chose to remain away. The Choctaw chiefs knew that in a face-to-face confrontation, Jackson would force them to give up their country, and they also knew that their people would kill them if they did so.

On August 23 the President met at the Presbyterian church with the Chickasaw delegation. Twenty-one chiefs and their agent, Colonel Benjamin Reynolds, assembled before their "Father." After a brief and formal welcoming ceremony the President gave the Indians one of his celebrated "talks."

"Friends and brothers," he began, "Your Great father is rejoiced once again to meet and shake you by the hand, and to have it in his power to assure you of his continued friendship and good will. He can cherish none but the best feelings for his red children, many of whom, during our late war, fought with him in defence of our country." He went on to tell them that Congress had given him power to extend justice to the Indians, to grant them lands in the west, to pay the expenses for removal, and to support them for a year. This was the reason he had asked them to come to Franklin and meet him in council, "to point you to a course which cannot fail to make you a happy and prosperous people. Hear and deliberate well," he said, "and under the exercise of your own reason and matured judgment, determine what may appear to you to be done for the benefit of yourselves and your children."

This "talk," which was published in all the newspapers, was intended to reach beyond the Indians to the American people so that they might better understand his purposes. Therefore Jackson chose his words very carefully. He wanted nothing in the text to appear threatening. No coercion or sign of force must be intimated. Yet the coercion was there.

> Brothers:—You have long dwelt upon the soil you occupy.... Now your white brothers are around you. States have been created within your ancient limits, which claim a right to govern and control your people as they do their own citizens, and to make them answerable to their civil and criminal codes. Your great father has not the authority to prevent this state of things.

Were they ready to submit to the laws of Mississippi if they chose to stay? for this they must in fact do.

> Brothers, listen:—To these laws, where you are, you must submit;—there is no preventive—no other alternative. Your great father cannot, nor can congress, prevent it. The states only can. What then? Do you believe that you can live under these laws? That you can surrender all your ancient habits, and the forms by which you have been so long controlled? If so, your great father has nothing to say or to advise.... His earnest desire is, that you may be perpetuated and preserved as a nation; and this he believes can only be done and secured by your consent to remove to a country beyond the Mississippi.... Where you are, it is not possible you can live contented and happy.

The "great father" promised that no force would be used to compel them to consent to removal. The decision was theirs alone. He said he understood fully their feeling about leaving the land of their birth. He knew how painful it would be to bid goodbye forever to the graves of their ancestors. But survival necessitated this move. Annihilation was the alternative.

"Old men!" he called, addressing the ancient chiefs. "Arouse to energy and lead your children to a land of promise and of peace before the Great Spirit shall call you to die." Then turning to the younger warriors, the President renewed his plea. "Young chiefs! Forget the prejudices you feel for the soil of your birth, and go to a land where you can preserve your people as a nation." It was a powerful appeal. It deeply affected the Indians.

The "great father" closed with a warning, thinly disguised: "Reject the opportunity which is now offered to obtain comfortable homes, and the time may soon pass away when such advantages as are now within your reach may again be presented." If you reject this opportunity, "call not upon your great father hereafter to relieve you of your troubles. . . ." If you choose to stay be advised that you are subject to state laws and state regulations. In a few years, he further warned, "by becoming amalgamated with the whites, your national character will be lost . . . you must disappear and be forgotten."

The Indians cried out their dismay when they heard these crushing words. The President paused to let his words sink in. After a moment he began again. This calamity can be avoided, he concluded. If you are willing to remove, say so and state your terms, and my friends Major Eaton and General Coffee, who are authorized to talk to you, will "act candidly, fairly and liberally towards you."

Thus spake the "great father." After hearing him out the Chickasaws withdrew to council among themselves. His words left them shaken and morose. They needed time to talk out their concerns and fears. They needed time for reflection. Four days later they returned with their answer. They met the President, Eaton, and Coffee at the Masonic Hall. The President seated himself in the center of a square formed by the chiefs. One of the chiefs, the secretary of the delegation, approached Eaton with a sheet of paper in his hand. The chief extended his free, right hand which Eaton took and shook. Then the Major was asked to read the paper to the President. He took the sheet, turned to his superior and began:

Franklin, August 27, 1830

*To our great father the president.* Your red children, the chiefs and head men of the Chickasaws, have had under consideration the talk of our father. . . . On the decision we this day make and declare to you and the world, depends our fate as a nation and as a people.

Father, you say that you have travelled a long way to talk to your red children. We have listened—and your words have sunk deep into our hearts. As you are about to set out for Washington city—before we shake our father's hand, perhaps with many of us for the last time—we have requested this meeting to tell you, that after sleeping upon the talk you sent us, and the talk delivered to us by our brothers, major Eaton and gen. Coffee, we are now ready to enter into any treaty based upon the principles communicated to us by major Eaton and gen. Coffee. Your friends and brothers.

(Signed etc.)

The "great father" smiled with satisfaction. He told the chiefs how much they had gladdened his heart and how good it was to have this "talk" with them. Many of the chiefs, he said, had known him a long time, a friendship that would never be interrupted. He would remember them always. He hoped —and as he spoke the next words his voice choked with emotion—the "Great Spirit above would take care of, bless, and preserve them." Jackson was so moved by the sight of these "gentle children" that he rose from his chair and bade them all an affectionate farewell. The Chickasaws were deeply touched by this unexpected and genuine show of emotion. Suddenly, one of the principal chiefs rushed forward and grasped the President with both hands. "God bless you, my great father," he exclaimed. Then, overcome by the intensity of his feeling, the chief turned away. The President and all the other chiefs stood perfectly still, too affected to say or do anything.

The emotional level of the scene reached an excruciating pitch. The father casting out his children. Each knew his role and what was happening. The Chickasaws loved their father as dutiful children, and yet he was saying goodbye to them forever. He was, said one reporter, "by them so much beloved," still he was telling them they must leave "the land of their youth, where the bones of their fathers reposed." They were all choked dumb by their feelings.

The President could not remain to negotiate the final terms of the treaty with the Chickasaw Nation. He had already stayed eight days with the Indians and it was time for him to return to Washington. Eaton and Coffee had excellent credentials; they enjoyed the President's total trust and the Chickasaws had agreed to negotiate with them. On August 31, 1830, they signed a treaty with the Indians embracing the main principles contained in the President's "talk." The Chickasaws agreed to give up their land, "cross the Mississippi," and find a new home in the west.

Jackson saw this victory as something won against the machinations of dark and hidden forces. The "opposition" had schemed to keep the southern tribes from meeting him in order to create havoc and discord. At least the Chickasaws had responded and yielded to his entreaties. This encouraging beginning, he felt, would draw other treaties after it. "Thus far we have succeeded, against the most corrupt and secrete combination that ever did exist," he snorted, "and we have preserved my Chickasaw friends and red brethren." Unfortunately, for a number of technical reasons, the Senate later refused to ratify this initial treaty and it was renegotiated by Coffee and signed on October 30, 1832.

As for the other southern tribes, Jackson predicted a less happy future. The Cherokees and Creeks had opted to sue in the courts and had placed themselves in the hands of William Wirt, the former United States Attorney General. The Creeks added insult to their other outrages by informing their "great father" that they would not meet him in Franklin. "We have answered," the President growled, "that we leave them to themselves, and to the protection of their friend Mr. Wirt . . . to whom they have given a large fee to protect them in their rights as an independent Nation; and when they find that they cannot live under the laws of Alabama, they must find, at their own expence . . . a country, and a home." As for Wirt, "he had been truly wicked" and will surely bring about "the distruction of the poor ignorant Indians." If only these meddlers would keep out of it and leave Indian removal to him. "I have exonerated the national character," intoned the great father, "and now leave the poor deluded Creeks and Cherokees to their fate, and their anihilation, which their wicked advisers has induced."

The Choctaws also rejected Jackson's invitation at first. They had been expected on August 25 but Greenwood LeFlore, a mixed-blood leader of the tribe, informed Eaton that his warriors were fiercely opposed to attending a convention at Franklin. The "lives of the chiefs and head men of the nation," he wrote, "would be in great danger if they propose of selling the country." Not that they rejected a discussion outright. LeFlore assured the "great father" that the Choctaws would listen most carefully to whatever he chose to tell them. "We wish our father the President would send us a talk by some good men, who will give us time to call a full council, and who will explain to us the views of the government on the subject of the removal of our people west of the Mississippi."

Angered at first by the Choctaw refusal to meet him, Jackson soon recognized that LeFlore's words left open the possibility of future removal. And if both the Choctaws and Chickasaws agreed to migrate, the state of Mississippi would be virtually emptied of Indians, thus tightening the nation's military grip on the lower Mississippi valley and increasing America's security against possible foreign invasion. So the President wrote a cordial acceptance of the offer and appointed Eaton and Coffee to present his "talk."

The commissioners met with the chiefs and headmen at Dancing Rabbit Creek on September 15, 1830. The policy of removal was explained simply as the President wished. Would the Choctaws migrate west and sign a treaty with the United States as evidence of their good faith? If not, they must submit to state law; and if they refused to submit to state jurisdiction, armed force would be used against them. Neither Eaton nor Coffee had Jackson's charisma with the Indians, so they offered bribes to induce agreement. The bribes rarely failed, and on September 27 a treaty was signed. As it turned out this was the first treaty to be signed and ratified by the Senate to implement the removal policy. The earlier Chickasaw treaty had served a valuable purpose, however. It demonstrated the President's willingness to intervene personally to achieve removal of all the southern tribes.

According to the Treaty of Dancing Rabbit Creek, the Choctaws agreed to evacuate all their land in Mississippi and emigrate to an area west of the Arkansas Territory to what is now Oklahoma. In addition the Indians would receive money, household and farm equipment, subsistence for one year, and reimbursement for improvements on their vacated property. In effect the Choctaws ceded to the United States 10.5 million acres of land east of the Mississippi River. They promised to emigrate in stages: the first group in the fall of 1831, the second in 1832, and the last in 1833.

Jackson immediately submitted the treaty to Congress when it reconvened in December, 1830, and Eaton, in his annual report, assured the members that agreement was reached through persuasion only. No secret agreements, no bribes, no promises. Everything had been open and aboveboard! The Senate swallowed the lie whole and ratified the treaty on February 25, 1831, by a vote of 35 to 12. Said one Choctaw chief: "Our doom is sealed."

Since the Treaty of Dancing Rabbit Creek was the first to win Senate approval the President was very anxious to make it a model of removal. He wanted everything to go smoothly so that the American people would understand that removal was humane and beneficial to both the Indians and the American nation at large. Furthermore, he hoped its success would encourage other tribes to capitulate to his policy and thereby send a veritable human tide streaming across the Mississippi into the plains beyond.

The actual removal of the Choctaw Nation violated every principle for which Jackson stood. From start to finish the operation was a fraud. Corruption, theft, mismanagement, inefficiency—all contributed to the destruction of a once-great people. The Choctaws asked to be guided to their new country by General George Gibson, a man they trusted and with whom they had scouted their new home. Even this was denied them. The bureaucracy dictated another choice. So they left the "land of their fathers" filled with fear and anxiety. To make matters worse the winter of 1831–1832 was "living hell." The elements conspired to add to their misery. The suffering was stupefying. Those who watched the horror never forgot it. Many wept. The Indians themselves showed not a single sign of their agony.

Jackson tried to prevent this calamity but he was too far away to exercise any real control, and the temptations and opportunities for graft and corruption were too great for some agents to resist. When he learned of the Choctaw experience and the suffering involved, Jackson was deeply offended. He did what he could to prevent its recurrence. He proposed a new set of guidelines for future removals. He hoped they would reform the system and erase mismanagement and the opportunity for theft.

To begin with, the entire operation of Indian removal was transferred from civilian hands to the military. Then the office of commissioner of Indian affairs was established under the war department to coordinate and direct all matters pertaining to the Indians. In large part these changes reflected Jackson's anguish over what had happened to the Choctaws, but they also resulted from his concern over public opinion. Popular outrage could kill the whole program of removal. . . .

The experience of removal is one of the horror stories of the modern era. Beginning with the Choctaws it decimated whole tribes. An entire race of people suffered. What it did to their lives, their culture, their language, their customs is a tragedy of truly staggering proportions. The irony is that removal was intended to prevent this calamity.

Would it have been worse had the Indians remained in the East? Jackson thought so. He said they would "disappear and be forgotten." One thing does seem certain: the Indians would have been forced to yield to state laws and white society. Indian Nations *per se* would have been obliterated and possibly Indian civilization with them.

In October, 1832, a year and a half after the Choctaw treaty was ratified,

General Coffee signed a treaty with the Chickasaws that met Jackson's complete approval. "Surely the religious enthusiasts," wrote the President in conveying his delight to Coffee, "or those who have been weeping over the oppression of the Indians will not find fault with it for want of liberality or justice to the Indians." By this time Jackson had grown callous. His promise to economize got the better of him. "The stipulation that they remove at their own expence and on their own means, is an excellent feature in it. The whole treaty is just, we want them in a state of safety removed from the states and free from colision with the whites; and if the land does this it is well disposed of and freed from being a corrupting source to our Legislature."

Coffee's success with the Chickasaws followed those with the Creeks and Seminoles. On March 24, 1832, the destruction of the Creek Nation begun with the Treaty of Fort Jackson in 1814 was completed when the chiefs signed an agreement to remove rather than fight it out in the courts. The Seminoles accepted a provisional treaty on May 9, 1832, pending approval of the site for relocation. Thus, by the close of Jackson's first administration the Choctaws, Creeks, Chickasaws, and Seminoles had capitulated. Of the so-called Five Civilized Tribes only the Cherokees held out.

Not for long. They found small consolation from the courts. The Cherokees' lawyer, William Wirt, sued in the Supreme Court for an injunction that would permit the Indians to remain in Georgia unmolested by state law. He argued that the Cherokees had a right to self-government as a foreign nation and that this right had long been recognized by the United States in its treaties with the Indians. He hoped to make it appear that Jackson himself was the nullifier of federal law. In effect he challenged the entire removal policy by asking for a restraining order against Georgia.

Chief Justice John Marshall in the case *Cherokee Nation* v. *Georgia* handed down his opinion on March 18, 1831. He rejected Wirt's contention that the Cherokees were a sovereign nation. He also rejected Jackson's insistence that they were subject to state law. The Indians, he said, were "domestic dependent nations," subject to the United States as a ward to a guardian. They were not subject to individual states, he declared. Indian territory was in fact part of the United States.

The Indians chose to regard the opinion as essentially favorable in that it commanded the United States to protect their rights and property. So they refused to submit—either to Georgia or to Jackson. Meanwhile, Georgia passed legislation in late December, 1830, prohibiting white men from entering Indian country after March 1, 1831, without a license from the state. This was clearly aimed at troublesome missionaries who encouraged Indians in their "disobedience." Samuel A. Worcester and Dr. Elizur Butler, two missionaries, defied the law; they were arrested and sentenced to four years imprisonment in a state penitentiary. They sued, and in the case *Worcester* v. *Georgia* the Supreme Court decided on March 3, 1832, that the Georgia law was unconstitutional. Speaking for the majority in a feeble voice, John Marshall croaked out the court's decision. All the laws of Georgia dealing with the Cherokees were unconstitutional, he declared. He issued a formal mandate two days later ordering the Georgia Superior Court to reverse its decision.

Georgia, of course, had refused to acknowledge the court's right to direct its actions and had boycotted the judicial proceedings. The state had no intention of obeying the court's order. Since the court adjourned almost immediately after rendering its decision nothing further could be done. According to the Judiciary Act of 1789 the Supreme Court could issue its order of compliance only when a case had already been remanded without response. Since the court would not reconvene until January, 1833, no further action by the government could take place. Thus, until the court either summoned state officials before it for contempt or issued a writ of habeas corpus for the release of the two missionaries there was nothing further to be done. The President was under no obligation to act. In fact there is some question as to whether the court itself could act since the existing habeas corpus law did not apply in this case because the missionaries were not being detained by federal authorities. And since the Superior Court of Georgia did not acknowledge in writing its refusal to obey, Marshall's decision could not be enforced. Jackson understood this. He knew there was nothing for him to do. "The decision of the supreme court has fell still born," he wrote John Coffee, "and they find that it cannot coerce Georgia to yield to its mandate."

It was later reported by Horace Greeley that Jackson's response to the Marshall decision was total defiance. "Well: John Marshall has made his decision: *now let him enforce it!*" Greeley cited George N. Briggs, a Representative from Massachusetts, as his source for the statement. The quotation certainly sounds like Jackson and many historians have chosen to believe that he said it. The fact is that Jackson did not say it because there was no reason to do so. There was nothing for him to enforce. Why, then, would he refuse an action that no one asked him to take? As he said, the decision was stillborn. The court rendered an opinion which abandoned the Indians to their inevitable fate. "It cannot coerce Georgia to yield to its mandate," said Jackson, "and I believe Ridge [leader of the Cherokee party who held out against removal] has expressed despair, and that it is better for them [the Cherokees] to treat and move."

Even if Jackson did not use the exact words Greeley put into his mouth, even if no direct action was required at the moment, some historians have argued that the quotation represents in fact Jackson's true attitude. There is evidence that Jackson "sportively said in private conversation" that if summoned "to support the decree of the Court he will call on those who have brought about the decision to enforce it." Actually nobody expected Jackson to enforce the decision, including the two missionaries, and therefore a lot of people simply assumed that the President would defy the court if pressured. In the rush to show Jackson as bombastic and blustery, however, an important point is missed. What should be remembered is that Jackson reacted with extreme caution to this crisis because a precipitous act could have triggered a confrontation with Georgia. Prudence, not defiance, characterized his reaction to both the challenge of Georgia and later the threat of nullification by South Carolina. As one historian has said, Jackson deserves praise for his caution in dealing with potentially explosive issues and should not be condemned for his so-called inaction.

Still the President had encouraged Georgia in its intransigence. He shares responsibility in producing this near-confrontation. He was so desperate to achieve Indian removal that he almost produced a crisis between federal and state authorities. Nor can it be denied, as one North Carolina Congressman observed, that "Gen Jackson could by a nod of the head or a crook of the finger induce Georgia to submit to the law. It is by the promise or belief of his countenance and support that Georgia is stimulated to her disorderly and rebellious conduct."

Jackson chose not to nod his head or crook his finger for several reasons, the most important of which was his determination to remove the Cherokees. But he had other concerns. As the time neared for the Supreme Court to reconvene and deliberate on Georgia's defiance, a controversy with South Carolina over nullification developed. Jackson had to be extremely careful that no action of his induced Georgia to join South Carolina in the dispute. Nullification might lead to secession and civil war. He therefore maneuvered to isolate South Carolina and force Georgia to back away from its position of confrontation. He needed to nudge Georgia into obeying the court order and free the two missionaries. Consequently he moved swiftly to win removal of the Indians. His secretary of war worked quietly to convince the legal counsel for the missionaries and the friends of the Cherokees in Congress, such as Theodore Frelinghuysen, that the President would not budge from his position nor interfere in the operation of Georgia laws and that the best solution for everyone was for the Indians to remove. Meanwhile the Creeks capitulated, and a treaty of removal was ratified by the Senate in April, 1832.

Although Senator Frelinghuysen "prayed to God" that Georgia would peacefully acquiesce in the decision of the Supreme Court he soon concluded that the Cherokees must yield. Even Justice John McLean, who wrote a concurring opinion in the *Worcester* case, counseled the Cherokee delegation in Washington to sign a removal treaty. Van Buren's Albany Regency actively intervened because of their concern over a possible southern backlash against their leader. Van Buren himself encouraged his friend Senator John Forsyth to intercede with the newly elected governor of Georgia, Wilson Lumpkin, keeping Jackson carefully informed of his actions. More significant, however, were the letters written by the secretary of war to Lumpkin. These letters pleaded for a pardon for the two missionaries and stated that the President himself gave his unconditional endorsement of the request. Finally Forsyth conferred with William Wirt who in turn conferred with a representative of the two missionaries, and they all agreed to make no further motion before the Supreme Court. That done, Governor Lumpkin ordered the "keeper" of the penitentiary on January 14, 1833 to release Worcester and Butler under an arrangement devised by Forsyth. Thus, while the President held steady to his course and directed the activities of the men in contact with Lumpkin, both the problem of Georgia's defiance and the fate of the two missionaries were quietly resolved without injurious consequences to the rest of the nation. It was one of Jackson's finest actions as a statesman.

Ultimately, the Cherokees also yielded to the President. On December 29, 1835, at New Echota a treaty was signed arranging an exchange of land. A protracted legal argument had gained the Indians a little time but nothing else. Removal now applied to all eastern Indians, not simply the southern tribes. After the Black Hawk War of 1832 Jackson responded to the demands of Americans in the northwest to send all Indians beyond the Mississippi. A hungry band of Sac and Fox Indians under the leadership of Black Hawk had recrossed the Mississippi in the spring of 1832 to find food. People on the frontier panicked and Governor John Reynolds of Illinois called out the militia and appealed to Jackson for assistance. Federal troops were immediately dispatched under Generals Winfield Scott and Henry Atkinson. A short and bloody war resulted, largely instigated by drunken militia troops, and when it ended the northwestern tribes were so demoralized that they offered little resistance to Jackson's steady pressure for their removal west of the Mississippi. The result of the Black Hawk War, said the President in his fourth message to Congress, had been very "creditable to the troops" engaged in the action. "Severe as is the lesson to the Indians," he lectured, "it was rendered necessary by their unprovoked aggressions, and it is to be hoped that its impression will be permanent and salutary."

It was useless for the Indians to resist Jackson's demands. Nearly 46,000 of them went west. Thousands died in transit. Even those under no treaty obligation to emigrate were eventually forced to remove. And the removal experiences were all pretty much like that of the Choctaws—all horrible, all rife with corruption and fraud, all disgraceful to the American nation.

The policy of removal formed an important part of Jackson's overall program of limiting federal authority and supporting states' rights. Despite the accusation of increased executive authority, Jackson successfully buttressed state sovereignty and jurisdiction over all inhabitants within state boundaries. This is a government of the people, Jackson argued, and the President is the agent of the people. The President and the Congress exercise their jurisdiction over *"the people of the union*. Who are the people of the union?" he asked. Then, answering his own question, he said: "all those subject to the jurisdiction of the sovereign states, none else." Indians are also subject to the states, he went on. They are subject "to the sovereign power of the state within whose sovereign limits they reside." An "absolute independence of the Indian tribes from state authority can never bear an intelligent investigation, and a quasi independence of state authority when located within its Territorial limits is *absurd*."

In addition to establishing the removal policy Jackson also restructured the bureaucracy handling Indian problems. Since 1824 a Bureau of Indian Affairs headed by Thomas L. McKenney had supervised the government's relations with the Indians. By the time Jackson assumed the presidency the Bureau had become an "enormous quagmire" from an administrative point of view. McKenney was retained in office to take advantage of his reputation to win passage of the Removal bill. Once Removal passed, McKenney was dismissed. (For one thing he had supported Adams in 1828.) Then the Bureau was reorganized. On June 30, 1834, Congress passed the necessary legislation establishing the Office of Indian Affairs under an Indian commissioner, and this administrative machinery remained in place well into the twentieth century. The Indian service was restructured into a more cohesive operation than had previously been the case. It regularized procedures that had been practiced as a matter of custom rather than law.

Ultimately Jackson's policy of removal and reorganization of the Indian service won acceptance by most Americans. The President was seen as a forceful executive who addressed one of the nation's most bedeviling problems and solved it. Even Americans who fretted over the fate of the Indians eventually went along with removal. The policy seemed enlightened and humane. It seemed rational and logical. It constituted, Americans thought, the only possible solution to the Indian problem.

## FURTHER READING

Angie Debo, *The Rise and Fall of the Choctaw Republic* (1961)

Arthur H. DeRosier, Jr., *The Removal of the Choctaw Indians* (1970)

Richard Drinnon, *Facing West: The Metaphysics of Indian-Hating and Empire Building* (1980)

Jack E. Eblen, *The First and Second United States Empires* (1968)

Arrell M. Gibson, *The American Indian* (1980)

Reginald Horsman, *Expansion and American Indian Policy, 1783–1812* (1967)

Francis P. Prucha, *American Indian Policy in the Formative Years: Indian Trade and the Intercourse Acts, 1790–1834* (1962)

———, "Andrew Jackson's Indian Policy: A Reassessment," *Journal of American History*, 56 (1969), 527–539

John K. Mahon, *History of the Second Seminole War, 1835–1842* (1967)

Michael Paul Rogin, *Fathers and Children: Andrew Jackson and the Subjugation of the American Indian* (1975)

Malcolm J. Rohrbough, *The Trans-Appalachian Frontier. People, Societies, and Institutions, 1775–1850* (1978)

Ronald N. Satz, *American Indian Policy in the Jacksonian Era* (1975)

Lyman S. Tyler, *A History of Indian Policy* (1973)

Glyndon G. Van Deusen, *The Jacksonian Era, 1828–1848* (1963)

Wilcomb E. Washburn, *The Indian in America* (1975)

Grace S. Woodward, *The Cherokees* (1963)

Mary E. Young, "Indian Removal and Land Allotment: The Civilized Tribes and Jacksonian Justice," *American Historical Review*, 64 (1958), 31–45

———, *Redskins, Ruffleshirts, and Rednecks: Indian Allotments in Alabama and Mississippi, 1830–1860* (1961)

# Manifest Destiny and the War with Mexico

# 8

*The 1840s witnessed an expansionist surge that netted the United States new territories. Texas, Oregon, and the California territory, after the use or threat of force and much debate, became parts of the expanding American empire. Expansionism was certainly not new to the United States in the 1840s. From infancy the nation had been expansionist and, between the Louisiana Purchase of 1803 and the treaty ending the war with Mexico in 1848, the United States had moved steadily westward, enlarging its territory, pushing out its boundaries, and removing Native Americans. The 1840s, however, were particularly active. What explains this burst of territorial acquisitiveness? James K. Polk as President? A cumulative and traditional American expansionism? Idealism? Racism? Commercial interest? The answers vary, as the selections in this chapter make evident.*

## DOCUMENTS

John L. O'Sullivan is credited with having popularized the idea of Manifest Destiny. As editor of the *Democratic Review,* he flamboyantly sketched an unbounded American future of democratic mission and territorial expansion. The first document is selected from his "The Great Nation of Futurity," published in 1839. James K. Polk became President in 1845. An avowed expanionist, he eyed Mexican lands and disputed territories in the Southwest and Northwest. His Inaugural Address of March 4, 1845, made the case for absorbing Texas and Oregon. The third document is Polk's War Message of May 11, 1846, in which he asked Congress to declare war against Mexico and presented United States grievances against its southern neighbor.

The outbreak of war, American territorial ambitions, and the ultimate American triumph aroused considerable debate. The Wilmot Proviso, drafted by Representative David Wilmot of Pennsylvania, was an attempt to keep slavery out of any territory won from Mexico. Although the House passed this amendment to an appropriations bill in 1846 and 1847, the Senate turned it down, exposing deep differences over whether limits ought to be placed on expansion. The fifth document is a strongly worded anti-war resolution penned by Charles Sumner and passed in 1847 by the Massachusetts legislature. The final selection is the statement of some Mexican editors who believed that a rapacious United States provoked war and wronged the Mexican people.

---

# John L. O'Sullivan on Manifest Destiny, 1839

The American people having derived their origin from many other nations, and the Declaration of National Independence being entirely based on the great principle of human equality, these facts demonstrate at once our disconnected position as regards any other nation; that we have, in reality, but little connection with the past history of any of them, and still less with all antiquity, its glories, or its crimes. On the contrary, our national birth was the beginning of a new history, the formation and progress of an untried political system, which separates us from the past and connects us with the future only; and so far as regards the entire development of the natural rights of man, in moral, political, and national life, we may confidently assume that our country is destined to be *the great nation* of futurity.

It is so destined, because the principle upon which a nation is organized fixes its destiny, and that of equality is perfect, is universal. It presides in all the operations of the physical world, and it is also the conscious law of the soul—the self-evident dictates of morality, which accurately defines the duty of man to man, and consequently man's rights as man. Besides, the truthful annals of any nation furnish abundant evidence, that its happiness, its greatness, its duration, were always proportionate to the democratic equality in its system of government. . . .

What friend of human liberty, civilization, and refinement, can cast his view over the past history of the monarchies and aristocracies of antiquity, and not deplore that they ever existed? What philanthropist can contemplate the oppressions, the cruelties, and injustice inflicted by them on the masses of mankind, and not turn with moral horror from the retrospect?

America is destined for better deeds. It is our unparalleled glory that we have no reminiscences of battle fields, but in defence of humanity, of the oppressed of all nations, of the rights of conscience, the rights of personal enfranchisement. Our annals describe no scenes of horrid carnage, where men were led on by hundreds of thousands to slay one another, dupes and victims to emperors, kings, nobles, demons in the human form called heroes. We have had patriots to defend our homes, our liberties, but no aspirants to crowns or thrones; nor have the American people ever suffered themselves to be led on by wicked ambition to depopulate the land, to spread desolation far and wide, that a human being might be placed on a seat of supremacy.

We have no interest in the scenes of antiquity, only as lessons of avoidance of nearly all their examples. The expansive future is our arena, and for our history. We are entering on its untrodden space, with the truths of God in our minds, beneficent objects in our hearts, and with a clear conscience unsullied by the past. We are the nation of human progress, and who will, what can, set limits to our onward march? Providence is with us, and no earthly power can. We point to the everlasting truth on the first page of our national declaration, and we proclaim to the millions of other lands, that "the gates of hell"—the powers of aristocracy and monarchy—"shall not prevail against it."

The far-reaching, the boundless future will be the era of American greatness. In its magnificent domain of space and time, the nation of many nations is destined to manifest to mankind the excellence of divine principles; to establish on earth the noblest temple ever dedicated to the worship of the Most High—the Sacred and the True. Its floor shall be a hemisphere—its roof the firmament of the star-studded heavens, and its congregation an Union of many Republics, comprising hundreds of happy millions, calling, owning no man master, but governed by God's natural and moral law of equality, the law of brotherhood—of "peace and good will amongst men." . . .

Yes, we are the nation of progress, of individual freedom, of universal enfranchisement. Equality of rights is the cynosure of our union of States, the grand exemplar of the correlative equality of individuals; and while truth sheds its effulgence, we cannot retrograde, without dissolving the one and subverting the other. We must onward to the fulfilment of our mission—to the entire development of the principle of our organization—freedom of conscience, freedom of person, freedom of trade and business pursuits, universality of freedom and equality. This is our high destiny, and in nature's eternal, inevitable decree of cause and effect we must accomplish it. All this will be our future history, to establish on earth the moral dignity and salvation of man—the immutable truth and beneficence of God. For this blessed mission to the nations of the world, which are shut out from the life-giving light of truth, has America been chosen; and her high example shall smite unto death the tyranny of kings, hierarchs, and oligarchs, and carry the glad tidings of peace and good will where myriads now endure an existence scarcely more enviable than that of beasts of the field. Who, then, can doubt that our country is destined to be *the great nation* of futurity?

## James K. Polk on Texas and Oregon, 1845

I regard the question of annexation as belonging exclusively to the United States and Texas. They are independent powers competent to contract, and foreign nations have no right to interfere with them or to take exceptions to their reunion. Foreign powers do not seem to appreciate the true character of our Government. Our Union is a confederation of independent States, whose policy is peace with each other and all the world. To enlarge its limits is to extend the dominions of peace over additional territories and increasing millions. The world has nothing to fear from military ambition in our Government. While the Chief Magistrate and the popular branch of Congress are elected for short terms by the suffrages of those millions who must in their own persons bear all the burdens and miseries of war, our Government can not be otherwise than pacific. Foreign powers should therefore look on the annexation of Texas to the United States not as the conquest of a nation seeking to extend her dominions by arms and violence, but as the peaceful acquisition of a territory once her own, by adding another member to our confederation, with the consent of that member, thereby diminishing the chances of war and opening to them new and ever-increasing markets for their products.

To Texas the reunion is important, because the strong protecting arm of our Government would be extended over her, and the vast resources of her fertile soil and genial climate would be speedily developed, while the safety of New Orleans and of our whole southwestern frontier against hostile aggression, as well as the interests of the whole Union, would be promoted by it.

In the earlier stages of our national existence the opinion prevailed with some that our system of confederated States could not operate successfully over an extended territory, and serious objections have at different times been made to the enlargement of our boundaries. These objections were earnestly urged when we acquired Louisiana. Experience has shown that they were not well founded. The title of numerous Indian tribes to vast tracts of country has been extinguished; new States have been admitted into the Union; new Territories have been created and our jurisdiction and laws extended over them. As our population has expanded, the Union has been cemented and strengthened. As our boundaries have been enlarged and our agricultural population has been spread over a large surface, our federative system has acquired additional strength and security. It may well be doubted whether it would not be in greater danger of overthrow if our present population were confined to the comparatively narrow limits of the original thirteen States than it is now that they are sparsely settled over a more expanded territory. It is confidently believed that our system may be safely extended to the utmost bounds of our territorial limits, and that as it shall be extended the bonds of our Union, so far from being weakened, will become stronger.

None can fail to see the danger to our safety and future peace if Texas remains an independent state or becomes an ally or dependency of some foreign nation more powerful than herself. Is there one among our citizens who would not prefer perpetual peace with Texas to occasional wars, which so often occur between bordering independent nations? Is there one who would not prefer free intercourse with her to high duties on all our products and manufactures which enter her ports or cross her frontiers? Is there one who would not prefer an unrestricted communication with her citizens to the frontier obstructions which must occur if she remains out of the Union? Whatever is good or evil in the local institutions of Texas will remain her own whether annexed to the United States or not. None of the present States will be responsible for them any more than they are for the local institutions of each other. They have confederated together for certain specified objects. Upon the same principle that they would refuse to form a perpetual union with Texas because of her local institutions our forefathers would have been prevented from forming our present Union. Perceiving no valid objection to the measure and many reasons for its adoption vitally affecting the peace, the safety, and the prosperity of both countries, I shall on the broad principle which formed the basis and produced the adoption of our Constitution, and not in any narrow spirit of sectional policy, endeavor by all constitutional, honorable, and appropriate means to consummate the expressed will of the people and Government of the United States by the reannexation of Texas to our Union at the earliest practicable period.

Nor will it become in a less degree my duty to assert and maintain by all constitutional means the right of the United States to that portion of our territory which lies beyond the Rocky Mountains. Our title to the country of the Oregon is "clear and unquestionable," and already are our people preparing to perfect that title by occupying it with their wives and children. But eighty years ago our population was confined on the west by the ridge of the Alleghanies. Within that period—within the lifetime, I might say, of some of my hearers—our people, increasing to many millions, have filled the eastern valley of the Mississippi, adventurously ascended the Missouri to its headsprings, and are already engaged in establishing the blessings of self-government in valleys of which the rivers flow to the Pacific. The world beholds the peaceful triumphs of the industry of our emigrants. To us belongs the duty of protecting them adequately wherever they may be upon our soil. The jurisdiction of our laws and the benefits of our republican institutions should be extended over them in the distant regions which they have selected for their homes. The increasing facilities of intercourse will easily bring the States, of which the formation in that part of our territory can not be long delayed, within the sphere of our federative Union. In the meantime every obligation imposed by treaty or conventional stipulations should be sacredly respected.

# Polk's War Message, 1846

The existing state of the relations between the United States and Mexico renders it proper that I should bring the subject to the consideration of Congress. . . .

The strong desire to establish peace with Mexico on liberal and honorable terms, and the readiness of this Government to regulate and adjust our boundary and other causes of difference with that power on such fair and equitable principles as would lead to permanent relations of the most friendly nature, induced me in September last to seek the reopening of diplomatic relations between the two countries. . . . An envoy of the United States repaired to

Mexico with full powers to adjust every existing difference. But though present on the Mexican soil by agreement between the two Governments, invested with full powers, and bearing evidence of the most friendly dispositions, his mission has been unavailing. The Mexican Government not only refused to receive him or listen to his propositions, but after a long-continued series of menaces have at last invaded our territory and shed the blood of our fellow-citizens on our own soil.

It now becomes my duty to state more in detail the origin, progress, and failure of that mission. In pursuance of the instructions given in September last, an inquiry was made on the 13th of October, 1845, in the most friendly terms, through our consul in Mexico, of the minister for foreign affairs, whether the Mexican Government "would receive an envoy from the United States intrusted with full powers to adjust all the questions in dispute between the two Governments," with the assurance that "should the answer be in the affirmative such an envoy would be immediately dispatched to Mexico." The Mexican minister on the 15th of October gave an affirmative answer to this inquiry. . . . On the 10th of November, 1845, Mr. John Slidell, of Louisiana, was commissioned by me as envoy extraordinary and minister plenipotentiary of the United States to Mexico, and was intrusted with full powers to adjust both the questions of the Texas boundary and of indemnification to our citizens. The redress of the wrongs of our citizens naturally and inseparably blended itself with the question of boundary. The settlement of the one question in any correct view of the subject involves that of the other. I could not for a moment entertain the idea that the claims of our much-injured and long-suffering citizens, many of which had existed for more than twenty years, should be postponed or separated from the settlement of the boundary question.

Mr. Slidell arrived at Vera Cruz on the 30th of November, and was courteously received by the authorities of that city. But the Government of General Herrera was then tottering to its fall. The revolutionary party had seized upon the Texas question to effect or hasten its overthrow. Its determination to restore friendly relations with the United States, and to receive our minister to negotiate for the settlement of this question, was violently assailed, and was made the great theme of denunciation against it. The Government of General Herrera, there is good reason to believe, was sincerely desirous to receive our minister; but it yielded to the storm raised by its enemies, and on the 21st of December refused to accredit Mr. Slidell upon the most frivolous pretexts. These are so fully and ably exposed in the note of Mr. Slidell of the 24th of December last to the Mexican minister of foreign relations, herewith transmitted, that I deem it unnecessary to enter into further detail on this portion of the subject.

Five days after the date of Mr. Slidell's note General Herrera yielded the Government to General Paredes without a struggle, and on the 30th of December resigned the Presidency. This revolution was accomplished solely by the army, the people having taken little part in the contest; and thus the supreme power in Mexico passed into the hands of a military leader.

Determined to leave no effort untried to effect an amicable adjustment with Mexico, I directed Mr. Slidell to present his credentials to the Government of General Paredes and ask to be officially received by him. There would have been less ground for taking this step had General Paredes come into power by a regular constitutional succession. In that event his administration would have been considered but a mere constitutional continuance of the Government of General Herrera, and the refusal of the latter to receive our minister would have been deemed conclusive unless an intimation had been given by General Paredes of his desire to reverse the decision of his predecessor. But the Government of General Paredes owes its existence to a military revolution, by which the subsisting constitutional authorities had been subverted. The form of government was entirely changed, as well as all the high functionaries by whom it was administered.

Under these circumstances, Mr. Slidell, in obedience to my direction, addressed a note to the Mexican minister of foreign relations, under date of the 1st of March last, asking to be received by that Government in the diplomatic character to which he had been appointed. This minister in his reply, under date of the 12th of March, reiterated the arguments of his predecessor, and in terms that may be considered as giving just grounds of offense to the Government and people of the United States denied the application of Mr. Slidell. Nothing therefore remained for our envoy but to demand his passports and return to his own country.

Thus the Government of Mexico, though solemnly pledged by official acts in October last to receive and accredit an American envoy, violated their plighted faith and refused the offer of a peaceful adjustment of our difficulties. Not only was the offer rejected, but the indignity of its rejection was enhanced by the manifest breach of faith in refusing to admit the envoy who came because they had bound themselves to receive him. Nor can it be said that the offer was fruitless from the want of opportunity of discussing it; our envoy was present on their own soil. Nor can it be ascribed to a want of sufficient powers; our envoy had full powers to adjust every question of difference. Nor was there room for complaint that our propositions for settlement were unreasonable; permission was not even given our envoy to make any proposition whatever. Nor can it be objected that we, on our part, would not listen to any reasonable terms of their suggestion; the Mexican Government refused all negotiation, and have made no proposition of any kind.

In my message at the commencement of the present session I informed you that upon the earnest appeal both of the Congress and convention of Texas I had ordered an efficient military force to take a position "between the Nueces and the Del Norte." This had become necessary to meet a threatened invasion of Texas by the Mexican forces, for which extensive military preparations had been made. The invasion was threatened solely because Texas had determined, in accordance with a solemn resolution of the Congress of the United States, to annex herself to our Union, and under these circumstances it was plainly our duty to extend our protection over her citizens and soil.

This force was concentrated at Corpus Christi, and remained there until after I had received such information from Mexico as rendered it probable, if not certain, that the Mexican Government would refuse to receive our envoy.

Meantime Texas, by the final action of our Congress, had become an integral part of our Union. The Congress of Texas, by its act of December 19, 1836, had declared the Rio del Norte to be the boundary of that Republic. Its jurisdiction had been extended and exercised beyond the Nueces. The country between that river and the Del Norte had been represented in the Congress and in the convention of Texas, had thus taken part in the act of annexation itself, and is now included within one of our Congressional districts. Our own Congress had, moreover, with great unanimity, by the act approved December 31, 1845, recognized the country beyond the Nueces as a part of our territory by including it within our own revenue system, and a revenue officer to reside within that district has been appointed by and with the advice and consent of the Senate. It became, therefore, of urgent necessity to provide for the defense of that portion of our country. Accordingly, on the 13th of January last instructions were issued to the general in command of these troops to occupy the left bank of the Del Norte. This river, which is the southwestern boundary of the State of Texas, is an exposed frontier. From this quarter invasion was threatened; upon it and in its immediate vicinity, in the judgment of high military experience, are the proper stations for the protecting forces of the Government. In addition to this important consideration, several others occurred to induce this movement. Among these are the facilities afforded by the ports at Brazos Santiago and the mouth of the Del Norte for the reception of supplies by sea, the stronger and more healthful military positions, the convenience for obtaining a ready and a more abundant supply of provisions, water, fuel, and forage, and the advantages which are afforded by the Del Norte in forwarding supplies to such posts as may be established in the interior and upon the Indian frontier.

The movement of the troops to the Del Norte was made by the commanding general under positive instructions to abstain from all aggressive acts toward Mexico or Mexican citizens and to regard the relations between that Republic and the United States as peaceful unless she should declare war or commit acts of hostility indicative of a state of war. He was specially directed to protect private property and respect personal rights.

The Army moved from Corpus Christi on the 11th of March, and on the 28th of that month arrived on the left bank of the Del Norte opposite to Matamoras, where it encamped on a commanding position, which has since been strengthened by the erection of fieldworks. A depot has also been established at Point Isabel, near the Brazos Santiago, 30 miles in the rear of the encampment. The selection of his position was necessarily confided to the judgment of the general in command.

The Mexican forces at Matamoras assumed a belligerent attitude, and on the 12th of April General Ampudia, then in command, notified General Taylor to break up his camp within twenty-four hours and to retire beyond the Nueces River, and in the event of his failure to comply with these demands announced that arms, and arms alone, must decide the question. But no open act of hostility was committed until the 24th of April. On that day General Arista, who had succeeded to the command of the Mexican forces, communicated to General Taylor that "he considered hostilities commenced and should prosecute them." A party of dragoons of 63 men and officers were on the same day dispatched from the American camp up the Rio del Norte, on its left bank, to ascertain whether the Mexican troops had crossed or were preparing to cross the river, "became engaged with a large body of these troops, and after a short affair, in which some 16 were killed and wounded, appear to have been surrounded and compelled to surrender."

The grievous wrongs perpetrated by Mexico upon our citizens throughout a long period of years remain unredressed, and solemn treaties pledging her public faith for this redress have been disregarded. A government either unable or unwilling to enforce the execution of such treaties fails to perform one of its plainest duties.

Our commerce with Mexico has been almost annihilated. It was formerly highly beneficial to both nations, but our merchants have been deterred from prosecuting it by the system of outrage and extortion which the Mexican authorities have pursued against them, whilst their appeals through their own Government for indemnity have been made in vain. Our forbearance has gone to such an extreme as to be mistaken in its character. Had we acted with vigor in repelling the insults and redressing the injuries inflicted by Mexico at the commencement, we should doubtless have escaped all the difficulties in which we are now involved.

Instead of this, however, we have been exerting our best efforts to propitiate her good will. Upon the pretext that Texas, a nation as independent as herself, thought proper to unite its destinies with our own she has affected to believe that we have severed her rightful territory, and in official proclamations and manifestoes has repeatedly threatened to make war upon us for the purpose of reconquering Texas. In the meantime we have tried every effort at reconciliation. The cup of forbearance had been exhausted even before the recent information from the frontier of the Del Norte. But now, after reiterated menaces, Mexico has passed the boundary of the United States, has invaded our territory and shed American blood upon the American soil. She has proclaimed that hostilities have commenced, and that the two nations are now at war.

As war exists, and, notwithstanding all our efforts to avoid it, exists by the act of Mexico herself, we are called upon by every consideration of duty and patriotism to vindicate with decision the honor, the rights, and the interests of our country.

## The Wilmot Proviso, 1846

*Provided,* That, as an express and fundamental condition to the acquisition of any territory from the Republic of Mexico by the United States, by virtue of any treaty which may be negotiated between them, and to the use by the Executive of the moneys herein appropriated, neither slavery nor involuntary servitude shall ever exist in any part of said territory, except for crime, whereof the party shall first be duly convicted.

## Massachusetts Protests the Mexican War, 1847

Resolves. Concerning the Mexican War, and the Institution of Slavery.

*Resolved,* That the present war with Mexico has its primary origin in the unconstitutional annexation to the United States of the foreign state of Texas while the same was still at war with Mexico; that it was unconstitutionally commenced by the order of the President, to General Taylor, to take military possession of territory in dispute between the United States and Mexico, and in the occupation of Mexico; and that it is now waged ingloriously—by a powerful nation against a weak neighbor—unnecessarily and without just cause, at immense cost of treasure and life, for the dismemberment of Mexico, and for the conquest, of a portion of her territory, from which slavery has already been excluded, with the triple object of extending slavery, of strengthening the "Slave Power," and of obtaining the control of the Free States, under the Constitution of the United States.

*Resolved,* That such a war of conquest, so hateful in its objects, so wanton, unjust, and unconstitutional in its origin and character, must be regarded as a war against freedom, against humanity, against justice, against the Union, against the Constitution, and against the Free States; and that a regard for the true interests and the highest honor of the country, not less than the impulses of Christian duty, should arouse all good citizens to join in efforts to arrest this gigantic crime, by withholding supplies, or other voluntary contributions, for its further prosecution; by calling for the withdrawal of our army within the established limits of the United States; and in every just way aiding the country to retreat from the disgraceful position of aggression which it now occupies towards a weak, distracted neighbor and sister republic.

*Resolved,* That our attention is directed anew to the wrong and "enormity" of slavery, and to the tyranny and usurpation of the "Slave Power," as displayed in the history of our country, particularly in the annexation of Texas and the present war with Mexico.

## A Mexican Perspective, 1849

To explain then in a few words the true origin of the war, it is sufficient to say that the insatiable ambition of the United States, favored by our weakness, caused it. But this assertion, however veracious and well founded, requires the confirmation which we will present, along with some former transactions, to the whole world. This evidence will leave no doubt of the correctness of our impressions.

In throwing off the yoke of the mother country, the United States of the North appeared at once as a powerful nation. This was the result of their excellent elementary principles of government established while in colonial subjection. The Republic announced at its birth, that it was called upon to represent an important part in the world of Columbus. Its rapid advancement, its progressive increase, its wonderful territory, the uninterrupted augmentation of its inhabitants, and the formidable power it had gradually acquired, were many proofs of its becoming a colossus, not only for the feeble nations of Spanish America, but even for the old populations of the ancient continent.

The United States did not hope for the assistance of time in their schemes of aggrandizement. From the days of their independence they adopted the project of extending their dominions, and since then, that line of policy has not deviated in the slightest degree. . . .

The American Minister, Mr. Shannon, whether from his really believing that the war was positively to be undertaken, or because a pretext was sought to compel Mexico to declare hostilities against the United States, and to make us appear as aggressors, transmitted an official note. In it he made known in the name of his government, that its policy had always been directed to the incorporation of Texas into the American Union, and the invasion which was proposed by Mexico against that Department would now be deemed an offence to the United States.

In this celebrated communication, which will disgrace for ever the diplomatist who subscribed it, a protest was entered against a war with Texas, while the project of annexation was pending. Here the confession had been made, important for us, that the scheme to obtain this part of our territory had been invariably pursued by all parties, and nearly all the administrations of the Republic of North America, for the space of twenty years. The facts which we have mentioned, with others, passed in silence, being less interesting, and, for the sake of brevity, prove by good evidence that this plan existed, and was of longer standing than had been said. But the explicit avowal of the Minister Shannon, not denied nor contradicted by the authorities of his country—this avowal, we say, is of the greatest importance, coming from the very mouths of the usurpers who style themselves the most honest before all civilized nations.

Again, Mexico ought at this time to have broken completely with her deceitful neighbor, and made war wherever her forces would have permitted. Temporizing, however, throughout, our government, in conformity with the justice on which it is founded and guided, hoped that the American Senate would decide upon the project of annexation. As the decision of this body had then been favorable, it continued an intercourse disturbed at present, but still existing, between our Republic and the one at Washington. The most that was done was to protest that annexation would be considered as a declaration of war, for it would come to this extremity if it should thereby heap upon us contempt and degradation.

At this time, more properly than before, it would have been exact justice to have immediately made war on a power that so rashly appropriated what by every title belonged to us. This necessity had increased to a point, that the administrations which had successively been intrusted with our affairs, upon consideration, had all agreed in the principle, that a decree of annexation should be viewed as a *casus belli*—a cause of war. But while this new injury was being suffered, without deciding anything, but keeping diplomatic relations suspended between both countries, our minister, General Almonte, retired from Washington, and the one from the United States did the same from Mexico.

At the close of the year 1844, a new revolution having overturned the government of General Santa Anna, intrusted in the interim to General Canaliso, elevated to power D. José Joaquin de Herrera, the President of the Council. The famous decree of the 29th of November of that year had ended in disgracing the public officers who had framed it. It had established an unlimited dictatorship, and the war with Texas was, as it had been at other times, the gloss of justice with which they tried to conceal the attack directed against the constitution. A majority of the people distrusted the sincerity of the government, recollecting that the national and indispensable war which they ought to have made in that separate Department had not been preferred to Yucatan, which, without any beneficial result, had been the sacrifice of so many men and so with it, the decree of the 6th of July was passed. By it the government was authorized to use the natural defences of the country to repel aggression committed against many of the departments, and to make known to friendly nations the justifiable causes which obliged it to defend its rights by repelling force by force.

While the United States seemed to be animated by a sincere desire not to break the peace, their acts of hostility manifested very evidently what were their true intentions. Their ships infested our coasts; their troops continued advancing upon our territory, situated at places which under no aspect could be disputed. Thus violence and insult were united: thus at the very time they usurped part of our territory, they offered to us the hand of treachery, to have soon the audacity to say that our obstinacy and arrogance were the real causes of the war. . . .

From the acts referred to, it has been demonstrated to the very senses, that the real and effective cause of this war that afflicted us was the spirit of aggrandizement of the United States of the North, availing itself of its power to conquer us. Impartial history will some day illustrate for ever the conduct observed by this Republic against all laws, divine and human, in an age that is called one of light, and which is, notwithstanding, the same as the former—one of *force and violence.*

---

# ESSAYS

Historians have probed extensively the causes of the expansionist surge of the 1840s under the mantle of Manifest Destiny. Reginald Horsman of the University of Wisconsin-Milwaukee emphasizes Anglo-Saxon racism, a central ingredient in the ideology of expansionism. Norman A. Graebner of the University of Virginia concentrates not on ideology or the dreams of empire, but on the concrete interests American leaders sought and the force they were willing to use to gain them. He studies means as much as goals and, in the second selection, explains American efforts to take Texas and California. The closing essay by David M. Pletcher of Indiana University asks whether the war with Mexico was necessary and explores alternatives. He appraises the leadership of James K. Polk and assesses the costs and consequences of the President's aggressive diplomacy.

# Anglo-Saxon Racism

REGINALD HORSMAN

The decisive years in the creation of a new Anglo-Saxon political ideology were from the mid-1830s to the mid-1840s. In these years American politicians and the American population were overwhelmed by a variety of influences, both practical and theoretical, which inspired a belief that the American Anglo-Saxons were destined to dominate or penetrate the American continents and large areas of the world. Americans had faith that they would increase in such numbers that they would personally shape the destiny of other areas.

The catalyst in the overt adoption of a racial Anglo-Saxonism was the meeting of Americans and Mexicans in the Southwest, the Texas Revolution, and the war with Mexico. In confronting the Mexicans the Americans clearly formulated the idea of themselves as an Anglo-Saxon race. The use of *Anglo-Saxon* in a racial sense, somewhat rare in the political arguments of the early 1830s, increased rapidly later in the decade and became commonplace by the mid-1840s. The manner in which the Anglo-Saxon race was being isolated from other peoples was stated with clarity by Senator Benjamin Leigh of Virginia in January 1836 when opposing the abolitionist petitions. After pointing out that his fellow Congressmen had only to remember how the mobs of Cincinnati, Philadelphia, and New York had dealt with the few free Negroes in their midst to appreciate what would follow general emancipation, he candidly sketched the problem: "It is peculiar to the character of this Anglo-Saxon race of men to which we belong, that it has never been contented to live in the same country with any other distinct race, upon terms of equality; it has, invariably, when placed in that situation, proceeded to exterminate or enslave the other race in some form or other, or, failing in that, to abandon the country."

The idea of the Anglo-Saxon race as a distinct, all-encompassing force was expressed with increasing frequency in the late 1830s. In February 1837 William Gilpin wrote to his father from New Orleans that while the town was still Gallic in character the "Anglo-Saxon is pushing aside the

Frenchman and eating him up. The big steamers . . . are Anglo-Saxon, the huge stores and warehouses into which [goods] are piled have an Anglo-Saxon look and an Anglo-Saxon ship bears them hence. [Of] all the new part of the city, the only decent part is English." When Horace Bushnell, in August 1837, delivered an oration on the principles of national greatness, he used old and familiar arguments concerning America as a land saved for events of world significance; however, he used a new precision in writing of the origin of the people for whom the New World had been preserved. "Out of all the inhabitants of the world," he said, ". . . a select stock, the Saxon, and out of this the British family, the noblest of the stock, was chosen to people our country." In contrast, the Mexican state, he said, had started with fundamental disadvantages in the character of its immigrants. If the quality of the British people was changed into that of the Mexican, "five years would make their noble island a seat of poverty and desolation." For Bushnell, God had reserved America for a special people of Saxon blood.

By the 1830s the Americans were eagerly grasping at reasons for their own success and for the failure of others. Although the white Americans of Jacksonian America wanted personal success and wealth, they also wanted a clear conscience. If the United States was to remain in the minds of its people a nation divinely ordained for great deeds, then the fault for the suffering inflicted in the rise to power and prosperity had to lie elsewhere. White Americans could rest easier if the sufferings of other races could be blamed on racial weakness rather than on the whites' relentless search for wealth and power. In the 1830s and 1840s, when it became obvious that American and Mexican interests were incompatible and that the Mexicans would suffer, innate weaknesses were found in the Mexicans. Americans, it was argued, were not to be blamed for forcibly taking the northern provinces of Mexico, for Mexicans, like Indians, were unable to make proper use of the land. The Mexicans had failed because they were a mixed, inferior race with considerable Indian and some black blood. The world would benefit if a superior race shaped the future of the Southwest.

By the time of the Mexican War, America had placed the Mexicans firmly within the rapidly emerging hierarchy of superior and inferior races. While the Anglo-Saxons were depicted as the purest of the pure—the finest Caucasians—the Mexicans who stood in the way of southwestern expansion were depicted as a mongrel race, adulterated by extensive intermarriage with an inferior Indian race. Travelers delighted in depicting the Mexicans as an unimprovable breed and were particularly scathing about the inhabitants of Mexico's northern provinces. T. J. Farnham in 1840 wrote of the Californians as "an imbecile, pusillanimous, race of men, and unfit to control the destinies of that beautiful country." No one who knew "the indolent, mixed race of California," he argued, could believe they would long populate much less govern, the region. The mixed white and Indian races of California and Mexico "must fade away; while the mingling of different branches of the Caucasian family in the States" would produce a race which would expand to cover all the northern provinces of Mexico. "The old Saxon blood must

stride the continent," wrote Farnham, "must command all its northern shores
. . . and . . . erect the altar of civil and religious freedom on the plains of the
Californias." . . .

The American dismissal of the Mexicans as an inferior, largely-Indian
race did not pass unnoticed in Mexico. Mexican ministers in the United
States warned their government that the Americans considered the Mexicans
an inferior people. The Mexicans realized both that their neighbors to the
north were likely to invade their northern provinces, and that they would
claim that this was justified because they could make better use of the lands.
Mexicans who served as diplomatic representatives in the United States were
shocked at the rabid anti-Mexican attitudes and at the manner in which
Mexicans were lumped together with Indians and blacks as an inferior race.

The Texas Revolution was from its beginnings interpreted in the United
States and among Americans in Texas as a racial clash, not simply a revolt
against unjust government or tyranny. Thomas Hart Benton said that the
Texas revolt "has illustrated the anglo-Saxon character, and given it new
titles to the respect and admiration of the world. It shows that liberty, justice,
valour—moral, physical, and intellectual power—discriminate that race wherever it goes." Benton asked "old England" to rejoice that distant Texas
streams had seen the exploits of "a people sprung from their loins, and carrying their language, laws, and customs, their *magna charta* and all its glorious
privileges, into new regions and far distant climes."

In his two terms as president of Texas, Sam Houston consistently thought
of the struggle in his region as one between a glorious Anglo-Saxon race
and an inferior Mexican rabble. Victory for the Texans and the Americans
in the Southwest would mean that larger areas of the world were to be
brought under the rule of a race that could make best use of them. Houston
was less imbued with the harsh scientific racial theories that carried most
Americans before them in the 1840s than with the romantic exaltation of
the Saxons given by Sir Walter Scott and his followers.

Houston's inaugural address in October 1836 contrasted the harsh, uncivilized warfare of the Mexicans with the more humane conduct of the
Texans. He conjured up a vision of the civilized world proudly contemplating "conduct which reflected so much glory on the Anglo-Saxon race."
The idea of the Anglo-Saxons as the living embodiment of the chivalric ideal
always fascinated Houston; the Mexicans were "the base invader" fleeing from
"Anglo-Saxon chivalry." In fighting Mexico the Texans were struggling to
disarm tyranny, to overthrow oppression, and create representative government: "With these principles we will march across the Rio Grande, and . . .
ere the banner of Mexico shall triumphantly float upon the banks of the
Sabine, the Texian standard of the single star, borne by the Anglo-Saxon
race, shall display its bright folds in Liberty's triumph, on the isthmus of
Darien."

While conceiving of the Texas Revolution as that of a freedom-loving
Anglo-Saxon race rising up to throw off the bonds of tyranny imposed by
a foreign despot, Houston was also fully convinced of the inevitability of

general American Anglo-Saxon expansion. To him "the genius as well as the excitability" of the American people impelled them to war. "Their love of dominion," he said, "and the extension of their territorial limits, also, is equal to that of Rome in the last ages of the Commonwealth and the first of the Caesars." The people of the United States, he argued, were convinced that the North American continent had been bestowed on them, and if necessary they would take it by force. He told one correspondent in 1844 that there was no need to be concerned about the population said to occupy the vast area from the 29th to the 46th latitude on the Pacific: "They will, like the Indian race yield to the advance of the North American population."

For the most part Houston was content to exalt the Anglo-Saxons as a chivalric, freedom-loving, and expansionist race without launching bitter attacks on the capacities of other races. But the image he helped to create of a gallant band of Anglo-Saxon freemen struggling to throw off the yoke of Mexican oppression, and the more general image of the Mexicans that was present in the United States from the mid-1830s, helped breed a callousness toward the Mexicans as a people. The Alamo, the massacre at Goliad, and, later, the fate of the Texas-Santa Fe expedition received wide publicity in the United States and increased the venom with which the Mexican race was condemned. Hearing that those on the Texas-Santa Fe expedition had been captured and sent on a long march to Mexico City, the *Mobile Register and Journal* prophesied that a flame of resentment would sweep the United States which "will bring upon that feeble and treacherous race, a dreadful retribution for a long career of perfidy and cruelty." Increasingly Mexicans were lumped with the blacks and the Indians. One man who had been on the Texas-Santa Fe expedition wrote of soon being able to have his turn "with the yellow skins" and said that though he did not think of himself as being much of a soldier he would risk his life in resisting "such beings as the Mexicans." By the early 1840s few were willing to acknowledge that the Mexicans had anything to commend them as a race. . . .

The racial affinity of Americans and Texans was constantly on the lips of those who favored the annexation of Texas. Levi Woodbury of New Hampshire stated that the Texans had "a body of intelligent and talented men of the true Saxon race. And if all these do not constitute a state, what does?" He thought it was much more the duty of the United States to receive these Saxons into the union than it had been to receive the French of Louisiana or the Spanish of Florida. To Woodbury the Texans had been decoyed to their country by liberal colonization laws, then their rights and privileges invaded, "and their Saxon blood humiliated, and enslaved to Moors, Indians, and mongrels." David L. Seymour of New York saw annexation as "the easy and natural union of two contiguous nations, both founded by the Anglo-Saxon race, both organized upon the same basis of popular rights and republican equality." The Texans were a superior people. "They are of the Americo-Anglo-Saxon race," said Whig Alexander H. Stephens of Georgia. "They are from us, and of us; bone of our bone, and flesh of our flesh."

Although many southern supporters of the annexation of Texas saw it as a means of protecting slavery and the interests of the slave states, there were supporters of annexation all over the country who saw the slavery question as irrelevant. They believed that the expansion of the Anglo-Americans into Texas was part of an inevitable movement of the American people, and that while the immediate effect might be the extension of slavery, the most important result would be the extension of the progressive power of the American race. As the blacks were more and more viewed as a race apart, whatever the fate of slavery, it was possible to conceive of an expansion which both extended slavery and the current boundaries of American settlement as being for the absolute good of the world. William J. Brown of Indiana was unwilling to accept the argument that the Rio Grande formed the natural boundary between races. To discuss whether or not the American advance should stop there was irrelevant, he argued, for "it *will not*. A half a century will not roll around before it will cover all Mexico; nor a century pass by before it will find its way to Patagonia's snow-invested wilds." He was uncertain how many republics would be carved from this area, but he had no doubt that their destinies "would be guided by Anglo-Saxon hands."

The opponents of the annexation of Texas were unable to prevent it. The measure was firmly supported both in Congress and in the nation, and it was difficult to deny the argument that this was merely a reuniting of Americans who wished to be reunited. Although some objected to expansion that would mean the extension of slavery, practically all viewed the Southwest as an area that eventually would be transformed by Anglo-Saxons. It seemed that no human agency could stop the predestined outward thrust of the American people.

It was in commenting on the annexation of Texas that Democratic politician and publicist John L. O'Sullivan coined the phrase *Manifest Destiny* to describe the process of American expansion. In the early 1840s O'Sullivan, in editing the *Democratic Review,* had not accepted the most virulent of the new racial theories. Although he acknowledged black inferiority, he was generally reluctant to condemn all other races as being incapable of improvement. He had as much in common with the expansionists of the Jeffersonian generation as with those who seized on his phrases at mid-century, and he was more confident of general human improvement than most expansionists of the 1840s. Yet O'Sullivan was convinced that without violence America's population would expand outward in ever-increasing numbers, and though he had at first advised caution on the Texas issue, he was happy to accept the annexation of Texas. His qualms over methods were subsumed in his delight that his vision of American expansion was being realized.

O'Sullivan first used the phrase Manifest Destiny in criticizing other nations for attempting to interfere with a natural process: other nations had intruded, he said, "for the avowed object of thwarting our policy and hampering our power, limiting our greatness and checking the fulfillment of our manifest destiny to overspread the continent allotted by Providence for the free development of our yearly multiplying millions." Slavery had nothing to do with the annexation, he argued, for slaves would be drawn off to the South.

Texas had been absorbed as part of the fulfillment of "the general law" which was sending a rapidly increasing American population westward. California would probably soon follow Mexico within the American orbit: "The Anglo-Saxon foot is already on its borders. Already the advance guard of the irresistible army of Anglo-Saxon emigration has begun to pour down upon it, armed with the plough and the rifle, and marking its trail with schools and colleges, courts and representative halls, mills and meeting houses." There was to be no balance of power on the American continent: Spanish America had demonstrated no ability for growth; Canada would break away from England to be annexed by the United States; and no European power could contend "against the simple, solid weight of the two hundred and fifty, or three hundred millions—and American millions—destined to gather beneath the flutter of the stripes and stars in the fast hastening year of the Lord 1945!" In his enthusiasm O'Sullivan had put a touch of Carlyle into his style.

The initial use of the phrase Manifest Destiny in the summer of 1845 attracted no particular attention, but in December of that year O'Sullivan used it again, this time in his newspaper, the *New York Morning News*. O'Sullivan was now concerned with the Oregon question. He maintained that although America's legal title to Oregon was perfect, its better claim was by "the right of our manifest destiny to overspread and to possess the whole of the continent which Providence has given us for the development of the great experiment of liberty and federated self-government entrusted to us." A week later Representative Robert C. Winthrop of Massachusetts referred to the phrase in Congress. It immediately became the subject of debate and inspired both praise and censure. In the following years it was referred to frequently both by advocates and opponents of expansion.

O'Sullivan was able to meld the Texas and Oregon crises in his general assumptions of overriding American destiny, but in Congress discussions of the racial implications of the two controversies differed sharply. In discussing Texas and Mexican rule Congressmen drew few distinctions between Mexicans and their government. It was argued that the instability and ineffectiveness of the Mexican government stemmed from the inadequacies of an inferior population. In discussing Great Britain and Oregon even those Congressmen who were most critical of the British government usually made a clear distinction between the British government and the English race. The English were respected as fellow Anglo-Saxons who were not to be swept out of Oregon as an inferior breed; and those who opposed war with England frequently discussed the disastrous effects of a clash between the two great branches of the Anglo-Saxon race. The sense of Anglo-Saxon racial community, combined with a respect for British power and ability, helped mute the most strident demands for war. While the Texas issue had provided an opportunity for accentuating the differences between superior Americans and inferior Mexicans, the Oregon crisis stimulated a public avowal of the common roots of the American and English peoples. . . .

That the Oregon question was settled peacefully and the southwestern problem resulted in war with Mexico stemmed partially from the differences in strength between Great Britain and Mexico. But it also arose from the obvious fact that many American politicians were reluctant to clash with their Anglo-Saxon brethren, whereas they thought as little of clashing with the Mexicans as they did of clashing with the Indians. The Oregon debates revealed the extent to which the British government was hated by some Americans and the extent to which British imperial ambition was feared; but they also revealed a basic admiration for the English people and a pride in belonging to a common Anglo-Saxon stock. . . .

Along with the exaltation of a particular race came a new sense of urgency and ultimately a willingness to admit the necessity of force—when the ends were so sublime, could one continually quibble about the means? Anglo-Saxons, through the expansion of England and the United States, were visibly taking over the world, and by the 1840s only a few in the United States were prepared to suggest that this was not for the good of the world. Some even began to welcome force rather than regret its necessity. George O. Sanders of Kentucky, later a leader of the political Young America group, wrote in 1844 in regard to the Texas question that "the Americans are everywhere awake. They are booted and spurred, and are panting for the contest." Representative Charles G. Ferris of New York noted that America's "march is *onward, onward.*" The United States was springing forward "to greatness and empire." The imagery of American expansion no longer simply emphasized "spreading"; it stressed "marching." John Reynolds of Illinois thought that the Americans by 1890 would extend through Canada and would have large cities on the Pacific and extensive commerce across that ocean: this was the "onward march of the United States to her high destiny, which no foreign nation can arrest." In this mood the Americans were ready to take what the Mexicans would not sell. Many had convinced themselves that what they wanted was for the good of the world as well as themselves. . . .

The contradictions which had long been implicit in America's sense of mission became explicit at the time of the Mexican War. It became obvious in these years that the United States had now rejected the idea that most other peoples of the world could share in the free government, power, and prosperity of the United States. To sow the seeds of freedom and republicanism over an ever-widening area was not enough to secure world progress, because Americans now believed that these seeds were falling on barren ground. Most peoples, they believed, lacked the innate abilities to take advantage of free institutions. Some races were doomed to permanent inferiority, some to extinction.

While faith in general human improvability was often lost, faith in the expansive power of the American branch of the Anglo-Saxon race increased. The Americans were destined to continue to increase rapidly in numbers and to spread far and wide. But if other peoples could not be instructed in the establishment of free republican states, what would happen to the population in the areas into which the American Anglo-Saxons were expanding? The Americans had two immediate racial models—the Indians and the blacks. Wherever the whites had moved in large numbers the Indians had disappeared, and it was assumed that as the American population expanded its settlements to the Pacific the Indians would be eliminated. The blacks were not disappearing but were increasing in numbers. They were surviving, argued the advocates of slavery, because they had been totally subordinated to a superior race. Even many of those who opposed slavery believed that free blacks could not survive and prosper in close proximity to the white race.

The most irrational American expansionists in the 1840s appeared to believe that the Anglo-Saxons would actually replace numerous world peoples in the course of progress. The practical realities embodied in the idea of "the survival of the fittest" were made use of in America well before they were embodied in a statement of general principle. Some Americans believed that their problems would be solved by having other races, like the Indians, melt away before the American advance. The American Anglo-Saxons would not teach or rule other peoples—they would replace them.

For some, southern slavery taught that another route to a free, prosperous society was the total subordination of the inferior to the superior race. Perhaps this could be the future pattern of the American advance. Mexicans and others might not be enslaved, but they would be subordinated to the rule of a superior people. Military success in Mexico led some Americans to argue that the United States should enforce a military, colonial-style government. They asserted that this would bring prosperity to Mexico, more power and wealth to the United States, and would hasten the time when the whole world would become progressive. The United States would become a colonial power.

This last suggestion brought a crisis in American thinking on expansion. There were many in the United States who believed that the trappings of colonialism would ruin the republic. But they did not want to bring large numbers of non-Anglo-Saxon peoples as equal citizens within the American union. They thought such inferior peoples would also ruin the republic. This dilemma quickly produced strong opposition to immediate expansion. If Americans believed that other peoples would not disappear before the American advance, if they also thought that colonialism would corrupt the nation, and if they believed that other races were incapable of participating in a free government, then opposition to a further extension of territory became their only hope of preserving a free American Anglo-Saxon republic. It meant resisting those who were now convinced that the United States should rapidly assume political control over vast new areas. Yet the expansionists were to be resisted not because this would mean the degradation of other peoples, but because the presence of other races would ruin the society created in the United States.

The general low regard in which the people of Mexico were held by the government and people of the United States helped to precipitate the outbreak of war. Since the time of the Texas Revolution the Mexicans had been repeatedly attacked in the United States as a degenerate, largely Indian race unable to control or improve the territories they owned. Only a minority of Americans felt a sense of guilt in waging war on such a people. Indeed, faced by a people considered so feeble and lacking in self-respect, Polk's administration hoped to achieve the annexation of Texas and the purchase of California without resorting to overt force.

The American minister in Mexico, Wilson Shannon, commented to Calhoun in October 1844 that "I see it is predicted in some of the papers in the U.S. that Mexico will declare war against the U.S.; there is as much probability that the Emperor of China will do so." Because the Mexicans were held in contempt, it was assumed that firmness would force them to yield to American wishes. Unlike the English in Oregon, the Mexicans were neither praised as fellow members of a special race, nor respected as a potentially formidable foe. Before going to Mexico in the fall of 1845 envoy John Slidell told Secretary of State James Buchanan that he did not believe that the Mexicans would go to war: "The truth is that although I have no very exalted idea of Mexican intellect, yet I cannot imagine that any one who could by possibility be elected president, could have so small a modicum of sense as to think seriously of going to war with [the] United States." Secretary of War William L. Marcy as late as July 1845 expressed the opinion that he had at no time felt that war with Mexico was probable "and do not now believe it is." Secretary of State James Buchanan had a particularly low opinion of Mexican character and talents and for much of the war balked at the idea of annexing territory that contained any large number of Mexicans. In his official instructions to Slidell he asked his envoy to be as conciliatory as possible and patiently to endure any unjust reproaches. "It would be difficult," he said, "to raise a point of honor between the United States and so feeble and degraded a Power as Mexico."

The general assumption in the cabinet that Mexico would not fight the United States, or at worst could easily be defeated, was reflected in public opinion throughout the country. Although a few prominent individuals, including Senator Benton, warned that Mexico would fight valiantly to protect its lands, the general assumption was that a weak and degraded Mexico could offer no real resistance to the United States forces. It was even assumed at the beginning of the war that a Mexican population oppressed by the military, the clergy, and a corrupt government would welcome the invading armies. Throughout the conflict some argued that the United States was carrying freedom to the Mexicans, and that a true regeneration of the Mexicans was to take place. But it soon became apparent that most Americans believed that the Mexicans lacked the innate ability to benefit from the opportunity to be given them by liberating American armies.

The older idea of Americans actually carrying the seeds of free institutions to Mexicans who would throw off their bondage and create a sister republic was expressed most often at the beginning of the war in the writings of America's patriotic poets. Many obviously found their inspiration in the older tradition of the widening arc of free institutions. One poet envisioned the stars in America's flag increasing "Till the world shall have welcomed their mission sublime / And the nations of earth shall be one." Another, in leaden verse, sang that "The world is wide, our views are large / We're sailing on in Freedom's barge / Our God is good and we are brave / From tyranny the world we'll save." The sentiment that the United States' flag would be the flag of the world when tyranny had perished was a common one, and many united in conceiving of the invasion as a war of liberation. The inhabitants of Mexico were expected to welcome the Saxons with open arms. A New York poet in May 1846 conjured up an image of Mexicans joyously shouting "The Saxons are coming, our freedom is nigh."

Yet while many poets wrote in an older, idealistic tradition, some reflected the prevailing racial stereotypes of the Mexicans and added sexual overtones to the image of the liberating drive into Mexico. A poem published in Boston in June 1846 and entitled "They Wait for Us" foreshadowed the views of those expansionists who later in the war argued that the American Anglo-Saxons would simply absorb and eliminate what was left of the Mexican population. Neither this poet nor the later politicians had any doubt that extinguishing the remnants of the Mexican race was to be accomplished by a union of American men and Mexican women:

> The Spanish maid, with eye of fire,
> At balmy evening turns her lyre
> And, looking to the Eastern sky,
> Awaits our Yankee chivalry
> Whose purer blood and valiant arms,
> Are fit to clasp her budding charms.

> The *man,* her mate, is sunk in sloth—
> To love, his senseless heart is loth:
> The pipe and glass and tinkling lute,
> A sofa, and a dish of fruit;
> A nap, some dozen times by day;
> Sombre and sad, and never gay.

The image of lazy Mexican men and available Mexican women had already been established by the accounts of American travelers. Dana, in his *Two Years before the Mast,* had written of "thriftless, proud, extravagant" California men and of women with "a good deal of beauty" whose morality was "none of the best." Kendall, who was on the Texas-Santa Fe expedition, dismissed Mexican men in the usual fashion, but was obviously fascinated by the women. The "Anglo-Saxon traveler" entering New Mexico, he said, "feels not a little astonished at the Eve-like and scanty garments of the females he meets." He went on to describe the beauty of Mexican women and was obviously delighted that "the forms of the gentler sex obtain a roundness, a fulness, which the divinity of tight lacing never allows her votaries." His general characterization of the women was in striking contrast to his dismissal of Mexican men: the women of northern Mexico "are joyous, sociable, kind-hearted creatures almost universally, liberal to a fault, easy and naturally graceful in their manners." Kendall's distinction between Mexican men and women was commonplace in the travel narratives. "The ladies," Rufus B. Sage wrote, "present a striking contrast to their countrymen in general character, other than morals." The stereotype of exotic, receptive

Mexican women and lazy, inept Mexican men was to sink deep into American racial mythology. . . .

Some, in the heat and emotion of the conflict, wavered between faith in the improvability of mankind and the new racial pride. Walt Whitman, then editor of the *Brooklyn Daily Eagle,* argued that American expansion was for the good of the whole world: "We pant to see our country and its rule far-reaching," he wrote, "only inasmuch as it will take off the shackles that prevent men the even chance of being happy and good." Yet while Whitman generally attacked the Mexican government rather than the Mexican people, he could not free himself from the prevailing racial interpretation of events. "What has miserable, inefficient Mexico . . . to do," he asked, "with the great mission of peopling the New World with a noble race?" General Zachary Taylor's capture of Monterey in September 1846 was welcomed as "another clinching proof of the indomitable energy of the Anglo-Saxon character." Whitman now wanted peace and the cession of large areas by Mexico. This would be for the good of mankind. . . .

After the Mexican War it was clear that if American expansion was to continue into populous areas it either had to be through colonial rule or economic penetration. The American republican government was not a government for all races and all colors—federalism had its limits. Yet Americans were determined to participate fully in shaping the economic future not only of the American continents but also of the world. A search for personal and national wealth was put in terms of world progress under the leadership of a supreme race. In thrusting into the Pacific, Americans revived arguments that the American advance would bring freedom and civilization to all peoples; but the reality of attitudes toward neighborhing peoples in the years of the Mexican War made nonsense of the claims that the American penetration of Asia was intimately connected with the regeneration of other races.

## Concrete Interests and Expansion

NORMAN A. GRAEBNER

Manifest destiny, a phrase used by contemporaries and historians to describe and explain the continental expansion of the United States in the 1840's, expressed merely a national mood. The belief in a national destiny was neither new nor strange; no nation or empire in history has ever been totally without it. But for its proponents of the 1840's the meaning conveyed by the phrase was clearly understood and peculiarly American. It implied that the United States was destined by the will of Heaven to become a country of political and territorial eminence. It attributed the probability and even the necessity of this growth to a homogeneous process created by certain unique qualities in American civilization—the energy and vigor of its people, their idealism and faith in their democratic institutions, and their sense of mission now endowed with a new vitality. It assigned to the American people the obligation to extend the area of freedom to their less fortunate neighbors, but only to those trained for self-government and genuinely desirous of entering the American Union. Expansionists of the forties saw this self-imposed limitation on forceful annexation as no serious barrier to the Republic's growth. It was inconceivable to them that any neighboring population would decline an invitation to enter the realm of the United States. Eventually editors and politicians transformed the idea of manifest destiny into a significant expression of American nationalism.

Such convictions of destiny came easily to the American people in the midforties, for they logically emerged from the sheer size and dramatic achievements of the young Republic. From New England and Pennsylvania, reaching on into the Ohio Valley and the Great Lakes region, an industrial revolution was multiplying the productive resources of the United States. New forms of transportation, made possible by the efficient application of steam, rendered the national economy greater than the sum of its parts. Steamboats transformed the Mississippi and Ohio rivers—with their many tributaries—into a mighty inland system of commercial and human traffic. Railroads had long since left the Atlantic seaboard and were, by the forties, creeping toward the burgeoning cities of the Middle West. Asa Whitney had already projected a railroad line from Lake Michigan to the Pacific Northwest. Samuel F. B. Morse's successful demonstration of the magnetic telegraph in 1844 assured almost instantaneous communication across the entire continent. "What mighty distances have been overcome by railroads," exclaimed the *Southern Quarterly Review* (October, 1844), "and, stranger than all, is the transmission of intelligence with the speed and with the aid of lightning!" . . .

Never in history could a people more readily accept and proclaim a sense of destiny, for never were a people more perfectly situated to transform their whims into realities. Expansion was rationalized so effectively at each point of conflict that it seemed to many Americans an unchallengeable franchise. Confronted by problems neither of conscience nor of extensive countering force, the American people could claim as a natural right boundaries that seemed to satisfy the requirements of security and commerce. Expanding as they did into a vacuum—vast regions almost devoid of population—they could conclude that they were simply fulfilling the dictates of manifest destiny. For them the distinctions between sentiment and action, between individual purpose and national achievement, appeared inconsequential.

Historians, emphasizing the expansive mood of the forties, have tended to identify the westward extension of the United States to the Pacific with the concept of destiny itself. Such identifications are misleading, for they ignore all the genuine elements of successful policy. Those regions into which the nation threatened to expand were under the legal jurisdiction of other governments. Their acquisition required the formulation of policies which encompassed both the precise definition of ends and the creation of adequate means. Manifest destiny doctrines—a body of sentiment and nothing else—avoided completely the essential question of *means,* and it was only the absence of powerful opposition on the North American continent that permitted the fallacy that power and its employment were of little consequence. Occupying a wilderness created the illusion that power was less important than moral progress, and that expansion was indeed a civilizing, not a conquering, process.

Jeremy Bentham once termed the concept of natural right pure nonsense, for the claims of nations were natural only when supported by superior force. The natural right of the United States to a continental empire lay in its power of conquest, not in the uniqueness of its political institutions. American expansionism could triumph only when the nation could bring its diplomatic and military influence to bear on specific points of national concern. What created the easy victory of American expansion was not a sense of destiny, however widely and dramatically it was proclaimed, but the absence of powerful competitors which might have either prevented the expansion entirely or forced the country to pay an exorbitant price for its territorial gains. The advantages of geography and the political and military inefficiency of the Indian tribes or even of Mexican arms tended to obscure the elements of force which were no less real, only less obtrusive, than that employed by other nations in their efforts at empire building. It was no wonder that British and French critics concluded that the American conquest of the continent was by pick and shovel.

Concepts of manifest destiny were as totally negligent of *ends* as they were of means. Expansionists agreed that the nation was destined to reach its natural boundaries. But what were these natural frontiers? For Benjamin Franklin and John Adams they comprised the Mississippi River. But when the United States, through the purchase of Louisiana, crossed the Mississippi, there was no end in sight. Expansionists now regarded Florida as a natural appendage—belonging as naturally to the United States, declared one Kentucky newspaper, as Cornwall did to England. John Quincy Adams observed in his diary that the acquisition of Florida in 1819 "rendered it still more unavoidable that the remainder of the continent should ultimately be ours." Eventually Europe would discover, he predicted, that the United States and North America were identical. But President James Monroe revealed no more interest in building a state on the Pacific than had Jefferson. Equally convinced that the distances to Oregon were too great to be bridged by one empire, Thomas Hart Benton of Missouri in 1825 defined the natural boundary of the United States as "the ridge of the Rocky Mountains. . . . Along the back of this ridge, the Western limit of this republic should be drawn, and the statue of the fabled god, Terminus, should be raised upon its highest peak, never to be thrown down." President John Tyler, in his message of December, 1843, perpetuated this limited view of the nation's future. And as late as 1845 Daniel Webster continued to refer to an independent republic along the distant Pacific coast. Meanwhile expansionists could never agree on the natural boundaries of Texas. Representative C. J. Ingersoll of Pennsylvania found them in vast deserts between the Rio Grande and the Nueces. For others they comprised the Rio Grande itself, but James Gadsden discovered in the Sierra Madre mountains "a natural territorial boundary, imposing in its Mountain and Desert outlines." . . .

If the ultimate vision of American destiny in the forties comprised a vast federal republic that boasted continental dimensions and a government based on the principle of states rights, the future boundaries of the United States, as determined by the standards of geographical predestination, never seemed to possess any ultimate logic. Boundaries that appeared natural to one generation were rejected as utterly inadequate by the next. It was left for Robert Winthrop, the conservative Massachusetts Whig, in January, 1846, to reduce the doctrine of geographical predestination to an absurdity:

> It is not a little amusing to observe what different views are taken as to the indication of "the hand of nature" and the pointings of "the finger of God," by the same gentlemen, under different circumstances and upon different subjects. In one quarter of the compass they can descry the hand of nature in a level desert and a second-rate river, beckoning us impatiently to march up to them. But when they turn their eyes to another part of the horizon the loftiest mountains in the universe are quite lost upon their gaze. There is no hand of nature there. The configuration of the earth has no longer any significance. The Rocky Mountains are mere molehills. Our destiny is onward.

Democratic idealism was even less precise as a guide to national action than the doctrine of geographical predestination. By 1845 such goals of reaching the waters of the Pacific were far too limited for the more enthusiastic exponents of the new expansionism. As they interpreted the expression of democratic idealism, the dogma represented an ever-expanding force. Indeed, for some it had no visible limit at all. It looked beyond the North American continent to South America, to the islands of the Pacific, and to the Old World itself. One editorial in the New York *Herald* (September 15, 1845), declared, "American patriotism takes a wider and loftier range than heretofore. Its horizon is widening every day. No longer bounded by the limits of the confederacy, it looks abroad upon the whole earth, and into the mind of the republic daily sinks deeper and deeper the conviction that the civilization of the earth—the reform of the governments of the ancient world—the emancipation of the whole race, are dependent, in a great degree, on the United States." This was a magnificent vision for a democratic purpose, but it hardly explains the sweep of the United States across the continent. It bears no relationship whatever to the actual goals which the Tyler and Polk administrations pursued in their diplomacy with Texas, Mexico, and England.

Texas provided the necessary catalyst which fused all the elements of manifest destiny into a single national movement. When, in 1844, the annexation issue suddenly exploded on the national scene, the expansionist front had been quiescent for a full generation. The twenties and thirties had been years of introspection. The changing structure of American political and economic life had absorbed the people's energies and directed their thoughts inward. Yet the same inner-directed concerns which rendered the country generally oblivious to external affairs promoted both the sense of power and the democratic idealism which, under the impetus of expansionist oratory, could easily transform the nation's mood and forge a spirit of national destiny. . . .

California no less than Oregon demanded its own peculiar expansionist rationale, for its acquisition confronted the United States with a series of problems not present in either the Texas or Oregon issues. If the government in Mexico

City lacked the energy to control, much less develop, this remote province, its title was still as clear as its hold was ephemeral. The annexation of this outpost required bargaining with its owner. Even that possibility seemed remote in 1845, for the Mexican government had carried out its threat to break diplomatic relations with the United States rather than condone the American annexation of Texas. For a decade American citizens had drifted into the inland valleys and coastal villages of California, but in 1845 they still comprised an infinitesimal number, even when compared to the small Mexican and Indian population.

Obviously the United States could not achieve its continental destiny without embracing California. Yet this Mexican province had never been an issue in American politics; its positive contribution to American civilization had scarcely been established. California, moreover, because of its alien population, was by the established principles of American expansion less than acceptable as a territorial objective. American acquisitiveness toward Texas and Oregon had been ethnocentric; it rejected the notion of annexing allegedly inferior peoples. "There seems to be something in our laws and institutions," Alexander Duncan of Ohio reminded the House of Representatives early in 1845, "peculiarly adapted to our Anglo-Saxon-American race, under which they will thrive and prosper, but under which all others wilt and die." He pointed to the decline of the French and Spanish on the North American continent when American laws had been extended to them. It was their unfitness for "liberal and equal laws, and equal institutions," he assumed, that accounted for this inability to prosper under the United States.

Such inhibitions toward the annexing of Mexican peoples gradually disintegrated under the pressure of events. The decision to annex Texas itself encouraged the process by weakening the respect which many Americans held for Mexico's territorial integrity, and thus pointed the way to further acquisitions in the Southwest. Having, through the annexation of Texas, passed its arm "down to the waist of the continent," observed the *Dublin Freeman,* the nation would certainly "not hesitate to pass it round." That the United States was destined to annex additional portions of Mexican territory seemed apparent enough, but only when its population had been absorbed by the Anglo-Saxons now overspreading the continent. As early as 1845 the rapid migration of pioneers into California promised to render the province fit for eventual annexation. In July, 1845, the *Democratic Review* noted that Mexican influence in California was nearing extinction, for the Anglo-Saxon foot was on its border.

American acquisitiveness toward California, like that displayed toward Texas and Oregon, progressed at two levels—that of abstract rationalization and that of concrete national interest. Polk alone carried the responsibility for United States diplomacy with Mexico, and interpreted American objectives in the Southwest—like those in Oregon—as precise and determined by the sea. Travelers and sea captains of the early forties agreed that two inlets gave special significance to the California coast—the bays of San Francisco and San Diego. These men viewed San Francisco harbor with wonderment. Charles Wilkes assured the readers of his *Narrative* . . . that California could boast "one of the finest, if not the very best harbor in the world." It was sufficiently extensive, he added, to shelter the combined navies of Europe. Thomas J. Farnham, the American traveler and writer, called it simply "the glory of the Western world." All who had visited the bay observed that it was the unqualified answer to American hopes for commercial greatness in the Pacific. To the south lay San Diego Bay—the rendezvous of the California hide trade. Here, all Boston firms maintained their coastal depots for cleaning, drying, and storing the hides until a full cargo of thirty to forty thousand had been collected for the long journey to Boston. The processing and storing of hides required a warm port, free from rain, fog, and heavy surf. San Diego alone met all these require- ments. This beautiful bay, so deep and placid that ships could lie a cable's length from the smooth, hard-packed, sandy beach, became the chief point of New England's interest on the California coast. The bay was exposed to neither wind nor surf, for it was protected for its entire fifteen-mile length and possessed a narrow, deep entrance. Richard Henry Dana observed in *Two Years Before the Mast* (1840) that San Diego harbor was comparable in value and impor- tance to San Francisco Bay. The noted sea captain, Benjamin Morrell, once termed San Diego "as fine a bay for vessels under three hundred tons as was ever formed by Nature in her most friendly mood to mariners."

During the autumn of 1845, even before his administration had disposed of the Oregon question, Polk embarked on a dual course to acquire at least a por- tion of California. English activity in that distant province convinced him that, in Great Britain, the United States faced a strong and determined competitor for possession, in particular, of San Francisco Bay. Thomas O. Larkin, an Amer- ican merchant at Monterey, reported that the French and British governments maintained consuls in California although neither nation had any commercial interests along the Pacific coast. "Why they are in Service their Government best know and Uncle Sam will know to his cost," Larkin warned in July, 1845. Larkin's reports produced a wave of excitement in the administration. "The appearance of a British Vice Consul and French Consul in California at this present crisis without any apparent commercial business," Secretary of State James Buchanan answered Larkin, "is well calculated to produce the impression that their respective governments entertained designs on that coun- try...."On October 17, 1845, Buchanan drafted special instructions to Larkin:

> The future destiny of that country is a subject of anxious solicitude for the government and people of the United States. The interests of our commerce and our whale fisheries on the Pacific Ocean demand that you should exert the greatest vigilance in discovering and defeating any attempts which may be made by foreign governments to acquire a control over that country. . . . On all proper occasions, you should not fail prudently to warn the government and people of California of the danger of such an interference to their peace and prosperity; to inspire them with a jealousy of European domination, and to arouse in their bosoms that love of liberty and independence so natural to the American continent.

Polk appointed Larkin as his confidential agent in California to encourage the Californians, should they separate from Mexico, to cast their lot with the United States. "While the President will make no effort and use no influence to induce California to become one of the free and independent states of the Union, yet," continued Buchanan's instructions, "if the people should desire to unite their destiny with ours, they would be received as brethren, whenever this can be done without affording Mexico just cause of complaint." Larkin was told to let events take their course unless Britain or France should attempt to take California against the will of its residents.

During November, 1845, Polk initiated the second phase of his California policy—an immediate effort to purchase the province from Mexico. On November 9, William S. Parrott, a long-time resident of Mexico now serving as Polk's special agent at the Mexican capital, returned to Washington with confirming information that the officials in Mexico City would receive an American envoy. As early as September Polk and his cabinet had agreed to tender such a mission to John Slidell of Louisiana. In his instructions to Slidell, dated November 10, Buchanan clarified the administration's objectives in California. In a variety of boundary proposals Polk was adamant only on one—the Rio Grande. Those that applied to California were defined solely in terms of Pacific ports. They started with San Francisco and Monterey, the capital of the province, but they included also a suggested boundary line which would reach westward from El Paso along the 32nd parallel to the Pacific, this extended as far as the harbor of San Diego. Unfortunately Slidell was not received by the Mexican government. The administration's program of acquiring at least one of the important harbors along the California coast by purchase from Mexico had failed.

From the defeat of their diplomacy to achieve a boundary settlement with Mexico Polk and his cabinet moved early in May, 1846, toward a recommendation of war, employing as the immediate pretext the refusal of the Mexican government to pay the claims of American citizens against it for their losses in Mexico. Before the cabinet could agree on such a drastic course of action, Polk received word that a detachment of General Zachary Taylor's forces stationed along the disputed Rio Grande boundary of Texas had been fired upon by Mexican forces. Armed with such intelligence, the President now phrased his message to obtain an immediate and overwhelming endorsement for a policy of force. Mexico, he charged, "has passed the boundary of the United States, has invaded our territory and shed American blood upon American soil." War existed, in short, by act of Mexico. Polk explained that his action of stationing Taylor on the Rio Grande was not an act of aggression, but merely the attempt to occupy a disputed territory. Yet the possibility that the President had sought to provoke a clash of arms left sufficient doubt in the minds of his Whig opponents to permit them to make the Mexican War the most bitterly criticized in American history.

During the summer of 1846 the rapid American conquest of California quickly crystallized the expansionist arguments for the retention of the province. Indeed, California suddenly appeared totally satisfactory as a territorial addition. Amalgamation of the Mexican population no longer caused anxiety, for, as Andrew J. Donelson predicted, within five years the Anglo-American people would be dominant in the province. Lewis Cass in February, 1847, still believed any amalgamation between Americans and Mexicans quite deplorable. "We do not want the people of Mexico either as citizens or subjects," he warned, but then he added reassuringly with special reference to California, "all we want is a portion of territory which they nominally hold, generally un-inhabited, or, where inhabited at all, sparsely so, and with a population which would soon recede or identify itself with ours." Buchanan, opposing the ex-tension of the United States to the Sierra Madre Mountains, asked: "How should we govern the mongrel race which inhabit it?" Like Donelson and Cass, he harbored no fear of annexing California, for, he added, "The Californias are comparatively uninhabited and will therefore be almost exclusively colo-nised by our own people."

There was little sentimentality in the *Democratic Review*'s prediction in March, 1847, that American pioneers in California would dispossess the in-habitants as they had the American Indians. It declared that evidently "the process which has been gone through at the North of driving back the Indians, or annihilating them as a race, has yet to be gone through at the south." Sim-ilarly the *American Review* that same month saw Mexicans giving way to "a superior population, insensibly oozing into her territories, changing her cus-toms, and out-living, out-trading, exterminating her weaker blood. . . ."

California's immense potential as the seat of a rich empire, contrasted to its backwardness under Mexican rule, added a new dimension to the doctrine of manifest destiny—the regeneration of California's soil. . . .

Polk, adequately supported by the Democratic expansionists in Congress, ra-tionalized the American retention of California, not with references to the doc-trine of regeneration, but with the principle of indemnity. "No terms can . . . be contemplated," O'Sullivan argued in July, 1846, "which will not require from [Mexico] indemnity . . . for the many wrongs which we have suffered at her hands. And if, in agreeing upon those terms, she finds it more for her in-terest to give us California than to satisfy our just demands in any other way, what objection can there be to the arrangement . . . ?" Unfortunately for the President, indemnity, clearly recognized as a legitimate fruit of victory by the law of nations, was acceptable to only those Americans who placed responsibil-ity of the war on Mexico. To those Whigs who attacked the war California constituted conquest, not indemnity, and therefore was scarcely an acceptable objective to be pursued through the agency of war. . . .

During December and January, with Congress in session, Democratic orators seized control of the all-of-Mexico movement and carried this new burst of expansionism to greater heights of grandeur and extravagance. Their speeches rang with appeals to the nationalism of war and the cause of liberty. Cass ob-served that annexation would sweep away the abuses of generations. Senator Ambrose Sevier of Arkansas pointed to the progress that awaited the most degenerate Mexican population from the application of American law and education. In January, 1848, the Democratic Party of New York, in conven-tion, adopted resolutions favoring annexation. The new mission of regenera-tion was proclaimed everywhere in the banquet toasts to returning officers.

At one Washington dinner in January Senator Daniel Dickinson of New York offered a toast to "A more perfect Union: embracing the entire North American continent." In Congress that month Senator R. M. T. Hunter of Virginia commented on the fever annexationism had stirred up. "Schemes of ambition, vast enough to have tasked even a Roman imagination to conceive," he cried, "present themselves suddenly as practical questions." Both Buchanan and Walker of the cabinet, as well as Vice President George M. Dallas, openly embraced the all-of-Mexico movement.

That conservative coalition which had upheld the Oregon compromise combined again early in 1848 to oppose and condemn this new crusade. This powerful and well-led group feared that the United States, unless it sought greater moderation in its external policies, would drift into a perilous career of conquest which would tax the nation's energies without bringing any commensurate advantages. Its spokesmen doubted that the annexation of Mexico would serve the cause of humanity or present a new world of opportunity for American immigrants. Waddy Thompson, the South Carolina Whig who had spent many years in Mexico, warned in October against annexation: "We shall get no land, but will add a large population, aliens to us in feeling, education, race, and religion—a people unaccustomed to work, and accustomed to insubordination and resistance to law, the expense of governing whom will be ten times as great as the revenues derived from them." Thompson, joined by Calhoun and other Southern antiannexationists, warned the South that no portion of Mexico was suitable for slavery. Mexico's annexation would merely endanger the South's interests with a new cordon of free states. In Congress Calhoun acknowledged the dilemma created by the thoughtless decision to invade Mexico and recommended that the United States withdraw all its military forces to a defensive line across northern Mexico and maintain that line until Mexico chose to negotiate a permanent and satisfactory boundary arrangement with the United States.

Neither the mission of regeneration nor its rejection by conservatives determined the American course of empire. The great debate between those who anticipated nothing less than the achievement of a continental destiny and those who, in the interest of morality or from fear of a bitter controversy over slavery expansion, opposed the further acquisition of national territory, was largely irrelevant. Polk and his advisers pursued a precise vision, shared by those expansionists who searched the Mexican borderlands for the American interest. In the mid-forties, when the nation's agricultural frontier was still pushing across Iowa and Missouri, the concern of those who knew California lay less in land than in the configuration of the coastline and its possible relationship to America's future in the entire world of the Pacific. If American continentalism during the war years provided a substantially favorable climate for the acquisition of Mexican lands, it contributed nothing to the actual formulation of the administration's expansionist program.

During the early weeks of the Mexican War the President noted repeatedly in his diary that he would accept no treaty which did not transfer New Mexico and Upper California to the United States. It was left only to hammer out his precise war aims. Initially, Polk and his cabinet were attracted to San Francisco and Monterey. Several days after the outbreak of war George Bancroft, Secretary of the Navy, assured the Marblehead merchant, Samuel Hooper, that by mid-June the United States flag would be floating over these two northern California ports. "I hope California is now in our possession, never to be given up," he added. "We were driven reluctantly to war; we must make a solid peace. . . ."

But Hooper did not rest at Bancroft's promise. He prodded the administration to look southward along the California coast. Settlement at the thirty-second parallel, Hooper informed Bancroft, would secure both Los Angeles and the bay of San Diego. Such a boundary, moreover, would encompass all the Anglo-American population in the province and remove future annoyance by leaving a barren wilderness between Upper California and the larger Mexican cities to the south. Should the United States acquire San Diego as well as Monterey and San Francisco, continued Hooper, "it would insure a peaceful state of things through the whole country and enable [the Americans] to continue their trade as before along the whole coast. . . ." Thereafter the administration looked to San Diego. Bancroft assured Hooper in June, 1846, that the administration would accede to New England's wishes. "If Mexico makes peace this month," he wrote, "the Rio del Norte and the Parallel of 35° may do as a boundary; after that 32° which will include San Diego." This harbor remained the ultimate and unshakable territorial objective of Polk's wartime diplomacy.

Eventually the President achieved this goal through the efforts of Nicholas P. Trist. Unable after almost a year of successful fighting in Mexico to force the Mexican government to sue for terms, Polk, in April, 1847, dispatched Trist as a secret diplomatic agent to join General Winfield Scott's army in Mexico and await any sudden shift in Mexican politics. Trist's official baggage contained detailed instructions and the *projet* for a treaty which aimed pointedly at the acquisition of the entire coast of California to San Diego Bay. Trist's subsequent negotiations secured not only a treaty of peace with Mexico which terminated the war but also the administration's precise territorial objectives. Manifest destiny fully revealed itself in the Mexican War only when it clamored for the whole of Mexico, but even that final burst of agrarian nationalism was killed effectively by the Treaty of Guadalupe Hidalgo. American victories along the road to Mexico City were important only in that they created the force which permitted the President to secure through war what he had once hoped to achieve through diplomacy alone. It was Trist, working alone and unobserved, who in the final analysis defined the southern boundary of California. . . .

Manifest destiny, in its evolution as a body of American thought, expressed a spirit of confidence and a sense of power. It set forth in extravagant language a vision of national greatness in territorial, political, or diplomatic concerns. It proclaimed a national mission to the downtrodden and oppressed, designed to rationalize in terms of a higher good the nation's right, and even its duty, to dispossess neighboring countries of portions of their landed possessions. But whatever its form and strength, manifest destiny was purely the creation of editors and politicians, expounded to churn the public's nationalistic emotions for the purpose of reaping larger political harvests. Those who preached the crusade created fanciful dreams of the Republic's future; they ignored specifics and were unmindful of means. They were ideologues, not statesmen.

Even their success in converting the nation to the wisdom or feasibility of their views was doubtful. It was the consideration of national interest alone that carried the annexations of the forties through Congress. In the case of Texas, where the final decision conformed to the will of the expansionists, the victory came hard. The Senate overwhelmingly rejected the Texas treaty of 1844, and only after months of intense party and sectional maneuvering—during which time the Texas issue became nationalized—was the joint resolution of annexation adopted by the narrow vote of 27 to 25. Where the nation would expand after Texas was the business of the national executive as the wielder of the nation's diplomacy, and the territory which the United States opened up across the continent to the Pacific satisfied a series of traditional and limited national interests. National growth itself had little or no connection with the continentalism which dominated the language of manifest destiny in the forties and which cloaked American expansionism with universal goals —abstract rather than precise. Manifest destiny created the sentiment that would underwrite governmental policies of expansion; it could not and did not create the policies themselves.

The Senate approved the Oregon Treaty of 1846 with an ample margin, but it was the minority of fourteen senators—the die-hard proponents of the whole-of-Oregon movement—who represented the cause of manifest destiny. The Oregon Treaty was a triumph for the moderates. Again, in 1848, the Senate agreed to the nation's expansion by accepting the Treaty of Guadalupe Hidalgo. But the Senate resolution which demanded more than California and New Mexico from the defeated enemy represented a futile effort to convert the all-of-Mexico sentiment into policy. It lost by eleven votes. The persistent failure of Democratic orators to achieve their declared political and diplomatic goals with appeals to both the emotions of patriotism and the actual record of American expansion culminated in their inability to elect their leading expansionist, Lewis Cass, to the White House in 1848.

Except for the Gadsden Purchase in 1853, a quiet transaction that responded to the needs of railroad building, the nation failed to expand between 1848 and 1860. However, manifest destiny suffered one last and glorious revival when, as late as 1859, James Buchanan sparked another burst of expansionism toward Cuba. But whatever the appeal of such sentiment in Washington, it had no influence in Madrid. Without the physical coercion of Spain there could be no expansion, and even those Americans who would accept the doctrine that the ends justified the means could not discover the "occasion"—at least one acceptable to the majority of United States citizens—for bringing the overwhelming power of the United States to bear on the weakening Spanish rule in Cuba.

American expansion before the Civil War, like all successful national action abroad, required specific and limited objectives, totally achievable within the context of diplomacy or force, whether that force be displayed or merely assumed. After national interest and diplomatic advantage combined, during the forties, to carry the United States to the Pacific, the necessary elements of policy and policy formulation never reoccurred to extend boundaries further. Perhaps it mattered little. The decade of the fifties—for the United States a decade of unprecedented internal development—amply proved the contention of the antiexpansionists that the country's material growth was not dependent upon its further territorial advancement.

# Polk's Aggressive Leadership

### DAVID M. PLETCHER

Shortly after the Mexican War the American Peace Society offered a $500 prize for the best study of the recent conflict "on the principles of Christianity, and an enlightened statesmanship." Abiel A. Livermore, a Unitarian minister from New Hampshire, won the prize with a manuscript setting forth the thesis that the war and the preceding annexation of Texas had been parts of a plot by Polk, Tyler, Calhoun, and the South for the extension of slavery. Another entry in the contest by the Rev. Mr. Philip Berry, a Presbyterian, was less to the judges' liking, perhaps because it criticized the war not as immoral but as unnecessary: "Tested by the principles which have ordinarily governed the civilized world in its international relations [it] was . . . one of the most *just* wars that have blotted with gore the history of man—a war that might nevertheless have been avoided by the United States, had they been so disposed, probably without diminution of an inch of territory."

Livermore's blast was an opening gun in a long historiographical battle over the legal and moral validity of American actions, which lasted well into the twentieth century, but Berry's arresting statement drew no answering fire from the defenders of the war and the annexations. Was the war, in fact, necessary? More broadly expressed, did Tyler, Polk, and other policy makers of the mid-1840s carry through their program of territorial expansion in such a way as to minimize dangers, loss, and general tension? Did the annexations cost the United States too much? Speculative questions such as these cannot be finally answered, but they may serve as a point of departure for appraising policies and actions.

The first step in such an appraisal is to draw up a balance sheet of American gains and losses resulting from the war and from the Texas and Oregon treaties. Some gains are obvious to anyone who can read a map. Between 1845 and 1848 the United States acquired more than 1,200,000 square miles of territory, just over a third of its present area, including Alaska and Hawaii—a vast domain almost as large as all the countries of Free Europe after World War II. During the Mexican War some Whigs were inclined to write off California and Oregon as worthless, save for a few Pacific harbors, but the gold rush of 1849 quickly

Reprinted from *The Diplomacy of Annexation: Texas, Oregon, and the Mexican War* by David M. Pletcher, by permission of the University of Missouri Press. Copyright © 1973 by the Curators of the University of Missouri.

put an end to such skepticism. After the news of the gold strikes reached Mexico City, Consul John Black, once more at his old post, overheard a Mexican in a restaurant remark bitterly, "Ah, . . . the Yankees knew full well before they commenced the war, what they were going to fight for, they knew the value of that country better than we did."

Other American gains were more intangible—for example, the increasing respect of Europeans. Impressed by the show of power, Old World statesmen and publicists recognized that the United States would now dominate the north Pacific coast and the Gulf of Mexico. After the American occupation of California was confirmed, the London *Times* commented, "From so favorable a harbour the course lies straight and obvious to Polynesia, the Philippines, New Holland, and China, and it is not extravagant to suppose that the merchants of this future emporium may open the commerce of Japan."

To be sure, European efforts against American expansion did not entirely cease after 1848, but never again did their agents act so boldly and so close to American borders as had Captain Charles Elliot, the British consul in Texas. Indeed, in 1848, as revolution spread over Europe, the democratic republicanism that most persons identified with the United States seemed close to a final triumph on both sides of the Atlantic. The irrepressible George Bancroft rejoiced that "the struggles of Europe . . . will not rest, till every vestige of feudal nobility is effaced; and the power of the people shall have superseded that of hereditary princes." In these struggles, he added, the United States would be the model. To Bancroft's dismay, reaction soon triumphed over the Revolution of 1848, but American successes in the New World remained to raise the discouraged spirits of Old World liberals and democrats.

More immediately important to the United States, the Mexican War helped to shift the balance of power in the Western Hemisphere. In January 1848 the Earl of Ellenborough, who had wanted San Francisco for a British naval base, wrote gloomily to his former chief, Sir Robert Peel, that the only hope for Anglo-American peace was the indefinite occupation of Mexico by the United States, since this would keep the Americans too busy to seize Canada. Probably to his surprise, when the war ended a few weeks later the troops were immediately brought home and mustered out. Nevertheless, the American lodgement on Puget Sound and the American performance in the Mexican War emphasized more firmly to succeeding British administrations that Her Majesty's Canadian subjects were hostages to American good will.

As a result of the war, the British government also gave up any remaining hopes of political influence around the Gulf of Mexico. In 1848 it declined to guarantee the new Mexican boundaries, sponsor a Tehuantepec transit route, or set up a protectorate over Yucatán. The Americans then pursued the British into Central America, which became a field of intrigue for rival diplomatic agents during the late 1840s. Both sides accepted a temporary stalemate in the Clayton-Bulwer Treaty of 1850, which placed the United States for the first time on an equal basis with Great Britain in that area. During the following decade the British gradually abandoned political aspirations in Central America too, content to compete for economic gains with the potent but unmilitary weapons of their factory system and their merchant marine. If the Mexican War alone did not accomplish this contraction of British influence in the Western Hemisphere, it surely hastened the process.

Against these American gains of territory and prestige, however, the appraising historian must charge certain losses. Some of these were the familiar costs of all wars: about 12,800 men dead out of 90,000 under arms and about $100 million in expenses, to which might be added the $15 million paid to Mexico under the peace treaty. The families and friends of the dead soldiers were the chief sufferers, for the growing nation hardly felt the expenditure of men and money. But, as with the gains, some of the most serious losses caused by the Western annexations and the war are impossible to measure exactly.

One part of this intangible deficit was a rising spirit of "lick all creation," an overblown chauvinism with strong hints of militarism and racism that coarsened democratic sensibilities and laid American ideologues open to charges of hypocrisy. Two examples of this national hubris will suffice. The last Texan secretary of state, Ashbel Smith, who had opposed annexation in 1845, saw in the Mexican peace treaty three years later only the first chapter of a long story:

> The Mexican War is part of the mission, of the destiny allotted to the Anglo Saxon race on this continent. It is our destiny, our mission to Americanize this continent. No nation once degenerate has ever been regenerated but by foreign conquest; and such is the predestined fate of degenerate Mexico. The sword is the great civilizer, it clears the way for commerce, education, religion and all the harmonizing influences of morality and humanity. . . . Palo Alto and Buena Vista, Cerro Gordo and Churubusco . . . will be the talismanic watchwords of freedom and security.

A little later, as Lieutenant Raphael Semmes USN looked back on his wartime service, he agreed:

> The passage of our race into Texas, New Mexico, and California, was but the first step in that great movement southward, which forms a part of our destiny. An all-wise Providence has placed us in juxtaposition with an inferior people, in order, without doubt, that we may sweep over them, and remove them (as a people) and their worn-out institutions from the face of the earth. We are the northern hordes of the Alani, spreading ourselves over fairer and sunnier fields, and carrying along with us, beside the newness of life, and the energy and courage of our prototypes, letters, arts, and civilization.

The rest of the world, long accustomed to American strutting, might well have discounted these predictions but for the amazing victories of Zachary Taylor and Winfield Scott and the persistent filibustering expeditions that Americans launched during the 1850s against Mexico, Cuba, and Central America. To Latin Americans the events of 1843–1848 revealed, perhaps for the first time, the aggressive potential of the United States. Sympathy for Mexico encouraged a widespread but disorganized sentiment for some sort of congress to unite Spanish-speaking peoples against their external enemies. The press of many South American countries reprinted the Whigs' speeches and editorials attacking Polk as evidence that the war was unpopular with the American people, but the onward march of the troops suggested that even public opinion could not halt the *yanqui* government. A stereotype began to take shape in Latin American writing about the United States—the Colossus of the North.

But the most alarming effects of Western annexations and the Mexican War developed within the United States. By the early 1840s many Whigs had come to believe that further expansion in any direction would place intolerable strains on national unity. For that reason Daniel Webster opposed acquiring Texas, and even the expansionist James Buchanan eventually came to think of it as a Trojan horse, for its annexation widened the sectional gap between North and South. To abolitionists Texas became a moral issue; as Charles Sumner put it, "By welcoming Texas as a Slave State we make slavery our own original sin."

In debating the Oregon question, Webster's Whigs also discouraged annexation, expecting that the American emigrants would form an independent, friendly nation on the Pacific coast. To annex it would be as preposterous as annexing Ireland. Nevertheless, the Democratic platform of 1844 and Polk's inaugural address reassured Northern and Western expansionists that the "clear and unquestionable" American title to all Oregon would maintain the balance of sections. The compromise at 49°, however reasonable in legal and practical argument, struck many of them as betrayal by the South. "We have been duped . . . ," declared an Ohioan. "Oregon & Texas should have went [*sic*] hand in hand, Oregon first."

Northern sectionalism undoubtedly encouraged the nation's desire for California, thereby reinforcing the prowar group within the Democratic party. But it also strengthened Whigs' opposition to the war, especially as the progress of Taylor's army suggested the annexation of territory to the southwest. The Northerners' feeling of betrayal crystallized in the Wilmot Proviso, first introduced by one of Polk's own Democrats, which completed the association of slavery and expansion and made the war seem, like Texas and Oregon before it, both a sectional and a moral issue. "It was conceived in sin . . . ," proclaimed the Albany *Evening Standard,* "not to promote any great principle; . . . but to conquer a neighboring republic to acquiesce in an attempt to extend the borders of slavery." "When the foreign war ends, *the domestic war will begin,*" warned the New York *Gazette and Times.* Ralph Waldo Emerson compared the Mexican War to a dose of arsenic, and he might well have applied the term to the acquisition of Texas and Oregon too.

No one would be so bold as to attribute Latin American Yankeephobia and the Civil War wholly or mainly to the annexations of the 1840s. It would be safer to argue that Texas, Oregon, and the Mexican War hastened and intensified trends that might have led to the same results eventually. But insofar as these annexations inflated American arrogance and spread hemispheric and national disunity, they exacted a heavy price, which a fair appraisal must somehow balance against the material gains and the rise in national prestige.

One may next ask whether the nation might have secured substantially the same territory at smaller cost. Brief examination of this question suggests that the alternatives multiplied as the expansion progressed. Given the situation of the early 1840s, the only way for the United States to acquire Texas was to negotiate an acceptable settlement with the Texan government. After the annexation, the United States had the choice of conciliating Mexico, perhaps by paying a disguised indemnity, or of ignoring her claims to the lost province, secure in the confidence that she would not or could not back them with force.

In the Oregon question the United States faced the alternatives of fighting Britain, negotiating with her, or waiting for American settlers to overrun the disputed territory. Controlling elements in both the American and British governments regarded the first option as a last resort, the unthinkable result of blundering rather than of a deliberate decision by either side. The other two options, both highly plausible, will be discussed later.

In the case of the Mexican War the choice was the most complicated of all, for at various points in their relations with Mexico, American leaders contemplated four different lines of action. One was the course actually followed, that of invading Mexico, compelling her to cede the desired territory in a treaty, and then withdrawing American troops at once. A second was the establishment of a temporary protectorate over all Mexico to regenerate that unhappy nation while the United States detached her northern provinces or even prepared her for total absorption. A third was passive military occupation of California, New Mexico, and parts of Chihuahua, Coahuila, Nuevo León, and Tamaulipas, the Army maintaining a chain of forts along the line of the Sierra Madre until Mexico gave up and recognized the *fait accompli*. The last course of action was not to declare war at all but to wait until American settlers could form a majority in California and possibly also in New Mexico, rebel, create an independent state, and enter the Union in the manner of Texas.

The alternative of establishing a protectorate and regenerating Mexico was a most unlikely one. In the first place, its plausibility was muddied by Americans' envy of Mexican natural resources, so that many who espoused it did so only as a rationalization for annexation. But even if the protectorate plan had been more fully worked out and less burdened with hypocrisy, it would still have been wholly impracticable on several counts. At the most abstract level, no one has ever convincingly demonstrated that democracy can be imposed from above. Waddy Thompson, ex-minister to Mexico and a comparatively enlightened commentator on the war, asked, "But of what avail are free institutions without the spirit of liberty amongst the people; or what avail are both without general intelligence and virtue?" Many Americans believed Mexicans to be sunk so deep in ignorance and reaction that if the United States tried to do more than set a good example, the effort would end by endangering this country's free institutions through militarism, bureaucracy, and executive tyranny.

Descending to more concrete levels, opponents of a protectorate could reasonably doubt that it would command the support of many Mexicans. To be sure, a group of *puros* expressed admiration for American institutions, especially control by the civil government over the military. But at the same time, another part of this faction, the followers of Valentín Gómez Farías, were proclaiming undying hatred of the *yanqui*. Assuming that a sizable group of Mexican liberals had initially supported a protectorate, the detachment of California and New Mexico would have disillusioned many of them.

Also, if a protectorate had been established, the American officials in charge of Mexico would quickly have had to deal with deep-seated internal problems —the powers of the Church, the ownership of land, the role of the army, and others. Whatever they did, these officials would have alienated large blocs of influential citizens. A cursory glance at the French protectorate of the 1860s, the well-meant but blundering leadership of Maximilian, and the everlasting guerrilla warfare fought by the *juaristas* suggests the staggering obstacles confronting even a temporary administration of Mexico. Finally, the protectorate plan would have done nothing to abate destructive sectionalism in the United States. Indeed, the rivalry of conservative and liberal policies in Mexico might have exacerbated the quarrels of North and South.

Another plan of action, somewhat less ambitious than the regeneration of all Mexico, was to occupy the northern territory which the United States wished to annex, establish a line of forts along the proposed new boundary, and wait for Mexico to abandon her efforts at reconquest. This idea seems to have occurred to many Americans at about the same time during the early autumn of 1846. By then Taylor had established his control along the lower Rio Grande, and Stockton and Frémont had taken over the principal settlements along the California coast. Although various versions of the partial occupation plan differed in details, most of them specified a line from Tampico to Mazatlán or San Blas, including several cities such as Monterrey and San Luis Potosí as well as many important silver mines. During the invasion of central Mexico and especially after the impasse had developed at Mexico City, some generals and civilians suggested withdrawal to a northern line. But by this time such a policy would have been most difficult to execute, for the evacuation of any territory whatever would have affronted American patriots, spread war weariness, and encouraged Mexican resistance.

Even if undertaken earlier in the war, the indefinite passive military occupation of northern Mexico would have presented serious obstacles. The advocates of this strategy counted heavily on local separatism and growing friendliness between the inhabitants and the occupying forces. But cities such as Tampico, Monterrey, and San Luis Potosí comprised fully developed Mexican societies and culture, as contrasted to the conglomerate, shallowly rooted settlements of California and the Rio Grande Valley. Sooner or later the relations of long-established Mexican groups with the Protestant, Anglo-Saxon Americans, each despising the strangeness of the other, would surely have produced chronic instability. Arguments over the introduction of slaves, economic and social rivalry between the lower classes of both countries, and differences concerning the position of the Church would probably have intensified sectional and partisan divisions within the United States. At the same time, the indefinite continuation of the war would have stimulated Polk's opposition—Whigs, abolitionists, and those who impatiently demanded bold attack and speedy victory. Once the war had gotten under way, it was hard to refute Thomas Hart Benton's argument that an overwhelming offensive was the surest route to peace.

But was it necessary to fight for the territory at all? The last alternative under consideration was for the United States to maintain "a wise and masterly inactivity" following the annexation of Texas—to parry British proposals for ending joint occupation in Oregon, station a defensive force at the western edge of effective Texan settlement, and wait for the movement of American pioneers to fill up the desired areas. If left to themselves, Californians would presumably declare their independence of Mexico, and the settlers in the Willamette Valley would expand northward to Puget Sound. Meanwhile, in both areas bonds of trade and kinship with the United States would develop. Eventually, the United States government would negotiate an annexation treaty with California; Britain would recognize the *fait accompli* in Oregon by splitting the territory at 49°; and Mexico would abandon her claims, perhaps in return for an indemnity.

This policy assumed that American expansion was inevitable and that the past would continue to repeat itself. Politicians and journalists were fond of proclaiming this assumption; as one of them declared in 1846, "No power on earth ... can check the swelling tide of American population. ... Every portion of this continent, from the sunny south to the frozen north, will be, in a very few years, filled with industrious and thriving Anglo-Saxons. ... This is the irresistible progress of our people. Like the flow of the ocean, it overcomes all opposition." Since its independence the United States had developed a flexible, effective procedure for acquiring territory with a minimum of risk. This procedure was to reinforce the "irresistible progress" with diplomatic and economic pressure or perhaps veiled threats and to exploit fully the disunity among European powers and their tepid interest in North America. In this manner the Americans had won first the navigation of the lower Mississippi, then Louisiana, then the Floridas, and finally Texas without an open declaration of war or serious fighting except against the Indians.

Why not use the time-proven procedure in Oregon and California? In 1843 Calhoun advocated exactly this strategy in Oregon, and he conducted cordial but indeterminate negotiations with Britain during his year in the State Department. The outstanding exponent of the same policy in California was Thomas O. Larkin, the leading American merchant and, after 1843, American consul in Monterey. Always maintaining friendly relations with native inhabitants and local governments, Larkin encouraged a movement for an independent republic in which natives, Europeans, and Americans would enjoy equal status. Eventually, he believed, all three groups would find it to their interest to enter the American Union. For a time Polk approved this policy. After the war began, he experimented with secessionism in northeastern Mexico, hoping to attract the inhabitants peaceably into the United States.

The policy of relying on migration and gradual assimilation of thinly populated areas faced certain obstacles. In northeastern Mexico the boisterousness of the new American arrivals irrevocably antagonized most upper-class Mexicans. In California the Bear Flag revolt showed that many pro-American inhabitants preferred action to persuasion; sometimes Larkin himself leaned in that direction. Another obstacle to gradualism was certain to be the stubbornness of the Mexican government. After resisting the recognition of Texan independence for nine years, it had yielded in 1845 only through British persuasion and in the desperate hope of preventing annexation by the United

States. The Mexicans might have resisted for a longer time if California had pulled away from their grasp, and subsequent annexation by the United States might have created a chronic, festering diplomatic problem. Polk might not have come to terms even with the independent Californian republic during his four years as President. Had gradualism won California to the Union, New Mexico might not have attracted enough American settlers to repeat the process, thereby leaving an inconvenient Mexican salient between Texas and the Pacific coast. The chances of delay and of creating an awkward boundary must be weighed against the dangers and cost of precipitate action.

From the viewpoint of Polk and his generation the most serious drawback to gradualism was the risk of British intervention. Persistent rumors throughout 1845 declared that the Mexican government would sell or mortgage California to Britain. British residents were said to be planning an invitation for a protectorate. The British warships that regularly visited the Oregon coast might be carrying on reconnaissance to the south at the same time. Even if Britain did not interfere with an independence movement in California, the partly known story of her activities in Texas furnished a precedent for fearing subsequent intrigue on the Pacific coast. To many Americans a short, decisive war seemed greatly preferable to another long series of negotiations with some Californian Sam Houston, "coquetting" at the same time with the wily Aberdeen or the daredevil Palmerston. . . .

If the Mexican War was indeed an unnecessary gamble, why did Polk undertake it? He and his supporters explained that he did so only as a last resort, in defense of American interests and honor after Mexico had ignored claims, rejected negotiation, and hurled insult and defiance at the United States. Many historians have applied their scholarship to defense of this viewpoint. But a considerable segment of antiwar opinion at the time proclaimed that Polk was waging a war of conquest, pure and simple, which he rationalized with sophistical arguments, so as to legalize the American occupation of California under the law of nations and set up such a barrier as the British would not dare cross. Pursuing the matter further, some of Polk's opponents accused him of "a deliberate contrivance to bring the war about in such a manner as to throw on Mexico the odium of its commencement." Since the 1880s a few historians have accepted this "plot thesis" and have applied it to all his policies from his inauguration to the beginning of the war.

None of these explanations is wholly convincing. The list of American claims and the story of the Slidell mission suggest that American grievances were bearable and that the United States government had not exhausted the possibilities of negotiation. Also, the opening hostilities took place on disputed ground to which Mexico had an arguable claim. But if Polk was waging simply a war of conquest, it is hard to understand why he did not plan it more comprehensively from the beginning and why he conducted it with spurts of action followed by long periods of stagnant delay. As for the "plot thesis," its supporters offer too little evidence and too much surmise in its defense. They ignore the administration's repeated predictions that war was neither likely nor desirable and the administration's failure to enlarge or overhaul the inadequate army until war had begun. Also, they fail to make clear why Polk should have provoked Britain to a war crisis at the same time that he planned to fight Mexico.

A more consistent explanation of Polk's foreign policies appears in several revealing statements he made about Britain and Oregon. Note his account of a conversation with a minor Democratic Congressman on January 4, 1846, during the Oregon debate:

> I remarked to him that the only way to treat John Bull was to look him straight in the eye; that I considered a bold & firm course on our part the pacific one; that if Congress faultered [sic] or hesitated in their course, John Bull would immediately become arrogant and more grasping in his demands; & that such had been the history of the Brittish [sic] Nation in all their contests with other Powers for the last two hundred years.

He put it even more succinctly to a friend: "Great Brittain [sic] was never known to do justice to any country—with which she had a controversy, when that country was in an attitude of supplication or on her knees before her." Accordingly, when he sent Buchanan or McLane to approach Pakenham or Aberdeen, Polk took a high hand, exaggerated his legal case and his demands, and regarded all suggestions of compromise as probes from Britain or American Anglophiles to find weak points in his armor.

Polk applied the same policy of aggressive negotiation to American-Mexican relations, with the difference that, instead of respectful suspicion toward a tough, tenacious power, he felt contemptuous impatience toward a weak, corrupt, disorganized government, much given to delay and evasion. Tight-mouthed, he let slip no revealing private remarks about the Mexican character such as his comments on Britain, but his public statements in his annual message of 1845 and especially in the war message give some idea of his underlying feelings. "A continued and unprovoked series of wrongs," hope for "a returning sense of justice," "frivolous pretexts," "the subsisting constitutional authorities . . . subverted," a "manifest breach of faith," "a government either unable or unwilling . . . to perform one of its plainest duties," a "system of outrage and extortion" —all these phrases suggest Polk's distaste for Mexico. Such a government, like that of Britain, would respond only to strong words and a show of force. He declared to his cabinet during the last weeks before the declaration of war that "we must treat all nations, whether great or small, strong or weak, alike, and that we should take a bold and firm course toward Mexico."

Thus, when Polk became President, he set forth on a foreign policy of strong stands, overstated arguments, and menacing public pronouncements, not because he wanted war but because he felt that this was the only language which his foreign adversaries would understand. Faced at his inauguration with the delicate final arrangements for the annexation of Texas, Polk had no desire to precipitate an immediate crisis with either Mexico or Britain. Accordingly, he sent a special agent to reconnoiter in Mexico City for a renewal of diplomatic relations and agreed to exchange views on Oregon with Britain. When Pakenham cut short this exchange, Polk, overreacting, jumped to the conclusion that he had been tricked. Breaking off the dialogue, he stiffly notified the British government that it must now make a concrete proposal which he might treat as he chose.

The strong stand toward Mexico was slower to develop. During the summer and autumn of 1845 rumors of Mexico's intentions to attack in the Rio Grande Valley or to reconquer California with British aid provoked Polk to station troops and ships where they would be useful in case of war and also to inaugurate a program of propaganda and intrigue among the natives of California. These preparations made, he sent Slidell to Mexico, with instructions to press Herrera not only for recognition of Texan boundaries but for the sale of California and New Mexico as well. In December his annual message summarized the strong stands toward both Britain and Mexico and added new arguments, such as the Monroe Doctrine, to earlier rationalizations.

Events during the winter of 1845–1846 forced Polk to modify his original plans. He had called on Congress to demonstrate unified support by quickly passing a firm resolution of notice to Britain on Oregon. But before doing so, in late April, the legislators spent four months in rancorous debate, thus threatening Polk's whole legislative program and the unity of his party. Meanwhile, the Mexican government refused even to receive Slidell, who finally returned home empty-handed. At some time during the last stages of the Oregon debate Polk became convinced that an actual war with Mexico would be necessary—not a major conflict, but a limited, short, decisive engagement in the Rio Grande Valley which would convince Mexico that the United States meant business. If the Mexicans began the fighting, their attack could be used to unify the Democratic party and confound the Whigs. If American forces could then occupy California and New Mexico, Mexico would be forced to negotiate and the United States could obtain title to the provinces, perhaps in return for a disguised indemnity to Mexico. By this time Britain would have decided to propose an Oregon settlement which the Senate would accept.

This version of Polk's policies explains his episodic method of waging war. During May and June he carried out much of his program through Taylor's victories in the Rio Grande Valley, the Oregon settlement, and the occupation of California—so much that, when the Mexicans continued to resist, Polk was firmly convinced that one more crushing victory would cause their collapse and bring peace. First, the Americans advanced to Monterrey, then to Tampico, while he let the apparently pliant Santa Anna slip through the blockade to return home. He then pressed Congress for a special fund of $3 million, which might be used as an inducement to Mexico to sign a proper peace treaty.

After waiting in vain for Santa Anna to negotiate, Polk decided to occupy Veracruz and then to advance into the fever-free interior, sending a minor diplomat, Nicholas P. Trist, to accompany the army and transmit correspondence. But even Scott's victory at Cerro Gordo, the most impressive of the entire war, failed to break the Mexicans' amazing will to resist. After pausing three months at Puebla, Scott moved into the Valley of Mexico—a dangerous advance, for he risked being cut off from his base. At this point one setback would have undone the effect of all previous victories. But the Americans continued to win battles. At one point peace talks actually got under way, but again Santa Anna did not choose or dare to submit, and Scott had to occupy Mexico City.

The war now threatened to get out of hand altogether, as a movement spread through the United States for extensive annexations in central Mexico or rule over the entire country as the only acceptable return for American losses. But Polk gave no evidence that he had lost his nerve or had changed his plans. Instead, learning of the fruitless peace talks, he recalled Trist. Apparently the President intended to take over direct control of negotiations and perhaps force the Mexicans to come to Washington if they wanted peace. However, his repudiated envoy spared him the need of testing his assumptions further by an act of courageous insubordination. Urged by British diplomats and merchants, Trist remained in Mexico and with their aid obtained a treaty along the lines of his original instructions. One might add that Polk's luck continued to hold, even in his failure to acquire Yucatán and Cuba after the war, for he was able to leave office without bequeathing to his successor half-realized annexations which were beyond the country's capacity at that time.

To the retrospective eye of the historian Polk's alarums and excursions present an astonishing spectacle. Impelled by his conviction that successful diplomacy could rest only on a threat of force, he made his way, step by step, down the path to war. Then, viewing the war as a mere extension of his diplomatic scheme, he proceeded as confidently as a sleepwalker through a maze of obstacles and hazards to the peace settlement he had calmly intended from the beginning.

Despite his boldness and his unshakable determination, Polk was at heart a cautious leader. His apparently most impetuous acts—the withdrawal of the Oregon offer to Pakenham, the bold stands of his first annual message, the declaration of war, and the occupation of Veracruz—were undertaken only after weeks or even months of meditation and discussion with his advisers. If he thought long and hard about his country's interests, he was even more careful when the interests of his party and himself were concerned, for he tried to associate Congress in some way with every important decision he made, in order to divert and disperse the wrathful lightning of his many opponents.

Nevertheless, for all his prudence, he clearly did not anticipate the rigors of a war crisis with Britain or a long-drawn-out invasion of Mexico. Why did he miscalculate so grossly? One reason was simple lack of up-to-date, accurate information. Dispatches from London or Mexico City required at least three or four weeks to reach Washington, and news from Oregon and California five or six months. Even the most experienced, trusted observers were sometimes highly unreliable. While Everett and McLane presented fairly exact pictures of British attitudes, Consul Black in Mexico City consistently misled the United States government about the Mexicans' support of the war, and Larkin's important dispatch of July 10, 1845, about the British threat to California was wrong on every count. During the critical weeks of April and May 1846 Polk and his cabinet learned about Mexican troop movements from rumors in the New Orleans newspapers or hearsay dispatches from Mexico City and Veracruz. When

Taylor marched into the lower Rio Grande Valley, his superiors provided him with an almost useless topographical map put together in Washington and with little more. In effect, both the administration and the general were feeling their way into unknown territory.

Polk's rigid determination to follow a course of aggressive diplomacy and war also rose from traits of his personality. His diary reveals that he could be insensitive to the ideals and convictions of others; this characteristic was dominant when he looked outward toward Europe or Latin America. He lacked a primary qualification of the diplomat—the ability to appreciate a foreign people's hopes, fears, and driving impulses and to see America and himself through their eyes. To him, Britain was a thieving bully, British appeals to national honor mere rationalizations, and British sentiments of democracy and friendship no more than traps for the unwary. Similarly, the Mexicans were a people hardly worthy of self government, unable to develop the borderlands that stood in the way of American expansion, and their clamorous boasts and appeals to patriotism mere mouth honor.

Polk's insensitivity toward Britain, though dangerous to American interests, was eventually nullified by countervailing factors. The more sophisticated Britons understood the President's personality, having seen its traits in some of their own politicians, and they made allowances for it, although they found it distasteful. Webster, Everett, Sturgis, and other American conciliators well known in London assured them by their demeanor that Polk represented only one aspect of the American character. Most important, perhaps, British leaders were perceptive enough to sense some of the possibilities for future Anglo-American cooperation and strong enough to defend British national honor with patience rather than with passion.

If such countervailing factors existed in American-Mexican relations, they are hard to discern. Mexicans had long regarded the United States with a combination of admiration and suspicion, and in the 1840s their rising anger was both complicated and frustrated by profound ignorance concerning American political and social institutions. Weak, disunited, repeatedly humiliated by revolutions, penury, and foreign slights, the Mexicans seemed to have nothing further to lose but national integrity. Remembering his experiences in Mexico City, Pakenham predicted that the Mexicans' sense of honor would require stubborn defense of their boundaries and that an American offer of money would probably intensify their resistance. A high British official, well acquainted with the Spanish character, once observed, "The Mexican is like a mule—if you spur him too much he will back off the precipice with you."

The most enlightened leaders of this quixotic people were far behind Peel and Aberdeen in training, perception, and firmness of purpose. Some, like Herrera and Cuevas, saw the need to restrain a national impulse toward self-immolation but did not know how. Others, like Gómez Farías, plunged into the flames with the rest. The master of Mexico during most of the war, Santa Anna, was even more inscrutable than Polk. Despite his postwar apologies and reams of Mexican writings, no convincing evidence has emerged to indicate that he ever seriously intended to reach an agreement with the United States. The record of his words and deeds suggests only that he was an incorrigible opportunist who improvised his plans from day to day without any guiding principle more sophisticated than self preservation.

Whatever the qualities of the Mexican leaders, their view of Polk and the United States was as simplistic as Polk's view of them, and the intermediaries between the two nations did little to correct the fault. Almonte's abilities might have been comparable to Pakenham's, but the Mexicans recalled him in 1845. Slidell might have been as persuasive as McLane, but the Mexicans would not receive him. As for unofficial go-betweens, Atocha and Beach are not comparable with Everett, Sturgis, or the Baring agents.

Polk's myopia and lack of empathy in relations with Britain and Mexico can also be attributed in large measure to his training and environment. From his mentor Andrew Jackson, he may have derived the models for his British and Mexican policies—the peremptory Jacksonian challenge to France over unpaid debts and the conniving mission of Anthony Butler to Mexico. In the challenge to France the threat of force, though later modified, had brought action; while the heavy-handed Butler was unsuccessful, Polk might reasonably have supposed that a more suave agent would prevail.

In a broader sense, whether Polk received from Jackson his suspicions of other nations and his techniques for dealing with them, he may be said to have epitomized the self-centered, aggressive nationalism prevalent in the Mississippi Valley during much of the nineteenth century. Remembering British-Indian intrigues and the War of 1812, Midwesterners easily envisaged the Hudson's Bay Company, the governor general of Canada, and the cabinet in London as deceitful bullies. Remembering how Spanish dons in Madrid and New Orleans had opposed American expansion, the inhabitants of the lower valley and their cousins, the transplanted Texans, easily attributed to Mexico the same sly, ceremonious evasion they had experienced earlier. During the first fifty years of the United States' national existence Presidents and secretaries of state had frequently displayed a sophisticated cosmopolitanism that mitigated or, in some instances, nullified American xenophobia. This restraining factor, however, almost disappeared with the generation of Madison and Monroe. Post-Jacksonian leaders were not always more free from international involvements than their predecessors, but with few exceptions they were certainly less citizens of the world.

If Polk shared the *Weltanschauung* of his people and times, what may be said of his other blind spot—failure to anticipate the disunity Oregon and the Mexican War spread among the American people? Ideological and sectional rivalry arising from the Texas question had nearly torn the Democratic party asunder in the campaign of 1844. Once in office, Polk could not avoid carrying through the immediate annexation of Texas, since Congress and Tyler had precipitated the action. But why did he not realize that internal suspicions and resentments made it expedient to halt the pressure on Britain and Mexico for the time being?

Polk's abolitionist opponents and some later pro-Northern historians answered this question by labeling him the tool of the blind, recklessly imperialist

Southern "slaveocracy." Years ago, American scholars punctured the thesis that the South monopolized or was even united behind southwest expansionism, although many Mexican writers still accept it as sound. Might Polk have wished to avoid a repetition of the sectional struggle over Texas and therefore set out to acquire Oregon, California, and New Mexico directly and quickly, so as to give sectionalism no time to develop? There is no evidence in his correspondence or diary to indicate this line of thought. Like many other Southerners, Polk regarded the "local institutions" of Texas as a matter of concern to the Texans alone. In his diary he had nothing to say about sectional agitation over slavery until the introduction of the Wilmot Proviso in the summer of 1846, when the war had already begun. Thereafter, he clearly looked on all attempts to link slavery and expansion as mischievous, wicked, and foolish —mischievous and wicked because his opponents were using the issues for partisan gain, foolish because the territory to be acquired would never support slavery.

Polk was not alone in his shallow, unenlightened view of the nation's most threatening problem, for other statesmen of the mid-1840s, older and more experienced than he, failed also to understand that sectionalism and expansion had formed a new, explosive compound. John C. Calhoun, deliberate and canny where Oregon was concerned, acted with reckless abandon in the Texas question when he answered Aberdeen's mild defense of abolitionism with a note gratuitously proclaiming what the North already suspected—that Calhoun wanted annexation in order to preserve slavery as a positive good. John Quincy Adams, who had reluctantly surrendered American claims to Texas in the Spanish treaty of 1819, threatened a secessionist movement in 1843 if Texas were annexed. Three years later he shifted back to expansionism and invoked *Genesis* to support the American claim to 54°40'. When one sees elder statesmen like these playing ducks and drakes with American passions, the insensitivity of younger men becomes more understandable.

In the effort to explain and appraise Polk's policies, one final element remains to be considered—his freedom of choice. To what extent were his decisions shaped or forced on him by circumstances beyond his control?

From 1845 to 1848 Polk seems to have experienced a phenomenon that diplomatic and military strategists of the mid-twentieth century have called *escalation*. This phenomenon is a process by which an initial set of decisions starts a chain of causes and effects, each more difficult to control than its predecessor. At the beginning of the chain the decision maker may have been presented with a fairly wide range of acceptable choices. The range is gradually reduced until at the end he has—or seems to have—none. In other words, events close in on him until he finds himself surrounded with dilemmas, all exits blocked.

Even at the beginning of his administration Polk did not have complete freedom of choice, for his party platform, the joint resolution of Congress, and Tyler's last-minute offer to Texas committed him to immediate annexation. This action, in turn, brought an unavoidable break in formal diplomatic relations with Mexico. Nevertheless, since that nation was in no position to launch a concerted attack, Polk could take stock of the situation, send a private observer to Mexico, and wait for the Mexicans' anger to subside. In the Oregon question he was limited only by an extremist plank in the Democratic platform and by the statements of Democratic congressmen during the winter debate of 1844–1845.

Polk might have taken stock of this question too, and perhaps he intended to do so. But he committed his first serious tactical error when he inserted into his inaugural address a restatement of the "clear and unquestionable" United States title—by implication to all Oregon—and thereby stirred up violent argument in Britain and in the American West. After this address, postponement of action was no longer possible, but for a time he considered private negotiations with Britain on the basis laid down by Calhoun in 1844. Pakenham rebuffed him; then, yielding to his own convictions about Britain, Polk committed his second major error by breaking off negotiations altogether and insisting that Britain must take the initiative to resume them. In less than six months he had abdicated nearly all choice concerning Oregon.

Until November 1845 Polk retained, almost unhampered, the power to determine the direction and timing of his Mexican policy. During the next two months, however, he seriously restricted his freedom of choice here as well. His instructions to Slidell and his annual message to Congress announced to Mexico and to the world at large that the United States would take an extreme position regarding its claims and objectives to the southwest. By thus proclaiming his intentions and by sending Taylor's army to the Rio Grande, Polk destroyed any hope of privately persuading Mexico. Meanwhile, his annual message again stimulated Western expectations for all of Oregon and formally transferred to Congress much of the responsibility for settling the question.

After January 1846 events began to drive Polk irresistibly. The long, raucous debate on Oregon encouraged the British government to postpone any useful initiative to resume negotiations. The debate and Mexico's rejection of Slidell induced Polk to plan for a short war with Mexico. But a short war turned into a long one, for the Mexicans now held the power of decision, and although repulsed or routed in every major battle, they determined to resist the invaders, supported by their formidable topography and climate.

Once war had been declared, Polk's policy choices were limited to alternate military strategies, attack of some sort versus a holding action. After the landing at Veracruz there remained only one way forward—up the foothills and across the mountains into the Valley of Mexico. When Scott captured Mexico City, Polk had exhausted the acceptable choices available to him, for further conquest, indefinite occupation, and retreat to a line across northern Mexico all presented insuperable difficulties. Fortunately, at this point conciliation and compromise, so foreign to Polk's nature, saved him.

All in all, an appraisal of the diplomacy of annexation brings the realization that annexation might have been less painful and costly if skillful diplomacy had been allowed to play a more vital role at several points. Diplomats drew up the basic terms for the incorporation of Texas, and the climactic victory of Donelson over Elliot was in large measure a diplomatic one. After a serious Anglo-American war crisis, it was the diplomacy of McLane that pointed the way to a settlement of the Oregon question. Similarly, after nearly two years of costly war with Mexico, it was the diplomacy of Trist, aided by British representatives, that laboriously untied the Gordian knot in Mexico City.

Could Polk have avoided the Oregon and Mexican crises by placing his chief reliance on conventional, professional diplomacy in the spring of 1845? The evidence suggests that he might have done so. In one of Tyler's last special messages, the outgoing President had reassured Congress about Oregon: "Considerable progress has been made in the discussion, . . . [and] there is reason to hope that it may be terminated and the negotiation brought to a close within a short period." Some such bromide, inserted into Polk's inaugural address, would probably have mollified most Western expansionists for the time being and would have allowed him opportunity to examine the files of the diplomatic correspondence before taking a stand.

At Polk's inauguration he had a nine-month period of grace before facing Congress—a period in which distribution of patronage, internal problems, and the Texas question were certain to occupy the public's attention. If he had set diplomats to work privately during this period, he might have been able to announce a viable solution of the Oregon question in his first annual message. The prospect of a peaceful settlement with Britain would then have immeasurably strengthened his hand in further diplomacy with Mexico. As the urgency of the Oregon question faded, Polk might have sent Slidell to Mexico as a special envoy, nominally to discuss Texan annexation but actually to present a confidential offer for boundary adjustments, while Taylor's army, still at Corpus Christi, mounted guard over the disputed zone without offering an overt threat that would goad the Mexicans to cross the Rio Grande.

By avoiding a crisis, Polk might have maintained this indeterminate but not uncomfortable position for a year or more, while the emigrants of 1845 and 1846 settled in central California. Tactful private warnings to Britain and the presence of Sloat's squadron cruising off the Mexican coast could have shielded an independence movement in California, which would establish a new state. At the least, an independent California could have maintained friendly relations for an indefinite period with the government at Washington. Eventually, the United States might have opened negotiations for annexation, choosing a time when Britain was fully involved in European affairs. As events developed, the revolutions of 1848 provided just such an opportunity, and there were others during the succeeding years.

Would this gradualism have satisfied Western expansionists? Probably not, but it is inconceivable that their protests could have been as divisive as the debates that took place over Oregon and the Mexican War. Indeed, their impatient outbursts might have been put to good use, for diplomats such as McLane or Slidell, their cunning sharpened by experience in American politics, would have known how to invoke Western extremism as a stimulus for lagging negotiations. If expansionist pressure became too great to resist, Polk would yet have retained his freedom to speak out; after initiating bona fide efforts toward peaceful settlement, his stirring pronouncements would probably have had more effect than they actually did. They might indeed have strengthened moderates in Britain or Mexico instead of repelling them.

Polk's background and character militated against such reliance on conventional diplomacy. Instead of carefully exploring issues and interests, he chose a policy based on bluff and a show of force. At the time it seemed an easier policy. In its constant appeals to Congress and the people it seemed more democratic. By goading British and Mexican nationalists, however, this policy raised obstacles, and as these obstacles increased, it proved impossible to reverse. No one can deny that Polk achieved his goals, but he was favored by good luck, by the steadfastness of American soldiers, and, at the end, by the long-neglected skill of his diplomats. For many persons his achievements justified themselves. But later generations might reasonably complain that he served his country ill by paying an unnecessarily high price in money, in lives, and in national disunity.

## FURTHER READING

Samuel Flagg Bemis, *John Quincy Adams and the Union* (1956)
Ray A. Billington, *The Far Western Frontier, 1830–1860* (1956)
Charles H. Brown, *Agents of Manifest Destiny* (1980)
Gene Brack, *Mexico Views Manifest Destiny, 1821–1846* (1975)
Richard Drinnon, *Facing West* (1980)
William Goetzmann, *When the Eagle Screamed* (1966)
Norman A. Graebner, *Empire on the Pacific* (1955)
——, "Lessons of the Mexican War," *Pacific Historical Review*, 57 (1978), 325–342
——, "The Mexican War: A Study in Causation," *Pacific Historical Review*, 59 (1980), 405–426
Neal Harlow, *California Conquered* (1982)
Ernest M. Lander, Jr., *Reluctant Imperialists: Calhoun, the Southern Carolinians, and the Mexican War* (1980)
Archie P. McDonald, ed., *The Mexican War* (1969)
Frederick Merk, *Albert Gallatin and the Oregon Problem* (1950)
——, *Manifest Destiny and Mission in American History* (1963)
——, *The Monroe Doctrine and American Expansionism, 1843–1849* (1966)
——, *The Oregon Question* (1967)
Julius W. Pratt, "The Ideology of American Expansion," in Avery Craven, ed., *Essays in Honor of William E. Dodd* (1935)
Glenn W. Price, *Origins of the War with Mexico: The Polk-Stockton Intrigue* (1967)
José Fernando Ramérez, *Mexico during the War with the United States,* ed. Walter C. Scholes (1950)
John H. Schroeder, *Mr. Polk's War* (1973)
Charles G. Sellers, *James K. Polk: Continentalist, 1843–1846* (1966)
Justin H. Smith, *The War with Mexico,* 2 vols. (1919)
Richard Van Alstyne, *The Rising American Empire* (1960)
Paul A. Varg, *United States Foreign Relations, 1820–1860* (1979)
Charles Vevier, "American Continentalism: An Idea of Expansion, 1845–1910," *American Historical Review*, 65 (1960), 323–335
Albert K. Weinberg, *Manifest Destiny* (1935)

# Civil War Diplomacy

# 9

*American expansionism faltered in the 1850s and 1860s when sectionalism bedeviled the nation. After Union and Confederate armies began to bloody themselves and ravage the countryside, expansionists of both sides worried more about their survival than about expanding empire. Southern diplomats busied themselves with the task of winning European favor for their secession and independence. Northern diplomats threw their energy into preventing European interference. Whereas Confederate leaders worked to internationalize the internecine conflict, Union leaders strove to contain the conflagration and to warn Europeans—including the French who meddled in Mexico—against taking advantage of American weakness to extend their interests in the western hemisphere.*

*The competition centered on Britain and cotton. Jefferson Davis's Confederacy sought to woo the British with "King Cotton" arguments, believing that British industry was dependent upon Southern cotton exports and could be persuaded to back Confederate independence because of economic self-interest. Abraham Lincoln's Union tried to foil such arrangements with a blockade of Southern ports, sparking controversy with London over maritime rights. The British building of war vessels for the Confederacy particularly angered the people of the North and rekindled Anglophobia. Whether Britain chose to limit itself to only recognition of belligerency and small amounts of military supplies because of Northern diplomatic skills, dependency on American foodstuffs, Southern ineptitude, the political influence of pro-American British citizens, or a cautious respect for Northern military power is the stuff of debate among historians.*

## DOCUMENTS

Secretary of State William H. Seward was such an ardent nationalist that he advised President Lincoln, in the first document, dated April 1, 1861, to take the drastic action of fighting either Spain or France so as to cause Southern secessionists to rally around the flag and rejoin the Union. Lincoln discreetly buried the proposal and reminded his impertinent secretary that the President was in charge. The second document is Lincoln's controversial proclamation of blockade, April 19, 1861. In the third document, Seward instructs Minister to England Charles Francis Adams to warn the British not to deal with the Confederate commissioners in London—"fraternize with our domestic enemy"—unless they wish an Anglo-American war. The Confederate faith in cotton as an inducement to a favorable British policy is illustrated well by the next document, a September 23, 1861, letter from Confederate Secretary of State R. M. T. Hunter to Confederate agent James M. Mason. In the fall of 1861, Mason and another Confederate agent were boldly seized from the British vessel *Trent* by Captain Charles Wilkes of the United States Navy. The British howled in protest, while Americans cheered Wilkes for his audacity. In the end, the agents were set free. On January 9, 1862, Senator Charles Sumner of Massachusetts made the best of it by slamming the Confederates, applauding Wilkes' noble if mistaken act, and ribbing the British for finally endorsing a traditional American principle against boarding neutral ships. The last document is Charles Francis Adams' firm protest to the British against their delivery of an "iron-clad" to the Confederate Navy: "This is war."

# William H. Seward's "Some Thoughts for the President's Consideration," 1861

I would demand explanations from *Spain* and France, categorically, at once.

I would seek explanations from Great Britain and Russia, and send agents into *Canada, Mexico* and *Central America,* to rouse a vigorous continental *spirit of independence* on this continent against European intervention.

And if satisfactory explanations are not received from Spain and France, Would convene Congress and declare war against them

But whatever policy we adopt, there must be an energetic prosecution of it.

For this purpose it must be somebody's business to pursue and direct it incessantly.

Either the President must do it himself, and be all the while active in it; or Devolve it on some member of his Cabinet. Once adopted, debates on it must end, and all agree and abide.

It is not in my especial province.

But I neither seek to evade nor assume responsibility.

# Lincoln's Proclamation of a Blockade, 1861

Whereas an insurrection against the Government of the United States has broken out in the States of South Carolina, Georgia, Alabama, Florida, Mississippi, Louisiana, and Texas, and the laws of the United States for the collection of the revenue cannot be effectually executed therein conformably to that provision of the Constitution which requires duties to be uniform throughout the United States:

And whereas a combination of persons engaged in such insurrection, have threatened to grant pretended letters of marque to authorize the bearers thereof to commit assaults on the lives, vessels, and property of good citizens of the country lawfully engaged in commerce on the high seas and in waters of the United States:

And whereas an Executive Proclamation has been already issued, requiring the persons engaged in these disorderly proceedings to desist therefrom, calling out a militia force for the purpose of repressing the same, and convening Congress in extraordinary session, to deliberate and determine thereon:

Now, therefore, I, Abraham Lincoln, President of the United States, with a view to the same purposes before mentioned, and to the protection of the public peace, and the lives and property of quiet and orderly citizens pursuing their lawful occupations, until Congress shall have assembled and deliberated on the said unlawful proceedings, or until the same shall have ceased, have further deemed it advisable to set on foot a blockade of the ports within the States aforesaid, in pursuance of the laws of the United States, and of the law of Nations in such case provided. For this purpose a competent force will be posted so as to prevent entrance and exit of vessels from the ports aforesaid. If, therefore, with a view to violate such blockade, a vessel shall approach, or shall attempt to leave either [sic] of the said ports, she will be duly warned by the Commander of one of the blockading vessels, who will endorse on her register the fact and date of such warning, and if the same vessel shall again attempt to enter or leave the blockaded port, she will be captured and sent to the nearest convenient port, for such proceedings against her and her cargo as prize, as may be deemed advisable.

And I hereby proclaim and declare that if any person, under the pretended authority of the said States, or under any other pretense, shall molest a vessel of the United States, or the persons or cargo on board of her, such person will be held amenable to the laws of the United States for the prevention and punishment of piracy.

# Seward Warns the British, 1861

... This government considers that our affairs in Europe have reached a crisis, in which it is necessary for it to take a decided stand, on which not only its immediate measures, but its ultimate and permanent policy can be determined and defined. At the same time it neither means to menace Great

Britain nor to wound the susceptibilities of that or any other European nation. That policy is developed in this paper. . . .

Mr. Dallas, in a brief dispatch of May 2, tells us that Lord John Russell recently requested an interview with him on account of the solicitude which his lordship felt concerning the effect of certain measures represented as likely to be adopted by the President. In that conversation the British Secretary told Mr. Dallas that the three representatives of the Southern Confederacy were then in London, that Lord John Russell had not yet seen them, but that he was not unwilling to see them unofficially. He further informed Mr. Dallas that an understanding exists between the British and French governments which would lead both to take one and the same course as to recognition. . . .

Intercourse of any kind with the so-called commissioners is liable to be construed as a recognition of the authority which appointed them. Such intercourse would be none the less hurtful to us for being called unofficial, and it might be even more injurious, because we should have no means of knowing what points might be resolved by it. Moreover, unofficial intercourse is useless and meaningless if it is not expected to ripen into official intercourse and direct recognition. . . . You will, in any event, desist from all intercourse whatever, unofficial as well as official, with the British government, so long as it shall continue intercourse of either kind with the domestic enemies of this country. When intercourse shall have been arrested for this cause, you will communicate with this department and receive further directions. . . .

As to the blockade, you will say that by our own laws and the laws of nature, and the laws of nations, this government has a clear right to suppress insurrection. An exclusion of commerce from national ports which have been seized by insurgents, in the equitable form of blockade, is a proper means to that end. You will not insist that our blockade is to be respected, if it be not maintained by a competent force; but passing by that question as not now a practical or at least an urgent one, you will add that the blockade is now, and it will continue to be, so maintained, and therefore we expect it to be respected by Great Britain. You will add that we have already revoked the *exequatur* of a Russian consul who had enlisted in the military service of the insurgents, and we shall dismiss or demand the recall of every foreign agent, consular or diplomatic, who shall either disobey the Federal laws or disown the Federal authority.

As to the recognition of the so-called Southern Confederacy, it is not to be made a subject of technical definition. It is, of course, direct recognition to publish an acknowledgment of the sovereignty and independence of a new power. It is direct recognition to receive its ambassadors, ministers, agents or commissioners, officially. A concession of belligerent rights is liable to be construed as a recognition of them. No one of these proceedings will pass unquestioned by the United States in this case.

Hitherto, recognition has been moved only on the assumption that the so-called Confederate States are *de facto* a self-sustaining power. Now, after long forbearance, designed to soothe discontent and avert the need of civil war, the land and naval forces of the United States have been put in force to suppress insurrection. The true character of the pretended new state is at once revealed. It is seen to be a power existing in *pronunciamento* only. It has never won a field. It has obtained no forts that were not virtually betrayed into its hands or seized in breach of trust. It commands not a single port on the coast nor any highway out from its pretended capital by land. Under these circumstances, Great Britain is called upon to intervene and give it body and independence by resisting our measures of suppression. British recognition would be British intervention, to create within our territory a hostile state by overthrowing this Republic itself. . . .

As to the treatment of privateers in the insurgent service, you will say that this is a question exclusively our own. We treat them as pirates. They are our own citizens, or persons employed by our citizens, preying on the commerce of our country. If Great Britain should choose to recognize them as lawful belligerents, and give them shelter from our pursuit and punishment, the laws of nations afford an adequate and proper remedy.

Happily, however, her Britannic Majesty's government can avoid all these difficulties. It invited us in 1856 to accede to the declaration of the Congress of Paris, of which body Great Britain was herself a member, abolishing privateering everywhere in all cases and forever. You already have our authority to propose to her our accession to that declaration. If she refuse it, it can only be because she is willing to become the patron of privateering when aimed at our devastation.

These positions are not elaborately defended now, because to vindicate them would imply a possibility of our waiving them.

We are not insensible of the grave importance of this occasion. We see how, upon the result of the debate in which we are engaged, a war may ensue between the United States and one, two, or even more European nations. War in any case is as exceptional from the habits as it is revolting from the sentiments of the American people. But if it come it will be fully seen that it results from the action of Great Britain, not our own; that Great Britain will have decided to fraternize with our domestic enemy either without waiting to hear from you our remonstrances and our warnings, or after having heard them. War in defence of national life is not immoral, and war in defence of independence is an inevitable part of the discipline of nations.

## The Confederacy Lures the British with Cotton, 1861

The enemy, with greatly superior numbers, have been routed in pitched battles at Bethel and at Manassas (in Virginia), and their recent defeat at Springfield, Mo., was almost as signal as that of Manassas. The comparatively little foothold which they have had in the Confederate States is gradually being lost, and after six months of war, in which they employed their best resources, it may be truly said they are much farther from the conquest of the Southern States than they seemed to be when the struggle commenced. The Union feeling supposed to exist largely in the South, and which was known to us to be imaginary, is now shown in its true light to all mankind. Never were any people more united than are those of the Confederate States in their purpose to maintain their independence at any cost of life and treasure, nor is there a party to be found anywhere in these States which professes a desire for a reunion with the United States.

Nothing could prove this unanimity of feeling more strongly than the fact that this immense army may be said to have taken the field spontaneously, and faster almost than the Government could provide for its organization and equipment. But the voluntary contributions of the people supplied all deficiencies until the Government could come to their assistance, as it has done with the necessary military establishments.

And what is perhaps equally remarkable, it may be said with truth that there has been no judicial execution for a political offense during the whole of the war, and, so far as military offenses are concerned, our prisons would be empty if it were not for a few captured spies. Under these circumstances it would seem that the time has arrived when it would be proper in the Government of Great Britain to recognize our independence. If it be obvious that the Confederate States cannot be conquered in this struggle, then the sooner the strife be ended the better for the cause of peace and the interests of mankind. Under such circumstances, to fail to throw the great moral influence of such a recognition into the scale of peace, when this may be done without risk or danger, may be to share in the responsibility for the longer continuance of an unnecessary war. This is a consideration which ought, perhaps, to have some weight with a nation which leads so largely as does that of Great Britain in the progress of Christian civilization. That the British people have a deep political and commercial interest in the establishment of the independence of the Confederate States must be obvious to all. Their real interest in that event is only a little less than our own. The great question of cotton supply, which has occupied their attention so justly and so anxiously for some years past, will then be satisfactorily settled. Whilst the main source of cotton production was in the hands of such a power as that of the United States, and controlled by those who were disposed to use that control to acquire the supremacy in navigation, commerce, and manufactures over all rivals, there was just cause for anxiety on the part of nations who were largely dependent upon the source of supply for the raw material of important manufactures. But the case will be far different when peace is assured and the independence of the Confederate States is acknowledged. Within these States must be found for years to come the great source of cotton supply. So favorable a combination of soil, climate, and labor is nowhere else to be found. Their capacity for increased production has so far kept pace with the increased demand, and in time of peace it promises to do so for a long while to come. In the question of the supply of this great staple there is a worldwide interest; and if the nations of the earth could choose for themselves a single depository for such an interest, perhaps none could be found to act so impartially in that capacity as the Confederacy of Southern States.

Their great interest is, and will be for a long time to come, in the production and exportation of the important staples so much sought by the rest of the world.

It would be long before they would become the rivals of those who are largely concerned in navigation, manufactures, and commerce. On the contrary, these interests would make them valuable customers and bind them to the policy of free trade. Their early legislation, which has thrown open their navigation, foreign and coasting, to the free competition of all nations, and which has imposed the lowest duties on imports consistent with their necessary revenue wants, proves the natural tendency of their commercial policy. Under such circumstances the supply of cotton to Great Britain would be as abundant, as cheap, and as certain as if these States were themselves her colonies.

The establishment of such an empire, committed as it would be to the policy of free trade by its interests and traditions, would seem to be a matter of primary importance to the progress of human industry and the great causes of human civilization. It would be of the deepest interest to such a Government to preserve peace and to improve its opportunities for the pursuit of the useful arts. The residue of the world would find here, too, sources of supply of more than the great staples in which manufactures and commerce are most deeply interested, and these sources would probably prove to be not only constant, as being little likely to be troubled by the chances of war, but also of easy access to all who might desire to resort to them. In presenting the great importance of this question to the Government of Great Britain in its connection with their material interests, you will not omit its bearing upon the future political relations between the Old and the New World.

With a balance of power established between the great Confederacies of the North American Continent, the fears of a disturbance of the peace of the world from the desire for the annexation of contiguous territory on the part of a vast and overshadowing political and military organization will be dissipated. Under the former Union the slaveholding States had an interest in the acquisition of territory suitable to their institutions, in order to establish a balance of power within the Government for their own protection. This reason no longer exists, as the Confederate States have sought that protection by a separation from the Union in which their rights were endangered. It is manifest, from the nature of its interests, that the Southern Confederacy, in entering as a new member in the family of nations, would exercise not a disturbing but a harmonizing influence on human society; for it would not only desire peace itself, but to some extent become a bond of peace amongst other.

## Senator Charles Sumner on the *Trent* Affair, 1862

Two old men and two younger associates, recently taken from the British mail packet Trent on the high seas by order of Captain Wilkes of the United States Navy, and afterwards detained in custody at Fort Warren, have been liberated and placed at the disposition of the British Government. This has been done at the instance of that Government, courteously conveyed, and founded on the assumption that the original capture of these men was an act of violence which was an affront to the British flag, and a violation of international law. This is a simple outline of the facts. But in order to appreciate the value of this precedent, there are other matters which must be brought into view.

These two old men were citizens of the United States, and for many years Senators. One was the author of the fugitive slave bill, and the other was the chief author of the filibustering system which has disgraced our national name and disturbed our national peace. Occupying places of trust and power in the service of their country, they conspired against it, and at last the secret traitors and conspirators became open rebels. The present rebellion, now surpassing in proportions and also in wickedness any rebellion in history, was from the beginning quickened and promoted by their untiring energies. That country to which they owed love, honor, and obedience, they betrayed and gave over to violence and outrage. Treason, conspiracy, and rebellion, each in succession, have acted through them. The incalculable expenditures which now task our national resources, the untold derangement of affairs not only at home but also abroad, the levy of armies almost without an example, the devastation of extended regions of territory, the plunder of peaceful ships on the ocean, and the slaughter of fellow-citizens on the murderous battle-field; such are some of the consequences proceeding directly from them. To carry forward still further the gigantic crime of which they were so large a part, these two old men, with their two younger associates, stole from Charleston on board a rebel steamer, and, under cover of darkness and storm, running the blockade and avoiding the cruisers in that neighborhood, succeeded in reaching the neutral island of Cuba, where, with open display and the knowledge of the British consul, they embarked on board the British mail packet the Trent, bound for St. Thomas, whence they were to embark for England, in which kingdom one of them was to play the part of embassador of the rebellion, while the other was to play the same part in France. The original treason, conspiracy, and rebellion of which they were so heinously guilty, were all continued on this voyage, which became a prolongation of the original crime, destined to still further excess, through their embassadorial pretensions, which, it was hoped, would array two great nations against the United States, and enlist them openly in behalf of an accursed slaveholding rebellion. While on their way, the embassadors were arrested by Captain Wilkes, of the United States steamer San Jacinto, an accomplished officer, already well known by his scientific explorations, who, on this occasion, acted without instructions from his Government. If, in this arrest, he forgot for a moment the fixed policy of the Republic, which has been from the beginning like a frontlet between the eyes, and transcended the law of nations, as the United States have always declared it, his apology must be found in the patriotic impulse by which he was inspired, and the British examples which he could not forget. They were the enemies of his country, embodying in themselves the triple essence of worst enmity—treason, conspiracy, and rebellion; and they wore a pretended embassadorial character, which, as he supposed, according to high British authority, rendered them liable to be stopped. . . .

If this transaction be regarded exclusively in the light of British precedents; if we follow the seeming authority of the British admiralty, speaking by its greatest voice; and especially if we accept the oft-repeated example of British cruisers, upheld by the British Government against the oft-repeated protests of the United States, we shall not find it difficult to vindicate it. The act becomes questionable only when brought to the touchstone of these liberal principles, which, from the earliest times, the American Government has openly avowed and sought to advance, and which other European nations have accepted with regard to the sea. Indeed, Great Britain cannot complain except by now adopting those identical principles; and should we undertake to vindicate the act, it can be done only by repudiating those identical principles. Our two cases will be reversed. In the struggle between Laertes and Hamlet, the two combatants exchanged rapiers; so that Hamlet was armed with the rapier of Laertes and Laertes was armed with the rapier of Hamlet. And now on this sensitive question a similar exchange has occurred. Great Britain is armed with American principles, while to us is left only those British principles which, throughout our history, have been constantly, deliberately, and solemnly rejected. . . .

The seizure of the rebel emissaries on board a neutral ship cannot be justified according to our best American precedents and practice. There seems to be no single point where the seizure is not questionable, unless we choose to invoke British precedents and practice, which beyond doubt led Captain Wilkes to the mistake which he committed. In the solitude of his ship he consulted familiar authorities at hand, and felt that in following Vattel and Sir William Scott, as quoted and affirmed by eminent writers, reinforced by the inveterate practice of the British navy, he could not err. He was mistaken. There was a better example; it was the constant, uniform, unhesitating practice of his own country on the ocean, conceding always the greatest immunities to neutral ships, unless sailing to blockaded ports—refusing to consider dispatches as contraband of war—refusing to consider persons, other than soldiers or officers, as contraband of war; and protesting always against an adjudication of personal rights by the summary judgment of a quarter-deck. Had these well-attested precedents been in his mind, the gallant captain would not, even for a moment, have been seduced from his allegiance to those principles which constitute a part of our country's glory.

Mr. President, let the rebels go. Two wicked men, ungrateful to their country, are let loose with the brand of Cain upon their foreheads. Prison doors are opened; but principles are established which will help to free other men, and to open the gates of the sea. Never before in her active history has Great Britain ranged herself on this side. Such an event is an epoch. *Novus sæclorum nascitur ordo.* To the liberties of the sea this Power is now committed. To a certain extent this cause is now under her tutelary care. If the immunities of passengers, not in the military or naval service, as well as of sailors, are not directly recognized, they are at least implied; while the whole pretension of impressment, so long the pest of neutral commerce, and operating only through the lawless adjudication of a quarter-deck, is made absolutely impossible. Thus is the freedom of the seas enlarged, not only by limiting the number of persons who are exposed to the penalties of war, but by driving from it the most offensive pretension that ever stalked upon its waves. To such conclusion Great Britain is irrevocably pledged. Nor treaty nor bond was needed. It is sufficient that her late appeal can be vindicated only by a re- nunciation of early, long-continued tyranny. Let her bear the rebels back. The consideration is ample; for the sea became free as this altered Power went forth upon it, steering westward with the sun, on an errand of liberation.

In this surrender, if such it may be called, our Government does not even "stoop to conquer." It simply lifts itself to the height of its own original prin- ciples. The early efforts of its best negotiators—the patriot trials of its sol- diers in an unequal war—have at length prevailed, and Great Britain, usually so haughty, invites us to practice upon those principles which she has so strenuously opposed. There are victories of force. Here is a victory of truth. If Great Britain has gained the custody of two rebels, the United States have secured the triumph of their principles.

# Charles Francis Adams
## Protests the Iron Clads, 1863

At this moment, when one of the iron-clad vessels is on the point of depar- ture from this kingdom, on its hostile errand against the United States, I am honored with the reply of your lordship to my notes of the 11th, 16th and 25th of July, and of the 14th of August. I trust I need not express how profound is my regret at the conclusion to which her Majesty's government have arrived. I can regard it no otherwise than as practically opening to the insurgents free liberty in this kingdom to execute a policy described in one of their late publications in the following language:

"In the present state of the harbor defences of New York, Boston, Port- land, and smaller northern cities, such a vessel as the Warrior would have little difficulty in entering any of these ports and inflicting a vital blow upon the enemy. The destruction of Boston alone would be worth a hundred vic- tories in the field. It would bring such a terror to the 'blue-noses,' as to cause them to wish eagerly for peace, despite their overweening love of gain which has been so freely administered to since the opening of this war. Vessels of the Warrior class would promptly raise the blockade of our ports, and would even, in this respect, confer advantages which would soon repay the cost of their construction."

It would be superfluous in me to point out to your lordship that this is war. No matter what may be the theory adopted of neutrality in a struggle, when this process is carried on in the manner indicated, from a territory and with the aid of the subjects of a third party, that third party to all intents and purposes ceases to be neutral. Neither is it necessary to show, that any government which suffers it to be done fails in enforcing the essential conditions of national amity towards the country against whom the hostility is directed. In my belief it is impossible that any nation, retaining a proper degree of self-respect, could tamely submit to a continuance of relations so utterly deficient in reciprocity. I have no idea that Great Britain would do so for a moment.

## ESSAYS

Gordon H. Warren of Central Washington State University probes the "King Cotton" theory. He explains the economics of cotton, how Southerners came to exaggerate cotton's importance, and the ultimate failure of cotton diplomacy. In the other essay, Norman A. Graebner of the University of Virginia studies British and European caution in the face of Northern power and the Confederacy's inability to demonstrate its survivability. Graebner emphasizes a European commitment to power politics, rather than Northern diplomatic brilliance or Southern bungling.

# The King Cotton Theory

### GORDON H. WARREN

The antebellum South was a land of cotton where great fields stretched from South Carolina to Texas and slaves toiled from "day clean to first dark" to support the region's agricultural society. At the prewar height of production, in 1859, planters sent more than 4,000,000 bales to New England and European textile mills—a far cry from the day in 1784 when Liverpool customs agents had seized eight bags (about three bales) from an American ship, on the ground that so much cotton could not have been grown in the United States. Eli Whitney's invention of the cotton gin in 1793 had revolutionized an almost insignificant industry by enabling quick separation of short fiber from seeds. Eight years later cotton production had increased tenfold to 100,000 bales, to a million in 1835, to 2 million in 1842, and to 4.5 million on the eve of secession. By 1860 cotton shipments accounted for 60 percent of the value of all American exports. Proud of their success, Southerners developed a special relationship with their major cash crop, a kind of ethnocentric nature worship that evoked odes to cotton blossoms:

Gordon H. Warren, "The King Cotton Theory," from *Encyclopedia of American Foreign Policy: Studies of the Principal Movements and Ideas*, edited by Alexander De Conde. Copyright © 1978 Charles Scribner's Sons. Reprinted with the permission of Charles Scribner's Sons.

> First day white, next day red,
> Third day from my birth I'm dead;
> Though I am of short duration,
> Yet withal I clothe the nation.

Industrial centers all over the world relied upon Southern cotton to fuel their mills. Chief among them was Great Britain, whose largest industry, cotton manufacture, occupied 2,650 factories and many subsidiary establishments, employed 900,000 workers, and received 80 percent of its cotton from the South. Four million people, a fifth of the population of the British Isles, directly or indirectly depended on the industry. Although other European nations, especially France, operated fewer mills, they, too, bought almost entirely from the United States; the remaining cotton supply, of low quality and high cost, came from the East Indies and West Indies, Egypt, India, and Brazil. In the United States the Northern cotton textile industry, the nation's largest and most profitable manufacturing operation, acquired all of its supply from the South. Throughout much of the transatlantic world, cotton—Southern cotton—clothed, fed, and employed millions of people, constituted the bulk of manufactured goods, dominated exports, and duly enriched national treasuries.

Gradually, and perhaps inevitably, Southerners came to exaggerate cotton's importance. Although lacking sufficient industry, a merchant marine, and capital reserves, the South could always "point to that little attenuated cotton thread, which a child can break, but which nevertheless *can hang the world.*" For twenty years prior to the Civil War, Southerners watched Britain futilely attempt to end reliance on American cotton by encouraging its cultivation in India. Innumerable gloomy reports and speeches by British leaders convinced planters that Europe's industrial fate was inextricably linked to the American South. As sectional crises buffeted the United States throughout the 1850's, Southerners developed a deep conviction that with cotton controlling American, British, and French destinies, their side would triumph.

Southern boosters never lost an opportunity to praise their region, illuminate flaws in Northern society, and stress European subservience. Their contentions gained support in the mid-1850's with publication of David Christy's *Cotton Is King,* which, while lacking new ideas, carefully and ably summed up conventional beliefs about the world's dependence on cotton. Christy twitted Northerners and Britishers who criticized slavery and pronounced them hypocrites, since they were profiting from the manufacture of raw cotton into finished goods. "COTTON IS KING," Christy declared, "and his enemies are vanquished." The catchphrase dramatized sectional egotism and encouraged the South's leading financial journal, *DeBow's Review,* to abandon its cautious opinion that cotton could not be king without commerce as its queen. The *Review* soon enjoined readers "to teach our children to hold the cotton plant in one hand and a sword in the other, ever ready to defend it as the source of commercial power abroad and through that, of independence at home."

It fell to Senator James H. Hammond of South Carolina to transform a sectional shibboleth into a challenge to the federal union. After William H. Seward of New York had prophesied slavery's extinction during the Kansas debates of March 1858, Hammond retorted that the South and its peculiar institution would be around for a long time. Southerners did not need Northern vessels to carry produce. If the federal government would only remove tariffs, the "whole world will come to us to trade." The South need never go to war. No sane nation would make war on cotton, he said, because "without firing a gun, without drawing a sword . . . we could bring the whole world to our feet." If planters chose not to export cotton for three years, England and the civilized world would fall. The South Carolina senator then threw down the gauntlet to all critics of the South's cotton culture: "No, you do not dare to make war on cotton. No power on earth dares to make war upon it. Cotton *is* King."

Events moved rapidly toward a climax. Many Southerners viewed Abraham Lincoln as the Northern embodiment of antislavery doctrine, and Lincoln's election to the presidency convinced them that life under Republican rule would be unbearable. During the winter of 1860–1861, South Carolina seceded from the federal union; and by February the rest of the states of the lower South had followed. At the Washington Peace Conference—a meeting of Northern and Southern leaders who attempted to reconcile the sections with a compromise proposal on the future admission of slave and free states —Southern delegates seemed possessed by the power of cotton. The South, they told anyone who would listen, "neither wished nor intended to be more prosperous now, or to produce anything but cotton." After the conference's failure there remained only the firing of the first shot at Fort Sumter in April 1861 before the upper South left the Union. The American Civil War had begun.

Prospects at the outset appeared grim for the self-styled Confederate States of America, for in comparison with the resources of the North, those of the South were scanty—an inferior transportation network, a smaller white population, little industry, few skilled workers, and no navy. Despite these shortcomings euphoria prevailed. The war correspondent for the *Times* (London), William R. Russell, found South Carolinians scornful of Yankee martial skills and confident that Britain would intervene by autumn. John Bull, Russell was told, would "make a great fuss about non-interference, but when he begins to want cotton he'll come off his perch." England had to recognize Confederate independence lest the cotton supply be shut off and the working classes revolt. "Look out there," one merchant said, pointing to a wharf piled high with bales, "there's the key will open all our ports, and put us into John Bull's strong box as well." Everyone knew the watchword: "Cotton at 12 cents a pound and we don't fear the world." The South, Russell concluded, saw the world through parapets of cotton bales and rice bags.

Thus, in 1861 the King Cotton theory was set out by publicists and popular notion: the cotton industry employed more workers and brought greater returns than any other business in the United States, Britain, and France; without a steady supply, economic ruin would follow and governments, lacking income from taxes, would be unable to control the ensuing social chaos; the South would not have to win independence on the battlefield because, even if Europe did not recognize the Confederate government, a sudden termination of cotton exports would compel intervention; European warships and Confederate armies together would break the Northern naval blockade, vanquish Union armies, and achieve nationhood for the South; if events developed according to this scenario, the war would end in six months or less. Cotton, as an instrument of national policy, seemed invincible.

The South held a curious attitude toward the purpose of a naval embargo, which in the nineteenth century constituted a form of reprisal or retaliation, one state coercing another into ceasing a harmful practice. The Confederate policy, however, aimed not at eliminating a detrimental practice but at producing a beneficial one. It was a measure of Southern optimism that officials chose the method least likely to force compliance of world powers that in the past had capitulated only to severe physical pressure, and then rarely. The cotton embargo, calling as it did for initiative by European governments, had almost no chance of success. This subtlety eluded Southerners.

Economic coercion had been a favorite weapon of the United States since the days of Thomas Jefferson, when the government first tried to gain the rewards of war by peaceful means. Designed to discourage British and French violations of American neutrality, the embargo of 1807–1809 on all exports was about 75 percent effective. The cessation of American cotton shipments at that time provided a temporary windfall for British and French manufacturers, who profited from the sudden increase in the value of their stocks. The working classes suffered in both countries but, of course, lacked the political power to change official policy. The failure of this first embargo apparently did not affect the thinking of Southerners fifty years later. Perhaps Confederate leaders had forgotten the disastrous Jeffersonian gambit, or they may have felt that during the intervening years Britain had grown too dependent on Southern cotton to survive an embargo. It was an interesting theory but, like its predecessor, it rested on the shaky hypothesis that the British government would allow itself to be blackmailed.

The obsession with King Cotton so deeply permeated every facet of Southern society that the historian Clement Eaton has compared it with "the belief of the French people prior to World War II in the impregnability of the Maginot Line." Ranking Confederate officials, who should have known better, subscribed to its tenets. President Jefferson Davis and his advisers believed cotton so powerful that "foreign recognition was looked forward to as an assumed fact."

In its instructions to commissioners abroad, the Confederate State Department repeated a familiar theme: Britain and France were so dependent on Southern cotton that terrible consequences would result if they permitted the Union blockade to stand. As early as March 1861, Secretary of State Robert Toombs suggested to the Confederacy's first diplomatic agents that they make "a delicate allusion to the probability of such an occurrence."

For a special reason the British had no intention of violating the blockade.

The American government, having long protested overbearing belligerent practices, particularly proclamation of a blockade manned by insufficient warships, had made elimination of "paper blockades" a national goal since the Revolution. The United States, however, had not been a party to the Declaration of Paris (1856), which declared them illegal. Five years later Lincoln inaugurated a paper blockade—forty-two vessels guarding 3,500 miles of Southern coast—which bore greater resemblance to a sieve than a stone wall. Nevertheless, the London government appreciated the precedent that the Lincoln administration was setting and later, during the period of America's neutrality in World War I (1914–1917), used it as precedent to meet American complaints against its blockade of Germany.

Southern public opinion overwhelmingly supported the nonexportation of cotton as a means to force recognition of Confederate independence. As early as March 1860 the *Charleston Mercury* had advocated withholding cotton from the market "to control the conduct of the people of the North and of foreign nations, to secure a peaceful result for our deliverance." Sentiment for a total embargo on cotton built rapidly until, by April 1861, talk of selling the crop verged on treason. Southerners had no intention of allowing Britain and France to lay in a cotton surplus and avoid intervention. The South would make the Union blockade so effective, induce such a cotton famine, that Europe would be rocked to its foundations. Planters permitted no cotton to leave their plantations; cotton exporters refused consignments; citizens' committees prevented British blockade-runners from loading cotton. The embargo, the historian Frank Owsley observed, was "as near air-tight as human effort could make it." The Confederate congress, however, never made the embargo official. Members often debated the subject, yet prohibited only exports to the North. They stopped short of enacting a complete embargo because President Davis, feeling it would alienate Europe, preferred to brandish it as a threat, the trump card to be played when all else failed.

Southerners did not confine restrictive activity to withholding cotton; they also burned it or curtailed its production. Newspapers and government officials urged planters to raise less cotton, and cultivate more corn to feed Confederate soldiers. "Plant Corn and Be Free," a Georgia paper warned, "or plant cotton and be whipped." Farmers who did not decrease cotton acreage or plow under a planted crop were publicly condemned; sometimes neighbors destroyed the cotton for them. State legislatures taxed seed cotton and set acreage limits; planting in excess of the limit was punishable by a fine. To pressure Britain and France, the Confederate congress passed a joint resolution recommending that no cotton be planted in 1862. The crop for that year was one-third the size of the 1861 harvest, and the 1863 crop only one-ninth. A more dramatic demonstration of Southern unity was an 1862 act of congress that allowed military forces to destroy all valuable property in imminent danger of capture. Zealots, interpreting the law liberally, sent millions of bales up in flames. Richmond authorities carefully notified foreign consuls.

Ironically, the less cotton was exported, the more binding the blockade appeared. In London the popular mood, which had once been pro-South, began to show a disturbing lack of sympathy with Confederate protests about the blockade's ineffectiveness. *Punch,* the weekly humor magazine noted for caustic political wit, deviated from its normal practice of mocking Union misfortunes and foibles to run a devastating cartoon entitled "King Cotton Bound; or, the Modern Prometheus." Looking for all the world like an angry cotton scarecrow, the helpless monarch lies manacled to a rock, straining to break the chains of the blockade, while the American eagle, talons digging into his leg, rips out great shreds of stuffing. The caricature of the Greek legend suggested no other parallels; there would be no miraculous rejuvenation of vital parts, no savior to break the chains. King Cotton's fate was sealed.

The success of Confederate diplomacy turned on the appearance of a cotton famine in Europe by the autumn of 1861 or, at least, the winter of early 1862. Unfortunately, the South had created conditions that worked against an early shortage. The years 1859–1860 had produced two bumper crops, totaling more than 8 million bales. Before proclamation of the Northern blockade, about 3.5 million bales of the 1860 crop had been exported, chiefly to Britain. A surplus of several hundred thousand bales crammed British warehouses as late as December 1861, even after some reshipment across the Atlantic to Northern factories. Moreover, quantities of manufactured cotton goods had accumulated in Britain as a result of overproduction, competition from linen and wool, and fewer American orders. The Civil War temporarily rescued British speculators and small manufacturers from impending bankruptcy, but their counterparts in France experienced harder times. French cotton reserves, never large, had declined so precipitously by September 1861 that the Foreign Ministry began to explore the possibility of joint Anglo-French recognition of the Confederacy and breaking of the blockade.

The cotton manufacturing districts in England—mainly Lancashire, Cheshire, and Derbyshire—did not begin to feel the full force of the embargo until April 1862, by which time production in the mills had fallen to half the rate for 1860. Over the preceding six months, cotton imports had dropped to less than 1 percent of the same period a year before. British reserves had plunged drastically by June 1862. With only a three-week supply (about 100,000 bales) on hand in September, cabinet officers in London discussed recognizing Confederate independence, upon the condition that General Robert E. Lee's invasion of Maryland was successful. But then Lee was repulsed at Antietam, and the British government held back.

During the winter of 1862–1863, the cotton famine rose to its peak; the mills did not close, however, since some cotton—admittedly not much—remained for manufacture, and inferior varieties from India, China, Brazil, and Egypt passed through British customs. American cotton also continued to arrive. With cotton selling at four times its previous average price, Southern merchants, speculators, planters, government agents, and thieves vied for the trade. Even the Confederate War Department exchanged staple goods for essential supplies from the North. Blockade-runners took 1.25 million bales to Europe, and almost another million was shipped North through Union lines at New Orleans and Memphis. The embargo had failed. "It is an error to say that 'Cotton is King,' " a Confederate diplomat declared on return from Europe. "It is not. It is a great and influential power in commerce, but not its dictator."

Richmond officials turned to new tactics. They had decided in the spring of 1862 to authorize their agent in Paris, John Slidell, to offer enormous amounts of cotton—more than 100,000 bales—to Emperor Napoleon III if he would break the blockade. It amounted to a bribe, a slight improvement over the previous tactic of extortion. Rejecting the proposal, the French foreign minister, Édouard Thouvenel, declared that his government would act only in accord with Britain. Since London would not move without Russian support, the French soon lost interest in intervention.

Extortion and bribery having failed to win the desired results, Southern officials turned belatedly to more practical measures. In December 1862 the Confederacy offered Britain the chance to conclude a massive barter agreement: to exchange $300 million in naval stores, cotton, tobacco, and other crops for a vast array of manufactured goods—upon conclusion of a peace treaty. Otherwise, Secretary of State Judah P. Benjamin declared, Confederate military authorities might have to destroy crops in order to prevent their capture, a policy that, of course, had already been implemented. An additional factor deserved consideration, he said. In the postwar period Northern merchants would swarm over the South, acquiring commodities and selling New England manufactured goods. Trade with Europe would remain "tributary to an intermediary," and the United States would reap all the profits. To avoid this predicament, neutral businessmen could purchase products in advance from the South and leave them "in depot till the ports are opened."

The British foreign secretary, Lord John Russell, was not interested. Thinking more of the empire's future glory than short-term economic benefits, he made it clear to even the most obdurate Confederate official that Britain would not intervene in the American Civil War unless critical national interests made it necessary. Thoroughly irritated by the counterproductive tactic of coercion, Russell remarked privately that it rubbed him the wrong way.

In desperation the Confederacy initiated its last cotton project. Following months of debate, the Confederate congress in January 1863 decided to put "the sacred King Cotton in hock" by selling an issue of cotton bonds worth $15 million to overseas investors. The issue had a double purpose: income from the bonds would purchase war matériel; and Europeans would acquire a small, though psychologically important, stake in Confederate fortunes. The sale netted more than $8.5 million for the Confederacy. Despite the success of the so-called Erlanger loan, the need for greater amounts of capital caused the Confederate government in 1864 to pressure blockade-runners to carry large amounts of cotton. Southerners had finally realized that if Europe would not come to cotton, cotton must go to Europe.

What had gone wrong? The fantasy of King Cotton reordering world politics had turned into a nightmare. Reflecting on the sad end of their dream, many Southerners sought to explain defeat by reverting to the persecution complex so characteristic of the antebellum psyche. An international anti-slavery conspiracy, orchestrated by Northern extremists, had prevented recognition, had enforced respect for the blockade, and had given moral support to the Union. The argument contained some truth but, like the King Cotton theory, was simplistic.

The embargo had failed to achieve its objectives. Although contemporary opinion blamed the distress of the cotton mills on a shortage of fiber, sufficient amounts were available at high prices that, according to Eugene Brady, resulted from *"expectations* of a future import shortage." The price of raw cotton climbed beyond reach of many British mills, and speculators actually increased reexports of cotton to France. Meanwhile, mills suffered at the outset of the Civil War from overproduction of cotton goods, which depressed prices and made manufacturing at the previous tempo a losing venture. High-priced cotton and low-priced manufactured goods brought misery to the mill districts. As predicted, discontent did mount among British and French mill operatives, who held protest meetings and signed petitions; but they had little political influence and could not force intervention, a fact apparently not appreciated by the Confederacy.

Seeking explanations for King Cotton's failure, historians have cited supplementary sources of cotton; profits in trade of noncotton textiles, munitions, commerce, and shipbuilding; economic ties to the North; and Confederate military defeats. Undoubtedly a combination of factors deterred European intervention. But one thing is clear: Confederate political and economic theorists erred in assuming that European prosperity rested on cotton. The British minister to the United States, Lord Richard B. P. Lyons, was struck by this misapprehension in 1860. "It is true that cotton is almost a necessity to us," he observed, "but it is still more necessary for them to sell it than it is for us to buy it."

The discrediting of the King Cotton theory reaffirmed the inherent difficulties of any nation seeking to achieve a political objective by economic means. Having based their ill-founded venture in foreign policy on the theory that a cotton embargo or cotton bribe could force Europe to recognize Southern sovereignty or break the North's blockade of the South, Confederate officials persisted in their course long after its futility became obvious. Once again the chimera of omnipotent economic coercion had led American statesmen to disaster. Rather than exporting cotton to establish international credit and to finance military and naval purchases, the leaders of the Confederacy had accepted the illusory notion held by so many Southerners that European dependence on the crop would bring intervention. That fundamental miscalculation surely contributed much to the failure of the South to achieve independence. Under the right circumstances—a Confederate victory at Antietam, the providential destruction of foreign cotton by insects—the King Cotton theory might have worked. But Providence did not smile on the Confederate States of America. Southerners who had placed so much faith in the "little attenuated cotton thread" that supposedly could hang the world discovered too late that they had fashioned a noose for themselves.

# Northern Diplomacy and European Realism

### NORMAN A. GRAEBNER

Major Robert Anderson's surrender of Fort Sumter in April, 1861, placed an unprecedented burden on American diplomacy. Not since the American Revolution had the foreign relations of the United States been reduced to a defense of the Republic's very existence. Diplomacy, to be sure, was only one element in the vast arsenal of resources upon which Northern leadership could draw to frustrate the South's determination to sever the Union, but from the outset of the struggle it assumed a primary importance. Even limited European power, thrown effectively into the scale against the North, could have rendered the Southern cause successful. The nation's future, therefore, rested on the efficiency of its diplomatic as much as its military corps.

Europe's involvement in the American Civil War comprised a persistent danger to the Union, for the Southern independence movement threatened all the fundamental power relationships between the Old World and the New. Despite its tradition of isolationism toward Europe, the American Republic had become by 1861 a significant force in world politics. Cassius Clay, President Lincoln's choice for the court at St. Petersburg, wrote in April, 1862, that it was "useless to deceive ourselves with the idea that we can isolate ourselves from European interventions. We became in spite of ourselves—the Monroe Doctrine—Washington's farewell—and all that—a part of the 'balance of power.' " To European leaders the United States was a nation of consequence in world affairs, but the relationship of American strength and American traditions to the precise interests of Europe varied from country to country.

London promised to become the focal point of all wartime diplomatic maneuvering, for Britain was the dominant power of Europe and her control of Canada and the sea lanes of the north Atlantic created extensive commitments in the New World. France was equally concerned over events in America but lacked the power to escape the British lead. Keeping such interested and calculating nations neutral became the chief task of Northern diplomacy.

Fortunately for the North, Anglo-American relations had never been more cordial than they were in 1861. But this was no guarantee of British neutrality. Britain's powerful conservative classes, always cynical toward the democratic experiment of the United States, recognized the fundamental meaning of the American Civil War. Democratic institutions were on trial.

"Northern Diplomacy and European Neutrality," by Norman A. Graebner in *Why the North Won the Civil War*, edited by David Donald (1960). Reprinted by permission of the author, Norman Graebner.

The United States as a nation had passed beyond the normal control of Old World power, but if the American people were determined to destroy their national greatness and demonstrate the failure of their institutions, the least that reactionary Europe could do was to encourage them in their effort so that the work of destruction might succeed. British aristocrats had long regarded the American democratic example as a threat to their estate. For them the breakup of the American Union would impede the expansion of democracy everywhere. In July, 1861, *Blackwood's Magazine* declared: "It is precisely because we do *not* share the admiration of America for her own institutions and political tendencies that we do not now see in the impending change an event altogether to be deplored."

British conservatives resented American power and truculence as much as American institutions. What disturbed them especially was the growth of the United States into a formidable maritime rival. Edouard de Stoeckl, the Russian Minister in Washington, lamented in January, 1860, that in approaching dissolution of the Union Great Britain would experience one of those "strokes of fortune" which occur but rarely in history. England, he predicted, would benefit more than any other nation from the disintegration of American power. "The Cabinet of London," he warned his government, "is watching attentively the internal dissensions of the Union and awaits the result with an impatience which it has difficulty in disguising." From St. Petersburg Cassius Clay warned Lincoln, "I saw at a glance where the feeling of England was. They hoped for our ruin! They are jealous of our power. They care neither for the South nor the North. They hate both."

Western Europe, moreover, had long been indignant at the American effort to keep the Western Hemisphere off limits for further European encroachment. For the ambitious Louis Napoleon of France, especially, events in America were encouraging, for they seemed to be rendering the Monroe Doctrine inoperative. No American fleet would block the contemplated movement of French troops to Vera Cruz or demolish his dreams of establishing a vassal empire in Mexico. A strong and friendly Confederate States of America would create a buffer between what remained of the United States and his new Mexican possessions. Secession appeared so consequential to Europe because it again exposed the western world to European partition. It was no wonder that Stoeckl advised his government in April, 1861, that "England will take advantage of the first opportunity to recognize the seceded States and that France will follow her."

In Washington, Henri Mercier, the French Minister, favored immediate action. He advised his government that in recognizing the Confederacy it would give the American conflict the character of a war and thereby extend to French seamen the benefit of neutral rights. The United States could not complain, he added, because it had recognized the revolutionary governments of Spanish America. Certainly this nation could not be offended merely because other nations accepted its democratic principles of self-determination. Yet Mercier was a realist. He admonished the French Minister in Paris to formulate his American policy only in agreement with the other powers of Europe.

Russia alone of the European states made the preservation of the Union a matter of conscious policy. For Stoeckl the destruction of the Union threatened the equilibrium of world politics. The United States, ran his argument, had become Europe's best guarantee against British aggression and arrogance. Traditional Russian-American friendship had been based on a mutual rivalry toward Great Britain. It had been the case of the enemies of a rival becoming friends. George Mifflin Dallas, when United States Minister at the Czar's court during the Van Buren administration, had recorded this significant phrase of Nicholas I, "Not only are our interests alike, our enemies are the same."

After the outbreak of the Civil War the *Journal of St. Petersburg,* official organ of the Czarist government, declared: "Russia entertains for the United States of America a lively sympathy founded on sentiments of mutual friendship and on common interests. She considers their prosperity necessary to the general equilibrium." Nothing, the Imperial Cabinet agreed, should be permitted to weaken this powerful counterpoise to England. Prince Gortchakov, the Russian Foreign Minister, instructed Stoeckl in July, 1861, to assure the American nation that it could assume "the most cordial sympathy on the part of our August Master, during the serious crisis which it is passing through at present." This *entente cordiale* between the world's greatest despotism and its leading democracy was *Realpolitik* at its diplomatic best, for despite the incompatibility of political principles, it served the best interests of both nations.

William H. Seward, Lincoln's Secretary of State, assumed the essential task of preventing the introduction of European power into the American Civil War. His diplomacy had but one objective—the preservation of the Union. Seward's devotion to this cause was so intense that in April, 1861, he recommended to Lincoln a foreign war, perhaps against Spain and France, to rally the seceded states around the American flag and thus reforge the Union. Lincoln tactfully ignored the proposal, but the Washington diplomatic corps was amazed. Lord Lyons, the British Minister, warned the Foreign Office in London that Seward would be "a dangerous foreign minister." Thereafter the British government regarded the American Secretary with suspicion. Charles Francis Adams, the American Minister in London, reported that Seward was viewed there as "an ogre fully resolved to eat all Englishmen raw." Lord John Russell, the British Foreign Secretary, addressed Lyons in February, 1861: "The success or failure of Mr. Seward's plans to prevent the disruption of the North American Union is a matter of deep interest to Her Majesty's Government." From the opening guns of the war Seward's leadership was a matter of grave concern to the chancelleries of Europe.

To forestall European interference in American affairs after the fall of Sumter, Seward denied officially the existence of any war between North and South. "There is here, as there always has been," he informed the British and French governments, "one political power, namely, the United States of America, competent to make war and peace, and conduct commerce and alliances with all foreign nations." What existed, he explained, was an armed sedition seeking to overthrow the government. Its suppression did not constitute a war or in any manner modify the character, rights, and responsibilities of either the United States or foreign nations in their diplomatic relationships. Seward admitted that international law permitted the recognition of established *de facto* governments; he merely denied that one existed in the South.

What endangered Seward's rigid position toward Europe was the rapid expansion of the conflict between North and South onto the Atlantic. It was fundamental in Lincoln's strategy to weaken and destroy the Southern economy by cutting off Southern shipments of cotton to Europe through a blockade of the Southern ports. Shortly after the crisis of Fort Sumter the Confederate government issued a proclamation calling for privateers, and Lincoln announced his blockade. Seward warned Lyons that the North would tolerate no further European commerce with the South, but he denied that a formal blockade destroyed his own claims that war did not exist. Yet the United States could hardly proclaim a blockade without declaring itself a belligerent and claiming rights over foreign vessels admitted only in time of war. Lyons was disturbed, for the blockade imposed on Europe the choice of recognizing the Confederacy or submitting to the interruption of its commerce with the South.

Britain, fearful of being trapped in a maritime war, took immediate steps to protect her commerce. On May 13, 1861, without awaiting the arrival of Minister Adams, Queen Victoria issued a declaration of neutrality which called upon British subjects to avoid hostilities between the North and South. Soon France, Spain, the Netherlands, and Brazil followed the British lead. This recognition of Southern belligerency granted to Southern ships the privileges in neutral ports accorded the ships of the Federal government.

Washington was shocked at this British action, for it not only suggested collusion between Britain and France but also presaged the diplomatic recognition of the South. Charles Sumner, the Massachusetts Senator, termed the Queen's proclamation "the most hateful act of English history since the time of Charles 2nd." Seward's reaction was even more violent. "They have misunderstood things fearfully, in Europe," he wrote home in May. "Great Britain is in great danger of sympathizing so much with the South for the sake of peace and cotton as to drive us to make war against her, as the ally of the traitors.... It will be dreadful but the end will be sure and swift." Through Adams in London, Seward warned the British government, "If any European power provokes war, we shall not shrink from it."

Similarly Seward advised Mercier that French recognition of the Confederacy would result in war with the United States. This nation might be defeated, he admitted bluntly, but France would know that she had been in a war. To William L. Dayton, the American Minister in Paris, Seward wrote: "Foreign intervention would oblige us to treat those who should yield it as allies of the insurrectionary party and to carry on the war against them as enemies.... The President and the people of the United States deem the

Union, which would then be at stake, worth all the cost and all the sacrifices of a contest with the world at arms, if such a contest should prove inevitable."

European interference meant war, but Seward offered the Old World powers the carrot as well as the stick. He reminded both Britain and France of their long tradition of friendship with the United States and assured them that this nation had cherished that peace. The American Republic, he instructed Adams, was "anxious to avoid all causes of misunderstanding with Great Britain; to draw closer, instead of breaking, the existing bonds of amity and friendship. There is nothing good or great," he added appealingly, "which both nations may not expect to attain or effect if they may remain friends. It would be a hazardous day for both branches of the British race when they should determine to test how much harm each could do the other." The Secretary extended similar assurances to the French: "We have no hostile or interested designs against any other state or nation whatever, and, on the contrary, we seek peace, harmony, and commerce with them all." Seward repeated ceaselessly his contention that the United States was one, and that the nations of Europe should not view themselves as neutrals between two imaginary belligerents in America, but as friends of the United States.

Seward's warnings were not without effect. When Lord Russell learned of the arrival in London of William L. Yancey, the Confederate Commissioner seeking recognition for his government, he wrote to Lyons in Washington: "If it can possibly be helped, Mr. Seward must not be allowed to get us into a quarrel. I shall see the southerners when they come, but unofficially and keep them at a proper distance." But even the unofficial reception of Yancey was too much for Seward. His next letter to Adams was so menacing that Lincoln revised certain passages and removed others. Nor would the President permit Adams to read the dispatch to Russell. Even in revised form the dispatch was little less than an ultimatum. It suggested that Adams break off his relations with the British government if Russell persisted in seeing the Confederate Commissioner. Not content with this warning, Seward invited William Russell, the noted Washington correspondent of the London *Times,* to his home and read to him deliberately the long dispatch with its insinuations that Britain would destroy the American Republic if she could. Russell, he hoped, would not keep his impressions to himself.

Adams regarded the Secretary's warning as little less than a declaration of war. "I scarcely know how to understand Mr. Seward," he admitted. "The rest of the Government may be demented for all I know, but he surely is calm and wise." Adams informed Lord Russell in London that further relations between the British government and the "pseudo-commissioners" of the Confederate States, whether unofficial or not, would be regarded as a manifestation of hostility by the United States. Lord Russell did not receive the Southern Commissioner again. In May the British Minister announced a hands-off policy: ". . . we have not been involved in any way in that contest . . . and for God's sake, let us if possible, keep out of it."

Through Dayton, Seward informed the French Minister that the United States would regard any further communications of his government with the Southern Commissioners as "exceptional and injurious" to American dignity and honor. Even an unofficial reception of the emissaries of disunion, he complained, would give them encouragement to prosecute their effort to destroy the American Republic. Perhaps a warning would be sufficient to relieve the United States of further action, for Seward declared that this nation could not tolerate, whatever the consequences of its resistance, the recognition of the Confederacy by the French government.

Mercier and Lyons in Washington, still determined to commit their nations to a settlement of the American conflict, suggested mediation, with their governments serving as umpires between North and South. Lord Russell judiciously declined and Seward caused the diplomatic corps abruptly to drop what remained of the scheme. In a statement to the governor of Maryland he made it clear that the Federal government would accept no foreign arbitrament in settling its differences with the Confederacy. The American Constitution, he reminded the Europeans, provided all the required means for surmounting internal disorders. Arbitration would endanger the nation's integrity by substituting non-Constitutional devices for the normal functioning of the American system.

United States relations with Britain were unnecessarily disturbed in December, 1861, when Captain Charles Wilkes of the Federal warship *San Jacinto* stopped the British mail steamer *Trent* off the coast of Cuba and removed two Confederate leaders, James M. Mason and John Slidell. These men, among the South's ablest, had been dispatched to London and Paris respectively to replace the earlier commissioners. To the zealous Wilkes their capture was an unprecedented coup, but unfortunately he had broken the cherished maritime principle for which this nation supposedly had fought the British in the War of 1812. In London Henry Adams, son of the American Minister, saw the issue clearly, writing to his brother: "Good God, what's got into you all? What do you mean by deserting now the great principles of our fathers, by returning to the vomit of that dog Great Britain? What do you mean by asserting now principles against which every Adams yet has protested and resisted?"

Seward was embarrassed. He faced the necessity of satisfying the British who were wronged and at the same time of protecting American prestige abroad. "If I decide this case in favor of my own government," he admitted, "I must disavow its most cherished principles, and . . . forever abandon its essential policy. The country cannot afford the sacrifice. If I maintain those principles, and adhere to that policy, I must surrender the case itself." Seward soon decided on the latter course and conceded to the British with remarkable grace, for nowhere did the *Trent* case challenge his Union policies. "In coming to my conclusion," he wrote to Adams, "I have not forgotten that if the safety of this Union required the detention of the captured persons it would be the right and duty of this government to detain them. But the effective check and waning proportions of the existing insurrection, as well as the comparative unimportance of the captured persons themselves, when dispassionately weighed happily forbid me from resorting to that defense." Federal officials released the two Confederates promptly and sent them on their way. Lord Russell was relieved. He wrote, "I do not believe that Seward has any animosity to this country. It is all buncom."

What gave the South the presumption of success in its effort to secure European recognition was the alleged economic power of cotton. Southern writers in 1861 assumed that Britain would break the Northern blockade to guarantee the flow of cotton into England. "Cotton," declared the Charleston *Mercury*, "would bring England to her knees." *De Bow's Review* in June predicted that a blockade of the Southern ports would be "swept away by the English fleets of observation hovering on the Southern coasts, to protect English commerce, and especially the free flow of cotton to English and French factories." If cotton were king, the South had only to place an embargo on that commodity to force Britain to destroy the blockade. "Foreign nations will not recognize the independence of the Confederate States," admitted one Southern governor realistically, "until commerce with the Confederate States will become not only desirable, but necessary to their own prosperity." The Confederate Congress refused to establish an embargo, but Committees of Public Safety in the Southern seaport towns effectively halted the export of cotton to Europe.

By the spring of 1862 King Cotton had compelled neither Britain nor France to recognize Southern independence or break the blockade. Confederate efforts to force action in the British government by depriving Lancashire of raw cotton actually had the opposite effect. As one British leader observed, "I wonder the South do not see that our recognition *because* they keep cotton from us would be ignominious beyond measure, & that no English Parlt could do so base a thing." But the British resolve not to break the blockade resulted from a far more fundamental motive than a willingness to dispense with cotton, for the blockade defied America's own precedents and doctrines of neutral maritime rights. In undermining the principle of the Declaration of Paris that blockades to be binding must be effective, the United States was releasing England in a future conflict from this burdensome feature of the past. American action weakened the stand of the smaller maritime powers in their perennial effort to force Great Britain to recognize neutral rights in time of war.

Historians have agreed that cotton failed as a diplomatic weapon because Britain enjoyed too much lucrative trade with the North, requiring especially huge quantities of Northern grain, and because the textile workers most affected by the cotton famine remained staunch friends of the Union. Professor Ephraim D. Adams has accounted for the allegiance of English workingmen to Lincoln's wartime leadership by citing the general threat to democratic progress imposed by Southern secession. Either the North would triumph or democracy everywhere would be in jeopardy. The eventual Northern success vindicated the democratic system so completely, says Adams, that it led directly to the British Reform Bill of 1867.

Lincoln's Emancipation Proclamation, although designed, at least partially, to influence European attitudes toward the Union cause, had little effect on European sentiment and none on European action. British conservatives thought it foolhardy and anticipated a servile insurrection. Even William E. Gladstone was unmoved by Lincoln's action, reiterating his conviction that "negro emancipation cannot be effected, in any sense favourable either to black or to white by the bloody hand of war, especially of Civil War." British liberals, abolitionists, and workingmen lauded the Proclamation, but these groups had always favored the Union because it represented the cause of democracy. None of these groups, moreover, wielded influence over British policy. Northern diplomatic success found its fundamental explanation less in specific interests and doubts than in a great diplomatic tradition.

Europe's diplomatic tradition cautioned against any recognition of the Confederacy until the South had demonstrated the power required to establish and maintain its independence. Without the assurance of ultimate Southern success, European involvement would assume the risk of either an eventual ignominious retreat from a declared diplomatic objective or an unlimited military commitment to guarantee the achievement of Southern independence. Confronted with Europe's traditional realism, the Southern diplomatic cause in London and Paris could be no more successful than the Southern military cause in Virginia and Pennsylvania. Diplomacy reflects the status of power, and Southern power never appeared greater than during the summer and autumn months of 1862.

News of General George B. McClellan's retirement from before Richmond in the early summer of 1862 merely confirmed a general European conviction that the American Union was doomed. To European military experts, diplomats, and statesmen, Northern power seemed incapable of overcoming the defensive nature of the Southern military commitment. The North, Europe understood, enjoyed an immense industrial superiority, but the advantages of strategy, terrain, and leadership appeared to lie with the South. Confederate armies had no obligation to conquer the North, but only to beat off the Union forces. This they appeared capable of doing. In June, 1862, the London *Times* broached the issue of European intervention, convinced that Southern independence was inevitable. "It is plain," said the *Times,* that the time is approaching when Europe will have to think seriously of its relations to the two belligerents in the American war. . . . That North and South must now choose between separation and ruin, material and political, is the opinion of nearly every one who, looking impartially and from a distance on the conflict, sees what is hidden from the frenzied eyes of the Northern politicians." Recognition of a successful cause could be both legitimate and effective.

For many British editors and politicians, McClellan's retreat from the peninsula during the summer of 1862 was like redemption. So dominant was the pro-Southern trend in British opinion that Henry Adams wrote from London, "There is no doubt that the idea here is as strong as ever that we must ultimately fail, and unless a very few weeks show some great military result we shall have our hands full in this quarter." Only a decisive Northern victory, he observed, could prevent European intervention. Public hostility, Charles Francis Adams wrote on July 18 to his son in America, was "rising every hour and running harder against us than at any time since the Trent affair." There was nothing to do but retreat. "I shut myself up," he lamented, "went to no parties and avoided contact with everyone except friends." Reports in the British press of the capture of McClellan's entire army, Adams believed, had been fabricated "to carry the House of Commons off their feet" as it commenced its crucial debate on William Shaw Lindsay's resolution calling for a more vigorous pro-Confederate British policy.

In defense of his resolution, Lindsay pointed to the inevitability of final separation between North and South. He declared that the Southern cause was just and that the North would now accept mediation. Lancashire was in distress. Lindsay quoted from a letter written by a mill hand, "We think it high time to give the Southern States the recognition they so richly deserve." Friends of the North were assured that the British Ministry would not be influenced by the parliamentary debate and therefore chose the strategy of permitting the pro-Confederates to wear themselves out against a stone wall of silence. After two days of verbal effort Lindsay asked for a postponement of his motion to "wait for king cotton to turn the screws still further." Somehow the debate created a strong impression in England that public opinion favored intervention.

That critical summer found the European diplomats confused and divided. Napoleon pondered the Southern victories, convinced that the moment for intervention had arrived. He informed the British Ministry that France would recognize Southern independence if the London government would follow. Edouard Antoine Thouvenel, the French Minister in Paris, did not share the Emperor's enthusiasm for intervention. He doubted that the French public had any interest in such involvement or that the Confederacy would win. He warned that French intervention, unless supported by both Britain and Russia, would result in an overcommitment of French power. Russia, he surmised, would reject every proposal for joint action. He was correct. Prince Gortchakov made it clear that his government would regard the dissolution of the Union as a catastrophe. In an interview with Bayard Taylor of the American Embassy in October, 1862, he said: "You know that the government of the United States has few friends among the Powers. England rejoices over what is happening to you; she longs and prays for your overthrow. France is less actively hostile; her interests would be less affected by the result; but she is not unwilling to see it. She is not your friend. . . . Russia, alone, stood by you from the first, and will continue to stand by you. We are very, *very* anxious that some means should be adopted—that *any* course should be pursued—which will prevent the division which now seems inevitable."

In Washington Mercier, still counseling mediation, stood alone. Lyons had no interest in confronting Seward with that issue again. To Stoeckl he observed, "We ought not to venture on mediation unless we are ready to go to war." Lyons did not share the European hostility toward the American

Union. During his visit to England in the summer of 1862 he wrote to the British chargé d'affaires in Washington, with reference to McClellan's defeat, "I'm afraid no one but me is sorry for it." He believed that the debate on British policy in Parliament was ill-timed. "I do not think we know here sufficiently the extent of the disaster [to McClellan] to be able to come to any conclusion as to what the European Powers should do," ran his warning. Stoeckl concluded that the ravages of war would prompt the North eventually to beg for mediation, but not yet. He doubted, moreover, that British or French recognition of the South would achieve anything. "It will not end the war and what is more," he predicted, "it will not procure cotton for them, and the distress of the manufacturing districts will not be lessened. It can be accomplished only by forcing open the Southern ports, thus leading to a clear rupture with the North."

In London Mason, misled by the public evidence of British interventionism and unmindful of the disturbing doubts in the Foreign Office, moved to drive home his apparent advantage. He dispatched a brief note to Lord Russell requesting an interview. This Russell refused, assuring Mason that no advantage would result from it. In a second dispatch the Confederate Commissioner phrased his position in great detail, but again Russell replied that the moment for recognition had not arrived. For Mason the official British position had suddenly become clear. The Ministry would not alter its policies until the South revealed its ability to gain and maintain its independence, and reports from America indicated that the South was faltering at New Orleans, Memphis, and Shiloh. From Vienna John Lothrop Motley observed with accuracy that diplomacy would continue to reflect the course of war in America.

In Paris Slidell met with equal opposition. Thouvenel convinced him that it would be unwise even to ask for recognition. France, he said, was involved in Italy, but Slidell understood clearly the cause for French hesitancy. To the Confederate government he wrote on August 24: "You will find by my official correspondence that we are still hard and fast aground here. Nothing will float us off but a strong and continued current of important successes in the field." England, he warned, would avoid intervention until the North and South had become entirely exhausted. "Nothing," he lamented, "can exceed the selfishness of English statesmen except their wretched hypocrisy. They are continually casting about their disinterested magnanimity and objection of all other considerations than those dictated by a high-toned morality, while their entire policy is marked by egotism and duplicity."

Despite the lack of conviction in Europe's judgment of Confederate prospects, Southern victories were prompting the British Ministry to consider intervention. Russell admitted that nothing less than further Confederate successes would force mediation on the North. "I think," he wrote to the Embassy in Washington, "we must allow the President to spend his second batch of 600,000 men before we can hope that he and his democracy will listen to reason." Russell was convinced privately that October, 1862, would be the anticipated time for action. Stonewall Jackson's victories in Virginia prompted him to inform Lord Palmerston, the Prime Minister, that "it really looks as if he might end the war." Palmerston agreed, writing on September 14: "The Federals . . . got a very complete smashing . . . even Washington or Baltimore may fall into the hands of the Confederates. If this should happen, would it not be time for us to consider whether in such a state of things England and France might not address the contending parties and recommend an arrangement upon the basis of separation." The British Cabinet awaited word from France.

Before Napoleon could commit France to intervention, the British government passed the moment of decision. The wise and respected British politician, Earl Granville, warned Russell that involvement would mean war. "I doubt," he cautioned, "if the war continues long after our recognition of the South, whether it will be possible for us to avoid drifting into it." If Granville's words lacked conviction, Northern arms did not. Before the end of September news reached London of McClellan's success at Antietam and Lee's retreat down the Shenandoah Valley. Russell, who had been the ministry's most vigorous spokesman for involvement, now admitted, "This American question must be well sifted." Palmerston's support of Russell's position had been conditioned on the Southern invasion of Maryland. Now on October 2 in a letter to Russell he also acknowledged the wisdom of Granville's argument. Since mediation would favor the Southern position, its acceptance in the North hinged on Southern triumphs. Ten days earlier the necessary conditions seemed impending; now Palmerston counseled delay. He had no interest in exposing Canada and British commerce to a war against the United States. Nor would he venture into a quarrel without the support of Frence and Russia. "The whole matter is full of difficulty," he concluded, "and can only be cleared up by some more decided events between the contending armies."

William E. Gladstone, Britain's liberal cabinet leader, continued to urge British involvement in the American conflict as a moral obligation. At Newcastle on October 7 he declared: "Jefferson Davis and the other leaders have made an army, they are making, it appears, a navy, and they have made what is more than either, they have made a nation." Gladstone denied that British mediation would be met by insult or war, for, he predicted in a memorandum to the Prime Minister, "America would feel the influence and weight of a general opinion on the part of civilized Europe that this horrible war ought to cease." Whatever the immediate Northern reaction, the British proposal would produce a powerful effect on opinion and alter affairs in America in favor of peace. But perhaps Gladstone was motivated by more than a moral revulsion to war. He had recently toured the North of England and was fearful that the unemployment in the cotton districts would produce a violent upheaval. By serving the cause of peace the great liberal might also serve the cause of the British cotton textile industry.

Palmerston, under pressure from the Cabinet, sought the advice of the Earl of Derby, leader of the opposition. Derby vigorously opposed both mediation and recognition. He reiterated the fundamental conviction of European conservatives that either action would merely irritate the North without advancing the cause of the South or procuring a single bale of cotton. Mediation, he added, would gain its apparent objective only if England were prepared to sweep away the blockade and invite a declaration of war from the Lincoln administration. Intervention was hopeless because there was no way in which England could influence events in America short of military involvement. Palmerston's decision reflected this fundamental reality. Britain, he informed Lord Russell, "could take no step nor make any communication of a distinct proposition with any advantage." The North, he pointed out, demanded no less than restoration of the Union and the South no less than independence. To offer mediation would merely pledge each party in the conflict more firmly to its uncompromising objective. Russell added his conviction that no British action would be effective unless it were supported by Russia, Prussia, Austria, and France. For nations of such diverse interests agreement on interventionist policy was impossible.

During the crucial months of October and November, 1862, Napoleon never disguised his sympathy for the Confederate cause. But sentiment and policy are not synonymous, and the French Emperor balked at involvement in the American conflict. He complained to Slidell of troubles in Italy and Greece and acknowledged his fear that if he acted alone England would desert him and would attempt to embroil him in a war with the United States. Slidell assured him that recognition would not be regarded by the North as a *casus belli* and that with his powerful navy he could defend French interests on the seas without difficulty. To Slidell joint mediation was worthless, for he had no faith in England or Russia. Napoleon answered with a proposal acceptable to the Southern Commissioner. France and Britain might seek a six-month armistice in the American Civil War in the interest of humanity. Napoleon's final program for joint action was dispatched to both London and St. Petersburg.

In London the tripartite proposal threw the Cabinet into confusion. Palmerston was displeased, for he no longer had any interest in European intervention. Lord Russell favored action provided European leaders could discover terms upon which the warring sections in America would agree. In lieu of this elusive formula he favored a Cabinet discussion of the French dispatch. At the Cabinet meetings of November 11 and 12 Russell conceded the issue to Palmerston. Reported Gladstone to his wife: "The United States affair has ended and not well. Lord Russell rather turned tail. He gave way without resolutely fighting out his battle." In its reply to the French government, the British Ministry declared that mediation in any form was useless since Lincoln would not accept it.

At issue in the final Cabinet decision was the attitude of Russia. As early as November 8, St. Petersburg had informed the Foreign Office that the Russian government had rejected Napoleon's proposal. Prince Gortchakov advised the French that it was "essential to avoid the appearance of any pressure of a nature to offend American public opinion, and to excite susceptibilities very easily roused at the bare idea of intervention." Russell yielded on this key question to Palmerston when he wrote, "We ought not to move at present without Russia." Russia's inflexibility created the basis for a harmonious decision within the British Cabinet, and even Gladstone could write, "As to the state of matters generally in the Cabinet, I have never seen it smoother."

Throughout the months of decision in Europe, Seward exerted relentless pressure on the British and French governments. When Mercier transmitted a French offer of mediation to him in July, 1862, the Secretary warned that "the Emperor can commit no graver error than to mix himself in our affairs. At the rumor alone of intervention all the factions will reunite themselves against you and even in the border states you will meet resistance unanimous and desperate." It was not in the French interest, he continued, to compromise the kindly feeling which the United States held for France. Mercier thereupon advised caution in Paris, adding that intervention could easily result in war. When Mercier apprised Seward of Europe's reaction to McClellan's withdrawal from Richmond, the Secretary again stormed back: "I have noticed it but as for us it would be a great misfortune if the powers should wish to intervene in our affairs. There is no possible compromise . . . and at any price, we will not admit the division of the Union." Seward acknowledged the kindly sentiments of Europe but replied that the best testimony of those sentiments would be Old World abstention from American affairs. When Mercier suggested that restoration of the Union was impossible, Seward told him: "Do not believe for a moment that either the Federal Congress, myself or any person connected with this government will in any case entertain any proposition or suggestion of arrangement or accommodation or adjustment from within or without upon the basis of a surrender of the Federal Union."

Above all Seward sought to disabuse European leaders of their conviction that a Northern victory was impossible. Nothing had occurred, he once wrote to Dayton in Paris, to shake the confidence of the Federal government in the ultimate success of its purpose. To those Europeans who insisted that the United States was too large for one nation, Seward retorted that it was too small for two. When Europe gave evidence of interventionist tendencies in August, 1862, Seward wrote to Adams: "The nation has a right and it is its duty, to live. Those who favor and give aid to the insurrection, upon whatever pretext, assail the nation in an hour of danger, and therefore they cannot be held or regarded as its friends. In taking this ground, the United States claim only what they concede to all other nations. No state can be really independent in any other position."

In denying Europe the right to intervene, Seward insisted that he was defending the principle of civil government itself, for at stake was nothing less than the existence of the United States. "Any other principle than this," he said, "would be to resolve government everywhere into a thing of accident and caprice, and ultimately all human society into a state of perpetual war." American policy was dictated by the law of self-preservation, and no nation, he added, "animated by loyal sentiments and inspired by a generous ambition can ever suffer itself to debate with parties within or without a policy of self-preservation."

Seward, therefore, instructed Adams not to debate, hear, or receive any communication from the British government which sought to advise the United States in its relations with the Confederacy. This nation was fighting for empire, he admitted in October, 1862, but it was an empire lawfully acquired and lawfully held. "Studying to confine this unhappy struggle within our own borders," he wrote to Dayton, "we have not only invoked no foreign aid or sympathy, but we have warned foreign nations frankly and have besought them not to interfere. We have practised justice towards them in every way, and conciliation to an unusual degree. But we are none the less determined for all that to be sovereign and to be free."

Seward's reaction to the British Cabinet debate of November revealed both confidence and dismay. It was not pleasant for a loyal American, he admitted to Adams, to observe an English cabinet discuss the future of the American Republic. But the United States, he added, enjoyed the right and possessed the power to determine its own destiny; never before was it better prepared to meet danger from abroad. The wheel of political fortune continued to turn. England had once desired American friendship; she would do so again. "Neither politicians nor statesmen control events," the Secretary concluded. "They can moderate them and accommodate their ambitions to them, but they can do no more."

After November, 1862, all wartime diplomacy receded into insignificance. Whatever Southern hopes of European intervention still remained were shattered by the Confederate disasters at Gettysburg and Vicksburg in July, 1863. In September Mason informed Russell by note that his mission had been terminated. The British Secretary replied coldly: "I have on other occasions explained to you the reasons which have inclined her Majesty's Government to decline the overtures you allude to. . . . These reasons are still in force, and it is not necessary to repeat them." Europe's final refusal to involve itself in the American struggle was nothing less than a total vindication of Seward's diplomacy. Whatever the North's diplomatic advantages, he had understood them and exploited them with astonishing effectiveness. He made it clear that any European nation which committed itself to the destruction of the American Union would pay dearly if it sought to fulfill that commitment.

In one sense there was nothing unique in the diplomatic issues raised by the American Civil War. Many nations in the past had undergone internal revolution in which elements seeking power had sought either to overthrow the established government or to establish the independence of some portion of its territory. Such uprisings had succeeded and failed, but when major power was involved they had demonstrated invariably that other nations, whatever their moral and material interests, really could not intervene diplomatically without running the risk of military involvement.

Unfortunately Union diplomacy after 1861 placed this nation in the unprecedented and embarrassing position of appearing to defy its own democratic principle of self-determination. Americans in the past, Europe recalled, had not only made declarations in favor of the Greek and Hungarian revolutions and applauded such revolutionary leaders as Louis Kossuth, but they had furnished them money for the declared purpose of assuring new disorders.

Now Americans were compelled to recognize what they had often denied Europe—that governments cannot exist without authority and that, to maintain their authority, they must resort to force. Cassius Clay, to explain American purpose, once declared that the United States was fighting for nationality and liberty. To this the London *Times* replied sarcastically that it was difficult to understand how "a people fighting . . . to force their fellow citizens to remain in a confederacy which they repudiated, can be called the champions of liberty and nationalism." The Confederates were fighting for their independence, observed the *Times,* adding, "But with the Northerners all is different. They are not content with their own. They are fighting to coerce others."

Europe might have recalled that idealism had never established the official diplomatic tradition of the United States toward revolution and oppression. Whatever the concern of individual Americans toward events abroad, the nation's dictum since Washington's presidency had been one of abstention. John Quincy Adams had given it classical form in his Marcellus letters of 1794: "It is our duty to remain, the peaceful and silent, though sorrowful spectators of the European scene." Again in July, 1821, Adams declared that "America is the well-wisher to the freedom and independence of all. She is the vindicator only of her own." All national leaders prior to the Civil War, when holding positions of responsibility, agreed that any foreign intervention in behalf of liberal causes might well commit the United States beyond its national interest. President James Monroe recognized this when he refused to render aid to the revolting states of Latin America. They would receive recognition, he informed them, when they had demonstrated sufficient strength to establish their own independence. Palmerston was merely reflecting this diplomatic tradition when he admitted in October, 1862, that Britain "must continue merely to be lookers-on till the war shall have taken a more decided turn."

Tangible British and French interests were involved in the Southern struggle for independence, and to that extent neither nation could ignore events across the Atlantic. But until the South could demonstrate, as did the Latin American republics, that it could overcome the power and purpose of the North, European recognition would have defied one of the most significant and thoroughly established traditions of modern diplomacy. Except for one fleeting period in 1862, neither Britain nor France revealed any serious intention of breaking from their own past and assuming commitments which would endanger their territorial and commercial interests in the New World. Had Europe given expression to its moral sentiment by supporting the cause of the seemingly oppressed, it would merely have magnified the horror and confusion. Of this Seward left no doubt. He warned Europe in May, 1862, that its involvement in the affairs of the United States would not serve the interests of humanity. "If Europe will still sympathize with the revolution," he wrote, "it must now look forward to the end; an end in which the war ceases with anarchy substituted for the social system that existed when the war began. What will then have become of the interests which carried Europe to the side which was at once the wrong side and the losing one? Only a perfect withdrawal of all favor from the insurrection can now save those interests in any degree. The insurrectionary states, left hopeless of foreign intervention, will be content to stop in their career of self-destruction, and to avail themselves of the moderating power of the Federal government. If the nations of Europe shall refuse to see this, and the war must therefore go on to the conclusion I have indicated, the responsibility for that conclusion will not rest with the government of the United States.''

Seward here touched the central issue of Europe's relationship to the conflict in America. If after the summer of 1862 it was still within the power of the Old World to bring injury to the North, it was beyond its power to bring salvation to the South. There were no inexpensive means available to Europe to achieve the liberation of the South against the North's determination to hold it. Those Europeans who sought to cast from the South the yoke of alien rule might have been moved by the moral sentiment of Gladstone, but they had no influence on Palmerston. And since the realities of power are always the determining factors in international affairs, a Gladstone in office, whatever his sentimentalism and faith in moral pressure, could have influenced the internal affairs of the United States, wrapped in civil war, with no more success than the masters of *Realpolitik* who rejected such purpose as a matter of principle.

---

# FURTHER READING

Ephraim D. Adams, *Great Britain and the Civil War* (1925)

H. C. Allen, "Civil War, Reconstruction, and Great Britain," in Harold Hyman, ed., *Heard Round the World: The Impact Abroad of the Civil War* (1969)

Stuart Anderson, "1861: Blockade vs. Closing of the Confederate Ports," *Military Affairs,* 41 (1977), 190–193

Stuart L. Bernath, *Squall Across the Atlantic: American Civil War Prizes and Diplomacy* (1970)

Henry Blumenthal, "Confederate Diplomacy," *Journal of Southern History,* 32 (1966), 151–171

Kenneth Bourne, *Britain and the Balance of Power in North America, 1815–1908* (1967)

Kinley J. Brauer, "The Slavery Problem in the Diplomacy of the American Civil War," *Pacific Historical Review,* 46 (1977), 439–469

Charles S. Campbell, *From Revolution to Rapprochement* (1974)

Lynn M. Case and Warren F. Spencer, *The United States and France: Civil War Diplomacy* (1970)

D. P. Crook, *Diplomacy During the American Civil War* (1975)

———, *The North, the South, and the Powers, 1861–1865* (1974)

Charles P. Cullop, *Confederate Propaganda in Europe* (1969)

Norman B. Ferris, *Desperate Diplomacy: William H. Seward's Foreign Policy, 1861* (1975)

———, *The "Trent" Affair* (1977)

Kenneth J. Hagan, ed., *In Peace and War: Interpretations of American Naval History, 1775–1978* (1978)

Brian Jenkins, *Britain and the War for the Union*, 2 vols. (1974–1980)

Frank J. Merli, *Great Britain and the Confederate Navy* (1970)

Jay Monaghan, *Diplomat in Carpet Slippers: Abraham Lincoln Deals with Foreign Affairs* (1945)

Kenneth Moss, "The United States and Central Europe, 1861–1871," *The Historian*, 39 (1977), 248–269

Frank L. and Harriet Owsley, *King Cotton Diplomacy* (1959)

Emory M. Thomas, *The Confederate Nation, 1861–1865* (1979)

Gordon H. Warren, *Fountain of Discontent: The* Trent *Affair and Freedom of the Seas* (1981)

Albert A. Woldman, *Lincoln and the Russians* (1952)

# Late Nineteenth-Century
# Expansionism and Economics

# 10

*The issue of slavery, sectionalism, and the Civil War interrupted the seeming relentlessness of American expansion. After the bitter North-South clash, expansionists once again took up the call. Secretary of State William H. Seward (1861–1869) became their leader and, under his stewardship, the United States acquired the large territory of Alaska and the tiny Midway Islands. Seward's other schemes for acquiring islands in the Caribbean were squelched by Congress. Still, from the 1860s to 1900 the United States became more active in affairs beyond its continental boundaries, participating in international conferences, sending American products into distant lands, enlarging its navy, extending its commercial and missionary interests in Asia, scolding European powers about their intrusions in Latin America by citing the Monroe Doctrine, intervening in inter-American squabbles, and launching Pan-Americanism. The relative importance of economic factors in this conspicuous nineteenth-century expansionism has long been debated by historians.*

## DOCUMENTS

The following documents represent some of the most prominent voices of late nineteenth-century expansionism. William H. Seward acquired Alaska in 1867. Two years later, on August 12, 1869, he visited his imperial prize and delivered an exuberant speech to the citizens of Sitka. President Ulysses S. Grant tried very hard to annex Santo Domingo, but the Senate eventually blocked his effort. In his message to Congress, dated May 31, 1870, the President itemized the reasons why the Caribbean nation should be attached to the United States.

In 1881 Secretary of State James G. Blaine wanted to hold a Pan American Conference, but he left office within a few months and his dream was foiled. In 1888, however, once again the Secretary of State, he organized a Pan American Conference, which met in Washington, D.C., from October 1889 to April 1890. Blaine's goals are spelled out in the congressional resolution calling for the meeting, reprinted here. Another spokesman for expansion was Captain Alfred T. Mahan. His teaching at the Naval War College and his publications, including *The Influence of Sea Power Upon History,* from which the fourth selection is chosen, encouraged a larger navy and active overseas involvement for the United States.

A voice from the pulpit, the Reverend Josiah Strong, also envisioned American greatness, but largely in religious and racial terms. The Anglo-Saxon race, he preached according to Social Darwinism, was destined to rule a world of inferiors. His book *Our Country,* first published in 1885, made the point in reverent tones, as the fifth selection illustrates. Ten years later a major dispute, the Venezuelan controversy, sparked Secretary of State Richard Olney to send Britain a haughty message, dated July 20, 1895, which President Grover Cleveland called a "twenty-inch gun." Britain and Venezuela had been arguing for years about disputed land near British Guiana. Olney decided to settle the annoying question and, in so doing, declared United States hegemony over the Western Hemisphere, as the last document demonstrates.

---

# William H. Seward on Alaska, 1869

Citizens of Alaska, Fellow-citizens of the United States:—You have pressed me to meet you in public assembly once before I leave Alaska. It would be sheer affectation to pretend to doubt your sincerity in making this request, and capriciously ungrateful to refuse it, after having received so many and varied hospitalities from all sorts and conditions of men. It is not an easy task, however, to speak in a manner worthy of your consideration, while I am living constantly on ship-board, as you all know, and am occupied intently in searching out whatever is sublime, or beautiful, or peculiar, or useful. On the other hand, it is altogether natural on your part to say, "You have looked upon Alaska, what do you think of it?" Unhappily, I have seen too little of Alaska to answer the question satisfactorily. The entire coast line of the United States, exclusive of Alaska, is 10,000 miles, while the coast line of Alaska alone, including the islands, is 26,000 miles. The portion of the Territory which lies east of the peninsula, including islands, is 120 miles wide; the western portion, including Aleutian islands, expands to a breadth of 2,200 miles. The entire land area, including islands, is 577,390 statute square miles. . . .

Of course I speak first of the skies of Alaska. It seems to be assumed in the case of Alaska that a country which extends through fifty-eight degrees of longitude, and embraces portions as well of the arctic as of the temperate zone, unlike all other regions so situated, has not several climates, but only one. The weather of this one broad climate of Alaska is severely criticised in outside circles for being too wet and too cold. Nevertheless, it must be a fastidious person who complains of climates in which, while the eagle delights to soar, the humming-bird does not disdain to flutter. . . .

It is next in order to speak of the rivers and seas of Alaska. The rivers are broad, shallow, and rapid, while the seas are deep but tranquil. Mr. Sumner, in his elaborate and magnificent oration, although he spake only from historical accounts, has not exaggerated—no man can exaggerate—the marine treasures of the Territory. Beside the whale, which everywhere and at all times is seen enjoying his robust exercise, and the sea-otter, the fur-seal, the hair-seal, and the walrus, found in the waters which embosom the western islands, those waters, as well as the seas of the eastern archipelago, are found teeming with the salmon, cod, and other fishes adapted to the support of human and animal life. Indeed, what I have seen here has almost made me a convert to the theory of some naturalists, that the waters of the globe are filled with stores for the sustenance of animal life surpassing the available productions of the land.

It must be remembered that the coast range of mountains, which begins in Mexico, is continued into the Territory, and invades the seas of Alaska. Hence it is that in the islands and on the mainland, so far as I have explored it, we find ourselves everywhere in the immediate presence of black hills, or foot-hills, as they are variously called, and that these foot-hills are overtopped by ridges of snow-capped mountains. These snow-capped mountains are manifestly of volcanic origin, and they have been subjected, through an indefinite period, to atmospheric abrasion and disintegration. Hence they have assumed all conceivable shapes and forms. In some places they are serrated into sharp, angular peaks, and in other places they appear architecturally arranged, so as to present cloud-capped castles, towers, domes, and minarets. The mountain sides are furrowed with deep and straight ravines, down which the thawing fields of ice and snow are precipitated, generally in the month of May, with such a vehemence as to have produced in every valley immense level plains of intervale land. These plains, as well as the sides of the mountains, almost to the summits, are covered with forests so dense and dark as to be impenetrable, except to wild beasts and savage huntsmen. On the lowest intervale land the cotton-wood grows. It seems to be the species of poplar which is known in the Atlantic States as the Balm of Gilead, and which is dwarfed on the Rocky Mountains. Here it takes on such large dimensions, that the Indian shapes out of a single trunk even his great war canoe, which safely bears over the deepest waters a phalanx of sixty warriors. These imposing trees always appear to rise out of a jungle of elder, alder, crab-apple, and other fruit-bearing shrubs and bushes. The short and slender birch, which, sparsely scattered, marks the verge of vegetation in Labrador, has not yet been reached by the explorers of Alaska. The birch tree sometimes appears here upon the river side, upon the level next above the home of the cottonwood, and is generally found a comely and stately tree. The forests of Alaska, however, consist mainly neither of shrubs, nor of the birch, nor of the cottonwood, but, as I have already intimated, of the pine, the cedar, the cypress, the spruce, the fir, the larch, and the hemlock. These forests begin almost at the water's edge, and they rise with regular gradation to a height of two thousand feet. The trees, nowhere dwarfed or diminutive, attain the highest dimensions in sunny exposures in the deeper cañons or gorges of the mountains. The cedar, sometimes called the yellow cedar, and sometimes the fragrant cedar, was long ago imported into China as an ornamental wood; and it now furnishes the majestic beams and pillars with which the richer and more ambitious native chief delights to construct his rude but spacious hall or palatial residence, and upon which he carves in rude symbolical imagery the heraldry of his tribe and achievements of his nation. No beam, or pillar, or spar, or mast, or plank is ever required in either the land or the naval architecture of any civilized state greater in length and width than the trees which can be hewn down on the coasts of the islands and rivers here, and conveyed directly thence by navigation. A few gardens, fields, and meadows, have been attempted by natives in some of the settlements, and by soldiers at the military posts, with most encouraging results. Nor must we forget that the native grasses, ripening late in a humid climate, preserve their nutritive properties, though exposed, while the climate is so mild that cattle and horses require but slight provision of shelter during the winter. . . .

After what I have already said, I may excuse myself from expatiating on the animal productions of the forest. The elk and the deer are so plenty as to be undervalued for food or skins, by natives as well as strangers. The bear of many families—black, grizzly, and cinnamon; the mountain sheep, inestimable for his fleece; the wolf, the fox, the beaver, the otter, the mink, the raccoon, the marten, the ermine; the squirrel—gray, black, brown, and flying, are among the land fur-bearing animals. The furs thus found here have been the chief element, for more than a hundred years, of the profitable commerce of the Hudson Bay Company, whose mere possessory privileges seem, even at this late day, too costly to find a ready purchaser. This fur trade, together with the sea fur-trade within the Territory, were the sole basis alike of Russian commerce and empire on this continent. This commerce was so large and important as to induce the Governments of Russia and China to build and maintain a town for carrying on its exchanges in Tartary on the border of the two empires. It is well understood that the supply of furs in Alaska has not diminished, while the demand for them in China and elsewhere has immensely increased. . . .

Alaska has been as yet but imperfectly explored; but enough is known to assure us that it possesses treasures of what are called the baser ores equal to those of any other region of the continent. We have Copper Island and Copper River, so named as the places where the natives, before the period of the Russian discovery, had procured the pure metal from which they fabricated instruments of war and legendary shields. In regard to iron, the question seems to be not where it can be found, but whether there is any place where it does not exist. Mr. Davidson, of the Coast Survey, invited me to go up to him at the station he had taken up the Chilcat River to make his observations of the eclipse, by writing me that he had discovered an iron mountain there. When I came there I found that, very properly, he had been studying the heavens so busily, that he had but cursorily examined the earth under his feet; that it was not a single iron mountain he had discovered, but a range of hills, the very dust of which adheres to the magnet, while the range itself, two thousand feet high, extends along the east bank of the river thirty miles. Limestone and marble crop out on the banks of the same river and in many other places. Coal-beds, accessible to navigation, are found at Kootznoo. It is said, however, that the concentrated resin which the mineral contains renders it too inflammable to be safely used by steamers. In any case, it would seem calculated to supply the fuel requisite for the manufacture of iron. What seems to be excellent cannel coal is also found in the Prince of Wales archipelago. There are also mines at Cook's Inlet. Placer and quartz gold mining is pursued under many social disadvantages upon the Stickeen and elsewhere, with a degree of success which, while it does not warrant us in assigning a superiority in that respect to the Territory, does nevertheless warrant us in regarding gold mining as an established and reliable resource. . . .

It remains only to speak of man and of society in Alaska. Until the present moment the country has been exclusively inhabited and occupied by some thirty or more Indian tribes. I incline to doubt the popular classification of these tribes upon the assumption that they have descended from diverse races. Climate and other circumstances have indeed produced some differences of manners and customs between the Aleuts, the Koloschians, and the interior continental tribes. But all of them are manifestly of Mongol origin. Although they have preserved no common traditions, all alike indulge in tastes, wear a physiognomy, and are imbued with sentiments peculiarly noticed in Japan and China. Savage communities, no less than civilized nations, require space for subsistence, whether they depend for it upon the land or upon the sea—in savage communities especially; and increase of population disproportioned to the supplies of the country occupied necessitates subdivision and remote colonization. Oppression and cruelty occur even more frequently among barbarians than among civilized men. Nor are ambition and faction less inherent in the one condition than in the other. From these causes it has happened that the 25,000 Indians in Alaska are found permanently divided into so many insignificant nations. These nations are jealous, ambitious, and violent; could in no case exist long in the same region without mutually affording what, in every case, to each party, seems just cause of war. War between savages becomes the private cause of the several families which are afflicted with the loss of their members. Such a war can never be composed until each family which has suffered receives an indemnity in blankets, adjusted according to an imaginary tariff, or, in the failure of such compensation, secures the death of one or more enemies as an atonement for the injury it has sustained. The enemy captured, whether by superior force or strategy, either receives no quarter, or submits for himself and his progeny to perpetual slavery. It has thus happened that the Indian tribes of Alaska have never either confederated or formed permanent alliances, and that even at this late day, in the presence of superior power exercised by the United States Government, they live in regard to each other in a state of enforced and doubtful truce. It is manifest that, under these circumstances, they must steadily decline in numbers, and unhappily this decline is accelerated by their borrowing ruinous vices from the white man. Such as the natives of Alaska are, they are, nevertheless, in a practical sense, the only laborers at present in the Territory. The white man comes amongst them from London, from St. Petersburg, from Boston, from New York, from San Francisco, and from Victoria, not to fish (if we except alone the whale fishery) or to hunt, but simply to buy what fish and what peltries, ice, wood, lumber, and coal, the Indians have secured under the superintendence of temporary agents or factors. When we consider how greatly most of the tribes are reduced in numbers, and how precarious their vocations are, we shall cease to regard them as indolent or incapable; and, on the contrary, we shall more deeply regret than ever before, that a people so gifted by nature, so vigorous and energetic, and withal so docile and gentle in their intercourse with the white man, can neither be preserved as a distinct social community, or incorporated into our society. The Indian tribes will do here as they seem to have done in Washington Territory, and British Columbia: they will merely serve their turn until civilized white men come.

You, the citizens of Sitka, are the pioneers, the advanced guard, of the future population of Alaska; and you naturally ask when, from whence, and how soon, reinforcements shall come, and what are the signs and guarantees of their coming? This question, with all its minute and searching interrogations, has been asked by the pioneers of every state and territory of which the American Union is now composed; and the history of those states and territories furnishes the complete, conclusive, and satisfactory answer. Emigrants go to every infant state and territory in obedience to the great natural law that obliges needy men to seek subsistence, and invites adventurous men to seek fortune where it is most easily obtained, and this is always in the new and uncultivated regions. They go from every state and territory, and from every foreign nation in America, Europe, and Asia; because no established and populous state or nation can guarantee subsistence and fortune to all who demand them among its inhabitants.

The guarantees and signs of their coming to Alaska are found in the resources of the territory, which I have attempted to describe, and in the condition of society in other parts of the world. Some men seek other climes for health and some for pleasure. Alaska invites the former class by a climate singularly salubrious, and the latter class by scenery which surpasses in sublimity that of either the Alps, the Apennines, the Alleghanies, or the Rocky Mountains. Emigrants from our own states, from Europe, and from Asia, will not be slow in finding out that fortunes are to be gained by pursuing here the occupations which have so successfully sustained races of untutored men. Civilization and refinement are making more rapid advances in our day than at any former period. The rising states and nations on this continent, the European nations, and even those of Eastern Asia, have exhausted, or are exhausting, their own forests and mines, and are soon to become largely dependent upon those of the Pacific. The entire region of Oregon, Washington Territory, British Columbia, and Alaska, seem thus destined to become a ship-yard for the supply of all nations. I do not forget on this occasion that British Columbia belongs within a foreign jurisdiction.

That circumstance does not materially affect my calculations. British Columbia, by whomsoever possessed, must be governed in conformity with the interests of her people and of society upon the American continent. If that territory shall be so governed, there will be no ground of complaint anywhere. If it shall be governed so as to conflict with the interests of the inhabitants of that territory and of the United States, we all can easily foresee what will happen in that case. You will ask me, however, for guarantees that the hopes I encourage will not be postponed. I give them.

Within the period of my own recollection, I have seen twenty new states added to the eighteen which before that time constituted the American Union, and I now see, besides Alaska, ten territories in a forward condition of preparation for entering into the same great political family. I have seen in my own time not only the first electric telegraph, but even the first railroad and the first steamboat invented by man. And even on this present voyage of mine, I have fallen in with the first steamboat, still afloat, that thirty-five years ago lighted her fires on the Pacific ocean. These, citizens of Sitka, are the guarantees, not only that Alaska has a future, but that that future has already begun. I know that you want two things just now, when European monopoly is broken down and United States free trade is being introduced within the territory: These are, military protection while your number is so inferior to that of the Indians around you, and you need also a territorial civil government. Congress has already supplied the first of these wants adequately and effectually. I doubt not that it will supply the other want during the coming winter. It must do this, because our political system rejects alike anarchy and executive absolutism. Nor do I doubt that the political society to be constituted here, first as a territory, and ultimately as a state or many states, will prove a worthy constituency of the Republic. To doubt that it will be intelligent, virtuous, prosperous, and enterprising, is to doubt the experience of Scotland, Denmark, Sweden, Holland and Belgium, and of New England and New York. Nor do I doubt that it will be forever true in its republican instincts and loyal to the American Union, for the inhabitants will be both mountaineers and seafaring men. I am not among those who apprehend infidelity to liberty and the Union in any quarter hereafter, but I am sure that if constancy and loyalty are to fail anywhere, the failure will not be in the states which approach nearest to the North Pole.

# Ulysses S. Grant on Santo Domingo, 1870

I feel an unusual anxiety for the ratification of this treaty, because I believe it will redound greatly to the glory of the two countries interested, to civilization, and to the extirpation of the institution of slavery.

The doctrine promulgated by President Monroe has been adhered to by all political parties, and I now deem it proper to assert the equally important principle that hereafter no territory on this continent shall be regarded as subject of transfer to a European power.

The Government of San Domingo has voluntarily sought this annexation.

It is a weak power, numbering probably less than 120,000 souls, and yet possessing one of the richest territories under the sun, capable of supporting a population of 10,000,000 people in luxury. The people of San Domingo are not capable of maintaining themselves in their present condition, and must look for outside support.

They yearn for the protection of our free institutions and laws, our progress and civilization. Shall we refuse them?

I have information which I believe reliable that a European power stands ready now to offer $2,000,000 for the possession of Samana Bay alone. If refused by us, with what grace can we prevent a foreign power from attempting to secure the prize?

The acquisition of San Domingo is desirable because of its geographical position. It commands the entrance to the Caribbean Sea and the Isthmus transit of commerce. It possesses the richest soil, best and most capacious harbors, most salubrious climate, and the most valuable products of the forests, mine, and soil of any of the West India Islands. Its possession by us will in a few years build up a coastwise commerce of immense magnitude, which will go far toward restoring to us our lost merchant marine. It will give to us those articles which we consume so largely and do not produce, thus equalizing our exports and imports.

In case of foreign war it will give us command of all the islands referred to, and thus prevent an enemy from ever again possessing himself of rendezvous upon our very coast.

At present our coast trade between the States bordering on the Atlantic and those bordering on the Gulf of Mexico is cut into by the Bahamas and the Antilles. Twice we must, as it were, pass through foreign countries to get by sea from Georgia to the west coast of Florida.

San Domingo, with a stable government, under which her immense resources can be developed, will give remunerative wages to tens of thousands of laborers not now on the island.

This labor will take advantage of every available means of transportation to abandon the adjacent islands and seek the blessings of freedom and its sequence—each inhabitant receiving the reward of his own labor. Porto Rico and Cuba will have to abolish slavery, as a measure of self-preservation to retain their laborers.

San Domingo will become a large consumer of the products of Northern farms and manufactories. The cheap rate at which her citizens can be furnished with food, tools, and machinery will make it necessary that the contiguous islands should have the same advantages in order to compete in the production of sugar, coffee, tobacco, tropical fruits, etc. This will open to us a still wider market for our products.

The production of our own supply of these articles will cut off more than one hundred millions of our annual imports, besides largely increasing our exports. With such a picture it is easy to see how our large debt abroad is ultimately to be extinguished. With a balance of trade against us (including interest on bonds held by foreigners and money spent by our citizens traveling in foreign lands) equal to the entire yield of the precious metals in this country, it it is not so easy to see how this result is to be otherwise accomplished.

The acquisition of San Domingo is an adherence to the "Monroe doctrine"; it is a measure of national protection; it is asserting our just claim to a controlling influence over the great commercial traffic soon to flow from east to west by the way of the Isthmus of Darien; it is to build up our merchant marine; it is to furnish new markets for the products of our farms, shops, and manufactories; it is to make slavery insupportable in Cuba and Porto Rico at once and ultimately so in Brazil; it is to settle the unhappy condition of Cuba, and end an exterminating conflict; it is to provide honest means of paying our honest debts, without overtaxing the people; it is to furnish our citizens with the necessaries of everyday life at cheaper rates than ever before; and it is, in fine, a rapid stride toward that greatness which the intelligence, industry, and enterprise of the citizens of the United States entitle this country to assume among nations.

# Call for a Pan American Conference, 1888

The Conference is called to consider—

*First*. Measures that shall tend to preserve and promote the prosperity of the several American States.

*Second*. Measures toward the formation of an American customs union, under which the trade of the American nations with each other shall, so far as possible and profitable, be promoted.

*Third*. The establishment of regular and frequent communication between the ports of the several American States and the ports of each other.

*Fourth*. The establishment of a uniform system of customs regulations in each of the independent American States to govern the mode of importation and exportation of merchandise and port dues and charges, a uniform method of determining the classification and valuation of such merchandise in the ports of each country, and a uniform system of invoices, and the subject of the sanitation of ships and quarantine.

*Fifth*. The adoption of a uniform system of weights and measures, and laws to protect the patent-rights, copyrights, and trade-marks of citizens of either country in the other, and for the extradition of criminals.

*Sixth*. The adoption of a common silver coin, to be issued by each Government, the same to be legal tender in all commercial transactions between the citizens of all of the American States.

*Seventh*. An agreement upon and recommendation for adoption to their respective Governments of a definite plan of arbitration of all questions, disputes, and differences, that may now or hereafter exist between them, to the end that all difficulties and disputes between such nations may be peaceably settled and wars prevented.

*Eighth*. And to consider such other subjects relating to the welfare of the several States represented as may be presented by any of said States which are hereby invited to participate in said Conference.

# Alfred T. Mahan on Sea Power, 1890

To turn now from the particular lessons drawn from the history of the past to the general question of the influence of government upon the sea career of its people, it is seen that that influence can work in two distinct but closely related ways.

First, in peace: The government by its policy can favor the natural growth of a people's industries and its tendencies to seek adventure and gain by way of the sea; or it can try to develop such industries and such sea-going bent, when they do not naturally exist; or, on the other hand, the government may by mistaken action check and fetter the progress which the people left to themselves would make. In any one of these ways the influence of the government will be felt, making or marring the sea power of the country in the matter of peaceful commerce; upon which alone, it cannot be too often insisted, a thoroughly strong navy can be based.

Secondly, for war: The influence of the government will be felt in its most legitimate manner in maintaining an armed navy, of a size commensurate with the growth of its shipping and the importance of the interests connected with it. More important even than the size of the navy is the question of its institutions, favoring a healthful spirit and activity, and providing for rapid development in time of war by an adequate reserve of men and of ships and by measures for drawing out that general reserve power which has before been pointed to, when considering the character and pursuits of the people. Undoubtedly under this second head of warlike preparation must come the maintenance of suitable naval stations, in those distant parts of the world to which the armed shipping must follow the peaceful vessels of commerce. The protection of such stations must depend either upon direct military force, as do Gibraltar and Malta, or upon a surrounding friendly population, such as the American colonists once were to England, and, it may be presumed, the Australian colonists now are. Such friendly surroundings and backing, joined to a reasonable military provision, are the best of defences, and when combined with decided preponderance at sea, make a scattered and extensive empire, like that of England, secure; for while it is true that an unexpected attack may cause disaster in some one quarter, the actual superiority of naval power prevents such disaster from being general or irremediable. History has sufficiently proved this. England's naval bases have been in all parts of the world; and her fleets have at once protected them, kept open the communications between them, and relied upon them for shelter.

Colonies attached to the mother-country afford, therefore, the surest means of supporting abroad the sea power of a country. In peace, the influence of the government should be felt in promoting by all means a warmth of attachment and a unity of interest which will make the welfare of one the welfare of all, and the quarrel of one the quarrel of all; and in war, or rather for war, by inducing such measures of organization and defence as shall be felt by all to be a fair distribution of a burden of which each reaps the benefit.

Such colonies the United States has not and is not likely to have. As regards purely military naval stations, the feeling of her people was probably accurately expressed by an historian of the English navy a hundred years ago, speaking then of Gibraltar and Port Mahon. "Military governments," said he, "agree so little with the industry of a trading people, and are in themselves so repugnant to the genius of the British people, that I do not wonder that men of good sense and of all parties have inclined to give up these, as Tangiers was given up." Having therefore no foreign establishments, either colonial or military, the ships of war of the United States, in war, will be like land birds, unable to fly far from their own shores. To provide resting-places for them, where they can coal and repair, would be one of the first duties of a government proposing to itself the development of the power of the nation at sea. . . .

The question is eminently one in which the influence of the government should make itself felt, to build up for the nation a navy which, if not capable of reaching distant countries, shall at least be able to keep clear the chief approaches to its own. The eyes of the country have for a quarter of a century been turned from the sea; the results of such a policy and of its opposite will be shown in the instance of France and of England. Without asserting a narrow parallelism between the case of the United States and either of these, it may safely be said that it is essential to the welfare of the whole country that the conditions of trade and commerce should remain, as far as possible, unaffected by an external war. In order to do this, the enemy must be kept not only out of our ports, but far away from our coasts.

## Josiah Strong on Anglo-Saxon Predominance, 1891

It is not necessary to argue to those for whom I write that the two great needs of mankind, that all men may be lifted up into the light of the highest Christian civilization, are, first, a pure, spiritual Christianity, and second, civil liberty. Without controversy, these are the forces which, in the past, have contributed most to the elevation of the human race, and they must continue to be, in the future, the most efficient ministers to its progress. It follows, then, that the Anglo-Saxon, as the great representative of these two ideas, the despositary of these two greatest blessings, sustains peculiar relations to the world's future, is divinely commissioned to be, in a peculiar sense, his brother's keeper. Add to this the fact of his rapidly increasing strength in modern times, and we have well-nigh a demonstration of his destiny. In 1700 this race numbered less than 6,000,000 souls. In 1800, Anglo-Saxons (I use the term somewhat broadly to include all English-speaking peoples) had increased to about 20,500,000, and now, in 1890, they number more than 120,000,000, having multiplied almost six-fold in ninety years. At the end of the reign of Charles II, the English colonists in America numbered 200,000. During these two hundred years, our population has increased two hundred and fifty-fold. And the expansion of this race has been no less remarkable than its multiplication. In one century the United States has increased its territory ten-fold, while the enormous acquisition of foreign territory by Great Britain—and chiefly within the last hundred years—is wholly unparalleled in history. This mighty Anglo-Saxon race, though comprising only one-thirteenth part of mankind, now rules more than one-third of the earth's surface, and more than one-fourth of its people. And if this race, while growing from 6,000,000 to 120,000,000, thus gained possession of a third portion of the earth, is it to be supposed that when it numbers 1,000,000,000, it will lose the disposition, or lack the power to extend its sway? . . .

America is to have the great preponderance of numbers and of wealth, and by the logic of events will follow the scepter of controlling influence. This will be but the consummation of a movement as old as civilization—a result to which men have looked forward for centuries. John Adams records that nothing was "more ancient in his memory than the observation that arts, sciences and empire had traveled westward; and in conversation it was always added that their next leap would be over the Atlantic into America." He recalled a couplet that had been inscribed or rather drilled, into a rock on the shore of Monument Bay in our old colony of Plymouth:

> The Eastern nations sink, their glory ends,
> And empire rises where the sun descends. . . .

Mr. Darwin is not only disposed to see, in the superior vigor of our people, an illustration of his favorite theory of natural selection, but even intimates that the world's history thus far has been simply preparatory for our future, and tributary to it. He says: "There is apparently much truth in the belief that the wonderful progress of the United States, as well as the character of the people, are the results of natural selection; for the more energetic, restless, and courageous men from all parts of Europe have emigrated during the last ten or twelve generations to that great country, and have there succeeded best. Looking at the distant future, I do not think that the Rev. Mr. Zincke takes an exaggerated view when he says: 'All other series of events—as that which resulted in the culture of mind in Greece, and that which resulted in the Empire of Rome—only appear to have purpose and value when viewed in connection with, or rather as subsidiary to, the great stream of Anglo-Saxon emigration to the West.' "

There is abundant reason to believe that the Anglo-Saxon race is to be, is, indeed, already becoming, more effective here than in the mother country. The marked superiority of this race is due, in large measure, to its highly mixed origin. Says Rawlinson: "It is a general rule, now almost universally admitted by ethnologists, that the mixed races of mankind are superior to the pure ones"; and adds: "Even the Jews, who are so often cited as an example of a race at once pure and strong, may, with more reason, be adduced on the opposite side of the argument." The ancient Egyptians, the Greeks, and the Romans, were all mixed races. Among modern races, the most conspicuous example is afforded by the Anglo-Saxons. . . . There is here a new commingling of races; and, while the largest injections of foreign blood are substantially the same elements that constituted the original Anglo-Saxon admixture, so that we may infer the general type will be preserved, there are strains of other bloods being added, which, if Mr. Emerson's remark is true, that "the best nations are those most widely related," may be expected to improve the stock, and aid it to a higher destiny. If the dangers of immigration, which have been pointed out, can be successfully met for the next few years, until it has passed its climax, it may be expected to add value to the amalgam which will constitute the new Anglo-Saxon race of the New World. Concerning our future, Herbert Spencer says: "One great result is, I think, tolerably clear. From biological truths it is to be inferred that the eventual mixture of the allied varieties of the Aryan race, forming the population, will produce a more powerful type of man than has hitherto existed, and a type of man more plastic, more adaptable, more capable of undergoing the modifications needful for complete social life. I think, whatever difficulties they may have to surmount, and whatever tribulations they may have to pass through, the Americans may reasonably look forward to a time when they will have produced a civilization grander than any the world has known."

It may be easily shown, and is of no small significance, that the two great ideas of which the Anglo-Saxon is the exponent are having a fuller development in the United States than in Great Britain. There the union of Church and State tends strongly to paralyze some of the members of the body of Christ. Here there is no such influence to destroy spiritual life and power. Here, also, has been evolved the form of government consistent with the largest possible civil liberty. Furthermore, it is significant that the marked characteristics of this race are being here emphasized most. Among the most striking features of the Anglo-Saxon is his money-making power—a power of increasing importance in the widening commerce of the world's future. We have seen . . . that, although England is by far the richest nation of Europe, we have already outstripped her in the race after wealth, and we have only begun the development of our vast resources.

Again, another marked characteristic of the Anglo-Saxon is what may be called an instinct or genius for colonizing. His unequaled energy, his indomitable perseverance, and his personal independence, made him a pioneer. He excels all others in pushing his way into new countries. It was those in whom this tendency was strongest that came to America, and this inherited tendency has been further developed by the westward sweep of successive generations across the continent. So noticeable has this characteristic become that English visitors remark it. Charles Dickens once said that the typical American would hesitate to enter heaven unless assured that he could go farther west.

Again, nothing more manifestly distinguishes the Anglo-Saxon than his intense and persistent energy, and he is developing in the United States an energy which, in eager activity and effectiveness, is peculiarly American.

This is due partly to the fact that Americans are much better fed than Europeans, and partly to the undeveloped resources of a new country, but more largely to our climate, which acts as a constant stimulus. Ten years after the landing of the Pilgrims, the Rev. Francis Higginson, a good observer, wrote: "A sup of New England air is better than a whole flagon of English ale." Thus early had the stimulating effect of our climate been noted. Moreover, our social institutions are stimulating. In Europe the various ranks of society are, like the strata of the earth, fixed and fossilized. There can be no great change without a terrible upheaval, a social earthquake. Here society is like the waters of the sea, mobile; as General Garfield said, and so signally illustrated in his own experience, that which is at the bottom to-day may one day flash on the crest of the highest wave. Every one is free to become whatever he can make of himself; free to transform himself from a rail splitter or a tanner or a canal-boy, into the nation's President. Our aristocracy, unlike that of Europe, is open to all comers. Wealth, position, influence, are prizes offered for energy; and every farmer's boy, every apprentice and clerk, every friendless and penniless immigrant, is free to enter the lists. Thus many causes co-operate to produce here the most forceful and tremendous energy in the world.

What is the significance of such facts? These tendencies infold the future; they are the mighty alphabet with which God writes his prophecies. May we not, by a careful laying together of the letters, spell out something of his meaning? It seems to me that God, with infinite wisdom and skill, is training the Anglo-Saxon race for an hour sure to come in the world's future. Heretofore there has always been in the history of the world a comparatively unoccupied land westward, into which the crowded countries of the East have poured their surplus populations. But the widening waves of migration, which millenniums ago rolled east and west from the valley of the Euphrates, meet to-day on our Pacific coast. There are no more new worlds. The unoccupied arable lands of the earth are limited, and will soon be taken. The time is coming when the pressure of population on the means of subsistence will be felt here as it is now felt in Europe and Asia. Then will the world enter upon a new stage of its history—*the final competition of races, for which the Anglo-Saxon is being schooled*. Long before the thousand millions are here, the mighty *centrifugal* tendency, inherent in this stock and strengthened in the United States, will assert itself. Then this race of unequaled energy, with all the majesty of numbers and the might of wealth behind it—the representative, let us hope, of the largest liberty, the purest Christianity, the highest civilization—having developed peculiarly aggressive traits calculated to impress its institutions upon mankind, will spread itself over the earth. If I read not amiss, this powerful race will move down upon Mexico, down upon Central and South America, out upon the islands of the sea, over upon Africa and beyond. And can any one doubt that the results of this competition of races will be the "survival of the fittest?" "Any people," says Dr. Bushnell, "that is physiologically advanced in culture, though it be only in a degree beyond another which is mingled with it on strictly equal terms, is sure to live down and finally live out its inferior. Nothing can save the inferior race but a ready and pliant assimilation. Whether the feebler and more abject races are going to be regenerated and raised up, is already very much of a question. What if it should be God's plan to people the world with better and finer material?"

# Richard Olney on the Venezuelan Controversy, 1895

That America is in no part open to colonization, though the proposition was not universally admitted at the time of its first enunciation, has long been universally conceded. We are now concerned, therefore, only with that other practical application of the Monroe doctrine the disregard of which by an European power is to be deemed an act of unfriendliness towards the United States. The precise scope and limitations of this rule cannot be too clearly apprehended. It does not establish any general protectorate by the United States over other American states. It does not relieve any American state from its obligations as fixed by international law nor prevent any European power directly interested from enforcing such obligations or from inflicting merited punishment for the breach of them. It does not contemplate any interference in the internal affairs of any American state or in the relations between it and other American states. It does not justify any attempt on our part to change the established form of government of any American state or to prevent the people of such state from altering that form according to their own will and pleasure. The rule in question has but a single purpose and object. It is that no European power or combination of European powers shall forcibly deprive an American state of the right and power of self-government and of shaping for itself its own political fortunes and destinies. . . .

Is it true, then, that the safety and welfare of the United States are so concerned with the maintenance of the independence of every American state as against any European power as to justify and require the interposition of the United States whenever that independence is endangered? The question can be candidly answered in but one way. The states of America, South as well as North, by geographical proximity, by natural sympathy, by similarity of governmental constitutions, are friends and allies, commercially and politically, of the United States. To allow the subjugation of any of them by an European power is, of course, to completely reverse that situation and signifies the loss of all the advantages incident to their natural relations to us. But that is not all. The people of the United States have a vital interest in the cause of popular self-government. They have secured the right for themselves and their posterity at the cost of infinite blood and treasure. They have realized and exemplified its beneficent operation by a career unexampled in point of national greatness or individual felicity. They believe it to be for the healing of all nations, and that civilization must either advance or retrograde accordingly as its supremacy is extended or curtailed. Imbued with these sentiments, the people of the United States might not impossibly be wrought up to an active propaganda in favor of a cause so highly valued both for themselves and for mankind. But the age of the Crusades has passed, and they are content with such assertion and defense of the right of popular self-government as their own security and welfare demand. It is in that view more than in any other that they believe it not to be tolerated that the political control of an American state shall be forcibly assumed by an European power.

The mischiefs apprehended from such a source are none the less real because not immediately imminent in any specific case, and are none the less to be guarded against because the combination of circumstances that will bring them upon us cannot be predicted. The civilized states of Christendom deal with each other on substantially the same principles that regulate the conduct of individuals. The greater its enlightenment, the more surely every state perceives that its permanent interests require it to be governed by the immutable principles of right and justice. Each, nevertheless, is only too liable to succumb to the temptations offered by seeming special opportunities for its own aggrandizement, and each would rashly imperil its own safety were it not to remember that for the regard and respect of other states it must be largely dependent upon its own strength and power. Today the United States is practically sovereign on this continent, and its fiat is law upon the subjects to which it confines its interposition. Why? It is not because of the pure friendship or good will felt for it. It is not simply by reason of its high character as a civilized state, nor because wisdom and justice and equity are the invariable characteristics of the dealings of the United States. It is because, in addition to all other grounds, its infinite resources combined with its isolated position render it master of the situation and practically invulnerable as against any or all other powers.

All the advantages of this superiority are at once imperiled if the principle be admitted that European powers may convert American states into colonies or provinces of their own. The principle would be eagerly availed of, and every power doing so would immediately acquire a base of military operations against us. What one power was permitted to do could not be denied to another, and it is not inconceivable that the struggle now going on for the acquisition of Africa might be transferred to South America. If it were, the weaker countries would unquestionably be soon absorbed, while the ultimate result might be the partition of all South America between the various European powers. The disastrous consequences to the United States of such a condition of things are obvious. The loss of prestige, of authority, and of weight in the councils of the family of nations, would be among the least of them. Our only real rivals in peace as well as enemies in war would be found located at our very doors. Thus far in our history we have been spared the burdens and evils of immense standing armies and all the other accessories of huge warlike establishments, and the exemption has largely contributed to our national greatness and wealth as well as to the happiness of every citizen. But, with the powers of Europe permanently encamped on American soil, the ideal conditions we have thus far enjoyed can not be expected to continue. We too must be armed to the teeth, we too must convert the flower of our male population into soldiers and sailors, and by withdrawing them from the various pursuits of peaceful industry we too must practically annihilate a large share of the productive energy of the nation. . . .

Thus, as already intimated, the British demand that her right to a portion of the disputed territory shall be acknowledged before she will consent to an arbitration as to the rest seems to stand upon nothing but her own *ipse dixit*. She says to Venezuela, in substance: "You can get none of the debatable land by force, because you are not strong enough; you can get none by a treaty, because I will not agree; and you can take your chance of getting a portion by arbitration, only if you first agree to abandon to me such other portion as I may designate." It is not perceived how such an attitude can be defended nor how it is reconcilable with that love of justice and fair play so eminently characteristic of the English race. It in effect deprives Venezuela of her free agency and puts her under virtual duress. Territory acquired by reason of it will be as much wrested from her by the strong hand as if occupied by British troops or covered by British fleets. It seems therefore quite impossible that this position of Great Britain should be assented to by the United States, or that, if such position be adhered to with the result of enlarging the bounds of British Guiana, it should not be regarded as amounting, in substance, to an invasion and conquest of Venezuelan territory.

## ESSAYS

Although scholars agree that the United States was an important foreign trader and that the late nineteenth century saw increased commercial expansion, they disagree on the relative importance of economic questions in American foreign policy. Put simply, are the nation's leaders influenced at all or primarily in their decision-making by economic considerations such as the exportation of goods, the importation of inexpensive raw materials, and financial investment abroad? Have American businessmen exerted pressure on Washington to intervene abroad in order to expand and protect their economic interests? Basically, how important is foreign trade to the security and prosperity of the United States?

In the first selection, Charles S. Campbell of the Claremont Graduate School suggests that commercial expansionism was quite important in the post–Civil War years, especially when the depression of 1893 struck. Robert L. Beisner of American University, although acknowledging that foreign trade was one of several inducements to expansionism and that the depression of the 1890s accentuated a drive for foreign markets, finds fault with a primary emphasis on economics.

## Commercial Expansionism and Empire

### CHARLES S. CAMPBELL

For several decades the settlement of the west coast had been turning American attention toward territorial expansion overseas—especially in Central America, the site of a potential canal; in the Caribbean Sea; and in the Hawaiian Islands. Over the same years economic developments were creating pressure for commercial expansion. During the decades after the Civil War the American economy was growing at a tremendous rate. The gross national product quadrupled, rising from $9,110,000,000 for 1869–1873 to $37,100,000,000 for 1897–1901. The gross farm product almost tripled, increasing from a value of $1,484,000,000 in 1860 to one of $3,799,000,000 in 1900. In 1865, 35,085 miles of railway were under operation; in 1899, 250,143. As for manu-

From pp. 84–87, 106, 140–147 in *The Transformation of American Foreign Relations, 1865–1900* by Charles S. Campbell. Copyright © 1976 by Charles S. Campbell. Reprinted by permission of Harper & Row, Publishers.

facturing, the production index jumped from 17 in 1865 all the way to 100 in 1900.

As one consequence of this extraordinary economic growth, exports mounted steadily. From 1865 to 1900 total exports increased in value from $281 million to $1,394 million. Exports to the United Kingdom rose in value from $103 million to $534 million; to Germany, from $20 million to $187 million; to France, from $11 million to $83 million; to Canada, from $29 million to $95 million; and to Cuba, from $19 million to $26 million. Imports, too, were increasing, though less rapidly. As is to be expected in the case of a new and underdeveloped country, imports had exceeded exports for many years; but the traditional pattern reversed itself in 1876, the centennial year, when merchandise exports first began to exceed imports consistently.

The historic change meant that the United States was producing a greater value of goods than she consumed. In the late 1870s and early 1880s informed people were becoming aware of this unfamiliar situation, a situation seeming to require the urgent cultivation of foreign markets. Thus as early as 1877 Abram S. Hewitt, a member of Congress from New York, thought that the country needed foreign markets "more than any other thing"; and in 1881 John A. Kasson (later on, the American delegate at the Samoan conference in Berlin) warned that if the United States did not find markets for her agricultural and industrial goods, "our surplus will soon roll back from the Atlantic coast upon the interior, and the wheels of prosperity will be clogged by the very richness of the burden which they carry, but cannot deliver." Secretary of State Evarts found that all thinking people were worrying about "how to create a foreign demand for those manufactures which are left after supplying our home demand"; and in 1880 he inaugurated monthly consular reports giving up-to-date information about trade openings. American participation in international exhibitions testified to the interest in foreign markets. Congress made appropriations for American displays at many exhibitions, at Vienna in 1873, Sydney in 1879, Berlin in 1880, Melbourne in 1880 and 1888, London in 1883, Barcelona and Brussels in 1888, and Paris in 1867, 1878, 1889, 1890, and 1900.

Export promotion was chiefly the occupation not of the government but of thousands of individual producers who turned to foreign markets to absorb the goods they did not sell at home. But increasingly as the post–Civil War years passed, the government, too, concerned itself in the matter; and because of the worry about the surplus (as it was beginning to be called), and also because of an economic depression in 1884, administrations in the late 1870s and especially in the 1880s made unprecedented efforts to expand exports. The worry about overproduction was considerably less than it was to become during the great depression of the 1890s, and consequently these early moves to foster exports occupied a relatively small part of official attention. Nonetheless, already in the 1880s commercial expansion in the New World, in Europe, and even in darkest Africa and little known areas in Asia was an important objective of United States foreign policy.

Some historians have strongly emphasized the agricultural and industrial surplus, with the consequent desire for commercial expansion abroad; they have depicted Washington, responsive to lobbying by special business interests, as preoccupied with commercial expansion—which frequently led also to territorial expansion; and they have argued that the foreign markets which were opened up to the burgeoning American exports constituted just as real an empire as if the Stars and Stripes had flown over these lands. Although throughout the ages commercial expansion has sometimes been the precursor of territorial expansion, it is an oversimplification virtually to equate these two types of expansion. The question of their relationship is a complicated one, but in the present context it is sufficient to say that the political control associated with colonization assures a degree of continuity and certainty in trade and other arrangements that is unobtainable in an informal commercial "empire." Thus the United States, as we shall observe, become dissatisfied with the commercial control of Hawaii given by the reciprocity treaty and decided that outright political control was essential.

At any rate American administrations during the 1880s, which on the whole opposed colonization on principle, did not consider commercial expansion as a substitute for territorial expansion, although a few individuals did, including, probably, Secretary of State Frederick T. Frelinghuysen. For various reasons these administrations looked to Mexico, the west coast of South America, and the Caribbean islands, as New World markets that should be cultivated. Whereas it was mainly for reasons of security and naval strategy (although the influence of trade was already great too) that Washington directed its attention to the potential canal, the Caribbean, Hawaii, and Samoa, the strategic consideration was less significant in policy toward Mexico and South America. As regards Mexico, America's main purpose was simply to protect the Texan border from marauders, but the wish to gain a new market became increasingly strong. As regards South America, both ideology and strategy were important—the feeling, strongly encouraged by the Monroe Doctrine, that by the nature of things, as well as for her national security, the United States rather than Europe should shape Latin American destiny; but for a time in 1881 and 1882 American party politics strongly influenced foreign policy, and at all times export promotion was a major consideration. . . .

It is clear that America's increasing agricultural and industrial output had a marked effect upon her foreign policy in the 1880s. The influence of the so-called surplus, which was already noticeable during the border-crossing dispute with Mexico and, again, during the War of the Pacific, became especially apparent when Arthur was President. So prudent a Secretary of State as Frelinghuysen made vigorous attempts to find markets not only in familiar places like the Caribbean Sea, Hawaii, and Europe, but even in distant Africa. Although, thanks to Cleveland, all his Caribbean reciprocity treaties failed, as well as the Congo General Act, Frelinghuysen's wide-ranging efforts to relieve the surplus must have given rise to an uneasy suspicion throughout the country that the United States was confronting a difficult situation that might soon become critical. When the great panic of 1893 struck the country, the business community had no doubt that overproduction was the root cause. Business leaders and government officials redoubled their efforts to find foreign markets, and this time they were more successful. . . .

By the 1890s the enormous growth in the American economy, which already in the 1880s had aroused considerable interest in commercial expansion, had convinced not only Washington but most business leaders and many publicists that it was essential to cultivate foreign markets. Arthur and Frelinghuysen had favored commercial expansion but had opposed territorial expansion; in the 1890s many Americans came to wonder whether exports could be significantly increased without the acquisition of colonies, which not only would themselves provide markets but, more important, would serve as points of strength for ensuring access to larger markets nearby. The new attention to territorial expansion resulted from the continuing economic growth at home, from changing policies abroad, and from new ideas and outlooks. We must examine these various matters.

The Arthur administration's attempts to boost exports had come to grief, for the most part, when Cleveland shipwrecked Frelinghuysen's reciprocity treaties and the Congo General Act. Under Benjamin Harrison the Republicans again experimented with reciprocity. By authority of the McKinley tariff act of 1890 they concluded reciprocity treaties with Austria-Hungary, Brazil, Santo Domingo, Spain (for Cuba and Puerto Rico), Salvador, Great Britain (for British West Indian islands and British Guiana), Nicaragua, Honduras, and Guatemala. But the familiar story repeated itself: Cleveland, again President in 1893 and still opposed to preferential tariff arrangements, terminated them all in 1894.

If export promotion was so important, why did not American business interests induce Washington to act more resolutely? The fact is that most businessmen were apathetic about exporting until the mid-1890s. The home market was, generally speaking, quite adequate for their needs—although we have observed the considerable interest in Mexican and South American markets, in pork exports to Europe, and in such remote places as Korea and the Congo. Moreover, most exports consisted of agricultural goods, notably wheat and cotton; in 1875 exports of these two items alone had a value of $251 million, as compared with $499 million for total exports; in 1881, $416 million against $884 million. For many years after 1874 crops were poor in Europe, where the great bulk of American agricultural produce went; in the "black year" of 1879 they were catastrophic. A British royal commission of 1879 and another of 1893 foresaw no end to the avalanche pouring in from the American plains and prairies. In these circumstances there was little reason for anxiety about foreign markets. No wonder that American consuls in the 1870s and 1880s were described as being "almost pathetic" in begging business interests back home to wake up to the trade opportunities theirs for the asking. Worry about exporting simply did not exist on a large scale until the 1890s.

During that decade a major change occurred in the trade balance of manufactured goods; and it not only transformed ideas about exporting, but it directly affected industrialists, a group that had much more influence in Washington than agriculturalists had. We have seen that a favorable balance of trade for all kinds of merchandise, agricultural as well as industrial, was first achieved on a continuing basis in 1876; but the balance of manufactures remained on the debit side. Trends of commerce, however, indicated an early reversal; and in 1894 exports of manufactures passed imports; they continued to be greater during the years to come. The reversal came mainly from the staggering increase in American industrial output; this gave rise, in turn, to an equally staggering increase in exports of manufactures: from $89 million in 1865 to $805 million in 1900. Contrasting with this more than ninefold rise was an increase in imports of manufactures from $174 million in 1865 to $470 million in 1900, less than a threefold rise.

It was highly gratifying, of course, to have such a booming economy; but at the same time it was worrying. For where could ever-expanding markets be found for the ever-increasing industrial output? The domestic market, businessmen believed, was not large enough. Nor were the traditional markets in industrialized Europe, which absorbed the American agricultural output, expected to take this quite different, industrial output. The lesson of the rising tide of manufactures seemed clear: somehow, and at all costs, the United States must increase her exports; otherwise the home market would become saturated with a mounting surplus.

Much of the alarm about the surplus is attributable to the panic of 1893 and the great depression that followed. These events rocked the country to its foundations. Not only was the economic distress severe, but social disorders and the rise of the Populist party appeared to portend dire calamity. For conservatives, everything was going alarmingly wrong. Catastrophic business conditions, widespread radicalism, violent strikes—such dreadful happenings seemed to presage the disintegration of the social structure itself. After a century of brilliant success, were American institutions and ideals about to founder in chaos?

What caused the depression? Farmers typically attributed it to a scarcity of money and prescribed the free coinage of silver. Most business leaders, on the other hand, put the blame on overproduction, particularly of manufactured goods, and prescribed not financial tinkering but exporting the surplus. The worst of the distress came during Grover Cleveland's second administration (1893–1897). A strong gold-standard, low-tariff man, the President attempted to restore the plummeting economy by acting on two fronts: one relating to the currency; the other, the tariff. Both had direct implications for exporting. To strengthen the currency he fought hard and successfully for the repeal in 1893 of part of the Sherman Silver Purchase Act, which required the government to buy large quantities of silver every month, and he also replenished the Treasury's gold holdings by selling bonds. Businessmen in general strongly applauded these steps, partly because they accepted the overproduction thesis with its corollary that the surplus must be exported. They and the administration were in full accord that the gold standard, which Cleveland's measures were supporting, provided the stable exchange rates necessary for thriving international commerce—and consequently for export expansion. This was the accepted, orthodox doctrine. It contrasted sharply with the beliefs of free-silverites, who generally put less emphasis on foreign markets because they thought that if more money was created, Americans could themselves purchase enough goods to prevent a surplus from arising. Some silverites, but fewer in number, agreed with the gold-standard advocates on the importance of foreign markets. In many cases highly respectable businessmen, they advocated bimetallism not through free silver but by international agreement; and every President from Hayes through McKinley sent missions to Europe or participated in bimetallic conferences in the vain hope of arranging European and American bimetallism—or at least of quieting the clamor for free silver.

Cleveland's second device for dealing with the depression—the Wilson-Gorman tariff of 1894—also brought up considerations of overproduction and overseas markets. The chief purpose of the McKinley tariff of 1890 had been to protect the home market, but it had also provided for the small measure of reciprocity we have noted. Republicans extolled reciprocity as an ingenious device to gain foreign markets while retaining protection against cheap foreign labor. Democrats scoffed at this view. They agreed, to be sure (at least before 1896), that foreign markets were essential in order to prop up the collapsing economy. But their prescription for exporting the surplus was not reciprocity but duty-free raw materials; and the contention that export promotion depended on cheaper raw materials furnished perhaps the main argument for the tariff of 1894. Thus Representative William L. Wilson, who had charge of the bill in the House, reported for the Ways and Means Committee that every duty on raw materials raised the price of the finished product and thereby narrowed export possibilities; and the Senate's leading supporter of the bill, Roger Q. Mills, argued: "It is the tax on the materials of manufacture alone that keeps us out of foreign markets. . . ."

The tariff measure as passed by the House on February 1, 1894, contained a long duty-free list that included many components of industrial exports. But the Senate, as a result of pressure from special interests, deleted everything on the list except wool, copper, and lumber, an altogether inadequate basis for export promotion. The Senate passed the emasculated bill on July 3, 1894; Cleveland reluctantly signed it the next month.

Cleveland Democrats backed both the gold standard and low tariffs; Republicans, although generally supporting the gold standard, advocated high tariffs and, in some cases, reciprocity. But Cleveland Democrats and Republicans alike typically attributed the depression to surplus production and emphasized the necessity of cultivating foreign markets—although for Republicans, maintaining high tariff rates had first priority. Commercial expansion became a much more important objective of policy than it had been in the 1880s.

Where were foreign markets to be found? For many years Americans had looked to Latin America and, even more, to the great potential market of China with its 400 million supposedly eager customers. And now the depression of the 1890s clarified and intensified these older views. So did other developments.

The fact was that Latin America and China were desirable not only on their own merits; they were desirable also because most other large markets seemed in danger of being closed to American exports. In the middle years of the century colonies had been unfashionable in Western countries—a "mill-stone round our necks," Benjamin Disraeli, soon to be a leading British imperialist, had called them as late as 1852. But in the 1880s the great powers of Europe, now including Germany, embarked again upon a race for colonies, and in the 1890s Japan joined them. Two new and powerful navies, the German and Japanese, made their appearance; and Japan's intentions in Hawaii came to seem to Americans as sinister as Germany's in Samoa.

By the late 1890s the slicing up of Africa among the great powers, with the consequent erection of discriminatory tariffs, had been practically completed. There were signs that even America's European markets might soon be walled in. In a much-noticed speech regarding the perils for Europe posed by the colossal American economic machine, Count Agenor Goluchowski, Foreign Minister of Austria-Hungary, warned: "The destructive competition with trans-oceanic countries...requires prompt and thorough counteracting measures.... The European nations must close their ranks in order successfully to defend their existence." This and other such remarks worried Americans. About that same time the most dynamic public figure in Great Britain, Colonial Secretary Joseph Chamberlain, was campaigning for imperial preference by which the British empire, hitherto open to world commerce, would erect a tariff wall against outside countries. Should the vast British world abandon free trade, American exporters would be hard hit. China, too, seemed in danger of being partitioned, but Americans could hope to influence events there more than in Africa, Europe, and the British empire.

For United States foreign policy, the lesson of these domestic and international economic trends of the 1890s was clear. Everyone agreed that, to be more competitive with her European rivals, the United States needed a shorter sea route between her industrial center in the northeast and her potential markets in China and on the west coast of South America. This an isthmian canal would provide. In short, the economic trends of the 1890s, now reinforcing the older strategic and geographic considerations attendant upon west coast settlement, pointed urgently to a canal and to the Caribbean and Hawaiian bases needed for its protection. As yet, however, there was nothing like a consensus for even these basic objectives, and the old-fashioned repugnance for anything smacking of territorial expansion overseas remained remarkably strong. Notwithstanding the historic shift to an export surplus of manufactured goods, and notwithstanding the depression of the 1890s and the ominous signs of closing markets around the world, both the government and the business community continued to have faith in commercial expansion, unaccompanied by territorial expansion, as adequate to relieve the surplus. The faith was somewhat old-fashioned in a world of high and proliferating tariff walls (outside the British empire); it had in fact been greatly weakened, and a canal and bases in the Caribbean and Hawaii had come much more into national favor. But not until the Spanish-American War did sentiment turn irresistibly to territorial expansion.

# The Limits of an Economic Interpretation

## ROBERT L. BEISNER

An economic interpretation of American expansionism goes back at least as far as the Englishman John Hobson, who argued in *Imperialism* (1902) that the origins of this impulse were to be found in the efforts of moneylenders to find profitable new areas in which to invest their surplus capital. But the idea that J. P. Morgan singlehandedly got the United States ensconced in Manila has always been too much to swallow, and American historians—aware that the United States was a net borrower of capital until World War I—have tended to emphasize the search for foreign markets for goods, not capital, as the economic impetus to American imperialism. The search was necessary, according to this argument, because American industrialization had led to a productive surplus that must be disposed of abroad if businessmen were to avoid the unpleasant alternatives: decreased production, which would reduce profits and increase unemployment and social unrest, or, worse still because it reeked of socialism, a redistribution of wealth on a scale to permit lower-wage workers to buy the surplus products themselves.

Since neither alternative was attractive, another path was chosen—the government would help businessmen sell their surplus in other parts of the world. Thus, in this view, America's policymakers began the process of shaping U.S. diplomacy to these economic ends, haltingly at first right after the Civil War, but more systematically later on when business effectively supplanted agriculture as the dominant political influence in Washington and the need for action became more obvious. The climax came in the mid-nineties, precipitated by a shattering panic and depression and the news of the apparent disappearance of America's safety-valve frontier (Frederick Jackson Turner, "The Significance of the Frontier in American History," *Annual Report of the American Historical Association for the Year 1893*). These blows fell on an already unnerved population that had been nurtured on the story that America's progress would be onward-and-upward-forever. The threats of recurrent crisis or stagnation somehow had to be avoided, and an aggressive search for new markets seemed to provide the way out.

Latin America and the Far East were considered especially suitable areas for the construction of escape routes. Administrations once depicted as presenting a record of unparalleled mediocrity were actually, so the argument goes, establishing a crucial foundation for future developments by using tariff reform, reciprocity agreements, antirevolutionary and anti-European interventions, and other means to insure the increase of American exports. That the process culminated in war and the consequent acquisition of an empire did not mean that American leaders wanted it that way; it meant only that in 1898–99 they saw no other way to get what they did want without adopting such drastic methods.

This economic interpretation of the foreign policy of the period is not bur-

Robert L. Beisner, *From the Old Diplomacy to the New, 1865–1900* (Copyright © 1975 by Harlan Davidson, Inc., Arlington Heights, IL), pp. 17–26. Reprinted by permission of the publisher.

dened with the cruder aspects of "left wing" history that have always been so easy to criticize. Such present-day exponents as Williams, LaFeber, and Thomas J. McCormick have not made the mistake of blaming American imperialism on Wall Street or attributing it to some kind of conspiracy but have argued instead that American foreign policy was the product of a consensus of businessmen, politicians, and intellectuals. They do not brand these men as ideological colonialists, but rather as individuals who, if events had gone the way they hoped, would gladly have settled for a few small island bases of use to American merchants and the navy assigned to protect their trade. The leaders of the United States wanted an "informal empire" created by the demand for American products, not a formal empire dependent on the weapons of war.

Critics of this line of argument are quick to point out the apparently meager results of commercial diplomacy. Although U.S. exports to China rose from $3 million in 1890 to $15 million in 1900, the latter figure represented only 1.1 percent of total American exports, hardly an imperial proportion. It has also been noted that only a small portion of the gross national product in the late nineteenth century was involved in foreign trade, that most of this modest portion was with Canada and Europe and little with the "imperial" areas of Asia and Latin America (e.g., in 1900 about 44 percent of all U.S. exports went to Great Britain and France, while 3 percent went to China and Japan), and that agricultural rather than manufactured products continued to account for the bulk of American exports to the very end of the century.

"Informal empire" historians have made a three-fold response to these criticisms. First, they assert that American trade statistics of the time are not as modest and unimportant as they appear at first glance. Relatively small percentage increases in exports could make the difference between stagnation and prosperity, both for an individual company and the economy at large. For some industries exports to particular regions were crucial; almost 50 percent of the exports of the American cotton textile industry, for example, were shipped to China in the late 1890s. Second, they argued that their thesis does not depend upon massive economic results, but evidence that American leaders *believed* in the urgency of increased exports and the shimmering China market. Third, William A. Williams, in *Roots of the Modern American Empire,* has met the agricultural issue head-on. He points out himself that Americans earned as much in 1869 from the export of animal tallow and butter as from iron and steel, evidence of the continuing vitality of trade in agricultural commodities. Giving this fact its due attention, he concludes that the American obsession with exports started in Jeffersonian times; that wheat farmers, cattle-raisers, cotton farmers, dairymen, food processors, and others in the agricultural sector long pushed for a commercially oriented foreign policy; but that at the end of the century "metropolitan" business and political leaders took control of the export drive and turned it to the needs of an industrial economy. Thus Williams makes a valiant attempt to incorporate both preindustrial pressures for foreign markets and the continuing importance of agricultural exports in his economic interpretation of late-nineteenth-century U.S. diplomacy. And, by focusing attention once more on ordinary farmers and their spokesmen instead of the industrial-political elite, he places renewed emphasis on the popular roots of American imperialism.

The economic approach to American foreign policy from 1865 to 1900 contains many strong points and has found widespread acceptance, in part because of its appeal to the numerous critics of contemporary American foreign policy. But though it is valuable in explaining some specific episodes, this view has serious shortcomings as a key to the whole period. Not only is it simplistic to suppose there was a generation of policymakers invariably motivated by rational and precise calculations of the nation's economic interests, but a thorough sifting of the evidence turns up far too many discrepancies for an endorsement of the economic interpretation.

Much evidence, in fact, points in contrary directions. In 1870 when Secretary of State Fish put before the Grant cabinet a dispatch urging a concerted effort to increase American trade and influence in Hawaii, he was met with total silence and "the subject [was] dropped." In the same era the United States willingly jeopardized prospects for important new trade with China because of hostility at home to Chinese immigrants. No one was more eager for the China trade than Californians, yet, as Alexander DeConde states in his useful textbook, *A History of American Foreign Policy* (2d ed., 1971), "they were willing to sacrifice benefits that trade would bring rather than continue to accept the Chinese." Jobs and racial tensions were more important issues than foreign markets. In 1884 the Arthur administration actively participated in the Berlin conference on the Congo, from which many trade benefits were expected to flow; but the incoming Cleveland administration withdrew the conference treaty from the Senate in 1885 because it conflicted with American isolation from Big Power affairs, a tradition more deep-rooted than the imperatives of foreign trade. Did President Harrison shake the mailed fist at Chile in 1891–92 . . . to open it up as a market for Connecticut locomotives, or was it to avenge an insult to the American uniform and counterbalance Great Britain's considerable influence in the Latin republic? The fact is that patriotic concerns and fear of European political influence in the hemisphere weighed more in Harrison's mind than commercial ledger sheets. James G. Blaine's vain attempt in 1881 to establish a Pan-American conference is often cited as a pioneering venture in market expansionism, but according to Russell H. Bastert he acted "from a mixture of many motives, probably least of all economic." His desire to be president was perhaps the most important ("A New Approach to the Origins of Blaine's Pan-American Policy," *Hispanic American Historical Review*, XXXIX, August 1959). Grover Cleveland's attempt to lower the tariff during the nineties was not a depression-induced maneuver to stimulate trade but the fulfillment of a political pledge he had made in 1887. He was responding to old Democratic party traditions and the ire of American consumers, not the needs of eastern industrialists (Paul S. Holbo, "Economics, Emotion, and Expansion: An Emerging Foreign Policy," in H. Wayne Morgan, ed., *The Gilded Age* [rev. ed., 1970]). Indeed, despite the calamitous depression of the nineties and the purported "consensus" on the wisdom of supporting all measures that would encourage exports, Congress quashed reciprocity agreements with Brazil, the Central American States, the British West Indies, Austria-Hungary, Germany, and Spain (involving Cuba and Puerto Rico). America's legislators apparently had not gotten the word.

One reason politicians did not take the foreign trade problem too seriously was that businessmen themselves set a bad example. Expansionist Brooks Adams complained bitterly of their "failure . . . to act intelligently and aggressively" in foreign markets. Milton Plesur has argued (*America's Outward Thrust: Approaches to Foreign Affairs, 1865–1890* [1971]) that American trade suffered constantly from plain old sloppiness and ineptitude in business practices—sending products abroad that were not only inferior, poorly packaged, and inappropriate for their designated markets, but in some cases unsafe as well (e.g., celluloid collars and cuffs made of harmful ingredients); poor timing (fur coats sent to Canada in July); and reliance upon incompetent or negligent local representatives. The general problem described by Plesur applied doubly in China, where commercial aspirations were supposedly greatest of all at the end of the century (Paul A. Varg, "The Myth of the China Market, 1890–1914," *American Historical Review,* LXXIII, February 1968). One historian notes that despite the urging of American political officials for special attention to be paid to area conditions, U.S. manufacturers "were slow to meet the trade demands of the Asian market" and "made little effort" to adapt their products to its needs (Marilyn B. Young, "American Expansion, 1870–1900: The Far East," in Barton J. Bernstein, ed., *Towards a New Past: Dissenting Essays in American History* [1968]; Young develops her argument more fully in *Rhetoric of Empire: American China Policy, 1895–1900* [1968]).

It is therefore highly misleading to think in terms of a unified American business community, backed by a determined government, striving unremittingly to break into the markets of Asia and Latin America. Most exporters still regarded trade as a matter between businessmen in any case; and of those who did believe that the government should have an active economic policy, most had in mind the protection of *home* markets by a high tariff wall, a strategy not designed to promote exports either in theory or practice. Protectionist sentiment remained intact throughout the Johnson-McKinley years, and free-trade views virtually disappeared from the expansionist Republican Party. Paul Holbo has pointed out that the annual debates in Congress on the tariff, far more passionate and rhetorical over the years than those aroused by foreign trade, spent their strength in arguments about workingmen's jobs, relief for consumers, and such ideological labels as "Americanism" and "Jeffersonianism"—not export strategy; and Tom E. Terrill, while generally supporting the economic interpretation, makes clear in *The Tariff, Politics, and American Foreign Policy, 1874–1901* (1973) how hard it was to turn attention from protection of the home market to expansion of foreign trade. As to the businessmen who were vitally interested in foreign sales, the great majority directed their attention to the profitable markets of Canada and Europe and failed to concentrate significantly on the undeveloped markets of Asia and Latin America until the era of Theodore Roosevelt and Woodrow Wilson (David E. Novack and Matthew Simon, "Commercial Responses to the American Export Invasion, 1871–1914: An

Essay in Attitudinal History," *Explorations in Entrepreneurial History,* 2d ser., III, Winter 1966).

The behavior of American officials and businessmen does not support the carefully measured, symmetrical case put forward by LaFeber, Williams, McCormick, et al. That the United States government should skillfully and knowingly formulate and execute a farsighted economic foreign policy flies in the face of evidence that most American "policymakers," at least until the nineties, were amateurish and often maladroit in their diplomatic conduct, ignorant of and not particularly interested in the affairs of other nations, and much more inclined to react in the accustomed way to outside events than to initiate well-defined new policies. Behavior, not occasional rhetoric, is the crucial test. What, in actual fact, did presidents and secretaries of state do through most of the years from 1865 to 1900? They revealed some interest in the expansion of foreign markets, of course, but they also revealed much faintheartedness or unconcern about such matters and consistently appointed to the field men who were poorly qualified for any grand economic promotional task. And Congress? It raised the tariff and rejected the principle of reciprocal trade treaties, sacrificed quality in the diplomatic service on the altar of thrift, and repeatedly put partisan concerns high above good relations with other nations. And businessmen? They concentrated overwhelmingly on selling to the ever-enlarging domestic market, and, when they did get into the export game, continued to look to the traditional and nonimperialistic markets of neighboring Canada and Europe. Tables I and II illustrate both points.

TABLE I   United States Exports as Percentage of Estimated Gross National Product in Selected Years

| Year | Total Exports | Pct. of GNP (est.) |
|------|---------------|--------------------|
| 1874 | $   606,000,000 | 8.1% |
| 1884 | 752,600,000 | 7.1 |
| 1889 | 762,700,000 | 6.4 |
| 1891 | 909,800,000 | 6.7 |
| 1893 | 862,300,000 | 6.5 |
| 1895 | 807,500,000 | 5.8 |
| 1897 | 1,051,000,000 | 7.5 |
| 1899 | 1,227,000,000 | 6.9 |
| 1900 | 1,394,500,000 | 7.5 |

This criticism does not mean the economic interpretation should be rejected out of hand, but it must be blended where possible with other views to create a useful synthesis. Historians have always noted, of course, that foreign trade and other economic factors have been important in American diplomacy. The problem has been that few writers, including the recent revisionists, have integrated these factors into a general framework or emphasized their significant political and ideological overtones. Agile politicians throughout the years have manipulated these economic currents for their own purposes; David Healy has argued that many statesmen with power and prestige uppermost in their minds used a rhetoric heavily dosed with "markets" talk to win support from a public more concerned with dollars and cents than glory (*US Expansionism: The Imperialist Urge in the 1890s* [1970]). Even more common than politicians who manipulated economic, political, and ideological issues were those who never dreamed of separating them. They might, for example, have wanted to increase American political influence in China during the 1890s, but for what purpose if not to open doors for U.S. exports? Or, conversely, they might have wanted to increase exports as a means of enhancing American political influence throughout the Far East.

TABLE II  Exports to Canada and Europe Compared with Exports to Asia and Latin America

| Year | Exports to Canada and Europe | Pct. of Total | Exports to Asia and Latin America | Pct. of Total |
|------|------------------------------|---------------|-----------------------------------|---------------|
| 1875 | $   494,000,000 | 86.1% | $  72,000,000 | 12.5% |
| 1885 | 637,000,000 | 85.8 | 87,000,000 | 11.7 |
| 1895 | 681,000,000 | 84.3 | 108,000,000 | 13.4 |
| 1900 | 1,135,000,000 | 81.4 | 200,000,000 | 14.3 |

Tables compiled from information in *Historical Statistics of the United States*, 1960; U.S. Department of Commerce, *Long Term Growth, 1860–1965*, 1966; National Bureau of Economic Research, *Trends in the American Economy in the Nineteenth Century*, 1960.

In short, as Marilyn B. Young has written, most Americans merged economics into a broader view "which saw a strong navy, trade, political power, and the territory necessary . . . to maintain both trade and power, as complementary factors contributing to the wealth and strength of the nation." Moreover, since the time of the Revolution, Americans have considered foreign trade to be not only a source of money profits, but a wellspring of social enlightenment and a beneficent bond between distant peoples (James A. Field, Jr., *America and the Mediterranean World, 1776–1882* [1969]). Foreign commerce was, in addition, a source of American pride; Paul A. Varg observes that it "flattered the ego of Americans to think of their country as the supplier of the world's market. . . ." Thus American interest in foreign trade has long transcended exclusively economic horizons, a fact that must be understood if we are properly to appreciate the actual role of economics in late-nineteenth-century American foreign policy.

# FURTHER READING

William H. Becker, *Industry, Government, and Foreign Trade, 1893–1921* (1982)

Benjamin F. Cooling, *Gray Steel and Blue Water Navy* (1979)

Robert B. Davies, *Peacefully Working to Conquer the World: Singer Sewing Machines in Foreign Markets, 1854–1920* (1976)

John A. Garraty, *The New Commonwealth, 1877–1890* (1968)

John A. S. Grenville and George B. Young, *Politics, Strategy, and American Diplomacy* (1967)

Kenneth J. Hagan, *American Gunboat Diplomacy and the Old Navy, 1877–1889* (1973)

Walter R. Herrick, *The American Naval Revolution* (1966)

Paul S. Holbo, "Economics, Emotion, and Expansion: An Emerging Foreign Policy," in H. Wayne Morgan, ed., *The Gilded Age* (1970)

Walter LaFeber, *The New Empire* (1963)

Lester D. Langley, *Struggle for the American Mediterranean* (1976)

Ernest N. Paolino, *The Foundations of the American Empire: William Henry Seward and U. S. Foreign Policy* (1973)

Thomas G. Paterson, "American Businessmen and Consular Service Reform, 1890s to 1906," *Business History Review*, 40 (1966), 77–97

Milton Plesur, *America's Outward Thrust* (1971)

David M. Pletcher, *Rails, Mines, and Progress: Seven American Promoters in Mexico, 1867–1911* (1958)

———, "Rhetoric and Results: A Pragmatic View of American Economic Expansionism, 1865–98," *Diplomatic History*, 5 (1981), 93–105

Emily S. Rosenberg, *Spreading the American Dream* (1982)

Howard B. Schonberger, *Transportation to the Seaboard* (1971)

Thomas D. Schoonover, *Dollars over Dominion* (1978)

Robert Seager, *Alfred Thayer Mahan* (1977)

Tom Terrill, *The Tariff, Politics, and American Foreign Policy, 1874–1901* (1973)

Robert Wiebe, *The Search for Order* (1967)

Mira Wilkins, *The Emergence of the Multinational Enterprise: American Business Abroad from the Colonial Era to 1914* (1970)

William A. Williams, *The Roots of the Modern American Empire* (1969)

———, *The Tragedy of American Diplomacy* (1962)

Marilyn Blatt Young, "American Expansion, 1870–1900: The Far East," in Barton J. Bernstein, ed., *Towards a New Past* (1968)

# The Spanish-American
# War and Empire

# 11

*In 1898 the United States and Spain went to war over Cuba. After the brief conflict, which saw military action in Asia as well as in the Caribbean, the United States demanded and achieved from a humiliated Spain the cession of the Philippines, Guam, and Puerto Rico and independence for Cuba. At about the same time, the United States annexed Hawaii and Wake Island. Two key questions arise: Why did the McKinley administration decide in favor of war? And how did a war, declared to liberate Cuba, become an imperialist venture with new territorial acquisitions? Contemporary anti-imperialists presented their answers and arguments, but lost the debate. Historians are still debating these issues.*

## DOCUMENTS

In his War Message of April 11, 1898, reprinted as the first document, President William McKinley explained why he thought the United States had to take up arms. Congress granted his request on April 19 and war was officially declared two days later. As the next two documents demonstrate, critics of the American imperial course—evident in the absorption of the Philippines and the subsequent military suppression of a Filipino Insurrection led by nationalist Emilio Aguinaldo—spoke vigorously against what they considered a gross violation of American principles. Philosopher William James's impassioned letter to the *Boston Evening Transcript* (March 1, 1899) and the program of the American Anti-Imperialist League (October 17, 1899) condemn the McKinley administration's foreign policy. A defender of

354

American imperialism, Senator Albert J. Beveridge of Indiana, gave an unabashed endorsement to overseas acquisitions in a 1900 speech, the last document.

## William McKinley's War Message, 1898

Obedient to that precept of the Constitution which commands the President to give from time to time to the Congress information of the state of the Union and to recommend to their consideration such measures as he shall judge necessary and expedient, it becomes my duty to now address your body with regard to the grave crisis that has arisen in the relations of the United States to Spain by reason of the warfare that for more than three years has raged in the neighboring island of Cuba.

I do so because of the intimate connection of the Cuban question with the state of our own Union and the grave relation the course which it is now incumbent upon the nation to adopt must needs bear to the traditional policy of our Government if it is to accord with the precepts laid down by the founders of the Republic and religiously observed by succeeding Administrations to the present day.

The present revolution is but the successor of other similar insurrections which have occurred in Cuba against the dominion of Spain, extending over a period of nearly half a century, each of which during its progress has subjected the United States to great effort and expense in enforcing its neutrality laws, caused enormous losses to American trade and commerce, caused irritation, annoyance, and disturbance among our citizens, and, by the exercise of cruel, barbarous, and uncivilized practices of warfare, shocked the sensibilities and offended the humane sympathies of our people. . . .

Our people have beheld a once prosperous community reduced to comparative want, its lucrative commerce virtually paralyzed, its exceptional productiveness diminished, its fields laid waste, its mills in ruins, and its people perishing by tens of thousands from hunger and destitution. We have found ourselves constrained, in the observance of that strict neutrality which our laws enjoin and which the law of nations commands, to police our own waters and watch our own seaports in prevention of any unlawful act in aid of the Cubans.

Our trade has suffered, the capital invested by our citizens in Cuba has been largely lost, and the temper and forbearance of our people have been so sorely tried as to beget a perilous unrest among our own citizens, which has inevitably found its expression from time to time in the National Legislature, so that issues wholly external to our own body politic engross attention and stand in the way of that close devotion to domestic advancement that becomes a self-contained commonwealth whose primal maxim has been the avoidance of all foreign entanglements. All this must needs awaken, and has, indeed, aroused, the utmost concern on the part of this Government, as well during my predecessor's term as in my own. . . .

The war in Cuba is of such a nature that, short of subjugation or extermination, a final military victory for either side seems impracticable. The alternative lies in the physical exhaustion of the one or the other party, or perhaps of both—a condition which in effect ended the ten years' war by the truce of Zanjon. The prospect of such a protraction and conclusion of the present strife is a contingency hardly to be contemplated with equanimity by the civilized world, and least of all by the United States, affected and injured as we are, deeply and intimately, by its very existence.

Realizing this, it appeared to be my duty, in a spirit of true friendliness, no less to Spain than to the Cubans, who have so much to lose by the prolongation of the struggle, to seek to bring about an immediate termination of the war. To this end I submitted on the 27th ultimo, as a result of much representation and correspondence, through the United States minister at Madrid, propositions to the Spanish Government looking to an armistice until October 1 for the negotiation of peace with the good offices of the President.

In addition I asked the immediate revocation of the order of reconcentration, so as to permit the people to return to their farms and the needy to be relieved with provisions and supplies from the United States, cooperating with the Spanish authorities, so as to afford full relief.

The reply of the Spanish cabinet was received on the night of the 31st ultimo. It offered, as the means to bring about peace in Cuba, to confide the preparation thereof to the insular parliament, inasmuch as the concurrence of that body would be necessary to reach a final result, it being, however, understood that the powers reserved by the constitution to the central Government are not lessened or diminished. As the Cuban parliament does not meet until the 4th of May next, the Spanish Government would not object for its part to accept at once a suspension of hostilities if asked for by the insurgents from the general in chief, to whom it would pertain in such case to determine the duration and conditions of the armistice. . . .

With this last overture in the direction of immediate peace, and its disappointing reception by Spain, the Executive is brought to the end of his effort. . . .

The grounds for . . . intervention may be briefly summarized as follows:

*First.* In the cause of humanity and to put an end to the barbarities, bloodshed, starvation, and horrible miseries now existing there, and which the parties to the conflict are either unable or unwilling to stop or mitigate. It is no answer to say this is all in another country, belonging to another nation, and is therefore none of our business. It is specially our duty, for it is right at our door.

*Second.* We owe it to our citizens in Cuba to afford them that protection and indemnity for life and property which no government there can or will afford, and to that end to terminate the conditions that deprive them of legal protection.

*Third.* The right to intervene may be justified by the very serious injury to the commerce, trade, and business of our people and by the wanton destruction of property and devastation of the island.

*Fourth,* and which is of the utmost importance. The present condition of affairs in Cuba is a constant menace to our peace and entails upon this Government an enormous expense. With such a conflict waged for years in an

island so near us and with which our people have such trade and business relations; when the lives and liberty of our citizens are in constant danger and
their property destroyed and themselves ruined; where our trading vessels are
liable to seizure and are seized at our very door by war ships of a foreign nation; the expeditions of filibustering that we are powerless to prevent altogether,
and the irritating questions and entanglements thus arising—all these and
others that I need not mention, with the resulting strained relations, are a
constant menace to our peace and compel us to keep on a semi war footing
with a nation with which we are at peace. . . .

In view of these facts and of these considerations I ask the Congress to authorize and empower the President to take measures to secure a full and final termination of hostilities between the Government of Spain and the people of
Cuba, and to secure in the island the establishment of a stable government,
capable of maintaining order and observing its international obligations, insuring peace and tranquillity and the security of its citizens as well as our own, and
to use the military and naval forces of the United States as may be necessary
for these purposes.

And in the interest of humanity and to aid in preserving the lives of the starving people of the island I recommend that the distribution of food and supplies
be continued and that an appropriation be made out of the public Treasury to
supplement the charity of our citizens.

The issue is now with the Congress. It is a solemn responsibility. I have exhausted every effort to relieve the intolerable condition of affairs which is at our
doors. Prepared to execute every obligation imposed upon me by the Constitution and the law, I await your action.

Yesterday, and since the preparation of the foregoing message, official information was received by me that the latest decree of the Queen Regent of
Spain directs General Blanco, in order to prepare and facilitate peace, to proclaim a suspension of hostilities, the duration and details of which have not
yet been communicated to me.

This fact, with every other pertinent consideration, will, I am sure, have
your just and careful attention in the solemn deliberations upon which you are
about to enter. If this measure attains a successful result, then our aspirations
as a Christian, peace-loving people will be realized. If it fails, it will be only
another justification for our contemplated action.

# William James on the Suppression of the Philippines, 1899

Here was a people towards whom we felt no ill-will, against whom we had not
even a slanderous rumor to bring; a people for whose tenacious struggle
against their Spanish oppressors we have for years spoken (so far as we spoke
of them at all) with nothing but admiration and sympathy. Here was a leader
who as the Spanish lies about him, on which we were fed so long, drop off, and
as the truth gets more and more known, appears as an exceptionally fine speci-

men of the patriot and national hero; not only daring, but honest; not only a fighter, but a governor and organizer of extraordinary power. Here were the precious beginnings of an indigenous national life, with which, if we had any responsibilities to these islands at all, it was our first duty to have squared ourselves. Aguinaldo's movement was, and evidently deserved to be, an ideal popular movement, which as far as it had had time to exist was showing itself "fit" to survive and likely to become a healthy piece of national self-development. It was all we had to build on, at any rate, so far—if we had any desire not to succeed to the Spaniards' inheritance of native execration.

And what did our Administration do? So far as the facts have leaked out, it issued instructions to the commanders on the ground simply to freeze Aguinaldo out, as a dangerous rival, with whom all compromising entanglement was sedulously to be avoided by the great Yankee business concern. We were not to "recognize" him, we were to deny him all account of our intentions; and in general to refuse any account of our intentions to anybody, except to declare in abstract terms their "benevolence," until the inhabitants, without a pledge of any sort from us, should turn over their country into our hands. Our President's bouffé-proclamation was the only thing vouchsafed; "We are here for your own good; therefore unconditionally surrender to our tender mercies, or we'll blow you into kingdom come."

Our own people meanwhile were vaguely uneasy, for the inhuman callousness and insult shown at Paris and Washington to the officially delegated mouthpieces of the wants and claims of the Filipinos seems simply abominable from any moral point of view. But there must be reasons of state, we assumed, and good ones. Aguinaldo is evidently a pure adventurer "on the make," a blackmailer, sure in the end to betray our confidence, or our Government wouldn't treat him so, for our President is essentially methodistical and moral. Mr. McKinley must be in an intolerably perplexing situation, and we must not criticise him too soon. We assumed this, I say, though all the while there was a horribly suspicious look about the performance. On its face it reeked of the infernal adroitness of the great department store, which has reached perfect expertness in the art of killing silently and with no public squealing or commotion the neighboring small concern.

But that small concern, Aguinaldo, apparently not having the proper American business education, and being uninstructed on the irresistible character of our Republican party combine, neither offered to sell out nor to give up. So the Administration had to show its hand without disguise. It did so at last. We are now openly engaged in crushing out the sacredest thing in this great human world—the attempt of a people long enslaved to attain to the possession of itself, to organize its laws and government, to be free to follow its internal destinies according to its own ideals. War, said Moltke, aims at destruction, and at nothing else. And splendidly are we carrying out war's ideal. We are destroying the lives of these islanders by the thousand, their villages and their cities; for surely it is we who are solely responsible for all the incidental burnings that our operations entail. But these destructions are the smallest part of our sins. We are destroying down to the root every germ of a healthy national life in these unfortunate people, and we are surely helping to destroy for one generation at least their faith in God and man. No life shall you have, we say, except as a gift from our philanthropy after your unconditional submission to our will. So as they seem to be "slow pay" in the matter of submission, our yellow journals have abundant time in which to raise new monuments of capitals to the victories of Old Glory, and in which to extol the unrestrainable eagerness of our brave soldiers to rush into battles that remind them so much of rabbit hunts on Western plains.

It is horrible, simply horrible. Surely there cannot be many born and bred Americans who, when they look at the bare fact of what we are doing, the fact taken all by itself, do not feel this, and do not blush with burning shame at the unspeakable meanness and ignominy of the trick?

Why, then, do we go on? First, the war fever; and then the pride which always refuses to back down when under fire. But these are passions that interfere with the reasonable settlement of any affair; and in this affair we have to deal with a factor altogether peculiar with our belief, namely, in a national destiny which must be "big" at any cost, and which for some inscrutable reason it has become infamous for us to disbelieve in or refuse. We are to be missionaries of civilization, and to bear the white man's burden, painful as it often is. We must sow our ideals, plant our order, impose our God. The individual lives are nothing. Our duty and our destiny call, and civilization must go on.

Could there be a more damning indictment of that whole bloated idol termed "modern civilization" than this amounts to? Civilization is, then, the big, hollow, resounding, corrupting, sophisticating, confusing torrent of mere brutal momentum and irrationality that brings forth fruits like this! It is safe to say that one Christian missionary, whether primitive, Protestant or Catholic, of the original missionary type, one Buddhist or Mohammedan of a genuine saintly sort, one ethical reformer or philanthropist, or one disciple of Tolstoi would do more real good in these islands than our whole army and navy can possibly effect with our whole civilization at their back. He could build up realities, in however small a degree; we can only destroy the inner realities; and indeed destroy in a year more of them than a generation can make good.

It is by their moral fruits exclusively that these benighted brown people, "half-devil and half-child" as they are, are condemned to judge a civilization. Ours is already execrated by them forever for its hideous fruits.

Shall it not in so far forth be execrated by ourselves? Shall the unsophisticated verdict upon its hideousness which the plain moral sense pronounces avail nothing to stem the torrent of mere empty "bigness" in our destiny, before which it is said we must all knock under, swallowing our higher sentiments with a gulp? The issue is perfectly plain at last. We are cold-bloodedly, wantonly and abominably destroying the soul of a people who never did us an atom of harm in their lives. It is bald, brutal piracy, impossible to dish up any longer in the cold pot-grease of President McKinley's cant at the recent Boston banquet—surely as shamefully evasive a speech, considering the right of the public to know definite facts, as can often have fallen even from a professional politician's lips. The worst of our imperialists is that they do not themselves know where sincerity ends and insecurity begins. Their state of consciousness is so new, so mixed of primitively human passions and, in political circles, of calculations that are anything but primitively human; so at variance, moreover, with their former mental habits; and so empty of definite data and contents; that they face various ways at once, and their portraits should be taken with a squint. One reads the President's speech with a strange feeling— as if the very words were squinting on the page.

The impotence of the private individual, with imperialism under full headway as it is, is deplorable indeed. But every American has a voice or a pen, and may use it. So, impelled by my own sense of duty, I write these present words. One by one we shall creep from cover, and the opposition will organize itself. If the Filipinos hold out long enough, there was a good chance (the canting game being already pretty well played out, and the piracy having to show itself hence-forward naked) of the older American beliefs and sentiments coming to their rights again, and of the Administration being terrified into a conciliatory policy towards the native government.

The programme for the opposition should, it seems to me, be radical. The infamy and iniquity of a war of conquest must stop. A "protectorate," of course, if they will have it, though after this they would probably rather welcome any European Power; and as regards the inner state of the island, freedom, "fit" or "unfit," that is, home rule without humbugging phrases, and whatever anarchy may go with it until the Filipinos learn from each other, not from us, how to govern themselves. Mr. Adams's programme—which anyone may have by writing to Mr. Erving Winslow, Anti-Imperialist League, Washington, D.C.— seems to contain the only hopeful key to the situation. Until the opposition newspapers seriously begin, and the mass meetings are held, let every American who still wishes his country to possess its ancient soul—soul a thousand times more dear than ever, now that it seems in danger of perdition—do what little he can in the way of open speech and writing, and above all let him give his representatives and senators in Washington a positive piece of his mind.

# Program of the American Anti-Imperialist League, 1899

We hold that the policy known as imperialism is hostile to liberty and tends toward militarism, an evil from which it has been our glory to be free. We regret that it has become necessary in the land of Washington and Lincoln to reaffirm that all men, of whatever race or color, are entitled to life, liberty and the pursuit of happiness. We maintain that governments derive their just powers from the consent of the governed. We insist that the subjugation of any people is "criminal aggression" and open disloyalty to the distinctive principles of our Government.

We earnestly condemn the policy of the present National Administration in the Philippines. It seeks to extinguish the spirit of 1776 in those islands. We deplore the sacrifice of our soldiers and sailors, whose bravery deserves ad-

miration even in an unjust war. We denounce the slaughter of the Filipinos as
a needless horror. We protest against the extension of American sovereignty
by Spanish methods.

We demand the immediate cessation of the war against liberty, begun by
Spain and continued by us. We urge that Congress be promptly convened to
announce to the Filipinos our purpose to concede to them the independence
for which they have so long fought and which of right is theirs.

The United States have always protested against the doctrine of international
law which permits the subjugation of the weak by the strong. A self-governing
state cannot accept sovereignty over an unwilling people. The United States
cannot act upon the ancient heresy that might makes right.

Imperialists assume that with the destruction of self-government in the Philippines by American hands, all opposition here will cease. This is a grievous
error. Much as we abhor the war of "criminal aggression" in the Philippines,
greatly as we regret that the blood of the Filipinos is on American hands, we
more deeply resent the betrayal of American institutions at home. The real
firing line is not in the suburbs of Manila. The foe is of our own household.
The attempt of 1861 was to divide the country. That of 1899 is to destroy its
fundamental principles and noblest ideals.

Whether the ruthless slaughter of the Filipinos shall end next month or next
year is but an incident in a contest that must go on until the Declaration of
Independence and the Constitution of the United States are rescued from the
hands of their betrayers. Those who dispute about standards of value while
the foundation of the Republic is undermined will be listened to as little as those
who would wrangle about the small economies of the household while the
house is on fire. The training of a great people for a century, the aspiration for
liberty of a vast immigration are forces that will hurl aside those who in the
delirium of conquest seek to destroy the character of our institutions.

We deny that the obligation of all citizens to support their Government in
times of grave National peril applies to the present situation. If an Administration may with impunity ignore the issues upon which it was chosen, deliberately
create a condition of war anywhere on the face of the globe, debauch the civil
service for spoils to promote the adventure, organize a truth-suppressing
censorship and demand of all citizens a suspension of judgment and their
unanimous support while it chooses to continue the fighting, representative government itself is imperiled.

We propose to contribute to the defeat of any person or party that stands
for the forcible subjugation of any people. We shall oppose for reëlection all
who in the White House or in Congress betray American liberty in pursuit of
un-American ends. We still hope that both of our great political parties will
support and defend the Declaration of Independence in the closing campaign
of the century.

We hold, with Abraham Lincoln, that "no man is good enough to govern
another man without that other's consent. When the white man governs himself,
that is self-government, but when he governs himself and also governs another
man, that is more than self-government—that is despotism. Our reliance is

in the love of liberty which God has planted in us. Our defense is in the spirit which prizes liberty as the heritage of all men in all lands. Those who deny freedom to others deserve it not for themselves, and under a just God cannot long retain it."

We cordially invite the cooperation of all men and women who remain loyal to the Declaration of Independence and the Constitution of the United States.

# Senator Albert J. Beveridge's Salute to Imperialism, 1900

Fellow citizens, It is a noble land that God has given us; a land that can feed and clothe the world; a land whose coast lines would enclose half the countries of Europe; a land set like a sentinel between the two imperial oceans of the globe, a greater England with a nobler destiny. It is a mighty people that he has planted on this soil; a people sprung from the most masterful blood of history; a people perpetually revitalized by the virile, man-producing workingfolk of all the earth; a people imperial by virtue of their power, by right of their institutions, by authority of their heaven-directed purposes—the propagandists and not the misers of liberty. It is a glorious history our God has bestowed upon his chosen people; a history whose keynote was struck by Liberty Bell; a history heroic with faith in our mission and our future; a history of statesmen who flung the boundaries of the Republic out into unexplored lands and savage wildernesses; a history of soldiers who carried the flag across the blazing deserts and through the ranks of hostile mountains, even to the gates of sunset; a history of a multiplying people who overran a continent in half a century; a history of prophets who saw the consequences of evils inherited from the past and of martyrs who died to save us from them; a history divinely logical, in the process of whose tremendous reasoning we find ourselves today. . . .

Shall the American people continue their resistless march toward the commercial supremacy of the world? Shall free institutions broaden their blessed reign as the children of liberty wax in strength, until the empire of our principles is established over the hearts of all mankind?

Have we no mission to perform, no duty to discharge to our fellowman? Has the Almighty Father endowed us with gifts beyond our deserts and marked us as the people of his peculiar favor, merely to rot in our own selfishness, as men and nations must, who take cowardice for their companion and self for their Deity—as China has, as India has, as Egypt has?

Shall we be as the man who had one talent and hid it, or as he who had ten talents and used them until they grew to riches? And shall we reap the reward that waits on our discharge of our high duty as the sovereign power of earth; shall we occupy new markets for what our farmers raise, new markets for what our factories make, new markets for what our merchants sell—aye, and, please God, new markets for what our ships shall carry?

Shall we avail ourselves of new sources of supply of what we do not raise or make, so that what are luxuries to-day will be necessities to-morrow? Shall our commerce be encouraged until, with Oceanica, the Orient, and the world, American trade shall be the imperial trade of the entire globe? . . .

For William McKinley is continuing the policy that Jefferson began, Monroe continued, Seward advanced, Grant promoted, Harrison championed, and the growth of the republic has demanded. Hawaii is ours; Porto Rico is to be ours; at the prayer of the people Cuba will finally be ours; in the islands of the East, even to the gates of Asia, coaling-stations are to be ours; at the very least the flag of a liberal government is to float over the Philippines, and I pray God it may be the banner that Taylor unfurled in Texas and Fremont carried to the coast—the Stars and Stripes of glory. . . .

The Opposition tells us that we ought not to govern a people without their consent. I answer, The rule of liberty that all just government derives its authority from the consent of the governed, applies only to those who are capable of self-government. I answer, We govern the Indians without their consent, we govern our territories without their consent, we govern our children without their consent. I answer, How do you assume that our government would be without their consent? Would not the people of the Philippines prefer the just, humane, civilizing government of this republic to the savage, bloody rule of pillage and extortion from which we have rescued them?. . .

And, now, obeying the same voice that Jefferson heard and obeyed, that Jackson heard and obeyed, that Monroe heard and obeyed, that Seward heard and obeyed, that Ulysses S. Grant heard and obeyed, that Benjamin Harrison heard and obeyed, William McKinley plants the flag over the islands of the seas, outposts of commerce, citadels of national security, and the march of the flag goes on! . . .

Distance and oceans are no arguments. . . .

Steam joins us; electricity joins us—the very elements are in league with our destiny. Cuba not contiguous! Porto Rico not contiguous! Hawaii and the Philippines not contiguous! Our navy will make them contiguous. Dewey and Sampson and Schley have made them contiguous, and American speed, American guns, American heart and brain and nerve will keep them contiguous forever. . . .

To-day, we are raising more than we can consume. To-day, we are making more than we can use. To-day, our industrial society is congested; there are more workers than there is work; there is more capital than there is investment. We do not need more money—we need more circulation, more employment. Therefore we must find new markets for our produce, new occupation for our capital, new work for our labor. And so, while we did not need the territory taken during the past century at the time it was acquired, we do need what we have taken in 1898, and we need it now.

Think of the thousands of Americans who will pour into Hawaii and Porto Rico when the republic's laws cover those islands with justice and safety! Think of the tens of thousands of Americans who will invade mine and field and forest in the Philippines when a liberal government, protected and controlled by this republic, if not the government of the republic itself, shall establish order and equity there! Think of the hundreds of thousands of Americans who will build a soap-and-water, common-school civilization of energy and industry in Cuba, when a government of law replaces the double reign of anarchy and tyranny! —think of the prosperous millions that Empress of Islands will support when, obedient to the law of political gravitation, her people ask for the highest honor liberty can bestow, the sacred Order of the Stars and Stripes, the citizenship of the Great Republic!

What does all this mean for every one of us? It means opportunity for all the glorious young manhood of the republic—the most virile, ambitious, impatient, militant manhood the world has ever seen. It means that the resources and the commerce of these immensely rich dominions will be increased as much as American energy is greater than Spanish sloth; for Americans henceforth will monopolize those resources and that commerce. . . .

Fellow Americans, we are God's chosen people. Yonder at Bunker Hill and Yorktown his providence was above us. At New Orleans and on ensanguined seas his hand sustained us. Abraham Lincoln was his minister and his was the Altar of Freedom, the boys in blue set on a hundred battlefields. His power directed Dewey in the East and delivered the Spanish fleet into our hands on the eve of Liberty's natal day, as he delivered the elder Armada into the hands of our English sires two centuries ago. His great purposes are revealed in the progress of the flag, which surpasses the intentions of Congresses and Cabinets, and leads us like a holier pillar of cloud by day and pillar of fire by night into situations unforeseen by finite wisdom, and duties unexpected by the un-prophetic heart of selfishness. The American people cannot use a dishonest medium of exchange; it is ours to set the world its example of right and honor. We cannot fly from our world duties; it is ours to execute the purpose of a fate that has driven us to be greater than our small intentions. We cannot retreat from any soil where Providence has unfurled our banner; it is ours to save that soil for Liberty and Civilization. For Liberty and Civilization and God's prom-ise fulfilled, the flag must henceforth be the symbol and the sign to all man-kind—the flag!—

> Flag of the free heart's hope and home,
>   By angel hands to valor given,
> Thy stars have lit the welkin dome,
>   And all their hues were born in heaven!
> Forever wave that standard sheet,
>   Where breathes the foe but falls before us,
> With freedom's soil beneath our feet
>   And freedom's banner streaming o'er us.

# ESSAYS

Richard Hofstadter's essay places the war and imperialism in the context of a "psychic crisis" in the 1890s, wherein tumultuous events such as the depression created a compulsion to lash out overseas. Walter LaFeber of Cornell University also sees the 1890s as a watershed, but places more emphasis on the quest for foreign markets as a major stimulant to war and imperialism. On the other hand, in his essay, Ernest R. May of Harvard University does not find the causes of war in the United States itself. Rather, he argues that American leaders temporarily borrowed ideas from European imperialists. One question, then, is whether foreign policy is influenced more by events abroad than by careful thinking and planning in Washington. Just how self-conscious, rational, and deliberate were Americans in their imperial thrust?

# The Psychic Crisis of the 1890s

### RICHARD HOFSTADTER

The taking of the Philippine Islands from Spain in 1899 marked a major historical departure for the American people, a breach in their traditions and a shock to their established values. To be sure, from their national beginnings they had constantly engaged in expansion, but almost entirely into contiguous territory. Now they were extending themselves to distant extra-hemispheric colonies. They were abandoning a strategy of defense hitherto limited to the continent and its appurtenances, in favor of a major strategic commitment in the Far East. Thus far their expansion had been confined to the spread of a relatively homogeneous population into territories planned from the beginning to develop self-government; now control was to be imposed by force on millions of ethnic aliens. The acquisition of the islands, therefore, was understood by contemporaries on both sides of the debate, as it is readily understood today, to be a turning point in our history.

To discuss the debate in isolation from other events, however, would be to deprive it of its full significance. America's entrance into the Philippine Islands was a by-product of the Spanish-American War. The Philippine crisis is inseparable from the war crisis, and the war crisis itself is inseparable from a larger constellation that might be called "the psychic crisis of the 1890's."

Central in the background of the psychic crisis was the great depression that broke in 1893 and was still very acute when the agitation over the war in Cuba began. Severe depression, by itself, does not always generate an emotional crisis as intense as that of the nineties. In the 1870's the country had been swept by a depression of comparable acuteness and duration which, however, did not give rise to all the phenomena that appeared in the 1890's or to very many of them with comparable intensity and impact. It is often said that the 1890's, unlike the 1870's, form a "watershed" in American history. The difference between the emotional and intellectual impact of these two depressions can be measured, I believe, not by the difference in severity, but rather by reference to a number of singular events that in the 1890's converged with the depression to heighten its impact upon the public mind.

First in importance was the Populist movement, the free-silver agitation, the heated campaign of 1896. For the first time in our history a depression had created a protest movement strong enough to capture a major party and raise the specter, however unreal, of drastic social convulsion. Second was the maturation and bureaucratization of American business, the completion of its essential industrial plant, and the development of trusts on a scale sufficient to stir the anxiety that the old order of competitive opportunities was approaching an eclipse. Third, and of immense symbolic importance, was the apparent filling up of the continent and the disappearance of the frontier line. We now know how much land had not yet been taken up and how great were the remaining possibilities for internal expansion both in business and on the land; but to the mind of the 1890's it seemed that the resource that had engaged the energies of the people for three centuries had been used up. The frightening possibility suggested itself that a serious juncture in the nation's history had come. As Frederick Jackson Turner expressed it in his famous paper of 1893: "Now, four centuries from the discovery of America, at the end of one hundred years of life under the Constitution, the frontier has gone, and with its going has closed the first period of American history."

To middle-class citizens who had been brought up to think in terms of the nineteenth-century order, the outlook seemed grim. Farmers in the staple-growing region had gone mad over silver and Bryan; workers were stirring in bloody struggles like the Homestead and Pullman strikes; the supply of new land seemed at an end; the trust threatened the spirit of business enterprise; civic corruption was at a high point in the large cities; great waves of seemingly unassimilable immigrants arrived yearly and settled in hideous slums. To many historically conscious writers, the nation appeared overripe, like an empire ready for collapse through a stroke from outside or through internal upheaval. Acute as the situation was for all those who lived by the symbols of national power—for the governing and thinking classes—it was especially poignant for young people, who would have to make their careers in the dark world that seemed to be emerging.

The symptomatology of the crisis would record several tendencies in popular thought and behavior that had previously existed only in pale and tenuous form. These symptoms were manifest in two quite different moods. The key to one of them was an intensification of protest and humanitarian reform. Populism, utopianism, the rise of the Christian Social gospel, the growing intellectual interest in socialism, the social settlement movement that appealed so strongly to the college generation of the nineties, the quickening of protest and social criticism in the realistic novel—all these are expressions of this mood. The other mood was one of national self-assertion, aggression, expansion. The motif of the first was social sympathy; of the second, national power. During the 1890's far more patriotic groups were founded than in any other decade of our history; the naval theories of Captain Mahan were gaining in influence; naval construction was booming; there was an immense quickening of the American cult of Napoleon and a vogue of the virile and martial writings of Rudyard Kipling; young Theodore Roosevelt became the exemplar of the vigorous, masterful, out-of-doors man; the revival of European imperialism stirred speculation over what America's place would be in the world of renewed colonial rivalries, and in some stirred a demand to get into the imperial race to avoid the risk of being overwhelmed by other powers. But most significant was the rising tide of jingoism, a matter of constant comment among observers of American life during the decade.

Jingoism, of course, was not new in American history. But during the 1870's and 1880's the American public had been notably quiescent about foreign relations. There had been expansionist statesmen, but they had been blocked by popular apathy, and our statecraft had been restrained. Grant had failed dismally in his attempt to acquire Santo Domingo; our policy toward troubled Hawaii had been cautious; in 1877 an offer of two Haitian naval harbors had been spurned. In responding to Haiti, Secretary of State Frelinghuysen had remarked that "the policy of this Government . . . has tended toward avoidance of possessions disconnected from the main continent." Henry Cabot Lodge, in his life of George Washington published in 1889, observed that foreign relations then filled "but a slight place in American politics, and excite generally only a languid interest." Within a few years this comment would have seemed absurd. In 1895, Russell A. Alger reported to Lodge, after reading one of Lodge's own articles to a Cincinnati audience, that he was convinced by the response that foreign policy, "more than anything else, touches the public pulse of today." The history of the 1890's is the history of public agitation over expansionist issues and of quarrels with other nations. . . .

Since Julius W. Pratt published his *Expansionists of 1898* in 1936, it has been obvious that any interpretation of America's entry upon the paths of imperialism in the nineties in terms of rational economic motives would not fit the facts, and that a historian who approached the event with preconceptions no more supple than those, say, of Lenin's *Imperialism* would be helpless. This is not to say that markets and investments have no bearing; they do, but there are features of the situation that they do not explain at all. Insofar as the economic factor was important, it can be better studied by looking at the relation between the depression, the public mood, and the political system.

The alternative explanation has been the equally simple idea that the war was a newspapers' war. This notion, once again, has some point, but it certainly does not explain the war itself, much less its expansionist result. The New Deal period, when the political successes of F.D.R. were won in the face of overwhelming newspaper opposition, showed that the press is not powerful enough to impose upon the public mind a totally uncongenial view of public events. It must operate roughly within the framework of public predispositions. Moreover, not all the papers of the nineties were yellow journals. We must inquire into the structure of journalistic power and also into the views of the owners and editors to find out what differentiated the sensational editors and publishers from those of the conservative press.

There is still another qualification that must be placed upon the role of the press: the press itself, whatever it can do with opinion, does not have the power to precipitate opinion into action. That is something that takes place within the *political* process, and we cannot tell that part of the story without examining the state of party rivalries, the origin and goals of the political elites, and indeed the entire political context. We must, then, supplement our story about the role of the newspapers with at least two other factors: the state of the public temper upon which the newspapers worked, and the manner in which party rivalries deflected domestic clashes into foreign aggression. Here a perennial problem of politics under the competitive two-party system became manifest again in the 1890's. When there is, for whatever reason, a strong current of jingoism running in the channels of public sentiment, party competition tends to speed it along. If the party in power is behaving circumspectly, the opposition tends to beat the drums. For example, in 1896, with Cleveland still in office, the Republican platform was much more exigent on the Cuba issue. When McKinley came into office and began to show reluctance to push toward intervention, the Democratic party became a center of interventionist pressure; this pressure was promptly supplemented by a large number of Republicans who, quite aside from their agreement on the issue, were concerned about its effect on the fate of their party.

When we examine the public temper, we find that the depression, together with such other events as the approaching completion of the settlement of the continent, the growth of trusts, and the intensification of internal social conflict, had brought to large numbers of people intense frustrations in their economic lives and their careers. To others they had brought anxiety that a period of stagnation in national wealth and power had set in. The restlessness of the discontented classes had been heightened by the defeat of Bryan in 1896. The anxieties about the nation's position had been increased among statesmen and publicists by the revival of world imperialism, in particular by the feeling that America was threatened by Germany, Russia, and Japan. The expansionist statesmen themselves were drawn largely from a restless upper-middle-class elite that had been fighting an unrewarding battle for conservative reform in domestic politics and looked with some eagerness toward a more spacious field of action.

Men often respond to frustration with acts of aggression, and allay their anxieties by threatening acts against others. It is revealing that the underdog forces in American society showed a considerably higher responsiveness to the idea of war with Spain than the groups that were satisfied with their economic or political positions. Our entry into the Philippines then aroused the interest of conservative groups that had been indifferent to the quixotism of freeing Cuba but were alert to the possibility of capturing new markets. Imperialism appealed to members of both the business and the political elites as an enlargement of the sphere of American power and profits; many of the underdogs also responded to this new note of national self-assertion. Others, however, looked upon our conduct in the Philippines as a betrayal of national principles. Anti-expansionists attempted to stir a sense of guilt and foreboding in the nation at large. But the circumstances of the period 1898–1900—the return of prosperity and the quick spectacular victories in war—made it difficult for them to impress this feeling upon the majority. The rhetoric of Duty and Destiny carried the day. The anti-expansionists had neither the numbers nor the morale of their opponents. The most conspicuous result of their lack of drive and confidence can be seen in the lamentable strategy of Bryan over the ratification of the treaty.

Clearly this attempt to see the war and expansion in the light of social history has led us onto the high and dangerous ground of social psychology and into the arena of conjecture. But simple rationalistic explanations of national behavior will also leave us dissatisfied. What I have attempted here is merely a preliminary sketch of a possible explanatory model. Further inquiry might make it seem more plausible at some points, more questionable at others.

## Preserving the American System

### WALTER LAFEBER

The "splendidlittlewar" of 1898, as Secretary of State John Hay termed it at the time, is rapidly losing its splendor for those concerned with American foreign policy in the 1960s. Over the past decade few issues in the country's diplomatic history have aroused academics more than the causes of the Spanish-American War, and in the last several years the argument has become not merely academic, but a starting point in the debate over how the United States evolved into a great power, and more particularly how Americans got involved in the maelstrom of Asian nationalism. The line from the conquest of the Philippines in 1898 to the attempted pacification of Vietnam in 1968 is not straight, but it is quite traceable, and if Frederick Jackson Turner was correct when he observed in the 1890s that "The aim of history, then, is to know the elements of the present by understanding what came into the present from the past," the causes of the war in 1898 demand analysis from our present viewpoint.

Historians have offered four general interpretations to explain these causes. First, the war has been traced to a general impulse for war on the part of American public opinion. This interpretation has been illustrated in a famous cartoon showing President William McKinley, in the bonnet and dress of a little old lady, trying to sweep back huge waves marked "Congress" and "public opinion," with a very small broom. The "yellow journalism" generated by the Hearst-Pulitzer rivalry supposedly both created and reflected this sentiment for war. A sophisticated and useful version of this interpretation has been advanced by Richard Hofstadter. Granting the importance of the Hearst-Pulitzer struggle, he has asked why these newspaper titans were able to exploit public opinion. Hofstadter has concluded that psychological dilemmas arising out of the depression of the 1890s made Americans react somewhat irrationally because they were uncertain, frightened, and consequently open to exploitation by men who would

Walter LaFeber, "That 'Splendid Little War' in Historical Perspective," *Texas Quarterly*, 11 (1968), 89–98.

show them how to cure their frustrations through overseas adventures. In other words, the giddy minds of the 1890s could be quieted by foreign quarrels.

A second interpretation argues that the United States went to war for humanitarian reasons, that is, to free the Cubans from the horrors of Spanish policies and to give the Cubans democratic institutions. That this initial impulse resulted within ten months in an American protectorate over Cuba and Puerto Rico, annexation of the Philippines, and American participation in quarrels on the mainland of Asia itself, is explained as accidental, or, more familiarly, as done in a moment of "aberration" on the part of American policy-makers.

A third interpretation emphasizes the role of several Washington officials who advocated a "Large Policy" of conquering a vast colonial empire in the Caribbean and Western Pacific. By shrewd maneuvering, these few imperialists pushed the vacillating McKinley and a confused nation into war. Senator Henry Cabot Lodge, of Massachusetts, Captain Alfred Thayer Mahan, of the U.S. Navy, and Theodore Roosevelt, Assistant Secretary of the Navy in 1897–1898, are usually named as the leaders of the "Large Policy" contingent.

A fourth interpretation believes the economic drive carried the nation into war. This drive emanated from the rapid industrialization which characterized American society after the 1840s. The immediate link between this industrialization and the war of 1898 was the economic depression which afflicted the nation in the quarter-century after 1873. Particularly important were the 1893–1897 years when Americans endured the worst of the plunge. Government and business leaders, who were both intelligent and rational, believed an oversupply of goods created the depression. They finally accepted war as a means of opening overseas markets in order to alleviate domestic distress caused by the overproduction. For thirty years the economic interpretation dominated historians' views of the war, but in 1936 Professor Julius Pratt conclusively demonstrated that business journals did not want war in the early months of 1898. He argued instead the "Large Policy" explanation, and from that time to the present, Professor Pratt's interpretation has been pre-eminent in explaining the causes of the conflict.

As I shall argue in a moment, the absence of economic factors in causing the war has been considerably exaggerated. At this point, however, a common theme which unites the first three interpretations should be emphasized. Each of the three deals with a superficial aspect of American life; each is peculiar to 1898, and none is rooted in the structure, the bed-rock, of the nation's history. This theme is important, for it means that if the results of the war were distasteful and disadvantageous (and on this historians do largely agree because of the divisive problems which soon arose in the Philippines and Cuba), those misfortunes were endemic to episodes unique to 1898. The peculiarities of public sentiment or the Hearst-Pulitzer rivalry, for example, have not reoccurred; the wide-spread humanitarian desire to help Cubans has been confined to 1898; and the banding together of Lodge, Mahan, and Roosevelt to fight for "Large Policies" of the late 1890s was never repeated by the three men. Conspiracy theories, moreover, seldom explain history satisfactorily.

The fourth interpretation has different implications. It argues that if the economic was the primary drive toward war, criticism of that war must begin not with irrational factors or flights of humanitarianism or a few stereotyped figures, but with the basic structure of the American system.

United States foreign policy, after all, is concerned primarily with the nation's domestic system and only secondarily with the systems of other nations. American diplomatic history might be defined as the study of how United States relations with other nations are used to insure the survival and increasing prosperity of the American system. Foreign policymakers are no more motivated by altruism than is the rest of the human race, but are instead involved in making a system function at home. Secretary of State, as the Founding Fathers realized, is an apt title for the man in charge of American foreign policy.

Turning this definition around, it also means that domestic affairs are the main determinant of foreign policy. When viewed within this matrix, the diplomatic events of the 1890s are no longer aberrations or the results of conspiracies and drift; American policymakers indeed grabbed greatness with both hands. As for accident or chance, they certainly exist in history, but become more meaningful when one begins with J. B. Bury's definition of "chance": "The valuable collision of two or more independent chains of causes." The most fruitful approach to the war of 1898 might be from the inside out (from the domestic to the foreign), and by remembering that chance is "the valuable collision of two or more independent chains of causes."

Three of these "chains" can be identified: the economic crisis of the 1890s which caused extensive and dangerous maladjustments in American society; the opportunities which suddenly opened in Asia after 1895 and in the Caribbean and the Pacific in 1898, opportunities which officials began to view as poultices, if not cure-alls, for the illnesses at home; and a growing partnership between business and government which reached its nineteenth-century culmination in the person of William McKinley. In April 1898, these "chains" had a "valuable collision" and war resulted.

The formation of the first chain is the great success story of American history. Between 1850 and 1910 the average manufacturing plant in the country multiplied its capital thirty-nine times, its number of wage-earners nearly seven times, and the value of its output by more than nineteen times. By the mid-1890s American iron and steel producers joked about their successful underselling of the vaunted British steel industry not only in world markets, but also in the vicinity of Birmingham, England, itself. The United States traded more in international markets than any nation except Great Britain.

But the most accelerated period of this development, 1873–1898, was actually twenty-five years of boom hidden in twenty-five years of bust. That quarter-century endured the longest and worst depression in the nation's history. After brief and unsatisfactory recoveries in the mid-1880s and early 1890s, the economy reached bottom in 1893. Unparalleled social and economic disasters struck. One out of every six laborers was unemployed, with most of the remainder existing on substandard wages; not only weak firms but many companies with the best credit ratings were forced to close their doors; the unemployed slept in the streets; riots erupted in Brooklyn, California, and points in between, as in the calamitous Pullman Strike in Chicago; Coxey's Army of broken farmers and unemployed laborers made their famous march on Washington; and the Secretary of State, Walter Quentin Gresham, remarked privately in 1894 that he saw "symptoms of revolution" appearing. Federal troops were dispatched to Chicago and other urban areas, including a cordon which guarded the Federal Treasury building in New York City.

Faced with the prospect of revolution and confronted with an economy that had almost ground to a stop, American businessmen and political officials faced alternative policies: they could attempt to re-examine and reorient the economic system, making radical modifications in the means of distribution and particularly the distribution of wealth; or they could look for new physical frontiers, following the historic tendency to increase production and then ferreting out new markets so the surplus, which the nation supposedly was unable to consume, could be sold elsewhere and Americans then put back to work on the production lines.

To the business and political communities, these were not actually alternatives at all. Neither of those communities has been known historically for political and social radicalism. Each sought security, not new political experiments. Some business firms tried to find such security by squashing competitors. Extremely few, however, searched for such policies as a federal income tax. Although such a tax narrowly passed through Congress in 1894, the Supreme Court declared it unconstitutional within a year and the issue would not be resurrected for another seventeen years. As a result, business and political leaders accepted the solution which was traditional, least threatening to their own power, and (apparently) required the least risk: new markets. Secretary of the Treasury John G. Carlisle summarized this conclusion in his public report of 1894: "The prosperity of our people, therefore, depends largely upon their ability to sell their surplus products in foreign markets at remunerative prices."

This consensus included farmers and the labor movement among others, for these interests were no more ingenious in discovering new solutions than were businessmen. A few farmers and laborers murmured ominously about some kind [of] political and/or economic revolution, but Richard Hofstadter seems correct in suggesting that in a sense Populism was reactionary rather than radical. The agrarians in the Populist movement tended to look back to a Jeffersonian utopia. Historians argue this point, but beyond dispute is the drive by farmers, including Populists, for foreign markets. The agrarians acted out of a long and successful tradition, for they had sought overseas customers since the first tobacco surplus in Virginia three hundred and fifty years before. Farmers initially framed the expansionist arguments and over three centuries created the context for the growing consensus on the desirability of foreign markets, a consensus which businessmen and others would utilize in the 1890s.

The farmers' role in developing this theme in American history became highly ironic in the late nineteenth century, for businessmen not only adopted the argument that overseas markets were necessary, but added a proviso that agrarian interests would have to be suppressed in the process. Industrialists observed that export charts demonstrated the American economy to be depending more upon industrial than agrarian exports. To allow industrial goods to be fully competitive in the world market, however, labor costs would have to be minimal, and cheap bread meant sacrificing the farmers. Fully comprehending this argument, agrarians reacted bitterly. They nevertheless continued searching for their own overseas markets, agreeing with the industrialist that the traditional method of discovering new outlets provided the key to prosperity, individualism, and status.

The political conflict which shattered the 1890s revolved less around the question of whether conservatives could carry out a class solution than the question of which class would succeed in carrying out a conservative solution. This generalization remains valid even when the American labor movement is examined for its response to the alternatives posed. This movement, primarily comprised of the newly-formed American Federation of Labor, employed less than 3 per cent of the total number of employed workers in nonfarm occupations. In its own small sphere of influence, its membership largely consisted of skilled workers living in the East. The AFL was not important in the West or South, where the major discontent seethed. Although Samuel Gompers was known by some of the more faint-hearted as a "socialist," the AFL's founder never dramatized any radical solutions for the restructuring of the economy. He was concerned with obtaining more money, better hours, and improved working conditions for the Federation's members. Gompers refused, moreover, to use direct political action to obtain these benefits, content to negotiate within the corporate structure which the businessman had created. The AFL simply wanted more, and when overseas markets seemed to be a primary source of benefits, Gompers did not complain. As Louis Hartz has noted, "wage consciousness," not "class consciousness," triumphed.

The first "chain of causes" was marked by a consensus on the need to find markets overseas. Fortunately for the advocates of this policy, another "chain," quite complementary to the first, began to form beyond American borders. By the mid-1890s, American merchants, missionaries, and ship captains had been profiting from Asian markets for more than a century. Between 1895 and 1900, however, the United States for the first time became a mover-and-pusher in Asian affairs.

In 1895 Japan defeated China in a brief struggle that now appears to be one of the most momentous episodes in the nineteenth century. The Japanese emerged as the major Asian power, the Chinese suddenly seemed to be incapable of defending their honor or existence, Chinese nationalism began its peculiar path to the 1960s, and European powers which had long lusted after Asian markets now seized a golden opportunity. Russia, Germany, France, and ultimately Great Britain initiated policies designed to carve China and Manchuria into spheres of influence. Within a period of months, the Asian mainland suddenly became the scene of international power politics at its worst and most explosive.

The American reaction to these events has been summarized recently by Professor Thomas McCormick: "The conclusion of the Sino-Japanese War left Pandora's box wide open, but many Americans mistook it for the Horn of Plenty." Since the first American ship sailed to sell goods in China in 1784, Americans had chased that most mysterious phantom, the China Market. Now, just at the moment when key interest groups agreed that overseas markets could be the salvation of the 1890s crisis, China was almost miraculously opening its doors to the glutted American factories and farms. United States trade with China jumped significantly after 1895, particularly in the critical area of manufactures; by 1899 manufactured products accounted for more than 90 per cent of the nation's exports to the Chinese, a quadrupling of the amount sent in 1895. In their moment of need, Americans had apparently discovered a Horn of Plenty.

But, of course, it was Pandora's box. The ills which escaped from the box were threefold. Least important for the 1890s, a nascent Chinese nationalism appeared. During the next quarter-century, the United States attempted to minimize the effects of this nationalism either by cooperating with Japan or European powers to isolate and weaken the Chinese, or by siding with the most conservative groups within the nationalist movement. Americans also faced the competition of European and Japanese products, but they were nevertheless confident in the power of their newly-tooled industrial powerhouse. Given a "fair field and no favor," as the Secretary of State phrased the wish in 1900, Americans would undersell and defeat any competitors. But could fair fields and no favors be guaranteed? Within their recently-created spheres of influence European powers began to grant themselves trade preferences, thus effectively shutting out American competition. In 1897, the American business community and the newly-installed administration of William McKinley began to counter these threats.

The partnership between businessmen and politicians, in this case the Mc-Kinley administration, deserves emphasis, for if the businessman hoped to exploit Asian markets he required the aid of the politician. Americans could compete against British or Russian manufacturers in Asia, but they could not compete against, say, a Russian manufacturer who could turn to his government and through pressure exerted by that government on Chinese officials receive a prize railroad contract or banking concession. United States businessmen could only compete against such business-government coalitions if Washington officials helped. Only then would the field be fair and the favors equalized. To talk of utilizing American "rugged individualism" and a free enterprise philosophy in the race for the China market in the 1890s was silly. There consequently emerged in American policy-making a classic example of the business community and the government grasping hands and, marching shoulder to shoulder, leading the United States to its destiny of being a major power on a far-Eastern frontier. As one high Republican official remarked in the mid-1890s: "diplomacy is the management of international business."

William McKinley fully understood the need for such a partnership. He had grown to political maturity during the 1870s when, as one Congressman remarked, "The House of Representatives was like an auction room where more valuable considerations were disposed of under the speaker's hammer than in any other place on earth." Serving as governor of Ohio during the

1890s depression, McKinley learned firsthand about the dangers posed by the economic crisis (including riots in his state which he terminated with overwhelming displays of military force). The new Chief Executive believed there was nothing necessarily manifest about Manifest Destiny in American history, and his administration was the first in modern American history which so systematically and completely committed itself to helping businessmen, farmers, laborers, and missionaries in solving their problems in an industrializing, supposedly frontierless America. Mr. Dooley caught this aggressive side of the McKinley administration when he described the introduction of a presidential speech: "Th' proceedin's was opened with a prayer that Providence might r-remain undher th' protection iv th' administration."

Often characterized as a creature of his campaign manager Mark Hanna, or as having, in the famous but severely unjust words of Theodore Roosevelt, the backbone of a chocolate eclair, McKinley was, as Henry Adams and others fully understood, a master of men. McKinley was never pushed into a policy he did not want to accept. Elihu Root, probably the best mind and most acute observer who served in the McKinley cabinets, commented that on most important matters the President had his ideas fixed, but would convene the Cabinet, direct the members toward his own conclusions, and thereby allow the Cabinet to think it had formulated the policy. In responding to the problems and opportunities in China, however, McKinley's power to exploit that situation was limited by events in the Caribbean.

In 1895 revolution had broken out in Cuba. By 1897 Americans were becoming increasingly belligerent on this issue for several reasons: more than $50,000,000 of United States investments on the island were endangered; Spaniards were treating some Cubans inhumanely; the best traditions of the Monroe Doctrine had long dictated that a European in the Caribbean was a sty in the eye of any red-blooded American; and, finally, a number of Americans, not only Lodge, Roosevelt, and Mahan, understood the strategic and political relationship of Cuba to a proposed isthmian canal. Such a canal would provide a short-cut to the west coast of Latin America as well as to the promised markets of Asia. Within six months after assuming office, McKinley demanded that the island be pacified or the United States would take a "course of action which the time and the transcendent emergency may demand." Some Spanish reforms followed, but in January 1898, new revolts wracked Havana and a month later the "Maine" dramatically sank to the bottom of Havana harbor.

McKinley confronted the prospect of immediate war. Only two restraints appeared. First, a war might lead to the annexation of Cuba, and the multitude of problems (including racial) which had destroyed Spanish authority would be dumped on the United States. Neither the President nor his close advisers wanted to leap into the quicksands of noncontiguous, colonial empire. The business community comprised a second restraining influence. By mid-1897 increased exports, which removed part of the agricultural and industrial glut, began to extricate the country from its quarter-century of turmoil. Finally seeing light at the end of a long and treacherous tunnel, businessmen did not want the requirements of a war economy to jeopardize the growing prosperity.

These two restraints explain why the United States did not go to war in 1897, and the removal of these restraints indicates why war occurred in April 1898. The first problem disappeared because McKinley and his advisers entertained no ideas of warring for colonial empire in the Caribbean. After the war Cuba would be freed from Spain and then ostensibly returned to the Cubans to govern. The United States would retain a veto power over the more important policy decisions made on the island. McKinley discovered a classic solution in which the United States enjoyed the power over, but supposedly little of the responsibility for, the Cubans.

The second restraint disappeared in late March 1898, exactly at the time of McKinley's decision to send the final ultimatum to Madrid. The timing is crucial. Professor Pratt observed in 1936 that the business periodicals began to change their antiwar views in mid-March 1898, but he did not elaborate upon this point. The change is significant and confirms the advice McKinley received from a trusted political adviser in New York City who cabled on March 25 that the larger corporations would welcome war. The business journal and their readers were beginning to realize that the bloody struggle in Cuba and the resulting inability of the United States to operate at full-speed in Asian affairs more greatly endangered economic recovery than would a war.

McKinley's policies in late March manifested these changes. This does not mean that the business community manipulated the President, or that he was repaying those businessmen who had played vital roles in his election in 1896. Nor does it mean that McKinley thought the business community was forcing his hand or circumscribing his policies in late March. The opinions and policies of the President and the business community had been hammered out in the furnace of a terrible depression and the ominous changes in Asia. McKinley and pivotal businessmen emerged from these unforgettable experiences sharing a common conclusion: the nation's economy increasingly depended upon overseas markets, including the whole of China; that to develop these markets not only a business-government partnership but also tranquillity was required; and, finally, however paradoxical it might seem, tranquillity could be insured only through war against Spain. Not for the first or last time, Americans believed that to have peace they would have to wage war. Some, including McKinley, moved on to a final point. War, if properly conducted, could result in a few select strategic bases in the Pacific (such as Hawaii, Guam, and Manila) which would provide the United States with potent starting-blocks in the race for Asian markets. McKinley sharply distinguished between controlling such bases and trying to rule formally over an extensive territorial empire. In the development of the "chains of causes" the dominant theme was the economic, although not economic in the narrow sense. As discussed in the 1890s, business recovery carried most critical political and social implications.

Some historians argue that McKinley entered the war in confusion and annexed the Philippines in a moment of aberration. They delight in quoting the President's announcement to a group of Methodist missionaries that he decided to annex the Philippines one night when after praying he heard a mysterious voice. Most interesting, however, is not that the President heard a reassuring voice, but how the voice phrased its advice. The voice evidently outlined the points to be considered; in any case, McKinley numbered them in order, demonstrating, perhaps, that either he, the voice, or both had given some thought to putting the policy factors in neat and logical order. The second point is of particular importance: "that we could not turn them [the Philippines] over to France or Germany—our commercial rivals in the Orient—that would be bad business and discreditable. . . ." Apparently everyone who had been through the 1890s knew the dangers of "bad business." Even voices.

Interpretations which depend upon mass opinion, humanitarianism, and "Large Policy" advocates do not satisfactorily explain the causes of the war. Neither, however, does Mr. Dooley's famous one-sentence definition of American imperialism in 1898: "Hands acrost th' sea an' into somewan's pocket." The problem of American expansion is more complicated and historically rooted than that flippancy indicates. George Eliot once observed, "The happiest nations, like the happiest women, have no history." The United States, however, endured in the nineteenth century a history of growing industrialism, supposedly closing physical frontiers, rapid urbanization, unequal distribution of wealth, and an overdependence upon export trade. These historical currents clashed in the 1890s. The result was chaos and fear, then war and empire.

In 1898 McKinley and the business community wanted peace, but they also sought benefits which only a war could provide. Viewed from the perspective of the 1960's, the Spanish-American conflict can no longer be viewed as only a "splendid little war." It was a war to preserve the American system.

# Influence from Abroad

### ERNEST R. MAY

In 1898–99 the United States suddenly became a colonial power. It annexed the Hawaiian Islands. Humbling Spain in a short war, it took Puerto Rico and the Philippines. In quick sequence it also acquired Guam and part of Samoa and, if the Danish Rigsdag had consented, would have bought the Virgin Islands. In an eighteen-month period it became master of empires in the Caribbean and the Pacific.

Viewing America's tradition as anticolonial, historians have found these events puzzling. The legislative resolution for war with Spain seemingly expressed this tradition. Calling for independence for Spain's Cuban colony, Congress disclaimed "any disposition or intention to exercise sovereignty, jurisdiction, or control over" Cuba. That the same body should have ended the war by annexing Puerto Rico and Spanish islands in the Pacific appears a paradox, and many historians see 1898–99 as, in Samuel Flagg Bemis' phrase, a "great aberration."

To be sure, Americans of the time were hustled along by events. The first

Ernest R. May, from *American Imperialism: A Speculative Essay.* Copyright © 1967, 1968 by Ernest R. May. Reprinted by permission of Atheneum Publishers.

battle of the war took place not in Cuba but in Spain's more distant Philippine colony. A spectacular success, in which Admiral Dewey's squadron overcame all opposition without losing a single ship or life, it surprised many Americans into their first awareness that the Philippine Islands existed and that Spain owned them. Soon, however, following reports that Dewey's victory had shaken Spain's control, American troops sailed to seize the colonial capital, Manila. On the ground that these troops would need a support base in mid-Pacific, Congress annexed the Hawaiian Islands. By war's end, therefore, the United States already had one Pacific colony, and debate centered on whether to acquire another in the Philippines.

Both Americans and Europeans assumed that the United States could dispose of the Philippines as it chose. Seeming alternatives included handing the islands back to Spain, arranging for transfer to a European power, insisting on independence, or annexing. Most Americans saw the first alternative as giving up a hard-won prize and, moreover, returning the Filipinos to virtual slavery; the second as throwing an apple of discord among European states, perhaps even leading to general war; and the third, given the low level of Philippine development, as infeasible. Annexation appeared the least unattractive course.

American politicians could reason so, however, only by assuming that annexation would not cost votes at home. The historical puzzle rises from the fact that politicians then in power apparently did not expect to pay a price at the polls. Why not? With anticolonialism as strong as the Congressional war resolution suggests, how could politicians conclude that a colonialist policy could safely be pursued?

In *Expansionists of 1898* Julius W. Pratt offers part of an answer. He shows that, after Dewey's victory, religious journals changed tone. The Baptist *Standard,* the Presbyterian *Interior* and *Evangelist,* the Congregationalist *Advance,* and the *Catholic World* all spoke of rule over the Philippines as America's Christian duty. Methodist, Episcopalian, and Campbellite organs said the same. Only Quaker and Unitarian papers stood unitedly in opposition.

Pratt also shows the business press following a similar pattern. Having in the past either opposed or said nothing about acquisition of new territory, business journals now talked of the advantages of expansion. . . .

Before finally making up his mind, President McKinley toured the Midwest. Standing before large audiences, he delivered equivocal speeches. Some lines hinted at a decision to annex the Philippines; other lines hinted the opposite. His staff took notes on the relative levels of applause and reported that pro-annexation words drew louder handclaps. Other public figures presumably had similar experiences. Politicians thus had before them persuasive evidence of a dramatic swing in public opinion.

Such evidence explains their behavior partly but not entirely. In the past they had had plenty of evidence of antiexpansionist feeling. Though knowing in 1890 that minor tariff changes could encourage Canadians to seek annexation, congressmen found so little public enthusiasm that they failed to enact the changes. When voting the war resolution, they evidently felt that the people would not want Cuba. One might suppose that politicians would have anticipated the public's recovery from a momentary fancy for Pacific colonies and its repudiation of the officeholders who had pandered to such a perversion. That politicians showed no such fear must mean that they had some basis for believing the whim would endure. They must have seen some impulse stronger than momentary excitement over victories in far-off places. What can it have been? What conditions existed conducive to a lasting popular movement in favor of imperialism?

This question has challenged historians. Setting aside versions that stress Providence, the westward trend, or inherent tendencies in capitalism, one can single out four major efforts to answer it. Each emphasizes a different factor.

Frederick Merk, the preeminent historian of American expansion in the 1840s, argues that a long-lived Manifest Destiny tradition offset the anticolonial tradition. In *Manifest Destiny and Mission in American History* he describes two schools of thought existing at the time of the Mexican War. One, he says, favored the acquisition of territory in order to increase the nation's wealth and power. The other laid more stress on America's mission as the exemplar of democracy and individual liberty. After the victories of Taylor and Scott, men in the first school favored taking all or most of Mexico. Those in the second school wanted only sparsely inhabited tracts which settlers could easily turn into other Kentuckys and Ohios. In an epilogue on the 1890s Merk suggests that the ideas of the first, or Manifest Destiny, school reappeared later as imperialism, while the idea of Mission persisted as anti-imperialism. The two traditions had had equal hardihood, and the circumstances of 1898-99 gave the expansionist tradition an edge.

Explaining the actions of McKinley and other politicians would be an awareness of the expansionist tradition and an assumption that the balance had tipped toward it and away from the tradition of Mission. For parallels one might think of politicians concluding in 1913 that the protectionist tradition had lost out to the free-trade tradition or, in 1964, that states' rights had lost out to civil rights. In Merk's view the Manifest Destiny tradition provides the key to understanding what happened in 1898–99.

Julius Pratt emphasizes Social Darwinism. In *Expansionists of 1898* and elsewhere Pratt describes the expansionism of the 1890s as having a different rationale from that of pre–Civil War days. It took from Herbert Spencer and other writers the idea of an endless struggle testing each nation's fitness to survive. On this premise the United States had to seize whatever share of the earth it could, for not to do so would give advantages to rivals and in the long run would lead to defeat, decay, and decline. Expansion presented itself not as an open choice but as a necessity dictated by stern scientific law.

The premise already had wide acceptance. Dealing with domestic economic and social issues, writers and clergymen commonly invoked such formulae as "struggle for survival" and "survival of the fittest." At an early point some Americans progressed to conclusions about how the United States should behave internationally. Pointing to the navy's shift from sail to steam, they argued that the United States would stand at a dangerous disadvantage without coaling stations in distant seas. The Spanish War then created opportunities for acquiring such stations, far out in the Pacific as well as in the Caribbean. It also placed in America's grasp territories which, if not seized, could go to potential rivals. And it offered a seeming chance for Protestant Christianity (also a species, by Social Darwinist canons) to score a gain in its struggle for survival against Catholicism and heathenism. In Pratt's view these Social Darwinist theses captured American public opinion. The anticolonial tradition would not have intimidated politicians, because they would have expected these new ideas to dominate future public thinking about foreign policy.

In *The New Empire,* a more recent book than either Merk's or Pratt's, Walter LaFeber stresses economic forces. Like Pratt, he regards post–Civil War expansionism as different from that of the prewar era, but different because businessmen now captained the country and set their sights on markets rather than land. Whether manufacturers, merchants, or investors, they feared lest America's multiplying factories produce more than Americans could buy. As European states laid on protective tariffs, their thoughts turned to colonies and spheres of influence. Politicians behaved as they did in the 1890s, LaFeber suggests, because they put the interests of business ahead of all else, assumed the electorate would do the same, judged colonial expansion to serve business, and counted on the public's coming to the same conclusion and endorsing their actions.

A fourth major interpretation of the period, that of Richard Hofstadter, describes expansionism as merely one manifestation of a widespread "psychic crisis." The rise of bigger, more powerful, and more bureaucratized business organizations produced protest in strikes such as those at Homestead and Pullman and political movements such as those of the Populists and Bryanite Democrats. These forms of protest failed. Meanwhile, with such savants as Frederick Jackson Turner warning that the free land frontier no longer existed to drain off the discontented, members of the urban middle class took alarm not only at the growth of big business but at the radicalism of the protesters. For Americans in all these groups, Hofstadter argues, war with Spain and annexation of distant islands represented an escape from reality—madcap behavior comparable to that of disturbed adolescents. Politicians presumably counted on the public's remaining in this state of mind and applauding the acquisition of new frontiers rather than swinging back to disapproval of expansion.

The interpretations of Merk, Pratt, LaFeber, and Hofstadter can be reconciled. One could picture LaFeber's businessmen as borrowers of the Manifest Destiny tradition, differing from expansionists of the 1840s in questing for consumers rather than resources and quoting Herbert Spencer instead of the Book of Genesis, and one could explain their success in the 1890s as due to the "psychic crisis." But even such a blend of interpretations leaves two questions unanswered.

The first has to do with process. Merk does not say how the Manifest Destiny tradition came temporarily to outbalance the tradition of Mission. Pratt does not show how the Social Darwinist prescription won acceptance. LaFeber fails to explain how businessmen came to see expansion as in their interest. Hofstadter offers no reason why men caught in a "psychic crisis" concluded that

Pacific islands would be good things to have. No one charts the phases through which the individuals making up the public might have passed as they changed their convictions about colonies.

The second open question has to do with timing. Why did the change take place when it did?

Through the 1870s and 1880s the tradition of Mission, as Merk interprets it, appeared to hold the field. The influence of Social Darwinism did not extend to thought about foreign policy, and businessmen gave few signs of seeing colonial expansion as an answer to overproduction. At the end of the eighties, reports that Germany was about to take over Samoa produced some discussion of America's interest in the islands. Though no one spoke as a full-fledged expansionist, not everyone adopted the doctrinaire view that the United States could not consider taking part of the archipelago.

When Americans in Hawaii overthrew the native ruler in 1893 and appealed for annexation by the United States, politicians and newspaper reporters detected a surprising degree of public support for such a step. Some historians have concluded that if President Grover Cleveland had been of a mind to acquire the islands, he could have carried Congress and the country with him. Thus, despite the public's show of disinterest in annexing Canada and despite the language in Congress' 1898 war resolution, some shift away from anticolonialism could be observed even before Dewey's victory and its sequel. Circumstances created by the war will not account entirely for the estimates of public opinion formed by McKinley and other politicians. One has to ask why an apparent change in public attitudes should have set in around the beginning of the nineties.

Merk does not deal with this question. Pratt does so only indirectly. Describing books and essays by Josiah Strong, John Fiske, John W. Burgess, Alfred Thayer Mahan, and Henry Cabot Lodge that appeared after 1885, he implies that these writings had continuing and growing influence. LaFeber has at least a partial answer. According to his reconstruction, the idea of colonial expansion as a partial solution to overproduction gained ground after 1879, when European states began putting up protective tariffs, and became much more attractive when the domestic market suddenly shrank in the panic of 1893. Hofstadter responds to the question by saying, in effect, that the turn to expansionism originated in the "psychic crisis" and that, since the "psychic crisis" occurred in the 1890s, it could only have come at that time.

But the timing of American imperialism has an aspect that neither LaFeber nor Hofstadter adequately explains. Change occurred after 1898 as well as before. After annexing the Philippines and negotiating treaties for acquisition of part of Samoa and all of the Danish West Indies, McKinley stood for reelection. He won by a larger margin than in 1896, in a contest characterized by his Democratic opponent as a referendum on imperialism. After his assassination in 1901 the presidency went to Vice President Theodore Roosevelt, who had been an ardent champion of colonial expansion. Yet the United States did not continue a career as an imperial power.

Not only did the American government make no efforts after 1900 to acquire new islands in the Caribbean or Pacific, it deliberately spurned opportunities to do so. Theodore Roosevelt rebuffed Haitians and Dominicans who dropped proannexation hints, and during nearly eight years as President he acquired only one piece of real estate—the ten-mile-wide Canal Zone in Panama. Though one may cite the Platt Amendment, as applied to Cuba, the acquisition of the Canal Zone, and the Roosevelt Corollary to the Monroe Doctrine as evidence that the United States still had a mild case of imperialism, the nation's expansion as a colonial power effectively came to an end as of 1899 or 1900.

After that date, moreover, politicians reverted to the working assumption they had employed before 1898. McKinley and Roosevelt took it for granted that public opinion would not approve keeping Cuba as a colony. They judged that acquisition of a leasehold in China or annexation of Haiti, Santo Domingo, or a portion of Central America would be unpopular. And no evidence contradicted these judgments. After 1900 scarcely a congressman or newspaper editor raised his voice in favor of further colonial extension. Imperialism as a current in American public opinion appeared to be dead.

None of the theories concerning the rise of the imperialist movement satisfactorily explains its sudden demise. While Merk may be right that, over the long term, Mission had more power than Manifest Destiny, such a hypothesis does not in itself explain why, in this instance, Manifest Destiny enjoyed such short-lived ascendancy. Social Darwinism, the factor stressed by Pratt, had as much currency in 1902 as in 1898, yet seemed not to work the same effect on thought about foreign policy. LaFeber's businessmen had the same standing as before and regarded overproduction with only a little, if any, less concern. No apparent economic factor would account for their having different feelings about colonies. If a "psychic crisis" actuated imperialism, then it must have been literally a crisis, followed by quick recovery.

None of these comments depreciates the work of Merk, Pratt, LaFeber, and Hofstadter: all historians leave some questions unanswered. Nor does the present essay pretend to prove any of the four wrong. To the factors they have stressed, it adds a fifth—the impact on Americans of English and European examples. It does not, however, assert that this influence dominated. As much synthesis as reinterpretation, this study endeavors to portray the public that would have had opinion about expansion and to indicate how tradition, Social Darwinism, market hunger, psychological turmoil, *and* awareness of foreign fashions combined to cause a shift away from the anticolonial tradition at about the beginning of the 1890s, an upsurge of genuine imperialism in 1898–99, and then an abrupt return to the earlier faith. . . .

Owing to historic factors, the pretensions of its old families, and an essentially mercantile economy, Boston and its suburbs had many residents equipped by education, attainments, and connections to lead opinion on the colonial issue.

Thomas Jefferson Coolidge typified this comparatively large foreign policy elite. His autobiography and collected private papers tell us a good deal about him, and from recent historical studies by Barbara Solomon, Arthur Mann, and Geoffrey Blodgett we know that he had little to do with molding public opinion on domestic issues. He thus exemplifies the specialized opinion leader

––a prototype member of what today we call the foreign policy establishment.

Born in 1831 into a securely rich family, Coolidge took his primary and secondary schooling in England and Switzerland and then attended Harvard. Entering business, he became, by his late forties, president of the Merchants Bank of Boston and a heavy investor in railroads, serving at one time as president of the Sante Fe and, at another, as a director of the Chicago, Burlington, and Quincy. Owning land in the center of Birmingham, Alabama, he built stores that prospered from Birmingham's sudden boom. Not all his gambles succeeded. An electric-light plant in Topeka, Kansas, for example, resulted in a loss. Its optimistic manager wrote, "A coupon cutter and a Dividend payer, are the next inventions I look for in connection with this versatile agent"; but he proved unable to deliver. Nevertheless, in association with other financiers, Coolidge made many a dollar from well-timed purchases and sales of bonds, stocks, lands, and buildings.

Owning most if not all the characteristics of a robber baron, Coolidge could write the following record of a conversation with a rental agent: "He said the woman who occupies the Anderson property cannot pay rent. I directed him to turn her out and I would make the house into two tenements which could be rented." On another occasion Coolidge advised a friend not to accept a certain mortgage, cautioning, "It is very hard to collect either interest or capital from the Church without putting your hand in your pocket to help the good cause." Property in Birmingham attracted him because of "the endless supply of black labor." When profit beckoned he speculated in any commodity, including opium.

In domestic politics Coolidge also showed the temper of a robber baron. One of his letters gave marching orders for the senators and representatives from Nebraska who "are obeying the C.B.&Q." As the largest shareholder in the Amoskeag Cotton Mills, he maintained an agent in Manchester, New Hampshire, who labored to prevent "radical legislation." He himself spent time in Washington lobbying for protective duties on textiles.

Yet the press quoted him, and politicians sought his views and estimates of public feeling only on foreign policy problems, and not even on cotton tariffs. Reporters for Boston papers and for the Springfield *Republican* sought him out during a crisis with Chile of 1891–92, a crisis with Britain four years later over the Venezuela-Guiana boundary, the blowing up of the *Maine,* war with Spain, and the question of whether or not to annex the Philippines. James G. Blaine, when Secretary of State for Benjamin Harrison, expressed interest in Coolidge's views on possible complications with Germany in the Pacific. Both of Massachusetts' senators solicited his reactions to their positions on other foreign policy issues, including colonial expansion. Journalists in his home community and politicians in Washington evidently attached special weight to Coolidge's views on foreign policy.

He possessed unusually wide knowledge of the world. Fluent in French and familiar with English and European culture from his early education, he subsequently traveled much, not only in Europe but also in out-of-the-way places, such as Alexandria and Port au Prince, which most Americans discovered only as datelines on crisis reports. In 1889 he served as a delegate to the first Pan American Conference. In 1892–93 he spent a year as United States Minister to France.

Partly as a result of his travels and his diplomatic experience, Coolidge knew leading figures abroad. He could speak familiarly of such English and French statesmen as Joseph Chamberlain, Arthur Balfour, Jules Ferry, and Gabriel Hanotaux. He could name for President Harrison the men in England who would hold the keys to an international agreement on bimetallism and advise Massachusetts' Senator George F. Hoar on whether a proposed emissary would have the proper entree to this group. Interested citizens and politicians probably looked to Coolidge as an opinion leader primarily because of his firsthand knowledge of foreign places and inside knowledge of foreign politics.

Coolidge's near contemporary, William C. Endicott, possessed comparable qualifications. A noted lawyer, onetime judge and holder of large and profitable railroad investments, he had been Secretary of War during Cleveland's first administration, and his daughter had married the celebrated English politician, Joseph Chamberlain. When in England, he met the great and near great, and through his daughter and her friends received inside news of British and European political developments. Like Coolidge, Endicott could set Washington straight as to who pulled strings in London, and both politicians and newspapermen looked upon him as an authority on foreign affairs.

Richard Olney did not have quite the background of Coolidge or Endicott. Though of an old family, he came from western Massachusetts, and he had a bachelor's degree from Brown rather than Harvard. A hardworking, somewhat solitary railroad lawyer, he traveled little and gained none of Coolidge's or Endicott's firsthand knowledge of foreign statesmen. Before the 1890s he could have qualified as a leader of opinion on certain domestic issues, but hardly on foreign policy. In Cleveland's second administration, however, Olney served first as Attorney General and then, for two years, as Secretary of State. Coupled with his professional distinction, this experience caused him too to become a target of reporters' questions and of inquiring letters from politicians.

The circle of foreign policy leaders in Boston probably included also President Charles W. Eliot of Harvard. Of a high-caste family and equipped, of course, with a Harvard diploma, Eliot had lived in France and Germany and made many trips to England. He could claim friendship with Bryce and other eminent Englishmen, and he could speak with authority not only on European education but also on English government and the English colonial system. . . .

Men such as Coolidge, Endicott, and Eliot had a sense of the nation's complex traditions. Most had some acquaintance with Darwinian ideas as applied to current problems, and two, Fiske and Savage, were leading Social Darwinist writers. As capitalists or corporation lawyers, Coolidge, Endicott, Olney, and Elder watched out not only for the interests of their own companies or clients but for the general welfare of American business. And some at least participated in what Holstadter calls the "psychic crisis." In 1891, when workingmen and agrarians had only begun to agitate, Coolidge prophesied darkly, "communism will in time destroy not only the stock capital, but the bonds which are . . . the accumulation of labor." The distinction between these men and others sensitive to tradition, imbued with Darwinism, concerned about business, or irrationally anxious about the future, lay chiefly in their having special familiarity with, even inside knowledge of, European politics. . . .

By focusing on leaders of opinion we do not necessarily commit ourselves to the proposition that only an elite counted. If, however, only a relatively small public concerned itself with foreign policy issues, its members would have known the special qualifications of certain individuals, and these individuals would have functioned in some sense as opinion leaders. By examining the influences working on these leaders we can perhaps come somewhat closer to understanding why opinion within the foreign policy public changed during the 1890s. . . .

Primarily the object of this essay is to set forth a synthetic interpretation of a single episode. Trying to take account of the easily forgotten fact that public opinion is seldom if ever opinion among more than an interested minority of the electorate, it has emphasized the small group of opinion leaders that gave this minority some guidance and, perhaps more importantly, provided political leaders with evidence as to how the interested public might bend.

Though these opinion leaders seemed for an interval not to be directing or representing the public, that interval was short. Most of the time the men whom we have described as members of the foreign policy establishment served as the voices of effective opinion, and their expressed views underwent changes. Through the 1870s and 1880s they opposed America's acquiring colonies. By 1893 they had adopted a different outlook and, by and large, approved of annexing Hawaii. Only from the outbreak of the Spanish war in 1898 to some point in 1900 or 1901 did they not either concur or divide along clear lines corresponding to party lines. After 1901 they agreed once again that the United States did not need and should not want colonial possessions. . . .

International fashions in thought and events on the world scene could have had a decisive influence on men of the establishment. Not that they attached more importance to keeping step with Europeans than to preserving tradition, furthering trade, obeying scientific laws, or preventing domestic upheaval. Quite the contrary. But knowledge of foreign thought affected their ideas about America's world mission and their understanding of Social Darwinism. Observation of foreign experience suggested to them alternative methods of promoting national prosperity and dealing with social discontent. Above all, the foreign scene provided models for imitation (reference groups and reference idols, in social science jargon). The well-traveled and well-read American could select a position on the colonial issue by identifying it with, on the one hand, Bright, Gladstone, Morley, and Richter or, on the other, Rosebery, Chamberlain, Ferry, Bismarck, or Wilhelm II. Neither the American past nor an assessment of American economic needs nor Social Darwinism nor the domestic political scene offered such guidance.

Men of the establishment belonged both to their own country and to a larger Atlantic community. Ordinarily they defined opinion for an interested public, most of whom had less familiarity with currents abroad. Probably this fact explains in part why, when the establishment ceased to be coherent and leadership dispersed, apparent public opinion on colonies became so simplistic and emotional. It may also explain why, when the interested public appeared to be expanding, many politicians took an antiestablishment tack: they realized that a gulf separated the citizen of the Atlantic community from the citizen whose outlook comprehended only his county or state. Currents running within the larger community help to account for American public opinion not so much because they influenced a large number of Americans as because they influenced the few who set styles within a normally small foreign policy public.

As stated in the beginning, this essay does not dispute what other historians have said. On the contrary, it seeks to draw together previous interpretations by means of hypotheses about late nineteenth-century public opinion, its manifestations, and the play within it of tradition, economic interest, Social Darwinism, and psychological malaise, together with awareness of ideas and events abroad. I hope others will advance alternative hypotheses, for my aim is not to close debate but rather to reopen it by prompting new questions about this and other episodes. In the literal meaning of the term, this work is an essay.

---

## FURTHER READING

Howard K. Beale, *Theodore Roosevelt and the Rise of America to World Power* (1956)

Robert L. Beisner, *From the Old Diplomacy to the New* (1975)

———, *Twelve Against Empire* (1968)

Charles S. Campbell, *The Transformation of American Foreign Relations, 1865–1900* (1976)

Richard D. Challener, *Admirals, Generals, and American Foreign Policy, 1898–1914* (1973)

James A. Field, Jr., "American Imperialism," *American Historical Review*, 73 (1978), 644–668

Philip S. Foner, *The Spanish-Cuban-American War and the Birth of American Imperialism* (1972)

Willard B. Gatewood, Jr., *Black Americans and the White Man's Burden, 1898–1903* (1975)

Lewis L. Gould, *The Spanish-American War and President McKinley* (1983)

Henry F. Graff, ed., *American Imperialism and the Philippine Insurrection* (1969)

John A. S. Grenville and George B. Young, *Politics, Strategy, and American Diplomacy* (1967)

David Healy, *U. S. Expansionism* (1970)

Walter LaFeber, *The New Empire* (1963)

Margaret Leech, *In the Days of McKinley* (1959)

Gerald F. Linderman, *The Mirror of War: American Society and the Spanish-American War* (1974)

Ernest R. May, *Imperial Democracy* (1961)

Stuart C. Miller, *"Benevolent Assimilation:" The American Conquest of the Philippines, 1899–1903* (1982)

H. Wayne Morgan, *America's Road to Empire* (1965)

R. G. Neale, *Great Britain and United States Expansion, 1898–1900* (1966)

Thomas G. Paterson, ed., *American Imperialism and Anti-Imperialism* (1973)

Bradford Perkins, *The Great Rapprochement* (1968)

Julius Pratt, *Expansionists of 1898* (1936)

Hyman G. Rickover, *How the Battleship Maine Was Destroyed* (1976)

Goran Rystad, *Ambiguous Imperialism: American Foreign Policy and Domestic Politics at the Turn of the Century* (1981)

Daniel B. Schirmer, *Republic or Empire* (1972)

E. Berkeley Tompkins, *Anti-Imperialism in the United States* (1970)

David F. Trask, *The War with Spain in 1898* (1981)

Richard E. Welch, *Response to Imperialism: The United States and the Philippine-American War, 1899–1902* (1979)

William C. Widenor, *Henry Cabot Lodge and the Search for an American Foreign Policy* (1980)

M. M. Wilkinson, *Public Opinion and the Spanish-American War* (1932)

R. Hal Williams, *Years of Decision: American Politics in the 1890s* (1978)

William A. Williams, *The Roots of the Modern American Empire* (1969)

———, *The Tragedy of American Diplomacy* (1962)

# The Open Door Policy and China

# 12

*In late nineteenth-century China, when Japan and the great powers of Europe began to carve the Celestial Empire into leaseholds and spheres of influence, America's traditional trading policy of commercial equality was challenged. The imperial powers practiced discrimination in tariff rates and other fees, to the detriment of American economic interests. China was too weak to halt this assault upon its sovereignty or to insist on uniform, non-discriminatory trading behavior. The British, who heretofore had dominated Asian markets, hoped America would protest the dismemberment of China and the economic restrictions. Shortly after the Spanish-American War, Secretary of State John Hay issued two notes that became known as the "Open Door Policy." What prompted the United States to intervene verbally in the Asian tumult? British influence? American business interests? The China market? Ideals of self-determination and equal trade opportunity?*

## DOCUMENTS

In the first Hay note of September 6, 1899, the Secretary of State appealed for an end to discrimination against foreign commerce in the various Chinese spheres and leaseholds. The responses from the great powers were evasive. The second note, dated July 3, 1900, written during the Boxer Rebellion and the threat of partition by the imperial powers, argued for the preservation of Chinese independence.

# The Open Door Note, 1899

At the time when the Government of the United States was informed by that of Germany that it had leased from His Majesty the Emperor of China the port of Kiao-chao and the adjacent territory in the province of Shantung, assurances were given to the ambassador of the United States at Berlin by the Imperial German minister for foreign affairs that the rights and privileges insured by treaties with China to citizens of the United States would not thereby suffer or be in anywise impaired within the area over which Germany had thus obtained control.

More recently, however, the British Government recognized by a formal agreement with Germany the exclusive right of the latter country to enjoy in said leased area and the contiguous "sphere of influence or interest" certain privileges, more especially those relating to railroads and mining enterprises; but as the exact nature and extent of the rights thus recognized have not been clearly defined, it is possible that serious conflicts of interest may at any time arise not only between British and German subjects within said area, but that the interests of our citizens may also be jeopardized thereby.

Earnestly desirous to remove any cause of irritation and to insure at the same time to the commerce of all nations in China the undoubted benefits which should accrue from a formal recognition by the various powers claiming "spheres of interest" that they shall enjoy perfect equality of treatment for their commerce and navigation within such "spheres," the Government of the United States would be pleased to see His German Majesty's Government give formal assurances, and lend its cooperation in securing like assurances from the other interested powers, that each, within its respective sphere of whatever influence—

*First.* Will in no way interfere with any treaty port or any vested interest within any so-called "sphere of interest" or leased territory it may have in China.

*Second.* That the Chinese treaty tariff of the time being shall apply to all merchandise landed or shipped to all such ports as are within said "sphere of interest" (unless they be "free ports"), no matter to what nationality it may belong, and that duties so leviable shall be collected by the Chinese Government.

*Third.* That it will levy no higher harbor dues on vessels of another nationality frequenting any port in such "sphere" than shall be levied on vessels of its own nationality, and no higher railroad charges over lines built, controlled, or operated within its "sphere" on merchandise belonging to citizens or subjects of other nationalities transported through such "sphere" than shall be levied on similar merchandise belonging to its own nationals transported over equal distances.

The liberal policy pursued by His Imperial German Majesty in declaring Kiao-chao a free port and in aiding the Chinese Government in the establishment there of a custom-house are so clearly in line with the proposition which this Government is anxious to see recognized that it entertains the strongest hope that Germany will give its acceptance and hearty support.

The recent ukase of His Majesty the Emperor of Russia declaring the port of Ta-lien-wan open during the whole of the lease under which it is held from

China to the merchant ships of all nations, coupled with the categorical assurances made to this Government by His Imperial Majesty's representative at this capital at the time and since repeated to me by the present Russian ambassador, seem to insure the support of the Emperor to the proposed measure. Our ambassador at the Court of St. Petersburg has in consequence been instructed to submit it to the Russian Government and to request their early consideration of it. A copy of my instruction on the subject to Mr. Tower is herewith inclosed for your confidential information.

The commercial interests of Great Britain and Japan will be so clearly served by the desired declaration of intentions, and the views of the Governments of these countries as to the desirability of the adoption of measures insuring the benefits of equality of treatment of all foreign trade throughout China are so similar to those entertained by the United States, that their acceptance of the propositions herein outlined and their cooperation in advocating their adoption by the other powers can be confidently expected. I inclose herewith copy of the instruction which I have sent to Mr. Choate on the subject.

In view of the present favorable conditions, you are instructed to submit the above considerations to His Imperial German Majesty's Minister for Foreign Affairs, and to request his early consideration of the subject.

Copy of this instruction is sent to our ambassadors at London and at St. Petersburg for their information.

## Circular Note to the Great Powers, 1900

In this critical posture of affairs in China it is deemed appropriate to define the attitude of the United States as far as present circumstances permit this to be done. We adhere to the policy initiated by us in 1857, of peace with the Chinese nation, of furtherance of lawful commerce, and of protection of lives and property of our citizens by all means guaranteed under extraterritorial treaty rights and by the law of nations. If wrong be done to our citizens we propose to hold the responsible authors to the uttermost accountability. We regard the condition at Pekin as one of virtual anarchy, whereby power and responsibility are practically devolved upon the local provincial authorities. So long as they are not in overt collusion with rebellion and use their power to protect foreign life and property we regard them as representing the Chinese people, with whom we seek to remain in peace and friendship. The purpose of the President is, as it has been heretofore, to act concurrently with the other powers, first, in opening up communication with Pekin and rescuing the American officials, missionaries, and other Americans who are in danger; secondly, in affording all possible protection everywhere in China to American life and property; thirdly, in guarding and protecting all legitimate American interests; and fourthly, in aiding to prevent a spread of the disorders to the other provinces of the Empire and a recurrence of such disasters. It is, of course, too early to forecast the means of attaining this last result; but the policy of the Government of the United States is to seek a solution which may bring about permanent safety and peace to

China, preserve Chinese territorial and administrative entity, protect all rights guaranteed to friendly powers by treaty and international law, and safeguard for the world the principle of equal and impartial trade with all parts of the Chinese Empire.

## ESSAYS

The essay by A. Whitney Griswold, selected from his *The Far Eastern Policy of the United States,* emphasizes British influence on the Open Door Notes. Thomas J. McCormick of the University of Wisconsin, on the other hand, points to the self-conscious quest by American leaders for the China market. The question, as in the case of the Spanish-American War and imperialism and other issues, is whether external or internal factors were most important in stimulating Hay's notes. In the final selection, Paul A. Varg argues that the China market was a myth and that Americans evinced little concrete interest, despite their rhetoric, in China's economic fortunes.

## The Open Door Notes and British Influence

### A. WHITNEY GRISWOLD

Business and diplomacy were not the only forces impelling Hay toward his fateful decision. American missionaries in the Far East had also been thrilled by the conquest of the Philippines. In 1899 there were between one thousand and fifteen hundred of them in China where they, and their predecessors, had early assumed a political importance out of all proportion to their numbers. Now their situation was very comparable to that of American businessmen in China. Just as they were rejoicing in the annexation of the Philippines for the aid and comfort they thought it would give their cause, they found themselves confronted by an anti-foreign movement stirred up partly by the concessions-scramble, partly by their own proselytizing, that was to culminate in the Boxer Rebellion. In 1899 they, too, wished the United States to show a strong hand in China.

So far the McKinley Administration had adhered strictly to precedent in the Far East. It had kept free of alliances or understandings with foreign powers. It had called the attention of Europe to the long-established interest of the United States in the open door and the preservation of existing treaty rights. From the two particular nations that caused it most alarm it had obtained assurances. The President had declared himself satisfied with these, and proved it by rejecting Pauncefote for the second time within a year. In spite of the concessions-scramble, American trade with China, small though it was, was actually increasing. If it appeared likely to certain business groups that Russia would some day close them out of Northern China, others contemplated great profit in the sale of products to Russia in the development of that region. As yet Germany had been no less hospitable to American trade and capital in Shantung than England had been in the Yangtse Valley. American fears of exclusion, like American hopes of gain, were all in the future. Up to the summer of 1899 neither had been strong enough to cause a departure from the diplomatic traditions and precedents of the past hundred years.

Then, in July and August, through informal, personal channels, the British influence was once more turned on Hay, this time with success.

Like most Secretaries of State, John Hay had only a superficial knowledge of conditions in the Far East. To advise him on this complicated subject he had chosen a friend and, as it happened, one of the best-informed authorities on China of his generation, William W. Rockhill. Born in Philadelphia in 1854, Rockhill's early youth was spent in France, where he completed his education at the military school at Saint Cyr, and where he acquired an interest in the Chinese language and literature. After three years of service as lieutenant in the French Foreign Legion in Algeria, he returned to the United States, and in 1884 procured an appointment as Second Secretary of the Peking Legation. The next year he was promoted to First Secretary. During the winter of 1886–1887 he served as Chargé d'Affaires at Seoul, Korea. He had entered the diplomatic service as a means of pursuing his Chinese studies. He resigned because of personal incompatibility with Denby. After two famous journeys of exploration through Mongolia and Tibet (1888–1889 and 1891–1892) he returned to the diplomatic service as Chief Clerk of the State Department in 1893. From February 14, 1896, to May 10, 1897, he served as Assistant Secretary of State under Olney, during part of which period (March 4 to May 10, 1897) he filled the gap between Olney and Sherman as Acting Secretary.

By this time Rockhill's scholarly writings and explorations had brought him membership in learned Oriental societies and scientific institutes all over the world. His wide experience in the Far East and in the Department of State had established his reputation as an expert on China and earned him the friendship and admiration of influential Republicans including Roosevelt, Lodge and Hay. When it became evident that Denby was to be replaced, Rockhill's friends urged McKinley to appoint him Minister to China, a post his training pre-eminently qualified him to fill. They were disappointed. Rockhill was sent to Athens as Minister to Greece, Roumania and Servia. It was from this post that Adee and Hay rescued him in April, 1899, by helping to secure his appointment as Director of the Bureau of American Republics in Washington, presumably in order to have the benefit of his counsel on affairs in Eastern Asia. In any event, Rockhill had no sooner assumed his new office (May 22) than the Secretary of State began to solicit his advice.

Rockhill, too, had his confidential adviser in Alfred E. Hippisley, a British subject and a member of the Chinese Imperial Maritime Customs Service. Hippisley was an old China hand. It should be recalled that the Chinese customs service was administered by the British, a privilege ultimately sanctioned by treaty in 1898 for as long as England's share of China's foreign trade should exceed that of any other nation. A member of this service since 1867, Hippisley had long followed political affairs in China with a sharp, intelligent eye. His acquaintance with Rockhill dated from the autumn of 1884 when the latter first joined the staff of the American legation in Peking. "In a small community such as that of Peking," wrote Hippisley many years later, "acquaintance quickly ripens into intimacy between persons who have similar tastes, and both Rockhill and I were deeply interested in China and Chinese politics, and in my case the intimacy was made the closer by my marriage in the following year with Miss Howard, a friend of long standing of Mrs. Rockhill's, who had accompanied the latter and her husband from Baltimore." What Rockhill was to Hay, Hippisley was to Rockhill: an old friend and trusted adviser on the Far East.

Mutual friendship—and fate—drew the three men together in the early summer of 1899. Simultaneously with Rockhill's inauguration as Director General of the Bureau of American Republics, a periodic leave of absence brought Hippisley to the United States on his way home to England. From about the middle of June to the end of July the Englishman visited his wife's family in Baltimore. He was pleased to renew his acquaintance with Rockhill, whom he had not seen for over ten years. "Naturally," he remembers, "I went over as frequently as I could to Washington to discuss the conditions in China with him and especially what could be done to maintain the 'open door' or equality of opportunity for all nations in that country." On one of these occasions Rockhill, deeply impressed by his friend's ideas, introduced him to the Secretary of State. Hay heard him expound, in outline, the scheme ultimately comprehended by the open door notes.

Throughout the informal negotiations of that summer, Hippisley was clearly the prime mover. Hay, though disposed to cooperate with England, was waiting for Rockhill to find a way to do it. Rockhill, who had been absent from China for seven years, was rusty on China. Hippisley came fresh from the scene, his mind brimming with images and theories of the concessions-scramble and how to deal with it. It was he who took the initiative, who supplied the concrete plans; nor did he lack encouragement. "China is, and will remain, the one absorbing subject," Rockhill told him, "so I am awfully anxious to have all the data you can give me on the subject, that I may not make any mistake, and that my conclusions shall be practicable."

When, about August first, Hay left Washington for his summer home in New Hampshire, and Hippisley departed Baltimore on a leisurely journey, *via* Lenox and Bar Harbor to Quebec (whence he would sail for England September seventh), Hippisley opened an active correspondence with Rockhill. "As I shall not now have an opportunity of seeing you before we start for Europe," he wrote July 25, "I write these lines to ask you to use your influence towards, if possible, inducing the govt. to do what it can to maintain the open door for ordinary commerce in China." . . .

Rockhill passed Hippisley's recommendations on to Hay after adding to their weight his own authoritative *imprimatur*. The same day he replied to Hippisley:

> You know what my views are about the position the United States should take in China; I would like to see it make a declaration in some form or other, which would be understood by China as a pledge on our part to assist in maintaining the integrity of the Empire. I fear, however, that home politics and next year's elections will interfere with this, for it might be interpreted by a large part of the voting population of the United States, especially the Irish and the Germans, as an adoption of the policy advocated by England, and any leaning towards England on the part of the administration would, at this time and for the next year to come, be dangerous, and might lose the President his nomination. I consequently fear that he will do absolutely nothing either on the lines you indicate, and which are clearly those most beneficial to our interests in China, or in any other which will commit us. We will simply continue drifting along.

Hay confirmed these doubts. "I thank you for your letter inclosing Mr. Hippisley's," he wrote, August 7. "I am fully awake to the great importance of what you say, and am more than ready to act. But the senseless prejudices in certain sections of the 'Senate and people' compel us to move with great caution."

Hippisley did not give up hope. His reason for "urging *prompt* action" along the lines of his last note was, he explained, "precisely to forestall any suggestion likely to prove injurious to the Administration that it was following the lead of or leaning towards England by inducing it to take the initiative itself; then if England took similar action, she would follow America's lead." The Englishman had developed a remarkable solicitude for the welfare of the United States. "I think it would be suicidal for America to drift and do nothing for another year," he warned.

> My latest advices from Peking say: "the activity of the Russians in Manchuria is simply wonderful. . . . The Russification of Peking and of North China will proceed as rapidly as has that of Manchuria." These are precisely the districts which are the great consumers of American textile fabrics, and I don't for a moment believe that American manufacturers will sit by with folded hands and see these districts closed without making an effort to retain them. Pressure will therefore be brought to bear upon the Administration and it may then have no option but to take such action as I have suggested, with possibly however the difference of following instead of leading England.

This time Rockhill's response was more encouraging. He had received "today," he wrote on the eighteenth, "pretty clear assurances from the State Department that it may take some action sooner than could be anticipated from the position it held until within a few weeks and which I gave you in my last letter." But Rockhill was not over-sanguine. Once more he showed himself to be in advance of Hippisley: he favored securing "tangible" assurances from the powers "as to their desire to maintain and insure the integrity of the Chinese Empire. . . ." This, he still believed the Administration was unwilling to consider; the best he and Hippisley could do was to "keep pegging away at it." The next day he submitted to Adee long extracts from Hippisley's last two letters.

Meanwhile two things had come to Hippisley's support. Almost simultaneously came the news of the return to the United States of Dr. Jacob Gould

Schurman, Chairman of the President's Philippine Commission, and the Czar's ukase of August 15 declaring Talienwan a free port. All that restrained Hay from embarking on the policy advocated by Hippisley, apparently, was the opposition to it of the President himself. Whatever the true source of this opposition—respect for tradition, the lingering influence of Sherman, sincere conviction or mere partisan expediency—it had tied the Secretary's hands since his assumption of office. Undoubtedly Hay had been converted as early as June, 1898, when he had written McKinley a personal letter from the London embassy, urging him to reconsider the first Pauncefote overture. More lately he had professed to be "more than ready to act" and lamented the "senseless prejudices" that restrained him. It is probable that, for the past year, whenever the occasion had offered, he had urged on the President some such policy as that now in the making. Dr. Schurman and the Czar seem to have knocked the last props from under McKinley's resistance. . . .

The Rockhill memorandum (dated August 28, 1899) appears to have been the final instrument of McKinley's conversion. For, on September 5, Rockhill composed the actual drafts of the open door notes themselves, which, after a few corrections by Adee, were despatched the following day, over the signature of the Secretary of State, to the American ambassadors in London, Berlin and St. Petersburg. The notes, like the memoranda from which they were written, and as their authors had privately agreed, eschewed the subject of China's territorial integrity. This Rockhill felt to be "still such a complex question that I do not think we have it in anything like a shape to discuss it advantageously . . . so awfully big, that I think for the time being we had better not broach it over here." But, he believed, the notes would have the desired effect of giving China breathing space, of promoting "a general line of policy which may be favorable to the maintenance and the strengthening of the Peking Government."

The notes were carefully worded. Their authors were aware of the exigencies of American politics that restrained their own personal desires. Accordingly they recognized the spheres of influence as existing facts, omitted any reference to mining and railway concessions, and the whole perplexing problem of capital investment, and specifically asked only for equal commercial opportunity within each sphere. Each power addressed was requested to give its formal assurances that it would observe the regulations presented by the notes *mutatis mutandis*. But that is not all the notes requested. In addition to its own assurances, each power was urged to cooperate with the United States in obtaining the assurances of all the other powers concerned. Thus the notes invoked not only the time-honored American principle of the open door, but also the so-called "cooperative policy." The combination of the two, applied to the current situation in China, made the notes something more than a mere iteration of the traditional Far Eastern policy of the United States. It made them a foray into World politics, an attempt to influence the foreign policies of the European powers in such a way as to establish free commercial competition in the region of Eastern Asia. It was an unusual thing for the United States to seek to influence the dispensations of international politics in regions outside its own hemisphere. . . .

A careful perusal of the replies to the open door notes shows Rockhill's assumptions, both as to the influence of the United States in the Far East and the effectiveness of the notes themselves, to have been unfounded. The replies to the notes were uniformly evasive and non-committal. The first and most satisfactory reply was the British, but even this left much to be desired. Though Lord Salisbury professed his enthusiasm for the open door principle, he was loath to apply it either to Hongkong or to Weihaiwei, contending that the former was a colony, the latter a leased territory, and opposing the application of the principle to areas in either of these categories.

The Prime Minister's attitude was "rather disappointing in view of his first reception of your proposition," Ambassador Choate wrote Hay. Moreover, Salisbury was of the opinion that "we are a little too sanguine in our expectations of obtaining Declarations from the other Powers." Nearly three months elapsed before Salisbury was willing to compromise, which he did grudgingly. Great Britain agreed to the application of the open door principle to Weihaiwei, and to all British leased territory and spheres of interest in China, present or future, the United States acquiesced in the exemption of Kowloon [Hongkong] from this rule. The entire British declaration was then emasculated by the proviso that it was "to be considered as dependent on similar assent by the other Powers in like circumstances."

The replies of the other powers were full of loopholes, Russia's amounting to a thinly disguised rejection of the whole proposition. Each of them, like the British, made its acceptance contingent upon the acceptance of all the others, which reduced everyone to the least common denominator, the Russian. Rockhill and Hay realized the situation perfectly and tried to meet it with bluff. Rockhill privately admitted to Hippisley that the Russian reply "has what we call in America a string attached to it"; but he thought it "prudent" to accept it none the less. "Our object," Hay wrote Tower, "is now to give the widest significance to the Russian reply of which it is capable. Without running the risk of bringing upon ourselves a contradiction of our assumptions, we want to take it for granted that Russia has acceded to our proposals without much qualification." At length, on March 20, the Secretary of State cavalierly announced that he had received satisfactory assurances from all the powers addressed, and that he regarded each as "final and definitive."

Hay had not long to wait to discover just how "final and definitive" they were. In June, not three months after his expression of satisfaction, a Chinese patriotic society known to the West as the "Boxers" stirred up an armed rebellion against foreign missionaries and concession-hunters and the Manchu Government that had truckled with them. Ripping up portions of the Tientsin-Peking Railway and destroying telegraph lines, the rebels cut off Peking from the outside world, murdered the secretary of the Japanese legation, and the German minister, and besieged the foreign legations in the city. An allied military force was hastily dispatched to the relief of the legations. From June 20 until August 14, the day the siege was lifted, the foreigners in Peking lived under fire in the legation compound, menaced by starvation and disease, their fate unknown either to their governments or to the troops marching to their rescue.

It was apparent to Hay from the outset that the disorders had provided certain of the powers not unwelcome pretexts for enlarging their spheres and extending their influence in China. Russia and Germany were on the march. Hay sensed the need—or opportunity—for more extensive measures than mere participation in the allied relief expedition. "We have no policy in China except to protect with energy American interests, and especially American citizens, and the legation," he had wired Conger, June 10. "There must be nothing done which would commit us to future action inconsistent with your standing instructions. There must be no alliances." When the Boxers moved on Peking he showed his hand more fully. On July 3, with the approval of McKinley, he despatched to the powers another circular defining American policy. Unlike the notes of the previous September, this circular asked for no assurances and, indeed, elicited none; it was merely submitted to the consideration of each of the powers addressed. Taking cognizance of the "virtual anarchy" existing in China it set forth the purpose of the United States to "act concurrently with the other powers" in restoring order and protecting the lives and property of its nationals and "all legitimate American interests." In its concluding sentence, however, it added to this purpose a momentous new objective, namely, "to seek a solution which may bring about permanent safety and peace to China, *preserve Chinese territorial and administrative entity,* protect all rights guaranteed to friendly powers by treaty and international law, and safeguard for the world the principle of equal and impartial trade with all parts of the Chinese Empire."

The United States had always stood for the "territorial and administrative entity" of China but in a purely subjective way. It had observed the principle itself; it had not assumed the function of persuading others to observe it. The notes of September 6, as we have seen, had accepted the impairment of China's territorial integrity as a *fait accompli.* They had taken it for granted that foreign spheres of influence and territorial concessions in China would continue to exist, and even to expand, as is proved by the fact that the notes asked for most-favored-nation treatment for American commerce in all future as well as present spheres and leased territories. But the circumstances attending the Boxer Rebellion, following the unfavorable reception of the September notes, led Hay to the conclusion that the maintenance of the open door in China depended on the maintenance of China's complete sovereignty over her own territories. In his circular of July 3, 1900, therefore, he went further than reiterating America's traditional policy of respect for China's integrity, further than asking the powers to observe the principle of equal commercial opportunity. He suggested a collective guarantee of both these conditions. To "preserve" Chinese integrity was something different from merely respecting it. Assuming, as did Hay himself, that the chief end of America's Far Eastern policy remained commercial, the circular of July 3 and the subsequent adherence of the United States to the principles it contained, appreciably altered the means to that end. He had committed the United States to the policy of striving to deter its competitors for the Chinese market from violating the territorial and administrative integrity of the Chinese nation.

Only Great Britain made response to Hay's circular, and this in the most casual manner. The other powers proceeded with their independent plans for obtaining satisfaction from, or taking advantage of, China. Russia continued to pour troops into Manchuria. That England had no faith in the Hay policy, and had decided to rely on means other than American note-writing to defend her interests in China, seems obvious. She had never banked wholly on American co-operation in the Far East, but had used this only as one of three instruments, the other two being outright participation in the concessions-scramble, and bilateral agreements with her rivals.

Hay need not have been puzzled (as he was) by Pauncefote's uncommunicative attitude during the summer of 1900; by Salisbury's intrigues with the other powers to permit Japan to send an expeditionary force into northern China; by the Anglo-German declaration of October 16, 1900, in favor of the open door and the territorial integrity of China. What these signs indicated was that Great Britain had turned to Japan as her partner in the Far East, her ally against Russia, and had resorted to bilateral negotiations to stay the advance of Germany.

It was in this manner that the partitioning of China was halted, temporarily, in 1900. The Boer War, the German navy, the maneuverings of the hostile European coalitions, the Czar, the Kaiser, Delcassé and Salisbury—these were the factors and agents that called the halt, not the diplomacy of John Hay. It was a case of political stalemate rather than conversion to principle. No power dared move further for fear of precipitating the universal *débâcle* that was destined to come a decade later, and so China was granted a brief respite.

Experience was disillusioning to the authors of the open door notes, as it was to Roosevelt in the case of the Philippines. No sooner had the rescue of the legations been effected than McKinley began to press for the withdrawal of the American troops from China. He feared their continued residence there as a political liability at home. Rockhill, who had done so much to launch the United States on its new policy, and who, in July, 1900, was sent to China as special commissioner to investigate the rebellion and represent his country at the peace settlement, readily confessed his discouragement. So did Hippisley. The excessive indemnities demanded of China, the latter wrote, after a long silence, in March, 1901, would have to be "liquidated by territorial concessions leading to partition and so ultimately to war among the Powers.

> The soldiers have committed atrocities horrible beyond description, and the Ministers of their nationals are all engaged in looting. While [*sic*] Russia working independently on her own account places Manchuria, Mongolia, and Turkestan under a protectorate, and throws the treaty rights of other nations into the dustbin. Right and reason disappear, and we return to the ethics of the Dark Ages. To an outsider it is all very sad and shows utter demoralisation."

Rockhill replied in the same gloomy vein. He was, he said, "sick and tired of the whole business and heartily glad to get away from it.

> I have been able to do something for commercial interests, and in a number of points have been able to carry out the Secretary's views, but have been practically alone in the negotiations. England has her agreement with Germany, Russia has her alliance with France, the Triple Alliance comes in here, and

every other combination you know of is working here just as it is in Europe. I trust it may be a long time before the United States gets into another muddle of this description."

Hay's disillusionment, though less outspoken, was if anything more complete. For in November, 1900, under pressure from the War and Navy Departments, he executed the surprising *volte face* of instructing Conger to endeavor to obtain for the United States a naval base and territorial concession at Samsah Bay in the Chinese maritime province of Fukien. The erstwhile champion of Chinese integrity, still outwardly loyal to the policy of his notes, had actually forsaken that policy and tried to enter the concessions-scramble. As it happened Fukien had already been pre-empted as a sphere of influence by Japan, whose treaty right in the province would be infringed by the American venture. Japan had to be consulted. It must have been embarrassing for Hay to read the Japanese reply, reminding him of his own admonitions against using the Boxer Rebellion as the opportunity for territorial aggrandizement, and reaffirming the Imperial Government's adherence to that principle.

Thereafter the Secretary of State trimmed the sails of his Far Eastern policy ever more closely to the wind. As Russia strengthened her hold on Manchuria, he gradually retreated to the position of his first open door notes, accepting the fact that Manchuria was no longer an integral part of the Chinese Empire, but rather a Russian province, in which open door treatment was to be bargained for with the Czar. "I take it for granted," he told Roosevelt in April, 1903, "that Russia knows as we do that we will not fight over Manchuria, for the simple reason that we cannot. . . . If our rights and interests in opposition to Russia in the Far East were as clear as noonday, we could never get a treaty through the Senate, the object of which was to check Russian aggression." To all intents and purposes Hay had abandoned the doctrine of the territorial integrity of China, at least to the extent of recognizing Manchuria as beyond the Chinese pale.

What, then, had the open door notes accomplished? They had not invented, or even promoted, a "co-operative" policy. There never had been a co-operative policy in Eastern Asia that rose above joint military expeditions, such as the Shimonoseki and Boxer, or identic notes of protest at anti-foreign riots. Only in common defense of their nationals did the powers stand together. As for co-operating among themselves, in the interest of collective security, fair play, free competition, equal opportunity, there was none of that; there never had been any. Japanese, Russian, British, German, French and American soldiers could all march together to Peking. But once the siege was raised and the diplomats had taken charge, every semblance of co-operation vanished.

It has been suggested that the Hay notes were part of a diplomatic trade by which the United States gained supremacy in the Caribbean, in return for co-operating with England in the Far East. But, in spite of intensive search, no evidence has been discovered that would remove the idea from the realm of conjecture. Chronology alone makes it plausible. By the Hay-Pauncefote Treaty of 1900 the United States gained from England the right to construct and maintain a canal across the Isthmus of Panama. At approximately the same time, America came to England's assistance in China. History abounds, however, with examples of the *post hoc* fallacy. Rockhill and Hippisley, at pains to exhaust every possible argument that might further their designs, never mentioned the connection between the Caribbean and the Far East, which Hippisley has since called "the product of lively but ill-balanced imagination."

England was scarcely in a position to exact any such price as that supposed to have been paid by Hay for her strategic retreat from the Caribbean. The Boer War, the growing power of the United States, not to recapitulate more of the many international factors already reviewed, were sufficient to account for that. Months before the open door notes were written, Salisbury had informed Hay (through Henry White) in so many words that he realized the United States would build the canal, that he approved, and that "the canal is of comparatively little importance to England now that they have the Suez Canal. . . ." Pauncefote and Salisbury did not receive the open door notes or the circular on China's territorial integrity as if they were collecting payment for value received.

Hay's claim that he had "accomplished a good deal in the East, but thus far without the expense of a single commitment or promise" is no less difficult to validate. Hay was technically correct: nothing had been "put in writing." Legally the United States was no more bound to pursue the policy of the notes than the powers which had, in varying degrees, evaded their demands. It was the style of the notes, the fact that they were promulgated in a manner deliberately contrived to mobilize public opinion and create the impression of an international commitment, and most important of all, the way Hay's successors practiced what he preached that molded American policy. It may be conceded that the Secretaries of State who followed John Hay did not adhere to the principles of the open door and the preservation of China's territorial integrity solely because he had done so, and at the same time, that tradition and precedent exert a powerful influence on foreign policy.

One thing is clear: Hay had not secured anything approaching an international guarantee of the open door or the "territorial and administrative entity" of China. He had merely oriented American policy toward a more active participation in Far Eastern politics in support of those principles. In so doing he had kept pace with the expansionist forces (of which he was as much product as cause) that had propelled the United States into the conquest and annexation of the Philippines.

# The China Market

### THOMAS J. MCCORMICK

One year after the armistice with Spain, America sent forth into the world the then-famous, now-denigrated Open Door Notes. In and of themselves, they established no new policy lines. Both Cleveland's response to the Sino-Japanese

War and McKinley's stance during peace talks with Spain make it abundantly clear that the open door in China was already cardinal American policy long before the 1899 notes appeared.

But the promulgation of the Hay Doctrine did pass the sceptre of open door champion from Great Britain to the United States. For a half-century the British had successfully used an open door policy to create and sustain their economic (and diplomatic) supremacy in the Chinese Empire; the Americans, as "hitchhiking imperialists," gathered the commercial leavings. Now, as Britain's power wavered—and with it her commitment to the open door, the United States made a concerted effort to adapt the nineteenth-century policy to the expansive needs of a twentieth-century industrial America.

This dramatic departure and its timing have long been the source of interpretive controversy. For example, George F. Kennan, in a capsule version of A. Whitney Griswold's work, has viewed the Open Door Notes as a rather haphazard product, sold by an English member of the Chinese Customs Service indirectly to a somewhat disinterested and quickly disillusioned Secretary of State. On the other hand, Charles S. Campbell, Jr., has stressed the midwife role played by special business interests in bringing the policy to life. Yet each analysis, in its own way, has trivialized an event of enormous importance. The first grossly overestimates the influence of a quite peripheral figure, whose ideas were wholly unoriginal (and well known to every journeyman diplomat) and whose efforts in no way affected the timing of the Open Door Notes. The other bases its provocative interpretation upon a too narrow segment of the national community. Both inadequately appreciate that the Open Door Policy accurately reflected the widely shared assumptions and analyses of most social elements in America (including many without special vested interests); that both individual and group pressures were at best minor catalytic factors. Both, by focusing on the particular, miss the really substantive thing about the Open Door Policy—that it represented America's basic response to the methodological question of how to expand. Instead of closed doors, open markets; instead of political dominion, economic hegemony; instead of large-scale colonialism, informal empire. In short, a most interesting hybrid of anti-colonialism and economic imperialism.

On October 19, 1898, President McKinley told a Citizens' Banquet of Chicago that "territorial expansion is not alone and always necessary to national advancement" and the "broadening of trade." Before another year had passed, his State Department was feverishly at work trying to transform this unilateral sentiment into a universally accepted tenet—at least so far as the Chinese Empire was concerned. Behind this belated effort to make the open door a multilateral vehicle were two seemingly contradictory factors: a sense of power and a sense of impotence.

Latter-day critics of the Open Door Policy have managed to evade one central truth—that the policy was one of strength as well as weakness. A less confident nation might easily have joined in the partitioning scramble in China, content to have an assured but fragmentary slice of the market. But America wanted more, much more than that, and was certain of her ability to get it.

When Brooks Adams wrote in 1899 that "East Asia is the prize for which all the energetic nations are grasping," few of his readers doubted who would win that prize. When William McKinley told Congress in that same year that "the rule of the survival of the fittest must be . . . inexorable" in the "rivalry" for "mastery in commerce," most of his listeners were doubtless sure who would be the fittest. In each instance, the certitude grew from that sense of American economic supremacy born in the export revival of 1897, nourished by the retooling and refinancing of American industry, and confirmed by the return of full prosperity. Viewed from this vantage, the open door became appropriate means for the most advanced and competitive industrial nation to grab the lion's share of the China market instead of settling for a pittance. No one saw this more clearly or said it more forcefully than the influential *Bankers' Magazine,* when it exclaimed that "without wars and without military aggression that nation will secure the widest and best markets which can offer the cheapest and best goods." "If China was open to trade with all the world . . . the United States and England need not be afraid of any competitors. But Russia, Germany and France . . . are more or less at a disadvantage when they meet either English or American goods. They therefore do not take the philosophical view at all."

The analysis was hardly an isolated one. In the private sector, for example, the Riverside, New York, Republican Club assured Secretary Hay that "the Chinese market . . . rightfully belongs to us and that in free and untrammeled competition we can win it." Old war-horse Joseph C. Wheeler, musing on his belief that "eight thousand miles of ocean could not stay the destinies of mankind," prophesied to President McKinley that the ultimate volume of American exports to China would reach $5.4 billion a year. The International Commercial Congress (an *ad hoc* meeting of Eastern manufacturers and merchants) wrote Far Eastern expert W. W. Rockhill that "no other market in the world [i.e., China] offers such vast and varied opportunities for the further increase of American exports." The NAM's journal, *American Trade,* reported authoritatively that "millions after millions are being invested in Southern mill property, solely in the faith of a continuation of trade . . . in the Chinese empire." Later *The Nation* nicely summarized general sentiments by predicting that "An open door and no favor infallibly means . . . the greater share and gain in the commercial exploitation of China."

Likewise, public officials expressed optimism about America's open door penetration of the China market. Cushman K. Davis, chairman of the Senate Foreign Relations Committee, proclaimed that our position in the orient was now such "that we can commercially [do] what we please" and predicted that the China trade "would put 18 millions of people on the Pacific coast within not many years and give its cities a preponderance like that of Tyron." Charles E. Smith, Secretary of Agriculture and informal adviser on foreign affairs, reported his impression that "the people of the West regard the Pacific as an American lake which should be covered with ships carrying the American flag" and added that "I don't know but they are about right." Administration trade expert Worthington C. Ford noted (with some reservations) that "the commercial future" of the China trade "is wonderful to think of"—a view based on an independent analysis that China could both double its population and living standards, "and this without any revolutionary change." Finally, even the cautious John Hay, in a public letter that coincided with the dispatch of the Open Door Notes, exclaimed that "in the field of trade and commerce we shall be the keen competitors of the richest and greatest powers, and they need no warning to be assured that in that struggle, we shall bring the sweat to their brows."

In view of subsequent developments, such glowing optimism about the future of the China trade appears naive, misguided, and grotesquely overdrawn— much flap about nothing. But the *potential* for trade expansion was real, and it remained so (enough to exercise vast impact upon American policy-makers for the four decades that preceded Pearl Harbor). In 1899 there were signs— however small—that the penetration of the China market was already underway. For one thing, in the relative sense, manufactured products began to account for more than 90 per cent of American exports to China—a fact of some significance to those preoccupied with *industrial* overproduction. (By 1906, 96 per cent of all United States exports to China were finished products, as compared to 27 per cent for Europe.) The absolute volume of manufactured exports also experienced a sharp rise (albeit from a small base), multiplying four times between 1895 and 1899, from \$3.2 million to \$13.1 million. (Seven years later, despite a Chinese boycott and persistent obstacles from both Russia and Japan, the total had reached nearly \$42 million.) Particularly blessed were the iron and steel industry and cotton textile enterprises, both key elements in the American economy. The latter's exports to China, for example, grew from less than \$2 million in 1895 to almost \$10 million in 1899 (and reached \$30 million by the Panic of 1907, accounting for 56.5 per cent of all American cotton textile exports). The figures lent an air of credence to one southern group's assessment that "[the China trade] is everything." All these facts were, to be sure, small straws in the wind and easily written off in retrospect. But in the expansionist psychology of the 1890's they were eagerly seized upon to bolster the widespread expectation that given equal, open door access, the United States could and would win economic dominion in China.

If American commercial ascendancy made the Open Door Policy a fruitful one, American weaknesses made it nearly unavoidable.

Political power was the prime deficiency. The Far East was no Latin America, where, after 1895, American hegemony was seldom challenged and usually acknowledged. In China the United States faced all the handicaps of the latecomer to a game already in play with a full lineup of great powers. America did have the capacity to play a significant role in Chinese affairs, and its words and acts now carried substantially more weight, thanks to the Spanish-American War. As the American Ambassador to France reported to McKinley: "we did in three months what the great powers of Europe had sought in vain to do for over a hundred years . . ." and "the most experienced statesmen here envy our transcendent achievements and see clearly the future benefits." Still, heightened power and all, the United States was in no position to issue any Olney Corollaries for the Chinese Empire; to make American word fiat; to manipulate with relative impunity and success. Here more subtle methods would be demanded.

The instances are many (and well known) of America's inability to control events in the western Pacific. Significantly, these failures came despite "the President's most serious consideration" of Chinese instability; despite Secretary Hay's "serious attention" to the famous petition of cotton textile spokesmen, exhorting that something be done to keep the door open in northern China; despite Hay's assurances to Paul Dana of the *New York Sun* that "we are keenly alive to the importance of safeguarding our great commercial interests in that Empire." For all this accumulated anxiety, America's newly won status in the Pacific could not prevent Germany's acquisition of Spain's old insular empire in Micronesia. It could not prevent Japan from occupying Marcus Island (a cable point upon which the American Navy had tentative designs) or from establishing an extraterritorial settlement in Amoy (important for its geographic relationship to Manila). It could do little to stop Russia's apparent drift toward trade discrimination in Manchuria. It could do nothing, one way or another, about the rumored impending war between Russia and Japan. Finally, it could not block Italy's far-reaching demands for a sphere of influence in San Mun Bay and Che-Kiang province—demands that ominously had the support of Great Britain; that threatened to set off another whole round of partitioning in China; that led the *New York Times* to conclude that the disintegration of China (and the open door) was "inevitable," and the *Chicago Inter-Ocean* to guess that "the end may be at hand." All the administration did was to watch, wait, and hope—a policy (better, a stance) that offered little hope for the future.

Financial weakness, another marked American liability, was in part an extension of political weakness. Simply put, American commercial expansion could not encompass financial expansion. In the realm of investments (chiefly railroads and mines) no open door existed, and no American syndicate seemed likely to compete on equitable grounds with its European peers. None of this was exactly new, of course; the move toward a "modified" open door (one that concerned only commerce, not investment) had begun in 1895 and, as already noted, accelerated sharply in 1898. But it did not reach its climax until the Anglo-Russian agreement of April 1899. In effect, Great Britain promised not to compete for railroad concessions north of the Great Wall, while Russia made a similar pledge for the Yangtze basin. All that remained between them for open competition was a buffer zone between the Russian and British spheres— and much of this was already covered by the earlier Anglo-German agreement.

This tightly constricted area of activity left American investors with little more than hope of a junior partnership with the British. This would be by no means inconsequential, and in early 1899 there was some optimism along these general lines. On February 1 the American China Development Company and the British and Chinese Corporation agreed on paper to share in each other's future concessions. One day later the *New York Times* reported that yet another British syndicate had agreed to give American capital a one-quarter share of investments in the railroads and mines of Szechwan province. But in fact British support was seldom vigorous, and American financiers fared poorly in competition with their politically and financially subsidized opponents. A prime example was the glaring failure of the American China Development Company to secure the Hankow-Canton concession, despite initially high hopes. The syndicate's inability to meet the rigorous Chinese terms was probably the major reason for the contract loss, but the company, in its frustration, blamed it on inadequate governmental support. In the end the concession "went that-away" while the State Department and the company engaged in futile backbiting as to why. Overall the episode was more souring than cathartic and played no small role in the administration's later attitude toward American investment in China.

A realistic foreign policy is an exact blend of means and ends—it knows what is vital to the national interest, whether that interest can be fulfilled within the framework of national power and ideology, and precisely how. By 1899 the makers of American foreign policy had long since defined marketplace expansion into China as an important element in their variegated effort to stabilize the political economy. But they had to adopt means that would make the best use of American commercial power while minimizing American liabilities: a still inadequate power base and financial frailty.

There were only three viable choices, and the McKinley administration considered them all. One obvious alternative was to accept the disintegration of China as inevitable (even beneficial) and join in the partitioning. In 1899 there were repeated rumors that the United States would take precisely this course. The *New York Times,* during the San Mun Bay crisis, reported that the administration had already determined to have Pechihli province for an American sphere, while at the same time the actions of the American Consul in Amoy seemed designed to convert that port and its environs into an American entrepôt. But the rumors were untrue and the American Consul's efforts repudiated, and both for the same reason: the administration felt that partitioning was an ineffectual vehicle for American trade expansion. For one thing, it would intensify anti-imperialist criticism while adding bureaucratic and military burdens that McKinley wished to avoid (a view shared with his anti-imperialist critics). For another, American sales and arteries of distribution were largely centered in zones controlled by Russia and Germany, and to relocate these in an American sphere would be expensive and time consuming— far better to keep open existing channels if possible. And finally, to re-emphasize an earlier point, a small slice of the pie (which is all partitioning could offer) held little attraction for men who wanted (and thought they could get) the major share of the market.

The second policy possibility was to make common cause with other open door supporters, presumably England and Japan, and use force if necessary to keep trade entrées open. This was the method that Theodore Roosevelt later tried informally, and it did have the merit of reflecting one vital truth—that in the last analysis only force could make the open door work. But this technique also raised basic objections which ultimately made it an impractical choice for the administration. To begin with, no military alliance (especially one with the English) was likely to enhance the political popularity of the McKinley administration. Moreover, such a formal commitment would deprive the United States of complete freedom of action, and the President (far more than his Anglophile Secretary of State) disliked tying American national interests too rigidly to the foreign policies of countries whose own shifting interests might not always coincide with those of the United States. He already had sufficient evidence (and more was to come) of British and Japanese ambivalence toward the Open Door Policy—enough to make them seem somewhat uncertain allies. Finally, any policy predicated upon the *possible* use of force might eventually require its *actual* use, and the use of force in China (save against Chinese themselves) was considered out of the question. A Far Eastern war would be an unpopular war; it might lead to the very consequence one wished to avoid—the fragmentation of China; and it might ignite the general world holocaust that all the great powers feared at the turn of the century. No, this would not do. What the United States wanted was not force but coexistence and economic competition for open markets; an "eat-your-cake-and-have-it-too" policy of peace and market domination. That America could not have both was, again, the certain fallacy of informal marketplace expansionism and the insoluble dilemma that American policy-makers vainly struggled with for the first half of the twentieth century.

There was of course some informal tripartite consultation and cooperation, and some public figures (generally outside the government) did refer to an "open door entente" of Great Britain, Japan, and the United States. But such collusion never aimed at the use of force, and moreover it was generally an on-again-off-again sort of thing, a tactical strategem employed when it was advantageous to American interests and ignored when it was not—which was frequently.

The third policy alternative—and the one embodied in the Open Door Notes—was to gain common agreement among a concert of powers that China would be exempted from imperial competition. This course obviously begged the whole question of force and has been rightly criticized on that ground. But, on the other hand, it was hardly the legalistic-moralistic anachronism that some have made it seem. On the contrary, as we shall see, it tried to make use of two very real and interrelated factors: (1) the *de facto* balance of power that existed between the Russo-French entente and the emerging Anglo-Japanese bloc; and (2) the intense fear of possible world war that preoccupied the foreign offices of Europe. In this framework of balance and fear, the policies of each power were likely to be flexible and even a bit tentative, for rigidity could be disastrous. (Certainly British action was chameleonic, and students of Russian policy in the Far East at the turn of the century find it so baffling and contradictory that there is doubt one existed.) Furthermore, any changes in the status quo were likely to be cautious ones, undertaken on a quid pro quo basis, lest imbalance lead to conflict. Under these circumstances, if a third force dramatically insisted that the status quo (the open door and Chinese sovereignty) be universally accepted, and if that force had the capacity to upset the delicate equilibrium of power (as the United States certainly had in Europe's eyes after 1898), then there was a good chance the powers would acquiesce. The agreement might be more rhetorical than real, but it would (and did) offer useful leverage in exploiting Europe's fears and occasionally manipulating the scale of power.

These were the realities that produced the Open Door Notes. Neither partitioning nor military alliance offered practical means to realize the desired American ends; only the consensus neutralization held any glimmer of hope. That such hope was illusory, that indeed it *had* to be illusory, is worth analyzing later at length. But for the moment it ought to be emphasized that, given America's commitment to economic penetration in China, given the peculiar combination of American strengths and weaknesses, the Open Door Policy was the most *realistic* one at hand.

# The Myth of the China Market

### PAUL A. VARG

The thrust into Asia owed much to that segment of the business community interested in the China market and to the publicists who linked prosperity with sales to China's four hundred million customers. The ardent proponents talked about the future rather than the present. Exports to China had increased sufficiently to provide a basis for their argument and those who wrote about the future never failed to cite statistics that supported their cause. Exports of cotton goods had increased dramatically, and most of these went to North China and southern Manchuria, the area threatened by Russian expansion. But there, sales, never more than a miniscule portion of total American exports, became the indices for measuring the potential of the China market for manufactured goods.

From the middle of the 1890's to 1906, exports to China showed only a modest rate of growth but were sufficient to maintain faith in the earlier predictions. No one challenged this optimistic view. However, from 1906 to the Chinese Revolution of 1911, when annual export figures moved both up and down, there were some second thoughts. Declines were readily explained as caused by temporary phenomena. In 1906, the unsettling effects of the Russo-Japanese War and the piling up of supplies in warehouses during the hostilities received much attention. In the next few years, the difficulties were explained as due to the instability of the Chinese currency. Both, unquestionably, did hamper trade but conditions in China of a more permanent character were of greater importance.

In this period, too, it became apparent that there was reason to question the generally accepted assumption that the nations establishing leaseholds and spheres of influence would utilize them to favor their own exporters. Therefore, these should be opposed as hostile to the commercial interests of the

Paul A. Varg, *The Making of a Myth: The United States and China, 1897–1912* (East Lansing, Mich.: Michigan State University Press, 1968), pp. 36–40, 40–42, 43–47, 48–52, 53.

United States. Other Governments did favor their own nationals, but in some cases, American sales increased within the spheres of influence due to the economic development fostered by the controlling nation. Sales of railroad equipment to Japan's South Manchuria Railway offered the best illustration.

The facts notwithstanding, the prospect of a large market for manufactured goods lost but little of its luster prior to the Chinese Revolution. This continued to serve as one of the major reasons for the United States to make its influence felt in Chinese affairs. But there is also cause for reflection as to the real meaning of the repeated reliance of the Department of State on the commercial argument whenever it confronted a development in the China crucible that it found objectionable. It was undoubtedly convenient to object to a particular move on the part of other nations on the ground that it would violate the rights of American business to an equality of commercial opportunity, but the argument served more than business interests. It provided a suitable basis for those responsible for the conduct of foreign relations to assert an interest and to convey to other Powers that the United States was an interested party. Not until 1909, when Philander Knox became Secretary of State, did the United States make a determined effort to initiate arrangements which would enlarge the prospects of American business. Even then, the political aim seems to have been as important as the commercial. However, these reflections pertain only to the thinking of statesmen. A segment of the business community entertained the prospect of a growing market in China and it was interested in business, not the political future of East Asia.

The most elementary facts contradicted the dream that China would, before long, provide a large market. The first of these was that only a small part of China, the coastal cities and a few ports on the rivers, was open to trade. In 1899, Rounseville Wildman, the U.S. Consul-General in Hongkong, wrote:

> Another great point that American exporters overlook is that 99 percent of China is still closed to the world. When the magazine writer refers in glowing terms to the 400,000,000 inhabitants of China, he forgets that 350,000,000 are a dead letter so far as commerce is concerned.

Burlingame Johnson, the Consul in Amoy, in 1901, called for treaty revisions which would permit businessmen to reside in the interior. Such action, he believed, would open the markets as far away "as 150 to 200 miles . . . whereas now even kerosene and flour seldom get further than fifty miles from open ports and few other goods that far."

The lack of a transportation system restricted the influx of western goods. Except for river traffic, transport was almost nonexistent. The Grand Canal, which, in the time of Marco Polo, carried large vessels over a six hundred and fifty mile stretch between Peking and Hangchow, was in disrepair and small junks now navigated it with difficulty. Of the roads, the U.S. Consul in Shanghai in 1895 reported:

> Their condition is such that passage over them is virtually stopped as the holes and ruts that deface them force travelers to desert them for the tracks by the

sides, although these in wet weather are but quagmires, and in dry weather, several inches in dust.

A survey of the roads in 1890 by the China branch of the Royal Asiatic Society led to this conclusion:

> Probably no country in the world, certainly none aiming at civilization even of the most rudimentary nature, has paid so little attention to roads and means of communication as had the Chinese empire; and it may be remarked at the outset that no road in the European acceptance of the term, as an artificially constructed viaduct, laid out with engineering skill even of the crudest description, exists from one end of China to the other.

Given these conditions, only a small part of the country was accessible to foreign goods.

Another formidable barrier stood in the way. Western goods fitted neither ancient Chinese preferences nor Chinese pocketbooks. Flour, cotton goods, kerosene and lumber jibed with the native consumer habits and did find a growing market, but the great variety of western goods ran counter to long-established ways of work and customs. In 1906, James L. Rodgers, the Consul-General in Shanghai, wrote: "It is perhaps needless to call attention to the antiquity of Chinese methods and habits, to the fact that traders have for centuries been trying to introduce new things, and that beyond some modern devices for using and making the necessities of life, one sees very few inroads upon established customs." Rodgers stated that the Chinese did buy foreign oil, flour, leather, lamps, clocks and some food stuffs, but, he warned, "it does not follow that there is a market for a foreign shoe, for an agricultural implement, for machinery of various kinds and for the infinite variety of manufactured goods which distinguish the industry of the United States, Great Britain, and Germany." A certain Occidental, Rodgers reported, had written home that there was a great market for windmills. Such an opinion ignored the fact that the Chinese had been raising water from one level to another by means of pumps and water wheels long before the Christian era began and they were not likely to change their methods. Even more important than the reluctance to change, he declared, was the fact that "a windmill would cost many rice crops, or perhaps the savings of a lifetime. . . ."

Rodgers, after an examination of the markets in the Chinese cities near Shanghai, noted that there were few foreign products and "you will hunt for a day before you will find in this section of China an agricultural implement of foreign make." He concluded: "Numberless instances might be cited to show how limited a Chinese market is for things which encroach upon their customs or which will supplant the articles handed down from generation to generation. . . ." In conclusion, he offered these words: "And all this is written not to discourage but to place that which is conceived to be plain truth before the minds of those who nowadays read in the newspapers glowing prophecies about the oriental trade, who then remember that there are said to be four hundred million Chinese and who are straightway moved to attempt an export business to China. . . ." Given the "present scheme of civilization" whereby the Chinese "are practically sufficient unto themselves," he warned, "China, even under the reformation now beginning, will take at first only in a small way of those things she does not seem to need. . . ."

The poverty of the Chinese constituted a further obstacle. When the Department of State, in 1898, instructed Consuls throughout the world to report on the possible outlets for the surplus products of soap manufacturers, E. T. Williams, then Vice-Consul-General in Shanghai, wrote:

> The people of China are extremely poor. Their wages are paid in copper cash, one of which equals one-twentieth of a cent. One hundred to one hundred and fifty of these cash, that is, from five to seven and a half cents, form the average daily wage of the ordinary working man. It is evident that such an article as soap, which from the Chinese point of view, is an article of luxury rather than necessity, however, much desired, can be purchased only when furnished at a very low price. . . .

Another deterrent to a market for American goods was the rapid development after 1894 of an unfavorable trade balance. Exports to China did increase but exports from China did not. A study of China's long-term trade developments made by the Imperial Maritime Customs Service in 1904 showed that China's imports had increased until they were a third greater than exports. Indemnities incurred as a result of the war with Japan and the Boxer Revolt had necessitated foreign loans thereby increasing the outflow of gold. These foreign loans, in 1904, called for payments upwards of forty-five million haikwan taels a year.

Within this market, so circumscribed by inaccessibility to the interior, by aversion to western style products, by poverty, and by an unfavorable balance of international payments, a dog-eat-dog fight for sales and contracts raged. Germany, Great Britain, France, Russia, and Japan were more dependent upon foreign markets than the United States; the Governments of these nations gave their business enterprises greater support than did the United States, and, most important, the business enterprises of these countries demonstrated greater energy and initiative in China. Consequently, American companies found the going rough.

The Standard Oil Company, oriented to foreign markets by long experience and by the fact that since the 1860's more than half of its major product, kerosene, was exported, eyed the Far East. As early as 1882, the company sent William Herbert Libby to explore possible markets in that part of the world. He made a careful study of the China situation and more particularly of the barriers to greater sales of kerosene. Beginning in 1890, Standard Oil, anxious to expand sales, departed from the practice of selling to merchants on the Atlantic Seaboard who then handled sales in China. Under the new system, it distributed its products through its British affiliate, the Anglo-American Oil Company. In the next two decades, sales increased but Standard Oil's hopes of dominating the market never came even close to realization. Russian oil enjoyed the advantages of lower production costs, shorter transportation routes, and benefited by the tariffs levied on value as opposed to volume. The competition of the Dutch operating out of the East Indies also cut seriously into Standard Oil's sales in China. Standard Oil, more than any other American company, adopted a system of distribution and sales that was efficient and well suited to success in China, but although sales became important, the competition of the Russians and the Dutch was so effective that, in the words of the historians of the company, its "efforts in the Far East proved relatively ineffectual."

These barriers to trade, although not readily surmountable, sometimes appeared minor in comparison to inveterate Chinese hostility toward the foreigner. Indeed, the one characteristic quality of the Chinese in relations with the outside world—whether political, economic, or religious—was an intractable opposition. The missionaries, more often exposed to antagonism because their efforts touched upon matters subject to deep emotional response and because they were often in the interior, were the most frequent targets of antiforeign disturbances. Business and government representatives enjoyed the protection of treaty ports, but they could not be protected from the Chinese aversion to them that found expression in delayed negotiations, the placing of obstacles in the way of land purchases, and the playing of one foreigner against another. . . .

Turning our attention to a second major aspect of the problem, the willingness of the Government in Washington to lend assistance to American business, we find that the support was usually little more than an expression of goodwill. Beginning in the late 1880's, the Department of Commerce and the Department of State were vigorous in asking their officers for reports on commercial opportunities for many different types of manufactured goods. Bulletins including the reports were issued in great numbers.

Both Denby and Conger believed that the investment of American capital would spur the sale of American goods and they therefore supported their fellow countrymen when they presented proposals. In April, 1898, Denby reported to Secretary of State Sherman that he had "devoted a great deal of time and labor to the promotion of railroad projects" presented by his countrymen. His successor, E. H. Conger, later in the same year wrote: "So long as I am at this legation, its aid will be cheerfully and actively given along these lines so far as is wise and proper; but experience has long since proven that neither legislation nor official aid can take the place of business enterprise in business affairs." It was also true "that one of the chief elements of foreign potency, is the leverage obtained from actual occupation or ownership of territory." This was Conger's observation in August of 1898. During the next few years, the reverse was also true on occasion. Americans received some advantage because their schemes were considered to be free of political ambitions. In the period 1894 to 1906, Washington, through its representative in Peking, struck the boldest pose at the time that the Chinese Government cancelled the contract of the American China Development Company for building the railroad from Hankow to Canton. The cancellation led to sharp diplomatic notes and the Minister, W. W. Rockhill, questioned the chief of China's Foreign Office in a most peremptory tone.

However, the promotion of economic interests was generally the function of the Consular Service rather than the Legation in Peking. If the degree of government support of the Consular Service is a fair measure of how seriously Washington took the promotion of interests in China, the conclusion can only be that interest approximated apathy. For years, the Consul-General in Shanghai protested that the American consular offices in that city were not only inadequate but reflected unfavorably upon the United States. As late as 1905, Consul-General Rodgers declared that they were the poorest of any foreign nation except Portugal. The inadequacy of consular offices had its parallel in a very small staff. Rodgers compared the failure to provide an adequate group of American officers with the elaborate efforts of Great Britain, Germany, France and Japan. In September, 1905, he reported:

> They know for instance that Great Britain has a force of Englishmen in the various departments of its representation; that Germany has not only a large number here, but also has men traveling on trade matters; that France is likewise provided and that Japan is represented elsewhere. They know that absolute count will show that in Shanghai where the United States has one employee, Great Britain and Germany have six, France about four and Japan counting only those in evidence, three.

All of the districts found reason to complain but no one demonstrated greater impatience than Edward Bedloe who was appointed Consul in Canton in the latter part of 1897. On arrival, he found the offices so inadequately furnished that he carried on business from his hotel room. When facing the necessity of giving a reception in the offices for Chinese officials and other Consuls, he borrowed furnishings from several friendly parties.

The importance of the Canton district seemed to justify better quarters and a more adequate staff. Eighty million people lived in the area. Some seven cities had been made into treaty ports in 1897 and both the British and Germans had an official at each. Consul Bedloe was the only officer representing the United States. When he first took over, he had no Vice-Consul or clerk. During his first several months he employed a clerk and paid him out of his own pocket. A Vice-Consul was appointed late in 1898 after a missionary group petitioned the Department of State. The inadequacy of staff, particularly the absence of Consuls in the interior, meant there was no official to protest against a variety of types of interference with shipments of American goods or to promote American commercial interests.

The U.S. Consulate in Amoy typified the general neglect and apathy. In the early 1890's Edward Bedloe, previous to his transfer to Canton, occupied the office. A German resident served for several months after Bedloe was transferred. Then Delaware Kemper took over. In June, 1897, Burlingame Johnson, an energetic young man from Colorado, replaced Kemper. Johnson immediately reported to the Department of State "that the condition in which the work of the office has been found is very unsatisfactory." The "property," he declared, "is in a most dilapidated condition." He added: "The verandas are falling, posts have rotted off, plastings (sic!) falling, and the roof needs thorough repairs." An official reading the letter noted: "He may have the flagstaff painted at once." Within a year seventeen hundred dollars were spent on renovations.

The work of the Amoy Consulate harmonized with the dismal surroundings. Burlingame Johnson informed the Department of State: "Notwithstanding this I find that absolutely no attention was given to the opening for American products by my predecessor and that for three years there has not been a single trade report to the Department calling attention of exporters to existing conditions." Johnson's initial enthusiasm found expression in a detailed report on missionary work, praising its philanthropic aspects and as an activity that opened the door to commerce, but his efforts in behalf of trade do not appear to have measured up to his own high hopes.

In April, 1906, the Consul in Hankow, William Martin, complained "that all the force in this office at present, capable of doing clerical work, consists of Mr. W. B. Hull, Student Interpreter, Mr. Kong Chen-ren, the Chinese writer and myself." He asked for a stenographer and a typewriter. He based his request on the sharp increase of Standard Oil's business but acknowledged that his plea had a more important basis, the great numbers of missionaries scattered over the district and the voluminous correspondence carried on with them. Samuel Gracey, after many years of service, in 1902, requested restoration of his salary to what it was previously, namely, thirty-five hundred dollars. John Fowler, a veteran officer stationed in Chefoo, one of the more important posts from the point of view of sale of cotton goods, received a raise to thirty-five hundred dollars in 1905. He noted: ". . . it is the smallest salary any professional Consul or Vice-Consul is receiving at this port, and all of my colleagues in course of time will retire on a pension larger than the salary of $3500." Fowler, a short time later, protested that his allowance of $1775 for contingent expenses fell far short of the average annual $3209.85 contingency expenses of the previous five years. He met the difference by dipping into his own pocket.

Of course, this penurious policy resulted in a rapid turnover of personnel and in much incompetence. The interest in foreign markets led to agitation for reform, but there was long delay because appointments to foreign service assignments were an important source of patronage for members of Congress. Not until 1906 did Congress provide for improvements. In a final speech in the House of Representatives supporting the bill, Robert Adams, of Pennsylvania, cited the fact that for "sixteen years efforts have been made to secure the proposed legislation." "The new legislation," he agreed, "will go a long way in the movement that is now occupying the time of our merchants for the enlargement of our foreign commerce, for these are our advance pickets, sent throughout the world to furnish the merchants the necessary information to enlarge their business abroad."

The new law establishing five categories of consular posts based on estimates of the commercial importance of the foreign city did indicate a degree of serious purpose concerning China. Shanghai and Hongkong were placed in the second category, Tientsin and Canton in the fourth and Amoy and Fuchow in the fifth among the Consul-General posts.

The improved Consular Service reflected the Government's increasing awareness of the importance of foreign trade. The importance of export markets in the eyes of Washington is also evidenced in the strong support given to economic interests in Cuba, Santo Domingo, and the Philippines after the war with Spain. The building of the Panama Canal was likewise, in part, an extending of the helping hand of government to commercial interests. Others have discussed the role of economic considerations in the move of the Taft Administration to neutralize the railroads of Manchuria. These were important but compared to the actions of some other Governments, Washington scarcely played the game in a daring manner.

We are here dealing with the market for goods rather than for investment, but the first cannot be treated without some reference to the other. The lack of investments, especially in railroads, was quite correctly viewed by contemporaries as one of the reasons why the sale of American goods was not greater. . . .

The policy of government aid certainly rested on wide agreement on the importance of exports, but its implementation fell somewhere beyond half-heartedness and considerably short of boldness. Wide agreement did not produce aggressiveness because the very economic interests that might be expected to spur government action were now concerned with other matters: expanding the tremendous home market and gaining tariff protection. In 1909, John Barrett, Director of the Bureau of American Republics, in an address before the National Association of Manufacturers, bemoaned the fact that in all the speeches in Congress over the new tariff bill, and in almost all the discussions in the newspapers, "there has been an absolute neglect of the effect the tariff may have on our export trade." In brief, in spite of a consensus of opinion on the importance of foreign trade, government action was moderated by concerns that evoked a much greater response.

Having examined the two questions of the strengths and weaknesses of the China market at the turn of the century, and the degree of support provided by the Government in Washington in efforts to capture this market, the next question is whether the American business community demonstrated energy and imagination. Some of the Consuls stationed in major ports took a deep interest in the business activities of their fellow nationals and they prepared lengthy reports and wrote frequent letters containing detailed observations on commerce, the opportunities at hand, the factors making for success and failure, and the nature of the competition. In the 1890's, a majority of them filed optimistic reports and heralded even minor advances in sales of American goods, but throughout the hundreds of these reports and letters there is a common complaint of the lack of assertiveness on the part of American business concerns.

The apathy of American business concerns showed itself in a variety of ways. Consul John Fowler, stationed in the port of Chefoo, complained of the failure of American concerns to provide credit facilities, of the failure to send representatives to promote sales, and of the poor packaging of American goods. These practices did not change. Eleven years later, in 1911, Consul George Anderson, in charge of the Consulate in Hongkong, attributed the decline in sales in recent years to the high prices of American goods, Japanese competition, failure to supply credit, poor packaging, and the lack of an effective sales organization. Another official cited the failure of Americans to invest in China and reminded his readers that trade follows investment. Vice-Consul-General Willard B. Hull, in Hankow, warned that American firms could not follow their present policies and hope to secure the business. "Nearly every American company represented in Hankow," wrote Hull, "has some European firm for its agent, and, naturally, American products will be sold only when these firms cannot secure the same things from their own country in Europe, thus keeping American goods, in most cases, as a second choice." Hull likewise advised that American manufacturers "must also count on giving longer credits if they wish to do business in this field." Vice-Consul-General Percival Heintzleman in Shanghai, in 1908, stated that the three greatest handicaps of U.S. trade were: (1) failure to extend credit; (2) failure to send representatives; and (3) failure to invest American capital. The Vice-Consul in Dalny, in 1909, deplored the failure to send representatives. American business, he observed, is in the hands of persons who are regarded as commercial rivals.

American business, with the notable exception of Standard Oil, made no great effort to do what was necessary to sell to China. One major reason seems to have been the greener pastures near at hand. Consul George Anderson reported:

> They state frankly here that the cotton-goods market in the United States is so great, its demands so steady, the prices it pays so good, and its consumption so broad, that American manufacturers will give no more than passing interest to any foreign market and will not make the effort necessary to secure foreign business until home conditions turn against them.

These observations lead to the conclusion that American business was apathetic or at least unimaginative in its methods.

United States Ministers in Peking often expressed regret over the lack of enterprise. In October, 1897, Charles Denby observed: "Unfortunately, our fellow-citizens have made no serious effort to avail themselves of the good will of China." Two years before a loan of one hundred million dollars had been offered to Americans, but he recorded: "I could find nobody in the United States that would touch it." American banking representatives had come to China but they were without authority to make a contract. Denby advised: "To accomplish anything here we must imitate the European powers and have fully authorized agents on the ground."

Denby's successor, E. H. Conger, reported that Europeans were active in studying opportunities for railroads and mines. "If our capitalists," wrote Conger, "really desire a share they must have brains and money here."

The apathy of American business in the China market did not correspond to their behavior elsewhere if we may assume that success in sales was a result of their initiative. Exports of manufactured goods increased dramatically. In 1890, they constituted only 12.48 percent of total exports; in 1900, they represented 31.65 percent of the total. In 1910, the value reached $767 million compared to $122 million in 1880.

An examination of figures on the China trade shows that it was limited to a very few commodities. Illuminating oil and cotton goods led the way by a wide margin. Tobacco and tobacco products ranked third and lumber was fourth. Analyzing these further, we find that unbleached cloth constituted the bulk of textiles. In the peak year, 1909, unbleached cloth exports totaled $6,983,774; bleached cloth was valued at $908,681 and colored cloth at $111,402. The total exports of these three varieties in 1910 were $10,098,985 of unbleached, $1,351,040 of bleached and $8,521,466 of colored; of the total, China took $5,762,318 or approximately twenty-seven percent. However, cotton textiles ranked eleventh among the exports of the United States in 1910 and accounted for only 1.95 percent of the value of all exports.

Sales of illuminating oil totaled $1,251,201 in 1900, reached a peak for this period of $8,499,279 in 1908, and declined again to $5,016,397 in 1910. In the latter year, total exports of illuminating oil were valued at $62,477,527 and the Chinese market accounted for eight percent.

The next most important item in the trade fell far below cotton cloth and oil. Exports to China of leaf tobacco amounted to $639,369 in 1906; dipped to $273,687 in 1909; and advanced to a peak of $653,496 in 1910. Exports of cigarettes reached a high of $1,393,051 in 1907 and then slipped to $793,381 in 1908. The chief lumber products exported to China were boards, deals and planes. These totaled $976,629 in 1907 but declined by fifty percent in 1909 and then recovered in part, amounting to $748,026 or two percent of total exports of these lumber items in 1910.

These major exports represent the great bulk of the trade, $13,003,470 of a total of $16,181,670 in 1910. Sales of other important items were either trivial or nonexistent. Railway cars, carriages and other equipment varied; totaling only $382 in 1906, mounting to $137,439 in 1909 and then falling to $17,204 in 1910. Sales of railway equipment to Japan in her sphere in China were greater. The rebuilding of the South Manchuria Railway, destroyed by the Russians during the war, was done largely with American-made equipment and in 1908 the sales totaled almost two million dollars. Rails, considered a separate item, were sold to Japan for use in China to the extent of $1,121,199. But in the case of both equipment and rails, sales were trivial in most years. Locomotives, also considered a separate item, likewise were sold in large numbers ($2,404,619 worth in 1910) in one year and scarcely any in most years.

The point that the sales of most manufactured items were small is well illustrated by the statistics for 1900. In that year, American manufacturers sold $292 worth of cash registers, $6,345 of electrical supplies, $2,102 of laundry machinery, $17,520 of pumps and pumping machinery, and $7,769 of sewing machines. These were not the only items sold but they are representative. Obviously, these sales were scarcely adequate to excite the interest of the industrialists.

Contemporary observers of the China trade saw that the availability of credit and investment of American dollars were necessary for increasing sales. Recognition of this interdependence of trade and investment eventually encouraged bankers to show an interest in China but they found domestic American opportunities—and a few selective foreign ones—more promising. That the

United States remained a debtor nation until World War I was, of course, of primary importance in explaining the absence of American capital in China. . . .

Measured against these actualities, the rhetoric concerning the China market was so wild as to suggest that it was in the nature of a myth. Indeed, the gap between the rhetoric and the actualities attained dimensions of such scope that one may assume that the sheer joy of the discussion and not facts sufficed as a propellant.

## FURTHER READING

Thomas A. Breslin, *China, American Catholicism, and the Missionary* (1980)

Charles S. Campbell, *Special Business Interests and the Open Door Policy* (1951)

——, *The Transformation of American Foreign Relations, 1865–1900* (1976)

Kenton Clymer, *John Hay* (1975)

Warren I. Cohen, *America's Response to China* (1980)

Michael H. Hunt, "Americans in the China Market: Economic Opportunities and Economic Nationalism, 1890s–1931," *Business History Review*, 51 (1977), 277–307

——, *Frontier Defense and the Open Door: Manchuria in Chinese-American Relations, 1895–1911* (1973)

——, *The Making of a Special Relationship: The United States and China to 1914* (1983)

Akira Iriye, *Across the Pacific* (1967)

George F. Kennan, *American Diplomacy, 1900–1950* (1951)

Robert McClellan, *The Heathen Chinee: A Study of American Attitudes Toward China, 1890–1905* (1971)

Peter W. Stanley, "The Making of an American Sinologist: William W. Rockhill and the Open Door," *Perspectives in American History*, 11 (1977–1978), 419–460

James C. Thomson, Jr., Peter W. Stanley, and John C. Perry, *Sentimental Imperialists* (1981)

Paul A. Varg, *Missionaries, Chinese, and Diplomats* (1958)

——, *Open Door Diplomat: The Life of W. W. Rockhill* (1952)

Marilyn Blatt Young, "American Expansion, 1870–1900: The Far East," in Barton J. Bernstein, ed., *Towards a New Past* (1968)

——, *The Rhetoric of Empire* (1968)

# Theodore Roosevelt, the Big Stick, and the Panama Canal

# 13

*Theodore Roosevelt dominated the landscape of American diplomacy in the early twentieth century. The moustachioed President (1901–1909) always spoke frankly and pursued political power with enviable energy. An indefatigable expansionist, he exploited new opportunities. A formidable diplomat, he exercised American influence worldwide. When, after the Spanish-American War, the Caribbean became an American "lake," it was Roosevelt who doggedly extended American interests, lectured Latin Americans and Europeans alike on the virtues of an American model for development, and declared the United States an "international police power." Through the Platt Amendment and military occupation he fixed American control on a reluctant Cuba. He intimidated other Latin American states through naval demonstrations and short-term military interventions. He imposed United States financial supervision on the Dominican Republic. And he helped sever Panama from Colombia to gain rights to a canal across the Isthmus. This was "big stick" diplomacy, championed by American nationalists, but resented by foreigners. Patriot or bully, cautious diplomat or reckless imperialist, Theodore Roosevelt has fascinated historians.*

## DOCUMENTS

In a 1903 treaty with Cuba, the United States placed restrictions on Cuban independence and gained the right to intervene in Cuban internal affairs. The Platt Amendment, written by a United States senator and attached to the Cuban Constitution, governed relations until 1934, when it was abrogated. The treaty of November 18, 1903, with Panama came after the United States encouraged Panamanian independence from Colombia. The pact granted the United States canal rights and a zone. Theodore Roosevelt's defense of United States actions came in his December 7, 1903 message to Congress, the third document. Colombia, in a communication to Washington dated January 6, 1904, listed its grievances against the United States. The last document is the famous Roosevelt Corollary to the Monroe Doctrine, part of the President's Annual Message to Congress, December 6, 1904.

## The Platt Amendment, 1903

**Article I.** The Government of Cuba shall never enter into any treaty or other compact with any foreign power or powers which will impair or tend to impair the independence of Cuba, nor in any manner authorize or permit any foreign power or powers to obtain by colonization or for military or naval purposes, or otherwise, lodgment in or control over any portion of said island.

**Article II.** The Government of Cuba shall not assume or contract any public debt to pay the interest upon which, and to make reasonable sinking-fund provision for the ultimate discharge of which, the ordinary revenues of the Island of Cuba, after defraying the current expenses of the Government, shall be inadequate.

**Article III.** The Government of Cuba consents that the United States may exercise the right to intervene for the preservation of Cuban independence, the maintenance of a government adequate for the protection of life, property, and individual liberty, and for discharging the obligations with respect to Cuba imposed by the Treaty of Paris on the United States, now to be assumed and undertaken by the Government of Cuba. . . .

**Article V.** The Government of Cuba will execute, and, as far as necessary, extend the plans already devised, or other plans to be mutually agreed upon, for the sanitation of the cities of the island, to the end that a recurrence of epidemic and infectious diseases may be prevented, thereby assuring protection to the people and commerce of Cuba, as well as to the commerce of the Southern ports of the United States and the people residing therein. . . .

**Article VII.** To enable the United States to maintain the independence of Cuba, and to protect the people thereof, as well as for its own defense, the Government of Cuba will sell or lease to the United States lands necessary for coaling or naval stations, at certain specified points, to be agreed upon with the President of the United States.

## The Panama Canal Treaty, 1903

**Article I.** The United States guarantees and will maintain the independence of the Republic of Panama.

**Article II.** The Republic of Panama grants to the United States in perpetuity the use, occupation and control of a zone of land and land under water for the construction, maintenance, operation, sanitation and protection of said Canal of the width of ten miles extending to the distance of five miles on each side of the center line of the route of the Canal to be constructed. . . .

**Article III.** The Republic of Panama grants to the United States all the rights, power and authority within the zone mentioned and described in Article II of this agreement and within the limits of all auxiliary lands and waters mentioned and described in said Article II which the United States would possess and exercise if it were the sovereign of the territory within which said lands and waters are located to the entire exclusion of the exercise by the Republic of Panama of any such sovereign rights, power or authority. . . .

**Article XIV.** As the price or compensation for the rights, powers and privileges granted in this convention by the Republic of Panama to the United States, the Government of the United States agrees to pay to the Republic of Panama the sum of ten million dollars ($10,000,000) in gold coin of the United States on the exchange of the ratification of this convention and also an annual payment during the life of this convention of two hundred and fifty thousand dollars ($250,000) in like gold coin, beginning nine years after the date aforesaid. . . .

**Article XVIII.** The Canal, when constructed, and the entrances thereto shall be neutral in perpetuity, and shall be opened upon the terms provided for by Section I of Article three of, and in conformity with all the stipulations of, the treaty entered into by the Governments of the United States and Great Britain on November 18, 1901. . . .

**Article XXIII.** If it should become necessary at any time to employ armed forces for the safety or protection of the Canal, or of the ships that make use of the same, or the railways and auxiliary works, the United States shall have the right, at all times and in its discretion, to use its police and its land and naval forces or to establish fortifications for these purposes. . . .

**Article XXV.** For the better performance of the engagements of this convention and to the end of the efficient protection of the Canal and the preservation of its neutrality, the Government of the Republic of Panama will sell or lease to the United States lands adequate and necessary for naval or coaling stations on the Pacific coast and on the western Caribbean coast of the Republic at certain points to be agreed upon with the President of the United States.

# Roosevelt's Case for Supporting the Panamanian Revolution, 1903

First, that the United States has for over half a century patiently and in good faith carried out its obligations under the treaty of 1846; second, that when for the first time it became possible for Colombia to do anything in requital of the services thus repeatedly rendered to it for fifty-seven years by the United States, the Colombian Government peremptorily and offensively refused thus to do its part, even though to do so would have been to its advantage and immeasurably to the advantage of the State of Panama, at that time under its jurisdiction; third, that throughout this period revolutions, riots, and factional disturbances of every kind have occurred one after the other in almost uninterrupted succession, some of them lasting for months and even for years, while the central government was unable to put them down or to make peace with the rebels; fourth, that these disturbances instead of showing any sign of abating have tended to grow more numerous and more serious in the immediate past; fifth, that the control of Colombia over the Isthmus of Panama could not be maintained without the armed intervention and assistance of the United States. In other words, the Government of Colombia, though wholly unable to maintain order on the Isthmus, has nevertheless declined to ratify a treaty the conclusion of which opened the only chance to secure its own stability and to guarantee permanent peace on, and the construction of a canal across, the Isthmus.

Under such circumstances the Government of the United States would have been guilty of folly and weakness, amounting in their sum to a crime against the Nation, had it acted otherwise than it did when the revolution of November 3 last took place in Panama. This great enterprise of building the interoceanic canal can not be held up to gratify the whims, or out of respect to the governmental impotence, or to the even more sinister and evil political peculiarities, of people who, though they dwell afar off, yet, against the wish of the actual dwellers on the Isthmus, assert an unreal supremacy over the territory. The possession of a territory fraught with such peculiar capacities as the Isthmus in question carries with it obligations to mankind. The course of events has shown that this canal can not be built by private enterprise, or by any other nation than our own; therefore it must be built by the United States.

Every effort has been made by the Government of the United States to persuade Colombia to follow a course which was essentially not only to our interests and to the interests of the world, but to the interests of Colombia itself. These efforts have failed; and Colombia, by her persistence in repulsing the advances that have been made, has forced us, for the sake of our own honor, and of the interest and well-being, not merely of our own people, but of the people of the Isthmus of Panama and the people of the civilized countries of the world, to take decisive steps to bring to an end a condition of affairs which had become intolerable.

## Colombia's Grievances, 1904

*First.* That the said note of the 30th of December from your excellency is regarded by my Government as an intimation that the Colombian forces will be attacked by those of the United States on their entering the territory of Panama for the purpose of subduing the rebellion, and that for that reason, and owing to its inability to cope with the powerful American squadron that watches over the coasts of the Isthmus of Panama, it holds the Government of the United States responsible for all damages caused to it by the loss of that national territory.

*Second.* That since the 3d of November last the revolution of Panama would have yielded, or would not have taken place, if the American sailors and the agents of the Panama Canal had not prevented the Colombian forces from proceeding on their march toward Panama, and that I, as commander in chief of the army of Colombia, would have succeeded in suppressing the revolution of Panama as early as the 20th of the same month if Admiral Coghlan had not notified me in an official note that he had orders from his Government to prevent the landing of Colombian forces throughout the territory of the Isthmus.

*Third.* That the charges officially made against the Government and Senate of Colombia that it was opposed to the work of the Panama Canal, and that its purpose was to obtain a greater amount of money from the American Government and to recover the concession of the French company are unfair and groundless, and the proof of this assertion is that the Colombian Senate refused to ratify the Hay-Herran treaty, not because a greater sum of money was demanded, but because the treaty was contrary to the constitution of the country, which prohibits the cession of sovereignty over national territory; but the necessity of the canal is so well recognized in Colombia that it was proposed, in the discussion of the Senate, to amend the constitution in order to remove the constitutional difficulty, and the minister of foreign relations, after the sessions of Congress were closed, directed the chargé d'affaires, Doctor Herran, to advise the Government of your excellency that that of Colombia was ready to enter into renewed negotiations for a canal convention, and that it purposed to remove the existing constitutional difficulties. The charge made against the Government of Colombia that it purposed to cancel the concession of the French company vanishes as soon as it be known that under the latest extension granted to it by Colombia the said concession would not lapse until the year 1910.

*Fourth.* That the failure of the Colombian Senate to ratify the Hay-Herran treaty, for the reasons above stated, can not be regarded as an act of discourtesy or unfriendliness, as the minister of foreign relations of Colombia, Señor Rico, told the minister of the United States, Mr. Beaupré, at Bogotá, because a treaty prior to its ratification is nothing but a project which, according to the laws of nations, neither confers rights nor imposes obligations, and therefore its rejection or delay in its ratification gives no ground for the adoption of measures tending to alter the relations of friendship between the two countries. If it were not so, the mere act of preparing a public treaty would be an occasion for serious danger instead of an element of peace and progress, which is the predicament in which Colombia finds herself at present, owing to her weakness.

*Fifth.* That while the treaty of 1846 gives to the Government of the United States the right to maintain and protect the free transit of the Isthmus at the request of Colombia and when the latter is unable to do so, it places it under the obligation of enforcing the respect of Colombia's sovereignty over the territory of the Isthmus, and that the American Government has now not only failed to discharge that duty, but has prevented the Colombian forces from recovering the national sovereignty on the Isthmus, and thus the said treaty of 1846 being in full force, Colombia holds that the Government of the United States has no other reason than that of its own strength and of Colombia's weakness for interpreting and applying it in the manner it has; that is to say, for availing itself of the advantages and rights conferred by the treaty, and refusing to fulfill the obligations imposed thereby.

*Sixth.* That it is known, from sworn statements, that the garrisons of Panama and Colon were bought with gold brought from the United States, toward the end of October, by the Panama revolutionists.

*Seventh.* That if these revolutionists had not relied, and did not now rely, on the armed protection of the United States, whose powerful squadrons on both the Pacific and Atlantic oceans have prevented, and are preventing, since the 3d of November, the Colombian army from landing its forces, the Panama revolution would have been foiled by Colombia in a few hours.

*Eighth.* That the Government of Colombia, holding a perfect right that the cession of the compact with the French canal company be not effected without its express consent, has instituted an action against the said company before the French courts and asked that the contract made with the American Government be declared null and void.

*Ninth.* That on the grounds above stated, the Government of Colombia believes that it has been despoiled by that of the United States of its rights and sovereignty on the Isthmus of Panama, and not being possessed of the material strength sufficient to prevent this by the means of arms (although it does not forego this method, which it will use to the best of its ability), solemnly declares to the Government of the United States:

(1) That the Government of the United States is responsible to that of Colombia for the dismemberment that has been made of its territory by the separation of Panama, by reason of the attitude that the said Government assumed there as soon as the revolution of the 3d of November broke out.

(2) That the contract made between the United States and the French canal company is null, since it lacks the consent of Colombia, and the latter has already brought suit against the said canal company before the French courts in the defense of its interests.

(3) That the Government of Colombia does not nor will it ever relinquish the rights it possesses over the territory of the Isthmus of which it is now despoiled by the American forces, and will at all times claim the said rights and try to vindicate them by every means within its reach, and that for that reason the title over the territory of the Isthmus that may be acquired by the United States for the opening of the canal is void, and Colombia reserves to herself the right to claim the said territory at any time.

(4) That if the work of the Panama Canal is undertaken and carried to completion in disregard and trespass of the rights of Colombia, the latter puts it on record that she was denied justice by the United States; that she was forcibly despoiled of the territory of the Isthmus in clear violation of the treaty of 1846, and that she does not relinquish the rights she possesses over the said territory, and holds the United States responsible for the damages caused to her.

(5) That Colombia, earnestly wishing that the work of the canal be car-

ried into effect, not only because it suits her interests but also those of the commerce of the world, is disposed to enter into arrangements that would secure for the United States the execution and ownership of the said work and be based on respect for her honor and rights.

(6) That the United States has never protected Colombia on the Isthmus of Panama against foreign invasion, and that when it has intervened to prevent the interruption of the traffic it has been in help, or be it at the suggestion of the Government of Colombia. In this one instance it did so on its own initiative, with the obvious purpose of protecting the secession of the Isthmus. The guarantee of neutrality, if it were privileged, would estop the sovereign of the land from maintaining order, which is contrary to the fundamental principles of every government; and

(7) That the course followed by the American Government at Panama at the time when Colombia enjoyed peace, after overcoming a revolution of three years' duration, which left her exhausted, is in favor of any rebellion, but not of the maintenance of order, which is contrary to the principles and antecedents of the policy of this great nation as established in the war of secession. . . .

# The Roosevelt Corollary, 1904

It is not true that the United States feels any land hunger or entertains any projects as regards the other nations of the Western Hemisphere save such as are for their welfare. All that this country desires is to see the neighboring countries stable, orderly, and prosperous. Any country whose people conduct themselves well can count upon our hearty friendship. If a nation shows that it knows how to act with reasonable efficiency and decency in social and political matters, if it keeps order and pays its obligations, it need fear no interference from the United States. Chronic wrongdoing, or an impotence which results in a general loosening of the ties of civilized society, may in America, as elsewhere, ultimately require intervention by some civilized nation, and in the Western Hemisphere the adherence of the United States to the Monroe Doctrine may force the United States, however reluctantly, in flagrant cases of such wrongdoing or impotence, to the exercise of an international police power. If every country washed by the Caribbean Sea would show the progress in stable and just civilization which with the aid of the Platt amendment Cuba has shown since our troops left the island, and which so many of the republics in both Americas are constantly and brilliantly showing, all question of interference by this Nation with their affairs would be at an end. Our interests and those of our southern neighbors are in reality identical. They have great natural riches, and if within their borders the reign of law and justice obtains, prosperity is sure to come to them. While they thus obey the primary laws of civilized society they may rest assured that they will be treated by us in a spirit of cordial and helpful sympathy. We would interfere with them only in the last resort, and then only if it became evident that their inability or unwillingness to do justice at home and abroad had violated the rights of the

United States or had invited foreign aggression to the detriment of the entire body of American nations. It is a mere truism to say that every nation, whether in America or anywhere else, which desires to maintain its freedom, its independence, must ultimately realize that the right of such independence can not be separated from the responsibility of making good use of it.

---

## ESSAYS

Historians have long been critical of Theodore Roosevelt's behavior, especially of his bold style and foreign interventionism. Frederick W. Marks, III, prefers a more positive interpretation. In a recent unabashed defense of Roosevelt, Marks argues that the President was a cautious and deft diplomat who believed in law and faithfulness to agreements, and who finally intervened in Panama because of Colombian ineptitude. Walter LaFeber of Cornell University, on the other hand, faults Roosevelt's heavy-handed diplomacy, use of force, and insensitivity to the nationalism of other peoples. In the case of Panama, Roosevelt is depicted as a plotter who conspired with private French interests to exploit Panamanian nationalism in order to gain American canal rights. Rather than the man of noble accomplishment sketched by Marks, Roosevelt, in LaFeber's view, "triggered the most ignoble chapter in United States-Latin American relations."

---

## The Cautious Diplomat

### FREDERICK W. MARKS, III

In the realm of foreign relations, Roosevelt believed that nations were bound by the same moral code as individuals, and that the United States should adhere to the Golden Rule as scrupulously as any of its citizens. He was realistic enough to see that the application of morality was not always the same for international as for interpersonal relations, but he believed the standard should be the same in both cases. A powerful nation should act with restraint toward a weaker one, even though weakness was no license for wickedness; imperialism could be justified only when it benefited the subject as much as it did the subjugator; and the United States owed a great deal more to its overseas territories than roads, schools, and hospitals. One of the most bitter and protracted struggles of his political career was his fight for congressional enactment of a tariff that would place the Cuban and Philippine economies on a more prosperous footing.

In keeping with his credo that responsibility goes hand in hand with power, he felt that the nation had a moral duty, noblesse oblige, to work actively in

Reprinted from *Velvet on Iron: The Diplomacy of Theodore Roosevelt* by Frederick W. Marks, III, by permission of the University of Nebraska Press. Copyright © 1979 by the University of Nebraska Press.

all parts of the world for justice as well as peace. On at least one occasion, he declined to aid a foreign ruler who sought power by corrupt means. President Amador Guerrero of Panama was pro-American, and, in the interest of stability, it might have been expedient to support him in spite of his dubious methods. But Roosevelt refused to compromise on the principle of honest elections, and the result was an executive turnover. In 1908, when he sent American troops to monitor a Panamanian election, he explained to Taft that "fraudulent methods which deny to a large part of the people opportunity to vote constitutes a disturbance of the public order which under Panama's constitution requires intervention, and this government will not permit Panama to pass into the hands of anyone so elected." The Roosevelt Corollary to the Monroe Doctrine was based on the same general line of thought—that no state should be permitted to plunder under cover of the American flag. Thus, if Europe was to keep "hands off" the Western Hemisphere, the United States would have to act as a self-appointed guardian of foreign life and property. Lawlessness was as deplorable in the Caribbean as it was in the Sudan, as frightful in America's back yard as it was on the plains of Armenia. One of Roosevelt's chief motives for favoring imperialism over self-determination was his belief that the colonial power often exerted a force for law and order. No person or nation deserved to be independent until it could maintain stability at home and carry out its international obligations. Self-reliance was a cardinal virtue for the group as well as for the individual. . . .

His insistence on the binding nature of even informal agreements sometimes led him to do things that might appear inexplicable under normal circumstances. Take, for example, the way in which he acquired the Panama Canal Zone—one of the most heavily criticized moves in the annals of American diplomacy. Failing, in sustained effort, to obtain the Zone by treaty with Colombia, he used force to prevent Colombian suppression of an Isthmian revolt and proceeded to negotiate directly with the newborn republic, leaving Colombia in a state of impotent rage. Descriptions range all the way from "rape of Colombia" to "cowboy diplomacy." Even Samuel Flagg Bemis, never one to dwell upon the negative side of American history, calls this "the one really black mark in the Latin American policy of the United States, and a big black mark." Almost every account of the incident stresses Roosevelt's "Big Stick" philosophy and maintains that the Colombians had every right to disapprove their treaty with the United States; that they were at a distinct disadvantage in a contest of strength with their northern neighbor; and that Roosevelt's personal prestige as well as the national interest was tied to the speedy acquisition of a canal zone at Panama. Only a few critics have taken the president at his word when he described the basis for his action as one of high moral principle.

Roosevelt's case is an interesting one, however. To begin with, it was well known at the time that the province of Panama had never been fully integrated into the workings of the Colombian government. It had always conducted its own postal relations with the outside world and never adopted the national paper money, preferring to rely on silver specie. Nor had Panama always been a province of Colombia. When it first obtained independence from Spain in 1821, it established its own government. Thereafter, it voluntarily entered the Granadian Confederation which in 1832 broke apart to form Equador, Venezuela, and New Granada (Colombia). Panama remained with New Granada until 1840, when she resumed independent status. From 1842 to 1855, she was again with the larger state. In 1855, the national constitution was amended to divide power more evenly between central government and provinces, and three subsequent constitutions adopted with the approval of Panama allowed still more local control. Panama thus existed as a virtually sovereign state in confederation with others for twenty-three years until in 1886 her legislature, along with the legislatures of other provinces, was abolished by decree of Bogotà, and she was summarily stripped of nearly all her autonomy. The two Panamanian delegates who attended the constitutional convention of 1886 were both appointed by Bogotà, and neither had ever lived in Panama. Nor was the new instrument of government ever submitted for approval to the Panamanian people.

With three-quarters of the people reportedly in favor of separation, the year 1885 saw the outbreak of the first in a series of three full-scale insurrections which led eventually to complete independence. Twice, the people fought to exhaustion only to be put down by United States marines. In the rising of 1901–1902, they outnumbered their opponents on the isthmus by seven thousand to four thousand and had routed them in battle before American forces intervened to frustrate their bid for final victory. The revolution of 1903 was therefore the third major effort on the part of the Panamanian patriots. It was also a revolution which, by democratic standards, had every right to succeed, since the relationship between central government and province had always been one of exploitation rather than of reciprocal benefit. For decades, Colombian politicians had derived a good portion of the national revenue from isthmian railway tools without returning a pittance for the building of schools, hospitals, and other public facilities. President Marroquín's apparent willingness to gamble with the economic future of the isthmus by trying to squeeze the United States and the New Panama Canal Company was thus only one more grievance on a list of many.

It should also be recalled that even in physical terms Bogotá was separated from the isthmus by impassable jungle and awesome mountain terrain. At an altitude of 8,700 feet, the capital could not be reached from the sea in less than twelve days, three by mule and nine by rail. Provincials could make the trip to Washington, D.C., more quickly than they could arrive at the seat of their own government.

Elihu Root summed up the ethical issue when he pointed out that a strong Colombia had long held a weak Panama "in unlawful subjection," and Roosevelt was able to note in his Annual Address of 1903 that Panama had experienced fifty-three outbreaks, rebellions, and revolutionary disturbances in the fifty-three years since the United States had agreed to guarantee free and open transit across the isthmus. In addition, it is clear that the Colombian government had requested the aid of American troops to enforce order on the isthmus at least six different times (Roosevelt mentioned only four).

At the very time the treaty talks were taking place, American marines were again in Panama on behalf of a Colombian dictator engulfed in the worst civil war of his nation's history and threatened with invasion by Venezuela. It would have been easy to take advantage of the situation, especially since the Panamanian rebels promised a liberal canal treaty. Nevertheless, Secretary of State Hay sustained negotiations with Colombia for over two years until the dictator, José Marroquín, triumphed over all his rivals. Several times during this period, Hay reluctantly agreed to pay higher sums of money for a treaty which included such minimum security provisions as control of local police and establishment of American courts. The Colombian minister to the United States had been instructed to accept all of Hay's terms except those relating to price. Money was therefore the main stumbling block at the beginning, as it was to be at the end.

The crux of the issue for both Roosevelt and Hay was the expectation that once Marroquín had committed himself to the treaty as the best obtainable in competition with Nicaragua, he would be honor-bound to recommend it to his countrymen. Technically, Colombia had the right to reject the treaty, since it was a sovereign state with a constitution requiring congressional approval under normal conditions. But the canal negotiations had been initiated by Colombia. Three Colombian ministers had urged the treaty upon the United States for two years. The United States had agreed to purchase the rights and property of the French New Panama Canal Company with the express consent of Colombia, which held one million francs' worth of stock in the company, and whose representative at a stockholders' meeting had voted accordingly. It was on such assurances that the United States had concluded its agreement with the French company and that Congress had reversed itself, under strong administration pressure, from its original decision to designate Nicaragua as the preferred site. Thus, as Hay indicated to the Colombian minister of foreign affairs, "the United States, in view of the foregoing facts and of the responsibilities which it has thus been induced to incur, considers that the pending treaty is in the nature of a conclusive agreement on the part of Colombia." Marroquín's support was, in other words, not only something that had been promised, but also a "warrantable expectation."

In actual fact, Marroquín acted from the moment the treaty was signed to mobilize opinion against it. He not only failed to endorse it in his New Year's Message of 1903 but encouraged open debate, saying he would let the masses decide. General Fernandez, minister of finance, issued a circular to the Bogotá press inviting public discussion and reaffirming that the government "had no preconceived wishes for or against." One of Marroquín's more obvious moves was to solicit the opinion of three well-known lawyers, who responded with a uniformly critical view. Certainly, for the victor of a Latin-American civil war that had claimed over one hundred and fifty thousand lives, this was tantamount to inviting the treaty's defeat. The British minister to Bogotá observed that "the measures employed by the Colombian government to prevent public discussion of affairs of state [over a period of many years] have had the effect of destroying anything like public opinion." And he was correct. What passed for "public opinion," said to be enthusiastic at first, now shifted quickly to the negative. The Marroquín government continued to claim that it had no feelings for or against the treaty, while the American minister in Bogotá reported nothing but criticism coming from a press which he described as having "suddenly sprung into existence." He could not find a single journal or newspaper willing to publish an article in favor of the treaty, even though the articles that did appear gave no hint of Nicaraguan competition in the bidding and ridiculously exaggerated the profits expected to accrue to the United States.

Equally significant is the fact that when the time arrived to elect delegates for a congress specially called to consider the treaty (and the first to meet since 1898), the governor of Panama, who was a Marroquín appointee, named an antitreaty man as government candidate for the congress. This individual was then declared elected, despite the fact that the overwhelming sentiment in the province of Panama favored the treaty.

Historians have claimed that Marroquín was not to blame because he was politically weak. But the truth of the matter was well put by the Colombian consul in New York, who insisted that there was no party in Colombia "strong enough to defeat the wishes of the President." As soon as the congress convened, Marroquín showed himself firmly in control by mustering a vote of thirty-eight to five against an opposition party motion demanding to see all executive correspondence on the treaty. Marroquín supporters were elected president and vice-president of the senate, and the government went on to carry every important question in the course of the debate. Secretary Hay suspected that Marroquín might submit the treaty without recommendation. But the Colombian president went considerably beyond this to stall the proceedings and pave the way for the treaty's defeat should the United States refuse to pay large additional sums of money. In his opening address, he announced that he would only suggest that Colombia was in a good position to demand better terms. He withheld the treaty for several weeks of debate and then cavalierly submitted it without his signature, an act unprecedented in Colombian history. Two weeks of debate thus revolved around the question of whether congress had the right to consider an unsigned document. In the meantime, he sought additional sums from representatives of both the United States and the French Panama Canal Company, intimating that this was the only way to ensure senate approval.

Mysterious things happened. There was a secret meeting on 30 June between the senate and Marroquín's foreign minister at which he revealed a strongly worded plea from the United States. There was also an unusual failure of telegraph service for three critical weeks during which a senate committee decided to attach nine amendments to the treaty, including a stipulation for more money. On 4 August, the committee issued its report;

on 5 August, telegraph service resumed, and the American minister was presented with an urgent and long-delayed wire from Hay. Other cables were unaccountably lost.

In the end, Marroquín's special congress voted unanimously to reject the treaty, and the Panamanians carried out their long-threatened revolt. Bogotá failed to send early reinforcements, despite Roosevelt's frank warning that in such a situation he would avail himself of his legal right to maintain peace along the Panama railroad and prevent all troops from landing within a radius of fifty miles. Four hundred of Marroquín's troops did manage to land at Colón before Roosevelt acted, but they could do little on their own and were actually saved from an encounter with eager Panamanian forces nearly four times as large when the American naval commander refused them access to Panama City.

The Colombian government now asked for American aid in putting down the revolt and offered, in return, to approve the ill-fated Hay-Terrán Treaty either by presidential decree or by summoning an extra session of congress with new and friendly members. This only confirmed T.R.'s suspicions of double-dealing and steeled him all the more in his support of Panamanian independence. It is unnecessary to recall the long history of Panamanian separatism, the periods when the province had enjoyed various degrees of autonomy, or the many times Colombian authorities had been unable to put down insurrection on the isthmus without American aid. Suffice to say that in the opinion of both Hay and Roosevelt, a failure to intervene would have resulted in "endless guerrilla warfare." Hay had advised Roosevelt that we "shall be forced" to do something "in the case of a serious insurrectionary movement in Panama to keep the transit clear. Our intervention should not be haphazard, nor this time should it be to the profit, as heretofore, of Bogotá." And the president, for his part, harbored a fear of intervention by some European power and appreciated his responsibility to protect the lives of American citizens.

Even more to the point, the issue was conceived in terms of moral principle. Roosevelt might have shifted the negotiations to Nicaragua; he might have discouraged revolutionary sentiment on the isthmus; he might even have helped Colombia put the revolution down. But, apart from political and practical considerations, such actions would have been entirely out of character. It would have earned him, in his own words, a place in Dante's inferno "beside the faint-hearted cleric who was guilty of *il gran rifiuto*." Marroquín's last-minute demands for more money struck him as outrageous, and he filled his personal correspondence with words such as "homicidal corruptionists," "extortion," and "blackmail." Marroquín, an absolute dictator with power to "keep his promise or break it," had "determined to break it." The Colombian congress was an assembly "of mere puppets," a "sham," and the country "had forfeited every claim to consideration." Nor was that "stating the case strongly enough; she had so acted that yielding to her would have meant on our part that culpable form of weakness which stands on a level with wickedness."

Roosevelt was so convinced, in fact, that Marroquín had broken faith and brazenly flouted his part of the agreement that he was ready to seek congressional support for a direct takeover of the Canal Zone. Had he decided to do so, he could have counted on the enthusiastic support of at least two powerful members of the Senate Foreign Relations Committee, Senator Shelby Cullom of Illinois, the chairman, and Senator Henry Cabot Lodge of Massachusetts. He would also have been backed by Prof. John Bassett Moore of Columbia University, the nation's leading scholar in the field of international law. Mild-mannered, gentlemanly John Hay thought even less than Roosevelt of Colombia's conduct, labeling Marroquín and his advisers "greedy little anthropoids" and railing against "the jack rabbit mind." On one occasion, he wrote the president that "the jack rabbits are in a great funk." On another, he declared that the Colombians "have had their fun— let them wait the requisite number of days for the consequent symptoms." As for a unilateral takeover, it might lead to war, but the war "would be brief and inexpensive."

Some of the most telling indictments of Marroquín came, not from Americans, but from Colombians. Miguel Antonio Caro, former president and leader of the senate opposition, not only charged the government with lack of good faith in not defending a treaty of its own making and "endeavoring to throw the whole responsibility for its failure on Congress"; he also accused Marroquín of stage-managing the proceedings in such a way as to make it seem that the senate had rejected the treaty as a result of American threats. In accordance with a motion made by Marroquín's son, who participated in the debate as a senator, some of the more pointed communications from Hay to Marroquín were read aloud to the full senate. This tactic, which had been employed once before at a critical moment during a secret session of congress, now evoked loud murmurs of disapproval from the gallery. British observers who had seats in the chamber agreed with Caro that Marroquín's men were trying to "exculpate themselves for their action by throwing the responsibility, as much as possible, on the United States Minister as being the result of his so-called undiplomatic action." This is how the scene looked as they saw it.

> Senator Caro rose and vehemently attacked the government for its attitude in the conducting of the whole negotiations. He also taunted the Minister for Foreign Affairs for his action in having the correspondence between the American minister and himself read aloud as an attempt to elude the responsibility resting on the government and cover it by courting the applause of the gallery as the champion of the rights of the Colombian Senate, which Senator Caro pointed out, had never been called in question by the American minister. The same attitude was taken by Senator Arango in a short speech.

José Concha, Marroquín's ambassador to the United States in 1902 and a former secretary of war, charged his chief with acting in bad faith when he led the United States to believe that he would support the treaty. "I have not believed," he wrote, "that just because the Colombian Congress has the right to approve or disapprove the treaty under consideration, an agent of the Executive Power can sign it in any form, exempting himself and his superiors from all moral and legal responsibility." It was Concha, incidentally, who had earlier assured Hay that the treaty would "not be hampered by pecuniary considerations." Tomás Herrán, Colombian chargé d'affaires and signer of the treaty, went even further. He asserted that the dispute had been sought by Marroquín's "imbecilic government." Finally, the people of Bogotá registered their dissatisfaction by parading the streets in large crowds, chanting "Down with Marroquín!" and stoning the home of Marroquín's son. . . .

We come, finally, to the question of what cautionary principles, if any, lay at the root of "Big Stick" diplomacy. One of the stranger paradoxes of American history is the sharp contrast between Roosevelt's impressive diplomatic record and the standard conception of him as reckless, bellicose, and overbearing. Broadway's popular *Arsenic and Old Lace* told the story of two maiden aunts who poisoned lonely old men as an act of mercy. In their spare time, they took care of an insane brother who imagined himself to be Theodore Roosevelt. He appeared on stage in the garb of a Rough Rider, began every other sentence with the word "Bully," and liked to bolt up a flight of stairs with sword drawn, shouting "Charge!" More recently, a motion picture based on the Perdicaris incident depicted Roosevelt as a man who spent much time at his rifle range and took more interest in a stuffed bear than he did in Morocco—a cautious elder statesman by the name of John Hay had to explain to him patiently that the Moroccan situation should not be taken lightly, that it might even lead to war.

Scholarly appraisals of the Rough Rider are replete with such terms as "megalomania" and "militarism." He is said to have had a "trigger-like willingness to use troops" and an "adolescent love of war." One account calls him a "born bully," another a "sophomoric" adventurer. His tactics have been labeled "impetuous." And Howard Beale, the leading student of his diplomacy, has written that he "romanticized war," "gloried" in it, and "craved" its excitement—it was "such fun to have a big navy." Beale concludes that "in the sense of power that ordering ships about gave him he found exhilaration and perhaps compensation for unfulfilled yearnings of a sickly boy whose boyish urges had been unsatisfied."

Some historians have allowed that Roosevelt mellowed beneath the weight of age and experience. Others have recognized his flare for *Realpolitik*. But few approach his record without sharp reservation. According to Beale, he was a shrewd tactician whose conduct of foreign relations was marred by racial arrogance and a taste for imperialism; he refused "to take seriously other methods than armed force in establishing international stability" and, in the end, "failed in his most important objectives." Dexter Perkins credits him with a rare grasp of the role of power in international relations but finds his view of war "juvenile and romantic." Robert Osgood admires his realism, yet faults him for being, at heart, a "romantic militarist, an aggressive national egoist."

At first sight, one is tempted to bridge the gap between Roosevelt's reputed bellicosity and his record of peace by attributing his success to the conservative influence of two fine secretaries of state. While it is not easy to measure the subtle effect of one personality upon another, Hay and Root were gentler than Roosevelt and more given to legal solutions. They were also far more cautious in their emotional makeup. Either of them could be viewed as the carrot to Roosevelt's stick, and the president may well have chosen them with this very idea in mind.

On the other hand, Roosevelt took firm charge of foreign policy from the moment he entered the White House. He sent troops to Alaska in the spring of 1902 against the advice of Secretary Hay and in October ordered Hay to adopt a harder line in negotiations with Cuba. When Hay fell ill during the critical interval 1903–1905, T.R. assumed complete responsibility for the talks leading to Portsmouth and Algeciras. Furthermore, when Hay offered his resignation in July 1903, because he objected to the sending of troops to Alaska and disapproved of the tremendous pressure Roosevelt was bringing to bear on Britain, the chief had his way, and the cabinet remained intact.

On another occasion, Hay pushed for a harder line than the Rough Rider was willing to grant in regard to Russian control of Manchuria: "If we give them [the Japanese] a wink, they will fly at the throat of Russia in a moment." Roosevelt, who had earlier said he wished to go to extremes with Russia, demurred when it came to an actual showdown, assuring Hay that continued patience would eventually be rewarded. T.R.'s later reference to Hay as a "fine figurehead" may have been somewhat harsh. Yet, in all three of the major crises of the period, not to mention the talks leading to peace in the Far East and a settlement in western Europe, Hay played a distinctly minor role. Even on the question of Panama, while Hay may have been optimistic about a treaty with Nicaragua, there is no evidence that he acted as a brake upon Roosevelt. Both he and Root were quite comfortable with the course finally taken.

No one is likely to forget what Root is supposed to have said during a cabinet meeting when Roosevelt demanded to know if he had not ably defended himself against all charges of wrongdoing in connection with Panama: "You have shown that you were accused of seduction and you have conclusively proved that you were guilty of rape." Unfortunately, the anecdote is as misleading as it is entertaining. Root was obviously speaking in jest, and his relationship with Roosevelt as secretary of state turns out to have been very much the same as Hay's. T.R. praised him for his statesmanlike qualities, credited him with important help on speeches, and claimed that when it came to Latin America, he had been given carte blanche. Root managed the American position at the second Hague Peace Conference as well as the campaign for arbitration treaties and a Central American court of justice. He followed Roosevelt's example of winning a Nobel Peace Prize. But this hardly warrants the conclusion that he was a significant "restraining" influence. Interestingly enough, when he first accepted the post of secretary, at least one commentator supposed Roosevelt to be the one who would exercise the restraining influence: *Le Matin* of Paris commented that when Root ran wild, there would be a strong hand to hold him in check. Only two serious crises remained to be settled after 1905. In the clinch with Japan, Roosevelt acted on his own; and during the initial stages of the Cuban crisis (20 September to 1 October 1906) Root was away on a good-will tour. Like Hay, Root argued unsuccessfully for a harder line on Russian occupation of Manchuria and exerted minimal influence on American Far East policy in general. If his counsel served as something of a check in connection with one or two incidents in the Caribbean, Roosevelt was equally inhibited by public opinion, for as he later wrote, with customary vehemence, the nation refrained from war "merely because our people declined to be irritated by the actions of a weak opponent."

The more closely one examines the record, the more apparent it becomes that the real controls on Roosevelt's policy are to be found within the man himself. Careful examination reveals a complex character with a wide range of ideas often obscured by the popular image. . . .

In only two countries did he initiate prolonged intervention: Cuba and the Dominican Republic. Both nations were caught up in the coils of civil strife and threatened by European intervention. Both actions, moreover, were preceded by a thorough investigation and carried out with extreme reluctance. "I loathe the thought" of military involvement, he wrote. In neither case was there loss of life or any decline in American popularity, since Roosevelt refused to take sides. He was so eager, in fact, to avoid even the appearance of partisanship that he allowed all factions in the Dominican war to fight to the death outside those towns where foreign life and property were concentrated, with the understanding that he would cheerfully hand over the urban areas to whatever side emerged victorious. His agreement to establish an American customs receivership was popular with most groups on the island since it removed the incentive for civil war and seemed the best alternative to military intervention by a more predatory European power. There was opposition, to be sure, but chiefly among chronic enemies of law and order. As the British consul general observed:

> No coercion seems to have been used although there was some discussion over minor points. The Dominican government was unanimously in favor of the American proposals, speaking in a general point of view. . . . The Dominican Minister of Finance . . . has the reputation of being a man of undoubted integrity and patriotism, and he expressed himself . . . as being well satisfied with the agreement, fully realizing that something of the kind could not be avoided.

In Cuba, American troops were landed so deftly that no one on the island knew whether or not Roosevelt was intervening, and if so, on which side. Charles Magoon, the genial midwesterner who governed the island from 1906 to 1908, ended his term without issuing a single death sentence and was actually criticized for granting too many pardons. The marines thus marched out of Cuba to the tune of friendly bands and cheering crowds— in marked contrast, one might add, to subsequent landings under Presidents

Taft and Wilson. Taft took a decidedly partisan position in several Caribbean upheavals, one of them implicating Americans in the death of a hundred natives, while Wilson's record was bloodier still. . . .

Another T.R. pronouncement frequently cited as evidence of a desire to jump headlong into the fray is his corollary to the Monroe Doctrine, whereby the world was given to understand that Washington would undertake hemispheric police duty in case of flagrant "wrongdoing or impotence." But here again there is another side to the story. The country had just emerged from an explosive confrontation with Britain and Germany over their blockade of Venezuela. The specter of European intervention seemed ready to rear its ugly head a second time on the coast of Santo Domingo, and Roosevelt clearly aimed to forestall any such eventuality. Some historians have called the corollary a new policy, a perversion of the Monroe Doctrine. They assume that Roosevelt sought to use the doctrine as a cover for imperial designs on Latin America. The reverse, however, is more nearly true. Under strong pressure from foreign chancelleries, Whitehall in particular, he volunteered American action to justify the doctrine. It was neither fair nor realistic, in his opinion, to expect Europe to keep "hands off" the Western Hemisphere when there were so many situations in which intervention would be both legal and moral, as well as a standing invitation to acquire a naval base athwart vital sea lanes. The only alternative to the corollary was the Drago Doctrine, which would have bound major powers to abjure force in the collection of debts and which received strong support both from Roosevelt in his Annual Message of 1905 and at the second Hague Peace Conference. But even this was not really an alternative to the corollary since it ignored the question of claims other than debts. . . .

That Roosevelt proved himself no mean player in the thrust and parry of diplomatic combat is a fact far better known than the explanation behind it. One will search many a page without encountering the cautious strategist who figures so prominently in the foregoing chapter. Historians have made a notable effort of late to separate the man from the myth. Yet there is much work still to be done.

So it is that we return to the paradoxical contrast between the man's record and his reputation. T.R.'s boyish enthusiasm caused Spring Rice to liken him to a six-year-old child; and an embittered quondam friend by the name of Maria Storer published a posthumous tract entitled *Roosevelt, The Child*. Although his closest associates testified that he frequently sought counsel and was eminently advisable, those less close to him gained the impression that he was impulsive. To John Davis Long, he was a "bull in a china shop." Lord Bryce feared his impetuosity during the Japanese war scare. The British foreign secretary, Lord Lansdowne, expressed even less confidence: "[he] terrifies me almost as much as the German emperor"—while Sir Mortimer Durand paid tribute to Hay's "restraining influence."

Neither Durand nor Lansdowne knew Roosevelt well. Neither of them ever gained his confidence. Still, their impression of him is the one that, in the main, has endured to this day, and it is difficult to find in this image the man who believed that force must be wielded with restraint and applied with courtesy, the man who reserved his greatest admiration, not for the plain warrior, but for the "just man armed who wishes to keep the peace." Somehow, the comic cartoon showing huge white teeth and a spiked club is what remains most vivid. Across the years, it is a personality which is remembered rather than a philosophy. The "Big Stick" is still viewed by many as a policy of unvarnished power, when, in fact, it was a series of cautionary principles. Roosevelt may well have flashed his teeth and waved his arms on the rostrum, and his prose undoubtedly owed much to the Old Testament; but juvenile he was not, reckless and bellicose he was not. In thought and action he was sufficiently cautious to merit the untrammeled peace which crowned his efforts both at home and abroad.

# Self-Appointed Policeman

## WALTER LA FEBER

The 1898 war introduced the United States as a great world power. Specifically, the conflict made the nation supreme in the Caribbean region. The country emerged from "the splendid little war," as Secretary of State John Hay aptly called it, with Cuba, Puerto Rico, a great (if little tested) fleet, and British recognition that the days of the Clayton-Bulwer treaty were numbered. The cry for a canal intensified. Brooks Adams, John Quincy Adams's brilliant if eccentric grandson, and close friend of arch-expansionists Theodore Roosevelt and Senator Henry Cabot Lodge, had prophesied North American "economic supremacy" in world markets. The apparent fulfillment of that prophecy after 1898, Adams bragged, "knocked the stuffing out of me." "America has been irresistibly impelled to produce a large industrial surplus," he argued. "The expansion of any country must depend on the markets for its surplus product." Since "China is the only region which now provides almost boundless possibilities of absorption," an isthmian canal "to the Pacific must be built."

President William McKinley was equally direct in his Annual Message of December 1898. A canal, McKinley observed, was "demanded by the annexation of the Hawaiian Islands and the prospective expansion of our influence and commerce in the Pacific." He emphasized the waterway must be controlled by the United States. Brooks Adams and other acute observers believed Great Britain actually had little choice but to become the junior partner in an Anglo-Saxon empire. Not only did United States power appear awesome, but the London government was increasingly preoccupied with a rising Germany and a rebellion in South Africa where the Boer farmers were unexpectedly humiliating British troops.

With Great Britain busy elsewhere, in 1900 the United States Senate considered a bill that would build a Nicaraguan canal without regard for the Clayton-Bulwer treaty. That threat prodded British officials to negotiate with Secretary of State Hay (a noted Anglophile), to work out an alternative. Hay finally agreed with British Ambassador Lord Pauncefote that under a new treaty the United States could build and control a canal, but would not fortify it. The Senate rebelled against the non-fortification pledge, as did a hero of the 1898 war, a self-proclaimed expansionist, and Republican candidate for Vice-President of the United States in 1900, Theodore Roosevelt. Though a close friend of Hay, Roosevelt warned that a fresh treaty was necessary. The Secretary of State threatened to resign, muttering privately that "There will always be 34 percent of the Senate on the blackguard side of every question," then thought better of it and negotiated a second treaty with Pauncefote. Hay warned friends that in dealing with the Senate one should not underrate "the power of ignorance and spite, acting upon cowardice," but this time he had nothing to fear. The agreement directly abrogated the 1850 pact and implicitly gave the United States the sole right to fortify a canal. The treaty was negotiated during the weeks that President William McKinley, who had been shot, lingered near death, and then passed away. The White House was now in the hands of that "wild man," as one of McKinley's advisers called Theodore Roosevelt.

The only remaining question concerned the location of the passageway. Since the 1870s most knowledgeable observers had assumed the site would be Nicaragua. In 1901 the Walker Commission, a group of engineers named by McKinley to examine the prospects for a canal, also reported favorably on the Nicaraguan route. That conclusion received strong endorsement from Senator Morgan. But the Walker Commission made the recommendation reluctantly, believing the Nicaragua river system too shallow for a large canal. The Commission agreed with most engineers (and Theodore Roosevelt) that the Panama route was preferable, especially since de Lesseps had completed part of the work on the Isthmus. The Commission nevertheless concluded that building the canal in Panama would be considerably more expensive than the Nicaraguan route, for the New Panama Canal Company— a group of Frenchmen who had bought out the ruined de Lesseps company —was asking $109 million for its assets and concessionary rights to build in Panama. . . .

At this juncture two remarkable men reversed the movement toward the Nicaraguan route. William Nelson Cromwell headed a New York City law firm prestigious in 1900 (and even more prestigious a half-century later when two of Sullivan and Cromwell's senior partners, John Foster Dulles and Arthur Dean, became important United States diplomats in the Cold War). In 1896 Cromwell emerged as the New Panama Canal Company's agent in the United States and served as legal counsel for the Panama Railroad Company. Four years later the forty-eight-year-old lawyer miraculously prevented the inclusion in the Republican Party platform of a plank favoring the Nicaraguan canal. His means for working the miracle were direct: he contributed $60,000 to the party through the party chairman, and confidant of McKinley, Senator Mark Hanna of Ohio. Cromwell later charged this and other expenses to the Canal Company and apparently collected nearly a million dollars in fees.

The exact amount of money involved in the canal transactions will never be known. Cromwell burned many of his papers and most of the remainder, particularly those relating to Panama, were destroyed by several of his surviving law partners, including Dulles. Cromwell nevertheless deserved whatever he was paid, for between 1896 and 1902 he single-handedly fended off the commitment to the Nicaraguan route. In 1913 the head of a congressional investigation into the canal transactions called Cromwell "the most dangerous man the country has produced since the days of Aaron Burr." His abilities were apparent in a description written by a New York reporter in 1908:

> Mr. Cromwell is about 5 feet 8 inches high, and medium in build. . . . He can smile as sweetly as a society belle and at the same time deal a blow at a business foe that ties him in a hopeless tangle of financial knots. . . . He is a wizard with figures and a shorthand writer of wonderful skill. . . . He is one of the readiest talkers in town. . . . He talks fast, and when he wishes to, never to the point. . . . [He] has an intellect that works like a flash of lightning, and it swings about with the agility of an acrobat.

In November 1901 Cromwell's wizardry with figures and politics convinced the anxious New Panama Canal Company in Paris to drop its price from $109 million to $40 million, thereby making the Panama route less expensive than the Nicaraguan. The Walker Commission now recommended Panama to the Senate as the better buy.

The New Panama Canal Company's decision to lower the price occurred after bitter debate. Arguments became so heated that Parisian police were called in to calm one meeting. In the end, however, a faction led by Phillipe Bunau-Varilla triumphed. "A somewhat picturesque personage," as a contemporary described him, the vain and trimly mustached Bunau-Varilla viewed "the earth . . . like a school globe which he, the teacher, made to revolve at his pleasure." At twenty-six, Bunau-Varilla was chief engineer on the de Lesseps project in Panama before falling victim to the fever. After returning to Paris he embarked upon a career of building railroads in the Belgian Congo, constructing flood controls in Rumania, serving as an editor of *Le Matin* in Paris, and, in 1893, playing a central role in the formation of the New Panama Canal Company.

Realizing that the company's rights would expire in 1904, Bunau-Varilla raced against time. In the mid-1890s he tried to convince Russians to buy the claims and build the canal. After all, he told them, if the Anglo-Saxons controlled Panama as well as Suez, they would rule the world's commerce. When the Czar's government did not respond, he used the same argument in discussions with the British, only transforming the reference to Anglo-Saxons into North Americans. Busy elsewhere, London officials were preparing to leave the Caribbean in Washington's hands. The second Hay-Pauncefote treaty made this clear to Bunau-Varilla, and in 1902 he left Paris to join Cromwell in the United States. Just before the Frenchman arrived, however, the House passed, by an overwhelming vote of 308–2, a bill sponsored by William P. Hepburn of Iowa which ordered the canal to be built in Nicaragua. The pro-Nicaragua lobby, led by Senator Morgan, had scored an impressive victory.

Reaching Washington in late January 1902, Bunau-Varilla joined Cromwell and Senator Hanna in pushing for an amendment sponsored by Republican Senator John C. Spooner of Wisconsin. When attached to the Hepburn bill, the Spooner amendment instructed President Roosevelt to buy the Canal Company's claims for $40 million and build the passageway in Panama if he could obtain a treaty from Colombia. If he failed, Roosevelt was to deal with Nicaragua. Within six months Bunau-Varilla, Cromwell, and Hanna collected the votes to pass the Spooner amendment. The trio was even blessed by an act of God. In May a volcano erupted on the Caribbean island of Martinique, covering a city of 30,000 inhabitants with hot lava. Bunau-Varilla immediately notified all Senators that Nicaragua could suffer the same disaster.

Nicaraguan authorities made the mistake of claiming publicly that no active volcanoes had shaken their country since 1835. Bunau-Varilla, however, knew that Momotombo had erupted just several months before, and that in 1901 the Nicaraguan government even issued a postage stamp showing Momotombo magnificently belching lava. The Frenchman bought out the Washington dealers' supply of these stamps, then placed one on each Senator's desk with the simple notation, "Official testimony regarding volcanic activity in Nicaragua." The Senate and House passed the Spooner amendment (the House so totally reversing itself that it passed the Panama bill 260–8), and Roosevelt signed the new measure into law on June 28.

Happily following instructions, Roosevelt and Hay opened negotiations with Colombia. In January 1903, after a good deal of arm-twisting, Hay convinced the Colombian ambassador in Washington to sign a treaty that gave the United States a 99-year lease on a six-mile-wide canal zone. In return, the United States would pay Colombia $10 million plus an annual payment of $250,000. The United States Senate ratified the pact, but in August 1903 the Colombian Senate not only rejected it, but did so unanimously. The Bogotá government wanted more money. A leading Colombian historian later wrote that his nation feared the loss of sovereignty in Panama to the powerful North Americans, and believed itself entitled to a larger sum, particularly since the United States-owned isthmian railroad had earned millions in profits of which Colombia receive nothing. Left unsaid was that the Colombians hoped to stall until October 1904 when the Canal Company's rights would expire. Colombia could then collect all of the $40 million ticketed for Bunau-Varilla's and Cromwell's organization.

Roosevelt was livid. During the next several months he exhausted his rich vocabulary, calling the Colombians everything from "inefficient bandits" to "a corrupt pithecoid community." The sardonic Hay hid an equal anger behind his condescending smile and sarcastic words. At one time in 1902 he considered outright purchase of Panama from Colombia, then dropped the scheme, agreeing with a visitor's comment that Colombians viewed Panama

"as a financial cow to be milked for the benefit of the country at large."
In August 1903 the Secretary of State wondered whether he should turn to
deal with Nicaragua or instead begin "the far more difficult and multifurcate
scheme of building the Panama Canal *malgré* Bogotá."

Roosevelt's mind began to move in the same direction. He would be
"delighted" if Panama became independent, TR wrote a friend in October,
but "I cast aside the proposition made at this time to foment the secession
of Panama. Whatever other governments can do, the United States cannot
go into securing by such underhand means, the secession." As usual, he
worked more directly. Roosevelt began drafting a message to Congress suggesting that the simpler method would be to send the navy to seize the
Isthmus. . . .

Roosevelt never sent that particular message, for Panamanian nationalists
had long been awaiting such an opportunity. These nationalists, contrary to
North American myths too long propagated in textbooks, did not suddenly
spring up full-grown at Roosevelt's command. The belief that Panama should
exist as a separate, independent country was neither artificially created suddenly in 1903 nor propagated in Washington before it took hold in Panama
City. The Panamanian nationalism of 1902–03 formed only one part of an
ancient story, although, as it turned out, the most important chapter.

The point demands emphasis. Nothing is more important in understanding
the 1960s–70s crisis in United States-Panamanian relations than to realize
that Panamanians are acutely conscious of their four centuries' long history,
and that their ardent nationalism arising from this consciousness developed
at the same time United States expansionism conquered a continent and,
while building a worldwide empire, laid claims on Panama itself. Throughout
the nineteenth century, the two nationalisms were on a collision course.

After Colombia declared its independence from Spain in 1821, it was
never able to control Panama completely. In part this failure was due to
the type of person the Isthmus attracted—the rootless, lawless, transient
who obeyed no authority. This element remained in Panama, as a later observer noted, becoming "a community of gamblers, jockeys, boxers, and cock-
fighters." At the other end of the social spectrum a small propertied elite—
an "oligarchy"—developed that resembled the North American elite of 1776:
both developed valuable economic and political interests apart from the
mother country, and neither saw any reason to share their wealth with colo-
nizers. Colombia, moreover, was separated from the Isthmus as the United
States was from England. The mountains and jungles in eastern Panama
that bordered Colombia were so dense that in 1903 North Americans could
reach Panama more easily and quickly by steamer than Colombians could
by horse. In the 1970s, despite new technology, the Inter-American Highway
had not breached those jungles after thirty years of intermittent effort.

Separated from the supposed mother country, holding a mobile, rebellious,
independent population, Panama never developed the quasi-feudal, mercantilist characteristics of neighboring Latin American nations. Movement and
trade were freer, liberalism seemed more natural. The land-owning oligarchs

notably profited from such laissez-faire sentiment, but it also shaped the thought of most politically active Panamanians. They were individualistic, nationalistic, and ripe for revolt.

They first rebelled against Colombia (then New Granada), in 1830, again in 1831, and as many as fifty times between 1840 and 1903. . . .

Colombia's claim [to control over Panama] had been proven wrong throughout the nineteenth century. Indeed the Bogotá government itself had admitted failure. At least four times (some historians say six) between 1846 and 1903 Colombia asked the United States to restore order on the Isthmus. The settlement of the Thousand Days' War aboard a United States warship in November 1902 was only the last in a long line of North American interventions into affairs between Colombia and its raucous, hell-bent-for-independence province. A distinguished Panamanian diplomat later remarked that his country emerged as an independent nation because of its geography, economy, history, and "the interest and the sentiments of the people of Panama"—not "the arbitrariness of Theodore Roosevelt." And Panamanian historian Ricaurte Soler has observed that by 1903 "a nation already existed and a Panamanian consciousness had already been formed."

That was one important lesson to be drawn from four hundred years of Panamanian experience. There were others. Panama's prosperity historically depended on traffic through the Isthmus. When the Spanish Empire prospered or the new railroad flourished, so did Panama, but at other times the country stagnated. Without vast arable lands or mineral wealth, the people's fortunes rose and fell with the use outsiders made of the major resource— geographical location. The Panamanians have been historically conditioned to think of this as the key to their welfare. That perception has been sharpened by the nationalist, anti-imperialist ideology that began to take hold in the mid-nineteenth century. In the end, Colombia could not control a nationalism that was rooted in the historical memory of four centuries and expressed in the demands of a revolutionary elite.

As Colombia's grip slipped, Roosevelt's hand began to close around the Isthmus. A long list—Balboa and Spain, Drake and England, de Lesseps and France, as well as many Colombian leaders—tried to claim this crossroads of the world. All failed. Roosevelt and the United States, with the confidence peculiar to expanding empires, now determined to try their luck. . . .

With an isthmian canal virtually within his grasp, Roosevelt refused to allow those "contemptible little creatures" in Colombia to frustrate his grand plan. But TR could not decide how to deal with the Colombians. He apparently held little hope the deadlock would be broken by a successful Panamanian revolt. As the President searched desperately for alternatives, Bunau-Varilla and the Panamanian nationalists were devising a solution. That solution, together with a 1904 agreement negotiated between Washington and Panama City by Secretary of War William Howard Taft, created the framework for sixty years of relations between the two countries and shaped the crisis of the 1970s.

Bunau-Varilla, with considerable help from top State Department officials, took the lead in solving Roosevelt's dilemma. During September and October 1903, the Frenchman held a series of talks with Hay, Assistant Secretary of State Francis B. Loomis (whom Bunau-Varilla had known since a meeting in Paris two years before), and John Bassett Moore, a former Assistant Secretary of State, renowned international lawyer, and confidant of TR. Out of the conversations grew Bunau-Varilla's conviction that if the Panamanians tried to declare their independence the United States would use force, ostensibly to uphold its 1846 commitment to maintain transit rights across the Isthmus, but in reality to prevent Colombia from quashing the revolution.

As early as August, Moore sent a memorandum to Roosevelt arguing that the 1846 pact gave the United States the right to construct a canal. Loomis, who spent many hours with Bunau-Varilla, apparently inspired the memorandum; in any case, it completely reversed Moore's previous opinion of the 1846 treaty. Later in the autumn Bunau-Varilla asked Loomis how the United States would respond to an outbreak on the Isthmus. The Assistant Secretary of State said he "could only venture to guess that this Government would probably do as it had done in the past under like circumstances." Bunau-Varilla agreed, hoping that the North Americans "might freely do more rather than less." The Frenchman received the same reply from Moore and on October 10, 1903, probably heard similar words from the ultimate authority, Roosevelt. As the President later remarked, Bunau-Varilla "would have been a very dull man had he been unable to make such a guess." The Frenchman was many things, including devious, scheming, ambitious, and money-hungry, but he was certainly not dull.

And if he had been, Bunau-Varilla needed no more hints after a candid talk with Hay in the privacy of the latter's home. "I expressed my sentiments on the subject some days ago to President Roosevelt," the Frenchman began, "the whole thing will end in a revolution. You must take your measures. . . ." Hay played the game perfectly: "Yes, that is unfortunately the most probable hypothesis. But we shall not be caught napping. Orders have been given to naval forces on the Pacific to sail towards the Isthmus." As Bunau-Varilla later editorialized. "It only remained for me to act."

He first contacted the head of the revolutionary junta, Dr. Manuel Amador Guerrero, a physician closely associated with the Panama Railroad, now owned by the New Panama Canal Company. Amador happened to be in New York City to obtain money and support for the plot. Bunau-Varilla contacted Amador none too soon, for the Panamian had just discovered that Cromwell, the New Panama Canal Company's lawyer, was growing fearful that the revolution would abort and his company's concessions seized by a vengeful Colombia. The story of Cromwell getting cold feet has been embroidered by Bunau-Varilla and so is highly suspect; in his memoirs the Frenchman, with spectacular condescension and malice, always calls him "the lawyer Cromwell." Much of the malice doubtlessly resulted from Bunau-Varilla's fear that Cromwell would someday receive as many lines in history texts as he. But it does seem that his report to Amador of the TR and Hay conversations revived sagging Panamanian hopes.

Plans again moved forward on the Isthmus. The revolutionaries comprised an odd but not illogical assortment, for a number of them had one association in common. Other than Amador (the Panama Railroad's physician), the group included José Agustín Arango (the railway's attorney), James R. Shaler (superintendent of the railway), and James R. Beers (the railway's freight agent). It might have been Beers who first assured Arango that a Panamanian revolt would be supported by the United States. Amador and Arango were joined by the oligarchy's leaders: C. C. Arosemena, Ricardo Arias, Federico Boyd, and Tomás Arias. Once free of Colombian control—once they could develop their already extensive economic and political power according to their own interests and without concern for Bogotá—these oligarchs, their sons, and grandsons dominated Panama for sixty years. The motives varied, but for good reasons the railway officials and the Panamanian nationalists remained closely allied. As Roosevelt understood, "You don't have to foment a revolution. All you have to do is take your foot off and one will occur."

As the zero hour approached, however, TR displayed more optimism than did people in Panama. In early October the commander of the *U.S.S. Nashville* visited Colon, then reported to Washington that although three-quarters of the people would support a leader who would build a canal, "such a leader is now lacking, and it isn't believed that in the near future these people will take any initiative steps." The junta was preparing to provide the leadership, but the timing would be crucial. Closely following ship movements in the newspapers, Bunau-Varilla learned on October 30 that the *Nashville* was leaving Jamaica for an unspecified port. He correctly guessed it was heading for Colon and would arrive in two or three days. Given the intimacy between the Frenchman and Loomis, this was perhaps a mere deduction, not a lucky guess. Bunau-Varilla wired this news to Amador, who had returned to the Isthmus to lead the revolt. Both men now believed the United States was moving into a position to support their revolution. Loomis, however, jumped the gun and the result was nearly farce. "Uprising on the Isthmus reported," the Assistant Secretary anxiously cabled the United States Consul in Panama on November 3. "Keep department promptly and fully informed." Maintaining his composure, the Consul replied, "No uprising yet. Reported will be in the night. Situation critical."

Late that day the Panamanians struck, quickly seizing control of the Isthmus. The governor appointed by Colombia to rule the province, José Domingo de Obaldía, had long been sympathetic to Panamanian autonomy and gladly joined the revolutionaries. For his understanding he became one of Panama's first Vice-Presidents. Colombian army detachments were apparently bought off by Cromwell and the New Panama Canal Company; the commander received $30,000, other officers $10,000, and rank-and file $50 each in gold.

Commander Hubbard aboard the *Nashville* received no orders regarding the uprising until late on November 2. Roosevelt and Loomis apparently did not trust the navy with their plans. Thus when 2500 Colombian soldiers appeared off Colon on November 2 to prevent the rumored revolution, a confused Hubbard allowed them to land. Shaler, the superintendent of the railway, saved the situation. He first moved his cars to the Pacific side of the Isthmus, 48 miles from Colon, so the Colombians could not use the railway. Then he talked the Colombian officers into traveling to Panama City, assuring them that their troops would soon follow. In reality, the soldiers next saw their commanders when all were packed aboard ships for the return trip to Bogotá. The next day U.S. sailors finally landed to ensure that the Colombian troops behaved. An independent Panama had already been proclaimed by Amador. A new nation the size of South Carolina was born, and the labor pains had been easy. None of the belligerents was killed. The only deaths were a Chinese citizen who had gotten trapped in some desultory shelling, a dog, and, according to some reports, a donkey. . . .

Roosevelt justified his aid to the revolutionaries by citing the 1846 commitment, a justification that had no legal or historical basis. The treaty certainly did not give the United States the right to use force against Colombia, with whom the pact had been made, in order to build a canal. Nor did it require Colombia to allow a canal to be constructed. The treaty indeed justified United States intervention in order to preserve Colombia's sovereignty on the Isthmus. TR intervened, however, to destroy that sovereignty.

But Roosevelt clung to the 1846 pact since he had little else. He was consequently interested when Oscar Straus, a New York lawyer and adviser of the President, suggested the 1846 treaty required the United States to intervene because it was not made merely with Colombia, but was "a covenant running with the land"—regardless of who happened to control the land. With delight, and doubtless a sense of relief, Roosevelt immediately ordered Hay to use this argument. The United States held to this interpretation even though John Bassett Moore (certainly the State Department's most distinguished lawyer) exploded Straus's sophistry and suggested that in TR's hands it actually amounted to a "covenant running (away!) with the land!!"

The President later argued that the seizure had been for the sake of "civilization," thereby adopting the proposition that since North American actions were justified morally they were justified legally. His Attorney-General, Philander C. Knox, offered the appropriate reply: "Oh, Mr. President, do not let so great an achievement suffer from any taint of legality." Knox's caustic advice was better than he knew, for soon Roosevelt began a campaign, backed by force, to compel Latin American governments to uphold their own legal obligations as he defined those obligations.

In one sense, TR acted quite uncharacteristically: he aided a revolution. For a man whose central political tenet was stability, and for a nation that had fought revolutionaries and secessionists at least since 1861, unleashing revolution marked an abrupt change. It was also a short-lived change. Roosevelt possessed his canal territory and recognized the new Panamanian government led by Amador, Pablo Arosemena, and Obaldía on November 6. But when the Panamanian army attempted to land at Colon to claim the city, TR stopped it. A little revolution was sufficient. Washington needed time to sort things out. The Panamanian government would have to wait a while before its army could enter the country's second largest city. In the first moments after recognition, Panama and the United States were at loggerheads.

Nor did Roosevelt try to reconcile the Colombians. On November 6 he told them he had intervened because "treaty obligations" and the "interest of civilization" required that the Isthmus not endure "a constant succession of . . . wasteful civil wars." TR urged Bogotá to recognize the new government. Colombia responded by sending to Washington its most distinguished citizen and former president, General Rafael Reyes, in an attempt to revive the Hay-Herrán treaty—the same pact which the Colombian Senate unanimously rejected several months before. Reyes was now prepared to lower the price. The welcome in Washington was cool. Hay advised Roosevelt that "the sooner you see him, the sooner we can bid him good-bye." But Reyes was a forceful, popular figure, and hired one of the most adept lobbyists in Washington to fight against a treaty with an independent Panama. Hay wrote TR, "I told [Secretary of War Elihu] Root I was going to see Reyes. He replied, 'Better look out. Ex-Reyes are dangerous.' Do you think that, on my salary, I can afford to bear such things?" Hay need not have worried. As Roosevelt later noted, he viewed Colombians as similar to "a group of Sicilian or Calabrian bandits. . . . You could no more make an agreement with the Colombian rulers than you could nail currant jelly to a wall."

TR and Hay focused on arranging the canal treaty with the Panamanians, or, more precisely, the Frenchman who had taken the opportunity to represent Panama. Bunau-Varilla engaged in a mini-power struggle with Arango, Tomás Arias, and Federico Boyd for control over negotiations in Washington. Since the three Panamanians were not yet in the United States, and because Bunau-Varilla convinced them he knew the political situation and financial channels, the Frenchman was empowered to initiate talks with Hay. Amador and Boyd left Panama on November 10 to join Bunau-Varilla.

The new government meanwhile instructed the Frenchman that the negotiations were to be guided by three principles. First, no deals could be made that affected "the sovereignty of Panama, which [was] free, independent, and sovereign." Second, the United States should pledge to uphold the new nation's "sovereignty, territorial integrity, and public order." That clause would place North American troops, if necessary, between Panama and a vengeful Colombia. Third, a canal treaty would be drafted, but only after consultation with Amador and Boyd. "You will proceed in everything strictly in agreement with them," the Frenchman was told.

The instructions did not reach Bunau-Varilla in time, nor did Amador and Boyd. The minister made certain of that. On Friday the 13th of November he began talks with Roosevelt and Hay. Bunau-Varilla emphasized that time was all-important. If the treaty was not rushed to completion, he argued, a number of events would occur, all of them bad: a restless United States Senate, under Morgan's lashing, might turn back to Nicaragua; Colombia might seduce Panama back into the fold (the suave Reyes was on his way to Panama City); and isthmian politics might turn chaotic, forcing delays in the talks. Implicitly, but obviously, Bunau-Varilla also wanted to pocket the $40 million for his New Panama Canal Company as quickly as possible. Nor would he mind going down in history as the lone negotiator on the Panamanian side who signed the epochal pact.

Heartily sharing the Frenchman's mistrust of the Senate, Hay quickly prepared a treaty draft. It was largely the Hay-Herrán agreement that Colombia had rejected. The draft explicitly recognized Panamanian sovereignty in a canal zone, and even went further than the Hay-Herrán agreement by increasing Panama's judicial authority in a zone. Panamanian troops would protect the canal, and United States forces would be used in the area only with Panama's consent. The proposed treaty would run 99 years, or until about 2002.

Then, in what proved to be one of the most momentous twenty-four-hour periods in American diplomatic history, Bunau-Varilla worked all night and all day on November 16 to rewrite Hay's paper. The minister was afraid that the draft would not sufficiently appease the Senate, at least not enough to have the body act quickly on the treaty. Bunau-Varilla also wanted to complete the treaty before Amador and Boyd arrived. They were in New York City, but Cromwell, for purposes of his own, had detained them. On November 17, Bunau-Varilla told the two Panamanians to remain in New York for another day, then rushed to the State Department to consummate the deal.

Hay could hardly believe his eyes. Bunau-Varilla's treaty ensured the canal's neutrality, proposed payment to Panama of an amount equal to that which the United States would have paid Colombia, and guaranteed Washington's protection of Panama's independence. The United States was to assume a virtual protectorate over the new country. But in return, the treaty gave the United States extensive powers in the Canal Zone, for Washington would have "all the rights, power, and authority within the zone . . . which the United States would possess and exercise if it were the sovereign of the territory within which said lands and waters are located to the entire exclusion of the exercise by the Republic of Panama of any such sovereign rights, power, and authority."

That was the most radical change, a change that has caused continual crises in U.S.-Panamanian relations for the next three-quarters of a century. But there was more. Bunau-Varilla surrendered Panamanian judicial power in the Zone, widened the zone area from ten kilometers (or six miles) to ten miles, and lengthened Hay's 99-year lease to "perpetuity." The astonished Secretary of State made only one change (the United States "leases in perpetuity" phrase was transformed into the more direct wording that Panama "grants to the United States in perpetuity the use, occupation, and control" of a canal zone). At 6:40 p.m. on November 18, the treaty was signed by the two men. Amador and Boyd arrived in Washington three hours later. Bunau-Varilla met them at Union Station, showed them the pact, and Amador nearly fainted on the train platform.

The Panamanian government angrily protested "the manifest renunciation of sovereignty" in the treaty. That protest echoed down through the years, becoming ever more magnified. If the new government rejected the pact, however, it faced bitter alternatives: the United States might seize the canal area without either paying for it or undertaking to protect the new republic, or Roosevelt might build in Nicaragua and leave the Panama City revolutionaries to the tender mercies of the Colombian army. In truth, the Panamanians had no choice.

They had leaped across an abyss to gain their independence, were hanging on the other side by their fingertips, and the United States held the rescue rope. Having helped put them in that position, Bunau-Varilla dictated the terms under which they could be pulled up to safety. Hay and Bunau-Varilla were too powerful and sophisticated to allow Panama to claim it accepted the treaty under duress, a claim that if declared legally valid could void the acceptance. Panama, however, did accept under duress. Having a French citizen disobey the Panamanian government's instructions, and then having no choice but to accept the Frenchmen's treaty, compounded the humiliation. In the 1970s a documentary film made in Panama about the 1903 affair was entitled, "The Treaty that No Panamanian Signed." . . .

For the revolutionaries humiliation was nevertheless preferable to hanging. Throughout the negotiations Bunau-Varilla had kept them informed of rising indignation in the United States over his and Roosevelt's management of the affair. The President soon had another revolt on his hands; this one was in the Senate and the country at large.

It was not a massive revolt, but a surprising number of Senators and important newspapers condemned TR's action. The division was partially along party lines. William Randolph Hearst's Democratic papers attacked the President's action as "nefarious." Hearst's Chicago *American* called it "a rough-riding assault upon another republic over the shattered wreckage of international law and diplomatic usage." Such widely circulated urban dailies as the *New York Times,* New York *Evening Post,* Philadelphia *Record,* Memphis *Commercial Appeal,* and *Springfield Republican* agreed with Hearst's assessment.

In the Senate the powerful Maryland Democrat, Arthur Pue Gorman, organized opposition to the treaty. That Gorman was an avowed candidate for the 1904 presidential run against Roosevelt made his opposition doubly significant. Holding 33 of the 90 Senate seats, the Democrats could theoretically prevent the necessary two-thirds of the Senate from ratifying the pact. And with Senator Morgan holding out for the Nicaraguan route, Gorman's chances for success seemed reasonable. Even the newspapers and public spokesmen who supported TR refused to justify his action on moral grounds. Instead, as *Public Opinion* noted, since the majority of the country wanted "an isthmian canal above all things," it was willing to overlook moral issues in order to justify taking the canal as strictly "a business question."

Roosevelt refused to take that approach. As have most rulers who aggressively used naked force, he wanted it masked with morality. In an outspoken special message to the Senate on January 4, 1904, the President submitted the treaty and justified his actions in November on the grounds of the 1846 pact, "our national interests and safety," and the usual Rooseveltian claim of "the interests of collective civilization." He suffered no doubts that the United States had "received a mandate from civilization" to build a canal, although he could not tell exactly how that mandate had been expressed. One problem, of course, was that "the interests of collective civilization" had never been seen or defined (was Colombia, for example, a part of "collective civilization"?). Like many Rooseveltian phrases, the term better fit the President's prejudices than any international legal or moral standard.

Yet TR won and Gorman lost. The prospects of a United States-controlled canal caused flutters of patriotism in too many hearts and the prospect of rich satisfaction in too many pocketbooks. In the Senate the Democrats split, with many southerners, who had long sought the project, joining the President. Led by the prestigious Atlanta *Constitution,* southern papers crossed party lines formed during the Civil War in order to back the treaty. Even Gorman admitted he wanted a canal constructed; he simply disliked Roosevelt's methods. Some skeptics were won over by the President's message. Noting that he had denied any wrong-doing, the Detroit *Free Press* believed that the word of a United States President "is as good as anybody else's word." The *New York Times,* the New York *Evening Post,* and the *Washington Post,* however, never surrendered, and the Chicago *Chronicle* (a Democratic paper) summarized their feelings by calling Roosevelt's appeal to "civilization" a "pitiful and alarming chapter in American government," a "tyrant's plea of necessity." The opponents were equally bitter over the South's defection to the President's side. As the *New York Times* editorialized. "This is the southern spirit of the slavery days," for like slavery, the canal to the South is "purely a question of profit in dollars and cents."

As Roosevelt and the Senate Republican leadership intensified the pressure, Gorman admitted his effort had "ended in smash." On February 23, 1904, he watched sixteen, or nearly half the Senate Democrats, join the Republicans to sweep the treaty through 66–14. Opposition came almost entirely from the Northeast, the Middle States, and pockets of the South. The Midwest, West, and much of the South supported the President. Gorman's presidential hopes sunk with his effort to stop the treaty. Running eight months later against the colorless Democrat, Alton B. Parker, Roosevelt understood how the opposition had been silenced. "Can you not tell our speakers to dwell more on the Panama Canal?" he wrote a campaign manager. "We have not a stronger card."

After early 1904, politicians who opposed United States control of the canal were committing political suicide. Bunau-Varilla had triumphed. Although, as the *Pittsburgh Post* remarked, TR's methods in Panama "were subversive of the best principles of the republic," the Frenchman had made the treaty so attractive that the United States, as he hoped, quickly chose power over principle. . . .

The Senate ratification marked a beginning, not the end, of the struggle over the treaty. With Article I placing them under Washington's protection ("The United States guarantees and will maintain the independence of the Republic of Panama"), the Panamanians immediately began protesting the mushrooming North American control over their country. A first clash occurred in early 1904 when the State Department insisted that Panama must acknowledge in its new constitution (and not merely in the treaty), the United States right of intervention. William Buchanan, the U.S. Minister, wanted the widest possible power to control "pests" through Panama, and brought great pressure to bear on the Panamanian constitutional convention. Finally, Article 136 gave the United States the right to "intervene, in any part of Panama, to reestablish public peace and constitutional order." The North Americans could apparently unilaterally determine when public peace and order were jeopardized. But this Article squeaked through the convention 17–14; leading Panamanians were already trying to contain United States influence. As Buchanan told Hay, "The fact that fourteen . . . voted against it," together with the appearance on the streets of handbills and newspapers condemning Article 136, "amply justified the wisdom of our having secured" it.

Article III of the treaty, however, has most disrupted relations. It gave the United States the rights, powers, and authority in the zone "as if it were the sovereign of the territory." From the outset Panama argued that it remained the actual sovereign in the area. Bunau-Varilla agreed, perhaps out of conscience. "The United States, without becoming the sovereign, received the exclusive use of the rights of sovereignty," the Frenchman wrote, "while respecting the sovereignty itself of the Panama Republic."

Such an arrangement was not unprecedented in 1903, although from the United States point of view the precedents were not happy. When Germany, France, and Russia forcibly took territory from an enfeebled China during the late 1890s, the treaties stipulated (to quote the words of the German-Chinese pact), that "in order to avoid the possibility of conflicts, the Imperial Chinese Government will abstain from exercising rights of sovereignty in the ceded territory during the term of the lease, and leaves the exercise of the same to Germany." The precedent was not a happy one, for Washington had vigorously opposed those treaties.

Yet the United States wanted to compromise none of the vast powers Bunau-Varilla wrote into Article III. Attempting to placate the Panamanians while retaining all the power, in 1904 John Hay coined the phrase "titular sovereignty" to describe Panama's rights in a canal zone. The phrase became a widely used and condescending description of Panama's sovereignty in the zone, but on October 18, 1904, Roosevelt recognized the limitations of United States rights in the canal area when he instructed Secretary of War William Howard Taft:

> We have not the slightest intention of establishing an independent colony in the middle of the State of Panama, or exercising any greater governmental functions than are necessary to enable us conveniently and safely to construct, maintain and operate the canal, under the rights given us by the treaty. Least

of all do we desire to interfere with the business and prosperity of the people of Panama.... In asserting the equivalent of sovereignty over the canal strip, it is our full intention that the rights which we exercise shall be exercised with all proper care for the honor and interests of the people of Panama.

Roosevelt's term, "the equivalent of sovereignty," and the limitations placed upon United States power before and after the phrase, indicated that the President interpreted his nation's right in the Canal Zone to be short of sovereignty itself.

After looking into the matter in Panama, Taft, who possessed a notable judicial mind, thought the issue inconsequential. His report to Roosevelt of December 19, 1904, became the standard view of the question:

The truth is that while we have all the attributes of sovereignty necessary in the construction, maintenance and protection of the Canal, the very form in which these attributes are conferred in the Treaty seems to preserve the titular sovereignty over the Canal Zone in the Republic of Panama, and as we have conceded to us complete judicial and police power and control of two ports at the end of the Canal, I can see no reason for creating a resentment on the part of the people of the Isthmus by quarreling over that which is dear to them, but which to us is of no real moment whatever.

Taft thus admitted the United States did not have full sovereignty over the new Canal Zone. It had "complete judicial and police power and control" at the vital points, but the "titular sovereignty" or residual sovereignty resided with the Panamanians. Some North Americans who insisted on total control over the Zone during the 1960s and 1970s argued that their country was "sovereign" in the Zone. They were wrong, if Hay, Roosevelt, and Taft, the three Washington officials who constructed the Panamanian-United States relations, are to be believed. From the start the question was not whether Panama had residual sovereign rights in the Zone, for it did, but what would happen in the distant future if the Panamanians tried to exert those rights against the full control exercised by the United States.

The North Americans, of course, never had sovereignty over the Canal Zone as they do over Alaska or Texas. They must pay an annual fee to Panama for the use of the Zone, and children born of non-North American parents in the Canal Zone are not automatically United States citizens as they are if born in Texas or Alaska. The $10 million paid to Panama in 1903 was for treaty rights, not the purchase of territory as in the Louisiana acquisition of 1803 or the Alaskan purchase of 1867.

The clash over sovereignty initially occurred because the United States acted as if it were sovereign throughout parts of Panama *outside* the Canal Zone. Article II of the treaty gave the United States the right "in perpetuity" to occupy and control any lands outside the Zone which it thought necessary for building or maintaining the canal. Related provisions of the treaty were breath-taking in their sweep of power granted Washington. Article IV gave the United States "in perpetuity" the right "to use rivers, streams, lakes, and other bodies of water" for any purpose relating to the canal. Article V granted the United States a "monopoly" over "any [sic] system of communication" in Panama. Article VII provided the power to take by right of eminent domain needed lands, buildings, or water rights in Panama City and Colon, and to intervene in those cities, if necessary, to preserve public order. The same article granted the United States the authority to create and enforce sanitary regulations in the two cities, a power which actually gave Washington the dominant voice in their political and financial affairs. Article XII surrendered to the Canal Company control over Panama's immigration.

These provisions made Panama a potential colony of the United States. Article II—giving Washington officials the right "in perpetuity" to occupy and control any lands outside the Zone which, in their own opinion, they needed—was a virtual blank check. The cost of the lands would be determined by a joint U.S.-Panamanian commission, but under no circumstances could it delay canal construction while deliberating. The North Americans seized large chunks of Panamanian territory. Numerous requests for additional land were made between 1908 and 1930. Fourteen military bases were ultimately established, ostensibly to protect the Canal although some were for purposes outside Panama; several of the bases occupied land outside the Zone. Panamanian protests grew with the development of the military complex, particularly when United States-owned land later prevented orderly growth of Panama City and Colon.

Panama officials also objected to the $10 million fee and the $250,000 annual annuity. They noted that in contrast with their $10 million, the redoubtable Bunau-Varilla and his company received $40 million, and they further observed in the 1920s that the United States apologetically paid Colombia $25 million (although, admittedly, Congress found the courage to pacify the Colombians only after Roosevelt died). The $250,000 annuity merely equaled the amount Washington paid Colombia for the railroad rights alone before 1903. Panamanians interpreted each North American demand for additional land as fresh evidence they were being cheated. . . .

In a country possessing little experience in democratic politics, but of which democratic procedures were somehow expected, the United States placed an elite white oligarchy firmly in control. Washington officials helped create the conditions for an economically bipolarized, undemocratic, and potentially unstable country. When Panama later appeared as bipolarized, undemocratic, and unstable, North Americans could not understand why. . . .

The implications of Bunau-Varilla's treaty were outrunning even Roosevelt's fertile imagination. It should be stressed, however, that the implications made a greater impact on Panama than on United States policy. Roosevelt was extremely active in the Caribbean region during these years, but his activity was not due solely to the newly acquired canal area. TR's policy was the logical continuation of a century-long North American involvement that was turning Washington into a self-appointed policeman in the Caribbean.

Since the eighteenth century the United States had been driving southward, first to conquer a continent, then, after the Civil War, to seize economic and strategic prizes. Its financial power increasingly penetrated the Caribbean area after the 1870s. Victory in the War of 1898 brought Puerto Rico and the Cuban naval base of Guantanamo. The Caribbean was becoming a North American lake, and obtaining the Canal Zone marked one more step in that direction.

Within a year after construction of the Canal began, however, Roosevelt announced a new policy, the so-called Roosevelt Corollary to the Monroe Doctrine. In his Annual Messages to Congress in 1904 and 1905, the President hoped that Latin American nations would be happy and prosperous, but he believed they could not share such joys "unless they maintain order within their boundaries and behave with a just regard for their obligations towards outsiders." To help them, the United States would become the policeman throughout the area. (Roosevelt privately understood that the primary police work would be in the smaller Caribbean and Central American countries, not the large nations on the South American continent.) The policeman, TR proclaimed, would ensure that the countries met their "obligations," so the "outsiders" would have no excuse to intervene. The "outsider" most feared in Washington was Germany, whose businessmen, diplomats, and naval officers seemed overly ambitious in the Western Hemisphere. Great Britain possessed a greater fleet, but it apparently had made its peace with North American expansion southward, most notably by agreeing to the second Hay-Pauncefote treaty.

The Roosevelt Corollary triggered the most ignoble chapter in United States-Latin American relations. Believing, as TR said, that "a civilized nation" such as the United States possessed the right to stop "chronic wrongdoing," North Americans sent troops into a half-dozen Caribbean nations during the next twelve years, and within two decades dominated at least fourteen of the twenty Latin American countries through either financial controls or military power—and, in some instances, through both.

Officials at the time argued that the Roosevelt Corollary was necessary to protect the new canal. As John Hay's successor in the State Department, Elihu Root, wrote a friend in 1905, "The inevitable effect of our building the Canal must be to require us to police the surrounding premises." It became an early version of the domino theory: if unfriendly, powerful Europeans settled in one part of the Caribbean, their influence could spread until the Canal would be endangered.

Root's explanation of the Roosevelt Corollary cannot withstand historical analysis. That the Canal increased United States interest in the Caribbean cannot be disputed. But the Corollary's principles were formed long before the Isthmus was seized—as early as the 1870s, 1880s, and 1890s, when such Washington officials as Ulysses S. Grant, "Jingo Jim" Blaine, and Richard Olney bluntly told Europeans that the Caribbean should be considered a North American lake. And the Corollary evolved quite independently of Canal Zone policy. To misunderstand this relationship is to misunderstand a most important chapter in United States-Latin American affairs.

TR's inspiration to act as a "civilized" policeman occurred before the Canal Zone was seized, and quite independently of events on the Isthmus. In 1900–1901, for example, the United States imposed on Cuba the Platt

Amendment, giving Washington the right to intervene any time at its discretion to maintain order in the newly independent island. The provision established a precedent and a rationale for the later Corollary. In 1902–03 Germany and Great Britain intervened in Venezuela to collect overdue debts. An uproar resulted in the United States, and the British shrewdly suggested to Roosevelt that if he did not want the Europeans to protect their legal rights in the Western Hemisphere, he should do it for them. Grumbling that "These wretched republics cause me a great deal of trouble," TR believed a second foreign intervention "would simply not be tolerated here. I often think that a sort of protectorate over South and Central America is the only way out."

His opportunity finally arose in Santo Domingo. For over five years New York City bankers had fought French and German financiers for control of the country's resources. By early 1904 Santo Domingo seemed to be moving toward a state of permanent revolutionary instability. Roosevelt ordered the navy to seize the country's customs houses, pay off the foreign debt, and under no circumstances allow any revolutionary activity to interrupt the country's development. He publicly rationalized the seizure by announcing the Roosevelt Corollary.

These affairs in Cuba, Venezuela, and Santo Domingo had little or nothing to do with the Isthmus. Taking the Canal Zone by no means led to the Roosevelt Corollary. Instead, Roosevelt's Panama policy can be interpreted as fitting into a larger Latin American policy that was evolving long before the Panamanian revolution. To confuse the Canal as the cause of the Corollary, therefore, is to confuse fundamental motivations of American foreign policy.

Two motives shaped Roosevelt's Corollary. First, he hated disorder, especially disorder that might lead to political bipolarization or an opportunity for European economic and/or political intervention. The Monroe Doctrine might act as a shield for Latin Americans against European imperialists, but Roosevelt would not allow the Doctrine "to be used as a warrant for letting any of these republics remain as small bandit nests of a wicked and inefficient type." That premise of the Corollary was easily extended to Panama. Taft's intervention in 1904 (and again in 1908), rested in part on that premise, and both the President and his Secretary of War would have agreed with a leading naval strategist in Washington who argued that "so-called revolutions in the Caribbean are nothing less than struggles between different crews of bandits for the possession of the customs houses—and the loot." A second motivation was Roosevelt's belief that the United States had been entrusted with a "civilizing" mission which it should bear proudly. This belief seemed particularly applicable to the Caribbean, including Panama, where the people were largely a mixture of Indian, Spanish, and black. This motivation, of course, had its ironies. As sociologist William Graham Sumner observed at the time, "We talk of civilizing lower races, but we have never done it yet. We have exterminated them."

If Taft and Roosevelt were so concerned about the Canal Zone's security (instead of their "civilizing mission" of imposing order on Latin America), they might have allowed the United States Navy to build a chain of bases in the isthmian area. They did not. After the Panamanian revolution, naval officials asked for three bases around the Zone, bases they had long sought from Colombia. Roosevelt rejected the request. When fortifications were planned for each end of the Canal, two military boards concluded that these, along with the Guantanamo base in Cuba, sufficiently protected the passageway. As President, Taft later upheld this decision and refused to spend $4 million on army barracks in Panama. If war began, he reasoned, troops could move to the Isthmus quickly enough from the United States. Taft thought the fortifications along the Canal primarily useful for stopping any unhinged Latin American dictator who might try to seize the waterway.

Building the Panama Canal did not cause the announcement of the Roosevelt Corollary. TR instead used the Isthmus as one of several areas for the exercise of his police powers. The President's Panama policy was a symptom, not a cause, of his larger Caribbean plans. The evolution of United States policy in Panama can consequently be interpreted as another manifestation of his racial, economic, and military views. How such perceptions affected Panamanians and helped create their growing animosity toward North Americans should be considered separately, not filtered through a supposed preoccupation on Roosevelt's part to provide security for a canal.

The failure to understand the demands, dynamics, and confusions of nationalism is hardly peculiar to TR, yet historical circumstances made him President precisely at the point when the European-dominated world system, which he so admired, was disintegrating. In 1904–05 Japan's dramatic victory over Russia surprised the white races and encouraged non-whites, especially those who lived in Asian and African colonial areas. The Chinese, Turkish, and Russian revolutions formed roots in those years. Roosevelt prided himself on his understanding of historical change and his sensitivity to the nuances of a global balance of power, but he never comprehended the significance of these shattering events. TR was unable to see that the world was comprised of more than simply the "civilized" versus the "wicked and inefficient types."

After he intervened in Panama in 1903, Roosevelt painstakingly explained his actions to the Cabinet, then demanded to know whether the explanation would silence his opponents. "Have I defended myself?" he asked. "You certainly have," replied a brave Elihu Root. "You have shown that you were accused of seduction and you have conclusively proved that you were guilty of rape." Roosevelt never understood how his policies and explanations worsened the problems in the Caribbean area that he tried to stabilize. He, Taft, and Bunau-Varilla were making Panama as well as the Canal Zone a virtual colony of the United States, but the North American leaders refused to assume even the responsibilities of enlightened colonialism, save that of using force or the threat of force to maintain order. That solution worsened, not ameliorated, Panama's problem and, consequently, Panamanian relations with the United States.

# FURTHER READING

Charles D. Ameringer, "The Panama Canal Lobby of Phillippe Bunau-Varilla and William Nelson Cromwell," *American Historical Review,* 68 (1963), 346–363

Howard K. Beale, *Theodore Roosevelt and the Rise of America to World Power* (1956)

Samuel Flagg Bemis, *The Latin American Policy of the United States* (1943)

John M. Blum, *The Republican Roosevelt* (1954)

David H. Burton, *Theodore Roosevelt: Confident Imperialist* (1968)

Miles P. DuVal, *Cadiz to Cathay* (1940)

Thomas G. Dyer, *Theodore Roosevelt and the Idea of Race* (1980)

Raymond A. Esthus, *Theodore Roosevelt and the International Rivalries* (1970)

William H. Harbaugh, *The Life and Times of Theodore Roosevelt* (1975)

David Healy, *The United States in Cuba, 1898–1902* (1963)

Warren G. Kneer, *Great Britain and the Caribbean, 1901–1913* (1975)

Walter LaFeber, *Inevitable Revolutions: The United States in Central America* (1983)

Lester D. Langley, *The United States and the Caribbean in the Twentieth Century* (1982)

David McCullough, *The Path Between the Seas: The Creation of the Panama Canal, 1870–1914* (1977)

Allan R. Millett, *The Politics of Intervention: The Military Occupation of Cuba, 1906–1909* (1968)

Dwight C. Miner, *The Fight for the Panama Route* (1940)

Dana Munro, *Intervention and Dollar Diplomacy* (1964)

Dexter Perkins, *The Monroe Doctrine, 1867–1907* (1937)

Whitney T. Perkins, *Constraint of Empire: The United States and Caribbean Intervention* (1981)

Henry F. Pringle, *Theodore Roosevelt* (1956)

Ramon Ruiz, *Cuba: The Making of a Revolution* (1968)

# Woodrow Wilson and the Mexican Revolution

# 14

*Why the United States intervened in Latin America—economic profit?
humanitarianism? mission? security?—becomes a persistent question when
the historian studies the administrations of Theodore Roosevelt, William
Howard Taft, and Woodrow Wilson in sequence. That is, Roosevelt's interventions became a pattern, seemingly qualified only by the different styles
of the Presidents. Roosevelt wielded the "Big Stick" but Taft, espousing
"dollar diplomacy," sent troops into Nicaragua and Cuba and continued the
financial supervision of the Dominican Republic. Woodrow Wilson came
into office in 1913 promising a new era in inter-American relations, but soon
sent American soldiers into Mexico, the Dominican Republic, Cuba, and
Haiti to restore economic and political order to those revolution-wracked
countries—actions sometimes called "missionary diplomacy" and "moral imperialism." Wilson spoke in lofty terms of teaching Latin Americans to behave
by constitutional procedures and civilized standards. "When properly directed,"
Wilson remarked in 1914, "there is no people not fitted for self-government."
Yet Wilson seemed unwilling to relinquish United States hegemony over
much of Latin America. His troubles with the Mexican Revolution, which
became increasingly anti-American in tone and disruptive of American
interests, provide a case study. Mexicans had rebelled in 1910 against the
long-term dictatorship of Porforio Diaz, and by the time Wilson entered
the White House Mexico was awash in civil war. Wilson believed that the
United States should direct the future course of the Mexican Revolution.
Why?*

## DOCUMENTS

In October 1913, Woodrow Wilson, a critic of "dollar diplomacy," suggested that Latin American nations could expect more United States "understanding" and more emphasis on "constitutional liberty." Like many Latin American nationalists, Francisco García Calderón, a Peruvian diplomat and writer who later represented his nation at the Paris Peace Conference of 1919, resented United States interventions, as the second document indicates. The third document is a transcript of Wilson's press conference of November 24, 1914, in which he explains why he sent American troops to Veracruz, Mexico. On June 21, 1916, Secretary of State Robert Lansing wrote the President advising him to avoid the word *intervention* when he explained why the United States had again sent military forces into Mexico, this time under the leadership of General John J. "Black Jack" Pershing. The closing selection is an excerpt from Mexican President Venustiano Carranza's September 1, 1919, message to the National Congress. He mentions some of his nation's complaints against the United States.

# Woodrow Wilson on Latin American Policy, 1913

The future, ladies and gentlemen, is going to be very different for this hemisphere from the past. These States lying to the south of us, which have always been our neighbors, will now be drawn closer to us by innumerable ties, and I hope, chief of all, by the tie of a common understanding of each other. Interest does not tie nations together; it sometimes separates them. But sympathy and understanding does unite them, and I believe that by the new route that is just about to be opened, while we physically cut two continents asunder, we spiritually unite them. It is a spiritual union which we seek.

I wonder if you realize, I wonder if your imaginations have been filled with the significance of the tides of commerce. Your governor alluded in very fit and striking terms to the voyage of Columbus, but Columbus took his voyage under compulsion of circumstances. Constantinople had been captured by the Turks and all the routes of trade with the East had been suddenly closed. If there was not a way across the Atlantic to open those routes again, they were closed forever, and Columbus set out not to discover America, for he did not know that it existed, but to discover the eastern shores of Asia. He set sail for Cathay and stumbled upon America. With that change in the outlook of the world, what happened? England, that had been at the back of Europe, with an unknown sea behind her, found that all things had turned as if upon a pivot and she was at the front of Europe; and since then all the tides of energy and enterprise that have issued out of Europe have seemed to be turned westward across the Atlantic. But you will notice that they have turned westward chiefly north of the Equator and that it is the northern half of the globe that has seemed to be filled with the media of intercourse and of sympathy and of common understanding.

Do you not see now what is about to happen? These great tides which have been running along parallels of latitude will now swing southward athwart parallels of latitude, and that opening gate at the Isthmus of Panama will open the world to a commerce that she has not known before, a commerce of intelligence, of thought and sympathy between north and south. The Latin American States, which, to their disadvantage, have been off the main lines, will now be on the main lines. I feel that these gentlemen honoring us with their presence to-day will presently find that some part, at any rate, of the center of gravity of the world has shifted. Do you realize that New York, for example, will be nearer the western coast of South America than she is now to the eastern coast of South America? Do you realize that a line drawn northward parallel with the greater part of the western coast of South America will run only about 150 miles west of New York? The great bulk of South America, if you will look at your globes (not at your Mercator's projection), lies eastward of the continent of North America. You will realize that when you realize that the canal will run southeast, not southwest, and that when you get into the Pacific you will be farther east than you were when you left the Gulf of Mexico. These things are significant, therefore, of this, that we are closing one chapter in the history of the world and are opening another, of great, unimaginable significance.

There is one peculiarity about the history of the Latin American States which I am sure they are keenly aware of. You hear of "concessions" to foreign capitalists in Latin America. You do not hear of concessions to foreign capitalists in the United States. They are not granted concessions. They are invited to make investments. The work is ours, though they are welcome to invest in it. We do not ask them to supply the capital and do the work. It is an invitation, not a privilege; and States that are obliged, because their territory does not lie within the main field of modern enterprise and action, to grant concessions are in this condition—that foreign interests are apt to dominate their domestic affairs, a condition of affairs always dangerous and apt to become intolerable. What these States are going to see, therefore, is an emancipation from the subordination, which has been inevitable, to foreign enterprise, and an assertion of the splendid character which, in spite of these difficulties, they have again and again been able to demonstrate. The dignity, the courage, the self-possession, the self-respect of the Latin American States, their achievements in the face of all these adverse circumstances, deserve nothing but the admiration and applause of the world. They have had harder bargains driven with them in the matter of loans than any other peoples in the world. Interest has been exacted of them that was not exacted of anybody else, because the risk was said to be greater; and then securities were taken that destroyed the risk—an admirable arrangement for those who were forcing the terms! I rejoice in nothing so much as in the prospect that they will now be emancipated from these conditions, and we ought to be the first to take part in assisting in that emancipation. I think some of these gentlemen have already had occasion to bear witness that the Department of State in recent months has tried to serve them in that wise.  In the future they will draw closer and closer to us because of circumstances of which I wish to speak with moderation and, I hope, without indiscretion.

We must prove ourselves their friends and champions upon terms of equality and honor. You can not be friends upon any other terms than upon the terms of equality. You can not be friends at all except upon the terms of honor. We must show ourselves friends by comprehending their interest, whether it squares with our own interest or not. It is a very perilous thing to determine the foreign policy of a nation in the terms of material interest. It not only is unfair to those with whom you are dealing, but it is degrading as regards your own actions.

Comprehension must be the soil in which shall grow all the fruits of friendship, and there is a reason and a compulsion lying behind all this which is dearer than anything else to the thoughtful men of America. I mean the development of constitutional liberty in the world. Human rights, national integrity, and opportunity as against material interests—that, ladies and gentlemen, is the issue which we now have to face. I want to take this occasion to say that the United States will never again seek one additional foot of territory by conquest. She will devote herself to showing that she knows how to make honorable and fruitful use of the territory she has, and she must regard it as one of the duties of friendship to see that from no quarter are material interests made superior to human liberty and national opportunity. I say this, not with a single thought that anyone will gainsay it, but merely to fix in our consciousness what our real relationship with the rest of America is. It is the relationship of a family of mankind devoted to the development of true constitutional liberty. We know that that is the soil out of which the best enterprise springs. We know that this is a cause which we are making in common with our neighbors, because we have had to make it for ourselves.

## Francisco García Calderón on American Imperialism, 1913

To save themselves from Yankee imperialism the American democracies would almost accept a German alliance, or the aid of Japanese arms; everywhere the Americans of the North are feared. In the Antilles and in Central America hostility against the Anglo-Saxon invaders assumes the character of a Latin crusade. Do the United States deserve this hatred? Are they not, as their diplomatists preach, the elder brothers, generous and protecting? And is not protection their proper vocation in a continent rent by anarchy?

We must define the different aspects of their activities in South America; a summary examination of their influence could not fail to be unjust. They have conquered new territories, but they have upheld the independence of feeble States; they aspire to the hegemony of the Latin continent, but this ambition has prevented numerous and grievous conflicts between South American nations. The moral pressure of the United States makes itself felt everywhere; the imperialist and maternal Republic intervenes in all the internal conflicts of the Spanish-speaking democracies. It excites or suppresses revolutions; it fulfills a high vocation of culture. It uses or abuses a privilege which cannot be gainsaid. The better to protect the Ibero-Americans, it has proudly raised its Pillars of Hercules against the ambition of the Old World.

Sometimes this influence becomes a monopoly, and the United States take possession of the markets of the South. They aim at making a trust of the South American republics, the supreme dream of their multi-millionaire *conquistadores*. Alberdi has said that there they are the "Puerto Cabello" of the new America; that is to say, that they aim, after the Spanish fashion, at isolating the southern continent and becoming its exclusive purveyors of ideas and industries.

Their supremacy was excellent when it was a matter of basing the independence of twenty republics of uncertain future upon a solid foundation. The neo-Saxons did not then intervene in the wars of the South; they remained neutral and observed the peace which Washington had advocated. They proclaimed the autonomy of the continent, and contributed to conserve the originality of Southern America by forbidding the formation of colonies in its empty territories, and by defending the republican and democratic States against reactionary Europe.

But who will deliver the Ibero-Americans from the excess of this influence? *Quis custodiet custodem?* An irresponsible supremacy is perilous. . . .

Interventions have become more frequent with the expansion of frontiers. The United States have recently intervened in the territory of Acre, there to found a republic of rubber gatherers; at Panama, there to develop a province and construct a canal; in Cuba, under cover of the Platt amendment, to maintain order in the interior; in Santo Domingo, to support the civilising revolution and overthrow the tyrants; in Venezuela, and in Central America, to enforce upon these nations, torn by intestine disorders, the political and financial tutelage of the imperial democracy. In Guatemala and Honduras the loans concluded with the monarchs of North American finance have reduced the people to a new slavery. Supervision of the customs and the dispatch of pacificatory squadrons to defend the interests of the Anglo-Saxon have enforced peace and tranquility: such are the means employed. The *New York American* announces that Mr. Pierpont Morgan proposes to encompass the finances of Latin America by a vast network of Yankee banks. Chicago merchants and Wall Street financiers created the Meat Trust in the Argentine. The United States offer millions for the purpose of converting into Yankee loans the moneys raised in London during the last century by the Latin American States; they wish to obtain a monopoly of credit. It has even been announced, although the news hardly appears probable, that a North American syndicate wished to buy enormous belts of land in Guatemala, where the English tongue is the obligatory language. The fortification of the Panama Canal, and the possible acquisition of the Galapagos Islands in the Pacific, are fresh manifestations of imperialistic progress.

The Monroe doctrine takes an aggressive form with Mr. Roosevelt, the politician of the "big stick," and intervention *à outrance*. Roosevelt is conscious of his sacred mission; he wants a powerful army, and a navy majestically sailing the two oceans. His ambitions find an unlooked-for commentary in a book by Mr. Archibald Coolidge, the Harvard professor, upon the United States as a world-power. He therein shows the origin of the disquietude of the South Americans before the Northern peril: "When two contiguous States," he writes, "are separated by a long line of frontiers and one of the two rapidly increases, full of youth and vigor, while the other possesses, together with a small population, rich and desirable territories, and is troubled by continual revolutions which exhaust and weaken it, the first will inevitably encroach upon the second, just as water will always seek to regain its own level."

He recognises the fact that the progress accomplished by the United States is not of a nature to tranquillise the South American; "that the Yankee believes that his southern neighbours are trivial and childish peoples, and above all incapable of maintaining a proper self-government." He thinks the example of Cuba, liberated "from the rule of Spain, but not from internal troubles, will render the American of the States sceptical as to the aptitude of the Latin-American populations of mixed blood to govern themselves without disorder," and recognises that the "pacific penetration" of Mexico by American capital constitutes a possible menace to the independence of that Republic, were the death of Díaz to lead to its original state of anarchy and disturb the peace which the millionaires of the North desire to see untroubled.

Warnings, advice, distrust, invasion of capital, plans of financial hegemony —all these justify the anxiety of the southern peoples. . . . Neither irony nor grace nor scepticism, gifts of the old civilisations, can make way against the plebeian brutality, the excessive optimism, the violent individualism of the [North American] people.

All these things contribute to the triumph of mediocrity; the multitude of primary schools, the vices of utilitarianism, the cult of the average citizen, the transatlantic M. Homais, and the tyranny of opinion noted by Tocqueville; and in this vulgarity, which is devoid of traditions and has no leading aristocracy, a return to the primitive type of the redskin, which has already been noted by close observers, is threatening the proud democracy. From the excessive tension of wills, from the elementary state of culture, from the perpetual unrest of life, from the harshness of the industrial struggle, anarchy and violence will be born in the future. In a hundred years men will seek in vain for the "American soul," the "genius of America," elsewhere than in the undisciplined force or the violence which ignores moral laws. . . .

In seeking to imitate the United States we should not forget that the civilisation of the peoples of the North presents these symptoms of decadence.

Europe offers the Latin-American democracies what the latter demand of Anglo-Saxon America, which was formed in the school of Europe. We find the practical spirit, industrialism, and political liberty in England; organisation and education in Germany; and in France inventive genius, culture, wealth, great universities, and democracy. From these ruling peoples the new Latin world must indirectly receive the legacy of Western civilisation.

Essential points of difference separate the two Americas. Differences of language and therefore of spirit; the difference between Spanish Catholicism and the multiform Protestantism of the Anglo-Saxons; between the Yankee individualism and the omnipotence of the State natural to the nations of the South. In their origin, as in their race, we find fundamental antagonisms; the evolution of the North is slow and obedient to the lessons of time, to the influences of custom; the history of the southern peoples is full of revolutions, rich with dreams of an unattainable perfection.

The people of the United States hate the half-breed, and the impure marriages of whites and blacks which take place in Southern homes; no manifestation of Pan-Americanism could suffice to destroy the racial prejudice as it exists north of Mexico. The half-breeds and their descendants govern the Ibero-American democracies, and the Republic of the [sic] English and German origin entertains for the men of the tropics the same contempt which they feel for the slaves of Virginia whom Lincoln liberated.

In its friendship for them there will always be disdain; in their progress, a conquest; in their policy, a desire for hegemony. It is the fatality of blood, stronger than political affinities or geographical alliances. . . .

The Monroe doctrine, which prohibits the intervention of Europe in the affairs of America and angers the German imperialists, the professors of external expansion, like Münsterberg, may become obsolete. If Germany or Japan were to defeat the United States, this tutelary doctrine would be only a melancholy memory. Latin America would emerge from the isolation imposed upon it by the Yankee nation, and would form part of the European concert, the combination of political forces—alliances and understandings—which is the basis of the modern equilibrium. It would become united by political ties to the nations which enrich it with their capital and buy its products.

## Wilson on Huerta and Veracruz, 1914

Q. Mr. President, what, in your opinion, has been the big thing achieved by the taking and the evacuation of Veracruz?

A. Well, now, do you mean my own? If I speak to you, not for publication, that is the only way I can speak about it, because in the first place we are in there because of the action of a naval officer. Understand that we didn't go in on the choice of the administration, strictly speaking; but a situation arose that made it necessary for the maintenance of the dignity of the United States that we should take some decisive step; and the main thing to accomplish was a vital thing. We got Huerta. That was the end of Huerta. That was what I had in mind. It could not be done without taking Veracruz. It could not be done without some decisive step—to show the Mexican people that he was all bluff, that he was just composed of bluff and showed that; and that is all they ever got. That part is not for publication. I am sure I can trust you. But it is important

From Arthur S. Link, ed., *The Papers of Woodrow Wilson, Vol. 31: September 6– December 31, 1914.* Copyright © 1979 by Princeton University Press.

that it should guide your own thought in the matter, because apparently we are in there for nothing in particular, and came in for nothing in particular, and I don't wonder that people who don't look beneath the surface couldn't see that the objective was to finish Huerta, and that was accomplished. The very important thing—the thing I have got at heart now—is to leave those people free to settle their own concerns, under the principle that it's nobody else's business. Now, Huerta was not the Mexican people. He did not represent any part of them. He did not represent any part. He was nothing but a "plug ugly," working for himself. And the reason that the troops did not withdraw immediately after he was got rid of was that things were hanging at such an uneven balance that nobody had taken charge; that is, nobody was ready to take charge of things at Mexico City. I have said all along that I have reason to feel confident, as I do feel confident, that nothing will go seriously wrong with Mexico City, so far as the interests we are surely responsible for are concerned. Of course, we can't protect Mexican citizens. That is another matter. That is the whole thing. I am very glad, in confidence, to let you know just what is in it.

# Secretary of State
# Robert Lansing on "Intervention," 1916

My Dear Mr. President: As there appears to be an increasing probability that the Mexican situation may develop into a state of war I desire to make a suggestion for your consideration.

It seems to me that we should avoid the use of the word "Intervention" and deny that any invasion of Mexico is for the sake of intervention.

There are several reasons why this appears to me expedient:

*First.* We have all along denied any purpose to interfere in the internal affairs of Mexico and the St. Louis platform declares against it. Intervention conveys the idea of such interference.

*Second.* Intervention would be humiliating to many Mexicans whose pride and sense of national honor would not resent severe terms of peace in case of being defeated in a war.

*Third.* American intervention in Mexico is extremely distasteful to all Latin America and might have a very bad effect upon our Pan-American program.

*Fourth.* Intervention, which suggests a definite purpose to "clean up" the country, would bind us to certain accomplishments which circumstances might make extremely difficult or inadvisable, and, on the other hand, it would impose conditions which might be found to be serious restraints upon us as the situation develops.

*Fifth.* Intervention also implies that the war would be made primarily in the interest of the Mexican people, while the fact is it would be a war forced on us by the Mexican Government, and, if we term it intervention, we will have considerable difficulty in explaining why we had not intervened before but waited until attacked.

It seems to me that the real attitude is that the *de facto* Government having attacked our forces engaged in a rightful enterprise or invaded our borders (as the case may be) we had no recourse but to defend ourselves and to do so it has become necessary to prevent future attacks by forcing the Mexican Government to perform its obligations. That is, it is simply a state of international war without purpose on our part other than to end the conditions which menace our national peace and the safety of our citizens, and that is *not* intervention with all that that word implies.

I offer the foregoing suggestion, because I feel that we should have constantly in view the attitude we intend to take if worse comes to worse, so that we may regulate our present policy and future correspondence with Mexico and other American Republics with that attitude.

In case this suggestion meets with your approval I further suggest that we send to each diplomatic representative of a Latin American Republic in Washington a communication stating briefly our attitude and denying any intention to intervene. I enclose a draft of such a note. If this is to be done at all, it seems to me that it should be done at once, otherwise we will lose the chief benefit, namely, a right understanding by Latin America at the very outset.

# Some Mexican Complaints
# Against the United States, 1919

Unfortunately, the Government of Mexico frequently receives representations, more or less energetic, from the Government of the United States, in the cases in which we desire to introduce innovations which injure the interests of some citizens of that country; these representations tend to restrict our liberty of legislation, and invade the right which we possess of self-development in accordance with our own ideas.

The most important case is that of the Richardson Construction Company, in which diplomatic representations were made against the raising of taxes on a great estate, notwithstanding that one of the causes of the Revolution was the great disproportion between the values of real estate and the taxes imposed thereon.

There have been other cases of representations, for example: because of tax increases or export restrictions on hides; because of export taxes on cattle; because of production taxes on metals and taxes on mining claims; because of the increase of export taxes on cotton produced in Lower California.

In all these cases, the argument used by the Department of State of the United States in official notes, or by the press when the action has assumed other characteristics, has been that the duties or taxes are "confiscatory," the word having been given so extensive a meaning that it is thought that by its use every restriction on our liberty of legislation is covered and justified.

The Government of Mexico hopes that the Republic of the North will respect the sovereignty and independence of Mexico, because to violate them on the plea of lack of guarantees for its citizens or of legislation injurious to their interests would constitute an unpardonable transgression of the principles of international law and morality, and would give proof that the greatest misfortune of a people is that of being weak.

Due to our geographical situation in respect to the United States of America, and the numerous commercial ties we have with them, various incidents of different kinds have arisen in the course of our international relations:

Last year, a group of soldiers of the United States crossed the frontier and entered our territory as far as the town of El Mulato, as a result of which shots were exchanged, resulting in the death of a citizen of the United States and in injury to a Mexican fiscal guard. Our Embassy made appropriate representations and the Government of the United States replied that, in truth, its soldiers were to blame for the incident, and that as a result of a court martial two of them had been sentenced to one year's imprisonment, two others to three years, and one to five years.

In the same year, a group of soldiers of the United States shot at Mexican farmers who were at work in our territory, in the Municipality of Villa Acuña, Coahuila, and killed the Mexican Angel Rangel. The corresponding representations being made, the Department of State informed our Embassy, through which they were made, that, in truth, three soldiers of the Army of the United States had fired, occasioning the death of Rangel, and that they would be court-martialed. No information has been received that the culprits have been punished.

In April last, our Embassy in Washington received a memorial signed by numerous Mexicans residing at Bartlesville, Oklahoma, complaining of the unjust persecutions of which they are the victims in that region, because on the 16th of April the Mexican David Cantú was assaulted without reason by five or six citizens of the United States. On April 18th various Mexicans who were at a reunion overheard a public official say that in his opinion Cantú should be beaten and hanged to a post, and so it happened that on the 22nd three citizens of the United States went to the place where Cantú worked, and hanged and beat him—all without any reason whatever.

---

# ESSAYS

Robert Freeman Smith, an historian of inter-American relations who teaches at the University of Toledo, explains Woodrow Wilson's interventions in Mexico within the larger context of United States interest in foreign economic development favorable to American interests. Smith sees a "developed" nation (the United States) at odds with an "underdeveloped" country (Mexico). The former sought an "order" the latter would not provide. The second essay, by Ramón Eduardo Ruíz, a scholar of Cuban and Mexican history, studies the Mexican perspective on Woodrow Wilson and United States intervention. The Mexicans struggled with the question of how to have their revolution and at the same time maintain peaceful relations with their giant neighbor. They found, as Ruíz has written, that "in twentieth century Mexico, no regime stood a ghost of a chance of surviving without Washington's embrace."

# Wilson's Pursuit of Order

### ROBERT FREEMAN SMITH

A combination of material interests and ideas about the conduct and status of so-called backward nations shaped the reaction of the United States to the upheaval, nationalistic aspirations, and reforms of the Mexican Revolution. Prior to 1910, North American officials, intellectuals, and businessmen had articulated, and begun to act upon, a multidimensional conception of the "backward," or underdeveloped, areas. This, in turn, became an integral part of their ideas on economic expansion and the strategic necessities imposed by the new frontiers of interests and ambitions. Woodrow Wilson stated these views in very clear terms when he wrote:

> Since trade ignores national boundaries and the manufacturer insists on having the world as a market, the flag of his nation must follow him, and the doors of the nations which are closed against him must be battered down. Concessions obtained by financiers must be safeguarded by ministers of state, even if the sovereignty of unwilling nations be outraged in the process. Colonies must be obtained or planted, in order that no useful corner of the world may be overlooked or left unused.

The most important elements of this world view were: (1) the resources of the underdeveloped countries must be made available to developed nations to provide the raw materials for their industrial and military systems; (2) the markets of these same countries must be open to the exports of the developed nations; (3) investments must be protected, since these are vital elements in trade expansion and overall national prosperity; (4) order and stability (meaning no upheavals and friendly treatment of foreign interests) are necessary for the expansion of trade and investment, which in turn reinforces these conditions; and (5) the industrial-creditor nations have the right and the duty to police the underdeveloped areas in order to secure their version of order and stability.

These elements were often mixed with the emotional rhetoric of expansionist ideology, which spoke in terms of a "civilizing mission," the "white man's burden," and "protecting rights." Racism combined with these rather well, since most of the inhabitants of the underdeveloped world were non-white. Thus a belief in the racial inferiority of the peoples concerned seemed to give added justification to policies of economic penetration and political control. This combination of beliefs and myths provided the emotional dynamic for the material ambitions of the United States. As the Reverend Josiah Strong wrote in his layman's guide to the theology of empire: "The world is to be Christianized and civilized. . . . And what is the process of civilizing but *the creating of more and higher wants?* Commerce follows the missionary." . . .

In spite of its concern over the effects of turmoil and minor restrictions on economic penetration and order, the United States—and the other developed nations—did not have to contend with any fundamental challenges to the industrial-creditor conception of property rights until the reformist nationalism of the Mexican Revolution began to affect government policies. Prior to this, however, several Latin American nations had tried to gain some protection from the police power of the developed nations by asserting two international doctrines of their own. The Drago Doctrine stated that powerful nations did not have the right to collect by force the foreign debts owed to their citizens. Luis Drago, the Argentine foreign minister, hoped that this would become a "corollary" of the Monroe Doctrine, which would prevent such intervention by all countries. This was not what the United States meant in the "Roosevelt corollary." Secretary of State Elihu Root did not want to antagonize the major Latin American nations by completely rejecting the Drago Doctrine, and he persuaded the Second Hague Conference to adopt a modified version. This still sanctioned intervention as a last resort, and Drago voted against it. The United States maintained its "right" to police and continued to exercise this as it saw fit.

The Calvo Doctrine was much more extensive, involving not only intervention but also the basic questions concerning the "rights" of resident foreigners. Carlos Calvo, an Argentine diplomat and commentator on international law, began with the premise of the equality of states and attacked the extraterritorial concepts of the powerful states. He wrote:

> It is certain that aliens who establish themselves in a country have the same right to protection as nationals, but they ought not to lay claims to a protection more extended. . . .
> The rule that in more than one case it has been attempted to impose on American states is that foreigners merit more regard and privileges more marked and extended than those accorded even to the nationals of the country where they reside.

Calvo argued that foreign residents were subject to the same laws and to the same judicial processes as the citizens of the country. Foreign businesses had no right of appeal to another legal system (extraterritoriality principle) and were to be treated as if they were owned by citizens of the country. All questions of economic policy involving foreign resident business would be domestic questions only, not subject to interference by foreign governments. In short, the international rules of the developed nations would no longer be the overriding mechanism through which they controlled the treatment of their citizens by underdeveloped countries. . . .

468 / Major Problems in American Foreign Policy

The contemporary ideas, beliefs, and prejudices of the developed nations shaped the reaction of the United States to the Mexican Revolution throughout the entire period from 1916 through 1932. Influential North Americans, in and out of government, generally agreed that internal order and stability must be maintained in underdeveloped nations in order to protect and advance their interpretations of the national interest. In addition, the underdeveloped countries must carry out their economic policies within the bounds of the system of industrial capitalism and the legal framework which had been erected to protect the property relationships of this system. The struggle to achieve these goals constitutes a basic unifying factor behind the Mexican policy of the administrations of Woodrow Wilson, Warren Harding, and Calvin Coolidge.

The basic dilemma, however, was how to achieve these goals, especially in a larger, and more belligerent, underdeveloped country such as Mexico. Thus the major controversies concerning the Mexican policy of the United States were over the tactics or methods to be used in restoring order and stability to Mexico and in keeping the reforms of the revolution within the bounds of the international legal order of the industrial-creditor nations.

Specific issues such as control of subsurface minerals, foreign debts, and agrarian reform complicated the task of developing tactical policies. Even within administrations, ideas about methods varied, and one of the key variables was the definition of the point at which a law or regulation passed from "legitimate" regulation to nationalization—that is, when a tax or the size and number of federal mineral reserves or the definition of subsurface claims became "confiscatory." Closely related to this definition was each policy maker's view of the Mexican Revolution. Those who believed that it was a devious conspiracy, either of radicals or corrupt politicians, tended to be dogmatic in their evaluation of Mexico's laws and to advocate a more uncompromising policy. On the other hand, those who viewed the revolution as a complex, tumultuous stage in Mexico's historical evolution tended to have less anxiety over every jot and tittle of Mexican law and to concentrate on establishing a working relationship with key officials of the Mexican government. These same variations existed among the representatives of the various private groups with economic interests in Mexico. The variegated array of informal working relationships between these men and government officials with similar views provided another element in the policy making process.

But the ideas, interests, and beliefs of the Mexicans also would influence the policies and actions of North Americans in various ways. Mexico was not Haiti or the Dominican Republic, and the "wind that swept Mexico" was far more than a "golpe de estado" or the aimless violence of "backward" Indians and sadistic *bandidos.* . . .

When Woodrow Wilson took office on 4 March 1913, he confronted a revived revolution in Mexico with all the attendant dangers to foreign lives and property. The new president was a firm believer in the industrial-creditor concept of order and stability, and he emphasized the role of Anglo-American political institutions in establishing these conditions. In his view, revolutions occurred either because bad men were trying to usurp power through unconstitutional means or because the people were unable to vote in free elections. Revolutions would not occur when elections were held, constitutional provisions were obeyed, and bad men were eliminated. Granting recognition to men who seized power or who did not follow correct constitutional practices would only encourage revolutions, since only bad men would refuse to support a government which held elections. Constitutional provisions should protect private property and all rights legitimately acquired—that is, under a correct legal system. In addition, Wilson's constitutionalist concept of freedom and democracy was intimately linked to his views on capitalism and private property; he noted, "If America is not to have free enterprise, then she can have freedom of no sort whatever." He believed that the right kind of institutions and laws—which were equated with the terms freedom and democracy—would eliminate instability and revolutions and that the end product would be a condition of "constitutional order" where legitimate business would flourish and the doors would be open to commerce.

Wilson shared the world view of those who believed that the mission of the United States was to spread the institutional prerequisites of order and stability to the underdeveloped world as a necessary concomitant of economic penetration. He sounded very much like Mahan when he expressed this theme in an *Atlantic Monthly* article in 1901:

> The East is to be opened and transformed . . . the standards of the West are to be imposed upon it; nations and peoples who have stood still the centuries through are to be quickened, and to be made part of the universal world of commerce and of ideas which has so steadily been a-making by the advance of European power from age to age. It is our peculiar duty, as it is also England's, to moderate the process in the interests of liberty: to impart to the peoples thus driven out upon the road of change . . . our own principles of self-help; *teach them order and self-control* in the midst of change.

Wilson, and almost all others in positions of authority, continually said that the teaching of order and self-control, through the inculcation or imposition of North American political institutions, was not based upon selfish interests but upon the desire to help the peoples concerned. These officials sincerely believed that what was good for the United States was good for others—especially for the underdeveloped and backward peoples. But in this context freedom and self-determination meant specific conditions of order and the right kind of laws and policies. Wilson was a true believer in the righteousness of this policy, but the rhetoric of morality should not obscure what actually happened. Robert Lansing, who was either more cynical or less concerned with moral justification, pointed out this situation to Wilson on one occasion when the president had prepared a glowing defense of the U.S. regard for freedom and self-determination in its relations with Mexico. The secretary wrote in the margin, "Haiti, S. Domingo, Nicaragua, Panama?" This particular speech was not delivered.

President Wilson did place much emphasis on rule by good men—which in practice meant men who followed constitutional procedures, enforced law and order, and were friendly to the United States. When Sir William Tyrrell, in November 1913, asked Wilson to explain his Mexican policy, the president replied: "I am going to teach the South American republics to elect good men." Perhaps one could also note that a good man was one who agreed with Wilson, and faced with the rising intensity of Mexican nationalism Wilson saw himself as a veritable Demosthenes bearing the lantern of North American truths in search of a just Mexican.

Wilson also applied the criterion of good and bad to businesses. He was firmly convinced that some bad businessmen stirred up revolutions and exploited people through dishonest practices. In addition, bad businessmen were those who called for an all-out invasion of Mexico—those who wanted limited intervention were not necessarily classified as bad. The president repeatedly stressed that his Mexican policy was not designed to protect property rights. In one sense this was true, since Wilson's primary concern was not the physical protection of each and every holding in Mexico, especially if this involved extensive military efforts. But one of the major emphases of his policy was to insure the kind of order and legal structure in which business could flourish. In fact, the Wilson administration went beyond this general point and did make numerous representations for specific interests. On the basis of the historical record, the Wilson administration did as much as—if not more than—the administrations of Taft, Harding, and Coolidge to protect North American property interests in Mexico. The Mexicans certainly recognized this, for they were constantly being reminded of it. For example, as Wilson said on one occasion:

> We should let every one who assumes to exercise authority in any part of Mexico know in the most unequivocal way that we shall vigilantly watch the fortunes of those Americans who can not get away, and shall hold those responsible for their sufferings and losses to a definite reckoning. That can be and will be made plain beyond the possibility of a misunderstanding.

Some have argued that the real test of Wilson's idealistic policy was his refusal to go to war with Mexico. Taft, Harding, and Coolidge also refused to step into this abyss, and they did not have to contend with the complications of a European war and the struggle for a peace treaty. All these administrations evidenced the combination of ideals and interests which was a part of their commonly shared world view. The economic penetration of the underdeveloped world and its defense by nonmilitary means, if at all possible, were basic elements of this world view. Secretary of State William Jennings Bryan succinctly expressed this combination of economic and idealistic expansion in the Western Hemisphere when he wrote in 1913 that these would "give our country such increased influence . . . that we could prevent revolutions, promote education, and advance stable and just government. . . . we would in the end profit, negatively, by not having to incur expense in guarding our own and foreign interests there, and positively, by the increase of our trade." . . .

During the summer of 1913 the Wilson administration began its campaign to eliminate the Huerta government. Various tactics were employed: offers of mediation, ultimatums, threats of force, loan proposals, and the occupation of the port of Veracruz (April 1914). The British government feared that this policy would not bring order to Mexico and might jeopardize British economic interests. Wilson sought to reassure British officials. After a conference in November 1913 with Sir William Tyrrell, the president wrote him a letter outlining U.S. policy. In it he said: "I beg that you will assure Sir Edward Grey that the United States Government intends not merely to force Huerta from power, but also to exert every influence it can exert to secure Mexico a better government under which all contracts and business concessions will be safer than they have been." Wilson also noted his hope that Grey could convey this message to British and Canadian investors.

The president forcefully reiterated this position in his "international note" of 24 November, which was sent to fifteen European states, Brazil, and Japan. This note provided a clear statement of the industrial-creditor concept of order, as well as Wilson's belief that the continued rule of Huerta was a fundamental threat to this concept:

> Usurpations like that of General Huerta menace the peace and development of America as nothing else could. They not only render the development of ordered self-government impossible; they also tend to set law entirely aside, to put the lives and fortunes of citizens and foreigners alike in constant jeopardy, to invalidate contracts and concessions in any way the usurper may devise for his own profit, and to impair both the national credit and all the foundations of business, domestic or foreign.
>
> It is the purpose of the United States, therefore, to discredit and defeat such usurpations whenever they occur.

In the meantime, Wilson promised that every effort would be made "that the circumstances permit to safeguard foreign lives and property."

The oil fields around Tampico were already being watched over by the U.S. Navy. Admiral Frank F. Fletcher warned the Constitutionalist forces not to attack the property of Lord Cowdray or to levy taxes on foreign oil producers. In reply to a request for protection by H. Clay Pierce, Secretary Bryan stated that the department would instruct its representatives to extend "all possible and proper protection."

The Huerta government had more staying power than Wilson or his advisers realized. By February 1914 the Constitutionalist forces had been halted by a resurgent Huerta. President Wilson now abandoned his plans for a provisional government and decided to give complete support to the Constitutionalists, at least until they had eliminated Huerta. This decision was aided when Luis Cabrera, Carranza's agent in Washington, provided satisfactory answers to questions concerning the future treatment of foreign interests. Cabrera stated that although radical social and economic reforms were planned, these would be accomplished by constitutional and legal means which would respect property rights, including "just and equitable concessions." Confiscation and anarchy would not be tolerated. The U.S. government then lifted the embargo on arms shipments to the Carranza forces, an act which the State Department counselor John Bassett Moore called "the first of the series of measures for playing off one Mexican military 'chief' against another."

The United States seized Veracruz in April 1914, and shortly thereafter Argentina, Brazil, and Chile offered their services as mediators between the United States and Mexico. But Wilson intended to use the mediation conference—which convened at Niagara Falls, Canada, in May 1914—to do far more than ease tensions. As Arthur Link succinctly describes it: "He [Wilson] meant to use the A.B.C. mediation, first, to eliminate Huerta, and, second, to establish a new provisional government in Mexico City that he could control."

The Constitutionalists, however, refused to fall into a trap which would make them in any way dependent upon or under obligation to the U.S. government. Carranza refused the mediation of the conference, and his representatives informed the U.S. delegates that Mexico would settle its own problems without interference from any source. Wilson, however, clearly intended to exercise some influence over Huerta's successors and was not eager to see either Villa or Carranza become president.

Shortly after the triumph of the Constitutionalists in July 1914, Wilson dispatched a detailed set of instructions for proper behavior to Carranza. Three "matters of critical consequence" were listed: "First, the treatment of foreigners, foreign lives, foreign property, foreign rights, and particularly the delicate matter of the financial obligations, the legitimate financial obligations, of the government now suspended. Unless the utmost care, fairness and liberality are shown in these matters, the most dangerous complications may arise." The other two dealt with the generous treatment which Carranza was expected to display toward political and military opponents and the Roman Catholic Church. In short, there was to be no revolution, since adherence to all these prescriptions would prevent any basic changes in the socioeconomic structure of Mexico. Carranza did state that foreigners would be protected and all legitimate—a term most productive of controversy—contracts and obligations respected. But he refused to give assurances about the opposition, and Wilson then sent a note hinting at the "fatal consequences" which might follow if his advice were spurned. Revolutionary nationalism and U.S. hemispheric hegemony now had completely locked horns.

For the next fifteen months the U.S. government followed a most tortuous and oft-times contradictory course in its attempt to mold Mexican political developments. The process of playing off one military chief against another became almost ludicrous as the opinions of U.S. officials seemed to shift with every contradictory report from the south. All agreed that Mexico should be stabilized under pro-U.S. leadership, but they held various opinions concerning which leader or coalition would most effectively accomplish this goal. The Wilson administration increasingly stressed a new coalition of the factions. By mid-1915, it seemed that the Villistas met the pro-U.S. requirement but held little promise in regard to stable leadership. Conversely, the Carranzistas appeared to offer the best hope for stability, but Carranza's intensely nationalistic posture rejected U.S. influence. The civil war between the factions made this dilemma even more complex, especially after April 1915, when the Carranza forces increasingly gained the ascendancy. . . .

The United States extended *de facto* recognition to the Carranza government on 19 October 1915. But the Wilson administration still tried to qualify this acceptance of Carranza. *De facto* recognition was a sort of "half-way house." The idea at this time was to withhold full *de jure* recognition until the new government demonstrated its "good behavior." The meaning of this behavior was spelled out in detail in a memorandum prepared by Leon J. Canova, head of the Division of Mexican Affairs, at Lansing's request. Some modifications were made, and the document was handed to Eliseo Arredondo when he presented his credentials to the State Department. He was instructed to use the memorandum when he saw Carranza, since these were matters which must be handled properly and effectively. Seven of the eighteen points in the document dealt with protection of foreign economic rights in Mexico —loans, property, and trade. The others concerned questions of religion, elections, and the treatment of the opposition—necessary accouterments of peace and order in the official U.S. view. Basically, this was an extended version of the U.S. demands of July 1914.

The U.S. government had made a limited, tactical withdrawal in the face of Carranza's strength. It had not given up the attempt to influence the Mexican Revolution, however. To U.S. officials, the revolution had ended and Mexico must now return to the ranks of the stable, well-behaved under-developed nations. But the stage was already set for renewed complications. As Wilson and Lansing soon discovered, the nationalism of the revolution was not a force which could be tamed simply by *de facto* recognition. The instructions for proper behavior were just as unpalatable to Carranza after 19 October as they had been in July 1914—perhaps more so, since he was now the victor. . . .

Reviewing the history of U.S.-Mexican relations from 1913 to 1926, the chief of the State Department's Mexican Division stressed their consistently tense nature. In his memorandum of 17 December 1926, R. C. Tanis explained the matter: "This state of affairs has resulted from the persistent efforts of Carranza and succeeding executives of Mexico to deprive American citizens of properties legally acquired by them under the Mexican laws in effect at the time of purchase, and from the fact that the Government of the United States has consistently opposed such efforts." Tanis then traced the history of U.S. protests over reforms and policies affecting the property of North Americans. The almost steady stream of protest notes reflected the steadily increasing importance of the second stage of the unfolding revolutionary process: the development of a reform impetus stressing national control over the resources of the country. For a time this process was entangled with the effect which disorder and violence had upon foreign lives and property. In terms of U.S. protests and policy these two aspects to a limited degree would remain entangled until 1920. But after 1915 the Mexican reforms and policies affecting foreign economic interests became one of the major problems in U.S.-Mexican relations, and by mid-1920 it was the paramount issue.

Between 1913 and 1916 the State Department received numerous reports and statements about the possibility of national and state reform legislation. Many of these dealt with the possible nationalization of petroleum, but this problem seemed to be relatively insignificant—at least as compared to some other problems faced by foreign property owners—until early in 1915. At that time the State Department received information that Carranza had issued a decree requiring the oil companies to obtain the permission of the Constitutionalist government in order to continue operations. This government approval would be issued after the companies agreed to abide by the new petroleum laws which were being prepared. To the State Department and the oil companies this seemed to be an attempt by the Constitutionalists to obtain advance acceptance of a kind of Calvo Doctrine regulation. The Carranza government did not push the issue, but it did expand its regulatory functions. Complaints by foreign businesses increased—as did rumors of nationalization. . . .

These initial regulatory actions were quickly overshadowed by Pancho Villa. The Santa Isabel massacre of fifteen North Americans on 10 January 1916 set the stage. Then, on 9 March, the Villistas attacked Columbus, New Mexico, in search of arms, ammunition, and booty. Ironically, Wilson's tortuous attempts to bring "order and stability" to Mexico helped to create this crisis. Villa felt that he had been used badly by the United States, and General Hugh L. Scott had predicted some reaction. "His bridle is off," Scott wrote to James R. Garfield in October 1915. Garfield prophetically replied, "Your expectations of trouble will be more than fulfilled." Indeed, when Villa needed arms and supplies it was only natural that he head north. Anger was involved, but U.S. meddling in Mexican affairs also helped to remove any inhibitions which Villa may have had concerning such a raid.

Hardline interventionists now clamored for military action, and even less militant persons attacked Wilson's Mexican policy. Wilson found himself in a dilemma. He had intervened at Veracruz in 1914 over a lesser pretext, and his consistency was being questioned in an election year. To Wilson and Lansing, Europe was now the main event. Mexico constituted an important problem, but the Villista raids were not considered the major element in it. They were an unpleasant side show that stole the headlines and diverted attention from the basic issues. But the national soil had been invaded, and some North Americans were peculiarly touchy about foreign forces inside their own country. Without enthusiasm—but perhaps in the belief that he would avoid demands for the complete Cubanization of Mexico—Wilson ordered General John J. Pershing to pursue Villa into Mexico. . . .

The Mexican government notified the other Latin American nations of the possibility of war between Mexico and the United States. The Mexican note bluntly stated that the basic reason for U.S. intervention was opposition to the Mexican policy of eliminating the privileged treatment of foreign capital. In conclusion, the Mexican government declared that the "foreign invasion" must be repulsed and Mexican sovereignty be respected.

The Wilson administration now realized that the United States stood on the brink of a full-scale war with Mexico, but it would be a war caused by an incident which was clouded by questions of responsibility. Wilson and his advisers regarded the border incursions as "a symptom of the deeply rooted internal disturbances" which had been aggravated by the economic policies and problems of the Carranza government. The Wilson administration had dispatched the Pershing expedition not only to eliminate this symptom by catching Villa, but also indirectly to pressure the Carranza government to maintain order and stability. The latter point was based upon the assumption of the Wilson administration that Mexican officials in fact had the capability to do this but refused to act because of their opposition to foreigners. The U.S. reply (20 June) to the Mexican note of 22 May explicitly stated these points:

> The Government of the United States has viewed with deep concern and in-creasing disappointment the progress of the revolution in Mexico. . . . For three years the Mexican Republic has been torn with civil strife; the lives of Americans and other aliens have been sacrificed; vast properties developed by American capital and enterprise have been destroyed or rendered non-produc-tive; bandits have been permitted to roam at will through the territory con-tiguous to the United States and to seize, without punishment or without effec-tive attempts at punishment, the property of Americans.

The Mexican government was further informed that recognition had been granted with the expectation that the government would speedily restore order, to provide the "Mexican people, and others . . . opportunity to rebuild in peace and security their shattered fortunes." The United States had ignored repeated provocations to restore order by force in northern Mexico and had "sought by appeals and moderate though explicit demands to impress upon the *de facto* Government the seriousness of the situation and to arouse it to its duty to perform its international obligations toward citizens of the United States who had entered the territory of Mexico or had vested interests within its boundaries." In conclusion the U.S. note stated that the protection of American lives and property in Mexico was, first, the obligation of Mexico and, second, the obligation of the United States. Thus, the United States declared that it was "duty bound" to maintain its "national rights" and warned Mexico that an "appeal to arms" would lead to the "gravest conse-quences."

In the note of 20 June Wilson and Lansing placed just as much emphasis upon protecting U.S. interests in Mexico as upon preventing raids across the border. In addition, they clearly indicated that the basis of conflict was the Carranza government's attitude and policies toward foreign lives and property. The Pershing expedition would remain in Mexico until Carranza provided concrete evidence that these had been altered to meet U.S. specifications. Raids across the border now were linked to internal questions of order and the protection of foreign interests. The original decision to send troops into Mexico may have been based solely upon Villa's attacks across the border, but by June 1916 the Pershing expedition had become a lever to induce changes in Mexican policy.

Wilson did not want to engage in a major war to pacify Mexico, although he did not dismiss the possibility; yet a limited conflict to prevent the expulsion of the Pershing expedition could quickly escalate to such an extensive campaign. If Pershing were driven out of Mexico, or if the United States immediately withdrew the expedition under pressure, the Mexican government might be encouraged to defy the United States on all issues. The dilemma of the Wilson administration was how to avoid a war and still settle the problems of safeguarding the border and protecting foreign interests in Mexico. The Mexican government also faced a dilemma—how to remove the Pershing expedition from Mexican soil without a major war and without accepting the dictates of the U.S. government in regard to internal policies or the legitimacy of its asserted "policing role in Mexico." . . .

Woodrow Wilson was in a rather petulant mood when the U.S. commissioners presented their report on 3 January 1917. They had prepared a press notice justifying the withdrawal of Pershing's force, but Wilson "very flatly declined to permit the issuance of this statement." Gray and Mott were angered by what they considered to be such shabby treatment, and both felt that the president no longer represented a spirit of generosity toward Mexico. In all probability Wilson was suffering from acute frustration because a major attempt to shape the Mexican Revolution had so obviously failed. In late December 1916, Rowe had told Lane that the trouble with so many Mexicans was that "they talk as if their country is a fully organized, highly developed sovereign state, dealing on a plane of equality with the other nations of the earth." Carranza seemed to have converted this talk to reality by refusing to accept anything but unconditional evacuation. The war in Europe and the deteriorating state of U.S.-German relations strengthened the Mexican position, especially since Wilson believed that a war with Mexico would involve at least 500,000 troops. Wilson had to choose priorities in January 1917, and at this point Europe took precedence over Mexico. The president was obviously irritated over the further assertion of Mexican independence, but, to give him due credit, he was realistic enough to see that under the circumstances he had little choice but to concede to Mexico a diplomatic victory. In addition, Wilson feared that a massive Mexican intervention (and war) would turn the other Latin American nations toward Europe for leadership, thus opening the way for "round-about flank movements" upon the "regnant position" of the United States in the hemisphere. On 28 January, the War Department formally announced the withdrawal of the punitive expedition, and by 5 February the last of the saddlesore troopers had crossed the Rio Bravo. On the same day the new Mexican constitution was promulgated, and the issue of foreign interests in Mexico moved into a new phase. . . .

The constitution of 1917 contained several provisions which—if enforced —would alter the status of foreign investments in Mexico. Various articles discussed foreigners and foreign interests, but the famous article 27 contained the most explicit formulation of the drive to assert national control over the economy—and especially the natural resources—of the country. This lengthy article has been summarized as follows:

The ownership of lands and waters in Mexico was vested in the nation which could and did transmit its title to private persons but under what limitations it pleased. Direct ownership of all subsoil was vested in the nation. Only Mexican citizens might own land or obtain concessions to exploit the subsoil; or if foreigners received the same right they must agree to be considered Mexicans in respect of such property and not to invoke the protection of their government in respect of the same. Religious institutions had no power to acquire real property. All places of public worship were the property of the nation. The surface of the land was to be disposed of for the public good, expropriated owners receiving compensation. All measures passed since 1856 alienating communal lands were to be null and void.

Two of the most significant principles embodied in this article were the assertion of national ownership (*dominio directo*) of the subsurface "minerals or other substances," and the application of the Calvo Doctrine. Both were basic elements in the attempt to "Mexicanize" the economy, and would be the focal point for much of the intensive legal debate between Mexico and the industrial-creditor nations.

The authors of article 27 went back to the pre-Díaz legal traditions of Mexico for their basic definition of the ownership of natural resources. The Spanish law of reversion (as embodied in the *Ordenanzas de Minería* of 1783 for New Spain) provided one of the most significant legal foundations for national control of resources. As Harlow S. Person notes, the concepts of ownership and possession in the law of reversion corresponds "more nearly to the concept of perpetual conditional custody and enjoyment of usufruct, and the right to sell and transfer these as conditioned." The oil companies asserted the right of absolute ownership of both surface property and subsurface resources, and as a corollary the right to determine the proper use of these properties. The nationalistic leaders of the revolution were convinced that the future of the nation lay in Mexico's ability to determine the policies for effective development of subsurface resources, policies based upon Mexican evaluation of developmental necessities and not on the international oil companies' worldwide juggling of production and profits. Since, by purchase, lease, or concession, the foreign oil companies controlled vast portions of the oil-bearing lands of the nation, the revolutionary leaders realized that the only way they could assert effective control over resource utilization was by replacing the nouveau-legal concept of absolute ownership with the older concept of ownership "vested in the nation." The principles of the Calvo Doctrine now became vital to obtain the compliance of the foreign oil companies with the revised legal order and their future participation in a Mexican oriented program of development. The other alternative was complete nationalization, by either expropriation or confiscation, which would have resolved the problem of forcing foreign companies to abide by Mexican laws and policies.

At the end of the convention, Deputy Juan de Díos Bojórquez stated: "The true work of the Revolution begins now—the Revolution is not over; now it ought to become most revolutionary, most radical, most unyielding." The ideals and aspirations had been codified; now the question became one of implementation and enforcement by the Carranza government. The president, however, was not very sympathetic with some of the reforms and did little to implement the agrarian and labor sections, although he had to make a few concessions to the agrarians. Carranza was a dedicated nationalist, however, and this provided a link with those men who were oriented to national control of resources and economic development. He understood the relationships between national control of the economy and the development of the strength and independence of the nation. Carranza and his advisers hoped to secure for Mexico a larger share of the wealth produced by the country, through increased taxation of foreign enterprises and policies aimed at promoting more Mexican participation in commerce and industry. In addition, they hoped to reduce foreign influence over the economic and political affairs of the country. . . .

Mexican leaders believed that the international power struggle between the developed nations could produce disastrous consequences for Mexico and other underdeveloped countries. They especially feared that U.S. involvement in the European war would lead to pressures for Latin American participation, thus further curbing their independence, and to major disruptions in foreign commerce. In an attempt to counter the pro-Allied drift of the United States, the Mexican government, in February 1917, tried to form a neutral bloc. Mexico sent a note to all neutral nations, including the United States, proposing an agreement over the absolute equality of treatment accorded the belligerent nations. This proposal also called for such a neutral bloc to offer "good offices" or "friendly mediation," and if these were refused then all the neutrals would take the necessary steps to limit the war to a "strict area" and would suspend commercial relations with the warring nations. The Mexicans hoped that if such actions could not bring peace, they would at least keep the Western Hemisphere (south of Canada) out of the war. In order to succeed in the latter course, they would have to involve the United States in the "common accord." The U.S. government, however, rejected the Mexican proposal, and in a petulant tone chided Mexico for not cooperating with the anti-German "neutrality" policy of the United States. To the State Department, the Mexicans were guilty not only of following an independent course of action but also of asserting a leadership role.

The Mexican government had stated in its note of 11 February that "peace is an imperative necessity for Mexico," and the country did remain neutral throughout the First World War. In adhering to this policy, Mexico was subjected to Allied diplomatic pressure, trade restrictions, and violations of her neutrality by military forces. To try to counter these influences, Mexican officials gave limited encouragement to German activities in the country, and some hoped to develop closer relations with Japan.

Carranza and some of his colleagues became increasingly concerned that after the war the developed nations would concentrate their attention on policing the underdeveloped areas. Since Mexico was the prime candidate for such disciplinary operations, these men hoped to develop a foreign policy which would relate revolutionary nationalism to the aspirations of the other

Latin American nations. In the process, they hoped to encourage unified hemispheric opposition to any U.S. intervention. The first indications of this development appeared in 1918. Ambassador Fletcher reported that the newspaper *El Pueblo* had called for a formal declaration of nonrecognition of the Monroe Doctrine, alliances with powerful nations in Europe and elsewhere, and the negotiation of treaties with Latin American nations to offset the influence of the United States.

By mid-1919, the Mexican press was elaborating in more detail a set of propositions labeled the "Carranza Doctrine" derived from the president's speeches and writings. The major theme was: "Our work of saving the nation has more importance yet that Mexico may be the soul of the rest of the nations that suffer the same evils." As presented in the press, the new doctrine contained the following points:

1. Individuals who go to other nations must conform to the consequences and must not have more guarantees and rights than the nationals have. They must accept the law of the country just as it is. In the words of *El Pueblo*: "No more bayonets, no more cannon, no more dreadnaughts to follow a man who, through commercialism, goes in search of fortune and to exploit the richness of other countries."
2. Little by little all privileges and monopolies must end. Free and universal commerce should prevail, and in like fashion the equality of all peoples wherever they go.
3. The nonrecognition of the Monroe Doctrine in that Mexico does not consent that her foreign and domestic business be subject to the scrutiny and approbation of the United States.
4. The establishment of a real solidarity with other Latin American nations based upon the mutual respect of the independence, the territory, the rights, and the interior organization of each country. Absolute nonintervention must be the basis for this solidarity, and these principles must be respected by all nations of the hemisphere.
5. Alliances should be negotiated with European or other countries, and a treaty system with Latin America. The promulgators of the Carranza Doctrine stated that this was a "brotherly" concept which embraced "all aspirations, all nations, and all races." . . .

The Carranza Doctrine presented a blend of the Calvo Doctrine, the Drago Doctrine, and Mexican revolutionary nationalism. It was not a chauvinistic outlook but one which stressed peace and cooperation with a strong universalist flavor. The doctrine proclaimed the equality of all nations and races and called upon the developed nations to respect the sovereignty of the underdeveloped nations. Mexico's call for a new international system constituted a direct challenge to the industrial-creditor nation concept of world order. In addition, the United States was asked to give more than lip service to the ideal of Pan-Americanism. The leaders of the Mexican Revolution had asserted the principles of national control over the economy in the constitution of 1917. Now they proclaimed a doctrine which they believed would protect Mexican revolutionary nationalism by asserting it as a basis of unity for Latin America and the foundation of a new pattern of relations between the developed and underdeveloped nations. . . .

Early in his first administration President Wilson had declared that one of the cornerstones of his Latin American policy was to put an end to revolutions. The Mexican Revolution, however, turned out to be a different kind of upheaval from the usual *golpe de estado* which Wilson had in mind. The issues were much deeper, the fires of national emotion more intense, and Wilson came to a realization that intervention in such a conflict would destroy the credibility of his administration's pronouncements about self-determination. This realization did not stop him from trying to shape the course of the revolution or the policies of the revolutionary government, but it did help to create his dilemma over the methods to be used and the intellectual justification for such interference in Mexico's internal affairs. Wilson, as most observers, could hardly deny that the people of Mexico had major grievances ranging from extreme poverty to illiteracy and that some changes were necessary. Díaz and the *científicos* could be faulted for not instituting some reforms, and thus for driving the people to revolution. But the lid had blown and the problem now was one of directing this upheaval into the paths of order, stability, and gradual reform, in order to prevent another revolution.

Wilson once described the philosophy of the French Revolution as "radically evil and corrupting." Such a revolution not only was disorderly but also produced rapid and violent changes in the socioeconomic system. To a man who criticized the "radicalism" of the Socialists and Populists in the United States, revolutionary change was compounded heresy. Firmly rooted in the inherent conservatism of mainstream Anglo-American liberalism, Wilson had no sympathy for fundamental socioeconomic change. Indeed, in his last effort at political writing, entitled "The Road Away from Revolution," he stressed the theme that revolutionary assaults against capitalism threatened civilization and democracy.

The revolutionary leaders refused to accept Wilson's guidance, would not settle down after the elimination of Huerta and become Anglo-American style constitutionalists, and pursued policies which seemed to threaten "legitimate" foreign rights. Under these circumstances, how could the United States insure the proper behavior (play "Big Brother" as Wilson called it) of Mexico without being accused of opposition to the aspirations of the people? The resolution to this intellectual dilemma was provided by two arguments. The first professed sympathy for the downtrodden majority of the people but explained that the revolution had been promoted by demagogues who had no intention of helping them. The second acknowledged, reluctantly in some cases, the "original" ideals of the revolution but charged that the revolution had been betrayed by its leaders, especially Carranza. Secretary Lansing and Senator Fall espoused the first position, and Lansing explained: "It [the revolution] is a conflict between military oligarchies, the great body of the contestants being merely pawns in the game, who will be no better off after the struggle than they were before, no matter which party is victorious." Senator Fall varied the argument slightly by blaming outside agitators for the "infection" in Mexico.

The "revolution betrayed" argument appealed to the more liberal North Americans, since it enabled them to support reform vocally while attacking the Mexican government. Secretary Houston, George Creel, Boaz Long, and President Wilson took this position and asserted that the Carranza government really did not speak for the people of Mexico. Increasingly, Carranza himself became the focal point for this argument. By mid-1918, Ambassador Fletcher attributed all the problems in U.S.-Mexican relations to the "First Chief." This argument in turn had a peculiar effect on the official perception of events in Mexico. By attributing so much power and influence to Carranza and his government, U.S. officials interpreted all anti-American pronouncements and acts against foreign interests by local and state officials as part of a uniform, centrally directed plot. Such interpretations vastly distorted the actual policies and pronouncements of the Carranza government.

The official U.S. interpretation of the revolution combined both arguments, although the "betrayal" theme predominated. Lansing explained this position to the Five-Power Conference in August 1915 as "that we recognized the right of revolution against injustice and tyranny; that we recognized that the *principle* of the revolution, the *restoration of constitutional government,* had triumphed a year ago; . . . that personal ambition and personal greed were the causes of the factions." The president supported this statement, which reflected his own political philosophy, and told Lansing that the Mexicans should be made to understand clearly what they could and could not do without the concurrence of the U.S. government.

This raises the question of just what specific reforms U.S. officials had in mind when they expressed sympathy for the Mexican people. Most were quite vague, unless they were attacking the policies of Carranza. The few positive prescriptions, besides constitutional government and order, stressed gradualism above all. Secretary Houston wrote that it would take "generations" to bring the Mexican people "very far along the road to self-government and higher living." What they needed, he said, was "a good police force . . . , a system which would give the masses an interest in the land and in their products, an elementary vocational educational system, and an agricultural agency such as our Federal Department." But Houston felt that Villa's agrarian program could not be carried out without "grave trouble," and that if the people were given an interest in the land they would probably "make little use of their opportunities." Lansing agreed with this argument, and cited the "general improvidence of the Mexican Indians," caused by "natural traits, environment and lack of education," as the reason why land reform was not expedient. Secretary Lane granted that Mexico needed a few reforms such as a land tax system and agricultural schools. Boaz Long doubted that anything could be accomplished by giving more income to the peons, since they were "naturally lazy" and inclined to dissipation. The peons did need a "certain amount of religious form or belief," however, to hold them "in check." But these officials could be very specific about the policies they disliked; at the top of the list were those which asserted national control of the economy and an independent position in international relations.

George Creel wrote that the culmination of Carranza's insolence and hatred came with the attempt (1918) to implement article 27 and confiscate U.S.-owned oil properties. In a long hymn of nostalgia for the good old days when Mexicans lived up to the motto "Respect for foreign rights constitutes peace," Boaz Long attacked the idea of "Mexico for the Mexicans." The "wildcat Constitution" of 1917, he argued, was part of a plot to destroy the economy of the United States. Ambassador Fletcher made a similar observation when he reported that the "radical anticapitalistic" proclivities of the revolutionary party were synonymous with an anti-British and anti-American position.

The official U.S. concern over confiscation had become almost paranoid by late 1916, and almost every action of the Mexican government dealing with taxation or regulation was denounced as such. For example, during the Joint Commission conference the American commissioners and State Department personnel were referring to the proposed new Mexican constitution as confiscatory. In point of fact, they were denouncing the constitution of 1857 (which U.S. officials later would praise in ritual fashion), since the famous revised article 27 was not even written until late in January 1917, and Carranza's draft constitution only slightly revised the 1857 document. Of course, U.S. oil and mining interests were also denouncing the radical provisions of the "new constitution" and sending memorandums on the subject to the State Department and the American Commissioners. One such memorandum, drafted by Chandler P. Anderson, Frederic Kellogg, and Judge Delbert J. Haff, stated that the draft of the new constitution confirmed all their fears concerning radicalism and confiscation. They specifically cited articles 27, 28, and 33; the last two were derived almost word for word from the constitution of 1857. The Mexican regulatory efforts had been judged and convicted in advance.

In a similar fashion, U.S. officials considered Mexico's neutrality during the war and the assertion of an independent diplomatic position in the hemisphere to be unfriendly acts. Ambassador Fletcher was quite candid about the criteria for "unfriendly" acts in Latin America:

> In the fear of the gradual extension of this American influence in Mexico, I think, will be found the master-key of Mexico's present attitude in the great world war. . . .
> I am convinced that President Carranza—and this means Mexico today—desires correct rather than cordial relations with the United States, and hopes to find in the victory or non-defeat of Germany in the great war, a defense or counterbalance of the moral and economic influence of the United States in Mexico.

If resisting the growing U.S. influence in Mexico was considered unfriendly, the Carranza Doctrine was seen as a major threat to the United States. Fletcher described it as the "international program" of the Mexican government, although he did not think of the label "Carranzaism," and warned:

The so-called Carranza doctrine is to replace the Monroe Doctrine. The hegemony of the United States on this continent is to pass away, and our trade and influence must pass with it; presumably to be replaced by things German, or at any rate Latin America is to break away from Pan-Americanism and the United States.

Fear of German "commercial, economic, and political exploitation after the war" was involved in official U.S. calculations. But fear that Mexico, and perhaps Latin America, would assert an independent position was just as important, perhaps even more so. Fletcher downgraded the role of German influence in Mexican policies, and frankly acknowledged the indigenous nature of these policies and ideas. "The least connection possible between Mexico and the United States is his [Carranza's] idea," the ambassador reported in June 1918, "and his official newspaper [El Pueblo] is preaching economic, financial, and diplomatic—every sort of independence of the United States."

Mexican resistance to the influence and guidance of the "Big Brother" north of the Rio Bravo sometimes revealed the elitist, and even racist, side of big-power paternalism. Wilson labeled Carranza a "pedantic ass," because the "First Chief" would not accept his version of U.S.-Mexican relations. To Boaz Long, the Mexican leaders were "an improvident lot of politicians" who were incapable of running a government "according to our standard." By 1919, the rhetoric of paternalism had become more edgy and Congressman Fiorello H. La Guardia declared: "Yes; I would go down with beans in one hand and offer help to the Mexican people, but I would be sure to have hand grenades in the other hand, and God help them in case they do not accept our well-intended and sincere friendship." Franklin K. Lane complained to Lansing: "I wish that you could be given a free hand in this matter [Mexico]. I know it would be a stiff hand, an authoritative hand, and that is what these people need. They are naughty children who are exercising all the privileges and rights of grown ups." Indeed, Lane complained that the Mexicans believed in the words of Thomas Jefferson (equality of men), Karl Marx ("private property is robbery"), and Woodrow Wilson (self-determination). In a sense Lane was correct; the underdeveloped countries were beginning to assert some of the principles which they found in the intellectual heritage of the developed nations. The industrial-creditor powers had had an impact which they did not expect.

## Mexico at the Whim of Washington

RAMÓN EDUARDO RUÍZ

The Yankee next door, Mexicans learned immediately, would not easily relinquish his stake in Mexico. To the contrary, investors and their government in Washington watched warily the course of the rebellion, and from the start,

Reprinted from The Great Rebellion, Mexico 1905–1924, by Ramón Eduardo Ruíz, by permission of W. W. Norton & Company, Inc. Copyright © 1980 by W. W. Norton & Company, Inc.

worked feverishly to keep it within the bounds of what they believed permissible. They distrusted social revolution and only belatedly tolerated halfway reform. With the Treaty of Bucareli of 1923, say many Mexicans, policy makers in Washington dealt a hammer blow to the hopes of reformers in Mexico. Whatever the truth, history amply documents sundry American efforts to impede and stifle change in Mexico. The claim of American innocence hardly stands scrutiny.

The American attitude, from the perspective of some Mexicans, helps explain why their country stopped short of having a revolution. Given this view, at least three interpretations, all logically defensible, merit careful consideration. Mexicans failed to carry out a revolution because the United States would not permit it. Secondly, in another Mexican version, Yankee attitudes, as understood by Mexicans, frightened sincere reformers into believing that any attempt to implement social change invited American intervention. Confronted with this harsh reality, Mexicans abandoned thoughts of drastic change. Finally, in a third view, the cautious and conservative Mexican chieftains exploited the bugaboo of Yankee intervention to hide their unwillingness to alter significantly the status quo; in their opinion, Mexico needed American investments and know-how for the prosperity of its capitalist system, and obviously, for their own well-being. To some extent, all three versions have merit.

From the start, it scarcely requires saying, Mexican rebels, as Porfirio Díaz before them, had to come to terms with their gargantuan neighbor. To deny it is to distort the history of Mexico's relations with the United States. To begin with, the wealth, power, and sheer physical size of the United States dwarfed Mexico. The country inherited by Francisco I. Madero had one-fifth of the territory, a fraction of the population, and a tiny slice of the agricultural and industrial capacity of its huge neighbor. By the same token, the Mexican army, small, ill-equipped and poorly led, hardly served as a barrier to Washington's designs. As Francisco R. Serrano, a *político* from Sonora, put it, an ill fate had willed that Mexico lie adjacent to the United States. To Jorge Vera Estañol, American influence had been "decisive" in shaping the destiny of Mexico, so much so that its "political and social structure" shook with every change in Washington's attitude. Any repudiation by a Mexican government of contracts earlier agreed to with American interests, giving them rights and property, brought "onerous . . . consequences." Our foreign problem, added Luis Cabrera, boils down to how Mexico safeguards the investments of foreigners. Intelligent Mexicans know, to quote Félix F. Palavicini, that "it is impossible to long maintain a hostile attitude towards the colossus, to close our doors to its commerce, or worse still, to enter into alliances with Europeans or Asians who, surely, will turn against us." Mexico must put its house in order, lest the United States intervene, if not militarily, with diplomatic measures that, warned Antonio Manero, "could well cost us a loss of territory."

But all the same, after years of pandering to foreigners, Mexicans wanted a "Mexico for the Mexicans." To Venustiano Carranza, perhaps its loudest voice in government circles, love of country meant respect for Mexican sovereignty, nonintervention by outsiders, and the right to deal with domestic questions in light of the national interest. Love of country was equated with antiforeign. Carranza, his disciples reminded him, stood for a unity of Latin Americans and for their right to live independently of the Yankee, the enemy of the Hispanic people. When the governor of Texas invited three counterparts from northern Mexican states to meet with him in Laredo, Gustavo Espinosa Mireles, chief of Coahuila, speaking for his companions, refused, saying that it would look bad for them to come running at the behest of an American politician.

The cardinal question for Mexico to resolve, explained Aarón Sáenz, subsecretary of foreign affairs under Alvaro Obregón, was how to have equitable relations with the United States. The attempt to liquidate economic and political inequities of the Old Regime had disturbed powerful foreign interests that, to defend their holdings, had suborned Mexicans, employed diplomatic blackmail to stop reform, and rode roughshod over Mexican sovereignty. Yet, to bring the Revolution to a successful conclusion, Mexico had to make private interests, both native and foreign, obey its laws. The concept of property rights outlined by Article 27, the crux of the national charter, intended to rescue for the nation title to property and natural resources, particularly mines and petroleum, exploited by foreigners.

However, every try at reform almost always brought Mexico face to face with its neighbor across the border. Prudence, the soul of practical politics, therefore, called for caution lest Mexico unduly antagonize the Yankee. One reason for not pushing ahead with drastic social change, Carranza explained, was because "common sense dictated a policy that would not alarm landlords, business people, and capitalists who would immediately unite to defend their interests, while the United States, to avoid having a socialist country next door, would have embraced Victoriano Huerta." In an effort to justify the slow pace of agrarian reform, Obregón, speaking in 1923, dwelt on the "formidable resistance of both national and foreign" groups. Because of it, Sáenz added, one element in the Ministry of Foreign Affairs had urged Obregón to scale down plans for land redistribution, particularly since foreigners wanted ready payment for lands taken from them. To satisfy the hunger for land, in brief, exacerbated Mexico's international situation due to the hostility of foreign powers.

An added concern that every administration had to live with was the likely possibility that dissident Mexicans would inevitably court Washington's benevolence. Many Mexicans, apparently, saw nothing incongruous in their demand that Carranza and Obregón behave with nationalistic aplomb while, at the same time, asking outsiders to meddle in Mexican affairs on their behalf. Even Obregón, complained Carranza, to hurt him politically at home had stooped to exploiting Washington's paranoia of Japanese activity in Lower California. Carranza, moreover, angrily castigated the schemes of Mexican exiles who, to feather their own nest, plotted the downfall of his regime with foreigners. He saw a sharp similarity between Mexico's situation in 1919 and that of Benito Juárez who, in 1860, had to deal with the disloyalty of Mexican exiles begging Britain, France, and Spain to invade their country.

Ironically, however, the men who led Mexico down the path of rebellion had no quarrel with the principle of foreign investment. Like the Porfiristas, the new masters believed that outside capital could help cure the ills of underdevelopment. Without the aid of industrialized nations, little could be done to rebuild and develop Mexico. "Our country," Mexico's consul in Detroit cautioned Adolfo de la Huerta in 1923, "needs foreigners to develop its natural resources." Obregón, particularly, believed inevitable, and perhaps even beneficial, Mexico's dependence on the United States. Leaders of Obregón's stripe merely wanted to end the blatant special privileges of foreigners. While welcomed, foreign investors must abide by national legislation, so that Mexicans might govern as they saw fit. At no time did the rulers of post-Díaz Mexico ask Americans to leave or to stop investing their money in Mexico. If Americans and other aliens did not challenge the supremacy of the state, the new rulers were satisfied. It was not their wealth that preoccupied Mexico's rulers, but the power of the United States, so ubiquitously at their beck and call. . . .

Wilson's dislike of Madero, Mexicans state, went to pathological extremes. Regardless of the cost, he wanted Madero out of the way. In the opinion of Cabrera, so distorted was Wilson's fear of the Mexican leader that he eventually became the "intellectual author" of the barrack's coup that toppled Madero. Further, Cabrera, along with every Mexican of his time, accused Wilson of helping Felix Díaz, nephew of don Porfirio, during the Tragic Ten Days of February 1913, and of engineering the Pact of the Embassy, where General Victoriano Huerta, entrusted with the defense of the government, embraced Felix Díaz and betrayed Madero. The plot, said Jorge Vera Estañol, had been hatched, "discussed, written, and signed by both military chiefs" in the American embassy. Able to protect the lives of Madero and José María Pino Suárez had he wanted to, Wilson arrogantly dismissed the pleas of the president's wife for his intervention and simply stood by while Huerta had them killed in cold blood.

Madero's death left a lasting imprint on Mexican attitudes. With disastrous consequences, the intervention feared by Don Porfirio and his advisers had come to pass. The American ambassador had publicly unmasked the ability of the colossus to unmake Mexican presidents and to manipulate disloyal and opportunistic Mexicans. Washington's big stick did not go unnoticed in the Mexican Congress. "I accuse Mr. Henry Lane Wilson, the ambassador of the United States in Mexico," said Congressman Luis Manuel Rojas in his famous *yo acuso,* "of the moral responsibility for the death of Francisco I. Madero and José María Pino Suárez." Huerta, Governor Carranza of Coahuila told his companions, had carried out the foul deed "with the help of a band of pampered foreigners who surrounded Wilson." It was perfectly clear to Carranza and his allies, states Arnaldo Córdova, that in the future nothing could be done without taking into account the unruly neighbor across the border.

For the Constitutionalists, a huge problem loomed ahead: how to defeat Huerta while courting American diplomatic recognition, but at the same time, keep Washington from meddling in Mexican domestic business. Fittingly, Huerta, eager for Washington's benediction, had instead to listen to President Woodrow Wilson condemn his regime and to watch American marines and sailors invade Mexican soil. To Huerta's allies, and perhaps also to Carranza, Woodrow Wilson appeared to be trying to turn Mexico into a protectorate of the United States. During the interval of Huerta's presidency, and later after Wilson saw fit to recognize the Constitutionalists, Carranza, his sympathizers say, had to put up with almost daily American interference and harassment. In one period, Cabrera recalled, the State Department and its representative in Mexico sent endless notes and telegrams demanding guarantees for foreigners in Mexico. They included complaints against the Carranza regime for its use of the railroads; against efforts to hold prices in check; against the censure of telegrams and mail; against sanitary measures; against everything, in short, that prevented foreigners from enjoying "a life of security . . . in a civilized nation." In Cabrera's opinion, J. R. Silliman, vice-consul and special representative of Wilson, was as likely to protest the death of a man in Chihuahua, who turned up very much alive a day or two later, as he was to ask for the return of a mule stolen in Tabasco, on behalf of Americans, Englishmen, Frenchmen, Germans and even Mexicans who flew the Stars and Stripes over their property.

To Mexicans, their country was seldom free of American intervention. Wilson compelled Carranza to lift the siege of the port of Progreso when it cut into the profits of American corporations in Yucatán. In June 1916, the director of Mexican customs reported that officials in Laredo and Eagle Pass, two key border towns in Texas, had arbitrarily banned the export of corn and other basic foodstuffs to Mexico. According to Mexican sources, two years later the United States closed its doors to imports of Mexican vanilla. Washington, said Ignacio Bonilla, Carranza's minister to the United States, had viewed as unfriendly plans by officials in Sonora in 1911 to cancel a concession for water given the Richardson Construction Company ten years earlier. In the fall of 1915, reported Cabrera, authorities in El Paso, Texas were opening Mexican mail to the United States. A month earlier, Ramón P. DeNegri, Mexican consul in San Francisco, had alerted Carranza to a flotilla of naval ships being readied in case armed intervention came about. Efforts by both the Republican and Progressive parties to discredit President Wilson's Mexican policy, reviewed in detail for Carranza by the Mexican consul in Philadelphia, cast a pall over the National Palace in Mexico. If Wilson's political enemies wanted a tougher stance taken against Mexico, what could Carranza expect of them should they capture the White House? No wonder that Mexican agents in the United States gleefully reported Wilson's growing involvement in the war in Europe.

To survive or perish at the whims of Washington—this, said Mexicans, was their fate. Struggle as they might to control their own destinies, Washington pulled the strings. The lament, voiced by Díaz, was subsequently echoed in the halls of the National Palace by his successors. Mexicans especially resented the arms policy of the United States, the handling of Mexican news by the American press, and for both Huerta and Carranza, the invasion of Mexican soil by Yankee soldiers and marines.

The need to rely on the sale of American arms, the key to military victories at home, particularly galled Mexicans, both rebels and government officials. To complicate life for them, Washington frowned on the purchase of arms in Europe or Japan. Yet, by withholding or not withholding permission to buy arms, Washington, for all intents and purposes, decided the outcome of domestic quarrels in Mexico. Díaz had confronted this harsh reality first when, despite Washington's supposed benevolence toward him, his enemies had easily acquired arms across the border. One witness told Manero that he had seen smugglers swim across the Río Grande with weapons in their hands while American soldiers, dispatched to guard the border, deliberately fired over their heads. Huerta watched Washington deny entry to his agents while allowing his enemies to buy guns and ammunition from American suppliers. To Vera Estañol, Huerta's angry cabinet officer, this policy invited civil war in Mexico. Still, when Wilson decided to destroy Huerta, he included all Mexican factions in his arms embargo, making it difficult, Obregón acknowledged, to buy guns "on the other side." Cabrera, Roberto Pesqueira, and an army of other Constitutionalists had to travel to Washington to beg its leaders to lift the embargo against them. The war in Europe, a glorious opportunity for American arms merchants to prosper, complicated the Mexican hunt for weapons.

The Constitutionalists joyfully greeted Washington's order canceling its embargo on the sale of guns to Huerta's enemies. Had Washington dealt with Carranza and Villa as rebels and not as "belligerents," it would have denied them the right to buy arms and condemned them to defeat by Huerta. For Villa, it meant that while he competed with Carranza for Wilson's favors he could buy guns across the border, talk to George C. Carothers, a special American emissary in his camp, and drive a Packard automobile Carothers had given him. Wilson's decision to back Carranza, on the other hand, cost Villa his chance at victory. Without sufficient arms and ammunition, Villa was defeated at Celaya. For Carranza, the lesson was dramatically clear: so long as his government had to depend on the good will of the United States for arms, it was at the mercy of its northern neighbor. By the same token, to obtain permission to buy weapons, Cabrera bitterly exclaimed, Carranza had not only to swear "not to reconquer Texas" but to "behave." Without Washington's benediction, Obregón concluded in 1923, he could not purchase arms across the border and without them he could not put down De la Huerta's revolt. . . .

To aggravate matters, Mexicans, as they interpreted events, had to watch helplessly while the American military, at the behest of Wilson, trampled the sovereignty and dignity of their country. The occupation of Veracruz and the invasion of Chihuahua by an army under General John J. Pershing, to which Carranza had to acquiesce, significantly added to the distrust and fear of the Yankee. Ostensibly designed to destroy Huerta, the capture of Veracruz actually nearly united Mexicans behind him. As General Juan Barragán pointed out, Mexicans, believing their independence endangered, rushed to enlist in Huerta's army. In Sonora, the home of Huerta's major enemies, state authorities recruited men, collected arms and munitions, and raised funds for what they thought was the coming Armageddon. Carranza vehemently objected to the invasion of Pershing, wrote Cabrera, "in every manner and tone once and a hundred times." To justify armed intervention, Wilson had used as an excuse his determination to punish Villa for his raid on New Mexico. But to Cabrera, this was just a pretext; Wilson, he thought, actually wanted to compel the Mexican government to endorse his version of Mexico's obligation to foreigners and their properties in Mexico.

Months earlier, Carranza had to ward off Wilson's attempt to meddle in Mexico by using Argentina, Brazil, and Chile to help pick Mexico's ruler. For his refusal to send delegates to the ABC peace conference, Carranza earned the plaudits of Mexicans. Even Mexican businessmen, who stood to lose by the factional quarrels, applauded. I congratulate you, said one of them, "for your correct, energetic, and above all, patriotic reply to . . . the United States." Carranza won even more support for his opposition to the Pershing expedition. Countless telegrams and letters swearing loyalty to Mexico and Carranza arrived at the National Palace. Many came from labor, a group generally distrustful of Carranza. A message from one group of railroad workers, who offered to contribute one-tenth of their wages to the defense of Mexico, ended with the cry "We are not living in '47," a reference to the defeat of a century before.

However, while Wilson's blatant intervention had rallied Mexicans together, his unilateral acts confirmed, in the eyes of Mexicans, the ability and willingness of the *gringo* to intervene in their private business. Carranza, the haughty champion of national dignity, had to stand by and see a foreign army invade his country. That knowledge was not lost on him, or on his successor, Obregón. Care had to be exercised in handling the arrogant neighbor, even at the cost of discarding internal reforms.

Equally ominous to Mexico was the bitter dispute with the petroleum corporation. The conflict flared when Mexico attempted to enforce Article 27, declaring the subsoil the property of the Mexican nation. To shield the foreign oil giants, say Mexicans, Washington employed the diplomacy of the big stick. Not to put teeth in Article 27, however, meant undercutting nationalistic goals, and specifically, land reform, the key plank in the Constitution of 1917. Further, the oil companies often refused to obey Article 123, the labor code.

On petroleum, Mexico found itself in a quandary. It wanted to control the subsoil but also needed the revenue from the sale of petroleum abroad. According to the petroleum magnates, Mexico could not enjoy both. While Mexicans battled each other, petroleum production had shot upward, from 3.6 million barrels in 1910 to 157.1 million barrels by 1920. In 1920–21, the peak year of production, Mexico produced 26 percent of the total world output of petroleum. Revenue from its exports helped it to weather the international depression of 1921 and drops in the price of metals and raw materials. Income from taxes on the production and export of petroleum totaled nearly 86 million pesos in 1922, and despite a sizeable drop, 60.6 million pesos the next year. From duties and taxes on the Standard Oil Company alone, the Mexican Treasury received 32 million pesos in 1923.

All told, revenues from petroleum represented nearly one-fifth of the entire national revenue. As one Mexican financial expert summed up the picture, the disappearance or decline of petroleum revenues spelled trouble for Mexico, even bankruptcy. Not surprisingly, the oil bonanza put Mexico at the mercy of the petroleum companies, further complicating the enforcement of Articles 27 and 123. As evidence of this, say Mexican leaders, the companies curtailed operations in 1920 and 1921. . . .

Carranza, highly nationalistic but realistic, Cabrera stated, never intended to prevent foreigners from exploiting the petroleum, or by ruling Article 27 retroactive, to deprive them of rights acquired earlier. To Carranza, Article 27 merely returned legal ownership of the subsoil to the nation; in the future, subsoil rights, in the form of special concessions, must be obtained from the Mexican government as in the case of mining. With this interpretation, Carranza tempered the "confiscatory nature" of Article 27. At this juncture, a delighted President Wilson extended Carranza *de jure* recognition. By 1918, the two leaders had worked out a *modus vivendi*. Carranza refused to modify the nationalistic character of Article 27 or to settle accounts with foreign investors; but, all the same, he left undisturbed the titles of Americans to property in Mexico, including the holdings of the petroleum companies. In the landmark Texas Company Case, another major concession, the Mexican Supreme Court, acting on behalf of the administration, confirmed the ownership of oil lands acquired prior to 1917. Ownership merely called for proof of a "positive act" that demonstrated intent to exploit the subsoil.

Obregón inherited a blighted economy and the traditional need to rely on petroleum revenues to float the budget. To his dismay, Washington refused to recognize his government, demanding in return for it that he sign a Treaty of Amity and Commerce "interpreting Article 27 in a nonconfiscatory, nonretroactive manner." To Alberto Pani, the treaty, by undermining the authority of the Constitution, asked that Mexican laws favor Americans over Mexicans. Washington, added Bassols Batalla, in return for blessing Obregón, wanted Mexico to safeguard the properties of the international petroleum monopolies, limit the future of agrarian reform, and dispel the notion that it viewed with distrust the role of foreign capital in its basic industries. Ironically, in the Texas Company Case, Mexico, through its Supreme Court, had more or less already met these conditions. Further, Obregón, in his initial address to Congress, had declared himself fully in accord with the ruling of the court. As Bassols Batalla indicated, the question of retroactivity was a red herring. Of the capital invested in oil, just 23 percent had entered Mexico before 1917. Article 27 antedated the bulk of the capital invested. Actually, said Bassols Batalla, foreign interests, with the backing of conservatives in the Obregón administration, had employed the issue of diplomatic recognition to halt reform. . . .

In twentieth-century Mexico, no regime stood a ghost of a chance of surviving without Washington's embrace. Until the pope in the White House conferred his benediction, no Mexican president could look to God for help. But the White House, and its advisers in the State Department, usually responsive to the wishes of their business and financial community, judged with suspicion governments out of step with the American dream. Mexican efforts to modify property rights, particularly those of American investors, were met with the wrath of these defenders of private enterprise. Efforts at radical reform, certainly anything that smelled of socialism, had the taint of treason. With conservatives of their own to please, Carranza and Obregón, hardly militants themselves, quickly learned that the successful wooer of Washington's love must exhibit a healthy respect for Western capitalist traditions. Both men, however, were oracles for Mexican nationalism, the goal of teaching Mexicans to run their own house. This meant eliminating the special privileges of foreigners in Mexico, and establishing Mexican ownership and control of the subsoil as a legal principle. On this issue Mexicans clashed with Washington.

From the Mexican perspective, Washington employed diplomatic recognition as a weapon to compel Mexican regimes to toe the line. To cite Querido Moheno, Huerta's minister of industry and commerce, the issue was not whether a Mexican president could govern, but whether he could get Washington's recognition, for without it he could not stay in office. Carranza knew by 1915 that to govern effectively by Washington's standards meant to be willing to guarantee the person and properties of foreigners in Mexico. Conversely for Mexicans, to rule successfully depended upon the willingness of the White House to grant recognition, a lesson mastered by Carranza after Wilson accepted him. Yet, to obtain recognition, Carranza had to publicize his decision to leave undisturbed the interests of foreigners in Mexico. Not until 1917, when Carranza undermined the "confiscatory nature" of Article 27, however, did Wilson extend *de jure* recognition. Mexicans supporting social reform judged Carranza's pledge a betrayal of national goals.

Obregón confronted a similar problem. In return for recognition, Washington wanted Obregón to sign a treaty of friendship and commerce that, in the judgment of Sáenz in Foreign Affairs, weakened or destroyed the Constitution. Such a treaty, he said, struck at the heart of Article 27, not only undercutting land reform legislation but violating the right of the Supreme Court to interpret Mexican laws. The treaty stipulated immediate payment for any property expropriated and asked Mexico to recognize the properties of foreigners acquired before May 1, 1917. These, of course, were the oil lands. To add insult to injury, the treaty contained a clause condemning Mexico's handling of the Catholic Church, under the guise of insuring freedom of religion. Obregón rejected the treaty, although he signed the Lamont-De la Huerta Agreements, pledging Mexico in 1922 to begin payment on its foreign obligations.

Fate, to the misfortune of Obregón, forced him to give up his game of watchful waiting. Mexican politics, in the shape of De la Huerta's uprising in 1923, made Obregón's courtship of Washington a matter of life and death. In the absence of recognition, the foreign bankers, upon whom Obregón depended for loans with which to buy weapons to defeat his rivals, would not open their purse strings. Either Don Alvaro won the battle of Washington or he lost his job in Mexico.

[I]n August 1923, at a meeting on Bucareli Street in Mexico City attended by delegates from both countries, Obregón received the endorsement he coveted. Obregón chose no revolutionaries to speak for him. Fernando Gonzáles Rosa, a lawyer for the Pierce Oil Company, had been judged unfit to be a delegate to the Constitutional Convention by its credentials committee. His companion, Ramón Ross, an old friend of Obregón's, was a businessman from Sonora. By the Treaty of Bucareli, Mexico made Article 27 nonretroactive, confirming the decision of the Mexican Supreme Court in the Texas Company Case, and acknowledged the validity of American financial claims dating from 1868. It vowed to respect subsoil rights acquired both before and after 1917. On the debt, it agreed to abide by the rulings of a special claims commission composed of one Mexican, one American, and a representative of a "neutral" country selected by the other two. Americans with claims against Mexico could submit their case to the tribunal where the defendant, Mexico, had only one vote. Further, González Roa and Ross, quoting a memorandum from Obregón, promised that Mexico would indemnify Americans for the loss of their lands, at the same time implying that agrarian reform had about run its course. The propertied classes in Mexico could sleep peacefully from then on.

To worshippers at the temple of nationalism, the Bucareli Treaty was a betrayal of their dreams. To stay in power, Obregón had sacrificed noble goals, one of which was national sovereignty. By appealing for help to the United States, Obregón had admitted that a Mexican regime could not alone police its own house, proclaimed General Cándido Aquilar. By the same token, by pledging to pay Mexico's foreign debt, lamented Marte R. Gómez, Obregón had mortgaged money set aside for social reform. One caustic critic, Salvador Diego Fernández, author of *Los Pactos de Bucareli* (Mexico, 1937), saw a striking connection between the terms of Bucareli and the earlier treaty of friendship and commerce, rejected as unacceptable by Obregón. By ruling Article 27 nonretroactive, in the view of Isidro Fabela, Obregón had exceeded his authority. Antonio Salas Robledo, in *Los Convenios de Bucareli ante el Derecho Internacional* (Mexico, 1938), viewed the ruling of the Supreme Court in the Texas Company Case—the basis for Obregón's decision not to make Article 27 retroactive—as a betrayal of national legislation in order "to meet the demands of foreign capital." To Bassols Batalla, Obregón and his cohorts had abandoned the field of battle to the State Department, foreign oil monopolies, and enemies of social change.

The hindsight of over half a century amply verifies the legitimacy of Mexican interpretations of American attitudes and goals. Mexicans had reason to be afraid. The powerful giant across the border was hostile and misunderstood the objectives of Mexican leaders. Washington displayed no tolerance for drastic social change in Mexico. Woodrow Wilson, at the helm of foreign policy during much of the crucial decade, may have stumbled when he tried to curtail violence in Mexico, says an American historian, but he fared "far better in blocking the consummation of revolutionary reform."

But Wilson neither initiated nor ended this sorry chapter in American relations with its smaller and weaker neighbor. His policies had beginnings in the Taft administration and they outlived his death. As Limantour suspected, Taft had dispatched 20,000 troops to the Mexican border not just to "hold up the hands" of Díaz but to the contrary, as Taft told Philander C. Knox, his secretary of state, "to place troops in sufficient numbers where Congress shall direct that they enter Mexico to save lives and property." The navy, Taft confided to Theodore Roosevelt, "is anxious for a contest, and has to be held in leash." Moreover, Henry Lane Wilson, a diplomat with the mentality of Rudyard Kipling, played a significant role in shaping the opinions of Taft. To the ambassador, Madero was "weak" and unresponsive to complaints on behalf of American investors. He warned Madero to give "more hearty consideration" to American business interests lest Taft convene Congress to ask for guidance on Mexican matters. The labor strikes in the textile mills in the days of Madero turned Ambassador Wilson's hair gray. When the army brass revolted in 1913, Wilson arrogantly prevailed upon the ambassadors of Great Britain, Germany, and Spain to support his demand that Madero resign.

Although he rid himself of the bigoted and ungenerous ambassador, President Wilson added a fatal dose of capitalist morality to Taft's diplomacy. He intended to keep alive Mexican capitalism and to defend the American stake in it. His first press release welcomed as "friends . . . those . . . who protect private property." With Huerta and his rivals at war, Wilson began to ponder military intervention, "including blockading Mexico's ports and sending troops across the border . . . to protect American lives and property." Determined to oust Huerta, Wilson lifted the arms embargo on Huerta's enemies; when that failed, he sent troops to invade Veracruz. But Wilson had more in mind than the demise of Huerta. He "wanted a much larger role in Mexican affairs . . . He desired control over Mexico's destiny," ultimately to mold the Mexican Revolution "according to the American experience." Wilson denied any intent to invade Mexico, but nevertheless, cautioned that if "the lives and properties of Americans and all other foreigners are [not] safeguarded . . . we shall be forced to it." His tardy and reluctant recognition of Carranza on October 1915, simply acknowledged the Constitutionalist's mastery of Mexico.

Wilson's pilgrimage to save democracy in Europe granted Mexico a brief respite. To start with, Wilson had to call Pershing home. Still, while the war kept Wilson busy in Europe, and demands for oil and henequen richly benefited both industries, economically Mexico suffered. To aid the allies [to] win the war, the United States upset established commercial patterns, including trade ties with Mexico. Washington barred the export of corn and pork to Mexico, despite surpluses in the United States and starvation in Mexico. The sale of arms to Mexicans was banned, while Mexican gold reserves in the United States were frozen "as hostages to Mexico's good conduct." Determined to protect American petroleum properties in Mexico, Wilson had decided to occupy them with troops if necessary. During the interval, his government helped preserve the status quo in Mexico by loudly protesting decrees tampering with property and subsoil rights. According to Washington, Mexico could not expropriate foreign properties legally acquired before the promulgation of the Constitution without immediate compensation in accordance with due process of law. . . .

Perhaps, without this record of American hostility, of meddling in Mexico's business, Carranza and Obregón, albeit recalcitrant reformers, might have accepted a larger dose of change? Had they done so, Mexico might possibly have enjoyed a modicum of Revolution.

---

## FURTHER READING

Richard Abrams, "United States Intervention Abroad: The First Quarter Century," *American Historical Review,* 79 (1974), 72–102

Peter Calvert, *The Mexican Revolution, 1910–1914* (1968)

Clarence C. Clendenen, *The United States and Pancho Villa* (1961)

Howard F. Cline, *The United States and Mexico* (1963)

John M. Cooper, Jr., " 'An Irony of Fate': Woodrow Wilson's Pre-World War I Diplomacy," *Diplomatic History,* 3 (1979), 425–437

Jules Davids, *American Political and Economic Penetration of Mexico, 1877–1920* (1976)

Mark T. Gilderhus, *Diplomacy and Revolution: U.S.-Mexican Relations Under Wilson and Carranza* (1977)

Kenneth J. Grieb, *The United States and Huerta* (1969)

Larry D. Hill, *Emissaries to a Revolution: Woodrow Wilson's Executive Agents in Mexico* (1973)

David Healy, *Gunboat Diplomacy in the Wilson Era* (1976)

Friedrich Katz, "Pancho Villa and the Attack on Columbus, New Mexico," *American Historical Review,* 83 (1978), 101–130

———, *The Secret War in Mexico* (1981)

Lester D. Langley, *The United States and the Caribbean in the Twentieth Century* (1982)

Arthur S. Link, *Wilson,* 3 vols. (1960–1965)

———, ed., *Woodrow Wilson and a Revolutionary World, 1913–1921* (1982)

———, *Woodrow Wilson: Revolution, War, and Peace* (1979)

Dexter Perkins, *The United States and the Caribbean* (1947)

Robert E. Quirk, *An Affair of Honor: Woodrow Wilson and the Occupation of Veracruz* (1962)

Karl M. Schmitt, *Mexico and the United States* (1974)

Hans Schmidt, *The United States Occupation of Haiti, 1915–1934* (1971)